KT-561-109

CONSTITUTIONAL AND ADMINISTRATIVE LAW

THIRD EDITION

Alex Carroll

Senior Lecturer in Law,
Manchester Metropolitan University

PEARSON
Longman

Harlow, England • London • New York • Boston • San Francisco • Toronto
Sydney • Tokyo • Singapore • Hong Kong • Seoul • Taipei • New Delhi
Cape Town • Madrid • Mexico City • Amsterdam • Munich • Paris • Milan

*For my late Mother and Father and for Frances and
'the boys' (Joe, Matthew, Daniel and Sam)*

Pearson Education Limited
Edinburgh Gate
Harlow
Essex CM20 2JE
England

and Associated Companies around the World

Visit us on the World Wide Web at:
www.pearsoned.co.uk

First published 1998
Second edition published 2002
Third edition published 2003

© Financial Times Professional Limited 1998
© Pearson Education Limited 2002, 2003

The right of Alex Carroll to be identified as
author of this work has been asserted by him in accordance
with the Copyright, Designs and Patents Act 1988.

All rights reserved. No part of this publication may be reproduced, stored
in a retrieval system, or transmitted in any form or by any means, electronic,
mechanical, photocopying, recording or otherwise, without either the prior
written permission of the publisher or a licence permitting restricted copying
in the United Kingdom issued by the Copyright Licensing Agency Ltd,
90 Tottenham Court Road, London W1T 4LP.

ISBN 0582 47343 8

British Library Cataloguing in Publication Data
A catalogue record for this book is available
from the British Library

10 9 8 7 6 5 4
09 08 07 06 05

Typeset in 10/12.5 Sabon by 68
Printed and bound in Malaysia, CLP
*The publisher's policy is to use paper
manufactured from sustainable forests*

CONSTITUTIONAL AND ADMINISTRATIVE LAW

Free updating service for this book
at www.booksites.net/carroll

THE FOUNDATION STUDIES IN LAW SERIES

Series Adviser – Paul Richards

The books in this series are written for law students for the foundation subjects required to be studied on both law degrees and postgraduate common professional examination courses. Each text concentrates on developing a basic framework for the subject and as such is designed to be accessible and readable, a format especially suitable for part-time courses, postgraduate diploma and distance-learning courses, as well as more traditional full-time courses where teaching is becoming increasingly student-centred and modularised. These basic texts are intended to be used in conjunction with other sources, such as law reports, case books and statutory materials.

Paul Richards, LLB, PhD, PGCE is Head of the Department of Law
at the University of Huddersfield.

LAW OF CONTRACT

CRIMINAL LAW

LAND LAW

LAW OF TORT

TRUSTS AND EQUITY

CONSTITUTIONAL AND ADMINISTRATIVE LAW

LAW OF THE EUROPEAN COMMUNITY

CONTENTS

PART 2 · PARLIAMENT AND THE EUROPEAN COMMUNITY

PART 3 · THE COMPOSITION AND WORKINGS OF PARLIAMENT

PART 4 · THE EXECUTIVE

PART 5 · JUDICIAL REVIEW OF ADMINISTRATIVE ACTION

PART 6 · HUMAN RIGHTS

PREFACE

This book has been written for students undertaking legal studies at undergraduate level and those pursuing similar courses which include constitutional and administrative law as a core component (e.g. the Postgraduate Diploma in Law). It is based on over twenty-five years' experience of teaching the subject at A-level, on undergraduate programmes and on postgraduate courses. Particular attention has been paid to the views of students concerning the strengths and weaknesses of existing textbooks in this discipline.

No attempt has been made to produce an exhaustive reference book covering all those issues which might conceivably fall within the boundaries of the subject. Rather the book concentrates on those topics which form the essential core of most constitutional and administrative law syllabi currently taught in further and higher education institutions.

Recent years have witnessed many significant changes to the law and practice of the British constitution. Detailed comment on these changes has been included notwithstanding that in some contexts, e.g. the House of Lords, the process of change is not yet complete. Hence, in addition to parliamentary reform, extensive coverage is given to such further innovations as the creation of regional assemblies for Scotland, Wales and Northern Ireland, developments within the European Union, changes to electoral law, the enactment and application of the Human Rights Act 1998 and the granting of even greater powers to the executive to deal with crime and terrorism.

As with most law books many of the legal principles included are explained by reference to particular judicial decisions. The approach taken here has been to discuss those cases which illustrate the principles in issue most clearly or those which exemplify their most recent application.

Constitutional and administrative law cannot be fully understood without reference to the nation's political history and its social and cultural development. The subject is also of great topical interest and is in a constant process of change and adjustment with many of its principles and cases resulting from, or relating to, recent political controversies. Hence, while every attempt has been made to explain the necessary principles as precisely and succinctly as possible, it has also been the author's intention to do so in a way which places these in their contextual framework. This approach gives some insight into the relationship between the subject and those political, historical and cultural factors which have influenced and shaped its nature and content.

The author is greatly indebted to all those who have helped in the book's compilation and production. Particular thanks are due to Mrs Linda Cork, and Mrs Gaynor Breach, administrative assistants at Manchester Metropolitan University. The author would also like to express belated thanks to Mr R H Buckley, one-time Principal Lecturer in Law at Manchester Metropolitan University, for all his help and advice over the years and for first exciting the author's interest in the subject. Thanks are also due to Mr Pat Bond of Pearson Education for his patience, support and understanding while the book was being written.

Alex Carroll

ACKNOWLEDGEMENTS

We are grateful to the following for permission to reproduce copyright material:

Tables 9.1, 9.2, 9.3 adapted from tables in *House of Commons Library Research Paper 00/61*, © Parliamentary copyright House of Commons Library 2000; Table 9.4 from table in *House of Lords Annual Report 1999/2000*, HMSO (2000), Parliamentary copyright is reproduced with the permission of the Controller of Her Majesty's Stationery Office on behalf of Parliament; Table 9.5 adapted from a table in *A Transitional House of Lords: The Numbers*, The Constitution Unit, University College London (1999); Table 9.6 and unnumbered table under the heading Parliament Act 1911 from information supplied by the House of Lords Information Office, Parliamentary copyright is reproduced with the permission of the Controller of Her Majesty's Stationery Office on behalf of Parliament.

In some instances we have been unable to trace the owners of copyright material, and we would appreciate any information that would enable us to do so.

SUPPLEMENT DOWNLOAD WEBSITE

A Supplement Download Website accompanies *Constitutional and Administrative Law*, 3rd Edition by Alex Carroll.

Visit the Foundation Studies in Law Website at www.booksites.net/fsls to find regular updates to ensure your knowledge is up-to-date.

TABLE OF CASES

TABLE OF STATUTES

Part 1

FUNDAMENTAL PRINCIPLES

Chapter 1

INTRODUCTION TO CONSTITUTIONAL AND ADMINISTRATIVE LAW

WHAT IS A CONSTITUTION

In a purely formal sense a constitution consists of the laws, rules (e.g. conventions) and other practices which identify and explain:

(a) the institutions of government;
(b) the nature, extent and distribution of powers within those institutions;
(c) the forms and procedures through which such powers should be exercised;
(d) the relationship between the institutions of government and the individual citizen, often expressed in terms of a 'Bill of Rights'.

Hence, for example, the first three articles of the constitution of the USA (1789) – the earliest and perhaps most revered of the modern world's written constitutions – provide for and specify the respective roles and powers of the Congress (Art I); the President (Art II); and the Supreme Court (Art III). The famous American Bill of Rights may be found in the same document in a series of later amendments to the original version. Thus, for example, Amendment I provides that 'Congress shall make no law respecting an establishment of religion, or prohibiting the free exercise thereof, or abridging the freedom of speech, or of the press, or the right of people peacefully to assemble, and to petition the Government for a redress of grievances'.

THE BRITISH CONSTITUTION

In the majority of nations, as in the United States, such constitutional prescriptions have been set down or 'codified' into a single written document. The constitution may be said, therefore, to exist in a physically tangible form. It is possible to go into a bookshop and buy a copy or to visit the museum or library where the original may be on display albeit closely guarded. This is not the case, however, in the United Kingdom. Here the constitution has simply evolved and been added to by Acts of Parliaments, judicial decisions and the growth of constitutional conventions and other political practices. The United Kingdom does not have a constitution, therefore, in the narrow sense of a formal document in which all the fundamental rules relating to the process of government are articulated. For all practical purposes, however, it does possess a body of legal and other rules by which that process is regulated and does, therefore, have a 'constitution' in the functional sense.

THE CULTURAL DIMENSION

Within the nation-state to which it applies, the constitution will usually be regarded as both the ultimate source of legitimacy and authority for the practice of government and as a framework for the application of that society's political beliefs concerning how the process of government should be conducted and by whom. Thus, except in those circumstances where a particular form of government has been imposed by force, perhaps by some external authority, a society's constitutional arrangements will, to a considerable extent, be a product of its political culture. Thus the constitution of the United Kingdom seeks to give expression and protection to many of the values and beliefs now generally associated with that form of government often referred to as liberal democracy. The values of liberal democracy may be summarised as freedom of thought, expression, association and assembly and a preference for limited representative and responsible government according to which those in power are answerable:

(a) in regular general elections: to a fully enfranchised adult population;
(b) on a day-to-day basis to a Parliament or representative assembly freely created by that electorate;
(c) in matters of law and jurisdiction, to an independent system of courts.

It follows that the authority and status of a constitution may usually be understood as having cultural as well as legal foundations. Hence, in addition to the legal duty of allegiance which it may impose, the constitution will be something which also attracts considerable respect and loyalty in a more personal sense. This will be so because the people in a particular society may often regard the constitution, or at least its physical manifestations – e.g. in the United Kingdom, the Monarch and Parliament – as part of their cultural heritage and identity.

Where it exists this sense of cultural affinity with the nation's constitutional arrangements will usually contribute to the general level of political stability and order. Perversely, however, this may make the constitution more difficult to change, at least in any abrupt or substantial way, as people tend to be more 'comfortable' with that with which they are familiar. This may help to explain, to some extent, the tensions currently being experienced in the United Kingdom concerning the constitutional implications of greater European integration.

Given the usual close relationship between a constitution and the political culture which it mirrors, it is axiomatic that few constitutions are static or immutable. As a society's expectations and beliefs concerning the process of government evolve, so must its constitution respond and develop. Otherwise it atrophies and becomes increasingly irrelevant to prevailing social and political attitudes. This in turn may lead to dissention and conflict over the validity of the very arrangements through which such dissent is supposed to be channelled and resolved.

THE EUROPEAN DIMENSION

The most significant domestic constitutional development in the twentieth century was undoubtedly effected by British membership of the European Community. As the

next millennium began the question of the United Kingdom's political and legal relationship with the rest of Europe remained the most divisive and controversial issue
on the nation's political and constitutional agendas. Already it has been suggested
that the United Kingdom has, in effect, two constitutions, viz. its own ancient and
unwritten version and the constitution of the European Community which has been
superimposed upon it. What cannot be denied is that, as a result of accession to
the Community, whole swathes of policy and law-making competencies in matters of
trade, commerce, fisheries, agriculture, etc. have been given up to the Community
institutions – principally the Council of Ministers and the European Commission.
Further, in its judicial capacity the House of Lords has ruled, or conceded, that in the
event of a conflict between an Act of Parliament and a directly effective Community
law, courts in the United Kingdom should apply the Community law in preference to
the statute.

The foundation for further convergence in political and economic matters by
European states was laid by the Treaty of European Union 1992 (the 'Maastricht
Treaty'). By this instrument member states agreed to make progress towards the
formulation of 'common' policies relating to home, judicial, defence and foreign
affairs and, subject to certain qualifying economic criteria, to the adoption of a single
European currency and monetary system (EMU).

Each such move will involve a greater 'pooling' and concentration of power within
the European supranational organisation and, to that extent, a diminution of national
political, legal and economic sovereignty. It is too early to say whether all of this will
lead eventually to a federation of European states, i.e. a single political entity having
ultimate authority in the key 'federal' issues of finance, defence and foreign affairs.
What can be said with some certainty, however, is that the British constitution is
currently going through the most fundamental process of change since the events of
the late seventeenth century.

Distinguishing between constitutional law and administrative law

Constitutional law deals with the legal foundations of the institutional hierarchy
through which the state is governed. It concentrates in particular on the rules, both
legal and conventional, which explain and regulate the composition, powers, immunities, procedures of, and relationships between, those institutions – hence, for example,
the subject's concern with the composition, workings and powers of Parliament, the
legal authority and immunities of the executive, and the balance of legal and political
power between the two.

Constitutional law also seeks to delineate those individual rights which, according
to cultural traditions, are the inalienable attributes of a genuinely free society and
upon which the state should not transgress except where an overwhelming public
interest so requires (e.g. the defence of the realm). Such rights would include the freedom of the person (i.e. from arbitrary arrest and detention), freedom of association
and assembly, and freedom of speech.

Administrative law, on the other hand, directs greater attention to the control and
regulation of government power by both public and private law and through the
workings of the various extra-judicial appeals and complaints procedures created in

recent times to supplement the judicial and political mechanisms for dealing with individual grievances against the state. Central to the subject, therefore, is the process of judicial review, whereby alleged abuses of government power may be brought before the courts and condemned as *ultra vires* and of no legal effect. The subject also deals, *inter alia*, with the jurisdiction and workings of statutory tribunals and inquiries which hear appeals against official decisions, and with the activities of the increasing number of 'ombudspersons' or complaints commissioners dealing with allegations of 'maladministration' in the public services and the execution of public policy.

THE TERMINOLOGY OF CONSTITUTIONAL AND ADMINISTRATIVE LAW

Not all of those who come to the study of constitutional and administrative law for the first time will be entirely familiar with its language and terminology. Thus, for example, difficulty may be found in giving exact definition to, and distinguishing between, such concepts as the Crown, the Monarch, the government, Parliament, etc. Such conceptual problems are understandable as not all of these are capable of being given entirely distinctive and particular meanings. It is hoped, however, that the pages that follow will help to dispel some of these uncertainties and make for greater comprehension of the institutional context in which the subject operates.

The Monarch

This is the person who occupies the throne and who, by virtue of which, is recognised by law and tradition as Head of State. The right of succession to the throne is determined both by traditional hereditary principles (i.e. is reserved to the eldest male heir and, in the absence of which, to the eldest female) and by conditions laid down by Parliament in various enactments – principally the Act of Settlement 1700. This provided that in the absence of any issue by Queen Anne (1701–14), the right of succession should be confined to the Princess Sophia of Hanover 'and the heirs of her body being protestants'. It was by virtue of this enactment that the first of the Hanoverian monarchs, George I (1714–27), succeeded to the throne after Queen Anne's death.

As Head of State, the executive, legislative and judicial functions of government are all performed in the Monarch's name and by his or her appointees. The Prime Minister and other members of the government are the King or Queen's Ministers. Law is made by the King or Queen in Parliament, i.e. with the consent of the Commons, Lords and Monarch. The same law is administered in the Royal Courts of Justice by the King or Queen's judges.

In this personal sense, it is still accepted that 'the King can do no wrong'. Hence the Monarch may not be prosecuted for any criminal offence or sued for breach of any civil obligation.

More will be said about the constitutional role and status of the Monarch in Chapter 2.

The Crown

As the following quotation explains, the term has been given various meanings.

> The expression 'the Crown' may sometimes be used to designate Her Majesty in a purely personal capacity. It may sometimes be used to designate Her Majesty in Her capacity as Head of the Commonwealth. It may sometimes be used to designate Her Majesty in Her capacity as the constitutional Monarch of the United Kingdom...The expression may sometimes be used in a somewhat broad sense in reference to the functions of government and the administration. It may sometimes be used in reference to the Rule of Law...The case for the prosecution is the case for the Crown (per Lord Diplock, *Town Investments Ltd* v *Department of the Environment* [1978] AC 359).

For all practical purposes, however, and in terms of everyday usage and understanding, it is the fourth of these meanings which should be preferred. Thus when 'the Crown' is spoken of in constitutional law, this is normally for the purpose of referring to all those institutions and, in particular, central government departments and those who work within them (civil or 'Crown' servants), who are responsible for managing public affairs at a national level.

> Where...we are concerned with the legal nature of the exercise of executive powers of government, I believe that some of the more Athanasian-like features of the debate in your Lordships' House could have been eliminated if instead of speaking of 'the Crown' we were to speak of the 'government' – a term appropriate to embrace both collectively and individually all the Ministers of the Crown and parliamentary secretaries under whose direction the administrative work of government is carried on by the civil servants employed in the various government departments...Execution of acts of government that are done by any of them are acts done by 'the Crown' in the fictional sense in which that expression is now used in English public law (*ibid.*).

In this institutional rather than personal sense, the Crown is a 'corporation sole'. This means that, unlike the Monarch, it has a definable legal capacity and may sue and be sued in the ordinary courts of law.

The Sovereign

The word 'Sovereign' is employed, generally, in one of two senses. First it may be used as a synonym for the Monarch – i.e. the person who, in purely legal terms, is at the apex of the constitutional pyramid. In this sense the word denotes little in terms of legislative or actual political power, but much in terms of status and symbolism. Second, it is also frequently used to mean that which in terms of legal or political authority has no superior. Hence, in the United Kingdom, Parliament has long been regarded as the 'sovereign' law-making body – i.e. the law as made by Parliament prevails over all other legal rules whatever their source. In the political sense, however, it is often said that it is 'the people' who are sovereign, i.e. the legislative power of Parliament and the authority of the government is derived from the 'will' of the people as expressed through the ballot box.

The state

English constitutional law contains no exact or fixed definition of the above term. Once again, therefore, a variety of meanings may be attributed to it.

It may be used, for example, to describe the geographical entity over which the institutions of government of a particular society exercise independent political authority. In this sense the state which is referred to as the United Kingdom would be said to consist of England, Wales, Scotland and Northern Ireland.

Alternatively the word may be used to characterise the entire structure of institutions and organisations through which a particular society is regulated and protected.

> The state is the whole organisation of the body politic for civil rule and government – the whole political organisation which is the basis of civil government. As such it certainly extends to local and...statutory-bodies in so far as they are exercising autonomous rule (per Lord Simon, D v *National Society for Prevention of Cruelty to Children* [1978] AC 171).

The realm

The fact that the concept of the state does not have any great political or legal significance in the language of English constitutional law is largely due to historical factors and to the ancient nature of the institutions around which the constitution has developed. Just as these have survived, so has the language of those earlier times in which such institutions were founded. Hence, according to what may be called the language of tradition, the territory over which the King or Queen (now the Crown in the form of the central government) exercised political power by right of succession and/or battle was properly referred to as 'the realm'. In constitutional law, therefore, the term has a similar meaning to that of 'the state' when the latter is used to describe the area over which the government has authority.

The government

This is yet another term capable of various meanings. It may be used, for example, as a collective noun for all those who hold ministerial office at any particular time. These will all be persons with seats in the House of Commons or House of Lords (most in the Commons). The number of ministers of which any government may consist is not fixed, but will usually be in the region of 100 to 130. These will range from the heads of major departments ('Secretaries of State'), to second-rank ministers, usually referred to as 'Ministers of State', down to the more junior ministers with titles such as 'Under Secretaries of State' or 'Parliamentary Secretaries'.

The 'government', in this sense, should not be confused with the political party which 'won' the last General Election and holds a majority of the seats in the House of Commons. Hence, after the 1997 General Election, the party 'in power' was New Labour with 419 MPs. Those given ministerial office by Mr Blair became members of the government. Those not chosen remained merely backbenchers of the parliamentary (New) Labour party.

The word government is also sometimes given a more extensive meaning which includes all of those institutions and persons at a national level who are concerned with the making and execution of policy. In this sense the term is not dissimilar to the institutional meaning of 'the Crown' and would encompass all those ministers and civil servants who comprise the central administration.

Government also has a functional meaning in that it may be used to refer to the process through which the nation's affairs are regulated and protected. In this sense government means an activity rather than a particular combination of individuals or institutions.

The Cabinet

This refers to that senior group of ministers (usually 20–24) who meet weekly or twice weekly with the Prime Minister to determine government policy and action. Most of these will be the heads of major government departments. Others will have responsibility for a variety of activities which must be discharged effectively if the government is to survive and prosper. Hence the Cabinet will usually include ministers with responsibility for managing government business in the House of Commons (Leader of the House of Commons) and in the House of Lords (Lord Privy Seal). The Lord Chancellor, who has overall responsibility for the legal system and the Chancellor of the Exchequer's 'No. 2' at the Treasury, the Chief Secretary to the Treasury, will also be included.

It should be noted, therefore, that not all members of 'the government' (i.e. all ministers) are members of the Cabinet. Nor is the Cabinet composed purely of those with responsibility for the major government departments (viz. Secretaries of State).

The executive

This is a term used collectively to refer to all those institutions and persons concerned primarily with the implementation of law and policy. Hence all central and local government departments would generally be included as would the police and the armed forces. Precluded from the definition are all those engaged in making law as opposed to enforcing it. Hence it would be improper to regard Parliament or the judiciary as falling within the term's usual meaning.

The legislature

When the term is used in domestic constitutional and administrative law, normally it may be understood as referring to the Parliament. For the purposes of enacting legislation the Parliament of the United Kingdom consists of the House of Commons, the House of Lords and the Monarch.

Not all law in the United Kingdom is made by Parliament. Many important legal rules are made by the judges and become part of the common law. Others are made by government ministers and local authorities under powers Parliament has delegated to them (delegated or subordinate legislation). In the context of their law-making functions, neither the judges, ministers nor local authorities should be understood as parts of the legislature. This remains the case notwithstanding that the most senior judges (the 'Law Lords') and all government ministers have seats in one or other House of Parliament.

The judiciary

In the United Kingdom all those who preside over courts of law may rightly be defined as members of the judiciary. Those who preside over administrative tribunals would not generally be regarded as falling within the definition.

There is no absolutely convincing formula for distinguishing between the functions of a judge and those who chair tribunals. The practice and procedure of some tribunals is almost indistinguishable from that typical of courts of law (e.g. the Immigration Appeals Tribunal). Those who preside will usually be required to have qualifications similar to those holding judicial office proper. In such cases to deny that the presiding official is 'a judge' probably has more to do with tradition than with functional accuracy. Other tribunals may conduct their proceedings more informally than courts of law and may be staffed by 'lay' persons with only the chairperson being legally qualified (e.g. Social Security Appeals Tribunals). Decision-making in others may involve the application of discretion and policy as well as legal rules (e.g. the Civil Aviation Authority). In such instances the logic for excluding those presiding from the definition of the word 'judiciary' may be more obvious.

Also, in many instances those who chair administrative tribunals are not accorded the same independence and security of tenure (i.e. legally guaranteed protection from executive interference) as is normally thought essential from those sitting in courts of law in the traditional sense.

Local government

Local government in England and Wales is the responsibility of the elected councils which direct the affairs of the various county, district and 'unitary' authorities in their provision of essential public services. Such authorities are created by and receive their powers from Acts of Parliament. The employees of local authorities are paid out of local funds and are not civil or crown servants.

Local authorities are funded by local taxation ('council tax'), government grants and through borrowing. In strict constitutional terms, such authorities are not under the direct control of central government. The latter does, however, exercise considerable influence over local government affairs through various statutory procedures, including the inspection of local government services, the requirements for ministerial consent prior to the implementation of certain decisions (e.g. the application of a compulsory purchase order or the closure of a school), the issuing of directions to authorities not fulfilling their statutory obligations and the power to assume responsibility for certain local government functions should an authority be found to be 'in default' (see Education Act 1944, s 199). The central government may also seek to exert its will through its control of Treasury grants to local authorities and its ultimate, albeit seldom used, power to withhold monies where dissatisfied by the standards of service provided by a particular authority.

To a considerable extent the structure of local government in England and Wales remains based on the reforms introduced in 1974 by the Local Government Act 1972. Outside the large conurbations these produced a simplified two-tier system with responsibility for the provision of services being divided between 47 County Councils and 333 District Councils. County Councils were given overall responsibility for such services as education, policing, planning, highways and personal social services. District Councils were to provide certain services in their own right (e.g. housing, public health, parks and cemeteries) with others being provided in partnership with and subject to the overall policy direction of the counties (e.g. local planning). The six major urban areas other than London (Manchester, Merseyside, West Yorkshire, South Yorkshire, West Midlands, Tyne and Wear) were put under the control of new Metropolitan County Councils, working again on a two-tier system with Metropolitan District Councils. This was modelled to a considerable extent on the system of local government for London introduced by the Local Government Act 1963 which created the Greater London Council (the 'GLC') and 32 London Borough Councils. This system of 'big city' government continued until 1986 when the GLC and the Metropolitan County Councils were dissolved and their functions largely devolved to the Metropolitan Districts which remained in existence (Local Government Act 1985). Where this was not feasible for strategic reasons, e.g. as in the case of the police, functions were devolved to joint committees consisting of councillors from the related Metropolitan Districts.

The system so prevailed until the passage of the Local Government Act 1992. This established a Local Government Commission for England and Wales to review existing boundaries and structures and gave the Secretary of State power by order made under s 17 of the Act to implement the Commission's recommendations. To date this power has been used most extensively in Wales where the pre-existing two-tier system of local government has been replaced by 22 unitary 'all-purpose' authorities. In England 46 such authorities have been created outside London, which has 33 boroughs, these exist alongside 238 District Councils and 36 Metropolitan District Councils.

Local government in London is founded currently on the Greater London Authority Act 1999. The system was approved in a referendum of London elections in May 1998.

The Act established the Greater London Authority with a separately elected Mayor and Assembly, each to serve for four years. The Mayor has responsibility for, *inter alia*, transport, planning, the environment, setting the Authority's budget and the approval of economic development and cultural strategies. He or she is elected by simple majority where there are only two candidates or by the additional member system where three or more compete.

The Mayor is accountable to the Assembly which may override his or her decisions by a majority of two-thirds or more of its total membership.

The Assembly consists of 25 members. Fourteen are elected from the London constituencies and eleven by the electorate of London as a whole. Voters have two votes – a constituency vote and a London vote. The latter may be cast for an individual London candidate or for a party list. Constituency members are returned by the simple majority system. London members are elected by the De Hondt formula (see Greater London Authority Bill, Explanatory Notes, paras 48–53).

Outside the Greater London area a framework for the discharge of local executive functions through elected mayors or other forms of local executives was introduced by the Local Government Act 2000. The Act requires local authorities to draw up proposals for the adoption of one of the following options:

(a) an elected mayor with two or more councillors chosen by him/her (a 'mayor and cabinet executive');

(b) a councillor elected by the authority (the 'executive leader') and two or more councillors (a 'leader and cabinet executive');

(c) an elected mayor and an officer of the authority (a 'mayor and council manager executive').

An executive headed by a directly elected mayor shall not be established unless this is the will of the local electorate expressed in a referendum. Such referendum should be held where:

• an authority's proposal includes a directly elected mayor;
• 5 per cent or more of the council's electorate petition for a directly elected mayor;
• the Secretary of State requires an authority to hold a referendum on any of the forms of executives available under the Act.

The purpose of the Act is to introduce a new system of decision-making into local government. This involves a distinct separation of personnel between those responsible for the formulation and implementation of policy and those engaged in the scrutiny of it.

Prior to the Act and since the inception of elected local government in the nineteenth century, local administration was the responsibility of committees of councillors (e.g. education committees, social services committees), either making decisions or submitting recommendations to the full council. This system is now perceived to be out of date. Under the new system an authority's policy framework and general budget proposals will be drawn up by the local executive and put before the full council for approval. It is claimed that this will lead to greater efficiency, transparency and accountability.

THE GEOGRAPHY OF THE CONSTITUTION

The constitutional principles explained in the pages that follow are those applicable to the geographical and political entity known as the United Kingdom. This consists of:

(a) England and Wales;
(b) Scotland;
(c) Northern Ireland.

Wales

From the time of the military defeat of the Welsh prince Llywelyn in 1282, English monarchs claimed political authority over Wales by right of battle. Initially, however, the Welsh retained their own language, laws and customs. By Act of Parliament in 1536 England and Wales were united into a single kingdom with English as the common and official language. In 1543 the English common law was extended to Wales. Thereafter England and Wales existed as a single political and administrative unit.

Scotland and the formation of Great Britain

At the time of the English and Welsh union, Scotland was a separate and independent 'state' with its own monarchy, Parliament, administrative and legal systems.

In 1603, Elizabeth I, the last of the Tudors and one of England's most renowned monarchs, died without issue. With her prior agreement the throne of England descended to James IV of Scotland. He became James I of England by right of succession owing to his direct descent from Henry VII, who was his grandfather. Scotland retained, however, its existing Parliament and systems of law and government. In strict constitutional terms, therefore, the Kingdom of England and Wales and the Kingdom of Scotland remained as separate political and administrative entities but with a shared monarchy.

Genuine political union between the two kingdoms did not occur until 1707. In that year Acts of Union were passed by both the English and Scottish Parliaments. Thus a single unified Parliament was created with authority over what was to be known thereafter as the Kingdom of Great Britain.

Ireland and the formation of the United Kingdom

The troubled political relationship between England and Ireland dates back to the twelfth century when English intrusion into Irish affairs, and attempts to exert political influence there, began. Initially, however, and despite the claim by Henry II (1154–89) and his successors to be 'Lords of Ireland', effective English government was largely confined to 'the pale', a strip of territory along Ireland's eastern seaboard that was most easily accessible from 'the mainland'.

Genuine military subjugation of Ireland was not effected until the end of the sixteenth century. This followed Henry VIII's decree in 1541 that he and his successors would be recognised, not simply in name but in political fact, as Kings of Ireland. Throughout the century that followed, therefore, each king occupied three separate thrones – those of England and Wales, Scotland, and Ireland. Ireland was allowed to retain its own Parliament and a limited measure of political autonomy. Roman Catholics and Protestant dissenters (i.e. the majority of the population), were, however, entirely excluded from the processes of government.

Political domination of Ireland was finally placed on a formal legal and institutional basis in 1800. In that year, following the precedent set in 1707, Acts of Union were passed by the Irish Parliament and by the Parliament of Great Britain. Thus the United Kingdom of Great Britain and Ireland was created. The Irish Parliament in Dublin was thereby extinguished. Thereafter, legislative authority in Ireland was to be exercised by the Parliament of the United Kingdom at Westminster to which Ireland would send its elected representatives.

Ireland in its entirety remained within the United Kingdom until the Irish Free State (Agreement) Act 1922. The Act gave effect to the political agreement (the 'Treaty') reached by nationalist leaders and the British government following 'the Troubles' or Irish War of Independence 1919–21. The Free State consisted of 26 of the 32 counties of Ireland. It was deemed to be a self-governing dominion within the British empire and given status similar to that of Canada, Australia and New Zealand. The Monarch continued to be recognised as titular head of state with his/her functions being performed by a Governor-General. In 1948 the new Irish State declared itself a Republic. Thereafter the position of head of state was filled by an elected President. All formal constitutional links with the United Kingdom were thus severed.

The six northern counties of Ireland excluded from the Free State in 1922 remained within the United Kingdom. Under the terms of the Government of Ireland Act 1920, Northern Ireland was to have its own government and Parliament with authority over domestic affairs but subject at all times to the 'supreme authority of the Parliament of the United Kingdom' (s 75). Excluded from the legislative and executive jurisdiction of the institutions thus created were, *inter alia*, all matters relating to defence, foreign affairs and the armed forces.

The experiment with self-government in Northern Ireland did not prove entirely successful. Due to the religious and political composition of the province's population, the institutions of government were at all times in the control of the Unionist party, supported by its largely Protestant electorate. Those of different political persuasions were thus doomed to permanent opposition and exclusion from the process of government. This was one of the reasons for the political discontent, and eventual disorder, which broke out in the late 1960s.

As the violence escalated, and increasing numbers of British military personnel were committed to the province, it was decided that the Northern Ireland government and Parliament should be abolished and that, henceforth, all matters concerning Northern Ireland should be determined by the central government in London ('direct rule'). This was effected by the Northern Ireland Constitution Act 1973.

Since that time a number of attempts have been made to restore to the province a measure of self-government. The latest of these was concluded in April 1998 by the Irish and UK governments and by the representatives of the rival political and paramilitary factions. It provides for an Assembly of 108 members elected by proportional representation. From this is drawn a 'government' headed by a First Minister and Deputy First Minister, with ten other ministers consisting of representatives from all the main political groups. The membership of the committees through which the Assembly operates is in numerical proportion to the elected representation of the parties on the floor of the Assembly. The Assembly has legislative authority in certain devolved matters (see Chapter 2). Voting is 'weighted' so that a measure of cross-party support will be needed before any proposal may be enacted.

In consultation and agreement with the government of the Irish Republic, the Assembly will seek to establish areas in which common policies or cooperation may be developed and, where appropriate, administered by bodies representing both the northern and southern governments. Ministers from the Assembly and the Irish government will also meet regularly in a new North–South Ministerial Council 'to develop...cooperation and action within the island of Ireland...on matters of mutual interest within the competence of the Administration's North and South'. Matters of common concern will also be discussed in a larger British–Irish Council consisting of representatives from the Assembly, the British and Irish governments, and the Parliaments of Scotland, Wales, the Isle of Man and the Channel Islands.

Further reading

Birch (1993) *The British System of Government* (9th edn), London: Routledge, Ch 1.

Chapter 2

THE CHARACTERISTICS
OF THE CONSTITUTION

INTRODUCTION

It is helpful to begin any examination of the constitutional law of the United Kingdom with a general survey of the various theories, principles and institutions of which the constitution itself is composed. This contributes to an understanding of how the various features relate to each other in a functional sense and how they operate collectively to achieve, however imperfectly, the liberal democratic objectives which underpin the present constitutional arrangement.

THE UNWRITTEN CONSTITUTION

Meaning

Although many of the rules of the British Constitution may be found in law reports and parliamentary enactments, it remains true to say that no comprehensive attempt has ever been made to collect and codify these into a single defining instrument. As has been the case for centuries, therefore, the constitution's principal contents may still be traced to what may sometimes seem to be a myriad of judicial decisions, Acts of Parliament and established political practices (conventions). It is in this sense, therefore, that the constitution may be defined as 'unwritten'.

General awareness of the constitution's comparatively disparate nature should not be allowed, however, to obscure the efforts made in recent times to consolidate or 'tidy up' those elements perceived to be particularly lacking in clarity. Hence, for example, by the end of the twentieth century much of the law relating to the relationship between the individual and state in matters pertaining to personal liberty had been cast into statutory form by a series of key enactments including the Obscene Publications Act 1959, the Police and Criminal Evidence Act 1984, the Public Order Act 1986, the Official Secrets Act 1989 and the Criminal Justice and Public Order Act 1994. Further codification in this general area has been effected by the Human Rights Act 1998, the Regulation of Investigatory Powers Act 2000 and the Terrorism Act 2000.

Reasons for

Only two other states in the world (Israel and New Zealand) have constitutions which may be described as unwritten. The reasons typically advanced for survival of such in the United Kingdom usually relate to the degree of political continuity evident in the development of the state and consist of a mixture of historical, social and cultural factors – all of which have combined to avoid the sort of cathartic political events (e.g. defeat in war or civil insurrection) which, in many other countries, have led to the abandonment and replacement of a pre-existing constitutional order.

Historical considerations

The 'mainland' of England was last invaded successfully in 1066 (the Norman Conquest). This can be explained, to some extent, by the country's geographical position and separation from Europe by the English Channel – a physical feature which has played no small part in maintaining the nation's political integrity. The last actual 'invasion' took place in 1745 when the Scottish Jacobite army led by the 'Young Pretender', Charles Stuart (grandson of James II), penetrated as far south as Derby. Subsequently, foreign troops entered the United Kingdom for belligerent purposes in 1798 when French troops landed on the west coast of Ireland to assist the rebellion there, and in 1940 when German forces occupied the Channel Islands.

English history could not, of course, be described as a complete continuum of peace and tranquillity. The seventeenth century, in particular, was a period of great constitutional crisis and witnessed two major rebellions or civil wars, both of which led to the demise of individual monarchs. Neither conflict, however, led to the adoption of a permanent written constitution in the modern sense. Indeed, many of the great doctrines and conceptions of the attributes of civil government, including notions of representation, freedom and equality which were to spur the American and French revolutions of the late eighteenth century, and to which their constitutions sought to give expression, had not yet been articulated. The English Civil Wars did, however, directly lead to the creation of the most significant statutory elements of the post-revolutionary constitutional settlement, viz. the Bill of Rights 1689 and the Act of Settlement 1700. These remain fundamental elements of the modern constitution and give practical effect to the principles of parliamentary sovereignty and constitutional monarchy.

Towards the end of the eighteenth century relative economic prosperity and the very real threat of invasion by France combined to reduce the potentially destabilising influences of the American and French revolutions. As the nineteenth century dawned and the social and economic deprivations of the Industrial Revolution produced conditions ripe for political disorder, the established order was initially maintained by a policy of oppression. From the 1830s onwards, however, a sufficient blend of self-interest and enlightenment amongst the landed and industrial establishment combined to facilitate the type of moderate political and social reforms necessary to ensure uninterrupted economic development within the established legal and constitutional arrangements. This pragmatic and expedient attitude, sometimes referred to as the philosophy of reform to preserve, helped to avoid duplication of the revolutionary crises encountered by more intransigent regimes elsewhere in Europe. Prominent amongst these nineteenth-century reforms were the Representation of the People Acts 1832, 1867 and 1884, which enfranchised the male rate-paying population, the repeal of the Combination Acts which prohibited trade unions, and the various social and economic measures, including Public Health, Local Government and Factories legislation which attempted to introduce some minimum standards in terms of health, sanitation and working conditions.

During the ensuing years the United Kingdom has survived two World Wars and serious domestic industrial unrest (including the General Strike in 1926, the depression of the 1930s and, more recently, the Miners' Strikes of 1974 and 1984), but without significant constitutional disruption or rearrangement. Where changes to the relationships and the distribution of power between the institutions of government have occurred, this has been achieved by modifications of the relevant conventional and legal rules (e.g. the removal of the House of Lord's legislative veto by the Parliament Acts 1911 and 1949), thereby allowing the traditional framework to remain in place.

It is, of course, implicit in the above that not all the nations of the world have enjoyed an equally uninterrupted process of political development. Thus, in many countries, older systems of government have been abandoned after wars, revolutions or decolonialisation. These have then been replaced by government according to the political principles of whichever force – external or internal, popular or sectional – has been able to exert its will. In such circumstances it has seldom been possible for the new regime simply to wait for the appropriate rules and institutions of government to evolve. In order to avoid the danger of continued instability and insecurity these have been created, and given the requisite degree of legal authority to ensure peace, order and the continuity of the new system. In the vast majority of cases this has been done through the adoption of a written constitution.

Examples of the institution of written constitutions in recent history in circumstances similar to those described would include that of the Federal Republic of Germany which came into effect in 1949 and recreated the German state after the fall of the Third Reich in 1945, and the constitutions recently or currently being devised for the various elements of the former Yugoslavia. It is also interesting and perhaps paradoxical to note that the government and Parliament of the United Kingdom were responsible for the formulation of a number of written constitutions, particularly in the 1960s, given to ex-colonial territories as part of their grants of independence (see, for example, the Independence Acts of Nigeria, Kenya and Malawi, 1960, 1963 and 1964 respectively).

Social and cultural factors

The relatively stable conditions in which the United Kingdom's unwritten constitution has developed are not something which can be explained, however, purely by reference to defining historical events or the lack of them. Social and cultural attributes have also had considerable influence in reducing the likelihood of political tensions. The dominant English society, it has been said, until recent times at least displayed a marked degree of homogeneity, particularly in the racial and religious senses. Such significant differences as existed tended to be confined to the geographical margins, i.e. to those places (sometimes referred to as the 'Celtic Twilight') to which English influence was extended in order to create the wider political community known as the United Kingdom.

Attention has also been drawn to the contribution of some of the innate cultural preferences which, it has been claimed, for so long typified the attitude of the indigenous majority in political matters. These would include:

(a) a considerable level of agreement concerning the role of government and a reluc-
    tance to allow political partisanship to interfere with personal relationships;
(b) a general tendency to favour gradual development and moderate change with a
    correlative suspicion of ideological or 'quick fix' solutions;
(c) a high level of deference towards those responsible for the nation's affairs, and a
    related respect for authority and its political symbols, e.g. the monarchy, which
    in turn has encouraged a greater sense of national identity and loyalty.

The certainty of some of these culture assumptions is, of course, now under question.
Racial and religious homogeneity has been affected by post-war immigration from
Commonwealth and former colonial territories. Trust in the political élite and even in
the monarchy has been diminished by scandals, sleaze and exposés by an aggressive
media. The parliamentary and party system is perceived by some as having 'failed to
deliver', and being 'out of touch' particularly in social, economic and environmental
terms. Individual 'cause' groups have increased in popularity at the expense of the
established political parties. The very structure of the United Kingdom itself has even
been challenged by a rise in nationalism.

All of this could, of course, be understood as demonstrating nothing more than the
fact that a society's political culture is inevitably in a constant state of change and
evolution. This might be to understate, however, the pressures to which the United
Kingdom's venerable constitution is currently exposed. Perhaps all that can be said at
present is that, although there is no clearly articulated popular campaign for radical
constitutional reform beyond that pursued by the post-1997 Labour government,
signs of dissatisfaction with the workings of the established political and constitutional order are apparent; perhaps no more so than in the turn-out for the general
election of 2001 which was the lowest since 1918 at just 58 per cent.

FLEXIBILITY

Meaning

There are three principal ways in which the British constitution may be changed:

(a) by legislation enacted according to normal parliamentary procedure;
(b) by judicial decisions;
(c) by a change in existing conventional practices.

It follows that the constitution has no entrenched provisions, i.e. fundamental or
basic laws which cannot be altered except in accordance with a special legislative procedure and/or approval in a referendum.

Entrenchment

Examples of this way of protecting constitutional fundamentals may be found in
many of the world's leading liberal democratic constitutions. In the United States the
requirement is that any amendment must be approved by majorities of two-thirds in
both Houses of Congress and by the legislatures of 'three fourths of the several states'
(Art V). Entrenchment is also commonplace in the constitutions of Europe. The

French prescription is for amendments to be passed by both Houses of Parliament (National Assembly and Senate) supported by a referendum. Alternatively amendments may be made by Parliament, without a referendum, providing these receive the support of three-fifths of the votes cast (Art 89).

The purpose of such entrenchment is to protect key provisions (e.g. those relating to basic civil liberties) from the passing whims and caprice of those who may hold political office from time to time. The degree of flexibility of written constitutions will therefore depend, to a considerable extent, on the method of entrenchment, if any, which is used. Hence, it is perfectly possible for a written constitution to have no entrenched provisions whatsoever and be subject, therefore, to amendment by ordinary legislative process or, at the other extreme, to contain clauses which are to be regarded as immutable (e.g. the basic human rights requirements of the 1949 German Constitution).

Evaluation

In the absence of such restraining procedures it is clear that the British constitution may be changed relatively easily and quickly and may be described, therefore, as having a greater degree of flexibility than many of its written counterparts. This ready susceptibility to change has, however, been both praised and criticised. Hence, those supportive of the existing model have tended to emphasise the way in which the constitution has been able both to adapt to changing times and expectations about the practice of government and, on occasions, to respond to the needs of moment; as in 1975 when the Labour Prime Minister, Harold Wilson, suspended the convention of collective ministerial responsibility to enable ministers to speak freely on the referendum concerning British membership of the European Community. More sceptical opinions have suggested, however, that unqualified assertions of the benefits of flexibility could be based on the possibly dubious assumption that governments can be trusted not to use their political control of Parliament (through their majority in the House of Commons) to impose constitutional change purely for reasons of political expediency or ephemeral ideology.

Much depends, therefore, on the view that is taken of the effectiveness of the domestic democratic process to deter politicians from unwarranted interference with the constitution's primary rules, i.e. those which underpin contemporary political values and those 'constituent' enactments which brought the state into existence, e.g. the Bill of Rights 1689, the Act of Settlement 1700 and the Acts of Union 1707. At present the assumption appears to be that those tempted to 'meddle' with these crucial provisions do so in the knowledge that this may excite the type of widespread and sustained opposition which is impossible to either ignore or overcome.

The ideal

All constitutions do, of course, need to be changed from time to time. If they are not, they atrophy and become irrelevant to the needs of the times. Radical alterations may then be occasioned by political tensions. The ideal appears to be, therefore, a constitutional arrangement which avoids 'the Scylla of total rigidity and the Charybidis of total flexibility' (Calvert, *An Introduction to British Constitutional Law*, 1985). Some constitutions, as illustrated, seek this through formal restraints. The British preference is for reliance more on informal political and cultural pressures. What really matters, however, is whether the correct balance is struck and that required constitutional change is able to take place within a framework which provides sufficient protection for those fundamentals which retain their functional and ideological validity.

UNITARY

Meaning

The principal distinction between unitary and federal systems of government is that in the former ultimate legal authority is not divided between the central and regional authorities.

The relationship between central and local government

In the United Kingdom all sovereign or ultimate legal power is vested in one omnipotent central legislative assembly, viz. the Westminster Parliament. There are, therefore, no regional or state assemblies possessing autonomous authority, i.e. that which cannot be overridden by Parliament.

Local government is conducted by county, district and unitary councils. These do not equate, however, with the regional bodies which might be found in a federal system. Local authorities in the United Kingdom are created by Parliament (the present local government structure deriving from the Local Government Acts 1972 and 1992) and receive their powers from Parliament (in Housing Acts, Education Acts, Highways Acts, etc.). Hence Parliament has the power to abolish all or any type of authority (e.g. Metropolitan County Councils by the Local Government Act 1985) and to make radical alterations – in recent years usually reductions – to the powers allocated to them. In a federal arrangement, by contrast, the existence and partial autonomy of the state's regional components will usually originate and receive protection from the founding constitutional document. In other words, the relevant provisions are entrenched 'so that they cannot be amended at the sole discretion of the federation or of any province or combination of provinces' (Hood Phillips and Jackson, *Constitutional and Administrative Law*).

Local authorities in the United Kingdom also have the power to make law (by-laws) for the good rule and government of the districts for which they are responsible. Again, however, such power is derived from Parliament and may be revoked or altered at any time. Also, any by-laws which are inconsistent with an Act of Parliament are deemed to be invalid.

Central government and the regions

The United Kingdom does, of course, consist of a number of regions or provinces in the geographical and ethnic sense (particularly Scotland, Wales and Northern Ireland). Prior to the recent creation of national assemblies in Scotland and Wales, only Northern Ireland had previously been allowed to have its own Parliament (located at

Stormont in East Belfast). It was created by the Government of Ireland Act 1920 but ceased to exist as a result of the Northern Ireland (Temporary Provisions) Act 1972. The existence of the Stormont Parliament was, therefore, at all times, subject to the will of the imperial Parliament at Westminster. Its legislative powers were contained in and delimited by the 1920 Act. Any legislation outside the prescribed limits or inconsistent with Westminster legislation was deemed to be invalid. This sole experiment in regional government in the United Kingdom did not represent, therefore, a significant departure from the essence of the unitary principle.

At the time of writing, Scotland, Wales and Northern Ireland each continue to elect and send representatives to the sovereign Westminster Parliament and are subject to its authority without any intervening layer of government. Each does have its own central government department (the Scottish, Welsh and Northern Ireland Offices). These again, however, are directly accountable to Westminster.

Attitudes to federalism

The unitary principle and its expression in the current structure of the United Kingdom is, of course, a matter of political and national preference. By definition, therefore, it is either partly or wholly inimical to the aspirations of nationalist movements. It seems likely, however, at least for the foreseeable future, that any grants of autonomy precipitated by nationalist pressures, at least in Scotland and Wales, will be effected within the parameters, both geographical and legal, of the unitary state and will, therefore, remain subject to the ultimate authority of Westminster (see below, however, for comments concerning the new Assembly for Northern Ireland).

The relevance of federalism to the United Kingdom was considered by the Royal Commission on the Constitution which reported in 1973 (Cmnd 5460). The essence of its conclusions were contained in the following paragraph of its report:

> Although there are some circumstances in which the benefits to be derived from federalism may outweigh those of any practical alternative, in our view such circumstances do not exist in the United Kingdom. We believe that to most people a federal system would appear strange and artificial. It would not provide continuity with the past or sufficient flexibility for the future. It would be dominated by the overwhelming political importance and wealth of England. The English Parliament would rival the United Kingdom Federal Parliament; and in the Federal Parliament the representation of England could hardly be scaled down in such a way as to enable it to be outvoted by Scotland, Wales and Northern Ireland. A United Kingdom Federation of the four countries, with a Federal Parliament and provincial Parliaments…is not, therefore, a realistic proposition (*ibid.*, paras 530–31).

Devolution to Scotland, Wales and Northern Ireland

As has already been explained, the government which took office following the General Election of May 1997 was committed to a programme of constitutional reform. Included in its agenda were proposals for the creation of elected assemblies in Scotland and Wales. Popular approval for these was secured in a series of referenda conducted in 1997 and 1998.

The Scottish Parliament

Background

The government's White Paper, 'Scotland's Parliament', was published on 24 July 1997. In a referendum of Scottish electors on its proposals, 74.3 per cent were in favour with 65.5 per cent also in favour of vesting the Parliament with limited tax-varying powers. The referendum turnout was 60.4 per cent. The first elections for the Scottish Parliament were held on 6 May 1999, with the first meeting of the Parliament taking place on 12 May.

Creation

Statutory authority for the establishing and working of the Scottish Parliament was provided by the Scotland Act 1998. The framework for Scottish self-government as contained therein is as follows.

Composition and election

The Parliament is composed of 129 members. Seventy-three are directly elected from existing parliamentary constituencies by simple majority vote (s 1). A further 56 members are elected by proportional representation from eight regional constituencies. These are the same constituencies used for elections to the European Parliament. Each regional constituency returns seven members (s 1 and Sched 1).

Electors cast two votes each – one for a constituency candidate and one for either an individual regional candidate or for a regional party list (ss 6, 7 and 8).

Persons disqualified from the House of Commons are disqualified from membership of the Scottish Parliament. Peers of the realm, ordained priests and ministers of religion are eligible, however, as are European Union citizens resident in the United Kingdom (ss 15 and 16).

Duration and dissolution

The Parliament will sit for fixed terms of four years. In between such 'ordinary' general elections an 'extraordinary' general election may occur where:

(a) the Parliament so resolves by a majority of two-thirds of its total membership;
(b) the First Minister resigns and is not replaced within 28 days (i.e. the Parliament is unable to form an alternative administration) (ss 2, 3 and 46).

Legislative authority

Laws enacted by the Scottish Parliament are valid only so far as they relate to matters within its legislative competence and are compatible with European Community law and the Human Rights Act 1998 (s 29). Issues put specifically beyond the competence of the Assembly are known as 'reserved matters'. These extend to the Crown, Parliament and the constitution, foreign and European affairs, defence and national security, and immigration and nationality. Beyond these limitations the validity of an enactment is not open to question solely on the ground of procedural error during its parliamentary stages (s 28).

Questions of competence and validity are determined by the Judicial Committee of the Privy Council upon reference thereto either by the Advocate-General for Scotland or the Lord Advocate (s 33).

Power is also given to the Secretary of State for Scotland to prohibit any Scottish Bill from being submitted for the Royal Assent where there are reasonable grounds to believe that it would be incompatible with any international obligations, the interests of defence or national security, or would have an adverse effect on the law relating to any reserved matter (s 35).

In terms of its internal proceedings the Parliament has power to require the attendance of any person to give evidence relating to any matter within its competence and to require the production of any documentation relating to the same over which the person has control (s 23).

The Scottish Parliament's proceedings and authorised publications relating thereto attract absolute privilege for the purposes of the law of defamation (s 41). Qualified privilege extends to fair and accurate reports of the same (Defamation Act 1996, s 15 and Sched 1).

The executive

This consists of:

(a)   the First Minister;
(b)   such other Ministers as he/she may appoint;
(c)   the Lord Advocate and the Solicitor-General for Scotland (s 44).

The First Minister is to be a person who commands a majority among members of the Parliament. He/she will appoint Ministers from members of the Parliament with its approval (s 47).

The activities of Scottish Ministers are subject to restrictions similar to those applying to the legislative power. Hence Scottish Ministers are forbidden from making any subordinate legislation or taking any other action incompatible with the law of the European Community or the Human Rights Act 1998 (s 57). In addition, the Secretary of State for Scotland is given authority to prohibit the making or execution of any decision or subordinate legislation reasonably believed to be incompatible with any international obligations and to revoke any subordinate legislation reasonably believed to be incompatible with the interests of defence or national security or which modifies and, which it is reasonably believed, has adverse effect on the law relating to any reserved matter (ss 57 and 58).

The Welsh Assembly

Background

The government's proposals for the above were published on 22 July 1997 in its White Paper, 'A Voice for Wales'. These were approved in a referendum on 18 September 1997. The first elections to the Assembly were held on 6 May 1999. Its first meeting took place on 12 May 1999. Authority for creation of the Assembly is contained in the Government of Wales Act 1998.

Composition, election and duration

The Welsh Assembly is composed of 40 constituency members and 20 regional members (s 2 and Sched 1). Elections take place every four years (s 3). Each elector casts two votes – one for a constituency member and one for either a regional candidate or a regional party list (ss 4 and 5). Constituency members are elected by the simple majority system. Regional members are returned by the additional member system of proportional representation (ss 6 and 7).

The general disqualifications applying to the House of Commons are applicable to membership of the Welsh Assembly (s 12). Disputes as to qualifications are dealt with by the High Court (s 14).

Powers and functions

The Assembly is not possessed of any primary legislative power but has the right to be consulted by the Secretary of State for Wales concerning any proposed legislation of the Westminster government which may have implications for Wales (s 31). Otherwise, the Assembly may have transferred to it:

(a) any function so far exercisable by a Minister of the Crown in relation to Wales, including powers to make subordinate legislation (s 22);

(b) any or all of the functions of a Welsh Health Authority or other public body specified in Sched 4 to the Act.

The Assembly has no power to make any subordinate legislation or take any other action incompatible with European Community law or the Human Rights Act 1998 (ss 106 and 107). Also, a Minister of the Crown may prohibit any proposed action incompatible with any international obligations (s 108).

The Welsh ombudsman has the power to investigate complaints relating to administrative action taken by the Assembly or other Welsh public authorities (s 111).

The Assembly has authority to require any person to attend its proceedings for the purpose of giving evidence and to require the production of documents relating to the same (s 74). Absolute privilege for the purposes of the law of defamation applies to its proceedings and to authorised reports of the same (s 77). Qualified privilege extends to other fair and accurate reports of its proceedings (e.g. newspaper reports) (s 77 and Defamation Act 1996, s 15 and Sched 1).

The executive

The Welsh executive committee consists of the Assembly First Secretary and other Assembly Secretaries appointed by him/her (s 56). The First Secretary is elected by the Assembly (s 53). In the areas for which they are responsible, the activities of each Assembly Secretary is scrutinised by Assembly subject committees which, in their composition, shall, 'so far as it is practicable', reflect the 'balance of parties in the Assembly' (s 57).

The committee system

In addition to the above, the Assembly is to establish and maintain committees for:

(a) scrutinising Welsh subordinate legislation (s 58);
(b) auditing the expenditure of finance under the Assembly's control (s 60);
(c) advising about matters affecting North Wales and the other Welsh regions when the boundaries of these have been drawn (s 61).

The Northern Ireland Assembly

Background

Creation of the Assembly was one of the central pillars of the Good Friday Agreement concluded on 10 April 1998. The Agreement was supported by 71.2 per cent of those voting in the referendum of 22 May 1998. The first meeting of the Assembly took place on 1 July 1998, when it elected its First and Deputy First Ministers.

The statutory framework for the Assembly was provided by the Northern Ireland Act 1998. The Act restated Northern Ireland's constitutional guarantee as part of the United Kingdom and provides that this status shall not be altered without the consent of a majority of the people of Northern Ireland voting in a border poll (s 1).

Election, composition and duration

The Assembly is composed of 108 members. Elections are to be held every four years (s 31). Within such periods, however, an 'extraordinary election' may take place if so resolved by at least two-thirds of the Assembly's membership (s 32). Members of the Assembly are elected from the existing eighteen Westminster constituencies. Each constituency returns six members according to the single transferable vote (s 33).

Disqualifications apply according to the provisions of the Northern Ireland Assembly Disqualification Act 1975 (s 36). Disputes as to qualification are to be dealt with by the Northern Ireland High Court (s 38).

Legislative and other powers

Legislation enacted by the Assembly is not valid if it is outside its competence as prescribed by the 1998 Act. That is, if it:

(a) relates to the law of any country or territory outside Northern Ireland;
(b) deals with an excepted or reserved matter (Scheds 2 and 3);
(c) is incompatible with the European Convention on Human Rights;
(d) is incompatible with European Community law;
(e) discriminates between persons on religious or political grounds (s 6).

Excepted matters are areas of legislative jurisdiction which are unlikely to be transferred to the competence of the Assembly. This list includes such matters as the Crown, Parliament and constitution of the United Kingdom; parliamentary elections, including those for the Assembly itself; international relations and those within the European Union; the defence of the realm; the armed forces; nationality and immigration; and national security.

Reserved matters are those which may be transferred by order of the Secretary of State to the Assembly depending on the political circumstances. The principal reserved matters are those relating to policing and the maintenance of law and order.

The Attorney-General for Northern Ireland may refer questions of validity for determination by the Judicial Committee of the Privy Council (s 11). The Assembly may also seek the opinion of the Northern Ireland Human Rights Commission as to the compatibility of particular Bills with the requirements of human rights obligations (s 13).

Bills passed by the Assembly are submitted for Royal Assent by the Secretary of State for Northern Ireland. A Bill may not be submitted if it appears to be outside the Assembly's competence or if it is the subject of a reference to the Privy Council. The Secretary of State may also refuse to submit any Bill which deals with an excepted or reserved matter (i.e. matters which, unlike excepted matters, may be transferred to the Assembly, see Sched 3) or which contains a provision which would be incompatible with any international obligations, the interests of defence or national security, the protection of safety or public order, or which would have an adverse effect 'on the operation of the single market in goods and services within the United Kingdom' (s 14).

Where 30 or more members of the Assembly so petition on any matter to be voted on (a 'Petition of Concern'), the vote on that matter requires 'cross-community support' (s 42), viz:

(a) a majority of all those voting and of both the designated Nationalists and Unionists voting; or
(b) 60 per cent of all those voting, including 40 per cent of the Nationalists voting and 40 per cent of the Unionists voting (s 4).

The Assembly is empowered to require any person to attend its proceedings to give evidence and to produce any documents relating thereto (s 44). Failure to do so constitutes an offence (s 45).

Absolute privilege in defamation applies to 'the making of a statement in the Assembly' and to 'the publication of a statement under the Assembly's authority' (s 50). Other fair and accurate reports of its proceedings are protected by qualified privilege (Defamation Act 1996, s 15 and Sched 1).

The executive

This is headed by a First Minister and a Deputy First Minister elected jointly with the support of:

(a) a majority of all Assembly members;
(b) a majority of Nationalist Assembly members;
(c) a majority of Unionist Assembly members.

Should either of the above Ministers resign, the other also ceases to hold office (s 16). The executive also includes ten other Ministers determined jointly by the First and Deputy First Minister and approved by the Assembly with cross-community support (s 18). Party representation in the executive reflects the principal political groupings in the Assembly according to the formula contained in s 18.

Members of the executive have no power to make any subordinate legislation or take any other action incompatible with European Community law or the European Convention on Human Rights (s 24). In addition, the Secretary of State may prohibit the making of any such legislation or any other action, which would not be consistent with any international obligations.

Ministers may be excluded from office, and entire political parties from the Assembly, if the Assembly resolves that the Minister or party 'is not committed to non-violence and exclusively peaceful and democratic means'. Such exclusion will be of twelve months' duration (s 30).

Human rights and discrimination

The Act creates two supervisory bodies in the area of human rights and discrimination. These are:

(a) the Northern Ireland Human Rights Commission (s 68);
(b) the Equality Commission of Northern Ireland (s 73).

The principal functions of the Human Rights Commission are to:

(a) keep under review the adequacy and effectiveness in Northern Ireland of the law and practice relating to the protection of human rights and to advise the Secretary of State and Assembly in related matters;
(b) to assist those bringing legal proceedings in human rights matters;
(c) to generally promote awareness and understanding of the importance of human rights (ss 68, 69 and 70).

The Equality Commission will take over the functions of the Fair Employment Commission for Northern Ireland, the Equal Opportunities Commission for Northern Ireland, the Commission for Racial Equality for Northern Ireland and the Northern Ireland Disability Council.

Further protection for human rights and equality issues is provided by s 75, which imposes a duty on all public bodies in Northern Ireland to have due regard to the need to promote equality of opportunity between persons of different religious belief, political opinion, racial group, age, marital status or sexual orientation, between men and women generally, between persons with a disability and persons without, and between persons with dependants and those without. Discrimination by a public body on the grounds of religion or politics is a civil offence remedied by damages and/or injunction (s 76).

CONSTITUTIONAL MONARCHY

Definition

The term refers to a monarchy which exercises its responsibilities subject to the constitution. In the British context this means that the monarchy accepts the limitations imposed upon it by statute, convention and the common law. It presupposes, therefore, a monarchy which retains its status and symbolic importance but which is no longer directly involved in the political process.

Evolution

It was not always thus. English monarchs were once very much involved in the practicalities of government. Even after the events of 1689 had demonstrated that the throne was held at the will of Parliament, individual monarchs continued to exercise considerable influence at least until the earlier part of the nineteenth century. Queen Victoria (1837–1901) also attempted to influence policy and appointments and was not averse to expressing partisan political views in matters relating to national affairs. As, however, the influence and status of Parliament increased with the extension of the franchise, and it became accepted that the prime political responsibility of ministers was owed to the representative assembly rather than the Monarch, the latter's political significance began to diminish. The change to genuine constitutional monarchy was therefore almost imperceptible and has never been recognised or expressed in any formal sense.

The Monarch's formal role

The residue of former days is that the Monarch is still recognised as Head of State, Head of the Commonwealth, Monarch of those Commonwealth countries which are not republics, Head of the Church of England and Commander-in-Chief of the armed forces. The terminology of monarchy also has continued to pervade the British system of government. Hence the government is Her Majesty's Government, its main parliamentary rival is Her Majesty's Loyal Opposition, ministers are the Queen's Ministers, central government employees are Crown servants and justice is dispensed in the Royal Courts of Law. Even the fiction that the government exists merely to advise the Monarch is preserved by the Prime Minister's weekly audiences with the Queen.

Constitutional crises and residual royal discretion

Despite the above, however, and the United Kingdom's modern status as a liberal democracy, the Monarch, in strictly legal terms, retains a great deal of power extending, *inter alia*, to appointing the Prime Minister, summoning and dissolving Parliament, assenting to legislation and to making declarations of war (for further details see Chapter 12: The Royal Prerogative).

The only significant reduction in the powers which attach to the Monarch (the royal prerogative) was effected by the Bill of Rights 1689 (see below). The expectation is, however, that the prerogative will be used in accordance with convention – the principal requirement being that the powers will be exercised on the advice of the Prime Minister speaking on behalf of the government. This, in turn, presumes that such advice will be given in ways which uphold the constitution and other vital national interests. Should this not be the case then it has been suggested that the Monarch might still retain a degree of personal discretion to use the prerogative in ways which best served these concerns. Given, however, that public trust and confidence in the institution depends on the Monarch remaining aloof from ordinary political issues, it is unlikely that such intervention would be contemplated except in the most extreme circumstances. Informed speculation about what these circumstances might be has tended to be restricted to the power to grant or refuse a dissolution of Parliament (the prerogative of dissolution). Here, although generally accepted that a decision to dissolve Parliament without or in opposition to prime ministerial wishes is now almost inconceivable, tentative support may be found for the view that a dissolution might still be refused if:

(a) an alternative and viable government could be formed from the existing Parliament (or at very least, the grant delayed while deliberations to this end were pursued);
(b) the request was to be made during a period of grave national emergency, e.g. war time.

It is also not beyond the bounds of remoteness that the Monarch could be drawn into the political process should the electorate return a 'hung' Parliament (i.e. one in which no single party had an overall majority). In this scenario the convention requiring the Monarch to appoint as Prime Minister the person commanding a majority in the House of Commons would not be immediately applicable. Royal participation, presumably with the support of advisers and senior representatives from the major parties, would therefore be necessary to broker some sort of coalition prepared to unite behind a person whose appointment as Prime Minister would then follow.

The Monarchy's modern relevance

Monarchy in the United Kingdom has both advocates and detractors. Those who tend to favour the institution stress what they perceive to be the crucial position of the Monarch, not just in the constitutional hierarchy, but also in the very social and cultural consciousness of the nation. The institution, it is said, has helped to sustain the traditional inclination towards strong central government. It has encouraged a sense of national identity and unity which transcends political divisions. In time of war and national emergency it has provided a focal point of patriotism and loyalty and, on a more continuous basis, has lent a sense of dignity to the process of government which has given added authority and status to those who carry it out. On a wider international basis it has provided a uniquely prestigious and dignified ceremonial figurehead around which Commonwealth nations can unite and which adds an extra dimension to the head of state's ambassadorial role.

In more tangible or practical political terms reference has also been made to the fact that the present Monarch has been served by no less than ten Prime Ministers in a reign which has extended over five decades. All of these administrations have, therefore, been able to benefit from her advice and experience. Direct influence is hard to prove but this may represent yet another of the many subtle forces in the constitution's complex and informal structure which underpin and reinforce its central cultural imperatives.

For the sake of balance, however, some attention should be given to those more critical perspectives. Hence the Monarch has been accused of personifying and symbolising the class structure and the belief that the right to participate in the process of government may be inherited rather than granted by popular will. Greater concentration on, and media exposure of the personal lives of members of the Royal Family, accompanied by a feeling in some quarters that not all its members have conducted themselves according to popular expectations, also appears to have damaged the mystique of monarchy and affected respect for it.

For all this, evidence to date suggests that any increased dissatisfaction has not yet crystallised into a significant level of popular support for replacing the monarchy with some other form of head of state (e.g. a presidency). Reform of the monarchy may therefore be on the agenda, but it appears that its abolition, as yet, is not.

In 1992, in response to some of these concerns and to criticisms of the Royal Family's financial status and immunities, it was announced that, in future, Civil List payments would be requested in respect of the Queen and Prince Philip only; further that the Queen would take responsibility for supporting the activities of other members of the Royal Family and that both she and the Prince of Wales would pay tax on their private incomes.

BICAMERAL SOVEREIGN PARLIAMENT

Meaning

A Parliament with two chambers or 'houses' may be described as bicameral. In the USA these are the House of Representatives and the Senate; in France, the National Assembly and the Senate; in the Republic of Ireland, the Dáil and the Seanad.

The two chambers of the United Kingdom Parliament are the House of Commons and the House of Lords – the unique feature being that the latter is entirely unelected and until the House of Lords Act 1999 the majority of members succeeded to their seats by right of birth. The elected chamber, the House of Commons, is regarded as having the greater authority. This is given constitutional recognition by the convention that, in the event of a conflict (e.g. concerning amendments to a Bill), the Lords should 'give way' and by the Parliament Acts 1911 and 1949 which allow Bills to be enacted without the consent of the upper chamber.

The word 'sovereignty' is generally understood as referring to an ultimate source of authority. In most democratic states it is possible to distinguish between what may be called political sovereignty and legal sovereignty. Political sovereignty or ultimate political power, it may be argued, remains with the people (or, at least, the electorate). Indeed, where a written constitution has been approved by referendum, it may be regarded as an expression of that sovereign will (viz. in terms of the way the people wish to be governed). Legal sovereignty, on the other hand, has a somewhat narrower meaning and is generally understood as referring to the location of supreme legal authority or legitimation within the state. In the United Kingdom this is Parliament or, in traditional language, the Queen in Parliament (i.e. Commons, Lords and Monarch). In some states, as in the USA, legal sovereignty may vest in the written constitution itself; hence the power of the US Supreme Court to invalidate legislative and executive actions, including those of the Congress and the President, inconsistent with the founding constitutional document. In others, as in France, the distinction between political and legal sovereignty may be more difficult to draw. Thus the French Constitution provides that 'national sovereignty belongs to the people which shall exercise it through its representatives and by way of referendums' (Art 3). This helps to explain the French tendency to refer major constitutional issues to the people in contrast to the British tradition of seeking no greater authority than that of Parliament.

REPRESENTATIVE DEMOCRACY

Meaning

This may be defined as a system of government in which the composition of the legislature and the political complexion of the executive are determined by the popular will expressed in regular and free elections and where, between elections, the government is expected to address popular concerns as expressed by elected representatives. Pure democracy, where all citizens are directly involved in political decision-making, for reasons of scale, is not possible in a modern state. Autocracy or, alternatively, government which represents only a small section of the populace (as in the United Kingdom prior to the extension of the franchise), is now culturally and ideologically unacceptable. Representative democracy may be seen, therefore, as an attempted compromise between these extremes.

The United Kingdom approach is for both the legislature and the executive to be reconstituted by each general election. These are not elected separately as in many other states. Successful candidates in general elections become Members of Parliament. None are directly elected to be head or members of the government. By convention the government is formed from the party or coalition which has won a majority of seats in the House of Commons (except in the rare cases where a minority government is formed from the largest single party without an overall majority). The leader of this party or coalition then becomes the Prime Minister and he or she chooses the other members of the government.

The effectiveness and validity of this system is underpinned by certain essential prerequisites.

Universal adult suffrage

The exact details of the franchise, i.e. those who have the right to vote, are set out below (see Chapter 6). Suffice to say for the moment that, subject to certain disqualifications found in the Representation of the People Acts, all British and Commonwealth citizens, and citizens of the Commonwealth and Irish citizens resident in the United Kingdom, have the right to vote.

Regular elections and secret ballot

Granting all citizens the right to vote is of little use unless the right can be exercised and in a way which reduces the fear of intimidation or reprisal. In the British system these needs are addressed by the Parliament Act 1911, which provides for elections at least every five years (previously every seven, Septennial Act 1714), and the Secret Ballot Act 1872.

Party political plurality and freedom of speech and assembly

Even the right to vote regularly and secretly is reduced in democratic value unless there is a free and wide choice of parties and representatives to vote for and those engaged in the political process are able to meet, debate and criticise each other's policies and objectives.

The general rule pertaining in the United Kingdom is that political parties and cause groups have the right to exist and participate in national and local affairs providing they do not seek to further their objectives by violent means. Membership of certain paramilitary organisations is, therefore, prohibited by the Terrorism Act 2000 (see Chapter 23).

It is also possible for political matters to be debated freely unless the words used might, *inter alia*, provoke violence, inflame racial hatred, incite disaffection amongst the police or members of the armed forces or amount to sedition, blasphemy, defamation, or contempt of court.

The extent of the freedom of assembly in the United Kingdom, i.e. the right to meet for the purposes of such debate, is a matter of greater uncertainty. This will be considered in more detail in the chapter devoted to civil liberties. However, the general premiss underlying the relevant legal rules is that the right exists unless serious disorder, damage to property or disruption to the life of the community is the likely result.

The electoral system

An obvious essential of representative democracy is a system of electoral law and practice which seeks to:

(a) control electoral abuses (e.g. bribery, intimidation, etc.);
(b) ensure that parties and candidates for election are given fair access to and treatment by the media;
(c) guarantee that the 'weight' or value of each vote is relatively equal;
(d) ensure that party political preferences expressed in the election are reflected in the composition of Parliament.

Electoral abuses in the United Kingdom are dealt with by the Representation of the People Acts (principally that of 1983) which specify a wide range of corrupt and illegal electoral practices. These are criminal offences for which the perpetrator may be fined or imprisoned, and, if committed by the successful candidate, may invalidate his or her election.

Provisions also exist to minimise bias and unfair discrimination by the broadcast media. These may be found in the Representation of the People Act 1983, the Broadcasting Acts 1990 and 1996, and the licensing conditions of the BBC. No such restraints, however, apply to the press or other written comment.

The problem of the differential weighting of votes was dealt with by the Boundary Commissions for England, Wales, Scotland and Northern Ireland, operating according to rules in the Parliamentary Constituencies Act 1986. The functions of the Boundary Commissions were transferred to the Electoral Commission by the Political Parties, Elections and Referendums Act 2000. Clearly, if there are 120,000 voters in one constituency and only 30,000 in another, votes in the latter have greater weight or value. Only 15,001 would secure an absolute majority; 60,001 would be required in the former. The Boundary Commissions, therefore, made recommendations for the redrawing of constituency boundaries every ten to fifteen years and, in so doing, attempted to ensure that the numbers of electors in different constituencies approximated to the electoral quota for their part of the United Kingdom (number of electors ÷ number of constituencies) and that 'excessive disparities' between the numbers of voters in different constituences was avoided. The work of the Boundary Commissions will henceforth be undertaken by four Boundary Committees under the directions of the Electoral Commission (*ibid.* s 6).

The method of voting in the United Kingdom is usually referred to as the simple majority or 'first past the post' system. It does not result in proportional representation, i.e. close proximity between the proportion of the vote cast for a particular party and the proportion of seats that party acquires in the new Parliament. This is an aspect of the United Kingdom's version of representative democracy which attracts particular controversy. The 1979, 1983, 1987 and 1992 elections were all 'won' by the Conservative party. On each occasion the party secured more than 57 per cent of the seats in the House of Commons. On no occasion, however, did the Conservatives poll more than 43 per cent of the votes cast or 32 per cent of the total votes of all the electorate. In the 1997 General Election the Labour party secured 63.5 per cent of the seats for just 43.2 per cent of the vote. In 2001, 42 per cent of the vote gave the same party 413 seats, equivalent to 62.7 per cent of the seats available. In purely representative terms, therefore, the voting system may be regarded as inaccurate.

Some alleged defects

Other criticisms of the United Kingdom's version of representative democracy have pointed to the powerful influences within the constitutional structure which have little to do with popular opinion. The Monarch, the House of Lords and the judiciary are all unelected. The civil service is said to have an undue influence on government policy and decision-making. The government is said to be unnecessarily secretive and to have at its disposal a wide range of powers which derive from the Monarch rather than Parliament (the royal prerogative) and which may be exercised, therefore, without parliamentary consent or approval.

RESPONSIBLE GOVERNMENT

Meaning

This should not be understood as suggesting that the British government can always be expected to behave in a sensible and reasonable way. It refers instead to the fact that the government in the United Kingdom is answerable to Parliament for its stewardship of the nation's affairs. This concept of responsibility is founded on two constitutional conventions: collective and individual ministerial responsibility.

Collective ministerial responsibility

This encapsulates the following rules.

(a) In Parliament and in public all ministers must support government policy. Should a minister feel unable to do so, and wish to speak freely on a particular issue, he/she is expected to resign.
(b) Ministers should not divulge the contents of Cabinet or ministerial deliberations.
(c) If defeated in a vote of confidence in the House of Commons, the government must resign.

This requirement that the government should resign if so defeated is part of the very essence of the British constitution and the relationship between government and Parliament. In states where the executive and parliament are elected separately (e.g. the USA and France), the tenure of the government may not be directly affected by adverse votes in legislature. In the United Kingdom, however, the government must maintain the confidence of the elected assembly which retains the ultimate power of dismissal over any administration whose competence or propriety is deemed beyond redemption.

It is, however, a power which, for party political reasons and the need for government stability, Parliament uses extremely sparingly. Only three governments resigned pursuant to adverse confidence votes in the twentieth century (in 1924 (twice), and 1979). On each of these occasions the government was in a minority. No majority government has been put out of office since 1885. It follows that a government with a secure majority is in little danger of dismissal. The power is, however, by no means obsolete or politically moribund. It remains a potentially potent reminder of the government's obligation to explain and justify its actions to the nation's representatives and to secure parliamentary legitimacy for the implementation of its policies and decisions.

Individual ministerial responsibility

This contains the rule that each minister is responsible to Parliament for the conduct of his/her department or sphere of responsibility and for all actions and decisions relating thereto. The minister is expected to 'take the blame' for mistakes and errors of judgement and not to 'point the finger' at individual civil servants. In the final analysis, in cases of significant failure, the minister is expected to resign.

It is increasingly apparent, however, that compliance with this convention is largely a matter of political expediency rather than of honour or constitutional propriety. Hence, if the government and its parliamentary party are prepared to support a minister who is 'under fire', it is unlikely that the minister will resign. If, however, for whatever reasons, and these may have little to do with the specific issue of controversy, this support is not forthcoming, the minister may feel little option but to leave the government.

THE SEPARATION OF POWERS

Meaning

Writing in 1748, the French jurist, Montesquieu, argued that 'there can be no liberty' and there would be an end of everything 'if the legislative, executive and judicial powers of government were to be exercised by the same person or authority' (*L'Esprit des Lois*, 1748). Similar sentiments had been expressed previously by the English political philosopher, John Locke. He wrote that it 'may be too great a temptation to human frailty...for the same person to have the power of making laws, to have also in their hands the power to execute them, whereby they may exempt themselves from obedience to the laws they make, and suit the law both in its making and execution, to make their own private advantage' (*Second Treatise of Civil Government*, 1690).

The American model

These teachings had a marked effect on the makers of the American Constitution of 1787. They sought to provide a constitutional framework which separated the composition and functions of the three principal organs of state (executive: the presidency; legislature: the Congress; judiciary: the Supreme Court) as far as was compatible with governmental practicability. Hence the President is not elected at the same time as the Congress. He does not have a seat in the Congress and is not directly answerable to it. By the same token, members of Congress are not appointed to the executive. The President's election is for a fixed term (two four-year terms maximum) with the result that the Congress has no power to remove him from office (unless through impeachment by the Senate for 'treason, bribery, high crimes or...misdemeanours': Art 2(4)). The President and his cabinet do not control the business of the Congress in the way that the government in the United Kingdom is able to dominate Parliament. He may recommend legislation but cannot ensure that it is enacted. He may veto legislation but such veto, may, in turn, be overridden by majorities of two-thirds in the House of Representatives and the Senate. Members of the Supreme Court are appointed by the President but his nominations may be overruled by the Senate. Supreme Court judges do not sit in Congress and may not be members of the executive. The Supreme Court, as stated, may invalidate unconstitutional acts of the President or Congress (*Marbury v Madison* (1803) 5 US (Cranch) 137).

The existence of rules regulating the relationships between President, Congress and Supreme Court and, in particular, giving the Congress ultimate power to overcome the President, illustrates that, although the United States model constitutes a clearer separation of powers than that pertaining domestically, absolute separation does not exist, nor was it ever intended. It can be seen, therefore, that the principal political difference between the American and British systems lies in the relationship between the executive and the legislature. Responsible government, in the British sense, is not replicated in the American system. On the other hand, unlike his British counterparts, an American President will seldom be able to regard the legislature as a compliant ally in the execution of his policies. Hence, if a President is to be anything more than a 'lame-duck', an effective working relationship with Congress is essential.

Negotiation and compromise is, therefore, built into the system; it is the only way it can work. The ideal of the separation of powers, viz. a balancing of the authority of state institutions is thus achieved in a way which is at least as effective as that in the United Kingdom.

The British model: limited separation of powers

To the extent that the United Kingdom has a separation of powers, it is much less distinct than that just described. Clear overlaps both in terms of personnel and function between the three organs of government may be discerned.

Principal overlaps in personnel

(a) The Lord Chancellor presides over the House of Lords in both its legislative and judicial capacities. He is also a Cabinet Minister. The other Law Lords likewise participate in both the judicial and legislative work of the upper House.
(b) The majority of government ministers will be members of the House of Commons (the Ministerial and Other Salaries Act 1975 restricts the number of MPs in receipt of ministerial salaries to 95). Other ministers will have seats in the House of Lords.

Restrictions, however, do exist. Thus both civil servants and members of the judiciary are disqualified from membership of the House of Commons. Also, by convention, lay members of the House of Lords may not participate in its judicial functions.

Principal functional overlaps

(a) By definition the Lord Chancellor and other Law Lords perform legislative and judicial functions. The Lord Chancellor in his executive guise is head of a large government department responsible, *inter alia*, for the administration of the courts and the legal aid scheme (thus involving him in decisions relating to public expenditure and 'value for money' in the public services). His patronage extends to the appointment of all lay and stipendiary magistrates, Recorders and Assistant Recorders (Crown Court judges). Circuit and High Court judges are appointed by the Monarch on the Lord Chancellor's advice. Court of Appeal judges (Lord Justices of Appeal) and Law Lords (Lords of Appeal in Ordinary) are appointed by the Monarch on the Prime Minister's advice but the Lord Chancellor will invariably be consulted.
(b) Government ministers direct the activities of central government departments and, it has been alleged, through their majority in the House of Commons exert a controlling influence over its timetable, business and legislative output (over 90 per cent of government Bills receive the Royal Assent). In addition the government legislates in the form of regulations contained in statutory instruments and Orders in Council issued under the authority of an enabling or 'parent' Act (delegated or subordinate legislation). Nor is the executive's judicial role confined to the activities of the Lord Chancellor since it is also heavily involved in the process of adjudication through the modern proliferation of administrative tribunals and inquiries (see Chapter 24).

Checks and balances

In response to these apparent contradictions of the doctrine, it has been argued that the restraints which operate between the different institutions of government (the 'checks and balances') are sufficient to guard against the types of abuse to which the separation of powers is directed.

Restraints on the executive

(a) Attention has already been drawn to the conventions of collective and individual ministerial responsibility and to Parliament's conventional authority to make a government resign.

(b) The use of statutory and prerogative powers by government ministers is subject to the supervisory jurisdiction of the courts. The validity of actions and decisions for which there is no legal authority or source (*ultra vires*) or which are taken in flagrant abuse of the requirements of procedural fairness (natural justice) may be challenged through an application for judicial review.

(c) The government must submit itself to the electorate at regular intervals. In theory, at least, this is expected to make ministers sensitive and responsive to public opinion.

(d) The House of Lords retains the power to veto any bill purporting to extend the life of Parliament (Parliament Act 1911, s 2(1)). This is to protect against government use of its Commons majority to enact legislation postponing the next election thereby keeping the government in power. The credibility of this 'check' is, however, qualified to some extent by the fact that the upper House is unelected and has a large 'built-in' Conservative majority.

(e) Subject to what has already been said about the meaning of constitutional monarchy, it remains legally possible for the Monarch to use the royal prerogative to deal with a government which is behaving unconstitutionally.

Restraints on Parliament

(a) Despite its legislative authority, Parliament is not, in a political sense, a unified body. Rather it is a crucible for conflicting political interests. This operates as a force for moderation for, without a considerable degree of 'behind the scenes' cooperation and compromise between political parties, Parliament would be unable to function effectively.

(b) The composition of the House of Commons is, of course, determined ultimately by the electorate.

(c) Following the decision *R v Secretary of State for Transport, ex parte Factortame Ltd (No. 2)* [1991] 1 AC 603, it now appears that English courts will refuse to apply Acts of Parliament which are inconsistent with European Community law.

(d) Acts of Parliament are subject to judicial interpretation; the assumption being that this is simply a matter of determining and applying Parliament's will. In this regard, however, the law reports are replete with examples of judicial 'creativity' – particularly in relation to loosely worded or ambiguous legislation. Many examples of this inarticulate legislative tension between Parliament and the courts are considered in the pages that follow.

Restraints on the judiciary

(a) Judicial decisions may be modified or rendered ineffective by legislation. Hence, when the House of Lords ruled that the Crown was bound to pay compensation for property destroyed by British Forces in World War II in order to deny it to the enemy (*Burmah Oil Co Ltd* v *The Lord Advocate* [1965] AC 75), this was quickly overturned by Act of Parliament (War Damages Act 1965).

(b) The final authority to dismiss a judge resides in Parliament since this can only be done with the consent of both Houses (see judicial independence, below).

An over-mighty executive?

Despite these various restraints, many still believe that the British constitution does not achieve an adequate balance between the three principal government institutions. Too much power, it is said, resides with the executive and is not subject to adequate controls. Parliament is dominated by the government which is drawn from the party with a majority in the House of Commons. There is no sovereign written constitution against which executive and legislative actions can be tested. There are, as yet, no regional assemblies and systems of administration exercising autonomous powers which might act as counterweights to the influence of central government. Also, in the absence of any genuine freedom of information ('sunshine') legislation, real decision-making is conducted in an atmosphere of remoteness and secrecy which inevitably hampers effective scrutiny by both Parliament and the media.

An independent judiciary?

According to the separation of powers and most contemporary concepts of liberal democracy, it is essential that judges are able to make their decisions free of political interference and fear of reprisal. If this is not so those who might wish to challenge the legality of executive actions would have little hope of their complaints being dealt with objectively.

This explains why the tenure and independence of senior judges is protected by the provisions in the Act of Settlement 1700, now re-enacted in the Supreme Court Act 1981, s 11 (for judges in the High Court and Court of Appeal) and the Appellate Jurisdiction Act 1876, s 6 (for the House of Lords), that judges hold office during good behaviour and may only be dismissed pursuant to resolutions (in the form of addresses to the Monarch) passed by both Houses of Parliament. Put simply, this means that although the executive appoints the judiciary it cannot, of its own volition, rid itself of a senior judge whose decisions and opinions may be regarded as an irritation.

Most commentators express Parliament's authority in this regard to be exclusive. It should be noted, however, that there are those (including the authors of Hood Phillips, *Constitutional and Administrative Law*) who suggest that the Crown might still be able to dismiss a judge without an address from Parliament for 'official misconduct, neglect of official duties, or (probably) conviction for a serious offence'.

The last and only occasion a judge was removed by parliamentary resolutions was in 1830 (Judge Jonah Barrington). This was for embezzling money which had been paid into court. The last time a motion for removal was put down was in 1973 and involved Sir John (now Lord) Donaldson, then President of the controversial and now defunct National Industrial Relations Court.

Judges may also lose office as a result of retirement (now set at the age of 70 by the Judicial Pensions and Retirement Act 1993), resignation, or incapacity (Supreme Court Act 1981, s 11).

The requirement for resolutions of both Houses of Parliament does not apply to the dismissal of judges below the High Court. Such judges may be dismissed by the Lord Chancellor but this discretion is used very sparingly.

The Act of Settlement reinforced judicial security of tenure by the requirement that judges' salaries should be 'ascertained and established' and not left to executive discretion. This is currently given practical effect by the Supreme Court Act 1981, s 12, which makes the moneys for judicial salaries a standing charge on the Consolidated Fund. In this way the payments are not subject to annual review or legislative renewal and are thus removed from the area of political controversy.

Rules underpinning judicial independence

(a) Stipendiary magistrates, circuit judges, and all those in the High Court, Court of Appeal and House of Lords are disqualified from membership of the House of Commons (House of Commons (Disqualification) Act 1975, s 1 and Sched 1).

(b) By convention ministers do not criticise judges or their decisions – although in recent times some have found it hard to resist doing so in response to parliamentary questions relating to controversial cases.

(c) The rules of debate in the House of Commons forbid criticism of a judge unless pursuant to a substantive motion for dismissal. Adverse comment on judicial decisions appears to be permissible providing this does not reflect on a judge's character or competence.

(d) Ministers and MPs are expected not to comment on that which is *sub-judice* (except where issues of major national importance are involved).

(e) Judges are immune from all civil liability in respect of what is said or done in the exercise of judicial functions (*Scott* v *Mansfield* (1868) LR 3 Ex 220).

(f) Any comment which impugns the impartiality of a judge may amount to a criminal contempt of court, as may any conduct or words calculated to interfere with the administration of justice.

Judicial neutrality

The existence of rules to protect judges from political interference does not guarantee that judicial decisions will be free from subliminal political influences. Judges, like the rest of us, are a product of their social environment and it is probably inevitable that their approach to certain issues will be influenced by the attitudes of the group from which their majority is drawn – in this case what has been called the social and educational élite.

This does not mean that they are prejudiced in a party political sense. It has been suggested, however, that they bring to bear on their decisions a political philosophy which prefers the existing distribution of social and economic influence.

> The judges here by their education and training and the pursuit of their profession as barristers, acquire a strikingly homogenous collection of attitudes, beliefs and principles, which to them represent the public interest. They do not always express it as such. But it is the lodestar by which they navigate (Griffith, *The Politics of the Judiciary*, 1991).

This is something which it is hard to prove or disprove. It cannot be denied, however, that judges in the United Kingdom are predominantly white, male and from the social and educational group indicated.

While of course it is impossible to eradicate entirely any effect such influences may have, certain rules do exist to try to preserve the necessary appearance of neutrality.

Rules underpinning judicial neutrality

(a) In addition to their statutory disqualification from the House of Commons, there is a convention that judges do not participate in political activities and (with the exception, of course, of the Lord Chancellor) refrain from expressing political views.
(b) Justice must be dispensed in public. The conduct of judges is, therefore, open to public scrutiny. Fair and balanced media reports of such proceedings are protected by the defence of qualified privilege.

THE RULE OF LAW

Meaning

This is neither a rule nor a law. It is now generally understood as a doctrine of political morality which concentrates on the role of law in securing the correct balance of rights and powers between individuals and the state in free and civilised societies.

Content

This has been variously described. In liberal democracies, however, the assumption is that adherence to the doctrine requires more than simply government according to law. Otherwise, in states where the executive controls the law-making process, it would be possible for the executive to secure whatever powers it saw fit and to have these phrased in the vaguest possible terms (see, for example, 'The Law for the Relief of the People and the Reich', 1933, which gave the Hitler regime the powers it needed to stifle free speech and opposition in order to enforce the policies of the Third Reich). Government according to law is, therefore, not necessarily equivalent to government under law and is perfectly compatible with the sort of ordered but unfree systems of government typical of dictatorships and military junta.

> Only in a country where the rule of law means more than formal, legal validity will subjects enjoy real protection from official tyranny and abuse (Mathews, *The Rule of Law in an Apartheid Society*).

Accordingly, some interpretations have sought to give the doctrine greater content. One approach has been to propose minimum standards in terms of the way laws are expressed and administered. Here the emphasis has tended to be on the need for rules and procedures which ensure that laws may be used for the protection of rights and not just as a means of legitimising the use of powers. Such conceptions may say very little, however, about the substantive nature and extent of the rights in question.

One of the most respected proponents of this approach is Joseph Raz. His procedurally orientated version of the doctrine, explained in 1977, contained eight postulates ('The Rule of Law and Its Virtues' (1977) 93 LQR 195).

1   The law should be general (i.e. not discriminate), prospective, open and clear.
2   The law should be relatively stable (i.e. should not be subject to frequent and unnecessary alteration).
3   Open, stable, clear and general rules should govern executive law-making (i.e. the law should identify the jurisdictional limits to the exercise of delegated legislative powers).
4   The independence of the judiciary should be guaranteed.
5   The application of the law should accord with the rules of natural justice (i.e. the rule against bias and the right to a fair hearing).
6   The courts should have a power of review over law-making and administrative action to ensure compliance with these principles.
7   The courts should be easily accessible (i.e. individual recourse to justice should not be hindered by excessive delays and expense).
8   The discretion of the crime preventing agencies should not be allowed to pervert the law (i.e. such agencies should not be able to choose which laws to enforce and when).

Other interpretations of the doctrine have gone beyond the requirements of form and procedure and have extended the doctrine to the recognition of certain liberal political values. Of these perhaps the most renowned was that propounded by the International Commission of Jurists in 1959 (usually referred to as the Declaration of Delhi). This declared that the purpose of all law should be respect for the 'supreme value of human personality' and that observance of the rule of law should entail:

(a)   the existence of representative government;
(b)   respect for the type of basic human freedoms contained in the United Nations' 1948 Universal Declaration of Human Rights and the 1950 European Convention on Human Rights;
(c)   absence of retrospective penal laws;
(d)   the right to bring proceedings against the state;
(e)   the right to a fair trial including the presumption of innocence, legal representation, bail and the right to appeal;
(f)   an independent judiciary;
(g)   adequate control of delegated legislation.

The 1959 Declaration also broke new ground by contemplating that, if the value of human personality was to be fully realised, it might not be enough to limit the protection of the law to traditional concepts of rights (i.e. freedom of the person, expression, association, etc.). It might also be necessary, it was suggested, for the state to have regard to man's 'economic and social needs in addition to his spiritual and political freedom'. Two years later, at their Lagos Conference in 1961, the International Commission gave more specific expression to these ideas.

> The Rule of Law is a dynamic concept which should be employed to safeguard and advance the will of the people and the political rights of the individual and to establish social, economic, educational and cultural conditions under which the individual may achieve his dignity and realise his legitimate aspirations in all countries, whether dependent or independent.

This clearly prescribes a contentious political role to the law and the law-making agencies and would appear to allow the judiciary the right to interpret legislation and formulate law in ways which might best achieve the objectives stipulated. This in turn, however, raises major questions about traditional conceptions of judicial neutrality and the extent to which judges are accountable for the exercise of their functions.

Dicey's conception

It is normal in studies of English constitutional law for the meaning of the rule of law to be considered by reference to the views of Professor A V Dicey published in 1885 (*Introduction to the Study of the Law of the Constitution*). He contended that the essential ingredients of the doctrine were already manifest in the British constitution. These were as follows.

Absence of arbitrary power

Arbitrary power is that which has no identifiable legal origins or limits. It is inherent in such notions as government by decree or the doctrine of state necessity. To Dicey such ideas were alien to the British constitutional tradition and had been roundly condemned as such in *Entick* v *Carrington* (1765) 19 St Tr 1030, where Cambden CJ refused to accept that a government minister, in the absence of any common law or statutory authority, had any power to grant warrants permitting entry and search of private premises. In more modern times this judicial aversion to arbitrariness was evident in the refusal by the Northern Ireland Court of Appeal to accept that British soldiers dealing with the emergency there should be exempt from the normal legal requirements for the execution of a valid arrest (*Kelly* v *Faulkner* [1973] NI 31).

Absence of wide discretionary power

Dicey felt that the powers of government should be clearly specified and predictable. He did not feel that public officials should be allowed a wide degree of choice in terms of when and how powers should be used. His was a *laissez-faire*, individualist view of the relationship between citizen and the state. To him the state was not simply a public benefactor. Except for its traditional responsibilities it represented a potential threat to the traditional personal and proprietary rights of the individual. Its activities were, therefore, to be confined as narrowly as possible while the individual was left to pursue his or her own destiny with the minimum of regulation and interference.

In the period Dicey expressed these views the positive role of the regulatory state was clearly not so well developed or understood as it was to become. It is generally accepted, however, that, even in his own time, Dicey understated the functions of both central and local government and the degree to which public officials were already engaged in the exercise of discretionary power – particularly in the spheres of housing and public health.

Dicey also appeared to underestimate the degree of discretionary power available to the government in the royal prerogative and paid little regard to the emergency powers for the government and containment of Ireland contained in a succession of nineteenth-century Coercion Acts.

Dicey's fears were not, however, completely without foundation. Hence, while it is clear that the modern state could not function efficiently without a wide range of discretionary powers, some of which may be phrased in wide subjective language, concerns remain over the extent to which such powers are subject to adequate parliamentary and judicial controls. As will become apparent, part of the modern problem relates to the inability of Parliament to scrutinise effectively the work of the vast departments of state and the reluctance of the courts to challenge the legality of executive decisions in certain areas of government activity, e.g. defence and national security.

No person to be punished except for a breach of law

This was another aspect of Dicey's rejection of arbitrary power. Penalties should only be imposed on an individual where a breach of an established legal rule had been proved in the ordinary courts of law. This was a proposition of considerable contemporary validity but again was affected by its author's rather idealistic view of the British system. By the time Dicey was writing, powers already existed to interfere with both personal and proprietary rights – regardless of the repository's behaviour – where this was in the public interest. These included the statutory powers of imprisonment without trial used in Ireland, those authorising the compulsory purchase of property for public works, and the wide prerogative powers relating to the keeping of the peace and the defence of the realm.

The notion that law-abiding citizens should be free of executive interference is still deeply embedded in the nation's political psyche. Statutory powers do exist, however, to detain terrorist suspects for up to seven days (Prevention of Terrorism Acts). Also the ultimate power of unlimited detention without trial has been used in both World Wars and in Northern Ireland; the last occasion being between 1971 and 1976. Compulsory detention of psychiatric patients is also authorised by the Mental Health Act 1983. Beyond this, the executive retains wide powers of compulsory purchase of property and the extensive prerogatives already mentioned.

The equal subjection of all classes to the ordinary law of the land

Dicey was implacably opposed to government officials having special legal privileges and immunities. He was particularly unimpressed by the French *droit administratif*, a separate system of administrative law and courts for dealing with alleged abuses by government personnel. Such matters, he felt, should be dealt with in the ordinary courts, thus avoiding partiality whether real or apparent.

It would not be true to say, however, either then or now, that English law treated those in government in exactly the same way as private citizens. Indeed, until the Crown Proceedings Act 1947, the Crown could not be sued in contract as of right (the government's permission was required (see Chapter 13)) and was not vicariously liable for the torts of its employees. Members of Parliament possessed, and still possess, extensive privileges, including complete legal immunity for that said in the conduct of parliamentary proceedings (see Chapter 10). Also, by virtue of the Diplomatic Privileges Act 1964 foreign diplomats in the United Kingdom are not subject to the full rigour of the law.

The constitution is the result of the ordinary law

Dicey's view was that civil liberties in the United Kingdom did not, as in many other states, derive from a constitutional document. They were, in effect, fundamental social traditions which had been recognised by the judiciary and given protection by the common law:

> ... with us the law of the constitution, the rules which in foreign countries naturally form part of a constitutional code, are not the source but the consequence of the rights of individuals, as defined and enforced by the courts.

He believed that it was this close link between the social origins of rights and their judicial articulation which gave the liberties of the subject in this country their necessary degree of permanence and stability. They were something which could not be interfered with except by a 'thorough revolution in the institutions and manners of the nation'.

As with the other elements of Dicey's understanding of the doctrine, these assertions have not met with universal approval. It has been said, for example, that Dicey underestimated the effectiveness of written constitutions in restraining executive power; also that he put too much faith in the ability and readiness of the judiciary to withstand a sovereign Parliament and to apply a positive libertarian perspective to the task of developing individual freedom. Thus it is not hard to find examples of major and permanent legislative incursions into the rights of individuals (e.g. the loss of the absolute right to silence occasioned by the Criminal Justice and Public Order Act 1994), or cases in which judicial protection of such rights has been criticised as ineffective or unimaginative (see *Malone* v *Metropolitan Police Commissioner* [1979] Ch 344; *Council of Civil Service Unions* v *Minister for the Civil Service* [1985] AC 374).

Practical impact of the rule of law

Despite any imperfections the importance of the rule of law is that it is a doctrine of considerable intellectual pedigree, dating back in embryonic form to the Greek city states, which provides a rational philosophical basis for the regulation of state power and the promotion of individual liberty. It represents, therefore, an ideological framework for the legislature and those who have to interpret the law. In this country it can be seen in particular operation in the principles of judicial review (see the finding of the House of Lords in *Roberts v Hopwood* [1925] AC 578, that there is no such thing in English law as an unfettered discretion) and in the judicial presumptions that, in the absence of a clear contrary intent, statutes should not be given retrospective effect or allowed to restrict established civil liberties.

It is also widely accepted that Dicey's understanding of the doctrine has reinforced suspicions about the ways in which other states deal with state power – particularly through written constitutions and specialised systems of administrative law.

References

Calvert (1985) *An Introduction to British Constitutional Law*, London: Financial Training.

Dicey (1989) *Introduction to the Study of the Law of the Constitution* (10th edn), ed. Wade, E.C.S., London: Macmillan.

Hood Phillips and Jackson (1997) *Hood Phillips and Jackson's Constitutional and Administrative Law* (8th edn), London: Sweet & Maxwell.

Locke (1956) *Second Treatise of Civil Government*, Oxford: Blackwell.

Montesquieu (1961) *L'Esprit des Lois*, Paris: Garnier Frères.

Raz (1977) 'The Rule of Law and its Virtues' (1977) 93 LQR 195.

Report of the Royal Commission on the Constitution 1973 (Cmnd 5460).

Further reading

Allen and Thompson (1996) *Cases and Materials on Constitutional and Administrative Law* (3rd edn), London: Blackstone, Chs 1 and 3.

Loveland (1996) *Constitutional Law: A Critical Introduction*, London: Butterworths, Chs 1 and 3.

Marston and Ward (1997) *Cases and Commentary on Constitutional and Administrative Law* (4th edn), London: Pitman Publishing, Chs 1 and 9.

Turpin (2002) *British Government and the Constitution* (5th edn), London: Butterworths.

Chapter 3

SOURCES OF CONSTITUTIONAL AND ADMINISTRATIVE LAW

INTRODUCTION

This chapter will concentrate on the constitutional source material provided by Acts of Parliament, judicial decisions and constitutional conventions. Reference will also be made to European Community law, the European Convention on Human Rights, the law and custom of Parliament and to books of authority.

Acts of Parliament and judicial decisions are the principal sources of the United Kingdom's system of constitutional and administrative law. Other important constitutional prescriptions may be found in conventions. Conventions are not laws. They are the non-legal rules of the constitution. Strictly speaking, therefore, they should be regarded as a source of the constitution but not of constitutional law.

LEGISLATION

Meaning

This consists of rules of law made by Parliament either directly in the form of statute (sometimes referred to as 'primary' legislation) or indirectly by those other authorities on which Parliament has conferred the power to legislate (delegated, subordinate or 'secondary' legislation).

It has been said that legislation is now the most important source of constitutional and administrative law. To the extent that this is so, it would tend to undermine many of the assumptions associated with the notion that the United Kingdom does not have a constitution in the formal written sense.

Classification

The following brief synopsis of some of the most important enactments in this context will serve to illustrate the significance of legislation in all major aspects of the constitution.

Statutes relating to the structure of the United Kingdom and Commonwealth

(a) Acts of Union with Scotland 1707: by which the pre-existing English and Scottish Parliaments both passed Acts of Union and brought into existence the Parliament of Great Britain.

(b) Acts of Union with Ireland 1800: by which the pre-existing English and Irish Parliaments passed Acts of Union bringing into existence the Parliament of the United Kingdom of Great Britain and Ireland.

(c) Government of Ireland Act 1920: which created the Parliament of Northern Ireland (Stormont) and vested it with control of Northern Ireland's internal affairs (replaced by direct rule from Westminster in 1972).

(d) Irish Free State (Agreement) Act 1922: which gave dominion status to 26 of the 32 counties of Ireland.

(e) Statute of Westminster 1931: which provided that the Westminster Parliament would not legislate for any dominion state except 'that that dominion has requested and consented to the enactment thereof' (s 4).

(f) European Communities Act 1972: which gave effect to European Community law in the United Kingdom.

Statutes relating to the Monarch and the royal prerogative

(a) Bill of Rights 1689: which provided, *inter alia*, that the Monarch could not tax, make law, or maintain a standing army in peacetime without parliamentary consent, and could not suspend or dispense with laws made by Parliament.

(b) Act of Settlement 1700: which settled the throne on the Electress Sophia of Hanover (granddaughter of James I) and the heirs of her body being communicants of the Church of England and provided, *inter alia*, that the prerogative to remove judges' commissions should be exercised only on addresses by both Houses of Parliament.

(c) Regency Act 1937: provided for the appointment and exercise of the Monarch's functions by counsellors of state in circumstances of illness or absence from the state and for the appointment of a Regent should the Monarch be incompetent through age (under 18 years) or 'infirmity of mind or body'.

(d) Crown Proceedings Act 1947: which provided that the Crown could be sued in contract and tort as of right.

Statutes relating to the election, composition and workings of Parliament

(a) Representation of the Peoples Acts 1983–2000: which enacted the current rules relating to the conduct of parliamentary and local elections, the franchise and the control of electoral abuses.

(b) Parliamentary Constituencies Act 1986 and Political Parties, Elections and Referendums Act 2000: which provided the rules to be applied by the Boundary Commissions (now Boundary Committees of the Electoral Commission) in determining the boundaries of electoral districts.

(c) Parliament Acts 1911 and 1949: which allowed that the Royal Assent could be given to a Bill not approved by the House of Lords.

(d) Life Peerages Act 1958: which allowed for royal creation of 'life peers'.

(e) Peerages Act 1963: which allowed that hereditary peerages could be disclaimed for life thus qualifying those affected for membership of the House of Commons.

(f) House of Lords Act 1999: which removed the hereditary element from the
     upper chamber save for a possible temporary remission for 90 'excepted
     peers'.

Statutes relating to the judicial system

(a) Supreme Court of Judicature Acts 1873–75 and Appellate Jurisdiction Act 1876:
     by which the pre-existing system of courts was rationalised into the High Court,
     Court of Appeal and House of Lords.
(b) Courts Act 1971: created Crown Courts to exercise the criminal jurisdiction
     previously dispensed by Assizes and Quarter Sessions.
(c) Supreme Court Act 1981: determined the current structure, personnel and
     powers of the Supreme Court of Judicature (High Court and Court of Appeal).

Statutes relating to civil liberties and human rights

(a) Habeas Corpus Acts 1640–1862: prohibited imprisonment without just cause.
(b) Race Relations Act 1976: prohibited racial discrimination in employment, educa-
     tion and the provision of goods and services.
(c) Obscene Publications Acts 1959 and 1964: limited the freedom of expression by
     prohibiting the publication or possession for gain of obscene articles.
(d) Official Secrets Acts 1911 and 1989: limited the freedom of movement in rela-
     tion to 'prohibited places' (viz. those having to do with defence and national
     security), and the freedom of expression in terms of the communication of infor-
     mation which could be prejudicial to certain key national interests (e.g. defence,
     national security and the investigation of crime).
(e) Prevention of Terrorism Acts 1974–89: restricted both the freedom of association
     by proscribing the existence and membership of organisations concerned in
     terrorism in the United Kingdom connected with Irish affairs and the freedom
     of movement by authorising the use of exclusion orders preventing persons
     from being in or entering Great Britain (England, Scotland and Wales) or
     Northern Ireland (now see Terrorism Act 2000).
(f) Police and Criminal Evidence Act 1984 and Regulation of Investigatory Powers
     Act 2000: codified and clarified the law relating to individual freedoms and
     police powers.
(g) Public Order Act 1986: extended the statutory limits on the freedom of assembly
     and codified the pre-existing common law, public order offences.
(h) Criminal Justice and Public Order Act 1994: removed the absolute right to
     silence in criminal proceedings and provided the police with further powers for
     the apprehension of offenders and the control of public order.
(i) Freedom of Information Act 2000 and Data Protection Act 1998: provided
     a right of access to information held by government agencies and control of
     the use of information of a personal nature.
(j) Human Rights Act 1998: extended the rights of the individual against the state
     by giving legal effect to the European Convention on Human Rights.

Statutes relating to the administrative process

(a) Statutory Instruments Act 1946: introduced procedures for improved publicity and parliamentary control of delegated or subordinate legislation.
(b) Tribunals and Inquiries Acts 1958–92: provided rules governing the composition and procedure of statutory tribunals and inquiries.
(c) Parliamentary Commissioner Act 1967: established a complaints procedure for those claiming injustice as a result of maladministration by a central government department (also see Local Government Act 1974 for complaints relating to local authorities and the National Health Service Reorganisation Act 1973 for those against the Health Service).

Statutes relating to local government

(a) Local Government Act 1972: established the basic structure and distribution of powers of the modern local government system, subject to subsequent alterations by the Local Government Act 1985 (abolition of metropolitan county councils) and the Local Government Act 1992 (creation of single-tier authorities).

JUDICIAL DECISIONS

Meaning

The judicial contribution to the formulation of constitutional and administrative law is performed through interpretation of statutory provisions having to do with the process of government and by the declaration and development of relevant aspects of the common law.

Statutory interpretation

The modern judicial approach to statutory interpretation is to seek to give effect to the literal meaning of the words used by Parliament except where this would produce an absurd result or is not possible due to uncertainty or ambiguity. In these circumstances the usual expectation is that the provision in question will be given a meaning which is compatible both with its linguistic content and the purpose which it appears designed to achieve.

To assist in this sometimes difficult task judges may sometimes have resort to a number of interpretative presumptions (i.e. normative judicial suppositions of parliamentary intention), some of which are of particular significance to constitutional and administrative law. These would include the presumptions that in the absence of express words or necessary implication Parliament does not intend to:

(a) alter the existing rights and privileges of the Crown (*Lord Advocate* v *Dumbarton DC* [1990] 2 AC 580);
(b) reduce or extinguish the pre-existing rights of the citizen (*Secretary of State for Defence* v *Guardian Newspapers Ltd* [1985] AC 339);
(c) impose any taxation (*Attorney-General* v *Wilts United Dairies* (1921) 37 TLR 884);

(d) restrict the citizen's access to the courts (*Chester v Bateson* [1920] 1 KB 829), or exclude the power of judicial review (*Anisminic Ltd v Foreign Compensation Commission (No. 2)* [1969] 2 AC 147);

(e) give retrospective effect to penal enactments (*Waddington v Miah* [1974] 1 WLR 683);

(f) extinguish proprietary rights without compensation (*Central Control Board v Cannon Brewery Co Ltd* [1919] AC 744);

(g) alter the constitution by a 'sidewind' (i.e. effect major changes indirectly or surreptitiously: *Nairn v University of St Andrews* [1909] AC 147).

Common law

This consists of rules of law formulated to deal with those disputes for which there are no statutory prescriptions. This remains a significant source of law in relation to certain elements of the constitution.

The royal prerogative

For nearly four hundred years since Coke CJ declared that the 'King hath no prerogative but what the law of the land allows him' (*Case of Proclamations* (1611) 12 Co Rep 74), the courts have claimed the authority to declare the content of the prerogative (i.e. the powers contained within it), the extent of particular prerogatives (*Burmah Oil v Lord Advocate* [1965] AC 75), and the relationship between prerogative and statute (*Attorney-General v De Keyser's Royal Hotel* [1920] AC 508).

Judicial supervision of executive action

Persons aggrieved by alleged unlawful uses of government power have long had a right of access to the courts to challenge the actions or decisions in question. The resulting judgments have led to the formulation of the rules which determine when authorities have abused their powers in both the substantive or procedural senses (i.e. acted *ultra vires* or in breach of the rules of natural justice). This body of law includes the basic principles that official decisions may be quashed for unreasonableness (*Associated Picture Houses Ltd v Wednesbury Corporation* [1948] 1 KB 223), or for unfairness if a person whose rights or interests were seriously affected was not given a fair hearing (*Ridge v Baldwin (No. 1)* [1964] AC 40).

Civil liberties

As illustrated, much of the law relating to the rights of the individual has now been cast into statutory form. Complete codification has, however, neither been achieved nor attempted. Some significant elements of constitutional law in this context may still be found, therefore, in the common law. These would include:

(a) the restrictions on the freedom of speech imposed by the tort of defamation and the criminal offences of blasphemy, sedition and conspiracy to corrupt public morals;

(b) the powers of the police to interfere with the freedoms of the person, assembly and movement in order to prevent breaches of the peace.

Reference should, perhaps, also be made to the developing doctrine of confidentiality which enables the courts to restrict the publication and dissemination of information entrusted in confidence to government employees and agents where this would damage the public interest.

Public interest immunity

This is a common law doctrine with implications for both the law of evidence and the freedom of information. Essentially it consists of a body of rules which enable any party, and this may often be the government, to withhold relevant evidence from legal proceedings if, once again, its revelation would damage the public interest.

Parliamentary privilege

As a result of Parliament being the sovereign body, the courts have no jurisdiction to question its decisions or the way it regulates its composition and proceedings. The common law which determines whether a dispute relates to the affairs of Parliament, and is, therefore, beyond the cognisance of the courts, comprises the rules of parliamentary privilege.

CONSTITUTIONAL CONVENTIONS

Some definitions

These include some of the constitution's most important rules. In *Reference re Amendment of the Constitution of Canada* (1982) 125 DLR (3rd) 1, the Canadian Supreme Court's view was that 'while they are not laws some conventions may be more important than laws'.

Dicey defined conventions as 'rules which although they regulate the conduct of the several members of the sovereign power, of the ministers or the other officials, are not in reality laws at all since they are not enforced by the courts'. He also said that conventions could be described as rules of 'constitutional morality'.

Despite its antiquity this definition makes two essential points. First, although conventions are rules, they do not impose legal obligations and no English court will grant a remedy in respect of non-compliance. Second, they should properly be regarded as constituting a value system for the guidance of those engaged in the process of government and politics.

The purpose of conventions

Consistent with Dicey's view of conventions as rules of 'constitutional morality', it has been said that they provide a 'moral framework within which government ministers or the Monarch should exercise the non-justiciable powers' of the constitution (Loveland, *Constitutional Law: A Critical Introduction*, 1996). This value-orientated perspective on conventions may also be found in the Canadian Supreme Court's view that the 'main purpose of conventions is to ensure that the legal framework of the constitution will be operated in accordance with the principal constitutional values or principles of the period' (re *Amendment of the Constitution of Canada* (above)). Hence, in the domestic context, the rule that a government which loses the confidence of the House of Commons must resign may be seen as an obvious requirement of a representative and responsible parliamentary system.

Conventions are also regarded as giving the constitution a necessary degree of flexibility. In particular, they allow it to change and develop without significant alteration of the existing legal rules – many of which are of ancient origins and, in isolation to conventional practice, of little modern relevance. Thus, for example, the legal rules relating to the summoning of Parliament require that it meets 'frequently' (Bill of Rights 1689) and at least once every three years (Meeting of Parliament Act 1694). Taken and applied literally these bare legal requirements would be wholly inimical to contemporary assumptions about the proper relationship between the executive and Parliament – particularly that the former should conduct its activities subject to constant supervision by the latter. Hence the convention that Parliament should be summoned annually.

Classification

Conventions regulating the exercise of the royal prerogative

As has been made clear, the law of the constitution continues to repose a great deal of legal authority in the person of the Monarch. This is, however, subject to the following conventions.

(a) The Monarch's prerogative to appoint the Prime Minister must be exercised in favour of the person who commands a majority in the House of Commons.
(b) The prerogative to appoint other members of the government must be exercised on the advice of the Prime Minister.
(c) The prerogative to grant or refuse the Royal Assent must be exercised in favour of all Bills approved by the Commons and the Lords.
(d) The prerogative to summon Parliament must be exercised annually.
(e) The prerogative to dissolve Parliament must be exercised on the advice of the Prime Minister – but note the ongoing discussion concerning the rare circumstances in which a request for a dissolution might still be refused, i.e. where this would do serious harm to the national interest.

The conventional regulation of royal power is not just of functional significance. It is this which has enabled the prerogative to remain largely intact and which has, therefore, preserved the Monarch's formal constitutional role (i.e. the Monarch assents to legislation, summons and dissolves Parliament, appoints the Prime Minister, etc.). Thus, in turn, has done much to sustain the credibility and status of the institution of Monarchy itself. It has also helped to synthesise, in a practical sense, two essentially incompatible political concepts, viz. monarchical and representative parliamentary government.

Conventions regulating the practice of Cabinet government

The law of the constitution makes only peripheral reference to the offices of Prime Minister and Cabinet (see Ministerial and Other Salaries Act 1975). Both exist by virtue of convention. Their powers, relationship and *modus operandi* are also determined by conventional rules, the principal ones being as follows.

(a) The Prime Minister decides national policy in consultation with a Cabinet (i.e. a committee of senior ministers).
(b) The composition of the Cabinet, and the distribution of portfolios within it, are determined by the Prime Minister.
(c) The Cabinet is chosen from MPs and peers who support the party or parties in power.
(d) The Prime Minister, Cabinet and government are collectively responsible to the House of Commons for their conduct of national affairs and must resign if defeated in a vote of censure or no confidence (last occurred in 1979).
(e) Ministers are individually responsible and answerable for the conduct of their particular departments or areas of responsibility and should be prepared to resign if they, their department, or any of their civil servants are guilty of any serious errors of judgement.
(f) The Prime Minister calls Cabinet meetings and determines their agenda.
(g) The Prime Minister determines the number, subject matter and composition of Cabinet committees.

Conventions regulating the work of Parliament

It is generally agreed that the rules of parliamentary practice and privilege, which are recognised and enforced by the Speaker, and which may be embodied in standing orders of either House, should properly be regarded as part of the law and custom of Parliament and, as such, not be classified as conventions. Subject to this, the following rules of parliamentary conduct are founded in conventions.

(a) The House of Lords should give way to the House of Commons.
(b) Financial measures should be introduced in the House of Commons and should not be altered by the Lords.
(c) The government arranges the business of the House of Commons in consultation with the parties in opposition, particularly Her Majesty's Official Opposition ('behind the Speaker's chair').
(d) The government always provides parliamentary time for opposition censure motions.
(e) Lay peers should not participate in the business of the House of Lords when it sits as a court of law.
(f) In the event of a 'tied' vote in the House of Commons, the Speaker's casting vote is cast for the government.
(g) The composition of parliamentary committees should reflect each party's representation in the House of Commons.

Conventions regulating the relationship between the United Kingdom and the Commonwealth

The following rules may be understood as deriving from agreements reached between the United Kingdom and the independent members of the Commonwealth.

(a) Any alteration relating to the Royal Style and Titles or the succession to the throne requires the assent of all the independent Commonwealth states in which the Monarch is the Head of State (e.g. Canada, New Zealand, Australia).

(b) The Governor-Generals of independent Commonwealth states are appointed by the Monarch on the advice of the Prime Minister of the state in question.

(c) Governor-Generals represent the Monarch but not the British government.

Rules of recognition

The fact that a particular political practice has been repeated over a period of time or in a given set of circumstances does not, of itself, elevate it to the status of convention. Thus the traditional ritualistic activities of the Chancellor of the Exchequer on budget day are too trivial and lacking in constitutional significance to merit the title of convention. Other 'usual' practices such as the expectation that the Prime Minister will include in the Cabinet persons from the various wings (left, right, centre, etc.) of the party in power, although of greater significance, may be regarded as too imprecise and laden with political discretion to be defined as 'rules'.

Various formulae have been offered, therefore, to assist in determining which political practices qualify to be treated as conventions. The most cited of these is that provided by Sir Ivor Jennings in *The Law of the Constitution* (5th edn), 1959. Jennings proposed three essential tests:

(a) are there sufficient precedents?
(b) did those involved believe they were bound by a rule?
(c) is there a good constitutional reason for the rule?

Few would dispute that the accepted practice of the Prime Minister having a seat in the House of Commons has acquired the status and force of convention. No peer has held the office of Prime Minister since Lord Salisbury resigned in 1902. The precedents usually cited for this convention normally relate to events that occurred in 1923 and 1940. In 1923, when the incumbent premier (Bonar Law) resigned for ill health, the choice was between Lord Curzon and Stanley Baldwin. The latter was chosen. In 1940 the choice appeared to be between Lord Halifax and Winston Churchill. Again it was the 'commoner' who was appointed.

The exact grounds for the 1923 decision remain unclear. It cannot be said, therefore, that it represented unequivocal recognition of the existence of a convention based on the diminished significance of the House of Lords following the Parliament Act 1911. It is generally accepted, however, that Lord Halifax' status counted against him in 1940. Halifax himself expressed the view that 'having no access to the House of Commons' he would have 'speedily become a more or less honorary Prime Minister living in a kind of twilight just outside the things that really mattered' (Lord Halifax, *Fullness of Days*, 1957).

Any remaining doubts about whether the 1923 and 1940 incidents had come to be regarded as binding political precedents appeared to have disappeared by 1963 when both Lords Home and Hailsham announced their intention to renounce their titles in order to compete for the vacant premiership (after the resignation of Harold Macmillan). Lord Home became Sir Alec Douglas-Home and was the successful candidate.

The reasons for this convention are immediately apparent. The United Kingdom is a representative democracy. The nation's representatives sit in the House of Commons. It is there that the government must account for its conduct of national affairs. As Halifax acknowledged, therefore, it is axiomatic that the leader of the government should be a member of the forum which Professor de Smith has described as the 'grand inquest of the nation'.

It is clear that conventions can also come into existence by agreement. The agreement in 1930 that the royal power to appoint the Governor-General of a dominion would be exercised exclusively on the advice of the government of the dominion concerned, is generally accepted to have created a convention to that effect. Hence it would be regarded as unconstitutional for the Crown to act in this matter without or contrary to such advice.

The relationship between law and convention

In a functional sense law and convention are very closely connected. Most conventions presuppose the existence of particular constitutional laws and have been formulated to regulate the way these legal rules are exercised. Hence Hood Phillips' statement that 'conventions would be meaningless without their legal context' (op. cit.).

There are also considerable similarities between the attributes of law and convention. Both are regarded as rules and make use of precedent for the purposes of validity. Those affected accept that both impose a degree of obligation and that adverse consequences may result from disobedience.

For all these jurisprudential musings, however, it remains clear that the courts will not enforce conventions and, where a convention and a legal rule conflict, courts will always apply the latter.

In 1965 Parliament enacted the Southern Rhodesia Act and did so in contravention of the convention that Parliament would not legislate for a dominion unless so requested by the dominion concerned. The Act was the UK's response to Rhodesia's unilateral declaration of independence. It declared that Rhodesia remained a British dominion and invalidated all legislation promulgated by the illegal regime. In *Madzimbamuto v Lardner-Burke* [1967] 1 AC 645, the complainant challenged the legality of his detention under Rhodesian emergency regulations. The Privy Council refused to accept the argument that the 1965 Act should not be applied because of the breach of convention or that 'moral, political and other reasons' presented any barrier to the enforcement of a valid legal rule. The 1965 Act was applied and the complainant's detention was found to be illegal.

A further useful example of judicial refusal to give effect to convention was provided by the decision in *Manuel v Attorney-General* [1983] Ch 77. On this occasion a group of Canadian Indians took exception to the Canada Act 1982. This conferred authority on the Canadian Federal Parliament to alter certain founding parts of the Canadian constitution contained in nineteenth-century British North America Acts. The Indians believed that this would endanger the protection given by these enactments to rights granted to them in treaties agreed with the original British colonial administration.

The case raised issues similar to those canvassed in *Madzimbamuto*. The Indians argued breach of a convention that the Westminster Parliament would not amend the Canadian constitution except with the consent of all the provinces and peoples of Canada including the Indian nations. The Court of Appeal was firmly of the opinion that it could not inquire into whether a particular convention had been complied with and that purported non-compliance was not something which could impair the effectiveness of that which had been approved by Commons, Lords and Monarch.

It is interesting to note that the same court did appear to contemplate enforcing a convention in *Attorney-General v Jonathan Cape* [1976] QB 752. On this occasion the decision was that a court could grant injunctive relief to prevent an ex-Cabinet minister from including details of Cabinet meetings in his memoirs. This opinion was founded principally, however, on the equitable doctrine of confidentiality (see the freedom of expression, Chapter 22) and should not be understood, therefore, as giving legal force to the convention of collective ministerial responsibility.

It would be misleading, however, to represent judicial refusal to enforce convention as symptomatic of a reluctance to recognise the existence and significance of non-legal rules in the workings of the constitution. Hence many examples exist of judges citing particular conventions in order to explain the general constitutional coherence of their decisions. Thus the convention of individual ministerial responsibility has frequently been referred to in a series of cases in which the courts have refused to question ministerial decisions relating to matters of national security. Here, judicial reservations about interfering with such sensitive policy issues have tended to be accompanied by references to the minister's conventional responsibility to Parliament – thus implying a preference for alleged abuses of such powers to be dealt with in the chamber of the House of Commons rather than in the courts.

Judicial recognition of the utility of convention in regulating ministerial powers was evident in the famous wartime decision of *Liversidge v Anderson* [1942] AC 206. On this occasion the House of Lords felt that during a national emergency it would be inappropriate for a court to question the reasonableness of the way the Home Secretary had used his power to intern any person believed to be 'of hostile origins or associations' (contained in reg 18B of the Defence Regulations 1939). Viscount Maugham's view was that 'the person who is primarily entrusted with these important duties is one of the principal Secretaries of State, and a member of government answerable to Parliament for a proper discharge of his duties'.

More recently during the Gulf Crisis of 1991 the Court of Appeal refused to question the grounds on which the Home Secretary had exercised his discretion to deport a person whose presence in the United Kingdom was deemed not to be 'conducive to the public good' (Immigration Act 1971, s 3). Lord Donaldson MR commented that the Home Secretary was 'fully accountable to Parliament for his decisions whether or not to deport'; thus demonstrating again the judicial preference for conventional control of ministerial powers in this politically delicate context (*R v Home Secretary, ex parte Cheblak* [1991] 2 All ER 319).

Reasons for obedience

Various theories have been advanced for the general level of compliance with convention. In any given circumstance obedience is probably secured through a combination of influences.

Moral opprobrium

As already explained, one of the main objectives of convention is to ensure that power is used in accordance with the ideological principles on which the constitution is based. By definition, therefore, the stability of the constitution is prejudiced by unconventional behaviour. It follows that those responsible risk the opprobrium both of colleagues and the media, and may incite the type of public criticism and disapproval which serves to reinforce the effectiveness of any value system and the social and political order which it seeks to sustain.

Breach of the law

Dicey's view was that a breach of convention 'would almost immediately bring the offender into conflict with the courts and the law of the land'. Most commentators would accept that this is a proposition of some validity but one which does not have universal application. Hence, if the Monarch were to renege on the conventional obligation to summon Parliament every year, the annual financial legislation legalising the collection and expenditure of revenue could not be enacted. The same consequence would probably follow if a government refused to resign after losing the confidence and support of the House of Commons. On the other hand, it is difficult to envisage what state of illegality would result if a lay peer was allowed to sit in judgment with the Law Lords or if a member of the government were to launch a verbal attack on the competence of a member of the judiciary.

Political difficulties

Jennings argued that conventions are obeyed 'because of the political difficulties which follow if they are not'. There is little doubt that breach of some of the major conventional rules would have substantial political ramifications. Thus, an immediate constitutional crisis would probably result if the Monarch attempted to use the royal prerogative without or contrary to ministerial advice. In the longer term, this would be bound to precipitate questions concerning the wisdom of retaining a constitutional monarchy that was not prepared to behave constitutionally. Similarly a government could hardly hope to survive and function effectively if ministers wantonly ignored the conventions of collective and individual responsibility.

Result in legislation

In addition to that proposed by Dicey, a further legal consequence of breach of convention may be that the rule in question will be given legislative force. This is illustrated by the events of 1909–11 when the House of Lords voted against the Finance Bill 1909 – a flagrant breach of the conventional rule requiring the unelected chamber to 'give way' to the House of Commons. The matter was dealt with by the Parliament Act 1911 which gave the rule legal force in respect of all Public Bills (except if designed to prolong the life of Parliament).

Self-interest

Ambition for high public office is rarely well served by refusal to comply with the ethics of the political and constitutional system. A minister may be tempted to 'put on record' a sense of dissatisfaction with the Prime Minister or other Cabinet colleagues but will be aware that this could presage the end of a promising political career. An aspirant to high judicial office will know that controversial extra-curial comment will do little for the cause of personal advancement. As in any organisation, participants cannot hope to progress within it unless they are prepared to accept the rules by which it is conducted.

Codification of conventions

At first glance it might not seem entirely satisfactory that so many of the constitution's primary rules are not subject to either judicial enforcement or definition. This state of affairs is, however, usually explained by reference to a number of practical justifications.

The most obvious of these is that any comprehensive transformation of conventions into legal rules would inevitably inhibit the constitution's traditional potential to respond to political experience and to changing beliefs about the practice of government. Legislative intervention would then be needed to deal with rules expressive of outdated constitutional values. Legal certainty and authority might be bought, therefore, at the price of flexibility and political relevance. Also, history shows that laws are often not changed until long after they have ceased to fulfil any useful function and even then may be defended for purely symbolic or sentimental reasons. In terms of the ideals of government, therefore, organic constitutional growth and legal specificity may not be entirely compatible notions.

A further consequence of converting convention to law would be that disputes or uncertainty as to the exact content and requirements of the rules in question would become legal rather than political matters. This would have the effect of drawing the judiciary into overtly political controversies – something which would appear to be in direct contradiction of British constitutional tradition. It is also difficult to imagine that those aggrieved or politically disadvantaged by judicial interpretation of contentious constitution rules would be able to desist from allegations, however veiled, of party-political bias.

It might be, of course, that the judges would simply refuse to get involved and would prefer instead to take the view that legal rules relating to high affairs of state and laden with political discretion should be regarded as non-justiciable (i.e. as matters falling outside the proper sphere of judicial competence), an approach which has already been adopted in relation to some of the more important prerogative powers (see the House of Lords in *Council of Civil Service Unions* v *Minister for the Civil Service*, above). This in itself, however, might be another reason for leaving conventions as they are, since, apart from the issue of clarity, there would appear to be little point in giving legal status to that which the judges might not be prepared to enforce.

These arguments notwithstanding, it still has to be conceded that some conventions are fraught with uncertainty and it is not possible to state the obligations they impose with any exactitude or confidence. Hence, for example, does the convention that the Monarch dissolves Parliament on the advice of the Prime Minister admit of any exceptions and, if so, what are they? And what are the conventional requirements resting on the Monarch when appointing a Prime Minister from a 'hung' Parliament?

As something of a compromise, therefore, between the present state of uncertainty and the disadvantages of over-formalisation, it has been suggested that conventions could be declared and clarified without alteration of their existing non-legal nature. This has been done, for example, in Australia, where a Constitutional Conference consisting of representatives from the federal and state Parliaments meets at regular intervals for this express purpose.

An alternative approach worthy of mention is that of the Canadian constitution. This gives the Supreme Court there the jurisdiction to pronounce on the existence and content of a convention but not to give it legal force or effect. In Canada, therefore, government action in breach of convention may not be defined as illegal but could be declared to be unconstitutional. The likelihood of breach of convention is thus diminished as no government in a democratic state relishes having its actions condemned by the supreme judicial authority.

Domestically, however, such classification of conventions is unlikely to take place in isolation from some more general programme of constitutional reform – perhaps as part of the replacement of the existing model by a comprehensive written document. At present this is not something which appears to be a matter of immediate political priority, and may yet be 'a bridge too far' in terms of the current state of the prevailing political culture.

EUROPEAN COMMUNITY LAW

Introduction

As a result of EC membership the United Kingdom is, in effect, subject to two constitutions, viz. its own unwritten constitution for those matters of law and government not falling within the competence of the Community, and the constitution of the Community for the increasing range of matters which do. As a source of domestic constitutional and administrative law the law of the Community would appear to be particularly important for the following reasons.

Redefinition of the scope of national constitutions

First, Community law defines the extent to which legislative, executive and judicial powers previously founded in the British and other national constitutions have been transferred to the Community's governing institutions. Of particular significance in this context is the fact that Community law is based on the premiss that the 'pooling' of national sovereignty by member states has created a superior legal order which has precedence over the law of domestic legal systems. In the United Kingdom this has already had major ramifications for judicial interpretation and application of the constitution's most fundamental rule, viz. the doctrine of parliamentary sovereignty – of which more will be said in Chapter 5.

Judicial review

Second, the transfer of powers to the Community has been accompanied and counter-balanced by the application of Community laws which provide substantive and procedural rules through which member states and individuals may challenge any actions or decisions by Community institutions which purport to have legal effect (see Art 173). The doctrines of legitimate expectation and proportionality are amongst the grounds of judicial review which have been formulated by the European Court of Justice in the exercise of this jurisdiction. More will be said about these below as both have already influenced the common law principles of judicial review currently applied in the United Kingdom.

Human rights

Third, Community law is expanding the range of fundamental human rights to which it is prepared to give recognition and protection; a development which some might say is a 'far cry' from the original economic purposes to which the Community was directed.

Certain of these basic freedoms may, of course, be traced, to the EC Treaty itself. These would include the prohibition of discrimination of all kinds in matters over which the Community has jurisdiction, especially where related to matters of 'sex and ethnic origin, religion or belief, disability, age or sexual orientation' (Art 6a) and the right of free movement of citizens within member states (Art 48).

Reference should also be made, however, to the European Court's formulation of a body of human rights case law based on the principle that those rights generally recognised by the constitutions of member states should be respected in the application of European law and policy:

> ...fundamental rights form an integral part of the general principles of law...In safeguarding these rights the Court is bound to draw inspiration from constitutional traditions common to Member States and it cannot therefore uphold measures which are incompatible with fundamental rights recognised and protected by the Constitutions of those states (*Nold* v *Commission of the European Communities* [1974] ECR 491).

Cases in which such fundamental rights have been identified and enforced this way would include *R* v *Kirk* [1985] 1 All ER 453, in which the European Court of Justice recognised the principle that penal laws (in this case an EC directive) should not be given retrospective effect, and *Beydoun* v *Commission* [1984] ECR 1509, where the Court stated that the principle of 'equal treatment of both sexes...forms part of the fundamental rights the observance of which the court has a duty to secure'.

It is significant in this context that, by the Treaty of Amsterdam 1997, the European Union confirmed its commitment to democracy and human rights by providing for sanctions to be imposed on member states which seriously and persistently act in breach of the same. The Treaty also makes adherence to such principles a condition of entry to the Union.

THE EUROPEAN CONVENTION ON HUMAN RIGHTS

This is an international treaty which was formulated by the European democracies in 1950. It was ratified by the United Kingdom in 1951 and came into effect in 1953. It is not a part of European Community law and, until the coming into effect of the Human Rights Act 1998, was not directly enforceable in the courts of the United Kingdom. Under international law, however, the United Kingdom was under an obligation to comply with its requirements. It, therefore, had a strong persuasive effect on the making and interpretation of domestic law.

Alleged breaches of the Convention by the United Kingdom and other signatory states could, however, be raised by individuals or national governments before the European Court of Human Rights. In cases where domestic legislation was found to be incompatible with the Convention, the expectation (usually honoured) was that the offending provision would be amended to secure compliance. This was done either through subordinate legislation or by securing the passage of a Bill through Parliament, viz. the enactment of the Interception of Communications Act 1985 following the decision in *Malone* v *United Kingdom* (1985) 7 EHRR 14.

By way of illustration, reference may be made to the well known cases of *Golder* v *United Kingdom* (1975) 1 EHRR 524, and *Malone* v *United Kingdom,* above. In *Golder* a prisoner in the United Kingdom complained about a provision in the Prison Rules (made under the Prison Act 1952) which restricted his access to legal advice for the purpose of commencing legal proceedings. This was found to be incompatible with Art 6 of the Convention and the Prison Rules were amended accordingly. In *Malone* the petitioner alleged that the Metropolitan Police had infringed his right to privacy (Art 8) by tapping his telephone. The court found in his favour on the ground that the power to tap telephones in the United Kingdom was not subject to any clearly definable legal restraints. Again, English law was then rectified accordingly, this time by the passing of the Interception of Telecommunications Act 1985.

The Convention was made directly enforceable in domestic courts by the Human Rights Act 1998 which became extensive on 2 October 2000. The Act imposed an obligation on all courts and tribunals to take into account the jurisprudence of both the European Court and the Commission on Human Rights when interpreting and applying Convention rights. This effective body of case law must be referred to, therefore, and will influence judgments throughout the various disciplines of English law whenever an issue to which the Convention relates arises.

THE LAW AND CUSTOM OF PARLIAMENT

This consists, in the main, of the rules which regulate the conduct of parliamentary proceedings, the behaviour and the activities of members of both Houses, and which also contain the powers of both Houses to deal with those who are guilty of breaches of parliamentary privilege or whose words or behaviour are contemptuous of either House.

The majority of these rules may be found in parliamentary standing orders, resolutions and rulings from the chair. These are matters which are generally recognised as being beyond the competence of the courts. Compliance is, therefore, a matter for parliamentary rather than judicial enforcement.

References

Halifax (1957) *The Fullness of Days*, London: Collins.

Hood Phillips and Jackson (1997) *Hood Phillips and Jackson's Constitutional and Administrative Law* (8th edn), London: Sweet & Maxwell.

Jennings (1959) *The Law of the Constitution* (5th edn), London: University of London Press.

Loveland (1996) *Constitutional Law: A Critical Introduction*, London: Butterworths.

Further reading

Allen and Thompson (1996) *Cases and Materials on Constitutional and Administrative Law* (3rd edn), London: Blackstone, Ch 4.

Marshall (1986) *Constitutional Conventions: The Rules and Forms of Political Accountability*, Oxford: Clarendon Press.

Monro (1987) *Studies in Constitutional Law*, London: Butterworths, Ch 3.

Turpin (2002) *British Government and the Constitution* (5th edn), London: Butterworths, Ch 1.

Part 2

PARLIAMENT AND THE EUROPEAN COMMUNITY

Chapter 4

THE EUROPEAN COMMUNITY: INSTITUTIONS AND SOURCES OF LAW

ORIGINS OF THE EUROPEAN COMMUNITY

In 1951 – by the Treaty of Paris – Belgium, France, Germany, Italy, Holland and Luxembourg formed the European Coal and Steel Community (ECSC). Six years later, by virtue of the Treaties of Rome, the same six nations created two further communities (i.e. integrated economic and industrial systems). These were the European Economic Community and the European Atomic Energy Community (EAEC or Euratom). The three organisations were referred to collectively as the European Economic Communities (EEC).

Their legal and executive institutions were merged by the Treaty of Merger 1965. Thereafter the Council of Ministers, the European Commission, the European Court of Justice and the European Assembly acted on behalf of all three organisations.

The United Kingdom joined the EEC by virtue of the Brussels Treaty of Accession 1972. Under the EEC Act 1972 EEC law was incorporated into the law of the United Kingdom. Both the Treaty and the Act became effective on 1 January 1973. The United Kingdom thus became a member of a supranational organisation with power to make law taking effect within the state without reference to Parliament. Thus was effected the most significant change to the British constitution since the Glorious Revolution of 1688.

The European Economic Community was renamed the European Community by the Maastricht Treaty on European Union 1992 (TEU). This gave express recognition to the fact that the legislative and policy-making activities of the organisation had developed and extended beyond purely economic matters. The Maastricht Treaty was given effect in English law by the European Union (Amendment) Act 1993.

The integrated institutions of the three European Communities (EC, ECSC and Euratom) now have extensive policy- and law-making powers and are responsible for the maintenance and implementation of the European legal order created by the founding treaties (i.e. TEU, EC Treaty, ECSC Treaty and Euratom Treaty). By virtue of post-Maastricht guidance from these institutions, the term European Community may now be understood as referring to all three European Communities.

The purposes of the Community are set out in Art 2 of the EC Treaty. These are 'by establishing a common market and an economic and monetary union...to promote throughout the Community a harmonious and well balanced development of economic activities, sustainable and non-inflationary growth...a high degree of convergence of economic performance, a high level of employment and of social protection, the raising of the standard of living and the quality of life, and economic and social cohesion and solidarity among members'. Article 3 of the Treaty makes it abundantly clear that the activities of the Community now extend well beyond purely economic and commercial matters and include 'a policy in the social sphere...a policy in the sphere of the environment...a contribution to the attainment of a high level of health protection...a contribution to education and training of quality and to the flowering of cultures of Member States'.

THE MAASTRICHT TREATY AND THE EUROPEAN UNION

The European Union was born out of the Treaty on European Union (the 'Maastricht Treaty') 1992 which came into effect on 1 November 1993. This provided for inter-governmental cooperation by the signatory states directed towards the development of common policies in relation to:

(a) foreign affairs and security;
(b) justice and home affairs.

It is now usual to describe the post-Maastricht European order as having three 'pillars' or competencies. The first and central pillar is the European Community with its laws and institutions. The second and third pillars are those described in (a) and (b) above deriving from the 1992 Treaty. The organisation or entity composed of all three pillars or competencies is the European Union. In relation to the European Union, it is important to note that:

(i) the Maastricht Treaty did not seek to confer on existing European institutions any law-making authority in the matters covered by the two new pillars;
(ii) the Treaty did not impose any obligation on signatory states to give effect in their domestic law to any developments, agreements or further treaties which may arise from the aforementioned government cooperation in these matters;
(iii) to the extent that the Treaty creates any legal obligations, these, and agreements under the two intergovernmental pillars, are binding in international law only between the parties to the Treaty and any such agreements;
(iv) the European Union does not have any international legal personality and is therefore not capable of making binding international agreements with other states or organisations of states.

It is clear from this that the European Union is essentially a political organisation through which member states will seek to progress towards greater integration in the matters covered by the Maastricht Treaty. Hence, in terms of law and law-making institutions, the pages that follow will concentrate on the jurisdiction of the European Community.

It should also be mentioned that the Maastricht Treaty:

(a) created the concept of citizenship of the European Union with the rights specified in Arts 17–22 of the Treaty;
(b) committed the European Community to economic and monetary union by 1999;

(c) added to the EC Treaty the Protocol on Social Policy (the 'Social Chapter') to be implemented by relevant legislation by the Community's law-making institutions;

(d) made substantial amendments to and altered the name of the founding treaty of the EEC (viz. the Treaty of Rome) to the EC Treaty.

THE TREATY OF AMSTERDAM

The Maastricht Summit concluded with a commitment to keep the future development of the Union under review to be considered further at the next intergovernmental conference (IGC). This was based on an awareness of the differing perspectives concerning the Union's future political direction, the pace of development and the problems of enlargement. At the Brussels European Council of December 1998 it was agreed that, within this general debate, key matters for consideration should include:

(a) the future role of the European Parliament in decision-making procedures;

(b) the implications of enlargement for the size and composition of the Commission and for voting procedures within the Council of Ministers;

(c) the general issue of how to reconcile the needs of democracy in an enlarged Union with those of institutional efficiency.

An agenda of potential options for reform was prepared by a 'Reflection Group' composed of representatives from the Council of Ministers, the Commissions and the Parliament.

The ensuing IGC was held in Amsterdam in 1997 and resulted in the Treaty of Amsterdam 1997. The Treaty took effect on 1 May 1999. Its principal effects were as follows:

(a) a wholesale renumbering of the Articles of the Treaty of Rome as amended by the Treaty on European Union;

(b) the third pillar of the Union entitled Justice and Home Affairs to be renamed Police and Judicial Cooperation in Criminal Matters and its provisions relating to aspects of the freedom of movement including visas, asylum and immigration to be transferred to the jurisdiction of the European Community (pillar no. 1) (EC Arts 61–69);

(c) the role of the European Parliament in the legislative process to be enhanced by a significant increase in the number of matters to be decided according to the Co-Decision procedure (see below);

(d) the Common Foreign and Security Policy pillar to be extended to include humanitarian and rescue missions and peacekeeping.

No firm conclusions were reached at Amsterdam concerning the implications of enlargement for institutional reform either in terms of composition generally or the weighting and distribution of votes within the Council of Ministers. These matters were to be taken forward by the next IGC. Its conclusions there and related matters contained in the Treaty of Nice 2000 are dealt with below.

SUBSIDIARITY

This is the principle embodied in the Maastricht Treaty which provides that, in matters relating to the implementation of Community law and policy, where exclusive jurisdiction does not vest in the Community's institutions, decisions should be taken at the lowest appropriate level of national government which is easily accessible to individual citizens. EC Art 5 of the Maastricht Treaty states that 'the Community shall take action in accordance with the principle of subsidiarity only if and so far as the objectives of the proposed action cannot be sufficiently achieved by member states and can, therefore, by reason of the scale or effects of the proposed action, be better achieved by the Community'.

The taking of any action by the Community within the jurisdictional limits imposed by the principle of subsidiarity is further restricted by the requirements of proportionality. Thus any action taken by the Community 'shall not go beyond what is necessary' to achieve the objectives pursued (*ibid.*).

The Treaty of Amsterdam 1997 provides that Community action should be confined to those circumstances where the objective is achievable by the Community, but not by a member state acting alone. In such circumstances the form of the Community action should be as simple or as general as possible, leaving the maximum legitimate scope for flexibility in national implementation.

Alleged breaches of the restrictions imposed by the rules of subsidiarity and proportionality by Community institutions may be brought before the European Court of Justice.

COMMUNITY INSTITUTIONS

By virtue of the EC Treaty there are five institutions through which the executive, legislative and judicial work of the Community is carried out.

These are:

(a) the Council of Ministers;
(b) the European Commission;
(c) the European Parliament;
(d) the Court of Justice;
(e) the Court of Auditors.

The Council of Ministers

This is composed of ministerial representatives from all member states. Its composition at particular meetings is determined by the subject matter for discussion. If dealing with matters of general substance and Community policy it will be attended by foreign ministers. If a more specific or limited Community competence is under consideration, say agriculture, it will be the states' ministers of agriculture who will be present.

The presidency of the Council 'rotates' and is held for six months by each member state in turn. The Council is the Community's primary executive and legislative body. In the latter context it makes law in the form of regulations, directives and legally binding decisions following, in most cases, proposals from the European Commission.

The Council makes its decisions by qualified majority votes, simple majority votes or unanimous votes, depending on the subject matter. Most decisions are taken by qualified majority. When the Council is deciding on a proposal by the Commission, a qualified majority consisting of at least 62 of the maximum 87 votes available is required. The votes of each state are 'weighted' according to its population. Hence the larger states (UK, France, Germany, Italy) each cast ten votes; Spain has eight votes; Belgium, Greece, Holland and Portugal have five each; Austria and Spain four; Ireland has three as has Denmark and Finland; and Luxembourg two.

The Council may decide through a simple majority when dealing with relatively minor matters, e.g. its procedural rules. Unanimous voting tends to be reserved for matters of constitutional importance (e.g. admission of a new member state or a change in the composition of a Community institution), or for those which may be politically sensitive (e.g. the harmonisation of indirect taxes).

The Council is aided in its work by a Committee of Permanent Representatives (COREPER). This consists of the member states' permanent representatives or ambassadors to the Community. The Committee is charged with 'preparing the work of the Council and…carrying out the tasks assigned to it by the Council' (EC Art 201). More specifically, one of its most important functions is to determine whether agreement can be reached concerning any policy or legislative proposals about to be considered by the Council. Where this is the case, such proposals may be formally adopted by the Council without further debate.

The Council of Ministers should not be confused with the European Council which consists of the heads of the various member states meeting on a bi-annual basis. The function of the European Council is to provide the European Union with the necessary impetus for its development and to define the political guidelines within which that should take place (EC Art 4). In the main, therefore, it is a political body with no formal law-making or executive authority under the Treaty.

The European Commission

The Commission is composed of twenty members. France, Italy, Germany, Spain and the United Kingdom have two Commissioners each. The other ten member states have just one Commissioner each. Appointments to the Commission are made every five years to coincide with elections to the European Parliament. This is done as follows:

(a) a president designate of the Commission is chosen by agreement amongst the governments of the member states and after consultation with the newly elected European Parliament;

(b) individual Commissioners are proposed by member states as above in agreement with the President designate;

(c) the European Parliament then votes on whether to accept the entire Commission as so constituted.

Individual Commissioners serve the Community and not the particular interests of their member states. They must be 'completely independent in the performance of their duties' and 'neither seek nor take instructions from any government or from any other body' (EC Art 213). Members of the Commission serve for five years and may only be dismissed by a decision of the Court of Justice pursuant to an application by the Council of Ministers or the Commission itself. The grounds for removal are incapacity or misconduct. Also the whole Commission may be put out of office by a vote of censure of the European Parliament carried with a two-thirds majority of all members.

The Commission's principal functions are:

(a) to act as 'guardian of the treaties' by ensuring that member states act in accordance with their legal obligations under the Treaty and, where this cannot be achieved by less formal means, by commencing legal proceedings before the European Court of Justice to secure compliance with the same;

(b) to initiate proposals for the making of secondary legislation (principally regulations and directives) by the Council of Ministers;

(c) to ensure compliance with policy decisions taken by the Council of Ministers;

(d) to represent and negotiate on behalf of the Community in its dealings with non-member states and other international organisations;

(e) to prepare draft Budget proposals for submission to the Council of Ministers and the European Parliament.

The European Parliament

This has 626 members (MEPs) elected by the votes of the various member states. Each state has a number of seats in the Parliament according to the size of its population. The largest number of members (99) is returned by Germany. The United Kingdom, France and Italy return 87 members each. Ireland has fifteen members. Members are elected for a term of five years. They tend to sit and vote in political rather than national groupings. Thus Labour MEPs from the United Kingdom will usually align themselves with MEPs from other moderate left of centre political parties.

At present the European Parliament has limited legislative competence and certainly does not have the type of law-making authority generally associated with national legislatures. It does not enact law nor does it formulate legislative proposals for the Council of Ministers. That is not to say, however, that the Parliament has no role to play in the Community's legislative process. Its powers in this context have gradually been expanded and are as follows.

Consultative and advisory procedure

In a limited number of matters the Treaty requires the Council of Ministers to consult the Parliament before making secondary legislation. Should this not occur the legislative measure in issue may be annulled by the European Court of Justice (*Roquette Frères v Council* [1980] ECR 3333). The procedure does not vest the Parliament with any power of veto or amendment. If the Parliament's opinion does not coincide with that of the Council attempts will be made to reach an agreed solution. In the unlikely event that this fails to produce any compromise, the Council retains the right to make the final decision.

The procedure represented the full extent of the European Parliament's role in the legislative process during the period before 1979 when it was not directly elected and, therefore, had no democratic status or mandate on which to base opposition to the agreed will of the sovereign governments represented in the Council. Following the introduction of direct elections in 1979, the Single European Act 1985 and the Treaties of Maastricht and Amsterdam all effected reductions in the numbers of Treaty articles employing this procedure. Its use is now restricted, principally, to certain aspects of the common agricultural policy and to those matters transferred to the Community's jurisdiction from the Union's Justice and Home Affairs pillar by the Treaty of Amsterdam (e.g. visas, asylum, immigration).

Cooperation procedure (EC Art 252)

Where the Treaty requires the use of this procedure for the making of legislation the process is:

(a) the Council, on receipt of a legislative proposal from the Commission, submits this to the Parliament for its opinion (sometimes referred to as the particular measure's 'First Reading');
(b) having considered the Parliament's opinion, the Council by qualified majority adopts a 'common position' which is returned to the Parliament with a statement of reasons ('Second Reading');
(c) if the Parliament approves the common position, the measure may be adopted by the Council;
(d) if the Parliament by absolute majority rejects the common position, the Council may not adopt the measure in question except by a unanimous vote (note again, however, that the final decision lies with the Council).

The procedure was introduced by the Single European Act to enhance the legislative role of the European Parliament known previously as the European Assembly. It was used for legislative decision-making under a wide range of articles extending to such matters as transport, the environment and health and safety. The importance of the procedure was, in turn, diminished by the TEU, also as part of the process of enhancing the role of the European Parliament. Many of the matters previously subject to it were, henceforth, to be determined according to the newly devised Co-decision procedure.

Co-decision procedure (EC Art 251)

This is currently the most extensively employed of the Treaty's decision-making processes and is applicable to, *inter alia*, the free movement of labour, the right of establishment, the internal market and consumer policy. It was introduced by the TEU to prevent measures in certain key areas being adopted without parliamentary approval. The most important aspect of co-decision is that it enables the European Parliament to veto or defeat legislative proposals made by the Council of Ministers but not to insist on amendments.

The process follows the same course as the cooperative procedure unless at the 'Second Reading' stage (i.e. when the measure is returned to the Parliament with a statement of the Council's common position and reasons), the Parliament rejects the common position or proposes amendments with which the Council cannot agree.

Should this occur a Conciliation Committee representative of Council members and MEPs will be established. If the committee is able to devise an agreed joint text, this will be adopted if approved by a simple majority in the Parliament and by a qualified majority in the Council. The measure cannot be adopted, therefore, should such majority in either or both institutions not be achieved. In the event that a joint text cannot be agreed, the Council may reinstate its original common position by majority vote. The measure may then be adopted and become law unless vetoed by an absolute majority in the Parliament.

Assent procedure

The Assent procedure is reserved for particularly important matters including the membership of new states (EC Art 49), the functioning and powers of the European Central Bank (EC Art 107(5)) and sanctions for serious and persistent breaches of human rights (EC Art 7). It prevents the Council of Ministers adopting a particular measure except with the consent of the Parliament. It does not include any provision for the making or agreeing of amendments.

Other powers

The European Parliament also has the power to:

(a) receive and debate annual general reports from the Commission and to question individual Commissioners;
(b) initiate legal proceedings in the Court of Justice in respect of any failure of the Council or Commission to fulfil their obligations under the EC Treaty;
(c) establish Committees of Inquiry to investigate alleged contraventions or mal-administration in the implementation of Community law;
(d) propose (but not insist on) amendments to budget proposals for 'compulsory expenditure' (i.e. that which the Community is obliged to spend to implement its laws and decisions) and, by a majority vote of all MEPs and two-thirds of the vote cast, to insist on amendments to budget proposals for 'non-compulsory expenditure' (i.e. discretionary expenditure);
(e) by the same majority, reject the budget proposals in their entirety and ask for different proposals to be submitted;
(f) appoint an Ombudsman to investigate allegations of maladministration by Community institutions;
(g) receive and consider petitions from natural or legal persons subject to its juris-diction concerning any aspect of Community law, policy or administration;
(h) debate and express its views on any economic, social or political issue of relevance to the Community.

The European Court of Justice (ECJ)

The Court consists of fifteen judges appointed by common accord of the member states. It functions through 'chambers' of three to five members. It is the practice that there will be one judge from each state. The judges of the Court appoint a President who then has overall responsibility for the proper disposal of the Court's judicial and administrative functions. Persons appointed to the Court must be qualified to hold senior judicial positions in their own countries or be 'jurisconsults' of recognised standing (e.g. eminent academic lawyers). They must also be persons whose 'independence is beyond doubt' (EC Art 223). Removal from office may only be effected by a unanimous decision of the other members of the court and the Advocates-General. There are nine such Advocates-General. Their function is, at the conclusion of the parties' submissions, to present the Court with a reasoned opinion as to how the case might be decided:

> with complete impartiality and independence, to make...reasoned submissions...in order to assist the court in the performance of the task assigned to it (EC Treaty, Art 166).

The Court has jurisdiction to entertain proceedings:

(a) brought by the Commission or a member state alleging breach of Community obligations by another member state;
(b) brought by a Community institution or member state challenging the legality of any act or failure to act by the Council, Commissioner or Parliament;
(c) referred under EC Art 234 by a court of a member state seeking a ruling as to the proper interpretation of Community law relevant to a question before it;
(d) brought by member states and natural or legal persons seeking compensation in respect of the acts or decisions of Community institutions;
(e) appealing against a decision of the Court of First Instance.

The Court of First Instance

This was set up in 1988 to ease the burden of work on the Court of Justice. Under EC Art 225 the Council may transfer to it any matter within the jurisdiction of the Court of Justice. To date matters of importance remitted to it have included proceedings:

(a) brought by natural or legal persons against Community institutions;
(b) raising issues of competition law;
(c) arising out of disputes between Community employees and Community institutions.

Decisions of the Court of First Instance are appealable to the Court of Justice on points of law only. Both courts present their decisions in the form of single judgments. Dissenting judgments are not delivered. The Court of First Instance is bound by the decisions of the ECJ. Neither court, however, is bound by its own previous decisions.

The Court of Auditors

This is not so much a court as an audit commission. It has fifteen members appointed by the Council after consultation with the Parliament and is charged with auditing the Community's accounts and identifying any unlawful use or mismanagement of Community resources. Its findings are published in an annual report.

THE TREATY OF NICE

The Treaty was signed on 26 February 2001. It represents the outcome of the IGC opened on 14 February 2000. The principal objective of the Treaty is to reform the composition and decision-making processes in readiness for the biggest enlargement of the Union since its inception as the EEC by the Treaty of Rome in 1957. From 1 January 2004 the Treaty envisages a Union of 27 members, an increase of twelve from its present complement of fifteen.

The prinicipal reform to be effected by the Treaty will be as follows:

(a) The European Parliament
     Provisionally, and subject to accession negotiations, the European Parliament for the session 2004–09 will consist of no more than 732 members. Of these, 535 will be returned by the present fifteen member states and 197 by the newly acceded states.

     At present the European Parliament has 626 members. Implementation of the Treaty will thus mean a reduction of 91 in the number of seats currently occupied by the Union's fifteen members. These changes are to be effected in accordance with the democratic principles of proportionality and appropriate representation of the peoples of each member state.

     The exact distribution of seats in the Parliament at the time of writing is: Germany 99, France 87, Italy 87, United Kingdom 87, Spain 64, Netherlands 31, Belgium 25, Greece 25, Portugal 25, Sweden 22, Austria 21, Denmark 16, Finland 16, Ireland 15, Luxembourg 6.

     The provisional figures for 1 January 2004 are: Germany 99, France 72, Italy 72, United Kingdom 72, Spain 50, Poland 50, Romania 33, Netherlands 25, Greece 22, Belgium 22, Portugal 22, Czech Republic 20, Hungary 20, Sweden 18, Bulgaria 17, Austria 17, Slovakia 13, Denmark 13, Finland 13, Ireland 12, Lithuania 12, Latvia 8, Slovenia 7, Estonia 6, Cyprus 6, Luxembourg 6, Malta 5.

(b) The Council of Ministers
     The Council will continue to consist of one member for each contracting state thus taking its total complement after enlargement to 27 national ministerial representatives.

     The main changes to be effected by the Treaty relate to the composition of voting majorities necessary for approval of a Council decision.

     At present 73 Articles of the Treaty still require decisions to be taken by unanimity. Thirty of these provisions will in future be subject to decision by qualified majority. The Treaty will effect changes to the mathematics of the requirements and composition of a qualified majority and the numbers of votes to be cast by representatives of particular states. After accession of the twelve states the qualified majority threshold will be set at 255 out of 345 votes cast by a majority of states. A member state will be permitted to ask for verification that the qualified majority comprise at least 62 per cent of the Union's total population. If this is not so, the decision may not be adopted. The national allocation of votes will be: France 29, Germany 29, Italy 29, United Kingdom 29, Poland 27, Spain 27, Romania 14, Netherlands 13, Belgium 12, Czech Republic 12, Greece 12, Hungary 12, Portugal 12, Austria 10, Bulgaria 10, Sweden 10, Denmark 7,

Finland 7, Ireland 7, Lithuania 7, Slovakia 7, Cyprus 4, Estonia 4, Latvia 4, Luxembourg 4, Slovenia 4, Malta 3.

(c) The Commission

At present the Commission has twenty members, two Commissioners for each of the larger states and one each for the smaller ones.

From 1 January 2005, the Commission will consist of one Commissioner per member state. On the accession of all twelve new members the Council will decide on a reformed future composition to consist of fewer than 27 Commissioners determined by a system of rotation that will be fair to all countries. This decision will be taken by the Council voting unanimously.

(d) The Court of Justice

As a result of the heavy workload on both the Court of Justice and the Court of First Instance the average wait for a case to appear before the Court of Justice is at the time of writing 21 months. For the Court of First Instance the wait is, on average, 30 months. In order to avoid a worsening of this situation following enlargement the Treaty provides for a number of reforms including:

- the Court of First Instance to be enabled to hear direct actions;
- the creation of specialised chambers to relieve the Court of First Instance of cases in specific areas;
- allowing the Court of First Instance to give preliminary rulings in appropriate matters.

In the enlarged Union the Court will continue to consist of one judge from each state but may convene in a Grand Chamber of thirteen members rather than, at present, in plenary session attended by all members.

(e) The Court of Auditors

The Treaty requires that the Court will continue to consist of one officer for each member state appointed by the Council for six years by qualified majority vote. The Court will, however, be able to set up chambers to dispose of different aspects of its work.

SOURCES OF COMMUNITY LAW

Primary Community law

This is composed of the Articles of the various treaties on which the Community is founded – particularly the EC Treaty as amended. Treaty provisions are 'directly applicable' in all member states. As such they take effect without further legislative implementation by national Parliaments or governments (EC Art 249). Where such provisions are sufficiently 'clear and unconditional' so that they may be applied by national courts without unacceptably wide variations in interpretation, they are also said to be 'directly effective' – i.e. they create rights immediately enforceable by individuals. Such rights may be enforced:

(a) 'vertically', i.e. against the state (*Van Gend en Loos* v *Netherlands Fiscal Administration* [1963] CMLR 105);
(b) 'horizontally', i.e. between individuals (*Defrenne* v *SABENA* [1976] 2 CMLR 98).

Secondary Community law

Regulations

These are also directly applicable and 'binding in their entirety' (EC Art 249). Also, like Treaty Articles, where sufficiently precise, they are directly effective within member states both vertically and horizontally, as in (a) and (b) above. Hence in *Leonesio* v *Italian Ministry of Agriculture and Forestry* [1973] CMLR 343, the European Court of Justice explained that a regulation 'produces immediate effects and is, as such, apt to attribute to individuals rights which national courts must uphold'.

Directives

These are not directly applicable but are binding on states as to their objectives or the results to be achieved. Member states to which they are addressed are obliged to take legislative action (either primary or secondary) to give effect to them by the notified date or, in the case of directives applying to all member states where no particular date for implementation is given, within twenty days of the directive's publication.

A directive which has not been so implemented, or which has been implemented only partially or defectively, may still be capable of having direct effect – i.e. of conferring enforceable rights on individuals.

> A member state which has not adopted the implementing measures required by the directive in the prescribed period may not rely, as against individuals, on its failure to perform the obligation which the directive entails (*Publico Ministero* v *Ratti* [1980] 1 CMLR 96).

The circumstances in which this will pertain are as follows.

(a) The content of the directive is clear and concise and does not permit of any discretion in the manner of its implementation (*Van Duyn* v *The Home Office (No. 2)* [1974] ECR 1337).

(b) The directive is relied upon by an individual in proceedings against an 'emanation of the state' whether acting in its public or private capacity (*Marshall* v *Southampton and South-West Hampshire Area Health Authority (No. 1)* [1986] 1 CMLR 688). In addition to central and local government authorities, the term 'emanation of the state' has been held to extend to any 'body, whatever its legal form, which has been made responsible, pursuant to a measure adopted by the state, for providing a public service under the control of the state and for that purpose has special powers beyond those which result from the normal rules applicable in the relations between individuals' (*Foster* v *British Gas* [1990] 2 CMLR 833). This includes health authorities (*Marshall*, above), police authorities (*Johnston* v *Chief Constable of the Royal Ulster Constabulary* [1986] 3 CMLR 240), and service-providing public corporations (*Foster*, above). It is also probable that the Foster definition of emanations of the state is sufficiently wide to encompass 'privatised' public utilities (*Griffin* v *South West Water Services Ltd* [1995] IRLR 15). Directives, therefore, are capable of having vertical direct effect only. They are not enforceable by one individual against another – i.e. horizontally (*Johnston*, above) – and are not enforceable by the state against an individual (*Officier van Justitie* v

Kolpinghuis Nijmegen BV [1989] 2 CMLR 18). Note, however, the view of the European Court of Justice in *Marleasing SA* v *Comercial Internacional de Alimentación SA* [1992] 1 CMLR 305, that, even though no public body may be involved in a particular dispute, the relevant domestic legal principles should be interpreted to avoid any conflict with Community law including directives not yet implemented. In this sense, therefore, although the content of a directive not yet given effect by national law may not be used as a cause of action between individuals, it could affect the outcome of a case by influencing the domestic rules applied.

The fact that a directive which has not been transcribed into national law is not directly enforceable as between individuals does not mean that a person who has suffered financial loss through being unable to enforce the rights contained therein has no remedy. In such circumstances the individual may bring an action against the state in respect of loss incurred as a result of its failure to comply with its obligation under Community law to give effect to directives addressed to it within any prescribed date. Providing the directive in question was intended to confer rights on individuals, and there was a reasonable causal link between the state's failure and the loss suffered, such loss is recoverable (*Francovich* v *Italy* [1993] 2 CMLR 66).

National courts do not have the jurisdiction to rule over the validity of Community legislation. This power is reserved to the European Court of Justice. Moreover, where such issue is pending before that Court, a national court may not suspend the operation of national legislation giving effect to the impugned Community measure unless:

(a) there exists serious doubts as to the validity of the measure in question;
(b) not to suspend the operation would cause 'serious and irreparable damage' to the party seeking interim relief (*R* v *Secretary of State for Health, ex parte Imperial Tobacco* [2001] 1 WLR 127).

The issue of state liability for failure to implement, and breach of, Community law is dealt with in more detail in Chapter 13.

Decisions

These may be made by the Council or, with the Council's authority, by the Commission. They may be addressed to states, individuals or companies, and are binding in their entirety – i.e. no discretion is permitted in terms of their mode of application. Decisions may relate, for example, to implementation of EC competition policy or to whether member states are complying with Community obligations. Although this has not been settled unequivocally, it would appear that such decisions may be directly enforceable by individuals against those to whom they are addressed (*Franz Grad* v *Finanzamt Traunstein* [1971] CMLR 1).

Decisions of the European Court of Justice

These also constitute a secondary source of European Community law and are the means by which greater definition is given to the requirements of the EC Treaty and those regulations and directives made in pursuance of it. Although the ECJ need not follow its own decisions, these are binding on the Court of First Instance and on national courts in matters relating to the proper interpretations of European legal principles.

Further reading

Steiner and Woods (1996) *European Community Law* (5th edn), London: Blackstone, Chs 1, 2 and 3.

Turpin (2002) *British Government and the Constitution* (5th edn), London: Butterworths, Ch 5.

Vincenzi (1996) *Law of the European Community*, London: Pitman Publishing, Chs 1–5.

Chapter 5

THE LEGISLATIVE SOVEREIGNTY OF THE WESTMINSTER PARLIAMENT

INTRODUCTION

Definition

The theory of 'continuing' sovereignty, as explained by Professor Dicey, is that there are no limits to the legislative competence of Parliament. Each Parliament is absolutely sovereign in its own time and may legislate as it wishes on any topic and for any place. That which has been enacted by Parliament has supreme force and cannot be invalidated or changed by any other domestic or external authority.

The United Kingdom has no overriding written constitution against which the validity of Parliament's enactments may be tested. It follows that the function of the courts in relation to Acts of Parliament is limited to interpreting and applying that which has been placed before them bearing on its face the official consents of the Commons, Lords and Monarch.

> All that a Court of Justice can do is to look at the 'parliamentary role': if from that it should appear that a Bill has passed both Houses and received the Royal Assent, no Court of Justice can inquire into the mode in which was introduced in Parliament, not what was done previous to its introduction, or what passed in Parliament during its stages through both Houses (per Lord Campbell, *Edinburgh and Dalkeith Railway Co v Wauchope* (1842) 8 Cl & F 710).

It has also been said that even if 'an Act has been obtained improperly, it is for the legislature to correct it by repealing it: but so long as it exists as law, the courts are bound to obey it' (per Willis J, *Lee v Bude and Torrington Railway Co* (1871) LR 6 CP 577). The reluctance of the courts to 'go behind' how a statute was enacted is well illustrated by the facts of *Manuel v Attorney-General,* above. The case concerned a challenge made by representatives of the Indian nations of Canada to the Canada Act 1982. Their challenge was based, *inter alia,* on the Statute of Westminster, s 4, which provided that the Westminster Parliament would not legislate for a dominion 'unless it is expressly stated in the Act that the Dominion has requested, and consented to, the enactment...'. The Canadian Indians argued that as neither they nor all of the Canadian provinces had given their consent to the Canadian government's request for the legislation, the enactment was inconsistent with the 1931 Act and therefore invalid.

The argument did not convince the House of Lords. The Lords pointed out that all the 1931 Act required was that legislation affecting a dominion should simply *state* that it had been requested and consented to by the dominion concerned, and that a formula of words to this effect was contained in the preamble to the 1982 Act. It was not open to the court, therefore, to question the quality, validity, or even factual existence of this consent. If the Act stated that it had been given, that was not something a court could inquire into notwithstanding the substance of allegations to the contrary.

History

The doctrine of the unlimited sovereignty of Parliament really began to evolve in response to the political settlement of 1688. Prior to this, in a less secular society than exists today, examples may be found of judicial dicta suggesting that parliamentary enactments were subordinate to divine law or the law of natural reason.

> Whatsoever is not consonant to the law of God or to right reason which is maintained by scripture, be it Acts of Parliament, customs, or any judicial acts of the Court, it is not the law of England (per Keble J, *R* v *Lowe* (1853) 5 St Tr 825).

Other well-known cases in which courts claimed the authority to regard legislation as void if it offended against 'common right or reason' or against 'natural equity' would include *Dr Bonham's Case* (1610) 8 Co Rep 114, and *Day* v *Savadge* (1615) Hob 85.

The 'revolutionaries' of 1688 had, however, no intention of transferring sovereign power from the King to a Parliament genuinely representative of the people. Legal sovereignty was indeed to be vested in Parliament, but in a Parliament which, at the time, was returned by a tiny electorate consisting of the propertied and landed élite. Parliament's sovereign status did not, therefore, derive from its democratic authority in the modern sense.

The 1689 settlement did succeed, however, in establishing a 'balanced constitution' – that is, one dominated by a sovereign Parliament representative of the three principal estates or interests of the realm: Monarch, Lords and Commons. The enactment of valid legislation required the assent of each element. Hence no single estate could entirely dominate the others or legislate purely in its own interests.

Legal and political sovereignty distinguished

According to Dicey and others, while legal sovereignty or the power to issue commands in the form of laws which prevail against all others resides in Parliament, political sovereignty – particularly with the existence of universal adult suffrage – lies with the people. This is either expressed or generally implicit in the various doctrines of the social contract promulgated by Hobbes, Paine, Locke and others (see respectively *The Leviathan* (1615), *The Rights of Man* (1791), *The Treatises of Government* (1690)). The essence of the social contract is that individuals voluntarily submit themselves to the authority of government, and agree to limits on their freedom, in return for peace, order and a system of government which accords with the popular will. Should the government act in ways which abuse the trust and authority deposed in it, then 'the people have a right to act as supreme, and continue the legislative in themselves or place it in a new form, or new hands, as they think good' (Locke, *op. cit.*).

APPLICATION

Express repeal

Parliament is not bound by its predecessors and may amend or repeal any previous enactments by passing legislation stating its intentions to that end. Hence, were an Act to provide that it was not to be repealed, or to be repealed only according to some special parliamentary procedure, it is generally agreed that this would not bind a subsequent Parliament which could repeal or alter it in the normal way.

Implied repeal

As a general rule, if an Act is partially or wholly inconsistent with a previous Act, then the previous Act is repealed to the extent of the inconsistency. It does not matter that the later Act contains no express words to effect the repeal or alteration. This is known as the doctrine of implied repeal.

The doctrine of implied repeal was applied in *Vauxhall Estates* v *Liverpool Corporation* [1932] 1 KB 733. The plaintiffs claimed compensation for property which had been compulsorily purchased from them. According to the defendants, this was to be assessed in compliance with the Housing Act 1925. This was refuted by the plaintiffs. They argued that the assessment should be calculated according to the more generous terms contained in the Acquisition of Land (Assessment of Compensation) Act 1919 which stipulated expressly that its provisions were to prevail over any others passed or to be passed. The Court felt bound to apply the 1925 enactment. It was not within the competence of the Parliament of 1919 to impose fetters on the legislative authority of those which followed it. The fact that the 1925 Act made no express reference to the 1919 Act provisions was irrelevant. These had, by implication, been repealed.

The doctrine was given succinct expression in a much quoted dictum from a case with similar facts two years later:

> The Legislative cannot, according to our constitution, bind itself as to the form of subsequent legislation, and it is impossible for Parliament to enact that in a subsequent statute dealing with the same subject-matter there can be no implied repeal (per Maugham LJ, *Ellen Street Estates* v *Minister of Health* [1934] 1 KB 590).

Clearly, as was evident in the language of Maugham J, the doctrine as originally conceived was understood to permit of no significant exceptions. Recent developments suggest, however, that it should now be understood as describing a general rather than an absolute rule and that a major departure from it is in the process of development in relation to what have been called 'constitutional statutes'. The argument here appears to be that those statutes which were of fundamental importance in the shaping of the constitution and the rights guaranteed to those subject to it should only be repealed or altered by a clearly expressed intent to that end in subsequent legislation – an idea obviously premised on the view that, as the doctrine of sovereignty in general is judge-made, it remains open to the judges to adapt it to changing political and historical circumstances.

This modified version of the doctrine of implied repeal was articulated most clearly by Laws LJ in *Hunt* v *London Borough of Hackney; Thoburn* v *City of Sunderland;*

Harman v *Cornwall County Council; Collins* v *London Borough of Sutton* [2002] EWHC (Admin) 195 (the 'Metric Martyrs' case).

The case concerned a number of market traders who had been convicted of selling goods by imperial measurements, i.e. pounds and ounces, contrary to regulations made under the European Communities Act 1972, s 2 (ECA). These regulations gave effect to a European directive requiring the sale of goods in metric measurement only. By way of defence, the traders relied on the Weights and Measures Act 1985, which expressly permitted the use of both the imperial and metric systems. This, it was claimed, repealed impliedly any power in s 2 of the 1972 Act to make any regulations prohibiting the use of imperial measurements and to insist on pain of legal penalty that traders must use the metric system.

In terms of the traditional doctrine of implied repeal, this argument had much to commend it. Laws LJ, however, was of the view that the 1972 Act was a 'constitutional statute' and, as such, not subject to implied repeal. Given its clarity, significance and modernity, his reasons are worth quoting in full:

> In the present state of its maturity the common law has come to recognise that there exist rights which should be properly classified as constitutional or fundamental...We should recognise a hierarchy of Acts of Parliament: as it were 'ordinary' statutes and 'constitutional statutes...In my opinion a constitutional statute is one which (a) conditions the legal relationship between the citizen and the state in some general, overarching manner, or (b) enlarges or diminishes the scope of what we would now regard as fundamental constitutional rights...The special status of constitutional statutes follows the constitutional status of constitutional rights. Examples are the Magna Carta, the Bill of Rights 1689, the Act of Union, the Reform Acts which distributed and enlarged the franchise, the Human Rights Act 1998, the Scotland Act 1998 and the Government of Wales Act 1998. The ECA clearly belongs in this category. It incorporated the whole corpus of Community rights and obligations, and gave overriding domestic effect to the judicial and administrative machinery of Community Law. It may be that there has never been a statute having such profound effect on so many dimensions of our daily lives. The ECA is, by force of the common law, a constitutional statute...Ordinary statutes may be impliedly repealed. Constitutional statutes may not. For the repeal of a constitutional Act or the abrogation of a fundamental right to be effected by statute, the court would apply this test: is it shown that the legislature's actual – not imputed, constructed or presumed – intention was to effect the repeal or abrogation? I think the test could only be met by express words in the later statute, or by words so specific that the inference of an actual determination to the effect of the result contended for was irresistible.

Retrospective legislation

Parliament has the power to legislate retrospectively as well as prospectively. This means that Parliament can render illegal and impose penalties on actions which were perfectly lawful when they were committed. Also, actions which were unlawful at the time of commission, may be rendered lawful or not subject to any legal sanction or proceedings.

In *R* v *Londonderry Justices, ex parte Hume* [1972] NI 91, the Court of Appeal in Northern Ireland ruled that the Civil Authorities (Special Powers) Act 1922 (the principal emergency powers statute in force in Northern Ireland when the recent

'Troubles' began), conferred powers of arrest and detention on members of the RUC (the Northern Irish police) but not on British military personnel. This rendered illegal the arrests and detention of all those who had been taken into custody by the army – including those hundreds of suspects who had been 'rounded-up' in the internment operation of August 1971 and who were being held in internment camps. Within 48 hours of the decision the Westminster Parliament had enacted the Northern Ireland Act 1972. This provided that the armed forces were possessed of the necessary powers of arrest at the relevant time. The alternative would have been to release all the detainees.

Another famous example of legislative overruling of an 'awkward' judicial decision occurred in 1965. In *Burmah Oil* v *Lord Advocate*, above, the House of Lords held that the Crown was bound to compensate those whose property had been destroyed by British forces during the Second World War – except where this had occurred during the course of a battle. The decision would have resulted in a massive drain on the country's financial resources. Retrospective parliamentary intervention followed in the form of the War Damages Act 1965. The preamble to the Act recited that its purpose was to 'abolish rights at common law to compensation in respect of damage to property effected by the Crown during war'. Rights which existed prior to the Act were thus extinguished.

Retrospective legislation which imposes criminal penalties is inconsistent with the European Convention on Human Rights, Art 7, and with most modern conceptions of the rule of law. It contradicts the principle that persons should only be expected to regulate their conduct according to laws which are in existence and should not be punished 'on account of any action or omission which did not constitute a criminal offence...when it was committed' (Art 7). The constitutionally dubious nature of this type of legislation was recognised long before any of these more modern prescriptions were formulated. Hence in *Phillips* v *Eyre* (1870) LR 6 QB 1, Willes J stated that retrospective legislation was 'contrary to the general principle that legislation by which the conduct of mankind is to be regulated ought...to deal with future acts and ought not to change the character of past transactions carried on upon the faith of their existing law'. He also emphasised the still existing rule that a court 'will not ascribe legislative force to new laws affecting rights unless by express words or necessary implication it appears that such was the intention of the legislative'.

Acts of Parliament and international law

Parliament is not bound by international law. Should a parliamentary enactment be inconsistent with a rule of international law, the statute prevails. International treaties have only persuasive force in the United Kingdom. The judges assume that Parliament does not intend to legislate inconsistently with them. Hence ambiguities or uncertainties in English law will usually be interpreted in ways which accord with international rules. Where, however, there is a clear and unavoidable inconsistency, the parliamentary provision takes precedence. To the extent that customary international law (international common law) is part of the law of England, it, like any other common law provision, gives way to statute.

In *Mortensen* v *Peters* (1906) 14 SLT 227, the captain of a Norwegian trawler was convicted of fishing in the Moray Firth contrary to the Herring Fisheries (Scotland) Act 1889. The court felt bound to apply the Act even though it restricted fishing beyond the three-mile territorial limit recognised by international law.

A challenge to the validity of elements of the annual Finance Act was mounted in *Cheney* v *Conn* [1968] 1 All ER 779. The argument was that the Act authorised the collection of revenue some of which would be used for purposes contrary to the Geneva Convention 1957, viz. the construction of nuclear weapons. The Court's conclusion was:

> What the statute itself enacts cannot be unlawful, because what the statute says is itself the law, and the highest form of law, that is known in this country. It is the law which prevails over every other form of law, and it is not for the court to say that a parliamentary enactment...is illegal (per Ungoed-Thomas J).

Parliament's territorial competence

Parliament can and does legislate for places outside the executive competence of the British government. Jennings once said that Parliament could make it an offence to smoke in the streets of Paris. He was not suggesting that the British government could seek to implement domestic legislation in foreign jurisdictions but that the British courts and law enforcement agencies could enforce such legislation against allegedly guilty persons if, and when, they entered the United Kingdom.

Famous examples of statutes having extra-territorial effect would include the Continental Shelf Act 1964 which asserted British exploration and mining rights over the continental shelf beyond British waters, and the War Crimes Act 1991 which gave British courts the power to try war crimes committed outside the United Kingdom providing the accused had become a British citizen or was resident in the United Kingdom.

Parliament's extra-territorial competence was manifest as early as the fourteenth century in the Treason Felony Act 1351. This ancient statute, which is still in force, created the offence of adhering to the Crown's enemies in any place inside *or outside* the realm. The offence carries the death penalty. The Act was used in the two most famous treason trials of the twentieth century. In *R* v *Casement* [1917] 1 KB 78, the defendant, an Irish Nationalist and ex-member of the British diplomatic service, was convicted of treason and sentenced to death after he had tried to persuade Irish prisoners of war in Germany to join the German armed forces. The 1351 Act was also used to secure the conviction and execution of William Joyce (Lord 'Haw Haw') who was employed by the Germans to make propaganda broadcasts to the United Kingdom during the Second World War (*DPP* v *Joyce* [1946] AC 347).

In the case of some ex-colonies which were given their constitutions and independent dominion status by Acts of the Westminster Parliament, it was provided that alterations to key elements of those constitutions could be made only by further enactments from Westminster following a request from the dominion parliament concerned – according to the procedure in the Statute of Westminster Parliament 1931, s 4. Hence in relatively recent times the Westminster Parliament has, pursuant to the appropriate requests, legislated for both Canada (Canada Act 1982) and Australia (Australia Act 1986). In both cases the purposes of the legislation was to transfer ('repatriate') to the countries concerned the power to legislate in all matters relating to their own constitutions. These two enactments may be regarded, therefore, as examples of Parliament exercising its extra-territorial jurisdiction albeit, in both cases, for the purposes of surrendering that jurisdiction to the appropriate national assemblies.

The succession to the throne

Since the revolutionary settlement of 1688, Parliament has regulated the succession to the throne. This right was embodied in the Act of Settlement 1700 which, following the death of the childless Queen Anne (1702–14), conferred the succession onto the House of Hanover in the person of George I (1714–27). From subsequent events it would also appear that parliamentary consent is necessary for any alteration in the normal line of succession. Hence when Edward VIII decided that he wished to abdicate in order to marry the divorcee Mrs Wallis Simpson, this, and his replacement by his brother George VI, was authorised by His Majesty's Declaration of Abdication Act 1936.

> Immediately upon the Royal Assent being signified to this Act...His Majesty shall cease to be King and there shall be a demise of the Crown and accordingly the member of the Royal Family then next in succession to the throne shall succeed...

Defining the meaning of Parliament

Parliament is capable of redefining its constituent elements for the purpose of enacting legislation. Thus for most Bills Parliament will consist of the Commons, Lords and Monarch. By virtue of the Parliament Acts, however, a Bill rejected by the House of Lords in two successive sessions may go for the Royal Assent after one year has elapsed. 'Parliament', for such a Bill, would consist of the House of Commons and the Monarch – two elements rather than three. It has also been argued that, by the provision in the Statute of Westminster making a request from a dominion legislature a precondition to Westminster legislation affecting its territory, Parliament has again effectively redefined itself by adding a fourth element to its composition (viz. Commons, Lords, Monarch and the dominion parliament). Also note the provision in the Northern Ireland Constitution Act 1973, s 1, requiring the consent of the Northern Ireland people by referendum to any change in the province's constitutional status. This could be understood as redefining Parliament to include the Northern Ireland electorate for any relevant legislation.

Composition and membership

Parliament may decide who is and who is not qualified to sit and participate in its proceedings. This may be done by legislation or by mere resolution of either House. As such resolutions relate to the internal affairs of the sovereign body, they cannot be questioned by the courts. The measure which currently identifies those categories of persons disqualified from membership of the House of Commons is the House of Commons (Disqualification) Act 1975. Its precise content is set out in more detail below (see Chapter 7). The power of the House to exclude by resolution is also considered in greater detail in Chapter 10 dealing with parliamentary privilege. Statutes relating to the composition of the House of Lords – particularly the Life Peerages Act 1958 and House of Lords Act 1999 – are explained in Chapter 9.

Procedure

Parliament is master of its own procedure and may, therefore, change the procedural process according to which Bills are enacted or any other parliamentary business is conducted. Hence, if, for reasons of expediency, the House of Commons were to dispense with the Committee and Third Reading Stages of a Bill, it is unlikely that this would prevent the measure from becoming a valid Act of Parliament – providing, that is, it was approved by the House of Lords and received the Royal Assent. According to the enrolled Bill rule, a court would be limited to inquiring whether the Bill had been assented to by Parliament as currently defined and recognised by the common law, i.e. Commons, Lords and Monarch. To go beyond this would involve the court inquiring into the validity of the processes through which Parliament had exercised its sovereign legislative power.

In *Pickin v British Railways Board* [1994] AC 765, a challenge was made to the British Railways Act 1968. The Act sought to extinguish certain rights given to the owners of property on either side of a railway line. These rights had been granted by the Acts which had originally authorised acquisition of the land for the railway's construction. They provided that in the event of the line becoming disused, ownership of the land on which it ran should revert to the adjoining landowners. The standing orders of both Houses required that the promoters of Private Bills should give notice of the proposed legislation to any persons whose private interests would be affected thereby. Pickin alleged that this had not been done and that, as a result, the Bill had been put before and dealt with by Parliament, in error, as an unopposed Private Bill (i.e. according to the wrong procedure).

In a purely factual sense, *Pickin*'s case was not without substance. The House of Lords, however, could not be persuaded that it had any constitutional authority to investigate the allegations.

Length of existence

Each Parliament may determine the length of its own existence. Hence, although the Parliament Act 1911 provides that parliaments may continue in existence for a maximum period of five years (previously seven years by virtue of the Septennial Act 1714), twice in this century Parliament has continued without a dissolution beyond the five-year period. On both occasions this was to avoid the divisive effects of an election during wartime. Thus, the Parliament of 1910 continued until 1918 and the Parliament of 1935 until 1945 (Prolongation of Parliament Acts 1940, 1941, 1942, 1943, 1944).

Civil liberties

Since the United Kingdom has no overriding written constitution, Parliament, by ordinary legislative procedure, may alter or reduce that which might be regarded as the citizen's basic civil liberties or freedoms. This was done in both World Wars when the executive was given powers to intern without trial (Defence of the Realm Act 1914 and Emergency Powers (Defence) Act 1939). Similar powers of unlimited detention were provided by the Northern Ireland (Emergency Provisions) Acts. The power of detention in the Prevention of Terrorism Act 1989 was more limited (seven days in total). Other significant and relatively recent enactments restricting individual freedoms would include the Police and Criminal Evidence Act 1984, the Public Order Act 1986 and the Criminal Justice and Public Order Act 1994.

Parliament's sovereign status means that legislative curtailment of the freedoms of the individual is not a ground for judicial intervention (*R* v *Jordan* [1967] Crim LR 483).

Resolutions of the House and subordinate legislation

Mere resolutions of the House of Commons or the House of Lords do not make law and are not binding on the courts. Such resolutions are not made by Parliament as it is defined by the common law. In *Stockdale* v *Hansard* (1839) 9 Ad & El 1, the plaintiff sued for libel in respect of the contents of an official parliamentary report. The defendants pleaded a House of Commons resolution of 1839 to the effect that all such publications should be treated as absolutely privileged. The court refused to recognise the resolution as having any legal effect and awarded damages to the plaintiff. Lord Denham CJ explained the court's decision as follows:

> ...The House of Commons is not Parliament but only a co-ordinate and component part of the Parliament. That sovereign power can make and unmake the laws; but the concurrence of the three legislative estates is necessary; the resolution of any one of them cannot alter the law, or place anyone beyond its control.

This distinction between Acts of Parliament and parliamentary resolutions was also applied in *Bowles* v *Bank of England* [1913] 1 Ch 57. On this occasion it was held that the Bank was not entitled to deduct income tax from dividends owed to the plaintiff. The only authority for the tax in question was a Budget resolution of the House of Commons. For many years, and until this case, it had been the practice for tax proposals contained in the Budget (usually delivered in March) to be collected immediately or from the beginning of the new financial year and until the enactment of the annual Finance Act (late July/early August) merely on the authority of resolutions of the House. The court had no doubt that this was clearly unlawful and offended against the principle, recognised by the Bill of Rights, that taxation should not be imposed without statutory authority. The immediate result of the decision was the passing of the Provisional Collection of Taxes Act 1913. This gave legal effect to resolutions of the House approving variations of taxation during the period until the annual Finance Act came into force (see now, Provisional Collection of Taxes Act 1968).

The rule that the courts may not question or invalidate legislation applies only to Acts of Parliament or 'primary' legislation. Where, however, Parliament has delegated legislative power to subordinate bodies such as ministers or local authorities, legislation made by them ('secondary' legislation) is open to judicial review if it exceeds the powers delegated by the 'parent' or 'enabling' legislation (*Attorney-General* v *Wilts United Dairies* (1921) 37 TLR 881), or was not made according to the correct procedure (*R* v *Secretary of State for Social Services, ex parte Association of Metropolitan Authorities* [1986] 1 All ER 164).

Where secondary or subordinate legislation has been laid before and approved by Parliament, judicial intervention may appear to come close to questioning a decision of the Sovereign body. The rule here appears to be that review of such legislation is restricted to procedural error, bad faith, improper motive or manifest absurdity (*R* v *Secretary of State for the Environment, ex parte Hammersmith and Fulham LBC* [1991] 1 AC 521).

POSSIBLE LEGAL LIMITATIONS

The doctrine of manner and form

It has been suggested that, if a statute were to prescribe a particular procedure or 'manner and form' for its amendment or repeal, any subsequent legislative provisions seeking to achieve such alteration except by that method would be ineffective. This suggestion is sometimes said to be supported by the decisions in *Attorney-General for New South Wales* v *Trethowan* [1932] AC 526, and *Harris* v *Minister of the Interior* (1952) 2 SA 428.

The *Trethowan* case was concerned with the Constitution (Legislative Council Amendment) Act 1929, an Act of the New South Wales Parliament. The Act provided that the Parliament's upper House could not be abolished except by a Bill approved in a referendum after completing its parliamentary stages. In 1930, after an election in New South Wales had changed the political complexion of the state Parliament, a Bill to abolish the upper House was approved by both Houses but was not put to a referendum. An injunction was granted by the High Court of Australia and upheld by the Judicial Committee of the Privy Council to prevent the Bill going for the Royal Assent. It was held that since the Westminster Parliament was sovereign and had decreed in the Colonial Laws Validity Act 1865 that all colonial legislatures should legislate in accordance with 'such manner and form as might from time to time be required by an Act of Parliament or other law for the time being in force in the state', it was incumbent on the New South Wales Parliament to comply with the procedure contained in the 1929 Act.

In the *Harris* case, the South African Supreme Court refused to accept the constitutional validity of one of the pieces of legislation introduced by the post-1948 Nationalist government for the purpose of establishing apartheid. The modern state of South Africa was given its first constitution by the South African Act 1909, an Act of the Westminster Parliament. This Act sought to protect the political rights of black citizens in the Cape Province. Section 152 provided that they could not be removed from the electoral register except by a Bill passed by a majority of two-thirds of both

Houses of the South African Parliament sitting unicamerally. In 1951 the nationalist-dominated Parliament sought to remove this guarantee by the Separate Registration of Voters Act. The Act was passed by simple majorities in both Houses with the requirement in s 152 of the 1909 Act being simply ignored.

South Africa's most senior court held that since the South African Parliament had been created and given its powers by the 1909 Act, it was bound to exercise its legislative powers in accordance with the Act's requirements. Legislation seeking to alter the rights protected by s 152 was, therefore, invalid unless the prescribed procedure was adhered to.

These cases are direct authority for the principle that subordinate dominion Parliaments are bound to legislate within any constraints imposed on them by the mother Parliament at Westminster. Neither case, however, provides any genuine authority for the view that the Westminster Parliament may impose procedural fetters on itself. The British constitution does not recognise any superior Parliament or other legal authority which could impose similar restrictions on Westminster's freedom of action. From this it could be concluded that the doctrine of manner and form, at least as applied in the *Trethowan* and *Harris* cases, may be of limited validity in a purely domestic context.

The self-embracing theory of parliamentary sovereignty

More convincing and perhaps substantial – albeit purely academic – support for the relevance of the manner and form argument in the British context may perhaps be found in the 'self-embracing' theory of parliamentary sovereignty as originally advanced by Sir Ivor Jennings (*The Law of the Constitution* (5th edn), 1959).

According to this approach, and given the importance of statute as a source of English law, the common law requires and has developed a rule or formula for determining what constitutes a valid Act of Parliament. This had been referred to as the common law's 'rule of recognition' and is satisfied by that which has been consented to by the Commons, Lords and Monarch. Judicial statements that the court must simply interpret and apply that which had been so enacted, and may not question the procedure by which these consents were given, represent, therefore, no more than the rule of recognition in practice. It follows, according to Jennings, that if a statute were to prescribe an alternative definition of Parliament for the purpose of amending or repealing a particular enactment – say a requirement for two-thirds majorities in both Houses – this would lay down a new rule of recognition for the purpose of altering the Act in question. Moreover, since this would have been imposed by statute, it would be bound to prevail over the otherwise generally applicable common law rule. Essentially, therefore, the self-embracing theory of sovereignty is founded on the straightforward principle that the common law must give way to statute.

The essence of Jennings' theory is contained in the following statement:

> Legal sovereignty is merely a name indicating that the established legislature has for the time being power to make laws of any kind in the manner prescribed by law. That is, a rule expressed to be made by the Queen, 'with the advice and consent of the Lords spiritual and temporal, and the Commons in this present Parliament assembled...' will be recognised by the courts including a rule which alters this law itself. If this be so, the legal

sovereign may impose legal limitations upon itself, because its power to change the law includes the power to change the law affecting itself (*ibid.*).

Academics differ on the validity of this theory. Professor Wade has pointed out that its validity depends on the assumption that the rule of recognition is indeed nothing more than a common law principle. His view, explained in 1955, was that the supremacy of Parliament in its traditional and accepted form was of greater authority than that normally attributed to a common law rule and was one of the basic political facts which resulted from the 1688 revolution. This was then accepted and applied by the judiciary through the evolution of the doctrine of sovereignty in its traditional or continuing sense. As a result, only something equivalently momentous in the political sense – perhaps a further revolution or major constitutional rearrangement – would be sufficient to break the continuity of the post-1688 government order, and thus entrench and give constitutional authority to a redefined version of the power of Parliament (see 'The Basis of Legal Sovereignty' (1955) CLJ 172).

The Acts of Union

While most would accept that Parliament has the sovereign power to repeal and alter almost every other type of legislation, regardless of content, it has been suggested that this same legislative freedom might not apply to those major statutes which gave effect to the political settlements which brought the state and its existing constitutional arrangements into existence. In turn, this has led to considerable speculation about the position of the Acts of Union with Scotland (1707) and with Ireland (1800) which provide the legal basis of the political entity known as the United Kingdom. The issue for debate is whether these statutes may be amended or repealed in the normal way or whether their special constitutional status gives them added authority and, therefore, protection from parliamentary interference.

   Although the arguments in this context tend to be couched in legalistic terms, the issue is essentially political. Hence the particular perspective taken on whether such Acts are repealable tends to depend on the advocate's view of the validity of the present structure of the United Kingdom. It is not unusual, therefore, to find unionists – whether Scottish or Irish – taking the view that the Acts of Union are beyond the legislative competence normally attributed to the Westminster Parliament. Nationalists, on the other hand, may be more inclined to believe that Parliament has the legal authority to do that which its members regard as politically expedient in the circumstances and that the Acts in question, therefore, impose no absolute fetter on Parliament's authority to undo the Union.

Acts of Union with Scotland 1707

These were enacted by the pre-existing Parliaments of England and Scotland and brought into existence 'one Kingdom by the name of Great Britain' (Art 1). The Scottish and English Parliaments thus extinguished themselves and formed the Parliament of Great Britain sitting at Westminster. The Acts provided that the Union was to remain in being 'forever' (Art 1) and attempted to impose certain limits to the legislative competence of the Parliament thus created. In particular it was stipulated that the private law of Scotland was not to be altered except for the 'evident utility' of the Scottish people (Art 18). Other articles were to remain in force 'for all time coming'. These included provisions seeking to guarantee the separate existence of the Scottish courts and legal system (Art 19) and the position of the Presbyterian religion and Church of Scotland (Protestant Religion and Presbyterian Church Act 1707).

These prescriptions, it has been suggested, could be interpreted to mean that the Westminster Parliament was born 'unfree' and that its authority can be no greater than that allocated to it by its founding instruments. The limits on the Westminster Parliament's freedom should thus be understood as being the conditions upon which the two Parliaments, and particularly the Scottish one, agreed to abandon their separate identities. It is this which gives the Acts their special constitutional status and provides the guarantee for the provisions outlined above.

Whatever the weight of this argument, it has not proved entirely effective to give the Acts the type of protection which those responsible for their formulation might have intended. Hence a number of statutes have been passed which would appear to be inconsistent with the guaranteed provisions. The most notable of these was the Scottish Universities Act 1853. This reduced the special position of the Church of Scotland by abolishing the requirement that professors in Scottish universities should be members of the Presbyterian Church. It is not possible to say, however, at least with any certainty, that such post-1707 legislative intrusions have completely undermined the case for regarding the Acts of Union as being constituent or entrenched elements of the constitution. De Smith and Brazier, for example, have argued that, although it may be difficult to discern any strictly legal impediment to their repeal, the Acts may be regarded as the basis of a general conventional principle that Parliament will not enact legislation which substantially undermines their principal provisions, i.e. those relating to the Scottish Church and legal system. Nor is it possible to be absolutely sure about how the Scottish courts would react to such legislation if it were to be approved by the Westminster Parliament as presently constituted. Thus in *McCormick v Lord Advocate* 1953 SC 396, Scotland's most senior judge, the Lord President, opined that although the Scottish courts might be reluctant to question an Act of Parliament, this did not mean that such legislation would be regarded as constitutionally valid:

> The principle of the unlimited sovereignty of Parliament is a distinctively English principle which has no counterpart in Scottish Constitutional Law...Considering that the Union legislation extinguished the Parliaments of Scotland and England and replaced them by a new Parliament, I have difficulty in seeing why the new Parliament of Great Britain must inherit all the peculiar characteristics of the English Parliament but none of the Scottish Parliament as if all that happened in 1707 was that Scottish representatives were admitted to the Parliament of England. That is not what was done. Further, the Treaty and the associated legislation, by which the Parliament of Great Britain was brought into existence as the successor of the separate Parliaments...contain some clauses which expressly reserve to the Parliament of Great Britain powers of subsequent modification, and other clauses which contain no such power or emphatically exclude subsequent alteration by declarations that the provision shall be fundamental and unalterable in all time coming...I have not found in the Union legislation any provision that the Parliament of Great Britain should be 'absolutely sovereign' in the sense that Parliament should be free to alter the Treaty at will (per Lord Cooper).

To date, however, no Scottish court has crossed the rubicon (point of no return) and openly questioned the validity of any public general Act relating to the issues protected by the Acts of Union. In *Gibson v Lord Advocate* [1975] 1 CMLR 563, the Court of Session was asked whether permitting EEC nationals to fish in Scottish waters pursuant to the EEC Act 1972 could be for the 'evident utility of the Scottish people'. Lord Keith's opinion was that questions of this type should be resolved by political rather than legal means:

> I am...of the opinion that the question whether a particular Act of the United Kingdom Parliament altering a particular aspect of Scots private law is or is not for the evident utility of the subjects within Scotland is not a justiciable issue in this Court. The making of decisions upon what must essentially be a political matter is no part of the function of the court.

He was, however, more circumspect about how the Scottish courts would receive an Act seeking to alter substantially or irradicate the Union's essential provisions:

> I prefer to preserve my opinion on what the position would be if the United Kingdom Parliament passed an Act purporting to abolish the Court of Session or the Church of Scotland or to substitute English Law for the whole body of Scots Law.

Acts of Union with Ireland 1800

For a variety of reasons it is not possible to express similar reservations about the validity of legislation inconsistent with the Acts of Union with Ireland. These Acts created the United Kingdom of Great Britain and Ireland. They declared that the Union was to last forever and sought to guarantee the position of the Anglican Church in Ireland. Despite being adhered to by only a minority of the population, this was to remain the established church in Ireland 'forever', being deemed as an 'essential and fundamental part of the Union' (Art 5). The separate Irish Parliament was thereby extinguished and Ireland given increased representation in the United Kingdom Parliament at Westminster.

History proved, however, that the guarantees contained in the Acts of Union were inadequate to withstand the determination of the majority of Irish people to have a degree of political and religious freedom not envisaged when the Union was created. This may give support to the view that constitutions can do little more than recognise and give expression to political facts and cannot prevent political evolution from taking place. In 1869 the Irish Church Act disestablished the Church of Ireland. In *Ex parte Canon Selwyn* (1872) 36 JP 54, an attempt to question the validity of the Act was found to be non-justiciable. In 1922 the Irish Free State (Agreement) Act gave effect to the political settlement which brought to an end 'The Troubles' or Irish War of Independence 1919–21. The 26 southern counties were given dominion status and the Union, at least as envisaged in 1800, was effectively brought to an end. The Irish constitution of 1937 asserted that the country was a sovereign independent state. Its status as a republic was recognised by the Ireland Act 1949.

It is significant, however, that the 1949 Act provided that Northern Ireland – the six counties excluded from the Free State in 1922 – should not cease to be part of the United Kingdom without the consent of the Parliament of Northern Ireland. The Northern Ireland Parliament having been abolished in 1972, the Northern Ireland Constitution Act 1973 stipulated that Northern Ireland would remain in the United

Kingdom until a majority of its electorate should decide and vote otherwise. This guarantee was repeated in the Anglo-Irish Agreement 1985 and in the Joint Declaration of the British and Irish Governments on the Future of Northern Ireland in 1994.

The intention behind these guarantees appears to be that the unionist majority in Northern Ireland should be able to veto any proposed change to the status of the province which does not have their consent. How a court would, or should, view a statute affecting Northern Ireland's position in the United Kingdom and which was clearly opposed by the majority there remains, however, a matter of debate. The previous history of the Union and the events of 1922 clearly suggest that the traditional doctrine of absolute sovereignty would determine the issue. On the other hand, those with unionist sympathies might be tempted to argue that, for the purpose of altering the union with Northern Ireland, Parliament has changed the rule of recognition by adding the requirement of a referendum amongst the Northern Ireland electorate. It is, therefore, remotely conceivable that some judges might be reluctant to recognise legislation which blatantly ignored the requirement of consent which has been the basis of British policy towards Ireland since 1922. What is perhaps more certain is that the repeated assertions of the need for consent have established, at least for the time being, a convention that Parliament will not seek to legislate contrary to or without this requirement. As has been pointed out, however, conventions are flexible rules of political behaviour. They can and have been abandoned or modified when it was deemed politically expedient so to do. This may explain why there are those in the majority community in Northern Ireland who remain unconvinced as to the practical political reliability of the assurances which they have been given.

Constitutional statutes

The recent development of the concept of constitutional statutes was considered above in the context of the doctrine of implied repeal.

A constitutional statute is one which is of fundamental importance in the creation of the state and/or in determining the relationship between the state and the individuals within it. Examples have been said to include Magna Carta 1215, the Bill of Rights 1689, the Act of Union 1707, the nineteenth-century Reform Acts, the European Communities Act 1972, the Wales Act 1998 and the Scotland Act 1998 (Laws LJ, *Thoburn* v *City of Sunderland*, above). This list was not intended to be exhaustive and the concept would probably extend to such enactments as the legislation determining the relationship between Great Britain and Northern Ireland. In particular, given the importance of the political agreement to which it gave effect, it would be difficult to argue that the Northern Ireland Act 1998 does not also fall into this special category.

It is not argued that this special status leaves such enactments immune from repeal or amendment. Rather the contention is that, for this to be effected, express words must be used. In this way such basic constitutional prescriptions are given a degree of entrenchment. They may not be altered unless this is the open and declared intent of the legislation in question as formulated by governments in power at the time the issue arises.

International Transport Roth GmbH and Others v Home Secretary [2002] EWCA Civ 158, was one of the first cases in which the concept of constitutional statutes was considered by the Court of Appeal. On that occasion, with the Human Rights Act 1998 in mind, Law LJ put the emerging rule as follows: 'Here the courts protect the right in question, while acknowledging the legislative sovereignty of Parliament, by means of a rule of construction. The rule is that while the legislature possesses the power to override fundamental rights, general words will not suffice. It can only be done by express or specific provision.'

Political restraints

In an everyday sense, the forces which restrain Parliament from extreme uses of its sovereign power are essentially political. They are both subtle and diverse and thus beyond precise definition. Some of the more obvious factors, however, would include the following.

The party system

The House of Commons does not conduct its affairs as a united entity. It is composed of a variety of political parties within which there are further subdivisions on policy generally and on specific issues (e.g. European integration). It is necessary, therefore, for the government to maintain the support of the parliamentary majority and to keep its own party united if it is to get its legislative programme through Parliament. This, to some extent, operates as a restraining influence on the subject matter and content of legislation. Governments will be reluctant to propose measures so controversial as to precipitate dissention or even defection within their own ranks.

The electorate

There is no constitutional or political rule in the United Kingdom which formally inhibits Parliament from legislating contrary to the apparent wishes of the electorate nor is there any requirement for controversial measures to be put to a referendum. What Parliament is asked to do in the legislative sense is, however, affected by the government's knowledge that, as Dicey put it, ultimate political sovereignty lies with the people. The electorate may change the composition of Parliament when its opinion is sought at least once every five years. Too many unpopular legislative measures may be a factor in determining the opinion expressed by the electorate.

The doctrine of the mandate

The essence of this is that since the majority group in a particular Parliament has been elected to execute a declared political and legislative programme (the party 'manifesto'), it has no authority to introduce important measures not included therein. This is primarily a political argument of limited constitutional significance.

Governments must be free to respond to unforeseen and changing circumstances and to any emergencies which may arise by promoting the appropriate legislation. The argument may, however, have some validity in the early days of a new government and in relation to the making of major constitutional changes (e.g. leaving the European Union) without some further reference to the electorate (e.g. referendum).

Territorial competence and grants of independence

Despite what has already been said on this issue, Parliament is unlikely to enact legislation for places where the executive power of the British government does not operate. Hence, although in theory it could repeal the various statutory grants of independence to former colonial territories, it would do so in the sure knowledge that such legislation would be likely to be ignored.

The futility, if not the illegality, of such legislative action, and the fact that such grants of independence are now beyond Parliament's competence, has been recognised in judicial comment. Hence in *British Coal Corporation* v *The King* [1935] AC 500, the attitude of the Privy Council was that, while 'in abstract law' Parliament could revoke the undertaking in the Statute of Westminster 1931, s 4 not to legislate for a dominion without its consent, legal theory was bound to 'march alongside political reality'. This sentiment was repeated by Lord Denning MR, *Blackburn* v *Attorney-General* [1971] 1 WLR 1037.

> Take the Statute of Westminster 1931, which takes away the power of Parliament to legislate for the Dominions. Can anyone imagine that Parliament could or would reverse that statute? Take the Acts which have granted independence to the Dominions and territories overseas. Can anyone imagine that Parliament could or would reverse these laws and take away their independence? Most clearly not. Freedom once given cannot be taken away.

International law

Parliament is unlikely to enact legislation which, by contravening international legal standards, could cause diplomatic and political embarrassment in the United Kingdom's relationships with foreign states. When such legislation has been introduced, generally without intent to offend international rules, it has usually been amended forthwith (see *Golder* v *United Kingdom* (1975) 1 EHRR 524, *X* v *United Kingdom* (1981) 4 EHRR 188, and *Malone* v *United Kingdom* (1985) 7 EHRR 14).

This may be illustrated by the facts of *Dudgeon* v *United Kingdom (No. 2)* (1982) 4 EHRR 149, where the European Court of Human Rights found legislation in Northern Ireland criminalising homosexual relationships between consenting adult males to be contrary to the right to respect for private life in Art 8 of the European Convention on Human Rights. This was followed by the Homosexual Offences (Northern Ireland) Order 1982 which removed the offending restrictions.

THE RELATIONSHIP BETWEEN EC LAW AND ACTS OF PARLIAMENT

The EEC Act 1972

International treaties to which the United Kingdom is a party are binding on the state in international law only. They do not create legal obligations which are enforceable in the domestic legal system either between individuals or against the state. The content of a treaty may only become operative in domestic law if incorporated or given effect by an Act of Parliament. Hence the United Kingdom's signature of the Brussels Treaty of Accession in 1972 was, of itself, insufficient to implement the obligations contained therein and, in particular, that of giving effect to the Community legal order in the United Kingdom. This was done by the EEC Act 1972 which became effective on 1 January 1973. The concept of directly applicable EEC law is recognised by s 2(1) of the Act:

> All such rights, powers, liabilities, obligations and restrictions from time to time arising by or under the Treaties...are without further enactment to be given legal effect...in the United Kingdom.

Section 2(2) provides for the making of Orders in Council and statutory regulations for the purpose of implementing those European rules – particularly directives – which are not directly applicable.

Section 2(4) contains the key provision that any domestic legislation 'passed or to be passed' should be 'construed and have effect' subject to s 2(1) and (2), i.e. subject to all the 'rights, powers, liabilities, obligations and restrictions...arising...under the Treaties' including the obligation to give primacy to Community law (see below).

Section 3(1) states that the European Court of Justice should be recognised as the final arbiter concerning the meaning of EC law:

> ...for the purpose of all legal proceedings, any question as to meaning or effect of any of the Treaties or as to the meaning, validity or effect of any Community instrument shall be treated as a question of law (and if not referred to the European Court, be for determination as such in accordance with any principles laid down by the European Court or any court attached thereto).

Inevitably the incorporation of EC law into the United Kingdom's domestic legal system raised the question of how a court should react if dealing with a case to which both a rule of EC law and an inconsistent provision in an Act of Parliament appeared to be applicable.

National sovereignty and the ECJ

The European Court's attitude to the above question had been made abundantly clear well before the United Kingdom's accession to the Community in 1973. According to the Court, every member state by, and as a condition of, joining the Community had transferred legislative sovereignty to the Community in relation to those matters within the competence of the Community's law-making institutions.

By creating a Community of unlimited duration, having its own institutions, its own personality, its own legal capacity and capacity of representation on the international plane and, more particularly, real powers stemming from a limitation of sovereignty on a transfer of powers from the states to the Community, the members states have limited their sovereign rights, albeit within limited fields, and have thus created a body of law which binds both their nationals and themselves (*Costa* v *ENEL* [1964] ECR 585).

The principle of the supremacy of Community law was restated emphatically by the ECJ in *Internationale Handelsgesellschaft mbH* v *Einfuhr-und Vorrattstelle für Getreide* [1970] ECR 1125 ('the law stemming from the Treaty, an independent source of law, cannot by its very nature be overridden by rules of national law, however framed'), and in *Simmenthal SpA* v *Italian Minister for Finance* [1976] ECR 1871 ('every national court must…apply Community law in its entirety…and must accordingly set aside…national law which may conflict with it, whether prior or subsequent to the Community rule').

The ECJ has also made clear that the supremacy of Community law applies to entrenched and fundamental rights in national constitutions (*Hauer* v *Land Rheinland-Pfalz* [1979] ECR 3727).

The judicial approach in the United Kingdom

The doctrine of implied repeal

It was apparent from the outset that the views of the ECJ were incompatible with traditional domestic perceptions of the sovereign status of Parliament. This was not likely to cause difficulty in the event of an inconsistency between a rule of EC law and a provision in a statute enacted prior to the EEC Act 1972 itself. In such cases the problem could be disposed of by straightforward application of the doctrine of implied repeal – i.e. in so far as Parliament in the 1972 Act had stated that all legislation 'passed or to be passed' should have effect subject to Community law, this demonstrated a clear intent to repeal all inconsistent provisions in pre-1973 legislation.

The doctrine of implied repeal would not be applicable, however, if and when a statute enacted after 1 January 1973 was found to be inconsistent with either directly or indirectly effective Community law. This potentiality was not dealt with in explicit terms by the 1972 Act.

Section 2(4): a rule of constructions?

Although phrased in the rather cryptic terms which are so typical of domestic legislation, s 2(4) appeared to provide the only direct indication of Parliament's intentions in these matters. It soon became apparent that most judges were at least prepared to regard the section as imposing on them an obligation to construe words in domestic legislation in ways which accorded with the requirements of *directly effective* EC law and in this way to minimise the likelihood and incidence of conflict.

> …it is a principle of construction of United Kingdom statutes…that the words of a statute passed after the treaty has been signed and dealing with the subject of the international obligation of the United Kingdom, are to be construed, if they are reasonably

capable of being given such a meaning, as intending to carry out the obligation and not to be inconsistent with it (per Lord Diplock, *Garland* v *British Rail Engineering Ltd (No. 2)* [1983] 2 AC 751).

It was even suggested that statutory provisions should be given a meaning consistent with directly effective Community law albeit that this involved obvious departure from the literal meaning of the words used:

> ...a construction which permits the section to operate as proper fulfilment of the United Kingdom's obligations under the treaty involves not so much doing violence to the language of the section as filling a gap by an implication which arises not from the words used, but from...the manifest purpose of the legislation, by its history, and by the compulsive force of section 2(4)...(per Lord Oliver, *Pickstone* v *Freemans plc* [1989] AC 66).

Although *obiter* only, this appeared to be suggesting that judges should, in effect, be prepared to 'rewrite' statutes where, in the literal sense, these did not accord with Community law. According to this view, therefore, a judge should only be prepared to give a statutory provision a meaning inconsistent with Community law where the statute evinced an unequivocal intention to that effect. In other words, simple literal inconsistency with EC law in a post-1972 statute should not be regarded as sufficient to override the requirement in s 2(4) of the 1972 Act that future legislation should be construed in accordance with relevant EC provisions. Therefore, s 2(4) could not be overridden by mere implication.

Sovereignty 'surrendered'

From this it was only a 'short step' to the view that s 2(4) of the 1972 Act was not intended solely as a rule of construction but as an expression of Parliament's willingness to effect a voluntary surrender of its sovereign legislative power in those matters falling within the directly effective law-making competence of the Community. That such meaning could be given to the section had already been contemplated by the Court of Appeal in *Macarthy's Ltd* v *Smith* [1979] 3 All ER 325, where Cumming-Bruce LJ said that if the ECJ adjudged a statute to be incompatible with directly effective Community law 'the European law will prevail over that municipal legislation'.

The Factortame saga

This articulation of a further intent behind s 2(4) of the 1972 Act was finally confirmed by the House of Lords in the *Factortame* cases 1989–98.

A controversy arose when Spanish-owned trawlers were registered in the UK and began competing with British fishermen for the British 'quota', i.e. the limited weight of fish which, according to the Common Fisheries Policy, could be landed by the British fishing fleet (i.e. those vessels registered in the UK) on an annual basis. The British Merchant Shipping Act 1988 was the government's attempt to deal with the obvious concerns of the domestic fishing industry. The Act provided that foreign-owned vessels could not be registered in the UK. Hence their catches would not count against the British fishing quota.

In *R v Secretary of State for Transport, ex parte Factortame Ltd (No. 1)* [1989] 2 CMLR 353, the applicant contended that the 1988 Act violated its rights under Community law, particularly the right of establishment in Art 52 of the EC Treaty. The Divisional Court referred the question of the Act's compatibility with EC law to the ECJ under Art 177 and, pending the ECJ's decision, granted an interim injunction against the Minister of Transport, ordering that the Act should not be enforced. In effect, therefore, the court was claiming jurisdiction to suspend the operation of an Act of Parliament. This had not happened before and, according to the traditional doctrine of sovereignty, was not something which an English Court was competent to do.

The decision was appealed to the House of Lords ([1989] 2 All ER 692). Its decision was:

(a) the British Merchant Shipping Act 1988 should be read as including an implied clause rendering its interpretation as subject to s 2(4) of the EEC Act 1972, i.e. 'as if a section were incorporated in...the Act of 1988 which in terms enacted that the provisions with respect to the registration of British fishing vessels were to be without prejudice to the directly enforceable Community rights of nationals of any member state of the EEC';
(b) the Crown Proceedings Act 1947, s 21 expressly precluded the issuing of injunctions against ministers of the Crown acting in their official capacity (see Chapter 13);
(c) according to English law, it was not within the competence of the Divisional Court, or any other English court, to suspend or disapply an Act of Parliament.

The questions as to whether findings (b) and (c) offended Community law, and whether there was an overriding obligation on national courts not to give effect to national laws alleged to be incompatible with Community law pending a determination by the ECJ, were then referred to the ECJ under Art 177.

The ECJ's response came in *Factortame Ltd v Secretary of State for Transport* [1991] 1 All ER 70. It was as follows:

(a) national courts should grant interim relief for the purpose of suspending national legislation where this appeared to be in conflict with directly effective provisions of Community law;
(b) any rule of national law which sought to inhibit the granting of such relief – e.g. as in this case, the Crown Proceedings Act 1947, s 21 – was, therefore, inconsistent with Community law and should not be applied.

[A] national court which in a case before it concerning Community law considers that the sole obstacle which precludes it from granting interim relief is a rule of national law must set aside that rule.

The case was then remitted to the House of Lords for application of these principles. Its decision was that, as the applicant could show a strong prima facie case of inconsistency, the interim injunction should be issued to prevent the minister enforcing the relevant provisions of the 1988 Act (*R v Secretary of State for Transport, ex parte Factortame Ltd (No. 2)* [1991] 1 AC 603).

A short time later, the ECJ gave its ruling on the initial reference by the Divisional Court. It accepted the applicant's contention that the disputed provisions in the

Merchant Shipping Act 1988 were inconsistent with Community law and, in particular, the right of establishment. The Divisional Court then granted a declaration to that effect (*R v Secretary of State for Transport, ex parte Factortame (No. 3)* [1992] QB 680), following which the 1988 Act was duly amended (Merchant Shipping (Registration) Act 1993).

A breach of Community law having been established, the applicants made a claim for damages according to the principles laid down in *Francovich v Italy*, above. In *R v Secretary of State for Transport, ex parte Factortame (No. 4)* [1996] 2 WLR 506, the ECJ, in a preliminary ruling, held that a state may be sued for damages where this results from a serious breach of Community law by a national legislature. Such breach will be sufficiently serious for the purpose of attracting liability in damages where the legislature 'manifestly and gravely disregarded the limits of its discretion' (per Lord Hoffman, *R v Secretary of State for Transport, ex parte Factortame (No. 5)* [1999] 3 WLR 1062). In the same case the House of Lords went on to decide that by the enactment of the British Merchant Shipping Act 1988 which discriminated against 'community nationals on the grounds of their nationality…the legislature was, *prima facie*, flouting one of the most basic principles of Community law' (*ibid.*). The requirements for liability in damages were, therefore, established. The issue of state liability in damages for breach of Community law is dealt with in greater detail in Chapter 13.

Statute and indirectly effective Community law

The primary concern of the above cases was with the relationship between statutes and directly effective European provisions. As such, therefore, these cases did not decide how a domestic court should proceed if faced with an apparent inconsistency between a rule of indirectly effective Community law (e.g. a directive) and a provision in an Act of Parliament.

The attitude of the ECJ to this question would appear to be that all national authorities, including courts, are under an obligation to interpret national law in a way which, 'as far as possible', complies with Community rules, albeit that such rules are of indirect effect only and regardless of whether the national law in question was introduced to give effect to them (*Marleasing SA v La Comercial Internacionale de Alimentación SA* [1992] 1 CMLR 305).

So far as English courts are concerned there is House of Lords authority for the view that, where an inconsistency exists between a directive and a legislative provision intended to give effect to it, the legislative provision in question should be interpreted in a way which achieves that effect even though this involves some distortion of the literal meaning of the words used (*Pickstone v Freemans*, above; *Litster v Forth Dry Dock and Engineering Co Ltd* [1990] 1 AC 546). Where the inconsistency occurs between a directive and a legislative provision not specifically intended to give effect to it, the 'English' position would appear to be that the courts should seek consistency only so far as this is permitted by the words used in legislation in issue. This was the view taken by the House of Lords in *Webb v EMO Cargo (UK) Ltd* [1992] 4 All ER 929. In this case the House was of the opinion that it was for 'a United Kingdom court to construe domestic legislation in any field covered by a Community directive so as to accord with the interpretation of the directive as laid down by the European Court, if that can be done without distorting the meaning of the domestic legislation' (per Lord Keith).

In cases where construction in accord with indirectly effective EC law is not possible this may expose the state to legal proceedings by the Commission for failure to fulfil its obligations under the Treaty.

Absolute sovereignty retained – in theory

It is clear from the matters considered above that the attitude of English judges to the relationship between English statute and European Community law remains founded on an interpretation of Parliament's will as expressed in the EEC Act 1972, s 2(4). Hence, in construing legislation in accordance with Community law and, in the event of conflict, giving primacy to the same, the judges claim to be doing no more than was intended and authorised by the sovereign body. This is much different from (and falls far short of) recognising Community law as part of a superior constitutional and legal order to which the legislative sovereignty of the United Kingdom has been sublimated for so long as the Community remains in being. According to this English view of things, therefore, it remains possible for Parliament to reassert its sovereign power, even in relation to directly effective Community law, providing its intention to do so is clear and unequivocal.

> If the time should come when our Parliament deliberately passes an Act – with the intention of repudiating the Treaty or any provision in it – or intentionally of acting inconsistently with it – and says so in express terms – then I should have thought that it would be the duty of our courts to follow the statute of our Parliament (per Lord Denning MR, *Macarthy's v Smith*, above).

It should be remembered, however, that the doctrine of the unlimited legislative sovereignty of Parliament was formulated by the judges in response to the political events of the seventeenth century. The doctrine cannot be considered, therefore, to be immutable. It was formulated to recognise and give legal effect to a significantly altered constitutional order established by force of arms and in which the authority of the executive branch of government ('the King') was made subject to the overriding will of Parliament. In the same way, therefore, should the United Kingdom join with other states in the move towards greater European integration, leading perhaps towards a federation of European states, it remains possible for judges to redefine the doctrine of sovereignty to give legal expression and foundation to such fundamental political developments. Having formulated the doctrine to give effect to the constitutional restructuring and the shifts of power which took place around three hundred years ago, judges may presumably repeat the exercise to take account of the further restructuring and movements of political and legal power (i.e. from national governments to common European institutions) which appeared to be in train as the twenty-first century commenced.

References

Jennings (1959) *The Law of the Constitution* (5th edn), London: University of London Press.
Wade (1955) 'The Legal Basis of Sovereignty' CLJ 172.

Further reading

Allen and Thompson (1996) *Cases and Materials on Constitutional and Administrative Law* (3rd edn), London: Blackstone, Ch 2.

Heuston (1964) *Essays in Constitutional Law* (2nd edn), London: Stevens, Ch 1.

Loveland (1996) *Constitutional Law: A Critical Introduction*, London: Butterworths, Ch 2.

Marston and Ward (1997) *Cases and Commentary on Constitutional and Administrative Law* (4th edn), London: Pitman Publishing, Ch 5.

Steiner and Woods (1996) *European Community Law* (5th edn), London: Blackstone, Chs 3 and 4.

Turpin (2002) *British Government and the Constitution* (5th edn), London: Butterworths, Ch 5.

Part 3

THE COMPOSITION AND WORKINGS OF PARLIAMENT

Chapter 6

THE FRANCHISE AND
THE ELECTORATE

INTRODUCTION

The composition of the House of Commons is determined by the electorate voting in general elections at least once every five years and in by-elections. Subject to certain restrictions explained below, every British citizen of eighteen years and over resident in the United Kingdom has the right to vote. This is often referred to as 'universal adult suffrage'.

It has not always been thus. Until 1918 the right to vote was restricted to adult males (21 years and over) who owned property of a certain rateable value. The property qualification had been lowered incrementally in the nineteenth century (principally by the Reform Acts of 1832, 1867 and 1884) so that by the end of the century virtually all male householders had the vote. The property qualification was abolished by the Representation of the People Act 1918. The Act also extended the franchise to women of 30 years and over. Henceforth the only qualifications for the vote were in terms of age, citizenship and residence. Women of 21 years and over were enfranchised by the Representation of the People (Equal Franchise) Act 1928. The age qualification was reduced to eighteen years by the Family Law Reform Act 1969. The current law in relation to these matters is contained in the Representation of the People Act 1983 as amended and supplemented by the Representation of the People Act 2000.

The exact requirements of the citizenship and residence qualifications require some further explanation.

QUALIFICATIONS

Citizenship

The following categories of persons, if resident in the UK and of voting age, have the right to vote:

(a) British citizens;
(b) citizens of British dependent territories;
(c) British overseas citizens;
(d) Commonwealth citizens;
(e) citizens of the Irish Republic.

Citizens of other states may not vote in the UK regardless of how long they may have been resident here. Citizens of European Union states may vote in elections for the European Parliament and local government elections. They may not vote, however, in elections for the Westminster Parliament.

Residence

Prior to 1948 it was necessary to prove residence in the constituency for three months prior to the 'qualifying date' (the date by which completed electoral registration forms were to be returned). This remains the rule in Northern Ireland. For the rest of the UK, and until the Representation of the People Act 2000, the rule was that the person must have been registered on the qualifying date (10 October) in the constituency in which he/she wished to vote (Representation of the People Act 1983, s 1).

The requirement to show residence on a particular 'qualifying' date was removed by the Representation of the People Act 2000, s 1. The position now is that a person who does not suffer from any legal incapacity (see disqualifications below) and who satisfies the nationality and age requirements is entitled to be registered in the constituency in which he/she is resident at the time the application is made (RPA 1983, s 1, as amended by RPA 2000, s 1).

Section 3 of the RPA 2000 which inserts a new s 5 into the 1983 Act, sets out the matters to be taken into account or recognised by Electoral Registration Offices when determining whether a person should be regarded as resident in a particular constituency. A key factor to be considered is the reason for the person's presence at the address given. Simple absence from the address on the date of the application will not operate as a disqualification if it results from the 'performance of any duty arising from or incidental to any office, service or employment' or by reason of attendance at an academic institution, providing that the person intends to resume residence at the given address within six months or that address serves as his/her permanent address and is where he/she would be living but for the performance of the duty.

Where a person is staying at an address other than on a permanent basis, he/she may be regarded as resident there 'if he has no home elsewhere'.

The meaning of the residence qualification has also been considered in a number of judicial decisions.

In *Fox v Stirk* [1970] 2 QB 463, the question arose as to whether students in halls of residence at Bristol University could register to vote in the constituency where the halls were situated as well as in the constituencies where they otherwise lived. The Court of Appeal gave an affirmative answer and held that a person could register in any place where they were 'ordinarily resident' which included any constituency where they dwelt 'permanently or for a considerable time'. Therefore it was possible to have the right to vote in more than one place providing the person resided with a 'reasonable degree of permanence' in each.

In a number of other cases in which challenges have been made to exclusion from electoral registers it has been suggested that whether a person's residence is sufficient for the purposes of registration should be determined not only by the degree of permanence but also by reference to the nature, quality and purpose of the residence in issue. Hence in *Scott* v *Phillips*, 1974 SLT 32, it was held that residence in a holiday home for three and a half months per annum, although reasonably permanent, was residence for leisure and relaxation only and was, therefore, for functional purposes merely incidental to the place where the complainant lived for the rest of the year. This was consistent with the approach taken in *Ferris* v *Wallace*, 1936 SC 561, where it was decided that residence in a holiday home every weekend from April to September, and throughout the months of July and August, did not qualify. By contrast, in *Dumble* v *Electoral Registration Officer for the Borders*, 1980 SLT 60, it was held that weekend residence in a constituency to enable the complainant to fulfil his duties as a prospective Conservative party candidate was of a type which qualified him to be registered. Also, in *Hipperson* v *Newbury Electoral Registration Officer* [1985] QB 1060, the court was prepared to accept that women living in the Greenham Common Peace Camp were resident there for electoral purposes. Their presence in the camp was reasonably permanent, it was for a purpose not merely incidental to their other residences, and the fact that their residence in the camp might be illegal did not matter for electoral purposes: '...we reject the submission that the franchise is affected by the fact that the qualifying residence is illegal' (per Sir John Donaldson MR).

Note, however, that although a person may be eligible to vote in two or perhaps more constituencies, only one vote may be cast. Hence the person must decide in which constituency he/she wishes to exercise the right. It is an offence to vote in more than one constituency.

The register

The Representation of the People Act 2000, s 8 and Sched 1 amend the 1983 requirements for the drawing up and maintenance of the electoral register.

Each registration office is to carry out an annual canvass of the local population to establish who is resident in the constituency on 15 October (new s 10, RPA 1983). The register based on the canvass results should be published by 1 December or such other date as is specified in ministerial regulations (new s 13, RPA 1983). Other names may be added as and when application is made and revised versions of the register may be published from time to time. A revised register takes effect from the date on which it is published (*ibid.*).

An electoral registration officer has the authority to determine objections and claims concerning the content and accuracy of the register and to make alterations accordingly. Such determinations are subject to a right of appeal to a County Court (new ss 10 and 13).

The electoral register is treated for practical purposes as conclusive of eligibility to vote. Hence, although a person may satisfy all the substantive criteria of eligibility, viz. age, nationality and residence, no vote may be cast unless that person's name appears on the electoral register for the constituency in which it is to be used (RPA 1983, new s 1). Conversely, if a person is placed on there erroneously or, after being registered, becomes disqualified, it is unlikely that they will be prevented from voting. However, if a person does vote while under a disqualification, an offence is committed and the vote may be discounted.

Declarations of local connection

Certain categories of persons who may not be able to satisfy the normal requirements of 'residence' may still become entitled to vote by making a declaration of local connection. This applies to:

(a) persons in mental hospitals and remand prisoners who are unable to satisfy the criteria of residence for any place other than the one in which they are detained;

(b) homeless persons.

Such declarations must include:

*   the person's name;
*   an address for correspondence or an undertaking to collect such correspondence from the electoral registration office;
*   a statement that the person falls within one of the categories in (a) or (b) and which one;
*   in the case of mental patients and remand prisoners, the name of the institution where the person is detained and where the person would be living if not detained;
*   in the case of homeless persons, an address where, or near to, the person spends most of the time.

A person who has made a declaration of local connection may apply to be registered by being treated as if resident at the address given in the normal sense (RPA 1983, ss 7B and 7C, inserted by RPA 2000, s 6).

A person properly entered in the register has no right to have his/her name deleted (*Davis* v *Argyll Electoral Registration Officer* 1974, unreported).

DISQUALIFICATIONS

Any person falling into any of the following categories is disqualified from voting in parliamentary and local elections in the United Kingdom.

(a) Aliens (RPA 1983, s 1 as inserted by RPA 2000, s 1).

(b) Minors.

A person who is under eighteen years when the register is compiled or when the application to register is made, but who will reach the age of eighteen during the next twelve months, has the right to be registered and to vote in any election which occurs after the qualifying age has been attained (*ibid.*).

(c) Excepted hereditary peers and peeresses.

Until the House of Lords Act 1999, hereditary peers and peeresses could register and vote in European and local elections but were disqualified from voting in parliamentary elections. The 1999 Act, s 3, removes this disqualification save in the case of 'excepted' peers, i.e. those 92 hereditary peers who may sit in the House of Lords by virtue of the 1999 Act, s 2 (90 elected by all hereditary peers, plus the Earl Marshall and the Lord Chamberlain).

(d) Persons serving a sentence of imprisonment for a criminal offence.

The disqualification does not apply to remand prisoners. Remand prisoners may be registered in the constituency where the prison is situated if they are likely to be there for a period sufficient for them to be regarded as resident in that place or, alternatively, at the address they would have been living at but for the fact of the remand (RPA 1983, s 7A inserted by RPA 2000, s 5).

(e) Persons in mental hospitals.

Any person detained in a mental hospital as a result of criminal activity is disqualified from voting (RPA 1983, s 3A inserted by RPA 2000, s 2).

Otherwise both compulsory and voluntary patients are entitled to be registered. The patient may be registered in the constituency in which the hospital is situated if likely to be resident there for an extended period or, alternatively, at some other place, usually the person's normal place of abode (RPA 1988, s 7, inserted by RPA 2000, s 4).

SPECIAL CATEGORIES OF VOTERS

(a) Absent voters.

Since 1949 various categories of persons, including those suffering from blindness or other physical incapacity or those who could not reasonably be expected to be present during an election due to the nature of their occupation, service or employment, were entitled to register as absent voters and to vote by post or proxy. The Representation of the People Act 1985 added to these any person 'whose circumstances on the date of the poll will be or are likely to be such that he cannot reasonably be expected to vote in person' (e.g. those on holiday) (RPA 1983, Pt 1, as amended by RPA 2000, Sched 4).

(b) Overseas voters.

An overseas voter is:

(i)   a person who is resident overseas but who was resident and registered to vote in the United Kingdom at any time within the last twenty years; or,

(ii) a person who lived in the United Kingdom in the last twenty years when too young to vote with a parent or guardian who was a registered voter (RPA 1985, ss 1–3 as inserted by RPA 2000, Sched 2).

CASTING THE VOTE

A person may vote in person, by post or by proxy. Detained mental patients and remand prisoners must vote by post or proxy.

The RPA 2000 abolished most of the pre-existing restrictions on eligibility to vote by post. Hence, any person may now use a postal vote providing the application to do so is received on time, contains the required information and is genuine. Where a proxy is used that person must be a British, Commonwealth or Irish citizen of voting age who is not subject to any electoral disqualifications (RPA 2000, Sched 4).

Further reading

McEldowney (1998) *Public Law* (2nd edn), London: Sweet & Maxwell, Ch 6.

Rawlings (1988) *Law and the Electoral Process*, London: Sweet & Maxwell, Ch 3.

Chapter 7

THE HOUSE OF COMMONS: MEMBERS OF PARLIAMENT

DISQUALIFICATIONS

The following categories of persons may not sit in the House of Commons.

Minors

For the purposes of membership of the House of Commons persons under 21 years are minors (Parliamentary Elections Act 1965, s 7). This was not affected by the Family Law Reform Act 1969 which reduced the voting age to eighteen. Hence eighteen to twenty year-olds are old enough to vote but not to sit!

In *W, X, Y and Z v Belgium* (1975) 18 Yearbook 244, the European Commission on Human Rights concluded that Art 3 of the Convention guarantees the right to stand for election, but did not consider that the minimum age of 25 years for candidacy of the Belgium Parliament was 'unreasonable or arbitrary...or...likely to interfere with the free expression of the people in the choice of legislature'.

Aliens

This exclusion does not apply to Commonwealth and Irish citizens thus creating the anomalous situation in which Commonwealth citizens have no right of abode, but may be members of the United Kingdom Parliament. European Union nationals do have the right of abode but may not sit in the Westminster Parliament (British Nationality Act 1981, Sched 7).

Peers

Prior to the House of Lords Act 1999 all hereditary and life peers were excluded from the House of Commons. This prohibition continues to apply to all life peers but in relation to hereditary peers now affects only those who remain members of the transitional upper House, viz. the 90 'elected' hereditary peers (75 by all hereditary peers and fifteen by all peers) and the holders of the offices of Earl Marshal and Lord Chamberlain (1999 Act, s 3).

Clerics

The 26 senior bishops of the Church of England who comprise the spiritual element of the House of Lords are disqualified from membership of the House of Commons (House of Commons (Disqualification) Act 1975).

Prior to the House of Commons (Removal of Clergy Disqualification) Act 2001 clerical exclusions from the upper chamber extended also to the:

(a) priests and ministers of the Churches of England and Ireland (Anglican) and of the Church of Scotland (Presbyterian) (House of Commons (Disqualification) Act 1801);
(b) priests of the Catholic Church (Roman Catholic Relief Act 1829).

No such restrictions applied, however, to the priests of the Anglican Church in Wales (Welsh Church Act 1914), to the ministers of other Christian churches or to the priests and teachers of other faiths.

This anomalous situation was rectified by the 2001 Act. The Act removed the disqualifications on the Anglican priests of England and Ireland, ministers of the Presbyterian Church in Scotland and on Catholic priests (s 1). Eligibility for the House of Commons now extends to the clergy of all Christian churches and of all other faiths.

Psychiatric patients

Under the Mental Health Act 1983, s 141, if a member is ordered to be detained on the grounds of mental illness, the detention must be reported to the Speaker. If the member is still detained six months later (after a second medical report to the Speaker), the member's seat is declared vacant.

Bankrupts

A person who is declared bankrupt is ineligible for election to the House of Commons. A sitting member declared bankrupt becomes ineligible and their seat declared vacant if not discharged from bankruptcy before six months have elapsed (Insolvency Act 1986, s 427).

It appears, however, that, although declared bankrupt, a member is under no duty to make this known to the Speaker and may continue to sit until ordered to withdraw.

Persons convicted of corrupt or illegal electoral practices

A person convicted of a corrupt electoral practice (the more serious type of electoral offence) is disqualified from election for five years and from election in the constituency in relation to which the offence was committed for ten years (seven years if not personally guilty but guilty through their agent). A person guilty of an illegal electoral practice is disqualified from election for the constituency concerned for seven years (reduced to the duration of the Parliament for which the election was held if guilt is through their agent), but not, therefore, from election for an alternative constituency. The election of a successful candidate, guilty personally or through their agent is void (Representation of the People Act 1983, ss 159, 160, 173 and 174).

Prisoners

Persons sentenced to imprisonment for more than one year or any indefinite sentence are disqualified during their term of imprisonment. Further, any nomination or election of such person as a candidate is void (Representation of the People Act 1981, s 1). If a sitting member is so imprisoned his/her seat is vacated. These provisions were introduced as a response to the election of Bobby Sands in Fermanagh–South Tyrone in 1981. At the time Sands was a republican prisoner on hunger strike in the Maze prison near Belfast. His nomination and election aroused great passions and controversy on both sides of the Irish Sea. Subsequently Sands died after two months without food. Previously, if a member was sentenced to imprisonment for any period, the Speaker was informed of the offence and sentence, but the prisoner remained a member unless a motion was passed to exclude him.

If a sitting member is imprisoned for less than twelve months, unless for treason, he/she is not automatically disqualified but the House could vote for expulsion. A prisoner serving a sentence of less than twelve months is not disqualified from nomination or election but, of course, could not sit until the sentence has been served. Persons convicted of treason (Treason Forfeiture Act 1870) and sentenced to less than twelve months would be disqualified. Whatever the period of sentence, such persons remain disqualified until pardoned or their sentence expires.

Excess ministers

Not more than 95 holders of ministerial office may sit and vote in the House of Commons (House of Commons (Disqualification) Act 1975, s 2(1) and Sched 2). Hence if an MP is given a ministerial post in excess of the 95 he or she is disqualified unless and until another minister is removed or put into the House of Lords.

Members of other legislatures

This disqualification applies to the members of the legislative assemblies of all states outside the Commonwealth with the exception of the Irish Republic (House of Commons (Disqualification) Act 1975 as amended by the Disqualification Act 2000).

Holders of public office

This restriction extends to those who must be seen to be politically impartial, e.g. judges (but not lay magistrates), police, members of the armed forces. It also applies to those paid and appointed by the Crown (government) and therefore, susceptible to government influence or pressure – for example, civil servants, members of boards of public corporations and those with positions incompatible with attendance at Westminster such as members of foreign legislatures, ambassadors and high commissioners (House of Commons (Disqualification) Act 1975, Pt II, Sched 1).

Self-disqualification

Members of Parliament may also disqualify themselves by applying for any of the ancient offices of bailiff or steward of the Chiltern Hundreds or the Manor of North-stead. This is the method by which MPs resign (1975 Act, s 4).

Expulsion

The House may declare a disqualified member's seat vacant or may expel a member for whatever reason it pleases. Tony Benn's Bristol South-East seat was declared vacant after he succeeded to his father's peerage in 1961. In the subsequent by-election Benn (by now Lord Stansgate) was re-elected. The beaten Conservative then presented a successful election petition (*Re Parliamentary Election for Bristol South East* [1964] 2 QB 257) and was subsequently declared to have been elected. Benn later resigned his peerage under the provisions of the 1963 Peerage Act and regained his seat in 1964.

EFFECTS OF DISQUALIFICATION

(a) The House may declare the member's seat vacant (Benn Case, 1963).

(b) The House may request an advisory opinion from the Privy Council on the law relating to a particular issue of disqualification (Judicial Committee Act 1833, s 4; see *Re MacManaway* [1951] AC 161).

(c) The House may declare the seat vacant pursuant to the findings of an Election Court (two High Court judges) after consideration by the latter of an election petition (i.e. complaint by person aggrieved). This jurisdiction was given to the courts by virtue of the Parliamentary Elections Act 1868 and Parliamentary Elections and Corrupt Practices Act 1879. It is assumed that the House will comply with the Court's findings.

(d) The House may declare the seat vacant pursuant to a successful determination of an application alleging disqualification to the Privy Council (House of Commons (Disqualification) Act 1975, s 7).

ROLE AND FUNCTIONS OF MPs

Role

Members of Parliament each have at least four constituencies: their conscience, the party, their geographical constituency and, usually, an interest group. Perhaps a fifth constituency could be said to be in the public interest. Most MPs now appear to accept that their principal loyalty is to the party, but opinions have long differed concerning the extent to which (and how often) MPs should be free to voice their own opinions. It was once generally believed, prior to the advent of organised political parties (post-1832) that an MP's principal function was to speak for his constituents.

In the days when Parliament (or at least the Commons) existed largely to grant taxes to the monarch and occasionally, to present petitions for the redress of grievances, the primary loyalty of members was to those whom they represented. Members were seen as local representatives, living in the constituencies and often being maintained by them...The payment of members by their constituents tied them effectively to the interests of their paymasters (Radice, Vallence and Willis, *Members of Parliament*).

Later views, however, sought to reject the opinion that the MP should see himself as a mere delegate of his constituency electorate.

It ought to be the happiness and glory of a representative to live in the strictest union, the closest correspondence, and the most unreserved communication with his constituents. Their wishes ought to have great weight with him, their opinion high respect, their business unremitting attention. It is his duty to sacrifice his repose, his pleasures, his satisfaction to theirs; and above all, in all cases to prefer their interest to his own. But his unbiased opinion, his mature judgement, his enlightened conscience, he ought not to sacrifice to you, to any man, or to any set of men living...Your representative owes you not his industry only, but his judgement, and he betrays instead of serving you, if he sacrifices it to your opinion (Edmund Burke, Speech to the Electors of Bristol (1774) – see Bell, *The Works of Edmund Burke*).

Burke perceived MPs to be a socially and intellectually superior group of people well qualified to perform the functions of government.

Parliament is not a congress of ambassadors from different and hostile interests, which interests each must maintain as an agent and advocate against other agents and advocates; but Parliament is a deliberative assembly of one nation, with one interest, that of the whole, where not local purposes, not local prejudices ought to guide, but the general good resulting from the general reason of the whole. You chose a member indeed but when you have chosen him he is not the member for Bristol, but he is a member of Parliament (*ibid.*).

Sentiments of the Burkean tradition were evident in Churchill's famous exposition on the role of MPs.

What is the use of sending members to the House of Commons who say just the popular things of the moment and merely endeavour to give satisfaction to the government whips by walking through the lobbies oblivious to the criticism they hear. People talk about our parliamentary institutions and parliamentary democracy, but if these are to survive it will not be because the constituencies return tame, docile, subservient members, and try to stamp out every form of independent judgment.

For all this, even today, it could be dangerous for an MP to neglect the interests, views and problems of his constituents.

Indeed the more an MP takes an independent line at Westminster, the more he may need his local base, which must be both by rallying the troops against the political enemy and by pursuing local interests and solving local problems (Radice, Vallence and Willis, *op. cit.*).

Today, however, with a mass electorate, few MPs are elected because of their distinctive qualities or opinions. Most people vote for a party not for an individual and may be unaware, indeed may not even care, about the particular attributes of the individual for whom they vote. This, of course, strengthens the argument that MPs should sublimate the demands of conscience and constituency to those of the party.

Burke's claim to individual autonomy for the member is perhaps rather less compelling when put in the modern context of tight party discipline, where MPs owe their seats largely to their adoption by the particular party (*ibid.*).

Particular functions

(a) To provide a check on the power of governments. Perhaps the most effective constraint is the government's own MPs and not those of the opposition whose criticism is more ritualistic and less damaging.

> ...the real opposition of the present day sit behind the Treasury bench (Lord Palmerston, 1827).

> A government is more concerned to retain the loyalty and support of its own back-benchers than to placate the opposition. If disaffection should break out among its backbenchers the government's management of the House becomes difficult, the signs of disunity affect its reputation in the country, and it may suffer defeats in the House in circumstances of maximum publicity (Turpin, *British Government and the Constitution*).

(b) To represent interests and grievances of constituents. Most MPs hold local 'clinics' and remain 'in-touch' with local issues and concerns. These may be dealt with by asking questions in Parliament, by reference to the Parliamentary Commissioner or, more often, by informal contacts and lobbying.

(c) To represent interest groups, i.e. professional bodies and associations, trade unions, 'cause' groups (e.g. League Against Blood Sports, etc.), charities, business organisations (e.g. CBI, Institute of Directors).

(d) To represent and support the party thus preserving party unity, enhancing party credibility and thereby making it more effective in either government or opposition.

(e) To contribute to the effective working of Parliament (e.g. by working in standing and select committees, etc.).

(f) To prefer the interests of the nation to more narrow sectional causes in times of emergency (e.g. bipartisan approach during the Falklands War, towards Northern Ireland, and during the Gulf War).

THE RELATIONSHIP BETWEEN MP AND PARTY

Some general comments

The least conspicuous but most important role of the MP is that of party loyalist. Nearly all MPs are party loyalists when the whips are on. The typical loyalist supports the party position without argument, saying little in the Commons and attracting no attention to himself or herself. Loyalists see their role as maintaining party unity...An MP soon learns that his or her personal views are subject to the iron cage of party discipline. Because of the iron cage of party discipline, the government does not need to respond to MPs; it is confident of the outcome of votes in the Commons...The effectiveness of government in securing its legislation is virtually one hundred percent. It is far higher than what is normal in other democratic countries and qualitatively much greater than what a President achieves in Congress (Rose, *Politics in England*).

Factors contributing to party discipline

These include the following:

(a) *Benefits of party unity* It is accepted by most MPs that they were elected primarily to sustain the party and not to pursue their own or their constituency interest in preference to that of the party. Too many displays of independence may produce a disunited party which may damage the party's reputation and public confidence in it. Disunited parties tend not to win general elections and MPs, particularly those in marginal seats, risk losing their seats.

In addition, government backbenchers do not wish to make it difficult for ministers to manage the business of the Commons or to impede implementation of the government's legislative programme.

> If disaffection should break out among its backbenchers the government's management of the House becomes difficult, the signs of disunity affect its reputation in the country, and it may suffer defeats in the House on circumstances of maximum publicity (Turpin, *op. cit.*).

(b) *Danger of deselection* Too many incidents of disloyalty may result in an MP being deselected, i.e. the local constituency party may refuse to select the MP as its candidate for the next general election. Note that it is a convention in the Tory party for sitting members to be reselected. Since 1981, however, all Labour MPs have to go through the selection process each time a general election is called.

> All I say is watch it. Every dog is allowed one bite, but a different view is taken of a dog that goes on biting all the time. If there are doubts that the dog is biting not because of the dictates of conscience but because he is considered vicious, then things happen to that dog. He may not get his licence renewed when it falls due (Harold Wilson, *The Times*, 5 March 1967).

> An MP has to be very incompetent, quite exceptionally brave, or extremely lucky to be denied renomination. If he is rejected his exit is more likely to be caused by scandal, drink, unusual indolence, or some other personal disability, than by political differences with his local party (Gilmore, *The Body Politic*).

(c) *Desire for promotion*

> ...a body acting together must have the rewards of ambition, patronage and place always before their eyes and within their expectation and belief of grasping, as well as the fine expressions of love of their country and the patriotism which is a virtue (Lord Londonderry, 1837).

With the principal exception of Winston Churchill, very few politicians with a reputation for attacking the party leadership have achieved high political office.

(d) *Debt to party leader* If, as it is alleged, elections are widely perceived as contests between party leaders, it could be argued that many MPs on the government side may owe their seats to the popularity of their leader and are, therefore, honour bound to give him/her their support.

(e) *Loss of party whip* This is the ultimate disciplinary sanction and is seldom used as it is controversial and suggests party disharmony. An MP who suffers this fate may no longer be regarded as a member of the parliamentary party and, if not reinstated, would probably be deselected at the next general election.

(f) *Threat of dissolution*   It is sometimes said that a Prime Minister may threaten to dissolve Parliament, thereby putting MPs' seats at risk, in order to put pressure on MPs to give him/her their support. The use of this threat is only realistically possible when the government has a small and fragile majority when it may be used as a last resort to bring dissident MPs 'into line'. Many regard it as a power of dubious validity.

> As a footnote to the discussion of dissolution, it would be well to deal with a widely canvassed legend that has started a new academic hare, namely the power of the prime minister to bring his colleagues to heel by the unilateral threat of a dissolution…A prime minister who decided to act in such a way would be certifiable…The only consequence would be the image of a rattled prime minister and a split party (H Wilson, *op. cit.*).

References

Gilmore (1971) *The Body Politic*, London: Hutchinson.

Radice, Vallence and Willis (1987) *Members of Parliament*, London: Macmillan.

Rose (1980) *Politics in England* (3rd edn), London: Faber and Faber.

Turpin (2002) *British Government and the Constitution* (5th edn), London: Butterworths.

Wilson, *The Times*, 5 March 1967.

Further reading

Adonis (1990) *Parliament Today*, Manchester: Manchester University Press, Ch 3.

Brazier (1994) *Constitutional Practice* (2nd edn), Oxford: Clarendon Press, Ch 10.

Radice, Vallence and Willes, *ibid.*

Chapter 8

THE HOUSE OF COMMONS: PRINCIPAL FUNCTIONS

INTRODUCTION

The House of Commons consists of 659 members of diverse political opinions and allegiances. It does not 'govern' the United Kingdom in the sense of being responsible for the formulation and implementation of policy nor did it evolve for that purpose. The function of government is performed by central government departments and local authorities acting, in the main, through powers given to them by Act of Parliament.

Also, it is not the function of the House of Commons to 'control' the government of the day by dictating to it how the nation's affairs should be managed or inflicting regular defeats upon it. Were it otherwise the process of government and administration would become unstable and unpredictable as a result of frequent changes of government personnel and policy.

The principal function of the House of Commons is to subject the entire conduct of government to a continuous process of rigorous, critical inquiry.

> The only means of parliamentary control worth considering are those which do not threaten the...defeat of the government, but which help to keep it responsive to the underlying current and the more important drifts of public opinion. All others are purely antiquarian shufflings...Parliamentary control should not mislead anyone into asking for a situation in which governments can have their legislation changed or their lives terminated...Control means influence, but not direct power; advice not command; criticism not obstruction; scrutiny not initiation; and publicity of secrecy (Crick, *The Reform of Parliament*).

Academic analyses of the workings of the House of Commons often deal with its functions under the separate headings of legislation, scrutiny of the executive and financial proceedings (i.e. the voting of taxing and spending powers) and with the procedures through which each of these activities is conducted. It is important, however, that such categorisation and concentration on procedural detail should not be allowed to obscure the common or central theme with which all of these activities are concerned – the ability of the House of Commons to identify executive inadequacies and wrongdoings and to expose these to the light of day. Providing this is done effectively then the House can genuinely claim to be both a practical, democratic safeguard against the abuse of government power and an essential vehicle for conveying to the electorate the necessary material to make an informed judgement on the government's competence and fitness to continue in office.

The principal responsibility for laying bare the flaws of government lies, of course, with the parties in opposition. Thus the particular importance of 'Her Majesty's

Loyal Opposition' (the main or 'official' opposition party) in parliamentary and democratic processes. To some extent parliamentary procedures are only as effective as the use that is made of them. Hence a well-led and organised opposition may do much within the existing system to insist on government accountability to the elected chamber. By the same token, however, an opposition in disarray, perhaps after a particularly heavy election defeat, may be of little more than nuisance value as the government asserts its numerical majority in the business of the House.

Other more nebulous and covert political factors may also have their part to play in determining what is essentially a fluctuating relationship between government and Parliament. Hence even a government with a substantial majority may be affected and damaged by 'leaks', 'splits' over party policy, and challenges for the leadership of the party. Factors such as these may exacerbate discontent amongst the government's own backbenchers so that criticism comes from all sides of the House. Little wonder then that in Lord Palmerston's opinion the real opposition lay 'behind the Treasury Bench'; an opinion with which both Mrs Thatcher and Mr Major might readily agree.

LEGISLATION

Some basic definitions

Parliament legislates both directly and indirectly. It legislates directly in the form of Acts of Parliament. It legislates indirectly in the form of delegated or subordinate legislation. That which Parliament does directly is sometimes referred to as 'primary' legislation. That which it does indirectly may be referred to as 'secondary' legislation.

Primary legislation

During its procedural stages through Parliament a legislative proposal is known as a 'Bill'. In terms of its intended scope of application and the procedure for its enactment, a Bill may be:

(a)   a public Bill;
(b)   a private member's Bill;
(c)   a private Bill;
(d)   a hybrid Bill.

A public Bill is a legislative proposal intended to be of general application, i.e. one which will alter the law applicable throughout the realm and to all persons within it. In most cases it will have been formulated and put before Parliament by the government as part of its legislative programme for the session. A good example of the same would be the annual Finance Bill which gives the government the authority it needs to collect the revenues required in order to provide the moneys for defence, public services, etc. A public Bill may begin its parliamentary process in either the House of Commons or House of Lords. By convention, however, a Bill with significant financial or political implications will be introduced in the House of Commons.

A private member's Bill will, in most cases, also be 'public' or of general application in character. However, such a Bill will have been put before Parliament by an ordinary backbench MP and not by a government minister. Also, in some respects, the procedure for introducing and enacting a private member's Bill differs from that used for a public Bill proposed by the government. For these two reasons, therefore, a private member's Bill is often treated as a distinct type of legislative proposal. A good and relatively recent example of a legislative enactment of this type would be the Wild Mammals Protection Act 1996.

A private Bill is a legislative proposal of more limited application or scope. It will seek to have effect in a particular local government area or may relate to the activities of a particular statutory undertaker or company (e.g. a Water Co.). Where such a Bill is promoted by a local authority this will usually be to provide it with a power not available under general enabling legislation (e.g. education Acts, highways Acts, etc.). An example of this type of Bill would be the Greater Nottingham Light Rapid Transit Act 1994. It is common for such Bills to be referred to as local Bills.

Where a private Bill is promoted by a private company this will usually be for the purpose of enabling it to do that which may involve interference with private or public rights (see Lloyds Bank (Merger) Act 1985). On occasion, legislative changes relating to personal issues such as marriage or nationality may also be effected by this type of legislation (see Valerie Mary Hill and Alan Monk (Marriage Enabling) Act 1985; James Hugh Maxwell (Naturalisation) Act 1975). Private Bills of this type are sometimes referred to as personal Bills.

Secondary legislation

This is the general term used to describe legislation made by a subordinate authority (e.g. government minister or local authority) pursuant to a law-making power given to it by an Act of Parliament. As already indicated, such legislation may also be referred to as delegated or subordinate legislation. Secondary legislation made by a minister will usually be in the form of a statutory instrument. This will contain a set of regulations applicable to the particular subject area (e.g. road traffic regulations). Secondary legislation made by a local authority will usually be in the form of by-laws (e.g. those which regulate the use of public parks and amenities).

Public Bills

Formation

As already explained, the vast majority are formulated by the government. A Cabinet committee (legislation committee) will be responsible for managing the government's legislative programme for each session – i.e. for ensuring that Bills scheduled for a particular session pass through their required Commons stages within the time available. Providing the government has a sufficient majority, few such Bills will be lost (i.e. defeated by votes) or withdrawn. The Shops Bill 1986 was the last government Bill of any significance to be lost on the floor of the House (196 votes to 282). Depending on various factors – particularly the significance and complexity of the Bills proposed, and whether an election is pending – the number of Bills introduced in a particular session may be anything from 30 to 70. Some 2,167 public Bills were put before the House of Commons in the period 1945–87. Of these 2,102 were approved, some 97 per cent of the total.

Reasons for introduction

(a) implementation of party manifesto;
(b) response to lobbying by pressure/interest groups;
(c) implementation of recommendations of Royal Commissions, Tribunals of Inquiry (set up under Tribunals of Inquiry (Evidence) Act 1921), other non-statutory judicial inquiries (e.g. Scott Inquiry), departmental inquiries/committees, law commissions or parliamentary select committees;
(d) response to economic, social, industrial, public order or security problems perhaps not predicted in manifesto;
(e) response to political or other emergency (e.g. emergency legislation in wartime and at present in force in Northern Ireland);
(f) implementation of treaty obligations (e.g. EEC Act 1972).

Publication in draft

There is no general requirement that a Bill should be published in draft prior to being committed to its final form and submitted to Parliament. The practice does, however, have its benefits and found favour with the Select Committee on Modernisation of the House of Commons in its first report (1997–98, HC 190). In particular, it gives MPs the opportunity to comment on a Bill at its formative stage and at a time when the minister may be more amenable to suggested amendments or alterations.

> Once Bills are formally introduced they are largely set in concrete. There has been a distinct culture prevalent through Whitehall that the standing and reputation of Ministers has been dependent on their Bills getting through largely unchanged. As a result there has been an inevitable disposition to resist alteration not only in the main issues of substance, but also in matters of detail (para 7).

Immediately following this recommendation, three important Bills, the Pension Sharing on Divorce Bill, the Local Government Bill, and the Financial Services and Markets Bill, appeared in draft prior to the respective Bills being written. Four draft Bills were announced in the Queen's Speech for 1999–2000 and two in the speech for the 2001–02 sessions.

Parliamentary procedure

(1) First reading

This is most usually effected according to Standing Order no. 48. A 'dummy' copy (i.e. title only) is laid on the table of the House on the day scheduled for the Bill's introduction. At the completion of Question Time (circa 3.25 pm) the Speaker calls the sponsoring minister or whip acting on their behalf. A clerk then reads out the title of the Bill. This constitutes its First Reading. The minister is then required to name a date for the Bill's Second Reading. As this will usually not yet have been fixed, the practice is to give a purely nominal date, e.g. 'tomorrow'. The Bill is then ordered to be printed and published. No debate or division takes place at this stage. The House has, however, been given notice that the Bill has begun its parliamentary stages.

The actual text of the Bill is then presented to the Public Bill Office. There, the Clerk of Public Bills is responsible for ensuring that, *inter alia*, its text and content comply with the rules of the House; that its title adequately describes its content; that financial provisions requiring additional expenditure are printed in italics to indicate that financial resolutions will be required; and that it is genuinely a public and not a hybrid Bill (one which, in addition to its public general provisions, contains clauses which have a particular effect on some private or local interests).

(2) Second reading

On the day scheduled, and at the appointed time during public business (any time after about 3.20 pm), the order of the day for the Second Reading of the Bill is read out by the Clerk. The responsible minister then moves that the Bill now be read for a second time. He or she then speaks in favour of its general policy and content. Opposition spokespersons then respond, followed by a general debate by the whole House.

Detailed amendments may be suggested but not formally proposed at this stage. However, procedural amendments – e.g. that the Bill be read for a second time six months hence – may be taken. If carried, an amendment of this type would effectively defeat the Bill.

Since 1967 it has been possible for a minister to propose that a Bill be committed for its second reading debate to a second reading committee (16–50 members) providing not more than nineteen members object (usually non-controversial measures – on average about five per session).

A Bill relating exclusively to Scottish affairs may be referred for its second reading debate to the Scottish Grand Committee – providing not more than nine members object. The Committee is composed of all Scottish members. In addition to conducting such second reading debates, the functions of the Committee include:

(a) hearing oral questions to Scottish Office ministers and law officers;
(b) conducting general debates on Scottish issues;
(c) hearing ministerial statements relating to the same.

Similarly, a Bill dealing with Welsh affairs may be referred for its second reading to the Welsh Grand Committee. This consists of all Welsh members and five others. The Committee may also conduct general debates on Welsh affairs, hear oral questions to ministers and receive ministerial statements.

Albeit that a second reading debate has taken place in standing committee the actual vote or division on the Bill is taken in the whole House. Financial clauses must be further authorised by resolutions pursuant to motions introduced by the responsible minister between second reading and committee stage.

(3) Committee stage

After second reading most Bills will be referred to a 'Standing Committee' (about eighteen members nominated by the Committee of Selection) for detailed consideration and amendment. Some Bills may, however, by resolution be referred to a Committee of the Whole House or, more occasionally, to a Select Committee of the House or Joint

Select Committee consisting of members from both Houses. Consolidated Fund Bills (i.e. those authorising expenditure) will be dealt with in committee of the whole House as may minor Bills for which the committee stage is a pure formality, and, from time to time, Bills of major public importance (e.g. European Union (Amendment) Bill 1992 to give effect to the Maastricht Treaty). For a committee of the whole House the Speaker vacates the chair. Their place is then taken by the Chairman of Ways and Means (or deputy of same). The annual Finance Bill is, for purposes of expedition, considered partially on the floor of the House and partially in standing committee.

The composition of standing committees reflects party strengths in the House. Originally such committees were appointed to serve for the whole parliamentary session. Thus their membership 'stood' or remained the same for Bills dealt with during that period. Currently, however, such committees are reconstituted for the purposes of each Bill according to members' interests and qualifications. Ministers from the sponsoring department and opposition spokespersons will be represented. Given the composition of standing committees it is unlikely that major changes – amendments to clauses affecting the substance of the Bill or its policy objectives – will be made. Many other amendments may be made, however, and it is not unusual for the majority of these to be moved by the government – in response to pressure from within the party, views of interest groups, legal advice, etc.

The chairperson has a key role in expediting the business of the committee. He/she may eliminate amendments or proposals which are out of order or which are of a trivial or minor nature. The chair may also arrange for amendments of a similar content or intent to be considered collectively, and decide which amendments may be debated prior to a vote and which may be voted upon without debate.

On occasion, a Bill may be referred to a special standing committee. This is a type of hybrid between the more usual type of standing committee and the typical investigative select committee. Such committee commences its work with a limited number of evidence-taking sessions. As a general rule these should be completed within 28 days. The committee then proceeds to go through the Bill clause by clause, in the normal way, aided in the making of amendments by the evidence it has gathered.

A committee of this type will tend to be used for a Bill of great complexity or which may relate to unusual subject matter so that the taking of expert and other interested testimony may make a significant contribution to the examination and, possibly, alteration of the Bill's finer details. It is unlikely that a politically contentious Bill would be disposed of in this way. Such committees were first used in the 1980–81 session. Three Bills were dealt with in this way – the Criminal Attempts Bill, the Education Bill and the Deep Sea Mining (Temporary Provisions) Bill.

A Bill dealing exclusively with Scottish affairs may be referred to one of two Scottish standing committees.

(4) Report stage

A Bill considered by standing committee is then reported back to the House as amended or unamended. The House may accept or reject the amendments made but without further debate. New amendments and clauses may be proposed and considered. The Speaker will be careful to ensure that this stage is not used to rehearse arguments dealt with in committee.

Bills referred to standing committee or the Scottish Grand Committee for their second reading may remain in committee for their report stage.

Unamended Bills from committees of the whole House go straight to third reading – i.e. there is no report stage.

(5) Third reading
This is usually brief and formal except in the case of controversial measures. Only verbal amendments for the correction of errors are permitted. The opposition parties may or may not insist on a debate.

(6) Proceedings in the House of Lords
All Bills pass through similar procedural stages in the House of Lords, save that the Lords has no standing committees. The committee stage will usually be dealt with by committees of the whole House. Should the Lords amend a Bill, the amendments must be referred to and accepted, rejected or amended by the House of Commons. If there is disagreement the disputed amendments, with reasons, are referred back to the House of Lords. This exchanging of amendments, usually only in relation to controversial measures, may go on until agreement is reached. In the event of no such agreement and in very rare instances, the government may feel obliged to invoke the Parliament Acts 1911–49 which allow for Bills rejected by the Lords to go for the Royal Assent after at least one year has elapsed.

The upper House has no power to amend money Bills (i.e. those concerned wholly with finance). If such a Bill has not been passed by the Lords within one month of its receipt, it may proceed for the Royal Assent (Parliament Act 1911, s 1).

(7) The Royal Assent
By virtue of the Royal Assent Act 1967 this final stage of enacting a Bill may be either:

(a) announced by the Speaker in the House of Commons and by the Lord Chancellor in the House of Lords pursuant to authority granted to both by the Monarch in letters patent; or

(b) given by members of the upper House appointed as Lords Commissioners by the Monarch for the purposes of giving assent to a particular Bill or, more usually, a number of Bills.

Unless with the agreement of the House, a public Bill must receive the Royal Assent in the session it is put before Parliament. If not the Bill fails and will have to be reintroduced in the next session.

'Carrying over'
The Select Committee on Modernisation of the House of Commons in its third report for 1997–98 (HC 543), whilst recognising that the above rule acted as an important discipline on the government in terms of the effective disposal of its legislative programme, felt that it should be applied flexibly so that, in appropriate cases, and in the interests of more effective scrutiny, a Bill might be 'carried over' from one session to

another. This might be preferable, it was thought, to rushing important legislation through its final stages simply to meet the end of session deadline.

Shortly after publication of the Committee report, the Financial Services and Markets Bill 1997–98 was 'carried over' at its Committee stage.

Private members' Bills

Nature and subject matter

Private members legislation represents one of the few remaining processes through which the House and its members may exercise a truly creative and independent law-making function, i.e. one not dominated by the government.

Such Bills tend to relate to social, ethical, environmental or constitutional issues which the government may not have the time or – for a variety of reasons – the inclination to include in its legislative programme. Such reticence may be because:

(a) the matter is too sensitive and controversial (e.g. termination of pregnancy);
(b) it does not relate to party policy (e.g. animal research);
(c) there is no political gain to be made from the issues (family law reform, divorce, etc.);
(d) there is no clear party or public consensus relating thereto (e.g. pornography).

Some familiar examples of private members' Bills would include the Obscene Publications Act 1959, the Murder (Abolition of the Death Penalty) Act 1965, the Sexual Offences Act 1957 (legalisation of homosexual acts), and the Termination of Pregnancy Act 1968. Some interesting and more recent examples would include the Still-Birth (Definition) Act 1992, the Children and Young Persons (Protection from Tobacco) Act 1991, and the Welfare of Animals at Slaughter Act 1991.

In the last 50 years the average number of private members' Bills receiving the Royal Assent in each session has been thirteen.

Types of private members' Bills and procedure for enactment

(a) Ballot Bills

Standing orders of the House generally dedicate between ten and thirteen Fridays per session to the consideration of private members' Bills. On the second Thursday of each session a ballot is held to decide which members should be able to use the time available for the legislative measures of their choice. This is a matter of considerable interest to the majority of members. Four to five hundred will usually participate in the ballot. Ministers and government whips may not participate, nor, by convention, do opposition leaders and spokespersons. Twenty names only are drawn. Of these only the first six to ten have any realistic possibility of securing the passage of a Bill. Successful members may nominate a particular Friday for the second reading of their Bill (the first six being set aside for this purpose). Hence the MP who came first in the ballot may claim precedence on the first Friday and so on. These same Bills then have precedence for their remaining procedural stages and Lords amendments on the remaining Fridays set aside for private members legislation.

It is interesting to note that many members may not have a particular Bill in mind when they enter the ballot. When, as often happens, an 'undecided' member is drawn in the first twenty they will then be the subject of considerable lobbying from interest groups and other organisations – in the hope that they may introduce a Bill on their behalf. Also, the government may suggest a Bill to a successful MP. These will usually be minor measures which the government has been unable to fit into its legislative programme for that session. They are often referred to as 'handout' or 'whips' Bills.

Some members will decide, or may be persuaded, to introduce Bills which have little chance of success. They may do this simply to secure a debate and some publicity for a particular issue about which they have strong feelings. In recent years Bills of this type have raised such issues as abortion, embryo research, constitutional reform (freedom of information and the introduction of a Bill of Rights), smoking in public places, blood sports, etc.

A Bill given a second reading will then proceed to standing committee in the usual way. This will be a committee set up primarily to deal with private members' Bills. Some Bills, however, could be committed to other standing committees if these are not busy with government legislation. Having progressed through standing committee, private members' Bills return to the floor of the House for the report and third reading stages.

In order to secure the success of a Bill the sponsoring MP will have to negotiate a number of major procedural obstacles. First, the Bill may be defeated at second reading by hostile members. This will usually be the case if the Bill is opposed by the government. Although it is not usual for the government to formally oppose a private member's Bill (by imposing the 'whip'), communication to its backbenchers of government 'unease' about a particular measure will normally be sufficient to ensure its defeat. Second, a private member's Bill may simply be 'talked out'. In other words, members opposed to the Bill ensure that a particular procedural stage (usually second reading) has not been completed within the time available. Should this appear likely, the sponsoring member may propose the 'closure' (see below). This, of course, must be supported by a majority of members present. A simple majority, however (e.g. 26 for, 24 against), is not sufficient as, for the closure to be carried, at least 100 members must vote in favour. Since attendance at the House on Fridays is often low this is only likely in relation to those measures for which there is a considerable degree of backbench support. Also note that, as with all other proceedings on the floor of the House, a quorum of 40 is necessary if a vote is to take place.

(b) Ten-minute rule Bills

After Question Time on Tuesdays or Wednesdays, a member who has given at least five sitting days' notice may propose and speak for ten minutes in favour of a particular Bill. Any member opposed may have a similar period of time to speak against. There is no further debate. The House then divides on whether to give leave to introduce the Bill. If leave is given the Bill is deemed to have been read for the first time.

Ten-minute rule Bills have little chance of being enacted save in those rare cases where they are not opposed and sufficient time for their further procedural stages is either provided by the government – an unlikely event given the amount of government business to be conducted in each session of Parliament – or can be found during those Fridays dedicated to balloted private members legislation. Only 64 such Bills were enacted in the period 1949–99.

The purpose of introducing such a Bill is often to suggest a change in the law or to promote a particular cause. It also provides a member with the opportunity to test parliamentary opinion on a matter concerning which the member may wish to legislate in the future.

(c) Presentation Bills

Apart from using the ballot or ten-minute rule procedures, any member (having given notice) may put down a Bill for second reading on the day of their choice. Leave is not required. At least one day's notice must be given and the Bill then presented to the Clerk of the House. The Clerk reads out the short title of the Bill which is then deemed to have had its first reading. No further procedure is possible unless, that is, time for the further stages of the Bill can be found on those Fridays devoted to private members' Bills (when ballot Bills have precedence) or the government is prepared to make time available.

Some general comments

A private member's Bill may not be introduced if its primary objective is to require additional government expenditure. Where such expenditure is necessarily incidental to the main purposes of a Bill, a financial resolution or resolutions moved by a government minister would be required before the financial clauses could be considered in standing committee. Hence, without government support a Bill of this type could not proceed.

The sponsoring member is responsible for the drafting of a Bill. Parliamentary counsel are not normally available for this task – that is, unless the Bill has attracted government support. Financial and other assistance may, however, be provided by any supporting interest group. Also, since 1971, the MPs responsible for the first ten balloted Bills have been able to claim a small amount in expenses from public funds (£200).

Private members' Bills may also be introduced in the House of Lords. Where this occurs the Bill must then be sponsored by an MP to guide it through its Commons stages. As with other unballoted Bills, unless government or private members time can be found, there is little hope of such Bills progressing through the House.

In the ten parliamentary sessions between 1989 and 1999, 145 private members' Bills received the Royal Assent – an average of 14.5 per session. Of these, 88 were ballot Bills (8.8 per session), 21 were presentation Bills (2.1 per session) eight were ten-minute rule Bills (0.85 per session) and 28 were introduced in the House of Lords.

Private Bills

Nature and subject matter

Reference has already been made to the fact that such Bills do not attempt to make any change to the general law of the land but seek instead to make law for a particular local area, organisation (public or private), or individual.

In the eighteenth and nineteenth centuries Bills of this type tended to dominate the legislative work of Parliament. They were used particularly for such purposes as land enclosure (by extinguishing rights of common) and to acquire land for the construction of railways and canals. The role of the private Bill in this context has been revived in recent years as local authorities have sought statutory authorisation for the construction of rapid light transport systems (tramways) to relieve urban congestion. In the future, however, such projects will receive the necessary authorisation by ministerial Orders made under the Transport and Works Act 1992.

Procedure

As a general rule, notice of the intention to promote a private Bill should be given by public advertisement in newspapers and the *London Gazette,* and in writing to all persons whose rights or interests may be directly affected. When this has been done a petition signed by the promoters and a copy of the Bill must be presented at the Private Bill Office of the House of Commons by 27 November each year. This is to allow time for the Examiners of Private Bills to ensure that standing orders relating to the pre-parliamentary stages of private legislation have been complied with.

The Bill is presented to the House of Commons by being placed on the Order Table by a clerk from the Private Bill Office. This also operates as the Bill's first reading. At second reading a debate and division will occur only if a member has given notification of opposition. A Bill requiring government expenditure or imposing a tax will require the appropriate financial resolutions to be moved by a minister before it can proceed to its committee stage.

If a Bill has not been opposed it will be sent to an unopposed private Bill committee (four members). An opposed Bill will go to an opposed private Bill committee (seven members). Proceedings in the latter are 'quasi-judicial'. The promoters and their opponents argue their cases, often represented by counsel. Witnesses are examined on oath. Members of the committee should have no particular interest in the Bill's subject matter. In addition to considering individual clauses and suggested amendments, the committee will be concerned to see that the facts stated in the Bill's preamble (i.e. the introductory statement setting out the need for the Bill) are accurate and that the Bill is both in the local and national interest.

If the Bill is approved in committee it is reported to the House and then proceeds to its third reading (usually a formality) and thence to the House of Lords where it goes through much the same process.

Hybrid Bills

Definition

A hybrid Bill will be generally public in content but will contain provisions which affect particular private or local interests in a manner different from their effect on similar interests nationally (e.g. Channel Tunnel Act 1987).

Procedure

The procedure is similar to that for public Bills save that after second reading, if opposed, a hybrid Bill is referred to a small select committee of MPs. This deals with the 'private' aspects of the Bill. Those persons whose legal interests are affected by the clauses in question may place their objections before the committee. At this stage the general expediency of the Bill is not in issue nor does the committee concern itself with the Bill's public or general provisions.

The Bill then proceeds as normal to a standing committee and through its subsequent stages as if it were an ordinary public Bill.

Methods of curtailing debate

Reasons

If procedures for limiting discussion of particular Bills, particularly at second reading or in committee, were not available, it would be open for MPs to keep proceedings going for as long as possible thus interfering with the progress of particular Bills and causing problems for the whole of the government's legislative programme. Hence standing orders provide a number of procedural devices which may be used to expedite the business of the House. These devices were adopted at the end of the nineteenth century when Irish Nationalist MPs, in pursuit of Home Rule for Ireland, sought to put pressure on the government by disrupting the parliamentary process. Prior to these events proceedings in the House continued so long as any member had something relevant to say.

There is a danger, of course, that the devices mentioned below could be used to stifle informed debate and criticism and not simply as a means of ensuring parliamentary efficiency.

The closure

Any member either in the House or in committee may move that 'the question be now put' (e.g. that the Bill be read for a second time). The Speaker may or may not accept the motion depending on whether they think that the various interested opinions represented in the House have been given a fair opportunity to contribute to the debate. If the motion is accepted the House then divides. The motion is carried and the debate ended providing at least 100 MPs vote for the closure. The question which the House has been debating is then put to the vote – i.e. whether the Bill should be given a second reading.

The guillotine

This is properly known as the 'allocation of time motion' and is a procedure available to the government to secure the passage of legislation which it is anticipated may be vigorously opposed in the House. The motion, usually moved by a member of the government, seeks either to set a date by which the particular Bill must have completed its committee stage or to allocate a specific number of days to the Bill's various stages. Given the government's majority in the House such motions will normally be carried notwithstanding the expected protests of opposition members. As the Bill proceeds through the House and the time or times set for the completion of its various stages are reached, further debate is 'guillotined' or brought to an end with the Bill then proceeding to its next stage.

They may be regarded as the extreme limit to which procedure goes in affirming the rights of the majority at the expense of the minorities of the House and it cannot be denied that they are capable of being used in such a way as to upset the balance – between the claims of business and the rights of debate. But the harshness of this procedure is to some extent mitigated either by consultation between the party leaders or in the Business Committee in order to establish the greatest possible measure of agreement as to the most satisfactory disposal of the time available (May, *Parliamentary Practice*, p 409).

Programme motions

Both the closure and the guillotine are regarded as rather blunt instruments which are usually imposed on a resistant House of Commons. In more recent times, and particularly as a result of the urgings of the Select Committee on Modernisation of the House, greater emphasis has been placed on agreed programming whereby a timetable for a Bill's progress is agreed between party whips. When formulated, a programme motion will be put before the House after the Bill has been given its second reading. The motion will stipulate the date by which the Bill should complete its passage through standing committee and will state the time available for further discussion of the Bill during its report and third reading stages.

Programming is said to have the dual advantages of enabling the government to dispose effectively of its legislative agenda for the session at the same time as allowing opposition parties a greater opportunity of ensuring that important elements of a Bill are subjected to some genuine parliamentary scrutiny.

> In short, the government gets its legislation, the Opposition chooses what areas get the focus of debate, and individual members get some greater certainty about the progress of business and the timing of votes (1999–2000, HC 589).

The programming of legislation in response to these proposals began in the 1997–98 session. Some ten Bills were dealt with in this way, including the Scotland Bill, the Human Rights Bill and the Crime and Disorder Bill.

Delegated legislation

Numerous spheres of human activity are now regulated by various types of rules and orders made by subordinate authorities acting under legislative powers delegated to them by Act of Parliament. Indeed such is the volume of law made in this way, particularly by government departments, that this has become the most prolific source of legal rules operating in the United Kingdom. In historical terms the increase in the importance and use of delegated legislation is a relatively recent phenomenon and has been a feature of the development of the regulatory state.

Reasons for increased use

The particular reasons for this type of legislation are usually explained by reference to the following factors.

(a) Lack of parliamentary time

During the latter half of the nineteenth century as the state began to involve itself in such matters as public health, housing, education and safety at work, it became increasingly apparent that Parliament had neither the time nor the energy to enact all the legislation necessary for the detailed regulation of these activities. As a result, more frequent resort was made to the enactment of Bills setting out general policy objectives and standards, but which left the more detailed rule-making to government, both central and local.

The purpose and value of such delegation for the efficient functioning both of Parliament and of the process of administration was expressed thus in 1877:

> The adoption of the system of confining the attention of Parliament to material provisions only, and leaving details to be settled departmentally, is probably the only mode in which parliamentary government can...be carried on. The province of Parliament is to decide material questions affecting the public interest, and the more procedural and subordinate matters can be withdrawn from their cognizance the greater will be the time afforded for the consideration of the more serious questions involved in legislation (Lord Thring, *Practical Legislation*).

As the twentieth century progressed and the amount of delegated legislation – or executive law-making – increased some began to point to the dangers this posed for the preservation of the separation of powers. Fears were expressed that the legislative role of Parliament was being taken over by the executive:

> That there is in existence, and in certain quarters in the ascendant, a genuine belief that parliamentary institutions have been tried and found wanting, and that the time has come for the departmental despot, who shall be...a law to himself, needs no demonstration (Lord Hewart, *The New Despotism*, 1929).

This was one of the reasons for the creation of the Committee on Ministers' Powers (the Donoughmore Committee) which reported in 1932. In relation to delegated legislation its conclusion was that without it the legislative process would cease to function effectively but that the use of such law-making powers should be subject to effective parliamentary and judicial controls (see below).

(b) Complexity of subject matter

Parliament does not possess the expertise required to legislate effectively on many of the complex and technical issues which require legal regulation. Thus, for example, while many MPs might have general views on the risks associated with, say, the storage of dangerous chemicals or nuclear waste, it is not likely that these same persons would be possessed of sufficient relevant knowledge to be able to formulate a set of safety laws which would have any practical utility in these particular contexts.

The preparation of legislation on such issues requires detailed discussions between the relevant government department and experts in the field. There is little use in Parliament attempting to legislate specifically on matters which MPs do not understand, nor would the public interest be well served by legal rules which related only imperfectly to the matters to which they were directed.

> The details of such technical legislation need the assistance of experts and can be regulated after a Bill passes into an Act by delegated legislation with greater care and minuteness and

with a better adaption to local and other special circumstances than they can be in the passage of a Bill through Parliament (Select Committee on Procedure, Sixth Report, 1966/67).

(c) Speed

Regulations may be made more quickly than Acts of Parliament. The use of delegated legislation, therefore, enables the executive to act quickly and appropriately in terms of the legal rules needed to deal with pressing and unforeseen circumstances:

> for example, an increase in import duties would lose some of its effect if prior notice was given and importers were able to import large quantities of goods at the old lower rate of duty (*ibid.*).

(d) Flexibility

Acts of Parliament will frequently introduce schemes, particularly in the context of social welfare, which need updating from time to time. It would, for example, be extremely impractical and time-consuming if Parliament had to pass an Act every time it was decided to make a minor alteration to the levels of prescription charges, eligibility for legal aid, or any of the other numerous charges and benefits which the state administers. Such minor changes – providing these are consistent with the overall objectives of the enabling Act – are regarded, therefore, as the function of delegated legislation.

(e) Times of emergency

Despite the normative requirements of the rule of law and the separation of powers, it is generally accepted that a substantial degree of law-making authority should be entrusted to the executive when the state or the community is threatened by, *inter alia*, war, terrorism or natural disasters. The assumption here is that in such times those in government are best placed to judge what is required in terms of legislation for the protection of the state and its populace.

Dangers of delegated legislation

Delegated legislation may be an established and essential part of an efficient legislative and administrative process but, as its detractors in the early part of the twentieth century made clear, it has its dangers, particularly if no effective restraints on its abuse are in place. Some of the dangers to constitutional propriety usually associated with it are as follows:

(a) Government by decree

The fear is that a government could use its majority in Parliament to enact enabling legislation which authorised it to make law on matters of general principle or policy – i.e. not on matters of detail as is believed to be the proper domain of government law-making power. There is no formal control to prevent this nor are there any clear rules as to what is policy and what is detail.

(b) Imposition of taxation

It has been said that the use of delegated legislation to impose or alter rates of taxation is inconsistent with the requirement in the Bill of Rights 1689 that 'levying money for...the Crown...without consent of Parliament...is illegal'. This prescription is still adhered to in general terms. Hence the requirement of an annual Finance Act to effect major changes in matters relating to revenue and particularly to direct taxation.

Changes to indirect taxation of various types, including VAT, are now effected by virtue of delegated legislative powers. This would appear to be necessitated by the volume and complexity of the legislative rules operating in this context and by the need to have in place a system of law-making which permits ready application of the fiscal policies of the European Community.

(c) Alteration of Acts of Parliament

It is not unknown for an enabling Act to contain a clause which gives to the subordinate law-maker – usually a minister – the power to make legal rules which alter either the terms of the enabling Act itself or those in other Acts of Parliament. A provision of this type is sometimes referred to as a 'Henry VIII clause', so named because 'that King is regarded popularly as the impersonation of executive autocracy' (Donoughmore Committee, above).

Delegated legislation which permits ministers to amend primary legislation – that which has been enacted by Parliament – may be acceptable, so long as this is confined to matters of details. Cause for concern may arise, however, where such delegated power is used in relation to matters of substance.

(d) Retrospective effect

As a general rule retrospective legislation is contrary to the rule of law. It is most likely, therefore, that any retrospective provisions in a Bill would be the subject of adverse comment and debate in the House before the measure was enacted.

Delegated legislation is not subject, however, to such close parliamentary scrutiny nor does it attract great public awareness. The risk of retrospective legislation being introduced in this way, and going unnoticed or unchallenged is, therefore, increased.

(e) Exclusion of judicial review

The importance of this type of legislation, and the potential for abuse of such delegated powers, suggests that at all times it should be open to judicial review on both substantive and procedural grounds.

The availability and effectiveness of judicial control may be negatively affected, however, by:

- wide, subjectively worded enabling provisions – e.g. 'the Minister may make such regulations as he thinks fit';
- the inclusion of an express ouster clause (i.e. a clause stating that the validity of regulations made under the Act may not be questioned in the courts).

Principal categories of delegated legislation

(a) Statutory instruments

Statutes which confer legislative powers on specific ministers will usually provide that the minister in question may make law in the form of a statutory instrument. Some two thousand or more of these emanate from government departments annually. Each will contain regulations dealing with the subject matter of the enabling Act (e.g. Road Traffic).

(b) Orders in Council

Where it is the intention of an enabling Act to confer a legislative power on the government as a whole as distinct from an individual minister, the Act will usually provide that the power should be exercised by 'the Queen in Council'. Hence the provision in the Emergency Powers Act 1920 that when a proclamation of emergency has been made, it shall be lawful for His Majesty in Council, by Order, to make regulations for securing the essentials of life to the community.

As with Acts of Parliament, the Monarch's role in making such legislation is purely formal. The legislation will be formulated by the government. The Lord President of the Council (a senior Cabinet minister) then summons three or four other ministers to a meeting of the Privy Council presided over by the Monarch. The consent of the Monarch and the Council to the proposed legislation is automatic.

The Order in Council will contain a set of regulations relating to the matter covered by the enabling power. Delegated legislation by Order in Council tends to be reserved for matters of greater importance or constitutional significance than that which is thought to be the proper subject matter of ministerial regulations. Hence, for example, Orders in Council may be used to stipulate the date when an Act will take effect, to make changes to the boundaries of parliamentary constituencies (Parliamentary Constituencies Act 1986) or, as indicated, to effect emergency regulations, as under the Emergency Powers Act 1920. It is also possible for legislative authority conferred in this way to be exercised by whichever minister(s) appears to be appropriate.

For procedural purposes, Orders in Council are treated as statutory instruments and are, therefore, subject to the Statutory Instruments Act 1946.

Orders in Council made under an Act of Parliament should be distinguished from those issued under the royal prerogative. The latter are a type of primary legislation and are examples of the Monarch's remaining original legislative authority (nowadays limited to matters relating to the civil service and armed forces).

(c) By-laws

This is the name given to laws made by local authorities, public corporations or other companies vested with statutory powers.

The enabling power for by-laws made by local authorities is the Local Government Act 1972, s 235. This authorised district councils to 'make byelaws for the good rule and government' of the areas under their control. Such by-laws must be approved by a Secretary of State, usually the Secretary of State for the Environment.

Administrative and parliamentary controls

(a) Consultations

A frequent requirement in enabling Acts, particularly those giving the power to make law by statutory instrument, is that when formulating the regulations the minister responsible should consult with specified organisations and/or other organisations likely to be affected by the same.

The nature of the obligation imposed by a requirement to consult was explained in *R v Secretary of State for Social Services, ex parte Association of Metropolitan Authorities* [1986] 1 All ER 164:

> ...the essence of consultation is the communication of a genuine invitation to give advice and a genuine receipt of that advice. In my view it must go without saying that to achieve consultation sufficient information must be supplied by the consulting to the consulted party to enable it to tender helpful advice. Sufficient time must be given...to enable it to do that, and sufficient time must be available for such advice to be considered (per Webster J).

Even if an Act contains no obligation to consult it is usual administrative practice to consult those who may be involved in, or affected by, its implementation.

> No Minister in his right senses with the fear of Parliament before his eyes would even think of making regulations without...giving the persons who will be affected thereby...an opportunity of saying what they think about the proposal (Sir W G Harrison, *Evidence to the Committee on Ministers' Powers*, 1932).

(b) Publicity

The Statutory Instruments Act 1946, s 2(1), as amended by the Statutory Instruments (Production and Sale) Act 1996, provides that every statutory instrument (which definition includes Orders in Council) must be printed and sold by, or under the authority of, the King's printers of Acts of Parliament.

Where the contravention of a statutory instrument amounts to a criminal offence, it is a defence to prove that the instrument, or any relevant part of it, was not published and that no other reasonable steps had been taken to bring its content to the defendant's notice (s 3(2)).

(c) Parliamentary scrutiny

Most enabling Acts will require that statutory instruments made pursuant to them should be laid before Parliament (i.e. presented to the Votes and Proceedings Office in the House of Commons and the Office of the Clerk of the Parliaments in the House of Lords) according to one of the following procedures.

1. Laying subject to the negative resolution procedure

This is the procedure most commonly required by enabling Acts and is used for in excess of some 70 per cent of all statutory instruments.

The procedure's exact requirements are set out in the Statutory Instruments Act 1946, s 5. The instrument should be laid before Parliament for a period of 40 days. If either House passes an annulment or negative resolution in that period, the instrument ceases to have effect.

Note that (although there is some uncertainty on this point) a statutory instrument made according to this procedure probably takes effect at the time it is laid before Parliament. Thus it does not take effect as soon as it is made by the minister (i.e. before it is laid), nor does it have to wait to become effective until the 40-day laying period has expired.

This is the most favoured procedure as it preserves parliamentary control without any unnecessary wastage of time. This is because a debate and vote in either House is only necessary in relation to that small minority of instruments to which particular objection has been taken.

Where a member gives notice of intention to pray for the annulment of a particular resolution, the subsequent debate may take place in a standing committee. This was a new procedure introduced in the 1996–97 session.

2. Laying subject to the affirmative resolution procedure

This tends to be used for instruments which may relate to a matter of principle or possible political controversy – e.g. those which contain emergency regulations under the Emergency Powers Act 1920 or which give effect to legislation for Northern Ireland under the Northern Ireland Act 1974.

The enabling Act will specify the period for which the instrument must be laid before one or both Houses. An affirmative resolution or resolutions must then be passed within that period if the instrument is to take effect.

While this procedure preserves effective parliamentary control over the delegated legislation subject to it, its use involves the allocation of precious parliamentary time to each instrument laid in this way.

3. Laying in draft subject to negative or affirmative resolutions

An instrument laid in draft, subject to the negative resolution procedure, cannot be made or become effective until the draft has been laid before Parliament and 40 days have elapsed without an annulment resolution having been passed by either House.

An instrument laid in draft, subject to the affirmative resolution procedure, cannot be made or become effective until the required affirmative resolutions have been passed within the specified period.

All instruments laid before Parliament are subject to scrutiny by the Joint Committee on Statutory Instruments (seven members from each House). The committee is charged with deciding whether a particular instrument should be drawn to the attention of the House on any of the following grounds:

- it imposes a tax or charge on public revenues;
- the enabling Act seeks to exclude it from judicial review;
- it purports to have retrospective effect without clear authority in the enabling Act;
- there appears to have been unjustifiable delay in its publication or laying before Parliament;
- it may be *ultra vires* or appears to make an unusual or unexpected use of the enabling power;
- it appears to have been drafted defectively;
- it requires elucidation on any other ground.

Judicial supervision

A court may find a statutory instrument to be *ultra vires* and invalid on either substantive or procedural grounds.

An instrument will be *ultra vires* in the substantive sense if it deals with matters beyond the scope of the legislative authority conferred by the enabling Act. Particularly important in this context are certain judicial presumptions as to the intentions of Parliament when it confers delegated legislative powers. Thus it is presumed that, unless clear authority (by express words or necessary implication) is contained in the enabling Act, Parliament does not intend such powers to be used to:

- impose a tax (*Attorney-General v Wilts United Dairies Ltd,* above);
- deny or restrict the citizen's right of access to the courts (*Chester v Bateson,* above);
- make law having restrospective effect (*Malloch v Aberdeen Corporation* 1974 SLT 253);
- restrict basic civil liberties or human rights (*Raymond v Honey* [1983] 1 AC 1).

A statutory instrument may also be struck down for unreasonableness if it represents a use of the enabling power which is so outrageous or extraordinary that it could not have been intended by Parliament (*Sparks v Edward Ash* [1943] KB 223).

In the past courts have generally shown considerable reluctance to question instruments which have been laid before and approved by Parliament except in cases of extreme bad faith, improper purpose or manifest absurdity (*R v Secretary of State for the Environment, ex parte Hammersmith and Fulham LBC* [1991] 1 AC 521).

A statutory instrument may be *ultra vires* on procedural grounds if made in breach of a mandatory procedural requirement. Whether Parliament intended such requirement to be mandatory or merely directory is a matter of statutory construction (for distinction between mandatory and directory procedural requirements see coverage of procedural impropriety in Chapter 15). The preponderance of judicial and academic opinion suggests that a requirement to consult should be construed to be mandatory. Hence a failure to consult may result in the instrument in question being ruled to be invalid (*Agricultural, Horticultural and Forestry Industry Training Board v Aylesbury Mushrooms Ltd* [1972] 1 WLR 190).

The consequences of a failure to publish a statutory instrument or to lay it before Parliament, where so required, are not entirely clear. Judicial comment suggests that where an instrument is not published according to the Statutory Instruments Act 1946, s 2(1), and no other reasonable steps are taken to make its content known, the instrument is probably invalid or at least ineffective (*Johnson v Sargant* [1918] 1 KB 101). This implies, however, that if such reasonable steps have been taken then the instrument may be effective notwithstanding the failure to publish in the statutory or formal sense (*R v Sheer Metalcraft* [1954] 1 QB 586). It would appear, therefore, that the publication requirement imposed by the 1946 Act should be understood as directory only.

In relation to a requirement to lay an instrument before Parliament, there is judicial authority for the view that this also should be regarded as directory only (*Bailey v Williamson* (1873) LR 8 QBD 118). Such a view does not, however, sit particularly easily with the provision in the Statutory Instruments Act 1946, s 4 that an instrument which is required to be laid before Parliament does not come into effect until this has been done.

The above grounds of review apply particularly to statutory instruments. The validity of a by-law may be challenged if:

(a) in its terms and application it goes beyond the ambit of the delegated law-making power (*R* v *Reading Crown Court, ex parte Hutchinson* [1988] QB 384);

(b) it was made in breach of a mandatory procedural requirement, e.g. lack of ministerial consent (no case directly on this point);

(c) it is inconsistent with a provision in an Act of Parliament (*Powell* v *May* [1946] KB 330), or repugnant to a basic tenet of the common law (*London Passenger Transport Board* v *Sumner* (1935) 99 JP 387);

(d) it is unreasonable in the sense explained in *Kruse* v *Johnson* [1898] 2 QB 91, i.e. it is 'partial and unequal...as between different classes...manifestly unjust... disclosed bad faith...[or] involved such oppressive or gratuitous interference with the rights of those subject to them as could find no justification in the minds of reasonable men' (per Lord Russell CJ).

(e) it is so vague in its terminology that its exact meaning or scope of application cannot be readily ascertained (*Scott* v *Pilliner* [1904] 2 KB 855; *Percy* v *Hall* [1997] 3 WLR 573).

(f) it is inconsistent with European Community law (*Johnson* v *Chief Constable of the Royal Ulster Constabulary* [1987] QB 129 (ECJ).

Northern Ireland legislation

Since the introduction of direct rule in 1972, and except in relation to certain reserved matters, this legislation is now effected principally by Order in Council. The most important reserved matters are security, the administration of justice and taxation. Legislation for Northern Ireland in these matters should be by Act of Parliament (e.g. Northern Ireland (Emergency Provisions) Act 1996).

The Northern Ireland Act 1974, s 1 provides that Orders in Council which legislate for Northern Ireland should be laid in draft before both Houses of Parliament and approved thereby within 40 days. The procedure does, therefore, facilitate some measure of parliamentary scrutiny and debate of such legislation. However, Orders in Council must be simply approved or disapproved. Hence there is no opportunity for parliamentary revision or amendment.

European legislation

Much of the law made by the European Community takes effect automatically in the United Kingdom. In the language of the EC Treaty it is 'directly applicable' in member states. This applies to the Articles of the Treaty itself, and any amendments thereto, and to regulations made by the Council of Ministers.

Directives, however (as explained above), are binding only as to the result to be achieved. Hence they are not directly applicable as and when made. Domestic legislation is required to give effect to them. In the United Kingdom this is done by Act of Parliament or, as in the majority of cases, by subordinate legislation made under s 2(2) of the EEC Act 1972.

Parliamentary scrutiny of such legislation and Community affairs in general is exercised in a number of ways. First, government ministers – particularly in their capacity as members of the Council of Ministers – are answerable to Parliament in respect of matters relating to the Community. Such matters may be raised by written questions or – on the floor of the House – by oral questions or in debates concerning Community policy or the future development of the European Union. The House is assisted in these functions by six-monthly White Papers relating to European issues.

From 1974 detailed scrutiny of legislative proposals emanating from the Community was the responsibility of the Select Committee on European Legislation. Following the recommendations of the House of Commons Modernisation Committee in 1998, the select committee was given wider terms of reference and renamed the European Scrutiny Committee. It receives and considers all EU documents and legislative proposals together with information from the relevant departments explaining the implications of those which raise questions of legal or political importance. The committee may also recommend that particular proposals should be given further consideration by the House. The issues raised by such recommendations may be dealt with on the floor of the House or referred to one of three European standing committees.

SCRUTINY OF EXECUTIVE ACTION

Introduction

In addition to debating and amending the government's legislative proposals, the House of Commons is also concerned with the efficiency and propriety of the day-to-day working of the process of administration. Through a variety of procedures, therefore, the House seeks to examine the activities of those who are responsible for the making and implementation of government policy. The principal procedural devices used for this purpose are:

(a) Question Time;
(b) debates;
(c) select committees.

Question Time

This occupies 50–60 minutes on the floor of the House at the beginning of public business (2.35–3.30 pm) on each day from Monday to Thursday inclusive. Due to the constraints of time and government business, ministers appear by rota. This has the effect of bringing each departmental head to the dispatch box about once every three or four weeks.

Until 1962 there was no limit on the duration of Question Time or the number of questions a member could ask and no rota of ministers. As the volume of questions has increased, however, and in order to ensure proper expedition of other parliamentary business, rules regulating the use of the procedure have been introduced.

Types of questions

(a) Those requiring oral answers
These must be marked by an asterisk ('starred questions') when handed to the Clerk. No more than eight starred questions may be posed by any one member in any ten-day period and no more than two may be tabled for any one day. These latter two

cannot be put to the same minister. A member may ask one 'supplementary' question for each question posed. Further supplementaries may be put by other members at the discretion of the Speaker.

Around fifteen to twenty oral starred questions may be answered although it is not uncommon for many more to be tabled. Starred questions not answered orally receive written answers unless the MP wishes a question to be deferred for later oral answer. Questions to particular ministers are 'grouped' so that they may all be dealt with on the same day. About 3,000 questions of this type will be answered in any session.

A member gives notice of a question either by handing it to the Clerks in the Table Office (the place where, in addition to questions, motions and amendments are formally presented to the House) or to the Clerk at the Table of the House directly in front of the Speaker's chair. The Clerks ensure that questions comply with the rules of the House and advise on amendment where this is not the case.

Prime Minister's questions were introduced in 1961. Until 1997 these were put on Tuesday and Thursday from 3.15–3.30 pm. These are now taken on Wednesdays from 3.00–3.30 pm. This change was made to enable the Prime Minister to give more detailed answers where appropriate.

The order of priority amongst members who have tabled questions for the same day is determined by ballot, usually held ten days in advance.

The conduct of any Question Time owes much to the influence of the Speaker. If too many supplementaries are allowed the minister may be put under close scrutiny but many questions lower down in the priority list may go unanswered (in oral form at least). On the other hand, if too few supplementaries are called, the minister may not really be extended.

(b) Those requiring written answers

Answers to written questions are printed in *Hansard*. It is expected that written questions should be dealt with within three days unless marked with a 'W', in which case more immediate treatment is requested.

There is no limit on the number of written questions a member may put. It is commonplace for a member to put down dozens of questions for one Question Time all dealing with the same issue. As many as 250 may be tabled in a single day and about 50,000 may be tabled and answered in a session.

In respect of both oral and written questions at least two days' notice must be given.

(c) Private notice questions

These are concerned with urgent matters. They may be put without notice but only with leave from the Speaker. They are taken at the close of Question Time. At present about 40 per session are accepted.

Out of order questions

Questions may be ruled out of order on the following grounds:

- they do not relate to the exercise of the minister's statutory or prerogative powers;
- they involve discussion of the role or reputation of the sovereign;

- they request a statement of opinion of law;
- they constitute statements and not questions;
- they refer to issues dealt with during a debate in the current session;
- they refer to a matter which is *sub-judice*;
- the questions were asked in the previous three months;
- they relate to the date for dissolution;
- they relate to a matter pending in committee;
- they relate to a matter devolved to either the Scottish or Welsh Assemblies.

Other grounds for refusing to answer

Answers have been withheld on the following grounds:

- the cost of finding information would be excessive;
- providing the information could be damaging to national security;
- the question relates to confidential exchanges between governments;
- the question relates to matter of commercial or contractual confidentiality;
- the question relates to the details of arms sales;
- the question seeks to elicit details of budgetary proposals;
- the question relates to the private affairs of an individual (except where these are the cause of public mischief);
- the question seeks to elicit information concerning the existence of particular Cabinet committees.

Merits of Question Time

(a) It is the only regular occasion upon which the government is formally and con-stitutionally required and obliged to account to Parliament for its management of the nation's affairs.

(b) It provides an opportunity for the opposition to select issues which may embar-rass and discredit the government.

(c) It represents a formal manifestation and reinforcement of the convention of ministerial responsibility.

   If it were not for Question Time ministerial responsibility would be even more difficult to enforce. It represents the only procedural device which ensures that ministers appear regularly before the whole House to answer specific questions about current local, national and departmental affairs.

(d) It provides a rare opportunity for backbench MPs to question ministers on issues of their own choosing. Other proceedings are dominated by the front benches.

(e) It allows MPs to raise local and regional issues in full parliamentary session with the government present.

(f) It provides a test of ministerial competence and an opportunity for junior minis-ters to impress.

(g) It makes ministers aware of issues which otherwise might not have attracted their attention.

(h) It provides MPs with an opportunity to publicise incidents of government deceit.

The preparation of parliamentary answers takes precedence over all other departmental business. Permanent secretaries check and must approve all answers before submission to ministers. These prepared answers and statistical information will be studied by ministers to ensure that they are able to 'field' and deal competently with whatever supplementary questions may be put.

Demerits

(a) It lasts for 50–60 minutes only, four times a week.
(b) The operation of the rota limits the opportunities to question senior ministers.
(c) The restraints on time and the number of questions and supplementaries which may be asked makes 'in depth' questioning impossible.
(d) Questions on a wide range of sensitive issues may be ruled out of order. Frequently the spectre of national security or the *sub-judice* rule will be invoked to avoid having to give answers.
(e) Government backbenchers often 'feed' questions to ministers in order to:
   • reduce the time for opposition questions;
   • enable a minister to make an announcement or to provide information which may flatter the government (e.g. a fall in unemployment);
   • enable a minister to defend or explain a decision or policy initiative.
(f) Questions must relate to topics within the parameters of ministerial responsibility. Thus the 'day-to-day' activities of local authorities, nationalised industries and the police may not be raised.

Debates

The following constitute the major opportunities for the House to debate aspects of government policy.

• The second reading stage of the legislative process.
• Substantive motions for debate moved by the government where approval is sought for some aspect of government policy.
• Substantive motions for debate moved by the opposition, usually critical of some aspect of government policy, in the twenty Opposition Days (seventeen for topics chosen by the main opposition party and three for the topics selected by the second largest opposition party).
• The address in Reply to the Queen's Speech. The topics for debate are chosen by the opposition. This may go on for five or six days.
• The debate following the budget proposals. This may also continue for four to six days.
• The three Estimates Days.
• Adjournment debates immediately following the passage of Consolidated Fund Bills. Topics are chosen by backbenchers through ballot. These may entail all-night sittings.
• Recess adjournment debates. These debates take place on the last day before the House goes into recess. Topics are chosen by backbenchers subject to the discretion of the Speaker.

- Daily adjournment debates. These are held between 10.00 and 10.30 pm. Topics for debate are chosen by backbenchers through ballot or at the discretion of the Speaker in the case of the Thursday adjournment debate.
- Emergency adjournment debates under Standing Order (SO) 9. These are moved by any member after Questions and must raise specific and important matters that should have urgent consideration. If accepted by the Speaker the debate takes place on the following day or at 7.00 pm that same evening. Should 40 or more MPs support the motion the debate must take place. If supported by 10–40 MPs the House may decide by division.
- Motions of censure to which the government has submitted or which are forced upon it by defeat in the House.
- Government adjournment debates. A member of the government may move the adjournment of the House to facilitate a more wide-ranging general debate than is possible with a substantive motion.
- Private members' motions. These usually take place on eight Fridays per session and four other half-days (usually Mondays). The opportunity to table such motions is determined by ballot among MPs.

Merits

(a) They force ministers to explain and justify policy initiatives to the House.

> They may want to reveal as little as possible, but the government cannot afford to hold back too much for fear of letting the opposition appear to have the better argument (Norton, *The Commons in Perspective*).

(b) They provide an opportunity for the opposition to expose flaws in government policy/decisions and to present counter-arguments and suggestions for dealing with particular aspects of national affairs.

(c) They help to educate public opinion by presenting a variety of opinions and remedies for dealing with national concerns, e.g. the arguments for and against devolution to Scotland and Wales or charging students tuition fees.

(d) They provide an opportunity for disaffected members on the government side to display dissent, thus embarrassing the government and perhaps causing policy concessions to be made.

(e) They provide a platform for the enhancement and making of parliamentary reputations.

(f) They give MPs an opportunity to present the views of constituents and interest groups.

Demerits

(a) The parliamentary timetable is arranged by government in consultation with the opposition. In the main therefore it is the government, not Parliament, that decides what will be debated and when. Otherwise, the opposition has the twenty Opposition Days and three days for the Estimates when it is able to choose the subject for debate. Again, however, this is largely a matter for the Shadow Cabinet and not for opposition backbenchers.

(b) Most debates are dominated by frontbench speakers. Often MPs who wish to speak will not be called.

(c) Parliament lacks the time in any one session to:
  •   fully debate all issues of public concern;
  •   debate all crises or controversies as and when they arise;
  •   debate in detail all aspects and elements of new legislative measures.

(d) Many legislative debates are curtailed by the use of the 'guillotine' (allocation of time motion). The strange paradox is that the more significant and controversial a Bill is, the more likely it is to be guillotined.

(e) Debates appear to have very little immediate effect in terms of influencing government thinking or action.

(f) The content of debates appears to have very little effect on the way MPs vote. Most MPs will vote according to the 'whip', notwithstanding the quality of opposing arguments.

(g) They are often poorly attended as, in addition to the above:
  •   in any division or vote the government's majority will usually prevail;
  •   the primary role of backbench MPs, from the party's perspective, is to vote rather than speak – hence it is not unusual for MPs absent during debate to appear and vote when division bells ring;
  •   the quality of debate may be adversely affected by the practice of MPs reading prepared speeches rather than listening and responding to the different arguments used.

(h) They attract little public intention. Most people are largely unaware of what is happening in Parliament on a day-to-day basis. Only a minority of the electorate read the 'serious' newspapers which contain coverage of parliamentary proceedings. Also television coverage is limited and regulated by a strict code of conduct (imposed by both Houses) which restricts what programme makers may broadcast or record.

(i) Policy is formed and decisions are made before parliamentary debates take place. The government's perceived responsibility and role in debate is to defend its policies and decisions regardless of the merits of alternative proposals or the exposure of any defects in its own case. Hence, due to this adversarial approach, debates are not generally regarded as 'seminars' from which governments could learn and incorporate useful ideas into their own plans.

(j) It has been suggested that lobbying by interest groups may have greater impact on governments than views expressed during parliamentary debates.

Westminster Hall

In recent years the House of Commons has also held meetings on an experimental basis in an additional chamber known as Westminster Hall. This followed a recommendation of the Select Committee on Modernisation of the House in its 1998–99 report (HC 194) that a new parallel chamber would relieve pressure on the floor of the House and give ordinary MPs an increased opportunity to contribute to debates.

The first sitting of Westminster Hall took place on Tuesday, 30 November 1999. Sitting hours are Tuesdays and Wednesdays from 9.30 am to 2.00 pm and on Thursdays from 2.30 pm for up to three hours. Business on Tuesdays and Thursdays is usually devoted to private members debates while Thursday is generally used for discussion of select committee reports.

The Hall is laid out in an elongated horseshoe shape as part of a deliberate attempt to encourage a less partisan atmosphere than that prevailing in the House of Commons. Meetings in Westminster Hall are chaired by a deputy Speaker.

Select committees

Nature

These are smaller than standing committees and usually consist of up to fifteen MPs with the various parties being represented according to their proportion of seats in the House of Commons. They are given specific terms of reference (frequently to perform some type of inquiry or fact-finding exercise) and such other powers as the House considers appropriate. Such committees may be appointed from and by either House or joint committees from both Houses may be formed.

Types

(a) Ad hoc select committees
These are appointed to investigate and report on specific topics, e.g. the Joint Select Committee on Theatre Censorship (leading to the Theatres Act 1968).

The use of select committees for this purpose is now less common than in the nineteenth century. To some extent this is due to the increased use of Royal Commissions, Tribunals of Inquiry, departmental committees and other non-statutory committees of inquiry chaired by senior members of the judiciary (e.g. the Scott Inquiry into arms sales to Iraq).

(b) Regular or permanent select committees
The House of Commons has some 25 such committees which are appointed for every session. These include the Public Accounts Committee, the Select Committee on European Legislation, the Select Committee on the Parliamentary Commissioner and the Select Committee of Privileges (now Standards and Privileges).

Also falling within this category would be a variety of committees concerned with the internal affairs of the House, e.g. the select committees on services, selection, and Standing Orders.

(c) Departmental select committees
These scrutinise the activities of central government departments, each department being 'shadowed' by the appropriate select committee.

Usually in the region of sixteen to eighteen of these will be in operation at any one time. The exact number will vary as new government departments are established and others merged, etc.

History and development

Until 1914 select committees were used extensively for a variety of purposes. These included:

- the investigation of abuses or issues of controversy (see Putumayo Atrocities 1913; Marconi Affair 1914);
- inquiries into aspects of public policy or national affairs causing concern – often to prepare the ground for legislation, e.g. the Select Committee on Patent Medicines 1914 (after one G T Fulford made £1.1 million from marketing the useless 'Dr Williams's Pink Pills for Pink People');
- consideration of non-partisan Bills (e.g. trade marks, forgery, Sunday shopping);
- scrutiny of government finance and spending (the Public Accounts Committee was established in 1861 and the Estimates Committee in 1912).

The use of select committees declined after the First World War. The following factors contributed to this.

(a) With only minimal support in terms of research personnel and the extensive other demands on MPs' time, select committees were not a particularly efficient means of finding and collecting information.

(b) The growth of a powerful and effective bureaucracy with an independent and comprehensive fact-finding capacity.

(c) Their findings were sometimes influenced by party political considerations. This caused loss of confidence in the select committee as an independent and objective fact-finding technique.

(d) The increased effectiveness of the party 'machines' in the House of Commons in the twentieth century reduced the need for governments to involve and appease MPs in policy making.

(e) The size of central government bureaucracy and its inherent tradition of secrecy made it increasingly difficult for MPs to investigate the actions of government departments.

(f) It became increasingly rare for governments to entrust the committee stage of Bills to select committees.

(g) It also became less common for governments to submit questions to select committees as part of the preparatory legislative process. With increased party-political polarisation in the House of Commons, governments became less prepared to facilitate all-party backbench involvement in the formation of legislation.

In the years between 1920 and 1960 the influence and creativity of the House of Commons reached a low ebb. Increasingly the House became the place where policy and legislation, formed elsewhere, received legitimation.

In the 1960s, however, political and academic opinion began to express concern about the diminishing role of Parliament. The following factors contributed to the movement for reform:

(a) the domination of Parliament by the executive;
(b) the domination of MPs by their political parties;
(c) MPs' lack of access to departmental documentation and information;
(d) a feeling that attempts to halt the decline in the nation's international status and economic power might be enhanced by reform and improvement of the parliamentary system – particularly in relation to scrutiny of executive action.

The overall objective of this movement for change was to reassert the historic role and significance of Parliament within the British constitution.

When the 1964 Labour government came into office a number of sessional or permanent select committees were already operative. The most significant of these were:

- the Select Committee on Nationalised Industries
- the Joint Select Committee on Statutory Instruments
- the Select Committee on Procedure
- the Select Committee on Privileges
- the Public Accounts Committee
- the Estimates Committee.

This did not, however, constitute a systematic infrastructure for scrutinising the work of government departments.

The 1965 Select Committee on Procedure reported that lack of information and expertise amongst MPs constituted Parliament's main weakness *vis-à-vis* its function of scrutiny. The 1966–70 Labour government responded by establishing:

- the Select Committee on Agriculture, Fisheries and Food
- the Select Committee on Science and Technology
- the Select Committee on Education and Science
- the Select Committee on Overseas Development
- the Select Committee on Scottish Affairs
- the Select Committee on Race Relations and Immigration.

After the 1969 report of the Select Committee on Procedure it was decided to continue to extend the scrutinising function of select committees in an amended fashion. In 1971 the old Estimates Committee was replaced by a larger Expenditure Committee operating through six subcommittees each composed of eight MPs. These dealt with: (1) public expenditure; (2) trade and industry; (3) employment and social services; (4) defence and internal affairs; (5) education and the arts; (6) environment and the Home Office.

There also remained in place the Public Accounts Committee and select committees on statutory instruments, nationalised industries, the Parliamentary Commissioner, science and technology, overseas development, race and immigration and later the Select Committee on European Legislation.

These reforms were not particularly successful for the following reasons:

- uncertainty concerning the extent of the powers possessed by the committees, in particular their capacity to summon ministers and other senior public officials;
- no parliamentary time was set aside to debate their reports and recommendations;
- the government appeared to take little heed of their findings;
- they had insufficient resources to employ adequate research assistance.

In 1978 the Select Committee on Procedure declared:

The House should no longer rest content with incomplete and unsystematic scrutiny of the activities of the Executive merely as a result of historic accident or sporadic pressures, and it is equally desirable for the different branches of the public service to be subject to an even and regular incidence of select committee investigation into their activities and to have a clear understanding of the division of responsibilities between the committees which conduct it. We therefore favour a reorganisation of the select committee structure to provide the House with the means of scrutinising the activities of the public service on a continuing and systematic basis.

The Committee recommended:

(a) the creation of twelve department-related select committees;
(b) that these should have the power to summon ministers and civil servants and whatever research assistance they might need;
(c) that time on the floor of the House should be set aside for the discussion of their reports;
(d) that such committees should have powers of inquiry over all aspects of finance, administration, planning and policy in relation to their designated departments.

Of the existing select committees only the Public Accounts Committee and those dealing with statutory instruments and European legislation were to remain. Expenditure, overseas development, science and technology, nationalised industries, race relations and immigration, Parliamentary Commissioner were all to be abolished.

The Labour government was not sympathetic to the Committee's report and did not arrange for its debate on the floor of the House. During the 1979 General Election campaign, however, a pledge was made by the Conservative party that, if elected, they would allow the House to debate the report and vote for or against its implementation. After the election this pledge was honoured. The vote in favour was 248 for, twelve against.

Initially fourteen committees were created. According to SO 130, these were to 'examine the expenditure, administration and policy of the principal government departments ... and associated public bodies'. They were given the power to send for all 'persons, paper and records, to sit notwithstanding any adjournment of the House, to adjourn from place to place, and to report from time to time'. The recommendations that such committees should be able to insist on the attendance of ministers and that the House should be obliged to debate their reports were not accepted. However, the then Leader of the House (Norman St John Stevas) pledged that 'every Minister from the most senior Cabinet Minister to the most junior Under Secretary will do all in his or her power to cooperate with the new system of Committees and to make it a success'.

At the end of 2001 the sixteen committees were: Culture, Media and Sport; Defence; Education and Skills; Environment, Food and Rural Affairs; Foreign Affairs; Health; Home Affairs; International Development; Northern Ireland Affairs; Science and Technology; Scottish Affairs; Trade and Industry; Transport; Local Government and the Regions; Treasury; Welsh Affairs; and Work and Pensions.

In addition to the above there was also a significant number of 'domestic' and other non-departmental select committees, some representing joint committees with the House of Lords.

The domestic committees were: Accommodation and Works; Administration; Broadcasting; Catering; Finance and Services; and Information. The principal non-departmental committees were: Deregulation and Regulatory Reform; Environmental Audit; European Scrutiny; Modernisation; Procedure; Public Accounts; Public Administration; Standards and Privileges; and Statutory Instruments. Joint Committees with the House of Lords were: Consolidation Bills; Human Rights; Statutory Instruments; and Tax Simplification Bills.

Membership and workings of departmental select committees

Each committee has nine to thirteen members. These are chosen by the House after nomination by the committee of selection. Each committee then chooses its own chairperson. By convention all committee members will be backbench MPs.

The committees investigate matters of their own choosing. They issue annual and special reports. These may or may not be debated by the House. To date approximately 20–25 per cent have been debated.

Evidence and information is obtained from a wide range of sources, e.g. from ministers, civil servants, representatives of interest groups and public authorities, academics, members of the public, etc. Hearings are usually open to the public and sometimes away from Westminster (occasionally abroad). Hearings may be broadcast on radio or television.

Merits

(a) They provide a systematic infrastructure of committees for the detailed scrutiny of the conduct of government departments.

(b) They are the only parliamentary forum in which ministers and other public servants (including civil servants) may be questioned 'in depth' by backbench MPs on topics not predetermined by party leaders.

(c) To a greater extent than during proceedings on the floor of the House, MPs in select committees regard themselves as working for Parliament and not just for their party. Hence in committee the adversarial party-political atmosphere that pervades the House of Commons is not so evident. In select committees, MPs are more prepared to act collectively across party lines, and thus to pursue a more objective and, therefore, credible approach in their investigations.

(d) Departmental select committees are able to elicit information which otherwise would not have been made available to MPs. The information thus acquired enables MPs to be more informed during debates and to ask more incisive questions.

(e) The committees enable backbench MPs to develop expertise in a particular sphere of public policy which would otherwise have been difficult for them to acquire.

(f) Interest groups concentrate considerable attention on the numerous advisory committees working for government departments and, prior to 1979, had decreasing confidence in the ability of Parliament to influence government policy. However, increased lobbying of select committees suggests that many interest groups now regard the same as being a useful means of transmitting views and ideas to the policy-makers.

(g) Through their investigations and related research the committees have produced useful 'banks' of information for future reference by MPs, interest groups and the government itself. Thus the 1981 Defence Committee Report on Polaris replacement options (Trident) is regarded as a classic appraisal of the arguments for and against the nuclear deterrent.

(h) Many MPs appear to regard membership of select committees as a springboard to promotion. Accordingly, membership is sought after and attendance is high.

(i) The reports attract a considerable amount of media attention particularly when, as is often the case, they are critical of the government.

Demerits

(a) Select committees cannot impose any sanctions or other direct pressures on government as in the United States where Congressional Committees may withhold finance from Departments of State if dissatisfied with their conduct. It has been suggested that they should be empowered to reduce departmental estimates. At present, however, the report and its attendant publicity is their only weapon.

(b) Few of their reports are debated in Parliament. The 1978 Select Committee on Procedure recommended that eight days per session be allocated for consideration of reports. This has not been done.

(c) The Conservative administrations in power until 1997 did not accept that select committees could:
   (i) demand attendance of ministers;
   (ii) question the civil service about 'conduct' (i.e. individual actions and decisions), or about
      • interdepartmental exchanges
      • discussions in Cabinet committees
      • advice given by law officers
      • confidential information concerning private affairs of individuals or institutions
      • national security.

(d) Civil servants have also been told 'to avoid giving written evidence about or discussion of the following matters':
   • 'questions in the field of political controversy';
   • 'sensitive information of a commercial or economic character';
   • 'matters which may be the subject of sensitive negotiations';
   • 'matters which are *sub-judice*'
   (see *Guidance for Officials Appearing Before Select Committees*, 1980 – the 'Osmotherly Rules').

(e) They have inadequate numbers of research staff, resources and facilities. Parliament does not, like the US Congress, possess a 'counter-bureaucracy'.

Other relevant parliamentary procedures

Early day motions

Any member may table a motion asking for a debate in the near future of any national or local issue. These stand almost no chance of being allocated the necessary parliamentary time. Other members may sign or endorse such motions when they appear in the daily 'Votes and Proceedings' (the working papers issued to each member setting out the day's proceedings). These provide a means of notifying the government that a number of MPs are concerned about a particular issue. Both the responsible minister and the Leader of the House will be briefed on the issues raised by early day motions in case these are raised during Thursday's business questions when an MP may ask whether time will be set aside for a debate.

A List of Early Day Motions in the Votes and Proceedings thus serves both as noticeboard and a source of political intelligence (Philip Norton, *The Commons in Perspective*).

Private correspondence

Members' letters are dealt with at the highest levels within government departments. Ministers are aware that their answers may appear in the media or may be raised in the House. There is no limit on the number of supplementaries. It has been claimed that this is a more effective means of eliciting information than Question Time. Major public service departments may receive thousands of questions per month from MPs.

FINANCIAL PROCEEDINGS

History and significance

Governments cannot function without raising and spending money.

Parliament came into existence in the thirteenth century. From these earliest days one of its most important functions – indeed its *raison d'être* – was the granting of supply (money) to the executive ('the king'). Even in these times when monarchs were still immensely powerful, it had been realised that moneys might more easily be obtained from subjects with their consent rather than on demand.

Traditionally redress of grievances always preceded supply, thus symbolising the contract between government and the governed. According to this the latter would only provide the financial needs of the executive in return for government assurances that national and local grievances would receive attention. The executive's need to seek supply through Parliament provides the historical explanation and justification for Parliament's constitutional right to scrutinise and criticise government policy and action.

Financial proceedings in the House of Commons now provide a series of major opportunities for the opposition to debate and criticise the government's stewardship of the nation's affairs. These occasions include debates on the Estimates (spending proposals), the annual budget (taxing proposals), the parliamentary stages of the Finance Bill, Consolidated Fund Bills (i.e. those authorising expenditure), and financial resolutions authorising expenditure arising out of other general legislative measures (health, education, etc.).

In none of these proceedings is it possible for members to consider taxing or expenditure proposals in detail nor to amend the substance of any financial proposals. The Commons lacks the time and expertise to undertake meticulous scrutiny of government finance. Members are limited to debate of the general policy proposals to which the taxing and spending plans relate. Hence the idea that the Commons 'controls' government finance is somewhat notional. Note also that since 1911 the House of Lords has no veto or delaying power in relation to financial measures.

In the unlikely event that a government failed to get its financial measures through the House it would be forced to resign. Hence the resignation of the Liberal government in 1909 following the House of Lords defeat of the Finance Bill.

Article 4 of the Bill of Rights 1689 provides that taxation without parliamentary consent is illegal. This is enforced by the courts.

See:

- *Attorney-General* v *Wilts United Dairies*, above;
- *Congreve* v *Home Office* [1976] 1 All ER 697;
- *Bowles* v *Bank of England*, above;
- *Dyson* v *Attorney-General (No. 2)* (1912) 1 Ch 158;
- *Customs and Excise Commissioners* v *Cure and Deeley Ltd* (1962) 1 QB 340.

Some basic rules

(a) Spending and taxing proposals may not be implemented without legislative approval.

(b) Spending and taxing proposals must be moved or supported by the Crown (i.e. by a minister).

(c) Spending and taxing proposals must originate in the Commons.

(d) Estimates and related supply must be voted in the same session.

(e) Spending and taxing proposals must be approved by resolutions of the House of Commons. These are in addition to the normal stages in the legislative process. Such financial resolutions are usually taken after the second reading stage of the Bill containing the proposal in question.

Supply: procedure and scrutiny

The process for legitimising expenditure

Departmental estimates are prepared annually from autumn onwards for submission to the Treasury in December. After negotiation within the department and revision by the Treasury they are submitted to the House of Commons in February or March. Since 1982 three days have annually been set aside for debate of the Estimates. These debates must be concluded by 5 August.

When approved the estimates are embodied in the Annual Appropriation Bill, usually enacted towards the end of July or August. This gives the government legal authority to withdraw sums of money from the Consolidated Fund to finance its obligations and activities.

Terminology and particular procedures

(a) Votes on account

Prior to the beginning of the financial year, and in order to keep the government in supply pending enactment of the Appropriation Bill, the House will pass votes on account, to be embodied in Consolidation Fund Bills for enactment before 31 March, authorising withdrawals from the Consolidation Fund. These amounts will then be deducted from the main appropriate grant (Appropriation Act) in the following July or August.

(b) Excess votes

Where departments have overspent in the previous financial year the House may grant an excess vote which will then be included in a Consolidated Fund Bill to be enacted in the financial year immediately following the year in which the overspending occurred.

(c) Supplementary estimates

If departments have underestimated expenditure in any financial year, or if unforeseen causes of additional expenditure have arisen, supplementary estimates may be approved. These will be embodied in the main Appropriation Bill, if voted before July or, if later, then in subsequent Consolidation Bills.

(d) Consolidated Fund services

These are services financed out of the Consolidated Fund under the continuing authority of an Act of Parliament other than the Appropriation Act or Consolidated Fund Acts. For these purposes, therefore, annual grant of finance is not necessary. These services include payment of the judiciary and the various statutory ombudspersons. This helps to reinforce and guarantee the independence of those exercising judicial and related functions by exempting their financial remuneration from party-political debate.

(e) Supply services

These include the bulk of government supported public sector services. For these an annual submission of estimates and grant of supply is required. This applies, *inter alia*, to defence, health, social services, education, housing, etc.

Problems for parliamentary control

- The estimates are too detailed, complex, and voluminous to be fully comprehended by most MPs.
- There is insufficient time to consider the estimates item by item.
- MPs have no access to departmental documentation showing how the estimates were compiled.
- Most MPs do not have the expertise to identify or predict wastage, particularly where moneys are dedicated to complicated technical research and development projects.

Taxation: procedure and scrutiny

The Budget

The House must vote on the means by which the executive may acquire the amount of money needed to finance supply, i.e. its expenditure.

The Budget, containing taxation policy, is formulated by the Treasury under the political supervision of the Chancellor and the Prime Minister. This is not a Cabinet function. Other ministers will be consulted but not actually informed of exact Budget details until, at the earliest, the day before the Budget speech. As soon as the Chancellor's Budget speech is concluded, the House passes a series of financial resolutions authorising immediate alteration of existing rates of taxation. Pending enactment of the main Finance Bill, these are given legitimacy by the Provisional Collection of Taxes Act 1968.

The Budget proposals form the basis of the annual Finance Bill. This proceeds through Parliament in the normal way except that at the committee stage major or controversial items may be dealt with in committee of the whole House while the rest of the Bill goes in the normal way to a standing committee. Until 1967 the entire committee stage was taken on the floor of the House. This proved too time consuming, hence the procedural change.

Scrutiny of the financial aspects of government policy is now undertaken by the various departmental select committees. Scrutiny of Treasury affairs, and therefore taxation policy in particular, is the responsibility of the Treasury and Civil Service Committee.

Government finance and select committees

Various select committees are involved in scrutinising the government's financial policies and the use of public moneys. Thus, for example, the remit of the departmental select committees discussed above extends to the estimates and spending plans of the government departments falling within their jurisdiction. As already mentioned, scrutiny of Treasury affairs falls within the competence of the Treasury and Civil Service Commission.

Reference has already been made to the fact, however, that such committees have their limitations – particularly in terms of time and resources. Inevitably, therefore, their analysis and reporting of how spending decisions have been made, and whether public moneys are being used efficiently, is seldom sufficiently detailed or comprehensive to give the House of Commons an absolutely clear picture of how the government is managing the nation's financial affairs.

The Public Accounts Committee

This is one of the most important and prestigious of the House of Commons' sessional select committees. It was first appointed in 1861. Its principal functions are:

- to monitor and scrutinise government expenditure;
- to discover if public moneys have been used for unauthorised purposes (i.e. those for which there is no legislative authority);
- to highlight overspending and wastage of public funds.

The Committee consists of fifteen MPs. By tradition it is chaired by a senior member of the opposition. It conducts its investigations through examination of the reports and information laid before it by the Comptroller and Auditor General (see below). The Comptroller's reports are based on his perusal of the accounts of each government department. In this way the Committee is given a relatively detailed insight into the financial workings of government. The Committee is not concerned with the merits of government policy. Its sole concern is the legality and efficiency in the use of public funds. Due to lack of time, the Committee will normally direct its attention to a limited number of issues raised in the Comptroller's report. As a general rule the Committee produces unanimous reports. Most of these are debated on the floor of the House and will be responded to by the government.

It should be pointed out, however, that the Committee provides only an *ex post facto* method of control and is generally concerned with actions and decisions taken some eighteen months previously. Hence the Committee may only identify and condemn what has already occurred. It cannot prevent overspending or wastage from taking place – save to the extent that the Committee's very existence may have some precautionary effects. Also, not all of its members will be financial experts and, as ordinary backbench MPs, have many other calls on their time both in their constituencies and in Parliament.

The Comptroller and Auditor General

The Comptroller is an officer of the House of Commons. He is appointed by the Crown upon a resolution of the House of Commons. The resolution is moved by the Prime Minister with the approval of the chair of the Public Accounts Committee (National Audit Act 1983, s 1). The Comptroller's salary is paid by an annual charge on the Consolidated Fund. His security of tenure and independence is guaranteed by the provision that he may only be dismissed pursuant to resolutions of both Houses of Parliament (Exchequer Departments and Audit Act 1866, s 3).

The Comptroller is responsible for ensuring that all revenue raised by the government is duly lodged in the Consolidated Fund or the National Loans Fund at the Bank of England. Moneys cannot be withdrawn from either fund without his authorisation. This enables the Comptroller to monitor government expenditure as it occurs and to see that the government remains within the overall spending limits granted to it by Parliament. In his other capacity as Auditor General he also audits the accounts of each government department on an annual basis and is thus able to discern whether public moneys have been wasted or used for purposes other than those for which there is statutory authorisation.

By virtue of the National Audit Act 1983, the Comptroller is head of the National Audit Office (NAO). Those employed by the NAO are appointed by the Comptroller and are answerable to him. As such they are not civil servants and are not in any way subject to the control or influence of government ministers or departments. The NAO provides the Comptroller with the expertise and administrative support necessary for the effective exercise of his functions.

Although the Comptroller may not question the merits of departmental policies, the 1983 Act provides that he may pass comment on the 'economy, effectiveness and efficiency' with which a department has discharged its functions (s 6). This has been referred to as 'value for money' auditing.

The Comptroller's powers are not limited to central government departments. He may also audit the accounts of the National Health Service and any other body which receives 'more than half of its income from public funds' (s 7).

Problems for parliamentary control

- 'Although the tablets of stone on which the Finance Bill is written can be amended, in practice the Government's reputation is at stake and so major substantive amendments are rare' (Treasury and Civil Service Committee, 6th Report, 1982).

- Until 1993 and the introduction of the 'unified budget', the government's principal spending and taxing proposals (i.e. the Estimates and the Budget) were put to the House separately and at different times of the year (see below). This mitigated against effective evaluation and criticism of the relationship between taxation and expenditure. The pre-1993 procedure was reinstated in 1998.
- Government borrowing is not subject to any form of control in the House of Commons. Nor has the House any direct involvement in the spending proposals of local authorities or public bodies other than government departments.

Reform of financial procedure

The pre-1993 timetable

Unlike many other European states, the British approach was, for parliamentary purposes, to deal with taxing and spending proposals as two largely separate and unrelated processes. Hence, the Chancellor's Budget Statement (traditionally in March) – although accompanied by publication of a White Paper (the Financial Statement and Budget Report) containing general financial projections – tended principally to be concerned with the raising of revenue and not with how this could be related to particular spending plans. Following the Budget, as explained above, the Chancellor's announcements were either given immediate effect (by virtue of resolutions under the Provisional Collection of Taxes Act 1968) or came into effect as directed in the ensuing Finance Act embodying the Budget proposals. More detailed explanation of the government's spending plans, however, did not appear until the autumn. This would be contained in the annual Autumn Statement, usually published in November, setting out the Treasury's latest economic forecasts and resulting general allocations of finance for the next three years. These would be debated in the House and considered by the Treasury and Civil Service Select Committee (TCSC). From 1969 to 1988 the next 'event' in the financial calendar was the Public Expenditure White Paper, published usually in December or January, which sought to project the effect of existing policies on spending for the next three to four years and which, again, was subject to discussion in both the House and the TCSC. After 1988 these matters were dealt with in the Autumn Statement. Finally, then, in March, the main supply estimates for expenditure in the new financial year (commencing 6 April) would be published and presented to the House and embodied in the Appropriation Bill.

The reformed timetable 1993–97

In 1992 the government published a White Paper containing its proposals for a new timetable dealing with financial proceedings (Cm 1867, 1992). The most significant of these was that as from December 1993 (later changed to November) the Chancellor would make one Budget Statement a year to the House covering both the government's tax plans for the next financial year and its spending plans covering the next three years. This would replace both the Autumn Statement and the traditional March Budget and would be accompanied by publication of the detailed financial projections previously contained in the Autumn Statement and the Financial Statement and Budget Report including:

- a summary of the main taxing and spending changes;
- an analysis of departmental spending plans for the next three years;
- an explanation of the main tax and national insurance contributions changes and their consequences for the government's revenue;
- a statement of the government's medium-term financial strategy;
- a short-term economic forecast;
- detailed material on the likely out-turn for the public finances in the current year and the revenue forecasts for the year ahead;
- explanation of the cost of tax reliefs.

The annual Finance Bill would be brought forward to commence its parliamentary stages in January and to be enacted 5 May.

The Provisional Collection of Taxes Act 1968 was to be amended to give statutory authority to December Budget resolutions until 5 May pending enactment of the Finance Act. As originally drafted the Act gave authority to March/April Budget resolutions until 5 August (the previous date for enactment of the Finance Act). As before, the main supply estimates were to be published and presented to Parliament in March seeking authorisation for spending plans for the new financial year as announced in the November Budget. The government was to publish two short-term economic statements, one at the time of the Budget and the other in the summer.

Reasons for change

According to the 1992 White Paper these were:

(a) Announcing taxing and spending measures at the same time should facilitate greater parliamentary and public insight into the relationship between government expenditure and the means being adopted to pay for it: '...bringing together decisions on revenue and expenditure will make it easier to present the Government's fiscal proposals in a coherent and consistent way' (*ibid.*, p 2).
(b) This should 'contribute to more informed and focused debate in Parliament and among the general public on the choice and trade-offs between public expenditure, taxation and borrowing' (*ibid.*, pp 2–3).
(c) A unified Budget should make it easier for both employers and employees to assess and make provision for any changes in their financial obligations and give time for the Inland Revenue to make the necessary arrangements for implementation of fiscal changes well in advance of the forthcoming financial year.

Summary of reformed timetable

- November – the Budget, principal tax and spending changes announced.
- December – votes on account (authorised by a Consolidated Fund Bill) to allow the government to withdraw moneys from the Consolidated Fund from the beginning of the financial year until the enactment of the annual Appropriation Bill in July/August.
- January – introduction of the Finance Bill.
- February/March – spring supplementary estimates to permit expenditure beyond estimated departmental spending in the current financial year. Also possible

excess votes in respect of overspending in the previous financial year (all authorised by a Consolidated Fund Bill).

- March – main supply estimates (annual Appropriation Bill).
- July/August – three Estimates Days debates.
- November/December – winter supplementary estimates (Consolidated Funds Bill).

Current procedures

Despite its apparent virtues, the unified budget procedure did not survive the defeat of the Conservative government in the 1997 General Election. In the Budget Statement of 3 July 1997, the Chancellor of the Exchequer, Gordon Brown, announced that the next Budget would be in March 1998, thus indicating a reversion to the longstanding pre-1993 procedure and timetable (see above). Also since 1997, the Chancellor has issued a Pre-Budget Report in the autumn of each year to give the government's assessment of the state of the economy, to outline its Budget aims and to encourage informed debate on related issues.

OTHER FUNCTIONS

Provides personnel of government

It is a convention that the Prime Minister and most senior ministers have seats in the Commons.

The Commons does not choose members of the government. This is the function of the Prime Minister. It does, however, provide the people from which the choice is made. The Commons may also influence the choice of ministers since those MPs who show competence in parliamentary proceedings are more likely to be chosen.

Provides personnel of alternative governments

Her Majesty's Official or Loyal Opposition forms a 'Shadow Cabinet' which, through its activities in the House, attempts to establish itself as a credible and responsible alternative for which the electorate may decide to vote when a general election occurs.

Should it be necessary in time of national emergency to form an alternative administration, without resort to the divisiveness of a general election, the House can usually be relied upon to ensure the continuity of government. Alternative administrations (in both cases coalitions) were formed without elections in 1931, during a serious economic crisis, and in 1940 in the early years of World War II (after Chamberlain's resignation).

Legitimation

By convention the government's constitutional authority is dependent on maintaining the support of a majority of members. Should the House pass a resolution of no confidence, the government must resign from office. This happened only three times in the twentieth century and only to minority governments, i.e. governments which did not have an overall majority of seats in the Commons. Hence on no occasion in the twentieth century was a majority government forced to resign. March 1979 was the last instance of a government being put out of office by an adverse confidence vote in the House of Commons. James Callaghan's Labour government lost the confidence motion by just one vote but, accepting the convention, resigned forthwith.

Also, through the legislative process, the House of Commons is an essential element in providing legitimacy – i.e. providing the necessary statutory authority – for government policies. The rule of law rejects government by decree, hence specific legislative authority must precede the implementation of particular policies. Very occasionally this authority may be withheld (see Shops Bill 1986 which was intended to reduce restrictions on Sunday trading).

Note, however, that not all legitimacy for government action and decision is derived from Acts of Parliament. In certain contexts – particularly foreign affairs, defence, the maintenance of law and order and emergency powers – the royal prerogative remains an important source of authority for executive action.

Judicial powers

These include the following:

(a) The power to adjudicate and punish in matters of breach of privilege and contempt.
(b) The power to adjudicate between private and public interests during the committee stage of private Bills – particularly where these are opposed.
(c) The power of impeachment. Although perhaps now obsolete, this refers to the power of the Commons to bring judicial proceedings against any person 'accused of state offences beyond the reach of the law, or which no other authority in the state would prosecute' (Hood Phillips, *Constitutional and Administrative Law*, 5th edn). The power was last used in 1801. The Commons act as accusers and the Lords as judges of both fact and law. Trial by Parliament might still be used to deal with incidents of corruption or subversion of the constitution by MPs. It is now far more likely, however, that such misdemeanours would be dealt with through the ordinary criminal law and/or, in the case of ministers, by enforcement of the conventions of collective and individual ministerial responsibility.
(d) Act of Attainder. These were strictly legislative and not judicial acts.

> It was an Act of Parliament finding a person guilty of an offence, usually a political one of a rather substantial kind, and inflicting a punishment on him. The subject of the proceedings was allowed to defend himself… before both Houses (*ibid.*).

This method of dealing with political offenders has not been used since the early eighteenth century.

Disciplinary powers

The House may suspend a member for any period or expel a member for life. As decisions of the House of Commons are not justiciable, a member so treated has no legal redress. While suspension of a member is not uncommon, last century only two were expelled for life: Gary Allighan, Labour, in 1947 for gross contempt of the House (false allegations to the press about the behaviour of other members); Captain Barker, Conservative, in 1954 after a conviction for fraud.

References

Crick (1970) *The Reform of Parliament* (2nd edn), London: Weidenfeld & Nicolson.

Hewart (1975) *The New Despotism*, London: Greenwood Publication Group.

Norton (1982) *The Commons in Perspective*, Oxford: Robertson.

Hood Phillips and Jackson (1997) *Hood Phillips and Jackson's Constitutional and Administrative Law* (8th edn), London: Sweet & Maxwell.

May (1989) *Parliamentary Practice* (21st edn), London: Butterworths.

Thring (1902) *Practical Legislation.*

Further reading

Griffith and Ryle (1989) *Parliament: Functions, Practice and Procedures,* London: Sweet & Maxwell, Chs 6, 7, 8, 9, 10 and 11.

Hanson and Walles (1990) *Governing Britain, A Guidebook to Political Institutions* (5th edn), London: Fontana, Ch 4.

Punnett (1987) *British Government and Politics* (5th edn), Aldershot: Gower, Ch 8.

Walkland and Ryle (1981) *The Commons Today*, London: Fontana.

Chapter 9

THE HOUSE OF LORDS

COMPOSITION

As at June 2000 the new transitional House of Lords created by the House of Lords Act 1999 consisted of 695 members. Of these, only 91 held their seats by virtue of a hereditary peerage. The composition by different categories of members was as follows:

Table 9.1

Life peers (Peerage Act 1963)	578 (83%)
Hereditary peers (House of Lords Act 1999)	91 (13%)
Archbishops/bishops	26 (4%)
Total	695 (100%)

(Source: *House of Commons Research Paper 00/61*)

Tables 9.2 and 9.3 below show the composition of the transitional chamber by gender and party affiliation.

Table 9.2

Party	Women	Men and Women	% Women
Conservative	34	232	15
Labour	44	197	22
Liberal Democrat	14	63	22
Crossbench	18	164	11
Bishops	0	26	0
Other	1	13	8
Total	111	695	16

(Source: *House of Commons Research Paper 00/61*)

Table 9.3

Party	Number	%
Conservative	232	33
Labour	197	28
Liberal Democrat	63	9
Crossbench	164	24
Other	39	6
Total	695	100

(Source: *House of Commons Research Paper 00/61*)

Towards the end of the last session of the 'old' House of Lords, its membership stood at 1,290 divided between different categories as below.

Table 9.4

Hereditary peers	759	(59%)
Life peers	505	(39%)
Archbishops/bishops	26	(2%)
Total	1290	(100%)

(Source: *House of Lords Annual Report 1999/2000*)

The figures for party affiliation in Table 9.5 give some indication of the extent to which the political allegiances of peers in the unreformed chamber appeared to have as much to do with its history and traditions as with any rational scheme founded on principles of democracy and merit.

Table 9.5

Conservative	471
Labour	176
Liberal Democrat	66
Crossbench	325
Others	252
Total	1290

(Source: The Constitution Unit)

TYPES OF PEERS

Hereditary peers

All peers are created by the Monarch. For the creation of hereditary peerages the prerogative is exercised through the issue of a writ of summons or by letters patent. The writ of summons has, however, fallen into disuse. In modern times, therefore, all hereditary peerages have been created by letters patent issued on the advice of the Prime Minister. A peerage by writ descends to the heirs general, i.e. either male or female. A peerage created by letters patent – the more usual method in modern times – descends according to any limitations expressed in the patent which normally, but not invariably, restricts succession to male heirs.

No new hereditary peerages were created between 1964 and 1983 and it appeared that a convention against further appointments might be emerging. During Mrs Thatcher's premiership, however, the practice was revived. Hereditary peerages were conferred on William Whitelaw, the Conservative ex-Cabinet Minister (Viscount Whitelaw 1983); George Thomas, ex-Labour MP and Speaker (Viscount Tonypandy 1983); Harold Macmillan, Conservative Prime Minister 1957–63 (Earl of Stockton 1984); and the Duke of York (1986).

Hereditary peers may be divided into:

(a) holders of English peerages created before the Act of Union with Scotland 1707;
(b) holders of peerages of Great Britain created between 1707 and 1801;
(c) holders of peerages of the United Kingdom created since 1801;
(d) holders of Scottish peerages created prior to 1707 – originally limited by the Acts of Union to sixteen elected by all Scottish peers until the Peerage Age 1963 gave all such peers the right to sit.

Life peers

The Life Peerages Act 1958 permitted peerages to be conferred on persons of either sex for life. These attach to the particular individual only and do not pass to their heirs or successors.

Life peers are created by the Monarch on the advice of the Prime Minister (Life Peerages Act 1958, s 1). Appointment is by letters patent. Persons may be recommended as follows:

(a) as 'working' peers in the political sense from a list drawn up annually by the Prime Minister in consultation with other party leaders;
(b) by inclusion in the Queen's Birthday and New Year Honours Lists, again on the advice of the Prime Minister primarily for the purpose of recognising the achievements of those named rather than for any party-political reason;
(c) by inclusion in a dissolution of Parliament Honours List, normally drawn up at the beginning of each new Parliament on the Prime Minister's advice principally for the purpose of giving seats in the House of Lords to former ministers and MPs who did not seek re-election;
(d) by inclusion in a Resignation Honours List compiled by a Prime Minister who is resigning for reasons other than defeat in a General Election and who wishes to reward those to whom he/she feels some debt of gratitude;
(e) on the Prime Minister's advice so that those named may acquire a seat in Parliament and thus become eligible for ministerial office.

Although the 1958 Act was enacted during a period of Conservative government, its objective was to facilitate increased Labour representation in the upper chamber. This may, at first sight, appear somewhat paradoxical. It was done, however, to preserve the credibility of the House and thus reduce the case for abolition or major reform. Given that Labour had been one of the two main parties since the early 1920s, and had held a large majority in the House of Commons between 1945 and 1951, its level of representation in the Lords had become increasingly untenable. In 1955, shortly before the Act was passed, the Labour presence in the House of Lords was just 55. Of the rest, 507 were in receipt of the Conservative whip and 42 were Liberals (there was a further crossbench element of 251). Labour's position in the House of Lords was also improved by the parliamentary resolutions of 1957 permitting peers to claim expenses in respect of daily attendance. Prior to this time they received no recompense whatsoever for their parliamentary activities and to this day receive expenses only, unlike MPs who receive an annual salary. The provision of expenses has, however, been of some assistance to those peers unable to finance their political careers from other sources of income.

Spiritual peers

These consist of three groups:

(a) the Archbishops of Canterbury and York;
(b) the Bishops of London, Durham and Winchester;
(c) the next 21 diocesan Bishops of the Church of England in order of seniority of appointment.

These numbers were fixed by the Bishoprics Act 1847. A spiritual peer's entitlement to sit ceases on resignation or retirement (at 70 years) from the qualifying office.

It will be noted that such guaranteed religious representation extends only to the Church of England. No similar entitlement extends to other Christian denominations or other religious faiths. Leaders of such denominations and faiths may be given life peerages but this is entirely at the discretion of the Prime Minister.

Those holding the qualifying offices will, like all bishops, have been appointed by the Crown on the advice of the Prime Minister. The Prime Minister makes his recommendations from names submitted to him by the Church Commissioners (the two Archbishops, three clerics, three laymen and four representatives of the diocese concerned).

Law Lords

By virtue of the Appellate Jurisdiction Acts up to twelve senior judges may be given life peerages to perform the judicial functions of the House. This is in addition to the Lord Chancellor and Lord Chief Justice. On retirement from judicial office (aged 70), unlike spiritual peers, a Law Lord may continue to sit and participate in the work of the House.

These are also appointed by the Monarch on the Prime Minister's advice. Those eligible must be qualified according to the requirements in the Courts and Legal Services Act 1990, s 71 and Sched 10.

DISCLAIMER AND DISQUALIFICATION

Disclaimer

By virtue of the Peerage Act 1963, hereditary peers only (other than those of first creation), were enabled to disclaim their titles for life and thus become eligible for membership of the House of Commons. Such disclaimer is irrevocable and must be made within twelve months of succession or of coming of age (21 years). If the successor is already a member of the House of Commons the period for disclaimer is limited to one month only. The House of Lords Act 1999 does not prevent a hereditary who has disclaimed their title from being granted a life peerage and thus becoming eligible for membership of the upper House. As the disclaimer is for life only, the peerage is not extinguished and, on the death of the disclaimer, passes to the heir in the normal way.

As a general rule the facility to disclaim was left unaltered by the House of Lords Act 1999. It is, however, no longer a prerequisite of a hereditary peer's eligibility for membership of the House of Commons. The first hereditary peer to be elected to the House of Commons was the Earl of Caithness who was returned for Caithness, Sutherland and Easter Ross in the General Election of 2001. The 1999 Act does, however, appear to remove the right of disclaimer from those hereditary peers who remain in the House of Lords by virtue of election under s 2.

One of the principal reasons for the 1963 Act was the determination of the then Anthony Wedgwood-Benn not to become disqualified from membership of the House of Commons. A hereditary peerage (Lord Stansgate) had been conferred on Benn's father in 1940. This was done to increase Labour representation in the House of Lords during the period in office of the wartime coalition. Benn was aware, therefore, that on his father's death he would succeed to the title and be forced to vacate the Commons seat for Bristol South-East which he had won in 1951. To avoid this he attempted to secure the passage of a personal bill enabling him to renounce the unwanted title. All of this came to nought, however, and in 1960 Benn became Lord Stansgate. His nature being of the type not to give up readily, he then contested the subsequent by-election which he won with a massive and increased majority. Due to his disqualification, however, the second placed candidate (the Conservative) was declared to have been elected. In effect, therefore, Bristol South-East had to be content with the candidate who had 'lost' the election. It was to avoid any repetition of these events that the 1963 Act was passed. Its passage enabled Lords Home and Hailsham to contest the 1963 Conservative leadership election. Benn also renounced his title and was re-elected to the House of Commons in the 1964 General Election. The number of hereditary peers taking advantage of the facility provided by the 1963 Act has not been as great as expected. Only seventeen had done so by mid-1996.

Disqualifications

The following may not sit or vote in the House of Lords:

(a) aliens;
(b) bankrupts;
(c) persons under 21 years of age;
(d) persons sentenced to imprisonment for treason.

ATTENDANCE

Leave of absence

For each new Parliament a writ of summons will be issued to each person entitled to sit in the House. Any peer who does not intend or is unable to participate in the work of the House is expected to apply for leave of absence (to the Lord Chancellor) – a practice introduced in 1958.

Leave of absence may be granted for a session, for the remainder of a session, or for the remainder of the particular Parliament. At the beginning of each new session, peers given leave of absence for the session which has just come to an end will be asked if they wish the grant of leave to be renewed. The same question will also be put to those peers not granted leave for that session but who still failed to attend.

A peer granted leave of absence is expected not to attend proceedings in the period covered. This expectation is, however, binding in honour only. Hence a peer who is in receipt of a writ of summons and who has not become disqualified may not be prevented from attending. Leave of absence may be ended on one month's notice. The purpose behind the leave of absence procedure is to discourage attendance by 'backwoodsmen' – i.e. those who use their privilege of membership to enable them to attend and vote on major and (usually) controversial issues but who do not contribute to the work of the House on a regular basis.

Attendance figures

The average daily attendance of members of the House of Lords during the session 1951–52 was just 86. The House sat on 96 days and for a total of 292 hours. In the 1959–60 session, after the introduction of life peers, the figures increased to an average daily attendance of 136 with the House sitting on 113 days for 450 hours. Since then, as Table 9.6 shows, the figures have shown further improvement thereby creating a picture of a more active and well-patronised second chamber.

Table 9.6

Session	Sitting days	Average length	Average attendance
1959–60	113	3 hrs 59 mins	136
1964–65	124	4 hrs 47 mins	194
1971–72	141	5 hrs 46 mins	250
1975–76	155	6 hrs 15 mins	275
1980–81	143	6 hrs 43 mins	296
1985–86	165	7 hrs 21 mins	317
1994–95	142	6 hrs 22 mins	376
1995–96	136	6 hrs 53 mins	372
1996–97	79	6 hrs 40 mins	381
1998–99	163	7 hrs 26 mins	428
1999–2000	157	7 hrs 35 mins	434
2000–2001	169	7 hrs 28 mins	346

(Source: House of Lords Information Office)

The hereditary element in the unreformed House gave the Conservative party a substantial 'in-built' numerical advantage over all other political groups. In its final days some 40 per cent of its members accepted the Conservative whip. The second largest group was the Crossbenchers with nearly 30 per cent of members. The Labour party and Liberal Democrats could call on 15 per cent and 9 per cent of members respectively.

Evidence provided by incidence of government defeats in the House of Lords suggests, perhaps not surprisingly, that historically Labour administrations have had greater problems in convincing the upper chamber of the rectitude of their proposals. Hence the Conservative government of 1970–74 suffered just 26 defeats in the upper chamber. Its Labour successor, however, was outvoted in the Lords 344 times in the period from 1974–79.

In the light of these figures some comment has been made on the fact that the number of defeats inflicted by the Lords on Mrs Thatcher's governments was greater than might have been expected during a period of Tory domination. In explanation it has been suggested that during the Thatcher era there were, in effect, two Conservative parliamentary parties in existence. In the House of Lords the traditional and more liberal version of the party, as manifest during the premierships of Eden (1955–57) and Macmillan (1957–63), still maintained considerable influence. In the Commons, however, a new more radical and less patriarchal version of the party was in the ascendancy.

Whatever the truth of this, the tendency of the Lords to be troublesome to Conservative governments continued after Mrs Thatcher left office. The figures show that her administrations (1979–90) suffered 152 defeats in the Lords producing an average figure of 13.8 defeats per session.

Perhaps to nobody's great surprise, the unreformed House of Lords became even more 'active' in its last two years of existence after Labour was returned to power in 1997. It inflicted 39 defeats in the parliamentary session 1997–98 and 31 defeats in 1998–99.

POWERS

Introduction

Many of the facts and figures given below relate to the workings of the 'unreformed' House of Lords before its demise in 1999. It is as yet too early to form a meaningful assessment of how things will be done in the present 'transitional' House and, in particular, to what extent the removal of most of the hereditary element will affect the attitudes of members to the proper balance of power between the upper and lower chambers. Given, however, the temporary nature of the House created by the House of Lords Act 1999, it is unlikely that its members will feel it appropriate to act in ways which upset the established balance or depart significantly from the prevailing conventions in these matters.

The nineteenth century

Throughout the nineteenth century the House of Lords retained legislative powers which were coterminous with those of the House of Commons. Consequently any Bill which the Lords rejected at second reading could not pass into law. This power was, however, subject to the understanding that the Lords would refrain from defeating those measures for which the government had a clear electoral mandate.

In relation to financial measures the conventional understanding was that, while these should be introduced in the Commons and could not be amended by the House of Lords, the Lords could reject them outright.

The Parliament Act 1911

The Liberal administration which took office in 1906 was committed to a radical programme of social reform. Conflict with the House of Lords and the vested interests it represented was probably inevitable.

Matters came to a head when the Lords voted against the Finance Bill of 1909. This had proposed tax increases on income and property in order to finance the social legislation (including the introduction of old-age pensions and unemployment insurance) to which the government was committed. At the time the government had a huge majority in the House of Commons. The figures for the seats won by the main parties in 1906 were as laid out below (for a House of Commons consisting of 671 members).

Liberal	400
Conservative	157
Irish Nationalist	83
Labour	30

(Source: House of Lords Information Office)

As the Irish Nationalists and the Labour members generally supported the Liberals, this meant that the government had an effective Commons majority of some 356.

Despite this the Conservative party at large sought to justify the Lords' action on the ground that the government had no precise mandate for the financial proposals in issue. There was in this an obvious paradox in that an unelected second chamber was claiming to defend democratic principles by refusing to consent to measures supported by just over 76 per cent of the members of the elected House of Commons.

The immediate consequence of the 1909 Budget crisis was a general election early in 1910. The Liberals were returned to power, although with a reduced majority (with Labour and Irish Nationalist support this was in the region of 162 or 65 per cent of all MPs). The previously rejected Finance Bill was then enacted. Reducing the powers of the House of Lords and removing their legislative veto now became a government priority. Clearly it was unlikely that the Lords would readily accede to any legislative measure with this objective. The Prime Minister (Asquith) decided, therefore, to ask the King (George V) to create a sufficient number of peers to produce an overall majority in favour of reform (about four hundred in total). The King agreed to do so, providing the Liberal government could secure direct electoral support for their proposals. Accordingly a further general election was held (December 1910) and the Liberals were again returned to power (with an effective majority of 141). Faced with this apparent public support for a reduction in its powers and the threat of the creation of a large number of peers with Liberal sympathies – thereby eradicating its permanent Conservative majority – the House decided to 'cut its losses' and not to oppose the Parliament Bill which was enacted in 1911.

The 1911 Act had three main consequences. First, it removed the Lords' power of veto in respect of all public Bills with the exception of any Bill introduced to extend the life of a Parliament beyond the prescribed maximum period of duration (reduced from seven to five years by s 7). The House also retained its power of veto in relation to private Bills and subordinate legislation. Second, it replaced the Lords' veto in respect of public Bills with a delaying power of two years. Thereafter, any Bill passed by the House of Commons but rejected by the Lords in three successive sessions could be presented for the Royal Assent providing two years had elapsed between the Bill's second reading in the Commons in the first of those sessions and its third Commons reading in the third session. Third, it allowed Bills certified by the Speaker to be 'money Bills' to be presented for the Royal Assent if not passed by the House of Lords without amendment within one month of having been sent there from the House of Commons.

The Parliament Act 1949

Despite the removal of its veto, the 1911 provisions still left the Lords with the facility to seriously disrupt a government's legislative programme – particularly in the last two years of a Parliament when any Bill rejected by the Lords could not become law until after a general election. The Labour government which came into power in 1945 with a radical programme of industrial and social reform feared that, unless the delaying power was reduced, difficulties with the House of Lords might seriously interfere with the implementation of its policies.

The Parliament Act 1949 sought to deal with this problem. The Act reduced the delaying power to one year. The current position is that any Bill passed by the House of Commons but rejected by the House of Lords in two successive sessions may be presented for the Royal Assent providing one year has elapsed between its Commons second reading in the first session and its third reading in the same House in the following session.

FUNCTIONS

Protector of the constitution

It has been said that the powers of the Lords to reject any Bill to extend the life of a Parliament and to delay other controversial legislation represent the ultimate guarantees against executive exploitation of the unwritten constitution.

The life of Parliament was extended beyond the normal term of years on two occasions in the twentieth century. The Parliament elected in January 1910 continued until 1918 and that elected in 1935 continued until 1945. For obvious reasons it was thought unwise to divide the country for electoral purposes during time of war. Naturally, therefore, on these two occasions the question of the Lords vetoing the necessary statutory provisions did not arise. No other attempts to enact legislation for this purpose have been made.

Since it was introduced in 1911 the delaying power has been used against just five Bills emanating from the Commons. These were the Irish Home Bill 1912 and the Welsh Church Bill 1913 (both given the Royal Assent in 1914), the Parliament Bill 1947 (Parliament Act 1949), the War Crimes Bill 1990 (War Crimes Act 1991) and the Sexual Offences Bill 1999 (Sexual Offences Amendment Act 2000).

It is generally accepted that the unreformed House was deterred from more extensive use of the delaying power due to continuing reservations over the political propriety of overruling the elected chamber and from the realisation that this would be likely to precipitate even more strident calls for abolition or radical change to the upper chamber's composition.

The purpose of the delaying power is to cause governments to 'think again' and to facilitate greater public debate about controversial legislative proposals. This may be seen to be of particular value in a political system in which the elected chamber is usually dominated by a political party which is supported by less than half of the electorate. The problem is, however, that the credibility of the delaying power is based on the assumption that a parliamentary chamber still largely dominated by unelected members of the aristocracy is somehow best placed to judge when the government is acting against the interests of the constitution or the public.

Initiation of legislation

In discussing the legislative process it is usual to talk of Bills passing through the House of Commons and then going to the House of Lords. Both public and private Bills may, however, be introduced into the House of Lords. The idea is that such Bills, having been fully debated and amended in the Lords, may then pass relatively quickly through the House of Commons, thus providing the latter with more time for consideration of the government's main legislative proposals. There is, however, a convention that Bills which may be politically controversial should go to the Commons first.

Although most private members' Bills proposed in the Lords do not pass into law, the vast majority of government and consolidation Bills introduced there will proceed to receive the Royal Assent. Consolidation Bills are those for which the Lord Chancellor has special responsibility and are usually dealt with by the Lords first. These re-enact existing legislation in a consolidated form, perhaps with changes recommended by the appropriate Law Commission, or may be Bills to repeal obsolete enactments. Perhaps of greatest significance, however, is the number and proportion of government Bills introduced in the upper chamber. In recent sessions this has been 10–15 per cent of the government's legislative programme.

Revision of legislation

This is regarded by many as the most important function of the House of Lords and in any session will take up about half of its time. It is not unusual for the Lords to make over 2,000 amendments to public Bills in a session. The number of amendments made to government Bills in the unreformed House in its last year of operation was 2,972.

The procedural stages by which a public Bill goes through the House of Lords are broadly similar to those in the House of Commons:

First reading   – purely formal and no debate.
Second reading   – general debate on the Bill's main principles.
Committee stage – detailed consideration and amendment of individual clauses.
Report stage   – opportunity for further amendments to be moved.
Third reading   – opportunity for further brief debate and last minute amendments.

There are, however, a number of significant differences between the procedures of the two Houses. First, the Lords has no procedural mechanisms for curtailing debate (the guillotine and closure motions are not used). Second, there is no provision, as in the House of Commons, for the selection of amendments to be debated. Thus all amendments which have been tabled may be discussed. Third, as indicated above, further amendments may be made at the third reading stage.

Some comment should also be made about the various methods according to which the Lords committee stage of a Bill may be conducted. These are as follows.

(a) Committee of the whole House
For the majority of public Bills the House transforms itself into a committee so that the proceedings are conducted on the floor of the chamber. The House does not have a system of standing committees equivalent to that used in the House of Commons.

(b) Committee off the floor
This is a recent innovation and was first used for the Children (Scotland) Bill in the 1994–95 session. All Lords are free to attend and participate. The use of this type of committee allows the House to proceed with other business on the floor of the chamber.

(c) Public Bill committee
This type of committee is used infrequently – only one Bill was dealt with this way in the 1993–94 session (Trade Marks Bill) and none in 1994–95. A limited number of peers are selected to constitute the committee. Measures dealt with in this way are usually government Bills of a technical and non-controversial nature. Lords not selected for such a committee may attend and speak but may not vote.

(d) Special public Bill committee
This new type of committee was first used in 1994–95 for the Law of Property (Miscellaneous Provisions) Bill. A committee of this type may be selected for a Bill where it is felt that effective scrutiny and revision will be best effected by a limited number of members possessing relevant expertise. The committee is empowered to take written and oral evidence from interested parties prior to making any amendments. The procedure has been described as 'well suited to the proposals put forward by the Lord Chancellor to facilitate the introduction of certain legal and technical Bills, for example, certain Bills proposed by the two Law Commissions' (House of Lords Procedure Committee, Third Report, 1993–94).

(e) Select committee
A Bill may be committed to a select committee at any stage between its second and third readings. This type of committee is used most frequently for controversial private members' Bills (e.g. Laboratory Animals Protection Bill 1978–79; Infant Life (Preservation) Bill 1986–87; Dangerous Dogs (Amendment) Bill 1995–96). The committee may take evidence and recommends to the House whether the Bill should proceed or not. It may also amend the Bill prior to recommitting it to a committee of the whole House.

(f) Scottish select committee

This is another new procedure which allows a select committee to take evidence on a Scottish Bill before the Bill is committed to any of the above types of committee for possible amendment. The committee may sit in Scotland. Peers who are not members may attend and participate in its proceedings. Recent legislative proposals dealt with in this way included the Deer (Amendment) (Scotland) Bill and the Education (Scotland) Bill (both in 1995–96).

The incidence of Bills revised in the House of Lords would tend to indicate that simple abolition of the second chamber is not a realistic option. If this were done without radical reform of the existing parliamentary system – and perhaps even of the entire constitutional structure (e.g. by creation of regional legislative assemblies) – there is an obvious case for suggesting that the House of Commons would no longer be able to function effectively and certainly would not be able to produce legislation of the desired utility and clarity of purpose.

Forum for debate

For various reasons it has been claimed that debates in the House of Lords are of a higher standard and more informative than those in the Commons.

(a) The parliamentary responsibilities of the House of Lords are not so great as those laid upon the lower chamber, hence there is more time for full discussion of legislative proposals and other issues of public concern (as stated, the guillotine and closure procedures are not used in the upper House). Also the convention that a government should resign if defeated in a vote of confidence or on a major issue does not apply to proceedings in the House of Lords. Hence, although adverse votes and criticism may cause the government some embarrassment, it will not be so concerned with the enforcement of party unity and discipline as is the case in the lower House. This and the crossbench element makes, it is said, for a more open and less partisan approach.

(b) In addition, reference is usually made to the fact that many members of the House, particularly the life peers, will be persons of achievement and experience in politics, business, the professions, the church, etc. who are able to use these attributes to enhance the quality of proceedings.

Purely in terms of the time allocated to it, this function takes second place only to the Lords' consideration of public Bills. The figures show that in any given session debates will account for some 20–25 per cent of the business of the House.

It is, of course, extremely difficult to assess the effect such debates may have either on the government or on public opinion generally. At one level this may appear to be negligible as most members of the public probably have little idea of, or interest in, the daily business of the upper House. However, this may be missing the point, in the sense that in the short term it is not the public which makes policy. The House of Lords, on the other hand, operates in what has been called the 'rarified' political atmosphere of Westminster and Whitehall. The working members of the House will have close contacts with those in power. They are all part of the political élite. Therefore – within that select group – the opinions and deliberations of the House of Lords may assume a greater degree of significance than is sometimes recognised.

Scrutiny of government policy

All of the above functions may be regarded as mechanisms through which the second chamber seeks to check on the activities of the executive. This is also true of some of the House of Lords select committees which are considered below.

Another method of scrutiny used extensively by the Lords, as in the Commons, is the parliamentary question. At the beginning of each day's business (Monday–Thursday) in the House up to four oral ('starred') questions may be put to government spokespersons. A member may not pose more than two questions on the same day. Supplementaries may be asked by any member but there is no general debate.

Question Time in the House of Lords is shorter than in the Commons and lasts for about 30 minutes. Note that questions are put to the government (requiring information) rather than to individual ministers. Unstarred questions may be put at the end of the day's business. There is no time limit. The questions usually take the form of a speech and may be debated.

As with the House of Commons, peers may ask any number of written questions. Ministerial replies are normally given within two weeks.

The House of Lords also hears private notice questions. As in the Commons these are oral questions on matters of urgency and must be submitted to the Leader of the House (a government minister with a seat in Cabinet and who is responsible for the arrangement of business) before noon on the day they are to be asked. Usually, no more than two or three are posed per session.

Parliamentary questions are part of the general process whereby governments are made aware of the concerns of both those who support them and those who do not. They also help to elicit individual pieces of information from an executive prone to secrecy, all of which contributes to a broader impression of the government's competence and credibility.

Investigation by select committee

The House of Lords acquires information through a variety of sessional and *ad hoc* select committees. It does not, however, operate a system of departmental select committees equivalent to that established by the House of Commons in 1979.

Sessional select committees

The two most important permanent or sessional select committees are the Science and Technology Committee and the European Union Committee.

(a) The Science and Technology Committee

Set up in 1980, the Committee has the power to consider scientific and technological issues of particular social, political or environmental significance. The Committee usually has fifteen to twenty members including prominent scientists and engineers.

It conducts its work through three subcommittees. Subcommittees I and II carry out in-depth inquiries into specific issues. There is also a general purposes subcommittee which, *inter alia*, recommends topics for investigation and follows up the Committee's previous reports. Each inquiry lasts about a year. For the 1995–96 session subcommittee I was asked to consider fish stock conservation and management. Subcommittee II was allocated an investigation into the decommissioning of oil and gas installations. All reports are made in the name of the full Committee and are debated on the floor of the House. It is established practice for the government to issue a written response to each report.

Given the depth and detail of the Committee's reports, they are regarded as both authoritative and persuasive. It has been said of the Committee that it supports 'the non-political voice of the scientific community and that its procedures ensure that the government is reminded of what that voice is saying' (Griffith and Ryle, *Parliament: Functions, Practice and Procedures*, 1989).

(b) The European Union Committee

This was created in 1974. The Committee examines and reports on all European legislative proposals which may be of significance for the United Kingdom. It thus assists the government in determining what attitude to take to particular proposals when these are considered by the Council of Ministers.

The Committee has a membership of twenty. The work of the Committee is conducted though a number of subcommittees to which other peers may be co-opted. In the session 1999–2000 these committees were: Economic and Financial Affairs, Trade and External Relations; Energy, Industry and Transport; Common Foreign and Security Policy; Environment, Agriculture, Public Health and Consumer Protection; Law and Institutions; Social Affairs, Education and Home Affairs.

The Committee produces in the region of twenty reports per annum of which on average over half are debated on the floor of the House. Due to the time and expertise at its disposal, the Committee's reports are regarded by many as being of a higher quality than those produced by the equivalent committee in the House of Commons.

Ad hoc sessional select committees are set up in the House of Lords for a variety of other purposes. As explained above, this may be to consider a piece of proposed legislation. Alternatively, as in the Commons, a select committee may be established to inquire into a particular matter of public interest. Such committees usually have between ten to fifteen members and, in the past, have often taken at least two sessions to produce their reports.

All these committees, whether dealing with a Bill or a topic of controversy, have the benefit of being able to hear expert evidence and to have the assistance of specialist advisers. Examples of such topic-related *ad hoc* select committees would include those concerned with medical ethics (1993–94), sustainable development (economic and environmental) (1994–95), and relations between central and local government (1995–96).

Scrutiny of subordinate legislation

Enabling or parent Acts which permit the making of subordinate legislation by ministers may often provide for the 'laying' of such legislation before both Houses of Parliament subject to either the negative or affirmative resolution procedures. Negative resolution procedure, which is more frequently required, involves laying the instrument in which the regulations are contained for a prescribed period, usually 40 days. Should either House vote against the legislation within that period, it ceases to have effect. Where the affirmative resolution procedure is prescribed, the regulation may not take effect until approved by resolutions in both Houses. Both procedures, therefore, enable the House of Lords to veto any subordinate legislation laid before it.

Members of the House of Lords also participate in the work of the Joint Select Committee on Statutory Instruments. This considers all statutory instruments laid before Parliament and is empowered to draw Parliament's attention to any regulations which, *inter alia*, impose a tax, purport to have retrospective effect or which may appear to be *ultra vires*.

The powers of the House of Lords over subordinate legislation are not limited by the Parliament Acts. The convention is, however, that the Lords will not vote down an instrument which has the support of the House of Commons. In the entire twentieth century only one affirmative resolution was ever voted out (the Southern Rhodesia (United Nations) Order 1968). The Lords have never annulled an instrument laid according to the negative resolution procedure.

In the 1992–93 session the House of Lords set up the Delegated Powers Scrutiny Committee. The purpose of the Committee is to examine any Bill to see if it delegates greater legislative power to a minister than the circumstances would appear to demand or if the powers delegated are not subject to adequate parliamentary scrutiny and control. In May 1994 it was given the additional role of scrutinising deregulation proposals under the Deregulation and Contracting Out Act 1994.

Final court of appeal

The judicial function of the House is exercised by appellate committees consisting of five Law Lords. The convention that lay peers do not participate when the House sits as a court dates back to *O'Connell* v *R* (1844) 11 Cl & F 155, when several lay peers who wished to vote against Daniel O'Connell's appeal against conviction for conspiracy were persuaded to withdraw. The last occasion when a lay peer attempted to vote in judicial proceedings was in *Bradlaugh* v *Clarke* (1883) LR 8 App Cas 354. His vote was ignored.

PROPOSALS FOR REFORM

The problem

Despite the changes made by the Parliament Acts and the slight modifications effected by the Life Peerages Act 1958 and the Peerage Act 1963, the existence and composition of the House of Lords continued to attract controversy throughout much of the last century. The question was not so much whether the second chamber should continue to exist, but whether it should continue in its traditional form – particularly whether it should continue to be dominated by a hereditary, unelected element. It was clear, however, that the House of Lords still performs some important parliamentary functions and provides a useful complement to the work of the House of Commons. Were it to be abolished, radical reform of the functions and procedures of the House of Commons would be essential to maintain parliamentary efficiency. The real issue, therefore, was whether it would be possible for the work of the House of Lords to be undertaken by a reformed and more representative chamber without doing any undue damage to existing constitutional arrangements and to the capacity of Parliament to discharge its functions effectively.

The Bryce Conference 1917–18

This was established in the aftermath of the controversy surrounding the enactment of the Parliament Act 1911. The group convened had fifteen members (seven from each House) and was chaired by Viscount Bryce, a senior politician and eminent academic lawyer. Its report was issued in 1918 (*Report of the Second Chamber Conference*, Cd 9038). This contained the following principal recommendations.

(a) The House should consist of 246 members elected by panels of MPs representing different regions of the country and a further 81 members consisting of heredi- tary peers and bishops elected by a joint standing committee of both Houses. The Law Lords would sit *ex officio*.
(b) With the exception of the Law Lords, all members would hold their seats for up to twelve years with one-third retiring every four years.
(c) The reformed chamber would have a power of veto over non-financial legislation with disputes between the two Houses being referred to a free conference com- mittee consisting of up to 30 members of both Houses.

Perhaps inevitably, however, in a period of post-war reconstruction, parliamentary reform was not treated as an issue of great immediacy. It has also been suggested that the rise of the Labour party – which, by the 1920s had replaced the Liberals as the second major party – made the Conservative party increasingly uneasy about any diminution of their position in the Lords. Therefore, despite debates on the issue in 1922 and 1927, the Bryce proposals were never implemented.

The 1948 Conference of Party Leaders

When the House of Lords rejected the Parliament Bill 1947, the Labour government attempted to resolve the issue and secure some measure of agreement for reform by convening all-party talks. No consensus could be reached, however, on the powers to be left with the second chamber. As already explained, the government then pressed ahead with the Bill and secured its passage under the provisions of the Parliament Act 1911. The conference did, however, manage to agree a number of general propos- itions relating to the questions of membership and composition.

(a) No single party should have a permanent majority.
(b) The right to attend and vote should not depend on possession of a hereditary title.
(c) Members of the upper House should be termed Lords of Parliament and should be appointed on the basis of personal distinction or public service.

(d) Hereditary peers, other than those appointed Lords of Parliament, should be eligible to become MPs.
(e) Women should be eligible for membership of the upper chamber.
(f) Remuneration should be paid in order to avoid exclusion of those without private means.

The Parliament Bill 1968

With Labour out of power from 1951 to 1964 reform of the second chamber did not have a prominent place on the political agenda. In 1967, however, the Wilson government initiated further all-party talks which led to the Parliament Bill 1968. The measure was supported by the Conservative leadership at the time. Its principal objectives were the phasing out of the hereditary element of the House's composition and a reduction in its powers.

The composition of the House was to consist of voting and non-voting peers. Voting peers would be 230 life peers (created on the advice of the Prime Minister) and the first holders of new hereditary peerages. Other hereditary peers would make up the non-voting element – they would have the right to sit and speak but not vote. This right would not pass to their successors. The party in power was to be given a 10 per cent majority over all other parties represented in the House but, by inclusion of a crossbench element, would not be permitted an overall majority. The reformed House would have been left with a delaying power of six months in relation to non-financial public Bills. Its power over financial Bills was to remain unchanged.

Owing, however, to substantial opposition in the House of Commons and the government's fears for the rest of its legislative programme, the Bill was eventually withdrawn during its committee stage. It was opposed by Labour MPs in favour of more radical change (including outright abolition) and by Conservatives who felt that the Bill went too far in terms of reducing the rights and powers of the hereditary element thereby weakening the party's position in the upper House. There was also a more general feeling that the composition of the principal element of the House (i.e. the life peers) should not be simply a matter of prime ministerial patronage.

The House of Lords Act 1999

The government's proposals

In May 1997 the newly elected Labour government came into power with the stated intention of replacing the House of Lords with an elected second chamber with reduced powers. The delaying power was to be restricted to Bills relating to 'fundamental individual and constitutional rights'. The Lords would be able to delay these until the next election. In relation to other types of legislation, the power of the House would be limited to debate and revision. Public Bills would no longer be introduced in the second chamber.

The guiding principles and objectives behind the government's case for reform were explained in the White Paper, *Modernising Parliament: Reforming the House of Lords* (Cm 4183, 1999). These were as follows:

(a)   the United Kingdom needs a two-chamber legislature with a distinct role for the second chamber 'which must neither usurp, nor threaten, the supremacy of the first chamber' (Chap 2, para 6);

(b)   the institutions of government should 'reflect and serve the society which supports them' (Chap 2, para 10);

(c)   modernising the parliamentary system will enhance Britain's democracy, improve the connections between the people of Britain and those they put in place to represent them;

(d)   the continued question of the fate of the hereditary peers has in practice provided a distraction from full dispassionate consideration of what the United Kingdom actually wants and needs in its second chamber (Chap 2, para 2).

In essence the proposal was for a two-stage process of reform. Stage one would involve the creation of a transitional House of Lords from which the hereditary element would be removed and consisting, therefore, almost entirely of life peers. Stage two would be the creation of a new and permanent second chamber with its composition and powers based on the options presented by a Royal Commission.

The Bill to implement stage one was introduced in the parliamentary session of 1998–99. It passed into law with one amendment in November 1999. The main provisions of the Act were:

(a)   the removal of the right of any person to be a member of the House of Lords by virtue of a hereditary peerage (s 1);

(b)   the exemption from the above of 90 hereditary peers and the holders of the offices of Earl Marshal and Lord Chamberlain (s 2).

Such 'excepted' peers were to remain members of the House of Lords for life or until such time as Parliament enacted otherwise (*ibid.*). House of Lords Standing Order 9 (Election of Hereditary Peers) provided for 75 of the 90 excepted peers to be elected by and in proportion to the four main party groups into which the peers were divided at the time the transitional House came into existence, i.e. Conservative, Labour, Liberal Democrat and Crossbench. The election took place in October and November 1999. The number of excepted peers elected by party was Conservative 42, Crossbench 28, Liberal Democrat 3, Labour 2.

The remaining fifteen excepted peers were to be elected by the whole House to serve as Deputy Speakers and other office holders. The distribution of seats produced by this election was Conservative 9, Labour 2, Liberal Democrat 2, Crossbench 2.

Recommendations to the Monarch concerning the granting of non-political peerages in the transitional House were to be made by an independent Appointments Commission and not by the Prime Minister. The Prime Minister would, however, determine the number of non-party appointments to be made. The Commission is a non-statutory body and was established in May 2000.

The first annual report for the transitional House 2000–01 described it as one of the busiest parliamentary chambers in the world. The House sat for 169 days through a period of 40 weeks and for a record number of hours (1,261). There were 189 divisions, of which 36 were government defeats. By far the greatest amount of time in the

House was occupied by public Bills (800 hours) with 155 hours devoted to general debates. A total of 3,837 amendments to government Bills were made.

This creates an image of a very active and productive House, despite its transitional status. The figure of 36 government defeats is particularly significant, as it suggests that the elimination of the hereditary element has not produced a notably more subservient or quiescent chamber than that in existence at the time of reform.

The Royal Commission on Reform of the House of Lords

The Royal Commission under the chairmanship of Lord Wakeham was established on 1 January 1999. Its terms of reference were:

- 'having regard to the need to maintain the position of the House as a pre-eminent chamber of Parliament and taking particular account of the constitutional settlement, including the newly devolved institutions, the impact of the Human Rights Act and developing relations with the European Union';
- 'to consider and make recommendations on the role and functions of a second chamber';
- 'to make recommendations on the method or combination of methods of composition required to constitute a second chamber fit for that role and those functions'.

The Royal Commission's report, *A House for the Future* (the 'Wakeham Report', Cm 4534) was published on 20 January 2000. Its principal proposals were:

(a) the new second chamber to consist of around 550 members;
(b) an as yet unspecified minority of these would be elected (see below) with the rest appointed by an independent Appointments Commission;
(c) the distribution of seats by political allegiance should reflect the votes cast for each party at the last general election;
(d) a significant minority of members should be chosen on a regional basis which reflects the balance of political opinion within each of the nations and regions of the United Kingdom;
(e) the House to include a strong crossbench element of at least 20 per cent;
(f) at least 30 per cent of members to be women;
(g) the membership should represent a fair ethnic and regional balance;
(h) the Law Lords to remain in the upper chamber but the Church of England representation to be reduced from 26 to sixteen with fifteen seats for the representatives of other faiths (five for non-Anglican denominations in England; five for non-Anglican denominations in Scotland, Wales and Northern Ireland; five for non-Christian faith communities);
(i) members of the chamber would no longer be known as peers and qualification for membership would no longer be dependent on the grant of a peerage.

The Commission presented three possible models for determining the elected element.

Model A
A total of 65 regional members chosen at the time of each general election by a system of 'complementary election'. The proportion of the vote cast for the candidates of

each party in each region would determine the number of seats from the overall total of 65 to be allocated to each party in the second chamber.

Model B

A total of 87 regional members to be elected by a system of proportional representation. These elections would take place at the same time as elections to the European Parliament with one-third (29) being elected on each occasion.

Model C

A total of 195 regional members to be elected by thirds using a 'partially open' system of proportional representation at the time of each European parliamentary election.

As to the powers of the second chamber, the Royal Commission proposed that, in relation to public Bills and financial legislation, these should remain the same as those possessed by the unreformed House. The House should, however, lose its power of veto over subordinate legislation and be left with a delaying power of three months. New select committees should also be established dealing with the constitution, human rights and devolution.

The Commission's report was not received with universal acclaim. Principal criticisms were that it fell a long way short of providing the basis for a second chamber constituted on genuinely democratic principles and that it said little about ways in which a second chamber might be equipped to exercise a restraining influence over the excesses of a government-controlled House of Commons without challenging that chamber's primacy. Adverse comment was also made on the recommendation that the nation's most senior court should continue to be so closely linked to the legislature.

The government's response to the Commission's proposals was explained to the House of Lords in a debate on the Wakeham Report on 7 March 2000. It accepted 'the principles underlying the main elements' of the Commission's suggestions, in particular 'that the second chamber should clearly be subordinate, largely nominated, but with a minority elected element and with a particular responsibility to represent the regions'. It was also made clear that an attempt would be made to base any final proposals on cross-party consensus.

The government's White Paper: The House of Lords – Completing the Reform

In its manifesto for the 2001 General Election the government made the following pledge:

> We are committed to completing House of Lords Reform, including removal of the remaining hereditary peers, to make it more representative and democratic while maintaining the House of Commons traditional primacy. We have given our support to the report and conclusions of the Wakeham Commission, and will seek to implement them in the most effective way possible.

Six months later the White Paper 'The House of Lords – Completing the Reform' was produced (Cmd 5291). As indicated, in the government's manifesto, the White Paper was based largely on the findings of the Royal Commission but with a number of significant, detailed, departures.

The main proposals in the White Paper were as follows:

(a) no major changes should be made to the powers of the second chamber save as recommended by the Royal Commission in relation to subordinate legislation (see above);

(b) no group should have privileged access to the House;

(c) a majority of the reformed House should be nominated by the main political parties in proportion to their shares of the national vote in the last general election;

(d) there would be 'about' 120 appointed members with no particular political affiliations.

(e) a further 120 members should be elected by a party list system in large multi-member constituencies identical to those used for elections to the European Parliament;

(f) after the elapse of ten years from the enactment reforming legislation, the size of the House would be 'capped' at 600, 'with an interim House as close as may be to 750 members to accommodate existing life peers' (para 2);

(g) an Independent Appointments Commission would be created to appoint the 120 independent members and to decide the number of 'political' seats to which each party was entitled;

(h) the Church of England's representation would be reduced to sixteen but these would not be supplemented by a further fifteen religious members as recommended by the Royal Commission;

(i) judicial membership of the House would continue largely as before, with twelve full-time Lords of Appeal in Ordinary with an entitlement to remain members until the age of 75, whether or not still fully active judicially;

(j) members of the new House would be designated 'Members of the Lords' (ML).

The House so constituted would have three main elements consisting of not more than 332 members nominated by the political parties, 120 independent members appointed by the Appointments Commission and 120 elected members. Added to these would be the sixteen Bishops and at least twelve Law Lords.

The government's case against a mainly elected second chamber was:

• This could rival and 'usurp' the functions of the House of Commons and could be a recipe for damaging conflict in relation to which House had the final authority for determining the political legitimacy of the national government and the delivery of its legislative programme.

• Parliament would lose the contribution of those independent, non-professional members, who bring to the House 'the expertise and experience of those who are leaders in a wider range of national endeavours, including commerce, the voluntary sector, education, health, the armed forces and the faith communities' (para 4).

The main difference between the government's proposals and those of the Royal Commission related to the powers of the Appointments Commission. In essence, the government felt unable to accept the proposal that the Appointments Commission should choose those who would compile both the political (332 members) and the non-political (120 members) appointed elements. The Royal Commission's view was that, although it should receive and consider recommendations from the political parties in relation to the political element, it should have the final decision in all cases:

> The Appointments Commission should make all discretionary appointments to the second chamber and should make the final decision in all cases. The Appointments Commission should be able to appoint people with party affiliations whether or not these have the support of their political party (Cmd 4533, 2000, para 13.41).

As has been explained, however, the White Paper proposed that the power of choice of the Commission should be limited to non-political members only.

Beyond the White Paper

As with the Royal Commission's report, it was very soon apparent that the White Paper had its detractors in all of the major parties and in both Houses of Parliament. The main points of dissension related to the very small numbers of elected members which was proposed (just 20 per cent) and the resulting extensive degree of patronage in determining the composition of the House which would be placed in the hands of party leaders and, in particular, the Prime Minister. The government was accused of attempting to produce a second chamber with minimal political authority which would thereby be disabled from exercising any meaningful restraints on the possible excesses of a government dominated House of Commons. The overall result was described by one member of the House of Lords as 'an instrument of prime ministerial patronage hiding behind a fig leaf of token democracy' (Lord Strathclyde, HC Deb, 7.11.2001, C209).

By the spring of 2002 it was becoming apparent that the extent of opposition was causing the government to have second thoughts about the wisdom of pressing ahead with the White Paper's proposals. This suspicion was confirmed in May 2002 when the government announced plans for a joint committee of MPs and peers to devise options for reform which could be put before Parliament for consideration. The Committee, appointed in June 2002, consisted of twelve members from each House. The position taken by the government was that the issue of reform was now, ultimately, one for Parliament to decide and that the government would support whichever option emerged as the most favoured.

References

Griffith and Ryle (1989) *Parliament: Functions, Practice and Procedures*, London: Sweet & Maxwell.

Shell (1994) 'The House of Lords: Time for a Change', *Parliamentary Affairs*, vol. 94, p. 721.

Tivey (1995) 'Constitutional Reform, A Modest Proposal', *Political Quarterly*, vol. 66, p. 278.

Further reading

Brazier (1994) *Constitutional Practice*, Oxford: Clarendon Press, Ch 11.

Brazier (1991) *Constitutional Reform*, Oxford: Clarendon Press, Ch 4.

Shell (1992) *The House of Lords* (2nd edn), London: Harvester Wheatsheaf.

Chapter 10

PARLIAMENTARY PRIVILEGE

NATURE AND SOURCES

Definition

This consists of a body of rules which identify those special rights and legal immunities which are essential, it is claimed, if individual MPs and Parliament collectively are to be able to perform their functions fearlessly, independently and without outside interference:

> the sum of the peculiar rights enjoyed by each House collectively as a constitutional part of the High Court of Parliament and by Members of each House individually, without which they could not discharge their functions, and which exceed those possessed by other bodies or individuals (May, *Parliamentary Practice*).

Origins

Both Houses of Parliament constitute the High Court of Parliament. As such, in addition to legislating and scrutinising government activity, both have long claimed judicial and disciplinary powers in relation to their own members and other persons whose activities impinge on the workings of either House or a member of the same.

Particular sources

Parliamentary privilege is part of the 'law and custom of Parliament' and is found in:

1   written and unwritten parliamentary practices;
2   statute, e.g. Bill of Rights 1689, Parliamentary Papers Act 1840, Broadcasting Act 1990;
3   precedent, including judicial decisions in which particular privileges have been recognised or their extent considered (principal examples would include *Stockdale v Hansard* (1839) 9 Ad & E 1; *Prebble v Television New Zealand Ltd* [1995] 1 AC 321), and the various parliamentary resolutions adopted when issues of privilege have come before either House (see below, e.g. *Sandy's Case* (1938); *Browne's Case* (1947); the *Strauss Case* (1958)).

The various privileges

These are divided traditionally into two categories.

(a) Those claimed by the Speaker at the beginning of each new Parliament (the ancient and undoubted rights and privileges of the Commons):
  * freedom of speech;
  * freedom from arrest;
  * freedom of access to the Crown through the Speaker;
  * that the Crown will place the most favourable interpretation on deliberations in the House.

(b) Those not claimed expressly but now accepted as part of the law and custom of Parliament:
  * the right of the House to regulate its own internal composition;
  * the right of the House to regulate its own internal proceedings;
  * the right to punish for breach of privilege and contempt; ·
  * the right of impeachment;
  * control of government finance and the right to initiate all financial legislation.

FREEDOM OF SPEECH

History

During the conflict between the King and Parliament in the seventeenth century there were a number of celebrated incidents of royal interference in the business of the House of Commons. In 1629 three MPs who had criticised the King's government (Charles I), and who were prominent advocates of imposing limits on the royal prerogative, were arrested and sentenced to imprisonment for using 'seditious words' and causing 'tumult' in the House (*R v Eliot, Hollis and Valentine* (1629) 3 St Tr 294).

Charles I governed for the next eleven years without calling a Parliament. When Parliament was recalled in 1640 (in an attempt to raise money for defence purposes) he was once again subjected to determined opposition and criticism. His response was to march into the chamber of the House of Commons with 400 armed men in an attempt to arrest the leading anti-royalists (including John Hampden of the *Ship Money Case*). The House refused to identify the objects of the King's anger and the Speaker informed Charles: 'May it please your majesty, I have neither eyes to see or tongue to speak, in this place but as this House is pleased to direct, whose servant I am here.' The Civil War began in 1642.

After the Glorious Revolution in 1688, and as part of the redefinition of the royal prerogative and the relationship between King and Parliament, Parliament decided to embody its right to conduct its deliberations free from outside interference in the Bill of Rights 1689. Article 9 provided that 'the freedom of speech or debates in Parliament ought not to be impeached or questioned in any court or place out of Parliament'.

General scope of the privilege

It is generally understood to mean that no criminal or civil proceedings may be brought against a member of Parliament or any other person in respect of words used in parliamentary proceedings. Thus MPs and those giving evidence before select committees have complete legal immunity in respect of actions for defamation or prosecutions for criminal libel, sedition, blasphemy, breaches of the Official Secrets Acts, contempt of court, incitement to racial hatred, incitement to disaffection, etc.

Thus in *Dillon* v *Balfour* (1887) 20 Ir LR 600, the court refused to entertain an action for defamation in respect of a ministerial statement made during a parliamentary debate that the plaintiff, a midwife, had deliberately refused to attend a pregnant woman. Likewise, in *Goffin* v *Donnelly* (1881) LR 6 QBD 307, it was held that statements made to a parliamentary committee could not form the basis of an action for slander.

Even to attempt to institute legal proceedings in response to words used in Parliament would appear to amount to an interference with these protected parliamentary rights. In *Duncan Sandy's Case* (1937–38 HC Deb 146), an MP was informed that he might be prosecuted under the Official Secrets Acts after he had asked a parliamentary question which revealed a knowledge of sensitive defence information concerning the perilous state of the United Kingdom's air defence systems. The matter was considered by the House, which resolved that the threat to prosecute was a breach of privilege.

The privilege is absolute, which means it remains effective notwithstanding that the parliamentary statement in question was made maliciously, i.e. with intent to damage or with reckless disregard for the truth.

Absolute privilege also applies to statements made in judicial proceedings. It should be distinguished from qualified privilege which applies to a variety of communications providing these are made without malice. Qualified privilege is a defence to actions in defamation only.

Proceedings in Parliament

The term has never been precisely defined either by statute, the Commons or the courts but clearly applies to debates, speeches and questions in the House, deliberations and evidence given in committee, and actions taken by officers of the House in pursuance of its orders (see below, *Bradlaugh* v *Gossett* (1884) LR 12 QBD 271).

The extent to which other communications between ministers of Parliament, ministers and members of the public relating to parliamentary or public business are privileged remains a matter of some uncertainty. In this context the following findings and propositions are worthy of note:

(a) A letter from an MP to a minister relating to a matter of public concern within the minister's area of competence is not a proceeding in Parliament and, therefore, not absolutely privileged (*Strauss Case*, 1958 HC Deb 430). The common law defence of qualified privilege would, however, probably apply – but, as explained, this would give protection for actions in defamation only, providing such communication was not malicious.

The *Strauss Case* arose out of correspondence between George Strauss, a Labour MP, and the minister responsible for the electricity industry. The correspondence contained comments which were potentially defamatory of members of the London Electricity Board (a public corporation). After the minister had communicated these complaints to the Board's chairman, Strauss was informed that the Board intended to sue for libel unless the offending comments were withdrawn.

Strauss raised the matter in the House and claimed that the threat to sue constituted a direct infringement of his privileges as a member. The Committee of Privileges accepted his argument and recommended that such communications should be treated as parliamentary proceedings and, therefore, as absolutely privileged. Perhaps surprisingly, however, the full House rejected the Committee's conclusions (by 218 to 213) – the majority view being that the defence of qualified privilege provided sufficient protection for communications of this type.

Opinions on the *Strauss* decision differ. The Select Committee on Parliamentary Privilege (1966–67 HC Deb 34) felt that due to the amount of essential parliamentary and public business conducted by correspondence between members and ministers this should be covered by absolute privilege. The *Strauss* decision, it recommended, should be overruled by legislation. A different view, however, was taken by the Joint Committee on Parliamentary Privilege (1998/99 HL 43-I/HC 214-J) some 30 years later. Its opinion was that the 'exceptional protection' provided by the Bill of Rights, Art 9, 'should remain confined to the core activities of Parliament, unless a pressing need is shown for an extension'.

The Committee pointed out that, in the 40 years since the *Strauss* decision, the qualified privilege attaching to members' correspondence seemed 'to have enabled Members of both Houses to carry their functions out satisfactorily'. There was, therefore 'insufficient evidence of difficulty, at least at present, to justify so substantial an increase in the amount of parliamentary material protected by absolute privilege'. Given that the boundaries of privilege had 'to be drawn somewhere...the present boundary [was] clear and defensible' (1998–98 Report, paras 108–110).

(b) According to a Speaker's ruling of 1958, the definition of a parliamentary proceeding would extend to a communication between an MP and a minister following an invitation given by the minister in Parliament perhaps at Question Time or during a debate (1958 HC Deb 591).

Other communications between members or a member and a minister may be covered and, therefore, absolutely privileged if they are immediately related to a current, or imminent and scheduled, proceeding in the House. There is, however, no specific authority for this.

(c) By definition, therefore, communications and actions not related to current or imminent parliamentary business probably do not amount to proceedings in Parliament. Hence the ruling by the Select Committee of Privileges in 1987 that the showing of a film about the government's secret spy satellite project (Zircon) within the precincts of the House did not qualify. Those members responsible, therefore, were not immune from judicial sanction. Although an issue of public concern, the subject matter of the film did not relate to any item of parliamentary business being considered or about to be considered by the House.

This makes it clear that the term 'parliamentary proceedings' has no essential connection with the bricks and mortar of the Parliament buildings. Thus if a select committee travels overseas to conduct an investigation and take evidence, its formal sessions (wherever conducted) would, for the purposes of English law, be absolutely privileged.

(d)   If an MP repeats words used in Parliament in a later speech made elsewhere parliamentary privilege does not apply (*Aims of Industry Case*, 1973–74 HC Deb 246). Nor does it apply to the publication by an MP (perhaps to his/her constituents) of a speech made in the House (*R v Creevey* (1813) 1 M & S 278). Such communications are not parliamentary proceedings nor are they necessarily incidental to the same.

(e)   As indicated in relation to the *Strauss Case*, communications about public business between MPs and between an MP and a minister, if made without malice, would probably attract qualified privilege in relation to proceedings for defamation. Qualified privilege also applies to a letter from a constituent to an MP about a matter of public concern, local or national, or that which might reasonably be said to relate to the MP's functions and responsibilities as a constituency representative (*R v Rule* [1937] 2 KB 375; *Beach v Freeson* [1972] 1 QB 14).

If the constituent's letter raises a purely personal matter having nothing to do with any member of the House (e.g. a private person's alleged infidelity), it attracts no privilege whatsoever and it matters not that the letter was posted within the precincts of Parliament (*Rivlin v Bilainkin* [1953] 1 QB 485).

(f)   Although the absolute privilege attending parliamentary words gives an MP immunity from legal proceedings, it does not give any exemption from the penal powers of the House itself. A member could, therefore, be subjected to parliamentary sanctions (e.g. suspension) if it was felt that he or she was abusing the privilege of freedom of speech or using unparliamentary expressions.

Parliamentary papers

It had for long been accepted that at common law parliamentary privilege extended to papers circulated amongst MPs by order of the House. However, in *Stockdale v Hansard* (1839) A & E 1, it was held that privilege did not extend to such papers (in this case a report from the Inspectors of Prisons) when published generally outside the precincts of the House.

This led to the enactment of the Parliamentary Papers Act 1840. The Act conferred:

(a)   absolute privilege on the publication of reports, papers, votes or proceedings printed by order of, or under the authority of either House (s 1);

(b)   absolute privilege on correct copies of such authorised reports, papers, etc. (s 2);

(c)   qualified privilege on extracts from or abstracts of the above (s 3) – in this case it is for the defendant to show that publication of such extracts or abstract was bona fide and without malice (*Dingle v Associated Newspapers Ltd* [1960] 2 QB 405).

None of the above, however, applies to the type of reporting of events in Parliament which regularly appears in newspapers. Such reports are, however, protected by the common law defence of qualified privilege providing that they represent a fair and accurate record of what was said or done. This was made clear in *Wason* v *Walter* (1868) LR 4 QB 73, in which the plaintiff brought an action against the editor of *The Times* after it published a report of a debate in the House of Lords during which the plaintiff had been called a liar. It was felt that as the reporting of debates in Parliament was in the public interest, those responsible should be entitled to a degree of legal immunity:

> it is of paramount public and national importance that the proceedings of the Houses of Parliament should be communicated to the public, who have the deepest interest in knowing what passes within their walls, seeing that on what is then said and done, the welfare of the community depends (per Lord Cockburn CJ).

The defence has been given statutory reinforcement by the Defamation Act 1996, s 15 which gives qualified privilege 'to a fair and accurate report of proceedings in public of a legislature anywhere in the word'.

This does not mean that the report must simply précis the contents of the particular proceeding. It is sufficient that the report was 'fairly and honestly made' and is a 'fair presentation of what took place so as to convey to the reader the impression which the debate itself would have made on a hearer of it' (per Lord Denning MR, *Cook* v *Alexander* [1974] QB 279). Hence, if a newspaper were to report just one speech from a debate or concentrate entirely on one side of the argument only, the privilege would be unlikely to apply.

Beyond this, honest journalistic comment in the form of opinion on political issues and personalities generally (i.e. other than on parliamentary affairs specifically) founded on a reasonable basis of fact and published without malice, may attract the defence of fair comment on a matter of public interest. There is, however, no general defence of qualified privilege covering alleged misstatements of fact in the dissemination of 'political information'. Politicians are also entitled to legal protection of their reputations, and the measure of what is acceptable when publishing information about politicians is not something which should be left entirely to the exercise of professional ethics by journalists (*Reynolds* v *Times Newspapers Ltd* [1999] 3 WLR 1010).

Broadcast parliamentary proceedings

Qualified privilege extends to the use of extracts from, or abstracts of, a parliamentary paper in the making and broadcasting of radio or television programmes (Defamation Act 1952, s 9; Broadcasting Act 1990, s 203).

The protection is, however, confined to parliamentary papers – it does not appear to extend to live or recorded broadcasts of verbal exchanges during the conduct of general parliamentary proceedings, e.g. debates, Question Time, standing and select committees, etc. It is generally assumed, however, that a court would regard the qualified privilege extended to fair and accurate newspaper reports of parliamentary business to be also applicable to the broadcasting of similar material.

It should be emphasised again, however, that, as a general rule, qualified privilege is a defence to actions in defamation only. Hence television or radio networks which broadcast a parliamentary statement which amounted to a crime, e.g. a breach of the Official Secrets Act, would not be protected.

Parliamentary proceedings as evidence in court

As a general principle, official parliamentary records may be cited in legal proceedings for the following limited purposes only:

(a) 'as a guide to the construction of ambiguous legislation' (*Pepper* v *Hart* [1992] 3 WLR 1032);
(b) to clarify a statute's general or overall purpose (*Three Rivers District Council* v *Bank of England (No. 2)* [1996] 2 All ER 363);
(c) 'to prove what was done and said in Parliament as a matter of history' (*Prebble* v *Television New Zealand Ltd* [1995] 1 AC 321);
(d) in judicial review proceedings, for the purpose of citing a decision on policy statements announced in Parliament preparatory to challenging its validity (Joint Committee on Parliamentary Privilege, 1998–99 Report, paras 48 and 49).

This is based on the judicial acceptance that 'parties to litigation…cannot bring into question anything said or done in the House by suggesting that the actions or words were inspired by improper motives, or were untrue or misleading' (*ibid.* per Lord Browne-Wilkinson).

Hence, subject to what is said below, official parliamentary records or oral testimony as to what occurred during parliamentary proceedings should not be used to initiate or support:

(a) any civil cause of action (*Church of Scientology* v *Johnson-Smith* [1972] 1 QB 522; *Rost* v *Edwards* [1990] 2 All ER 641);
(b) any application for judicial review (*R* v *Secretary of State for Trade, ex parte Anderson-Strathclyde Plc* [1983] 2 All ER 233);
(c) any criminal prosecution (*ex parte Wason* (1869) LR 4 QB 573).

A major exception to the above was effected by the Defamation Act 1996, s 13. This qualified Art 9 of the Bill of Rights and allows an MP to waive the absolute immunity attending his/her words and actions in Parliament so that these may be used in any libel proceedings in which the member may be involved. The Act was precipitated, *inter alia*, by the decision in *Allason* v *Haines*, *The Times*, 25 July 1995, where the court struck out a libel action brought by an MP when it became apparent that the defence was based on the alleged impropriety of actions taken by the plaintiff in the course of a parliamentary proceeding. The view of the court was that under such circumstances, it would be manifestly unfair to allow the action to proceed. As a result, however, the MP was deprived of the opportunity to 'clear his name'.

The prohibition on the admission in legal proceedings of testimony touching on what was said, done or decided in Parliament was confirmed by the House of Lords in *Hamilton* v *Al Fayed* [2000] 2 All ER 224. It was made clear, however, that such prohibition does not apply in proceedings for defamation involving an MP who has waived the protection of privilege.

FREEDOM FROM ARREST

Scope

This protects an MP from arrest for any civil offence while Parliament is in session. The protection comes into effect 40 days before the session begins and continues for a further 40 days after it has ended. The purpose of the privilege was to ensure that no legal impediment could be used to prevent an MP journeying to and from and attending Parliament after being summoned by the King.

The privilege does not give any immunity in respect of criminal offences or detention without trial under emergency legislation (*Captain Ramsey's Case* (1940)). Nor does it prevent an MP from being arrested within the precincts of the House providing that the alleged crime was not said or done for the purpose of a parliamentary proceeding and that the permission of the House is given if it is a sitting day (*Lord Cochrane's Case* (1815)). There are also clear judicial dicta for the view that crimes committed in the House by an MP or any other person are justiciable in the ordinary courts.

The immunity is now restricted to civil contempt of court – the only civil offence which remains arrestable (*Stourton* v *Stourton* [1963] P 302). Civil contempt is committed by disobedience to an order of a court imposing a civil obligation (e.g. to pay damages).

Since the Debtors Act 1869, and the abolition of the power to arrest and imprison for debt, the privilege has ceased to give MPs any meaningful or necessary protection. In 1967 and 1977 the Select Committee of Privileges recommended its abolition. Its abolition was also recommended by the Joint Committee on Parliamentary Privilege in the 1998–99 Report. No such action has yet been taken.

MPs in prison

The House has the right to be informed of the arrest of an MP or his/her remand in custody or sentence to imprisonment and the reasons therefore. Such an MP could be expelled.

A convicted MP has no right to any special privileges while in prison. However, an MP merely remanded in custody should be allowed to fulfil as many of his/her representative functions as practicable (see Committee of Privileges Report, 1970).

MPs and legal proceedings

(a)   Service of a writ within the precincts of the House is a contempt.
(b)   A subpoena for an MP to give evidence during a parliamentary session is probably not enforceable when the House is in session.
(c)   MPs are exempt from jury duty (Juries Act 1974).

RIGHT OF THE HOUSE TO REGULATE ITS OWN COMPOSITION

History

Until the middle of the nineteenth century the House of Commons took the view that it had an exclusive right to adjudicate on all claims arising out of disputed elections (i.e. whether a particular candidate was disqualified or an individual was entitled to vote) and was not just restricted to deciding the competence or fitness of a particular member to sit. The right was conceded by James I after the events surrounding the election of Sir Francis Goodwin, an alleged outlaw (*Goodwin* v *Fortescue* (1604) 2 St Tr 91), and recognised by the House of Lords in *Barnardiston* v *Soame* (1674) 6 St Tr 1063; (1689) 6 St Tr 1119. In the nineteenth century, however, this jurisdiction was delegated to the courts (Parliamentary Elections Act 1868).

Present scope

The privilege now extends to the following:

(a) the right of the House to determine by resolution when the writ should be issued for the holding of a by-election;
(b) the right to determine whether a particular member is disqualified;
(c) the expulsion of a member deemed unfit to serve, for whatever reasons – e.g. conviction for a serious criminal offence (*Peter Baker's Case*, 1954) or contempt of Parliament (*Gary Allighan's Case*, 1947).

An MP aggrieved by such decision may not seek judicial redress. A decision to exclude constitutes a proceeding in Parliament and, as such, may not be questioned in a court of law. The House does not, however, have the power to prevent an excluded member from seeking re-election but could resolve that such person, if elected, should not be allowed to take his/her seat (*Wilkes' Case*, 1769–74; *Bradlaugh* v *Gossett* (1884) LR 12 QBD 271).

RIGHT OF THE HOUSE TO REGULATE ITS INTERNAL PROCEEDINGS

Scope

The House of Commons claims the exclusive and conclusive right to:

(a) decide what it will discuss or consider;
(b) settle or make rules for its own proceedings and determine whether such rules have been complied with.

Role of the courts

The courts must presume that the House discharges its functions 'properly and with due regard to the law' (Stephen J, *Bradlaugh* v *Gossett*, above) and, therefore, will not investigate or adjudicate upon alleged breaches of parliamentary procedure.

In the past the courts have refused to inquire into:

(a) alleged procedural defects in the passage of a Bill through Parliament (*Pickin* v *British Railways Board* [1974] AC 765);
(b) the conduct of proceedings in select committee (*Dingle* v *Associated Newspapers*, above);

(c)   the validity of reports laid before the House (*Harper* v *Home Secretary* [1955] Ch 238).

The courts also lack the competence to question the merits or procedural propriety of the House's disciplinary and domestic activities. In the famous case of *Bradlaugh* v *Gossett* (above), the House took the view that Charles Bradlaugh, who had been elected for Northampton, was disabled from swearing the required oath of allegiance because of his religious views (he was an atheist). It was resolved, therefore, that he should be excluded. The House would not accept the argument that the Parliamentary Oaths Act 1868 gave Bradlaugh the option of making a non-religious affirmation. Although it appeared that the House might have misconstrued the relevant statutory provisions, Bradlaugh's attempt to have the decision set aside was unsuccessful. The court was adamant that it could not question a parliamentary decision notwithstanding that it might be wrong in law:

> It seems to follow that the House of Commons has the exclusive power of interpreting the statute so far as the regulation of its own proceedings within its own walls is concerned; and that, even if that interpretation should be erroneous this Court has no power to interfere with it directly or indirectly (per Stephen J).

The same principle was applied in *R* v *Graham-Campbell, ex parte Herbert* [1935] 1 KB 594, where the court held that it had no jurisdiction to inquire into alleged breaches of the licensing laws by the House of Commons Kitchen Committee.

Exclusion of strangers

The Commons has always claimed the right to exclude non-members ('strangers') in order to ensure freedom of speech and to prevent interruption of proceedings. The procedure for exclusion is for a member to move 'I spy strangers'. The Speaker then puts to the vote the question that 'strangers do withdraw'. There is no debate on this issue. If carried the resolution operates for the remainder of that day. Further, the Speaker may, of his or her own volition, order strangers to withdraw.

Proceedings in camera

The House may also resolve to move into secret session for the remainder of a day's sitting. It would then be a contempt for a member to disclose anything said or done in that secret session unless the House otherwise resolved. The publication of any such matter would be a breach of privilege.

RIGHT OF THE HOUSE TO PUNISH FOR BREACH OF PRIVILEGE AND CONTEMPT OF PARLIAMENT

Breach of privilege is committed by abuse of, or interference with, any of the established privileges of the House. Any breach of privilege amounts to a contempt.

Contempt of Parliament is a more open-ended concept and consists of any act or omission which obstructs the House or its members or offends against the House or its dignity. Hence a contempt may be committed without any breach of privilege. Erskine May defines contempt as follows:

any act or omission which obstructs or impedes either House of Parliament in the performance of its functions, or which obstructs or impedes any Member or officer of such House in the discharge of his duty, or which has a tendency directly or indirectly, to produce such result may be treated as a contempt even though there is no precedent for the offence (*Parliamentary Practice*).

Examples of contempt

- Disorderly conduct in the presence of the House.
- Refusal to give or giving false evidence to the House or any of its committees.
- Interference with witnesses giving evidence to the House or its committees.
- Obstruction of MPs going to or from the House.
- Inclusion of falsehoods in any personal statement made to the House.
- Actual or attempted bribery and corruption by or of any member.
- Disobedience to the orders of the House or interference with officers, witnesses or proceedings before the House.
- False, perverted or unauthorised reports of parliamentary proceedings.
- Revealing details of confidential proceedings.
- Improper pressure on an MP to perform his duty in a particular way (see below, *Browne's Case* etc.).
- Molestation of an MP in relation to his conduct in the House (*Sunday Graphic Case*, 1956: contempt by national newspaper to print an MP's telephone number so that readers could contact him directly to protest against his views on the Suez Crisis – the MP was inundated with calls).
- Derogatory or contemptuous imputations damaging to the dignity of the House or any of its members (*Duffy's Case*, 1965: contempt to suggest that MPs had been 'half-drunk' during debates; *Junior's Case*, 1956: contempt to suggest that proposed petrol-rationing restrictions were unduly favourable to MPs; *Protestant Telegraph Case*, 1966: contempt to suggest that an MP was a traitor; *Ashton's Case*, 1974: contempt to suggest that MPs were prepared to surrender their independence for financial gain).

Financial inducements

It is a contempt to attempt to bribe an MP to influence his/her conduct in the House or to offer any other fee, reward or financial inducement to persuade an MP to advocate any matter in the House. It is also a contempt for an MP to accept the same.

In 1695 the House resolved that 'the offer of money, or other advantage to a Member of Parliament for promoting any matter whatsoever pending or to be transacted in Parliament is a high crime and misdemeanour'. Later, in 1858, the House resolved that it was improper for a member to promote any matter or cause in the House for which he had or was acting for any pecuniary reward. In 1945 the Committee of Privileges concluded that it would be a breach of privilege for money to be offered to a member or donated to any charity or local political party for the purpose of inducing a member to ask or pursue a particular question with a minister.

No contempt is committed, however, if an MP is offered and receives payment to represent the general interests of a particular organisation or concern – so long as no pressure is put on the MP to act, speak or vote in the House in a particular way and the contractual arrangement between the MP and the 'outside' interest does not seek in any way to limit the MP's freedom of action.

> ...this House declares that it is inconsistent with the dignity of the House, with the duty of a Member to his constituents, and with the maintenance of the privilege of freedom of speech, for any Member to enter into any contractual arrangement with an outside body, controlling or limiting the Member's complete independence and freedom of action in Parliament or stipulating that he shall act in any way as the representative of such outside body in regard to any matters to be transacted in Parliament (Resolution of the House, 15 July 1947).

Thus a decision by a trade union or professional association to terminate its relationship and financial support of an MP due to dissatisfaction with his/her general conduct as a member would not be a contempt (*Browne's Case*, 1947). However, a contempt would be committed were such organisation to seek to use its financial relationship with a member to influence their actions in the House in a specific way – e.g. by threatening to withdraw financial support unless the MP speaks or votes in accordance with that organisation's policies (*Scargill's Case*, 1975).

Pressure from party whips does not amount to a breach of privilege or contempt (Speaker's rulings, 1956 and 1975). Attempts by local political parties similarly to influence a member's actions in the House could, however, be contemptuous.

In 1975 the Commons adopted a resolution requiring MPs to disclose relevant pecuniary interest or benefits, whether direct or indirect, in any debate or proceedings of the House or its committees. Failure to disclose is a contempt.

The Register of Members' Interests

In the same year (1975) the House also resolved to establish a compulsory Register of Members' Interests. The object of the Register was 'to provide information of any pecuniary interest or other material benefit which a Member of Parliament may receive which might be thought to affect his conduct as a Member of Parliament or influence his actions, speeches or vote in Parliament'. Nine classes of pecuniary interest or other benefit were required to be registered:

- remunerated directorships of private or public companies;
- remunerated offices or employment (excluding ministerial positions);
- any remunerated trade, profession or vocation;
- names of clients for whom the MP has performed personal services relating to his/her membership of the House;
- financial sponsorships, support or other benefit in relation to a member's election expenses (if in excess of 25 per cent) or to assist a member in the performance of his/her duties (e.g. provision of research assistance);
- overseas visits relevant to membership of the House where the cost is not borne wholly by the MP or public funds;
- payments or other benefits received from any foreign government, organisation or person;

- land or property (other than the member's home) of substantial value from which a substantial income is derived;
- companies in which an MP and or their spouse or child hold more than 1 per cent of the issued share capital.

Registration is regarded as sufficient disclosure for the purpose of voting on matters to which the interest relates. Should, however, a member wish to speak in the antecedent proceedings – either in the House or in committee – the interest should be declared.

Failure to register a relevant interest may be regarded as a contempt. In 1990 John Browne MP was suspended and lost his parliamentary salary for fourteen days for omissions in this regard.

The Nolan Committee

Following the report of the Nolan Committee in 1995 (Committee on Standards in Public Life, Cm 2850) further measures were put in place to regulate the receipt of payments and other rewards by MPs in connection with services performed in their capacity as members.

> ...that is the political lobbying/consultancy/advice functions; work, generally paid, directly or otherwise, related to a Member's Parliamentary duties or their status as Members of Parliament, with all the access and influence in the legislative/government/policy networks that that position may bring (*House of Commons Research Paper*, 95/62).

The action taken (by resolutions of the House) to implement the Nolan recommendations was as follows.

(a) The creation in November 1995 of a Parliamentary Commissioner for Standards with responsibility:

- for the compilation and maintenance of the Register of Members' Interests;
- to advise members on matters relating to registration of individual interests;
- to advise the Select Committee on Standards and Privileges on the interpretation of the new Code of Conduct (see below);
- to receive complaints from MPs and members of the public concerning the registration of interests or other issues relating to the propriety of a member's conduct and to report to the above select committee.

(b) The creation of a new Select Committee on Standards and Privileges from the beginning of the 1995–96 session to take over the functions of the Select Committee on Privileges and in particular:

- to consider matters relating to privileges referred to it by the House;
- to oversee the work of the Parliamentary Commissioner for Standards;
- to consider alleged breaches of the members' Code of Conduct referred to it by the Commissioner.

(c) The creation of a Code of Conduct to ensure that all members are aware of the requirements of the rules concerning disclosure and conflict of interests.

(d) The amendment of the 1975 rules on declaration of interests so as to require members to declare any relevant interest when tabling written or oral questions or amendments to Bills (by use of the symbol [R]).

(e) Giving the 1947 resolution on conflict of interests greater specificity by adding the requirement that no MP or member of an MP's family shall receive any remuneration of any kind in connection with the raising of any issue in Parliament 'by means of any speech, Question, Motion, introduction of a Bill or amendment to a Motion or Bill'.

(f) The requirement that any agreement entered into by a member which 'involves the provision of services in his capacity as a Member of Parliament' should conform with the Code of Conduct and that a 'full copy of any such agreement including the fees or benefits payable' should by deposited with the Commissioner for Standards and registered in the Register of Members' Interests.

The role of the Commissioner for Standards and Privileges is analogous to that of an officer of the House of Commons. As such his decisions are not susceptible to judicial review (*R v Parliamentary Commissioner for Standards and Privileges, ex parte Fayed* [1998] 1 WLR 669).

Procedure for dealing with alleged breaches of privilege or contempt

In 1978 the House resolved that henceforth it would only entertain complaints about actions which threatened 'substantial damage' to the workings of the House or its members. An allegation of breach of privilege or contempt must be referred to the Speaker, in writing, as soon as is reasonably possible after the incident complained of. The Speaker must then decide whether the complaint:

(a) raises a matter of privilege or contempt;

(b) suggests that there has been substantial interference or damage;

(c) has been made as soon as reasonably practicable.

If these criteria are satisfied, the member who made the complaint will, as a matter of urgency, be allowed to move that the issue be referred to the Select Committee on Privileges and Standards. The resulting debate and vote will be given precedence over other business and will usually take place on the day following the Speaker's ruling.

The Select Committee is chaired by the Leader of the House. Other members will include the law officers and senior backbenchers from the government and main opposition parties. It has power to send for all persons, papers and records relevant to its inquiries. The committee, however, is not obliged to act judicially. Hence those against whom complaints have been made are not entitled to be heard or to be legally represented.

The committee reports to the House that a breach or contempt has or has not been committed. The report will then be debated in the House and its findings and recommendations may be accepted or rejected.

Punishments

(a) *Expulsion* – the ultimate sanction which may be imposed upon an MP for contempt or for general unfitness to serve. As indicated above, this penalty has only been imposed on two occasions since 1945. Only in *Allighan's Case*, however, was the punishment used to deal with an incident of contempt (false allegations by Allighan that MPs would provide confidential information to the press either for money or under the influence of drink). In *Baker's Case* expulsion was ordered after the MP was imprisoned for seven years for fraud.

(b) *Suspension* – the Speaker may order any member who behaves in a gross disorderly manner to be suspended for the rest of the day's sitting. In more serious cases, or where the MP refuses to submit to the Speaker's ruling, an MP may be 'named'. The House then decides whether the MP should be suspended. If the motion is carried, the member is suspended for five days. Where a member is 'named' for a second time in the same session, the period of suspension is twenty days. If named again, i.e. for a third time, suspension is for the rest of the session.

(c) *Censure by the Speaker* – the offender, if not an MP, is summoned to the Bar of the House to receive the 'dressing down'. A member is reprimanded or admonished in his/her seat. Since 1945 only two members and one journalist have been dealt with in this way.

(d) *Imprisonment* – Members are imprisoned in the Clock Tower while strangers are handed to the Sergeant-at-Arms who takes them to one of HM's prisons. Imprisonment is during the House's pleasure but cannot last beyond the end of the Parliamentary session. It has been suggested that this power is obsolete as it was last used in 1880. An alternative view is that imprisonment might still be imposed 'in extreme cases of disobedience if the general political sense so allowed' (Griffith and Ryle, *op. cit.*).

(e) *Fine* – the House last imposed a fine in *White's Case* (1666). The power was denied by Lord Mansfield in the latter half of the eighteenth century (*R v Pitt*; *R v Mead* (1763) 3 Burr 1335). It has also been suggested that at common law the House may have no power to fine as it is not a court of record.

THE COURTS AND PARLIAMENTARY PRIVILEGE

Established principles

The House has exclusive jurisdiction to determine whether a breach of privilege has been committed. It cannot, however, create new privileges by resolution. This can only be done by Act of Parliament (see Parliamentary Papers Act 1840, above; Parliamentary Commissioner Act 1967 – extended absolute privilege to communications between an MP and the Commissioner).

THE COURTS AND CONTEMPT

Established principles

It is for the House, not the courts, to decide what constitutes a contempt. The courts also recognise the right of the House to punish for contempt.

Matters of uncertainty

Doubt remains concerning the power of the courts to grant relief to a person committed to prison for contempt of the House. Where a person is so committed, but no reasons are given in the Speaker's warrant, it is unlikely that a court would grant *habeas corpus* (*Burdett* v *Abbott* (1814) 14 East 1; *Sheriff of Middlesex Case* (1840) Ad & E 273). Where, however, reasons are given and these show no just cause for the committal, then – according to Holt CJ in *Patsy's Case* (above) – *habeas corpus* could be issued.

References

Griffith and Ryle (1989) *Parliament: Functions, Practice and Procedures*, London: Sweet & Maxwell.

May (1989) *Parliamentary Practice* (21st edn), London: Butterworths.

Further reading

Bradley and Ewing (1997) *Constitutional and Administrative Law* (12th edn), London: Longman, Ch 11.

May, *ibid.*, Chs 5–9, 11.

Monro (1987) *Studies in Constitutional Law*, London: Butterworths, Ch 7.

Part 4

THE EXECUTIVE

Chapter 11

THE PRIME MINISTER
AND CABINET

INTRODUCTION

Not all Prime Ministers possess or even attempt to exercise the same degree of power. Much depends on a particular incumbent's personality and style, on political circumstances (e.g. the size of the majority in Parliament) and on good fortune (i.e. absence of scandals and incidents of misconduct by ministers). Hence Prime Ministers such as James Callaghan (1976–79) (with a very small majority and eventually with Liberal support), Harold Wilson (1964–70 and 1974–76), and Harold Macmillan (1957–63), are generally said to have been good 'chairmen' and conciliators rather than evangelical leaders. Wilson described the Prime Minister as being like a conductor of an orchestra, the orchestra being the various ministers, departments of state, etc. Macmillan pinned a quote from Gilbert and Sullivan's *The Gondoliers* on to the door of the Cabinet room. This said 'quiet calm deliberation disentangles every knot'. Mrs Thatcher's style was reputedly less discursive or collective. This would appear to have been due to her own personality and belief in 'conviction' politics plus the additional latitude given to her by large parliamentary majorities. 'It must be a conviction government. As Prime Minister I cannot waste time having any internal arguments' (*The Observer*, 25 February 1979). Mrs Thatcher reduced both the amount of time spent on Cabinet deliberations and the number of Cabinet committees. As a result there was an apparent increased incidence of decisions being taken without full Cabinet discussion. It was said she preferred to make decisions with small groups of ministers and other trusted advisers.

CHOOSING A PRIME MINISTER

The role of the Crown

According to convention the Monarch must appoint as Prime Minister the person who commands a majority in the House of Commons or who is in the best position to form and sustain a government in office. Hence, in theory, the Monarch's role is purely formal. She appoints but does not choose.

It has been suggested, however, that in certain circumstances the Monarch might still have to become involved in the decision-making process. This would be most likely to occur where an election produced a 'hung' Parliament, i.e. a Parliament in which no single party had an overall majority in the House of Commons.

The workings of the British electoral system render such indecisive results unlikely. Only five 'hung' Parliaments were returned in the twentieth century (January 1910, December 1910, December 1923, May 1929, February 1974). There are no specific rules that regulate how the Monarch should act in these circumstances. History and practice, however, indicate that the following approach might be thought appropriate.

(a) For the Monarch to allow the incumbent PM, now no longer with a majority, to be given an opportunity to form a further administration. This might be a minority government if the Prime Minister still leads the largest single party or a government with cross-party support – perhaps a coalition (see 1931 National Coalition).

(b) If this proves impossible, for the Monarch to invite the leader of the largest single party, if not the Prime Minister, to see if he or she is able to form a viable minority or cross-party majority administration.

(c) If this fails, for the Monarch, on advice, to invite any other party leader, or person capable of forming a government to see if an alternative administration may be formed.

(d) All of these possibilities having been considered or exhausted, to dissolve Parliament so that a further election may be held.

Party procedures for choosing a leader

Prior to 1981, the Labour leader was elected by simple majority vote amongst all members of the parliamentary party. In 1981, amidst much controversy, a new system was adopted. This involved choosing the leader through an 'electoral college'. According to this system, 40 per cent of the vote was cast by the trade unions, 30 per cent by the parliamentary party, and 30 per cent by the constituency parties. It was the introduction of this procedure which led four senior Labour members (David Owen, Shirley Williams, Roy Jenkins and Bill Rodgers – the 'gang of four') to leave the party and form the Social Democratic Party. This eventually fused with the Liberals producing the Liberal Democrats. In 1994 the electoral college approach was abandoned and replaced by a system of 'one man (person), one vote' ('OMOV') amongst all party members. Tony Blair was the first to be elected in this way.

The Conservative party did not adopt a procedure for electing its leaders until 1965. When a leader died or resigned it was assumed that a potential successor would automatically 'emerge' and be appointed on the basis of consensus following internal deliberations amongst party members. This system worked well enough but was found wanting after the resignations of Sir Anthony Eden in 1957 and Harold Macmillan in 1963. When Eden resigned after the Suez Crisis two possible successors 'emerged': R A Butler and Harold Macmillan. The Queen was forced to consult with senior Conservatives (including Churchill), and eventually opted for Macmillan. When Macmillan resigned in 1963 six possible successors 'emerged': Butler, Lord Hailsham, Lord Home, Reginald Maudling, Edward Heath and Ian McLeod. Once again the Queen was 'dragged' into the internal machinations of a divided Conservative party.

Sir Alex Douglas (Lord) Home was the eventual 'choice'. To avoid any repetition it was decided in 1965 that future leaders would be chosen by ballot amongst all members of the parliamentary party. This system remained in place untill 1997 when the franchise was extended to include both the parliamentary Conservative party and members of local Conservative constituency associations. According to this system the leading two candidates are identified by a series of ballots amongst Conservative MPs – the candidate with the least votes in each ballot dropping out until only two are left. The successful candidate is then chosen by simple majority in a ballot of all party members.

The Liberal Democrat leader is chosen by simple majority through a system of one person, one vote amongst all party members.

FACTORS CONTRIBUTING TO THE POWER OF THE PRIME MINISTER

The conventional power of patronage

Although in strictly legal terms it is the Monarch who appoints all members of the government and who makes many other appointments in both church and state, convention requires that all of these are made on the advice of the Prime Minister. Hence, the real power to 'hire and fire' belongs to the Prime Minister alone. But the power is not unlimited. In forming a government the Prime Minister must be aware of the need to preserve party unity and public confidence. Hence he or she may be constrained to include persons of ability, experience and stature from the various 'wings' of the party (hence the survival of prominent figures from the more liberal faction of the party in Mrs Thatcher's governments).

Excessive use of the power of dismissal may also have prejudicial effects on public confidence and the government's standing in Parliament. 'The electorate instinctively neglects any party which cannot form a government, and tends to despise a party that cannot form a united government' (Coote, *The Government We Deserve*). In total there were 129 ministerial resignations (for many types of reason) during Mrs Thatcher's period in office. By mid-1996 Mr Major's record appeared to be little better, 76 resignations having occurred since he became Prime Minister in 1990. In general, however, Mr Major's losses tended to be less high profile and acrimonious than some of those suffered by his predecessor. The bare figures also hide the fact that, in comparison to Mrs Thatcher, Mr Major often displayed a marked reluctance to sack ministerial colleagues and had little enthusiasm for large-scale Cabinet 'reshuffles'.

THE CONVENTIONAL POWER OF DISSOLUTION

Prime ministerial or Cabinet decision

Like so many aspects of the British constitution, the decision to ask for a dissolution of Parliament and the chronological incidence of general elections are not subject to precise legal prescriptions, save for the five-year rule contained in the Parliament Act 1911. Modern wisdom, however, tends to suggest that deciding the date of an election is largely a question for prime ministerial rather than Cabinet judgement and that whether or not Prime Ministers should consult their Cabinet colleagues is a matter of discretion and not obligation.

Background

The entrusting of this power to the Prime Minister is frequently claimed to date from the end of the First World War:

> Until the First World War no one doubted that the decision to advise the Crown to dissolve Parliament was a collective decision of the Cabinet, or at any rate of those members of it who sit in the House of Commons ... For reasons which are not wholly clear, the practice since 1918 has been for the decision to rest with the Prime Minister alone, taking such advice (or none) as he sees fit (Blake, *The Office of Prime Minister*).

This particular prime ministerial power is a double-edged sword. To get it wrong may well result in loss of office – a fate to which Ted Heath would no doubt testify. In the famous 'who runs the country election' in February 1974, called to secure a mandate for the government's battle with the miners, Mr Heath dissolved Parliament fifteen months earlier than necessary. His optimism was misjudged – his premiership was ended and by the end of 1975 so too his leadership of the Conservative party.

Despite her reputedly autocratic style, it would appear that Mrs Thatcher did consult before advising dissolutions in 1983 and 1987. On both occasions, however, it appears to have been accepted that the final decision was hers to make and that it was for her to inform rather than seek Cabinet support.

It has been said that the Prime Minister may use the threat of a dissolution to secure obedience in Cabinet and on the backbenches. Asquith said this was an 'essential' weapon. Harold Wilson's view, however, was that a premier who used the threat of dissolution to bolster his own position 'would be certifiable'. Others have expressed similar views: 'Since he wants to win he is hardly likely to enter an election campaign wielding the weapon of dissolution against his own party for the opposition will make much capital out of the splits' (Jones, *The Prime Minister's Power*). Note, however, that the threat was used by John Major in November 1994 prior to the second reading of a Bill to increase UK budgetary contributions to the European Community. It was generally agreed at the time, however, that – despite backbench dissension – the government was never in any serious danger of losing the vote.

The conventional powers in relation to the Cabinet

The Prime Minister determines the size and composition of the Cabinet and the number, subject matter and composition of Cabinet committees. He or she also determines when the Cabinet meets, the agenda for discussion, chairs Cabinet meetings and sums up whatever conclusions have been reached.

Traditionally the Cabinet meets twice a week. Mrs Thatcher, however, seldom called more than one Cabinet meeting per week. She also reduced the number of Cabinet committees and the number of occasions on which such committees met.

The Prime Minister has almost exclusive control over Cabinet agenda. It is not possible for ministers to insist on an item being included.

> ...the Prime Minister arranges the order of business, and can keep any item off the agenda indefinitely. It is regarded as quite improper for a Minister to raise any matter which has not previously been accepted for the agenda by the Prime Minister (King, *The British Prime Minister*).

But any persistent attempt to stifle debate of significant issues can lead to dissent and ultimately resignations. Thus Michael Heseltine resigned as Secretary of State for Defence in 1986 when Mrs Thatcher refused to permit further discussion of the decision to allow Westland Helicopters to be sold to Sikorski, an American enterprise, rather than a European consortium favoured by Heseltine.

The Cabinet rarely, if ever, votes. The sense of the meeting is 'summed up' by the Prime Minister.

> Ex Prime Ministers have confirmed – as I can – that in reaching a decision Cabinet does not vote, except to save time on minor procedural matters. On many issues, discussion is confined to one or two, or very few ministers, and, perhaps after suggesting a formula which appears to command assent, the Prime Minister asks 'Cabinet agree?' – technically a voice vote, sometimes a murmur. On a major issue, it is important not only to give the major protagonists their heads, but to ensure that everyone expresses an opinion, by going round the table to collect the voices. The Prime Minister usually keeps a tally of those for and against after which he records his assessment of the dominant view – or occasionally puts forward a suggestion of his own which all or nearly all, can support (Wilson, *The Governance of Britain*).

Most Prime Ministers in this century have used the devices of partial and inner cabinets to make decisions, thus avoiding full Cabinet discussion. Such decisions are then usually referred to Cabinet for approval or presented as *fait accompli*. A partial cabinet refers to a group of ministers selected to direct and co-ordinate government actions usually in relation to an urgent situation or national crisis (e.g. Falklands War). An inner cabinet refers to an informal and fluctuating group of senior ministers whom the Prime Minister trusts and favours and with whom major issues will often be discussed – and a common view formed – prior to Cabinet proceedings.

Support of the Cabinet Office or Secretariat

This is a body of senior civil servants whose formal task is to provide the Cabinet with administrative and secretarial support. One of its main functions is to prepare agenda and supply all other documentation and material necessary for the efficient disposal of business in Cabinet (also Cabinet committees). Surprisingly enough, prior to 1917 (when it was first created), no machinery existed for preparing Cabinet agenda and recording decisions. It has been said that, as a result, ministers were sometimes inadequately briefed prior to Cabinet meetings or, even worse, were sometimes unclear about what had been decided.

Other Cabinet Office functions include: summoning ministers to Cabinet and Cabinet committee meetings; taking and circulating Cabinet and Cabinet committee minutes; drafting reports of Cabinet committee recommendations for Cabinet discussion; filing and maintaining Cabinet papers and records.

Although dedicated to support of the whole Cabinet, the Secretariat provides the Prime Minister with access to a great deal of information and analysis without which his/her position would be weakened. Note that the Prime Minister does not have a department of his/her own and, therefore, could be at a disadvantage in relation to those ministerial colleagues able to rely on the extensive research facilities provided by large government departments.

The Secretariat is headed by the Cabinet Secretary. He or she is a very senior civil servant with whom the Prime Minister will be in regular personal contact for information and advice. It is known that Mrs Thatcher placed particular reliance on the counsel of her Cabinet Secretary, Sir Robert Armstrong, and regarded him as a source of support when dealing with tensions between herself and other ministers.

The Prime Minister's private office

This is divided into four sections and is staffed by a mixture of civil servants and political appointees. It has grown in size in recent years and now has a total of over 100 personnel (including messengers and clerical staff).

The private office

The major responsibility of this small group of civil servants (usually five or six) is to help the Prime Minister manage and prioritise the mass of paper work and communications with which they have to deal. The Private Office also co-ordinates the Prime Minister's diary, helps with the preparation of speeches and generally ensures that the Prime Minister is adequately briefed and prepared for both official and parliamentary business.

The No 10 policy unit

This body was established by Harold Wilson in 1974 and has been retained by his successors. Its members are political appointees (nine or ten usually). They are particularly concerned with the analysis and evaluation of policy proposals and with projecting the practical and political consequences of such proposals.

During Mrs Thatcher's tenure in office there occurred a number of much publicised inconsistencies between views emanating from such special advisers and those of members of the Cabinet. The most controversial of these were the differences of opinion between Nigel Lawson (then Chancellor of the Exchequer) and Professor Alan Walters over economic policy, which contributed to Lawson's eventual resignation.

The political office

Its principal function is to keep the Prime Minister in touch with opinion in the governing party and its organisations at both national and local level. It is composed of party members and not civil servants.

The No 10 press office

This has the important role of handling the Prime Minister's relationship and arrangements with the media. Normally its members are civil servants. This caused some controversy during the Thatcher years due to the allegedly proactive political role played by her Press Office Chief, Bernard Ingham.

Specialist advisers (the 'kitchen cabinet')

The term refers to a group of advisers, usually experts in a particular field and who are neither MPs nor permanent members of the civil service. These may be appointed by the Prime Minister or by other ministers. At the end of the first Blair administration there were alleged to be some 77 of these in Whitehall as a whole, of whom 28 were directly attached to No 10. Reliance on such experts has been alleged to be at odds with underlying constitutional values since it may appear to diminish the role of the Cabinet and allow national policy to be influenced unduly by persons with no democratic mandate or direct accountability.

Party loyalty and party discipline

The majority of government and party members will have no wish to antagonise the Prime Minister. Most will realise that their hopes of advancement are dependent on his/her favour, and that the Prime Minister will be able to claim some of the credit for the party's success in the last general election. It is also well appreciated that dissent and disunity do little for a party's public image and may adversely affect future electoral prospects.

Paradoxically, however, large parliamentary majorities – as Mrs Thatcher had after 1983, and as Mr Blair had after the 1997 and 2001 elections – tend to give MPs greater latitude for backbench revolts. 'A smallish working majority tends to keep a party *and* a government on its toes, a landslide is bad for party discipline, enabling rebellion with impunity' (Jenkins, *Mrs Thatcher's Revolution*). Note, however, that small majorities are no absolute guarantee of party unity – particularly where party managers have failed to convince backbenchers of the political or economic necessity of an unpopular proposal. Hence the failure of the Conservative government in December 1994 to defeat an opposition motion condemning increased VAT on domestic fuel.

The voting and two party systems

The current voting system tends to give the party with the largest minority of the vote a secure majority of parliamentary seats. Thus for 41.9 per cent of the vote in the 1992 General Election, the Conservatives gained 51.6 per cent of the seats in the House of Commons. In 1997 Mr Blair's New Labour party was rewarded with 63.5 per cent (419) of the seats for just 43.2 per cent of the vote. In 2001 it secured 62.7 per cent (413) of the seats for 43 per cent of the vote. The voting system also mitigates against the growth of smaller political parties and the formation of coalitions. Sustained by a single party with a safe majority in Parliament, the Prime Minister's position is inevitably enhanced.

Media exposure

In recent times coverage of political events has increasingly tended to concentrate on personalities rather than on the details of party policy. In all of this the Prime

Minister is given the limelight. His or her activities and utterances on both the domestic and international scenes are brought into people's homes on a daily basis. More than any other politician, Prime Ministers have the opportunity to convey their views to the electorate and to project and develop an image which will enhance their popularity.

The effect of two World Wars

Some have argued that the central and crucial role played by Lloyd George in the First World War and Churchill in the Second World War enhanced the prestige and power of the office. Powers assumed during these crises were not all surrendered during peacetime. It is generally agreed that Mrs Thatcher became more dominant after the Falklands War and the successful general election campaign which followed it.

LIMITS ON PRIME MINISTERIAL POWER

The Cabinet

Despite the Prime Minister's pre-eminent position in relation to other ministers, insistence on policies not fully supported in Cabinet tends to result in dissent and dissatisfaction (often revealed by 'leaks') and, possibly, in ministerial resignations – all of which damage the image of both the government and the Prime Minister. Towards the end of her premiership, it is generally accepted that Mrs Thatcher's power-base within the Conservative party and her image nationally were seriously damaged by her policy differences with, and the eventual resignations of, Sir Geoffrey Howe (Leader of the House of Commons and previously Foreign Secretary and Chancellor of the Exchequer) and Nigel Lawson (Chancellor of the Exchequer).

As indicated, although the Prime Minister has the power to deal with ministerial opposition by 'sacking' members of the Cabinet, too many sackings may give the impression of a divided government. There is also the danger that 'sacked' ministers may become the focus of discontent on the backbenches.

From time to time the Cabinet may be able to persuade the Prime Minister to change his/her stance in relation to a particular issue. In 1969, for example, the Cabinet combined to force Harold Wilson to abandon plans to place additional legal restraints on the activities of trade unions. It has also been claimed that the pro-European element in Mrs Thatcher's Cabinet successfully persuaded her to take a less sceptical attitude towards membership of the European Monetary System and to the general question of entrusting further and greater powers to the European Community.

Parliament

Government defeats, or the withdrawal of proposals because of parliamentary opposition, tend to damage the credibility of the Prime Minister and may create suspicions that he or she is no longer in effective control of the nation's affairs, i.e. that the government has 'lost its way'.

In the final analysis, of course, governments and Prime Ministers may be put out of office by adverse confidence votes in the House of Commons. The Labour Prime

Minister (James Callaghan) and government were forced to resign in 1979 after losing a confidence motion by just one vote. Also note that in 1940, although a vote of no confidence in the Prime Minister's handling of the war was defeated (by eight votes), the then Conservative premier, Neville Chamberlain, still felt compelled to resign. The fact that 33 of his own MPs voted against him and 40 abstained demonstrated a widespread and cross-party absence of support.

The parliamentary party

Lord Palmerston (Prime Minister from 1855–58 and 1859–65) once said that the real opposition sat 'behind the Treasury bench'. Criticism from opposition MPs is to be expected. It is almost ritualistic and, in the normal course of events, does little to damage either Prime Minister or government. Dissent on the government's own benches, however, can be far more detrimental. Backbench 'revolts' undermine the Prime Minister's authority and may cause difficulties for implementation of the government's legislative programme. In late 1994, for example, John Major's embarrassment was considerable when Conservative backbenchers opposed a number of key government initiatives. Due to overt backbench disaffection the second reading of the Bill increasing the UK's European budgetary contribution was made a matter of confidence (i.e. the government said it would resign if defeated) and shortly afterwards, as already mentioned, the government was defeated by an opposition motion condemning its planned increase in VAT on domestic fuel (fifteen Conservative MPs failed to obey the party whip). In addition, persistent backbench unrest concerning the government's attitude towards the European Union did little to enhance Mr Major's standing.

As indicated above, the Prime Minister's power of patronage in relation to ministerial appointments is constrained by the need to preserve party unity. It is generally accepted that ministerial appointments should recognise the existence of different views and factions within the party. A prudent Prime Minister will seek, therefore, to choose a government around which all the party can unite. A government chosen purely from the Prime Minister's particular persuasion or faction would inevitably have to deal with dissent from those elements of the party aggrieved by their exclusion.

Party conferences

The extent to which MPs are affected or influenced by the votes and opinions of party conferences is a matter of some uncertainty. This is not usually a problem for Conservative premiers as the Conservative party conference has no policy-making powers. Conservative conferences seldom vote and usually try to avoid open controversy or criticism of the party leadership. It follows, however, that when dissent is shown, this is something which the leadership would be unwise to ignore. The position is rather different in the Labour party. According to the party's constitution, the leadership is bound by resolutions supported by at least two-thirds of conference delegates. Labour Prime Ministers, however, have tended to take the view that their first loyalty is to the national interest (whatever they may perceive that to be) and not just to the rather narrower sectional views of the party. Hence, both Harold Wilson and James Callaghan maintained Britain's nuclear deterrent despite conference resolutions supporting unilateral nuclear disarmament.

The Monarch

In strict constitutional terms the Monarch still reserves the residual prerogative right to dismiss the Prime Minister. The power has not been used since 1783. As a result of the unwritten nature of the British constitution, no other formal legal procedure exists for removing a Prime Minister from office (the rule that a Prime Minister must tender his/her resignation if defeated in a vote of confidence or at a general election being purely conventional requirement). This being so, the prerogative power of the Monarch remains the only legal remedy for dealing with a premier who ignores conventional restraints or who, in some other way, behaves unconstitutionally or in a manner seriously damaging to the national interest. It is conceivable, for example, that the Monarch might be forced to act should a Prime Minister refuse to resign after losing the confidence of a majority in the House of Commons. Clearly, however, it is a royal power which would have to be reserved for the most extreme circumstances.

> The power is said to survive for use if a government should act to destroy the democratic or parliamentary bases of the constitution. But unless the Sovereign's judgment of the necessity to dismiss her ministers on these ground should be generally supported by public opinion, the monarchy itself would be placed in jeopardy (Turpin, *British Government and the Constitution*).

The civil service

It has been suggested that those in the senior echelons of the civil service regard themselves as the custodians of certain traditional views and values concerning the British system of government and that such attitudes, coupled with civil service responsibility for the implementation of policy, may be used to thwart prime ministerial and Cabinet intentions – particularly where these are of a radical nature. Such covert opposition to government policy may manifest itself in a number of ways including, *inter alia*, delay (both in terms of action and the provision of necessary information), the organisation of resistance amongst and within the departments of state involved, and the leaking of information to the media. Mrs Thatcher, on a number of occasions, made clear her displeasure concerning alleged civil service resistance to some of her policy objectives. One example was her concern about the 'Whitehall' ethos in relation to cuts in public expenditure. She is also said to have suspected pro-European elements in various departments, but particularly in the Foreign Office, Ministry of Defence, and the Department of Trade and Industry. This may explain why Mrs Thatcher was accused of attempting to 'politicise' the civil service, i.e. insisting on the appointment and preferment of persons likely to be sympathetic to her particular perspective.

Interest groups

The standing of a Prime Minister may also be damaged by determined and widespread opposition from those representing major interests within society. In the long term, for example, Mrs Thatcher's reputation was not helped by criticism from churches and charities concerning some of the alleged social consequences of monetarist policies. Nor would the fortunes of any Conservative government be well served by opposition from any of those organisations traditionally regarded as supportive of Conservative ideology, e.g. the CBI, Institute of Directors, National Farmers' Union, etc. In the same vein, a Labour premier and government at odds with traditional bastions of Labour support would be unlikely to prosper. Industrial unrest and trade union agitation in the winter of 1978–79 ('the winter of discontent'), for example, is generally agreed to have been a significant factor in Labour's defeat in the 1979 General Election.

Leaks

These have become an increasingly common tactical device to embarrass the Prime Minister and government. They are used by ministers to generate opposition to policy proposals to which they are opposed but cannot criticise due to the convention of collective ministerial responsibility.

> The unattributable leak involves the disclosure of matters that are secret only because of the doctrine of collective responsibility – such as the subject of Cabinet discussion, Cabinet decisions, views assigned to different Ministers, and the like. The leak gives information known only by Ministers. The main motives for leaks…became the desire to inform – or mislead – their followers in the parliamentary party about the stand they had taken in the Cabinet on a particular issue. Thus the doctrine of collective responsibility and the unattributable leak grew up side by side as an inevitable feature of the Cabinet in a mass two-party system. In every Cabinet the leak will be deplored and condemned, but it is para-doxically necessary to the preservation of the doctrine of collective responsibility. It is the mechanism by which the doctrine of collective responsibility is reconciled with political reality. The unattributable leak itself is a recognition and acceptance of the doctrine that members of a Cabinet do not disagree in public (Walker, *The Cabinet*).

By-election defeats

Sometimes these may be put down to a government's mid-term unpopularity (a frequent but not necessarily unavoidable feature of modern British politics). However, a succession of defeats – particularly if these continue after the mid-term period – will tend to have a detrimental effect on the Prime Minister's domestic standing and may cause backbench concern about the Prime Minister's suitability to lead the governing party into the next general election. Mrs Thatcher's position was considerably weakened by by-election defeats in the autumn of 1990 (Eastbourne and Bradford). The Eastbourne defeat was particularly damaging as this had previously been regarded as an absolutely safe Conservative seat.

The Major government was also adversely affected by a series of by-election losses. These not only had consequences for Mr Major's image, but by 1996 had reduced his majority from 21 to just one.

Public opinion polls

These contain regular assessments of the extent of the Prime Minister's popularity and, notwithstanding doubts as to their accuracy, may (if consistently detrimental), help to destabilise his/her position. It has been alleged, for example, that public opinion polls create an electoral momentum of their own. Put another way, they help to mould public opinion rather than simply measure it. Thus, if such polls repeatedly tell the electorate that the Prime Minister is unpopular and not regarded as a competent leader capable of winning the next election, this may further diminish his/her standing and influence electors to vote for an alternative party and leader. Gloomy public opinion polls may also be factors in creating backbench unease – possibly resulting in a leadership challenge, particularly once a government has passed its mid-term point and MPs begin to concentrate on the spectre of the next election.

External political and economic pressures

National governments are no longer able to exercise such exclusive control over their domestic economic affairs as once was the case. Changes in US or German interest rates, for example, may have immediate and not necessarily beneficial consequences for the United Kingdom's economy. Rates of taxation, particularly VAT, may be affected by membership of the European Union. Decisions by OPEC affecting the price of oil may have 'knock-on' effects for costs and inflation. The economy in general may be damaged by world-wide depression. These are just a few examples but they clearly illustrate the sort of external forces which, although not directly of its own making, can diminish public confidence in an administration and its leader. Little wonder, then, that sheer good luck is said to be one of the factors which Prime Ministers must have if they are to survive.

THE CABINET

Composition

Appointment to and allocation of portfolios within the Cabinet is entirely within the grant of the Prime Minister. These days the Cabinet will usually consist of 20–25 ministers, but again this is a matter for the Prime Minister. The heads of the major departments will be included, as will the Leader of the House of Commons (responsible for expedition of government business in the House), the Lord Chancellor, the Leader of the House of Lords (responsible for government business in the upper House), the Chancellor of the Duchy of Lancaster (responsibilities determined by Prime Minister – sometimes party chairman in Conservative governments), and the Chief Secretary to the Treasury (Chancellor of the Exchequer's 'No 2').

Note that not all ministers will be members of the Cabinet. Within each department there will be a 'team' of ministers junior to the departmental head or Secretary of State. Next in order of seniority are Ministers of State and, beneath them, Under-Secretaries of State and parliamentary private secretaries. The total number of ministers in a government, therefore, may be well in excess of 100. Mrs Thatcher's last administration had 129 members. Only 95 ministers may have seats in the House of

Commons (House of Commons (Disqualification) Act 1975). This is to minimise exploitation of the 'pay-roll vote', i.e. the number of MPs bound by the convention of collective ministerial responsibility and, therefore, obliged to support the government.

Functions

According to the 1918 Haldane Committee on the Machinery of Government (Cmnd 9230) the Cabinet has three major responsibilities:

...the final determination of policy to be submitted to Parliament;

...the supreme control of the national executive in accordance with the policy prescribed by Parliament;

...the continuous co-ordination and delimitation of the interests of the several departments of state.

The final determination of policy

Clearly the majority of major decisions concerning the management of parliamentary and national affairs are considered within Cabinet. However, due to reasons of time, and the size and complexity of modern government, it is not possible for the Cabinet in twice-weekly meetings to give its full attention to all issues relating to the formation and implementation of policy and to the multifarious other matters with which the government must deal. Inevitably, therefore, other mechanisms and procedures have been developed to expedite the process of policy- and decision-making.

(a) Cabinet committees

Until 1992 the exact number, designation and composition of these was not made public. Mrs Thatcher reportedly had some 25 such standing committees and another 110 *ad hoc* working parties. In May 1992 premier Major allowed the existence and composition of these committees to be made known. They are usually chaired by a Cabinet minister and will consist of other ministers, mostly not of Cabinet rank, from those departments with an interest in a particular committee's area of responsibility. Most are permanent but *ad hoc* committees may be set up to deal with or oversee a particular problem.

Their principal functions are to co-ordinate the activities of the various departments of state, to formulate policy suggestions or proposed courses of executive action (or oversee the same) for Cabinet consideration, and to deal with and make recommendations related to any other matter referred to them.

In 1992 the principal Cabinet committees included: economic and domestic policy (chaired by Prime Minister); defence and overseas policy (Prime Minister); nuclear defence (Prime Minister); European security (Prime Minister); Northern Ireland (Prime Minister); science and technology (Prime Minister); intelligence services (Prime Minister); industrial, commercial and consumer affairs (Leader of the House of Lords); home and social affairs (Leader of the House of Lords); local government (Leader of the House of Commons); Queen's speech and future legislation (Leader of the House of Commons); legislation (Leader of the House of Commons); civil service (Leader of the House of Commons).

(b) Inner and partial cabinets

As already explained, the term 'partial cabinet' refers to a group of Cabinet ministers selected by the Prime Minister to direct and co-ordinate some aspect of government action, often in relation to a matter of urgency or where expedition is needed to deal with an immediate and serious threat to the national interest. Note, for example, such use by Mrs Thatcher during the Falklands War (1982) and the periodic convening of a group of senior ministers (the 'Star Chamber') to mediate in the annual public expenditure negotiations between the Treasury and the main spending departments.

Such informal ministerial groups can be used to thwart or obstruct the plans of particular ministers. For example, after the inner city riots of 1981 Michael Heseltine (Minister for the Environment) proposed a major spending programme to deal with inner city dereliction.

> Mrs Thatcher convened an informal ministerial group, with a majority of members chosen by the Prime Minister who would be unsympathetic to Mr Heseltine's proposals. The extra spending which was ultimately authorised was on nothing like the scale urged by Mr Heseltine (Brazier, *Constitutional Practice*).

The 'inner cabinet', also referred to above, consists of that small group of particularly trusted senior ministers, usually holding key Cabinet posts, to whom the Prime Minister may refer for advice and support on an informal and confidential level. Although outnumbered by the rest of the Cabinet, decisions and courses of action proposed by such powerful groupings are unlikely to be defeated when and if put before a Cabinet meeting.

It has been claimed, for example, that no full Cabinet discussion took place before Neville Chamberlain's decision to meet Hitler in Munich in 1938 ('peace in our time') and, similarly, that the full Cabinet was not party to the decision to invade Egypt in 1956 (Suez Crisis).

(c) Matters outside Cabinet control

It appears to be accepted that, due to their special nature, certain specific government responsibilities are not subject to direct Cabinet control. Such matters would appear to include:

- the power of prime ministerial patronage;
- the power to advise a dissolution;
- the prerogative of mercy (largely a matter for the Home Secretary but note suggestions that the political sensitivity sometimes attaching to decisions to commute sentences or pardon or release persons in custody is such that some level of ministerial discussion would appear appropriate);
- the formation of the Budget (although most ministers will have some awareness of general budgetary policy and intentions, the details of the entire package are largely a matter for the Chancellor and the Chief Secretary to the Treasury in consultation with the Prime Minister and, perhaps, those ministers directly affected

by a particular proposal – otherwise most members of the government receive notification of the Budget only hours before it is put before the House).

Control of the national executive

Although in strict constitutional theory this remains a primary function of the Cabinet, for practical reasons the degree of control which it is actually able to exercise over the extensive machinery of central government is somewhat limited.

It is not possible for a body of some twenty to twenty-five persons which meets only once or twice per week to be fully appraised of, or make decisions in relation to, all those concerns of the various government departments. More detailed consideration and supervision of departmental activity and policy tends to be undertaken by Cabinet committees and subcommittees and in negotiations between Prime Minister, Chancellor, Cabinet Secretary and individual ministers.

As the size of government increased in the twentieth century, doubts began to emerge concerning the validity of the theory that ministers 'control' their departments and that collectively, in Cabinet, they exercise effective authority over the entire central government bureaucracy. Indeed, in more recent times, arguments relating to the size and complexity of government appear to have affected executive interpretation of the convention of ministerial responsibility. Hence it is now not uncommon for ministers to plead that they should not be expected to take the blame for the actions and decisions of civil servants which they had not directly sanctioned or were not aware of. This type of sentiment was evident in ministerial submissions to the 1995 Scott Inquiry which dealt with the extent of government knowledge concerning arms sales to Iraq immediately prior to the Gulf War.

Such concerns about the effectiveness of Cabinet and ministerial control of government departments (and the civil servants within them), and the extent to which ministers are able to account to Parliament for what goes on within them, has led in recent times to the introduction of mechanisms for the more rigorous scrutiny of executive activity. These include the appointments of the Parliamentary Commissioner (1967) and the Health Service Commissioner (1974), the creation of the system of departmental parliamentary select committees, and the setting up of the National Audit Office (1983) to give assistance to the work of the Comptroller and Auditor General.

Continuous co-ordination of the several departments of state

To a considerable extent, in day-to-day practical terms, this is one of the primary functions of Cabinet committees and subcommittees. The process of co-ordination is also assisted by the work of the Cabinet Secretariat (see above).

From time to time Prime Ministers have attempted to improve the extent of co-ordination by restructuring the departmental composition of central government. Departments may disappear altogether with their functions being transferred elsewhere or may be amalgamated into single 'giant' departments with Ministers of State responsible for the previously separate areas of responsibility. Hence the Department of the Environment (established in 1971, now known as DEFRA) encompassed local government, housing and planning, all of which (at various times) had the responsibilities of separate ministries.

Reasons for Cabinet confidentiality

This is supported by a variety of political, conventional and legal rules. In the narrow party-political sense it is clearly something which helps to preserve an image of a united and focused administration. Or, to put it more bluntly, it helps to hide mistakes and deceit. It also underpins various public interests including the need for candour and plain-speaking in ministerial deliberations, and the obvious benefits of a certain amount of secrecy in relation to defence, counter-subversion and sensitive aspects of foreign policy.

The principal conventional rules operating in this context are, of course, those of collective and individual ministerial responsibility which force ministers to either 'close ranks' and give unreserved support to all government actions and decisions or to relinquish office through resignation or dismissal. When faced with this choice of job or conscience, the trend in recent times has been for ministers to remain in office. This is something of a compromise which enables particular policy preferences to be pursued from within and, of course, does less immediate damage to hopes of political advancement.

The legal rules of most obvious relevance in this context are those relating to the equitable doctrine of confidentiality and to the common law concept of public interest immunity. Both are dealt with in greater detail below.

At the moment, suffice to say that ministers (or ex-ministers) may be restrained from publishing information entrusted to them in the course of their ministerial responsibilities if this would damage the public interest in government confidentiality or adversely affect national security (*Attorney-General* v *Jonathan Cape*, above). The rules of public interest immunity prevent the use of Cabinet papers in legal proceedings except in very limited circumstances (*Burmah Oil Co Ltd* v *Bank of England* [1980] AC 1090).

Nevertheless, as explained above, ministerial 'leaks' have become an accepted part of the British political process, and the written and broadcast media regularly publish information which could only have been gained from a source within government. How, then, is it possible to reconcile the incidence of leaks with the existence of rules designed to preserve confidentiality? This may be possible if the leak is understood as a tempering expedient which infuses the conventional and legal rules with a degree of flexibility and political efficacy without which meaningful extra-parliamentary debate of controversial issues would be inhibited to a degree not entirely compatible with the norms of democracy. The ideal, therefore, is a balance which preserves the integrity and effectiveness of Cabinet government without imposing undue fetters on the day-to-day functioning of the political process.

References

Blake (1975) *The Office of Prime Minister*, Oxford: Oxford University Press.

Brazier (1994) *Constitutional Practice*, Oxford: Clarendon Press.

Coote (1969) *The Government We Deserve*, Eyre and Spottiswood.

Jenkins (1989) *Mrs Thatcher's Revolution: The Ending of the Socialist Era*, London: Jonathan Cape.

Turpin (2002) *British Government and the Constitution* (5th edn), London: Butterworths.

Walker (1970) *The Cabinet*, London: Jonathan Cape.

Wilson (1976) *The Governance of Britain*, London: Weidenfeld and Nicolson.

Further reading

Brazier (1994) *Constitutional Practice* (2nd edn), Oxford: Clarendon Press, Chs 2–6.

Hennessy (1986) *The Cabinet*, Oxford: Blackwell.

Jennings (1969) *Cabinet Government*, London: Cambridge University Press.

Turpin (2002) *British Government and the Constitution* (5th edn), London: Butterworths, Ch 3.

Wilson (1977) *A Prime Minister on Prime Ministers*, London: Weidenfeld & Nicolson.

Chapter 12

THE ROYAL PREROGATIVE

NATURE AND SIGNIFICANCE

Terminology

In discussing the royal prerogative it will be necessary to make frequent reference both to the Monarch and to the Crown. In common parlance these terms tend to be used interchangeably. For students of the constitution, however, this can lead to confusion as, for all practical political purposes, the two terms have significantly different meanings. Hence when reference is made to the Monarch this is usually understood to mean the person who, through the formal ceremony of coronation has, for the time being, been recognised as the titular head of state. The concept of the Crown is, however, not so limited, transient or personal and is generally used to describe the sum of central government departments and agencies, presided over by the Prime Minister and Cabinet, through which the nation's national and international affairs are conducted.

In the context of the royal prerogative, the significance of this distinction lies in the fact that a limited number of prerogatives are, in formal terms at least, still exercised by the Monarch in person (principally appointment of the Prime Minister and the summoning and dissolution of Parliament), while most of the remainder are exercised by the Crown according to its impersonal and institutional identity as just defined.

Some definitions

The term royal prerogative applies to those ancient powers and immunities – once exercised or influenced by the Monarch personally and thought to be a natural attribute of the Monarch's constitutional and political pre-eminence – which were left untouched by the conflicts and political restructuring which occurred during the seventeenth century.

In the late nineteenth century Dicey described the prerogative as follows:

> The prerogative appears to be historically and as a matter of fact nothing else than the residue of discretionary or arbitrary authority which at any given time is legally left in the hands of the Crown...From the time of the Norman Conquest down to the Revolution of 1688, the Crown possessed in reality many of the attributes of sovereignty. The prerogative is the name of the remaining portion of the Crown's original authority ...Every act which the executive government can lawfully do without the authority of an Act of Parliament is done in virtue of the prerogative (Dicey, *The Law of the Constitution*).

A century earlier, another frequently cited definition had been provided by the eminent judge and jurist, Sir William Blackstone:

> By the word prerogative we usually understand that special pre-eminence, which the King hath, over and above all other persons, and out of the ordinary course of common law, in right of his regal dignity...It can only be applied to those rights and capacities which the King enjoys alone, in contradiction to others and not to those which he enjoys in common with any of his subjects, for if once any prerogative of the Crown could be held in common with the subject, it would cease to be a prerogative any longer (*Commentaries on the Laws of England*).

These two definitions are not coterminous. The definition provided by Dicey is clearly, in two important respects, less specific and therefore potentially more generous in terms of the amount of executive power it permits. First, it appears to suggest that if the Crown takes an action for which it has no specific authority, it may be presumed to be acting under the prerogative. This being so, the precise content of the prerogative must remain beyond definition and, in its starkest terms, would appear to mean that the prerogative allows the Crown to do whatever it likes providing it does not act illegally (i.e. in ways forbidden by existing common law or statute). Second, and by definition, it appears to infer that the prerogative is not limited, as Blackstone proposed, to the special rights and immunities peculiar to the Crown, but also extends to all that which it may do in common with ordinary citizens, e.g. the making of contracts.

Source

The royal prerogative is part of the common law. It represents those powers which, over the centuries, the courts have recognised as attaching to and emanating from the Monarch. The prerogative is available for use, therefore, without any grant of parliamentary authority or approval.

Much of the legal authority for modern government is, of course, now provided in legislation. However, the significance of these common law or prerogative powers should not be underestimated. Nor is it difficult to find recent examples of the courts referring to the prerogative as the source of power for executive action – sometimes controversial – not authorised by statute. Hence, in 1984, when Mrs Thatcher decided that those employed at the government's intelligence gathering and communications headquarters at Cheltenham should be required to terminate their membership of trade unions and professional associations, the decision was said to be authorised by the prerogative in relation to the management and conduct of the civil service (*Council for Civil Service Unions v Minister for the Civil Service*, above). Shortly afterwards the Home Secretary's decision to supply police forces with CS gas and plastic bullets was also justified by reference to the prerogative – this time the miscellaneous and indeterminate array of powers contained within the power to keep the Queen's peace (*R v Home Secretary, ex parte Northumbria Police Authority* [1988] 2 WLR 590).

The prerogative and convention

The use of all the major prerogatives is thus now regulated by constitutional convention. Principal amongst these is the rule that the prerogative to appoint the Prime Minister must be exercised in favour of the person who commands a majority in the House of Commons. Those other prerogatives in which the Monarch is still personally involved – for example, the dissolution of Parliament – should then be exercised on his/her advice. Others – for example, the prerogative in foreign affairs and to maintain the Queen's peace – are exercised by the government ('the Crown') on the Monarch's behalf.

Importance

As already indicated, the prerogative – despite its ancient origins – remains an important source of governmental power. It extends, *inter alia*, to the conduct of foreign affairs (including the making of treaties and declaring war and peace), the power of patronage, command of the armed forces, the summoning and dissolving of Parliament, giving the Royal Assent to legislation and the prerogative of mercy. Clearly, without it the process of government would be unable to function effectively and many of those powers currently provided by the prerogative would have to exist in statutory form.

HISTORY

The King, the prerogative and Parliament

After the Norman Conquest an effective system of central government in England was established by William the Conqueror and his immediate successors. From this time onwards, as head of state and feudal lord, the Monarch exercised extensive political administrative and legal power. The king had the right to demand military service, to impose and receive revenues and taxes, to make law and to dispense justice as well as exercising all those other powers necessary to defend the realm and preserve the peace.

Even in Norman times, however, it was customary for the Monarch to exercise these powers in consultation with the Curia Regis (the king's council) rather than in an entirely autocratic fashion. Also, from the thirteenth century onwards, it became common practice for the Monarch, from time to time, to summon Parliaments which, in return for granting the additional revenues required by the king ('supply'), claimed the right to debate and criticise the Monarch's stewardship of the nation's affairs. It is generally accepted, therefore, that although extensive, the powers of English monarchs were never despotic.

In the sixteenth century, under the Tudors, English monarchy probably reached its zenith in terms of power and prestige. For all this, however, the Tudors – particularly Henry VIII and Elizabeth I – tended to govern through and with Parliament rather than in conflict with it.

In 1603 Elizabeth I was succeeded by the first of the Stuart kings, James I. The views of the Stuarts concerning, in particular, the divine right of kings and the sympathies of James' successors (principally Charles I and James II), for Roman Catholicism – with all that that implied for the established protestant church and England's relations with other protestant states of Europe – soon led to domestic discontent and unease. What followed was a century punctuated by conflict concerning the proper constitutional relationship and balance of power between Monarch and Parliament and the extent of the royal prerogative.

The attitudes of the courts

Many of the disputes concerning the extent of the prerogative produced litigation in which individuals challenged the validity of royal actions and decisions. In other cases questions concerning the remaining scope of prerogatives were referred to the judges for their opinions. As (in those days) the king had the power both to appoint and dismiss members of the judiciary, it was perhaps not surprising that these decisions and opinions often favoured the royal perspective. However, some judges – particularly Coke CJ during the reign of James I – were prepared to resist Stuart claims and, in a number of famous cases, attempted to impose parameters to the use and content of royal power.

Cases decided for the king

Case of Impositions (Bates' Case) (1606) 2 St Tr 371 (*Held* that the king could impose taxes in the form of customs duties without parliamentary consent where this was done not for the purpose of raising revenue *simpliciter* but for the regulation of trade, and that the court could not question the king's assertion that this was the purpose of his actions).

Case of Ship Money (R v Hampden) (1637) 3 St Tr 825 (*Held* that the king could tax in time of emergency, without parliamentary consent, for the purposes of defending the realm; in this case increasing the navy – note, however, the Crown's concession that, in times of peace, Parliament's consent would be necessary).

Darnel's Case (The Five Knights' Case) (1627) 3 St Tr 1 (*Held* that the writ of *habeas corpus* was not sufficient to secure the release of a person imprisoned under the prerogative for failure to pay tax imposed without parliamentary consent).

Godden v Hales (1686) 11 St Tr 1165 (*Held* that the prerogative empowered the king to suspend or dispense with the operation of penal laws, including those contained in statute, where this was believed to be necessary in the interests of the state – which belief could not be questioned by the courts).

Cases decided against the king

Prohibitions del Roy (1607) 12 Co Rep 63 (Coke CJ, supported by all the common law judges, declared that the king could no longer dispense justice personally and that this could only be done through and by his judges).

Case of Proclamations (1611) 12 Co Rep 74 (Coke CJ again, supported by three other senior judges – in response to a request for clarification from the king's council – declared that the king could no longer change any part of the common law, statute or custom or create new offences by royal proclamation).

The Civil War and the Glorious Revolution

Charles I (1625–49) was unable to reach any effective understanding with an increasingly restless Parliament concerning the amount of influence it should have over the direction of the nation's affairs. The rift was exacerbated by the fact that by this time the House of Commons was dominated by protestant fundamentalists or 'puritans' who were opposed not only to the King's style of government but also to the dogma and government of the established Anglican Church (i.e. the bishops) of which the King was the head.

Weary of obstruction and parliamentary criticism, Charles governed for eleven years (1629–40) without summoning Parliament at all. It was eventually recalled in 1640 when additional revenues were needed to deal with insurrection in Scotland. By now, however, the extent of its demands for reform of church and state were far beyond anything Charles was prepared to contemplate. In an attempt to reassert the authority of the monarchy he resorted to arms. The Civil War lasted from 1642 to 1647. Charles was defeated and executed in 1649. England then became, in effect, a republic. The dominant figure in its government was Oliver Cromwell, who was given the title Lord Protector. So long as he was alive and supported by the military, this radical alternative to monarchy remained viable. On his death, however, in 1658, and in the absence of any other revolutionary leader of similar stature, the country began to drift into disorder as the government lost much of its authority and sense of direction.

Order and stability were preserved by the restoration of the monarchy in 1660 (Charles II 1660–85). The country then passed through a relatively settled period until Charles II was succeeded by his brother James II in 1685. James was autocratic in style and a Roman Catholic. His attempts to place catholics in prominent positions in the army and the government caused immediate resentment. However, as both his daughters from his first marriage (Mary and Anne) were practising members of the established protestant church, it was felt that in the long term the protestant succession and existing constitution were probably secure. This prospect was removed, however, in 1688 when James' second wife gave birth to a son and catholic heir.

Events then gathered pace. In November 1688 the protestant Dutch prince, William of Orange – husband of Mary Stuart, James' eldest daughter – landed with an armed force on the south coast. His purpose, he claimed, was to preserve the existing constitution and established church, not to drive James from the throne. James was, however, forced to abdicate after parts of his army defected to William. Parliament then offered the throne to William and Mary as joint monarchs. This was done on the understanding that they would concede to the restrictions on royal power contained in the Bill of Rights, formulated by Parliament early in 1689.

The Bill of Rights 1689

This remains in force today and, as already indicated, is one of the founding documents of the British constitution. The principal objective of the Bill was not to remove all royal power and influence but to radically reduce the Monarch's capacity to act in contravention of the wishes of Parliament. The Bill provided that the Monarch could not tax, make law, or maintain a standing army in peacetime without parliamentary consent.

The Bill of Rights did not deal directly with the question of the Monarch's religious affiliation. This was left to the Act of Settlement 1700 which limited the succession to protestant heirs and expressly excluded Roman Catholics.

The demise of royal power

Nearly three centuries have passed since these dramatic events. Since then, however, the prerogative has remained largely intact. The most significant change has been the evolution of those constitutional conventions already described which have minimised the extent of the Monarch's personal involvement in its use.

The extension of the franchise in the nineteenth century began the process of genuinely democratising the British constitution. This was reflected by the emergence of the central convention that the government should be formed from the elected majority in the House of Commons and that a government unable to maintain that majority had lost the right to remain in office. Royal influence over the formation, tenure and composition of governments was, thereby, radically reduced. Autocratic royal use of the prerogative in such changed political circumstances could not have been reconciled with the emerging expectations of responsible and representative parliamentary government. That this was accepted by the British monarchy was instrumental in securing its survival. Henceforth, therefore, the use of the prerogative was to be a matter for the Crown in the form of the elected government rather than for the Monarch in person.

PRINCIPAL REMAINING PREROGATIVES

Introduction

The prerogative remains an extensive mixture of rights, powers, duties and immunities operating in all three spheres of government (executive, legislative and judicial). An exhaustive coverage of its entire content is beyond the scope of this book. The following classification will serve, however, to provide some appreciation of its remaining utility in the modern state.

Executive prerogatives

Patronage

Elevation to most senior positions in church and state, including ministerial and judicial appointments and those in the armed forces, are made in the name of the Sovereign – as are the granting of peerages and preferment of honours. By convention this is now done on the advice of the Prime Minister or other ministers (e.g. Lord Chancellor in the case of certain judicial offices). Certain honours, however, remain within the Sovereign's personal grant. These are the Order of the Garter, the Order of the Thistle, the Order of Merit and the Royal Victoria Order (for personal service to the Sovereign).

Command and deployment of the armed forces

The Sovereign is Commander-in-Chief of the armed forces. Although some matters relating to the same are regulated by statute (e.g. military discipline), the authority for decisions concerning the use and deployment of such forces is still derived from the prerogative and not from Act of Parliament. Such matters may be raised and criticised during the course of parliamentary debate but no prior parliamentary authority or subsequent ratification is necessary for the commitment of British forces. The prerogative is also the authority for decisions relating to military procurement and weaponry. Hence whether or not British forces are armed with the nuclear deterrent is a matter for Her Majesty's Government in the exercise of Her prerogative and not something done under the authority of legislation. Also, decisions in these matters will clearly and frequently be of a sensitive political and security nature and, as such, beyond the scope of judicial review.

> The disposition, armament and direction of the defence forces of the State are matters decided upon by the Crown and are within its jurisdiction as the executive power of State ... If the methods of arming the defence forces and the disposition of those forces are at the decision of Her Majesty's Ministers for the time being, as we know that they are, it is not within the competence of a court to try the issue whether it would be better for the country that that armament or those dispositions should be different (*Chandler* v *Director of Public Prosecutions* [1964] AC 763, per Viscount Radcliffe).

Keeping the Queen's peace

The Court of Appeal in *R* v *Home Secretary, ex parte Northumbria Policy Authority* (above), recognised the existence of an executive prerogative 'to take all reasonable steps to preserve the Queen's peace' (per Purchas LJ). Hence, as explained above, the Home Secretary was empowered – whether or not so authorised by statute – to supply police forces with CS gas and plastic bullets. This prerogative is also the source of the authority exercised by police officers to do all that is reasonably necessary to prevent breaches of the peace.

Defence of the realm and emergency powers

The House of Lords in *Burmah Oil* v *Lord Advocate* [1965] AC 75, concluded that the prerogative 'certainly covers doing all those things in an emergency which are necessary for the conduct of the war' (per Lord Reid). In most modern wars or emergencies, however, the state has usually armed itself with an extensive array of special statutory powers (e.g. Defence of the Realm Act 1914; Emergency Powers (Defence) Act 1939; Prevention of Terrorism Acts 1974–1996). As a result, resort to the emergency prerogatives has been limited and, in the absence of usage, some doubt has arisen as to the exact content of the Crown's remaining powers in this context. At various times the following powers have been claimed:

(a) the right to requisition and destroy property;
(b) the right to enter upon land and construct fortifications;

(c)   the right to demand personal service within the realm;
(d)   the right to intern aliens.

It has been suggested that, strictly speaking, the first two of these should not be classi-fied as prerogatives. This is based on the proposition that in a genuine emergency such actions would probably not be illegal if taken by a private citizen. If so, and adopting Blackstone's general definition, they may not belong to 'those rights and capacities which the King enjoys alone'.

The conduct of foreign and colonial affairs

Most of that which is done by the government in the execution of British foreign policy or for the maintenance of British interests abroad receives its legitimacy from the prerogative. More specifically, and principally, the prerogative in foreign affairs encompasses:

(a)   declaring war and peace;
(b)   making treaties;
(c)   recognition of foreign states and government;
(d)   sending and receiving diplomatic representatives;
(e)   annexation and cessation of territory.

Actions taken against foreign nationals or their property outside the UK in pur-suance of British foreign policy are known as Acts of State and as such are non-justi-ciable. This means that the injured party will not be given redress in an English court. 'An act of state is essentially an exercise of sovereign power and hence cannot be challenged, controlled or interfered with by municipal courts' (*Salaman v Secretary State for India* [1906] 1 KB 613, per Fletcher-Moulton LJ). Act of State is, therefore, a complete defence to actions for damages arising out of the enforcement of foreign policy by the forces of the Crown or its servants. Hence, in *Buron v Denman* [1842] 2 Ex 167, the destruction of a Spanish national's slave-trading station on the West coast of Africa by a British naval officer was not actionable as it was done in the execution of government instructions to suppress the slave trade.

Note that the defence applies only where the action is taken against a foreign national who is *outside* the UK, its dominions or dependencies. Hence the Crown has no defence if, although the action was taken overseas and in pursuance of foreign policy, it occurred inside British territory and/or against a British subject. Thus, in *Walker v Baird* [1892] AC 491, Act of State was not available as a defence in respect of the seizure of the plaintiff's lobster factory by the British navy. Although done in pursuance of a fisheries agreement with France, the plaintiff was a British subject and the lobster factory was situated in the British dominion territory of Newfoundland.

Nor may the Crown rely on this immunity in respect of actions taken against a for-eign national if he or she was in British territory. This was the decision in *Johnston v Pedlar* [1921] AC 262, where Act of State was found to be no defence to the seizure by Crown forces of personal property belonging to an American citizen while he was in Ireland. In legal terms the plaintiff was a friendly alien within the United Kingdom and it mattered not that he was believed to be sympathetic to forces opposed to the maintenance of British government in Ireland.

Although the courts cannot question an Act of State, they do claim the authority to decide whether a particular action by Crown forces or servants is entitled to be recognised as such. Hence, in *Nissan* v *Attorney-General* [1970] AC 179, the House of Lords felt that damage caused to the plaintiff's hotel in Cyprus by British troops billeted there as part of a peace-keeping force did not qualify. Trivial acts of vandalism, which had no conceivable or practical connection with the principal policy reason for the troops' presence in Cyprus, could not be elevated into acts of the prerogative from which the Crown was immune from all liability (note also that the plaintiff was a British subject).

The judicial reluctance to interfere with issues relating to foreign policy was clearly evident in the Court of Appeal's decision in *R* v *Foreign Secretary, ex parte Butt* 9 July 1999, Smith Bernal Casetrack, which dealt with an application for judicial review of the Foreign Secretary's alleged failure to take sufficiently strong diplomatic action to persuade the President of Yemen to intercede on the part of UK citizens charged with terrorist offences in his country. The court held that 'policy decisions relating to Her Majesty's Government's relationships with friendly foreign states under royal prerogative were non-justiciable' as 'foreign policy is pre-eminently an area for the government and not for the courts' (per Henry LJ).

Management and regulation of the civil service

As in relation to the armed forces, decisions in this context are still, in the main, made under the authority of the prerogative – this includes matters relating to civil servants' pay and conditions of service. It is generally accepted that civil servants are employed at the Crown's 'pleasure' and that the Crown has the prerogative to dismiss them at will without incurring any common law liability (e.g. for breach of contract). The Crown is, however, bound by the Employment Rights Act 1996 and therefore may be liable for unfair dismissal.

This prerogative was the authority for the controversial decision taken by Prime Minister Thatcher in denying employees at the government's communications centre at Cheltenham (GCHQ) the right to be members of trade unions or professional associations. On that occasion the PM acted under an Order in Council (Civil Service Order in Council 1982) made, not under any statutory power, but in the exercise of the prerogative – thus illustrating that the Crown retains certain primary law-making powers.

> The Order in Council was not issued under powers conferred by any Act of Parliament. Like the provisions in Orders in Council on the same subject it was issued by the sovereign by virtue of her prerogative, but of course on the advice of the government of the day (*Council of Civil Service Unions* v *Minister for Civil Service* [1985] AC 374, per Lord Fraser).

Legislative prerogatives

Summoning, proroguing and dissolving Parliament

Historically, monarchs summoned and dissolved parliaments as they saw fit. As explained above, the determination of Charles I to govern without Parliament, and his resentment of the criticisms made therein, was one of the principal causes of the Civil War in the seventeenth century. Towards the end of the Stuart period, the Meeting of Parliament Act 1694 provided that Parliament should be summoned at least once every three years. The present position is that the Monarch dissolves Parliament on the advice of the Prime Minister. The proclamation effecting the dissolution also specifies the date for the meeting of the new Parliament.

The prerogative of prorogation, also exercised on prime ministerial advice, is used to terminate each parliamentary session. The prorogation usually lasts for only a few days – usually from a Thursday in late November until the opening of the new session the following Tuesday or Wednesday.

The Royal Assent

The Royal Assent by Commission Act 1541 authorised the giving of the Royal Assent by commissioners appointed for that purpose. This is the usual practice. The Royal Assent was last given by the Monarch personally in 1854. It was last refused by Queen Anne in 1707 (Scottish Militia Bill). It is known that in 1913 George V contemplated and took advice concerning the constitutional propriety of refusing his assent to the Irish Home Rule Bill 1912, but eventually conceded that he was bound to act, i.e. to consent, as advised by the Prime Minister (Asquith). Notification that the assent has been given to particular Bills is given to the House by the Speaker (Royal Assent Act 1967).

Legislation does not bind the Crown

Acts of Parliament do not apply to or bind the Crown in any way unless a contrary intention is clearly stated or is necessarily implicit from the words used.

> The modern rule of construction of statutes is that the Crown, which today personifies the executive government of the country and is also a party to all legislation, is not bound by a statute which imposes obligations or restraints on persons or in respect of property, unless the statute says so expressly or by necessary implication (*BBC v Johns* [1965] Ch 32, per Lord Diplock).

Note, however, the opinion expressed in the Scottish courts in *Dumbarton District Council v Lord Advocate, The Times*, 18 March 1988, later overruled by the House of Lords (*Lord Advocate v Dumbarton District Council* [1990] 2 AC 580), that the Crown should be regarded as bound by legislation except where this might prejudicially affect the Crown's existing rights, privileges, immunities or interests. This was consistent with the comment in Hood Phillips (*op. cit.*):

> The question of whether the Crown is bound by statutes is a matter of interpretation, but there is a presumption in favour of the prerogative of immunity. The general rule is subject to criticism. It has been suggested that the presumption should be reversed by legislation so that the Crown would be bound by statute unless it was expressly declared not to be bound, or public policy required the exemption of the Crown in a particular case.

Judicial prerogatives

The administration of justice

Although justice is still dispensed in the Queen's name, it has long been accepted (at least since the *Prohibition del Roy* (1607) 12 Co Rep 63), that the Monarch may no longer participate personally in the exercise of judicial power. It is also generally accepted that the Monarch has no remaining prerogative to create new courts, particularly if these are to be involved in the application of statutory rules. It has been suggested, however, that the prerogative might still extend to the creation of courts or tribunals concerned purely with the interpretation of rules emanating from the common law or the prerogative. Some support for this may be derived from *R v Criminal Injuries Compensation Board, ex parte Lain* [1967] 2 QB 864, where the Court of Appeal assumed that the Commission, which had not been established under any statute, must have been created under, and its authority derived from, the royal prerogative.

The prerogative of mercy

The power is exercised by the Home Secretary. It extends to the granting of full or conditional pardons and to the reprieve or remission of sentences. A pardon removes all those 'pains, penalties and punishments' which have resulted from a conviction. It does not, however, extinguish the conviction itself. This can only be quashed by a court (*R v Foster* [1985] QB 115). A conditional pardon usually involves the substitution of a lesser form of punishment (e.g. life imprisonment for the death penalty). A reprieve or remission is effected by the reduction of the whole or part of the sentence but again does not expunge the original conviction.

Protecting the public interest

At any time, the Crown, acting through the Attorney-General, may commence legal proceedings for the general public benefit – usually to restrain illegalities which could damage the public interest. The power may be used, for example, to initiate proceedings against a public body or statutory undertaker which is believed to be abusing its powers. A private citizen may only bring civil proceedings in respect of such abuse if he or she has sufficient interest or legal standing (*locus standi*), i.e. the individual's interests have been particularly and detrimentally affected by the alleged abuse (see *Gouriet v Union of Post Office Workers* [1978] AC 435): 'the Crown always has standing for this purpose, whereas a private individual might be refused relief on the ground that he had no more interest in the matter than any other member of the public' (Wade and Forsyth, *Administrative Law*).

Frequently the Attorney-General will become involved in such proceedings at the instigation or 'relation' of an individual who may lack sufficient standing to bring proceedings in his or her own name. This is known as a relator action. In practice, the case is brought and conducted by the concerned individual but the Attorney-General's consent and the lending of his or her name to the proceeding removes any problems of standing (see *Attorney-General, ex relator McWhirter v IBA* [1973] QB 629).

The prerogative also empowers the Attorney-General to discontinue indictable proceedings by entering a plea of *nolle prosequi* (to be unwilling to prosecute).

THE PREROGATIVE AND STATUTE

Since statute has supreme legal force and the prerogative is part of the common law, it is axiomatic that Parliament may abolish or modify the prerogative by express words or 'necessary intendment' (*De Morgan* v *Director General of Social Welfare* [1998] 2 WLR 427).

Where statute and the prerogative are coterminous or deal with the same subject matter – e.g. both provide a power to requisition property – the general principle is that the prerogative goes into abeyance. Therefore, the Crown is bound to use the power provided by Parliament.

This was established in *Attorney-General* v *De Keyser's Royal Hotel* [1920] AC 508. The Crown had requisitioned the plaintiff's hotel for use by the Royal Flying Corps during the First World War. After the war the plaintiff sued for compensation. A statutory power to requisition property had been provided by the Defence of the Realm Act 1914. The Act gave those affected a right to claim compensation. The Crown argued, however, that in requisitioning the hotel it had merely been exercising its prerogative for the defence of the realm and that it had not sought to use the power in the 1914 Act. Had the court accepted this, the plaintiff's action would have failed as it had never been established that the Crown was obliged to provide recompense for property requisitioned under the prerogative.

The House of Lords, however, was not prepared to accept that the Crown could 'pick and choose' a statutory or prerogative power depending on which one put it in the most advantageous position *vis-à-vis* the rights of the individual. What was to become known subsequently as the '*De Keyser's* principle' was summed up by Lord Atkinson:

> ...when such a statute, expressing the will and intention of the King and of the three estates of the realm, is passed, it abridges the royal prerogative while it is in force to this extent: that the Crown can only do the particular thing under and in accordance with the statutory provisions and that the prerogative power to do that thing is in abeyance.

More recent authority has suggested that the principle as thus articulated may be subject to the qualification that if the prerogative in question gives the citizen some positive benefit or protection it does not go into abeyance unless this is the clear intention of the statute with which the prerogative coincides.

In *R* v *Home Secretary, ex parte Northumbria Police Authority* (above), the Home Secretary decided to use the prerogative to maintain the Queen's peace to supply the police with CS gas and plastic bullets. In an application for judicial review it was argued that the power to decide how to equip police forces had been entrusted to individual police authorities by the Police Act 1964. Hence, by virtue of the *De Keyser's* principle, any ancient prerogative to do this had been displaced.

The judgment of Purchas LJ contained the proposed limitation to the *De Keyser's* principle mentioned above.

> Where the executive action is directed towards the benefit or protection of the individual, it is unlikely that its use will attract the intervention of the courts. In my judgment before

the courts will hold that such executive action is contrary to legislation, express and unequivocal terms must be found in the statute which deprive the individual from receiving the benefit or protection intended by the exercise of executive power.

Since no such 'unequivocal' terms could be found in the 1964 Act, the court assumed that it could not have been Parliament's intention to put the prerogative into abeyance.

If a statute which has put a prerogative into abeyance is eventually repealed, the restriction on the use of the prerogative is thereby removed. Being no longer in abeyance or a state of suspension, the particular prerogative may be resorted to once again. It has been suggested, however, that this should not apply in the case of minor prerogatives which are no longer necessary for the practice of effective modern government.

It is implicit in what has been said that the prerogative must not be used to thwart the exercise of a statutory power. Despite its importance, the prerogative is not something which the executive may use to avoid the wishes of Parliament (*Laker Airways v Department of Trade* [1977] QB 643). This was made abundantly clear by the House of Lords in *R v Home Secretary, ex parte Fire Brigades Union* [1995] 2 All ER 244. This concerned the criminal injuries compensation scheme which had been established in 1964 using powers contained in the royal prerogative (see above, judicial prerogatives). Nearly a quarter of a century later it was decided to put the scheme into statutory form. The necessary authority was provided by the Criminal Justice Act 1988. The Act provided that the relevant sections were to be brought into effect on a day appointed by the Home Secretary (s 171). Five years later, when this had still not been done, the minister decided to make changes to the original scheme which, it was believed, was proving too expensive. These changes were again to be effected under the authority of the royal prerogative.

Following an application for judicial review of the Home Secretary's actions, the House of Lords made the following findings.

(a) Where an Act of Parliament allows a minister a discretion as to when its provisions should come into operation, this does not permit the minister to decide that the Act, or any such provisions, should not take effect at all. It simply gives the minister the freedom to determine when the time is right, perhaps in terms of the availability of resources and facilities, for effective implementation of the legislation in issue.

(b) In the period after a statute has been enacted and before its coming into effect, it is not lawful for the minister to use the prerogative in a way which obviates the need for the statute to be implemented. It is for Parliament to repeal legislation and not the government under the royal prerogative.

THE PREROGATIVE AND THE COURTS

Limited judicial control

Reference has already been made to Coke CJ's assertion in the *Case of Proclamation* (1611) that the 'king hath no prerogative but what the law of the land allows'. This established the basic principle that it is for the courts and the courts alone to determine the powers contained within the prerogative. The courts have also long claimed the authority to determine the scope or limits of the prerogatives so identified. These principles made it clear that the judiciary was not prepared to allow the Crown to be the final arbiter as to the content and extent of its common law powers of government.

This was well illustrated by the decision in *Burmah Oil v Lord Advocate* (above). During the Second World War the plaintiff's oil installations in Rangoon had been destroyed by British forces as they evacuated the city and retreated from the Japanese. After the war the plaintiff claimed compensation. The Crown argued that its prerogative right to destroy property in time of war for the defence of the realm was not qualified by any liability to provide financial reparation. This argument was not accepted by the House of Lords. In its view the Crown was only exempt from paying compensation where the damage was done during the course of a battle ('battle damage'). No such exemption applied, however, where the property had been destroyed purely to prevent it falling into enemy hands ('denial damage').

However, until the watershed decision in the *GCHQ* case, such delineation of the content and scope of the prerogative was believed to represent the full extent of judicial authority in this context. The courts were not prepared, therefore, to review or question the prerogative's mode of exercise. The common law rules devised for judicial supervision of statutory powers (contained in the *Wednesbury* principles and the rules of natural justice) did not apply, therefore, to the use of the prerogative. The resulting position appeared somewhat incongruous. An individual aggrieved by alleged government abuse of a statutory power could apply for judicial review and perhaps have the offending decision overturned. If, however, the complaint related to the manner of use of a prerogative, then no such redress was available.

Hence in *Gouriet v Attorney-General*, above, the Court of Appeal (Lord Denning MR dissenting) felt that it was unable to question the decision of the then Labour Attorney-General not to commence legal proceedings to prevent what appeared to be illegal industrial action by the Post Office Workers Union. The allegation that the Attorney had reneged on his duty to protect the public interest for purely party-political interests (i.e. a desire not to antagonise the Trade Unions) was not something on which the court was prepared to comment. The Attorney-General had exercised a prerogative power and the propriety of his actions was not susceptible, therefore, to judicial inquiry.

Such refusal to inquire into the prerogative's mode of exercise reflected a deeply ingrained judicial deference towards the Monarch which continued to influence English law long after the revolutionary settlement of the late seventeenth century. The assumption was that, although the king was bound by law, he had to be trusted to act according to it (*Darnel's Case* (1627) 3 St Tr 1). Therefore, it was not for those subordinates to whom his judicial power had been entrusted to use that power against its source. The problem was, however, that this judicial temerity towards the prerogative continued in existence long after the Monarch had ceased to have any genuine influence over its use. As a result a whole range of powers now exercised by the government 'on the Monarch's behalf' remained exempt from judicial control – a state of affairs hardly consistent with some of the principal imperatives of Dicey's version of the rule of law.

Indications of a growing judicial awareness of what was becoming an increasingly anomalous and anachronistic state of affairs at last began to emerge in the 1970s. In particular, the then Master of the Rolls, Lord Denning, urged a change of approach.

Seeing that the prerogative is a discretionary power to be exercised for the public good, it follows that its exercise can be examined by the courts just as any other discretionary power that is vested in the executive (*Laker Airways* v *Department of Trade*, above).

GCHQ: Judicial control extended

These sentiments were finally given effect by the House of Lords in *Council of Civil Service Unions* v *Minister for the Civil Service*, above, on this occasion the view being that henceforth the way in which a particular prerogative had been used should be regarded as reviewable providing the power in issue could be treated as 'justiciable' or 'amenable to the judicial process'. In effect, this means that, henceforth, the courts could entertain challenges to the exercise of those prerogatives which do not relate to matters of 'high state policy' or to other matters so politically sensitive or contentious as to be outside the proper sphere of judicial inquiry: 'The courts are not the proper place wherein to determine whether a treaty should be concluded or the armed forces disposed in a particular manner or Parliament dissolved on one day rather than another' (per Lord Roskill). For the sake of greater clarification Lord Roskill went on to provide a list of those particular prerogatives which were to be regarded as 'non-justiciable'. These were the making of treaties, the defence of the realm, the prerogative of mercy, the grant of honours, the dissolution of Parliament and the appointment of ministers.

That the treaty-making power was unsuitable for review was confirmed shortly afterwards in *ex parte Molyneaux* [1986] 1 WLR 331, where the court felt unable to question the validity of the 1985 Anglo-Irish Agreement, and later in *R* v *Secretary of State for Foreign and Commonwealth Affairs, ex parte Lord Rees-Mogg* [1994] 1 All ER 457, in which the court declined any jurisdiction to question the government's decision to ratify the 1992 Treaty on European Union.

The reviewable prerogatives

Cases subsequent to *GCHQ* have made clear that the justiciable or reviewable prerogatives are those which have minimal political or policy content and which tend to be concerned with the regulation of individual rights, interests or legitimate expectations. The following are the prerogatives which, to date, have been held to be amenable to the judicial process.
(a) The refusal of a passport (*R* v *Secretary of State for Foreign and Commonwealth Affairs, ex parte Everett* [1989] QB 811).
(b) The regulation and management of the civil service (*Council for Civil Service Unions* v *Minister for the Civil Service*, above).
(c) The issuing of warrants to 'tap' telephones (*R* v *Home Secretary, ex parte Ruddock* [1987] 1 WLR 1482). This is now done under the authority of the Interception of Telecommunications Act 1985 and not under the prerogative.
(d) The Home Secretary's residual common-law powers in the sphere of immigration, including the power to expel friendly aliens (*R* v *Home Secretary, ex parte Beedassee* [1989] COD 525).

(e) The power to make *ex gratia* payment for criminal injuries compensation (*R v Criminal Injuries Compensation Board, ex parte Lain* [1967] 2 QB 864).

(f) The prerogative of mercy (*R v Home Secretary, ex parte Bentley* [1993] 4 All ER 442; *R (on the application of B) v Home Secretary* [2002] EWHC Admin 587).

The *Bentley* decision was concerned with one of the prerogatives said to be non-justiciable in *GCHQ*. However, given that those statutory powers relating to the administration of other aspects of the penal system raising similar types of policy issues (e.g. the granting of parole) had already been classified as review-able, the Divisional Court could see no good reason for treating the prerogative of mercy any differently.

The refusal of the court in *Bentley* to regard Lord Roskill's list as sacrosanct does not mean that it is only a matter of time before the power of review is extended to all the other prerogatives contained therein. Most of the decision-making powers referred to, e.g. the timing of a dissolution of Parliament, are so obviously political in nature as to remain entirely unsuitable for regulation by judge-made law – particularly in a constitutional framework founded, *inter alia*, on the belief that judges should leave the conduct of politics to the politicians.

(g) Exclusions of members from the armed forces where this is done primarily in the interests of maintaining good order and discipline and not for reasons of national security *simpliciter* (*R v Ministry of Defence, ex parte Smith* [1996] All ER 257).

References

Blackstone (1873) *Commentaries on the Laws of England*, London: Macmillan.

Dicey (1959) *An Introduction to the Law of the Constitution* (10th edn), ed. Wade, E.C.S., London: Macmillan.

Hood Phillips and Jackson (1997) *Hood Phillips and Jackson's Constitutional and Administrative Law* (8th edn), London: Sweet & Maxwell.

Wade and Forsyth (1994) *Administrative Law* (7th edn), Oxford: Clarendon Press.

Further reading

De Smith and Brazier (1994) *Constitutional and Administrative Law* (7th edn), London: Penguin, Chs 6 and 7.

Hood Phillips and Jackson (1997) *Hood Phillips and Jackson's Constitutional and Administrative Law* (8th edn), London: Sweet & Maxwell.

Loveland (1996) *Constitutional Law: A Critical Introduction*, London: Butterworths, Ch 4.

Monro (1987) *Studies in Constitutional Law*, London: Butterworths, Ch 8.

Chapter 13

CROWN PROCEEDINGS AND THE LEGAL LIABILITY OF THE CROWN AND PUBLIC AUTHORITIES

INTRODUCTION: THE LAW BEFORE THE CROWN PROCEEDINGS ACT 1947

The Crown's protected legal status

For many centuries it has been accepted that the Monarch in his or her personal capacity is completely immune from civil or criminal proceedings. This facet of the constitution found expression in such ancient legal maxims and principles as 'the King can do no wrong' and 'the King cannot be sued in his own courts'. Unfortunately, however, as the distinction between the Monarch in his or her personal and public capacities – i.e. between the Monarch and the Crown as the central government – became increasingly apparent, neither Parliament nor the courts changed the law accordingly. As a result, many of the immunities and privileges designed originally to protect the dignity and status of the person of Monarch became attached to the Crown as an institution. This meant that the ordinary private law dealings of the Crown with its subjects (e.g. in contract and tort) were not regulated solely by the generally applicable rules and procedures, but were subject to a set of principles – highly disadvantageous to the private litigant – designed for a political order which had ceased to exist.

The position remained the same until the Crown Proceedings Act 1947. By this time, of course, the Crown had become a major employer and contractor. The likelihood of other organisations or individuals having grievances against the Crown and wishing to seek legal redress was thus greatly increased. In such circumstances the Crown's special and protected legal position represented a major weakness in the British constitution. Once again, ancient legal principles had been allowed to survive into an age in which they had no practical relevance. The legal relationship between the Crown and its 'subjects' was thus clearly inconsistent with the rule of law and contained an obvious potential for injustice.

It should be conceded, however, that, even before the 1947 Act, attempts had been made to remedy this situation and to provide aggrieved citizens with ways of raising the Crown's alleged wrongdoings in the courts. These devices are explained under the subheadings immediately below. Reference should also be made to the long-established general principles that all persons, including Crown servants, are personally responsible for their own actions and that English law recognises no general doctrine of executive necessity nor the defence of superior orders. Hence it is, and was, not

open to a Crown servant to avoid the legal consequences of an unlawful act by pleading that it was done to protect some pressing state interest or in obedience to orders
from above. The Crown's immunities, therefore, did not attach to its servants but 'it
might however offer little satisfaction to an injured plaintiff to obtain judgement
against a penniless inferior, even a Minister of the Crown' (Calvert, *An Introduction
to British Constitutional Law*).

Liability in contract and the petition of right

Since the Crown is an institution, it can only make contracts through its servants.
According to the normal laws of agency this would have meant that – in respect of
contracts made on its behalf – liability for breach would have rested with the Crown,
as principal, and not with the individual Crown servant through whom the agreement
had been completed. Prior to 1948, however (when the 1947 Act took effect), the
strict legal position was that an aggrieved individual could not sue the Crown in contract *as of right*.

In order to proceed it was necessary for the individual to petition the Crown
through the Attorney-General (the Crown's senior law officer) for permission to pursue a judgment in the courts. The exact procedure was regulated by the Petition of
Right Act 1860 which simplified the pre-existing procedural rules. In effect, therefore,
the process involved the Crown voluntarily submitting itself to the jurisdiction of the
courts. However, as in any normal case permission was unlikely to be refused, so the
procedure did provide a generally effective means of seeking contractual redress
against government departments and agencies. In the case of a successful litigant, the
judgment took the form of a declaration of the contractual rights to which that individual was entitled. Although not legally enforceable by the individual against the
Crown, the latter would normally comply.

Liability in tort and the nominated defendant

Here the position of the aggrieved citizen was rather less satisfactory. No procedure
similar to the Petition of Right operated. As a result the Crown could not be sued
directly in tort nor could it be held vicariously liable for the torts of its employees.
Proceedings could, of course, be taken against the individual Crown employee and
tortfeasor but, for financial reasons – particularly in terms of recovering damages –
this might not have been particularly satisfactory for the person seeking redress. 'It is
beyond doubt that no claim in tort will lie against the Crown in respect of a wrongful
act done by its servants in the performance or approved performance of their duties'
(per Lord Thankerton, *Viscount Canterbury* v *Attorney-General* (1843) 1 Phillips 306;
12 LJ Ch 281).

To alleviate and circumvent the obvious injustice this immunity produced, two practices were evolved. The first of these involved the Crown 'standing behind' the individual Crown servant alleged to have committed a tort in the course of his/her
employment. This meant that if he or she were found liable the Crown would pay the
damages awarded to the plaintiff. Where, however, the particular employee allegedly
responsible for the tortious act was not identifiable, the practice was for the Crown to

nominate some other employee thought to be appropriate to act as the defendant. This would usually be a person with managerial or other responsibilities relating to the particular government activity in the course of which the act complained of was committed. The action would then proceed against such 'nominated defendant' on the fictional basis that they were, or had been, personally involved in the events which gave rise to the grievance. In reality the court would be concerned to discover whether a tortious act had been committed for which the Crown would have been responsible had the normal roles of vicarious liability been applicable. If so, the nominated defendant would be found liable and the damages, if awarded, paid by the Crown.

However, in respect of the Crown, this procedure provided no remedy where the liability of the employer, either under common law or statute, was direct rather than vicarious – e.g. as an occupier of property or under the Factories Acts. For this reason – and because in two well-known cases the courts decided that, henceforth, they would no longer entertain proceedings in which the defendant's role was purely fictional – parliamentary intervention became inevitable.

The first of these cases was *Adams* v *Naylor* [1946] AC 543. The case arose out of injuries caused to two boys who strayed into a wartime minefield with inadequate fencing and warning notices. An officer in the Royal Engineers was nominated to act as the defendant. It was not contended that he was personally responsible for the state of affairs which led to the injuries. In the event, the case was decided on the basis that liability for this type of injury had been excluded by the Personal Injuries (Emergency Provisions) Act 1939. However, the House of Lords expressed serious reservations about the practice of nominating defendants where no real 'culprit' could be found:

> The courts before whom such a case as this comes have to decide it as between the parties before them and have nothing to do with the fact that the Crown stands behind the defendant. For the plaintiffs to succeed...they must show that the defendant himself owes a duty of care to the plaintiff and has failed in discharging that duty (per Viscount Simon).

It was also made clear that, even without the statutory bar, the action would still have failed. The tort in issue was that of occupiers' liability at common law and, since the occupier of the land in question was the Crown, liability could not be imposed on any other defendant, fictional or otherwise.

Subsequently, in *Royster* v *Cavey* [1947] 1 KB 204, the Court of Appeal refused to impose liability for negligence and breach of statutory duty on the superintendent of an ordnance factory (a Crown employee) who was the nominated defendant in proceedings brought by an employee injured at work. The defendant had not been superintendent of the factory when the accident occurred. Also the Factories Act 1937, which imposed the duty in question, applied to employers only and could not, therefore, have imposed any liability on the defendant who, as stated, was himself also a Crown employee.

THE CROWN PROCEEDINGS ACT 1947

General objectives

Parliament's response to these difficulties was the passage of the 1947 Act. This removed many of the Crown's pre-existing immunities and, subject to a number of exceptions explained below, enabled proceedings in contract and tort to be brought against the Crown in the normal way. It would appear, however, that the Act applies only to wrongs committed in the course of the government of the United Kingdom (s 40). As a result, and providing a ministerial certificate is issued to this effect, the Crown's immunities in respect of actions committed in other contexts remain in place (*Trawnik* v *Lennox* [1985] 1 WLR 532).

Actions in contract

Section 1 of the Act provided:

> Where any person has a claim against the Crown...and, if this Act had not been passed, the claim might have been enforced, subject to His Majesty's fiat, by petition of right...then, subject to the provisions of this Act, the claim may be enforced as of right...

In effect this meant that thereafter, and subject to certain remaining exceptions and immunities, the Crown could be sued in contract in the normal way.

The old Petition of Right procedure was thereby abolished and the Crown thus bound by law to submit itself to the relevant jurisdiction of the courts.

It was not, however, the 1947 Act's intention to put the Crown in exactly the same position in terms of its contractual capacity as that of a private individual. There remained circumstances in which the public interest might still not be best served by holding the Crown or government to all its contractual obligations. These public policy exceptions to the Crown's capacity in contract had already been recognised by the law developed under the old Petition of Right procedure. Therefore, by providing that litigants could sue 'as of right' only in circumstances where an action could have been pursued under a Petition of Right, the Act made clear Parliament's intent that these pre-existing exceptions, considered below, should continue to operate in the Crown's favour.

Contracts that fetter future executive action

In *Rederiaktiebolaget Amphitrite* v *R* [1921] 3 KB 500, the owners of a Swedish ship brought a Petition of Right for breach of contract and damages after it had been detained in a British port in breach of an undertaking given by the government. The incident occurred during the First World War when all 'foreign' ships required official clearance before being allowed to leave the United Kingdom. The owners had been given an assurance that the necessary clearance would be given if the ship brought a certain type of cargo to this country.

The action was rejected for the following reasons:

> it is not competent for the government to fetter its future executive action, which must necessarily be determined by the needs of the community when the question arises. It cannot by contract hamper its freedom of action in matters which concern the welfare of the state (per Rowlatt J).

A similar approach was taken to a contractual fetter on emergency legislative powers entrusted to the Crown in World War II. Hence, in *Crown Lands Commissioners* v *Page* [1960] 2 QB 274, it was held that the Crown was entitled to requisition land which it had previously leased to the complainant if it was of the opinion that the land was needed for the purposes of defending the realm.

> When the Crown, or any other person, is entrusted by virtue of the prerogative or statute, with discretionary power to be exercised for the public good, it does not, when making a private contract...undertake...to fetter itself in the use of those powers, and in the exercise of its discretion.

This doctrine recognised that the Crown's contractual obligations may sometimes be inconsistent with its prerogative to protect the public interest. However, the notion that the Crown may not fetter its future executive action is both vague and problematical. Taken literally it could be understood to mean that the Crown may avoid any contract it chooses, since any agreement it has entered into will perforce have limited its freedom of action to the extent of the obligations thereby incurred.

This, presumably, is not what was intended when the *Amphitrite* case was decided – otherwise persons and organisations might be discouraged from contracting with the Crown, particularly if large sums of money were involved. This, in turn, might prejudice the Crown's efficiency by affecting its ability to acquire the goods and services needed to perform its functions. It is generally accepted that the *Amphitrite* rule does not apply to the Crown's ordinary commercial transactions and may only give exemption from liability where the demands of the public interest are both immediate and substantial.

An alternative view is that the case was wrongly decided and that the only immunity the Crown requires in order to satisfy the public interest is immunity from the remedies of specific performance and injunction (i.e. those which would hold the Crown to fulfil a contract) – but that the Crown should always be liable to pay damages where a contractual obligation was sacrificed for public interest reasons.

> The liability to pay damages would not prevent the Crown from taking action which was required in the public interest; it would simply require the Crown to pay the true cost of the action taken. In order to preserve its freedom of action, only one immunity is needed by the Crown, and that is immunity from the remedies of specific performance and injunction (Hogg, *Liability of the Crown*).

If accepted in future cases this would mean that legal remedies would not be available to hold the Crown to a contractual undertaking if this would be damaging to the public interest, but would allow the other contracting parties to secure financial reparation in respect of the breach. In this way both the public and private interests would be protected.

The *Amphitrite* rule is analogous to the rule that public authorities in general are not bound by contracts which fetter the exercise of their statutory powers. Such powers having been given for the protection of the public interest, it is axiomatic that no contractual or other limits should be imposed on the full extent of the discretion which Parliament has conferred for that purpose.

The application of this principle was well illustrated by the decision in *William Cory and Son v London Corporation* [1951] 2 KB 476. The plaintiffs entered into a contract with the Corporation to ship sewage down the Thames for disposal at sea. The contract imposed certain obligations in terms of the way the sewage was to be covered and contained during shipment. Some years later, and while the contract was still in operation, the Corporation introduced new by-laws which laid down even stricter requirements for the carriage of sewage by barge. The plaintiffs sought rescission of the contract and argued that it contained an implied term that the authority would not use its powers in ways inconsistent with its contractual obligations. The Court of Appeal held that the Corporation, as a public authority, was not competent to enter into agreements which fettered the future exercise of its legislative powers. When making by-laws it was bound, therefore, to regard the protection of the public interest as the paramount and overriding consideration.

The rule in Churchward's case

Where a contract states expressly or by necessary implication that Parliament is to provide the sum of money required by the Crown to enable it to perform the obligations imposed thereby, but Parliament refuses to supply those moneys, the contract becomes unenforceable. Parliamentary supply of the sum stipulated operates, therefore, as a condition precedent to the contract's effectiveness.

This principle is generally believed to be derived from the decision in *Churchward* v *R* (1865) LR 1 QB 173. The plaintiff entered into a contract with the Crown to carry mail to France. The contract stipulated expressly that he was to be paid out of moneys voted by Parliament for this specific purpose. When the contract had been in operation for some time, Parliament voted not to supply further sums for its continued performance. This was held to have rendered the contract to be unenforceable.

This does not mean, however, that to be effective, every contract made by the Crown has to be supported by a specific and related grant of money by Parliament. Indeed, in the course of conducting its normal commercial business, it is most unusual for the Crown, when making a contract, to stipulate that its performance will be paid for and is therefore dependent on parliamentary supply of the sum involved. This would, of course, be wholly impractical. Therefore, when a contract entered into with the Crown makes no reference to the supply of moneys by Parliament, it is generally accepted that the Crown is obliged to pay for the performance of its obligations out of those general sums of money voted annually by Parliament to each government department. In such cases 'the prior provision of funds by Parliament is not a condition preliminary to the obligation of the contract' (*New South Wales* v *Bardolph* (1934) 52 CLR 455).

In the extremely unlikely circumstances that such moneys were inadequate to pay for a contract when it fell due, the probability is that the court would regard the contract as unenforceable. In financial terms the Crown can only do that which it has been enabled to do by Parliament. The enforcement of contracts outside the Crown's financial capacity would, therefore, be inconsistent with this principle.

The Crown and its employees

The Crown may not be sued in contract in respect of the summary dismissal of a civil servant. Civil servants hold office at the Crown's pleasure and their services may be dispensed with as and when the Crown sees fit: 'Such employment being for the public good, it is essential for the public good that it should be capable of being determined at the pleasure of the Crown...' (per Lord Herschell, *Dunn* v *R* [1896] QB 116).

Note, however, that civil servants may bring proceedings in respect of alleged unfair dismissal under the modern employment protection legislation. This is, however, a statutory and not a common law remedy (see the Employment Rights Act 1996, s 191).

At one time the existence of a power to dismiss at pleasure was, in some quarters, taken to mean that civil servants did not have any sort of contact with the Crown whatsoever and, therefore, could not sue in respect of other types of dispute arising out of their relationship with their employer (see *Lucas v Lucas and High Commissioner for India* [1943] P 68).

The case law was, however, uncertain. Other decisions suggested that the existence of a power to dismiss at pleasure was not necessarily inconsistent with the existence of a contractual relationship and that aggrieved civil servants should at least be able to recover arrears of pay (see *Sutton v Attorney-General* (1923) 39 TLR 294; *Terrell v Secretary of State for the Colonies* [1953] 2 QB 482; *Kodeeswaran v Attorney-General of Ceylon* [1970] AC 1111).

The latter view has been given support by more recent authority. The courts now appear to accept that a contractual employer–employee relationship may exist between the Crown and its civil servants unless, in a particular case, it can be shown that this was not the Crown's intention. Hence, while for public interest reasons the Crown may still have the common law (i.e. prerogative) right to dismiss at pleasure, other grievances arising out of its legal relationship with its employees may be pursued by way of actions for breach of contract (see *R v Lord Chancellor's Department, ex parte Nangle* [1992] 1 All ER 897; *McClaren v Home Office* [1990] ICR 824; *R v Civil Service Appeal Board, ex parte Bruce* [1988] 3 All ER 686, per May LJ).

The Crown and the law of agency

Under the common law the Crown has unlimited contractual authority. The view that it may only enter into contracts incidental to the usual functions of government is not supported by authority. It is not open to the Crown, therefore, to seek to avoid a contract on the ground that it was beyond its powers. If, however, its contractual capacity in any particular context has been limited by statute, a contract made outside those limitations would be *ultra vires* and invalid.

Since the Crown is an institution and not an individual it cannot enter into contracts personally. This is done by ministers or civil servants on its behalf. To a considerable extent such contracts are regulated by the normal private law rules of agency. This means that the person who acted for the Crown is not personally liable for the contract's performance. It is the Crown as principal against whom the contract is actionable. This will be the case providing that the person who made the contract was acting within his/her actual, ostensible or usual authority. An agent's actual authority is that which was conferred on him/her by the principal (in this case a minister or other empowered superior). Ostensible authority is that which the principal by word or deed has represented ('held out') the agent to have, but which is beyond the latter's actual authority. Usual authority is that which an agent of the type in question would usually be expected to have but which, in a particular case, is greater than the actual authority conferred. This may arise where, for whatever reasons, a principal has imposed restrictions on the scope of authority normally conferred on agents operating in a particular sphere of trade and failed to take reasonable steps to make these known to those with whom the agent might be expected to deal.

In *Robertson v Minister of Pensions* [1949] 1 KB 227, a disabled ex-army officer made written enquiries about his eligibility for a pension to the government department which might usually have been expected to have dealt with such matters, viz. the War Office. He received a letter in return saying that he qualified for the type of pension in issue. Strictly speaking, however, he had applied to the wrong department as the authority to decide matters of this type had been vested in the Ministry of Pensions. When, however, the Ministry of Pensions sought to deny his eligibility, it was held that the Ministry could not change the decision and that the plaintiff was entitled to rely on the War Office having the authority which it had both assumed and which he might reasonably have expected it to have.

If, however, a Crown agent's authority is limited by legislation, the above common law rules cannot clothe the agent with a degree of authority in excess of such statutory restrictions. In these circumstances any contract entered into beyond the statutory restraints would be invalid and unenforceable (*Attorney-General of Ceylon v Silva* [1953] AC 461).

In *Silva* a Crown agent had legislative authority to sell any goods, except those belonging to the Crown, left unclaimed in a customs warehouse. A quantity of steel which had been stored in the warehouse and which belonged to the Crown was 'sold' to the plaintiff. When the steel was not delivered he sued for breach of contract. It was held that the contract was clearly outside the authority granted and that no concept of agency could give legitimacy to that which had been prohibited by legislation.

The normal rule is that an agent who makes a contract outside the scope of his authority may be sued for breach of warranty of authority. The person who has been misled into making an unenforceable contract is, therefore, provided some means of redress. It would appear, however, that such right of action is not available against Crown agents (*Dunn v MacDonald* [1897] 1 QB 401). This was said to be in the interests of public policy, otherwise 'no man would accept any office of trust under government'.

Liability in tort

Section 2 of the 1947 Act removed most of the Crown's immunity in tort and rendered it liable:

(a) vicariously, for the torts of its employees;
(b) in respect of those common law duties owed by an employer to its employees;
(c) in respect of those common law duties owed by the owners or occupiers of property (e.g. the rule in *Rylands v Fletcher* (1868) LR 3 HL 330).

Section 2(2) provided that the Crown could be sued in tort for failure to comply with any statutory duties imposed by statutes binding upon the Crown as well as upon other persons, e.g. Occupiers' Liability Act 1957.

The categories of persons coming within the definition of Crown servant or employee were defined by s 2(6). The definition extends to persons appointed directly or indirectly by the Crown and who are paid wholly out of the Consolidated Fund or other moneys provided by Parliament or from any other fund certified by the Treasury. The Crown is not vicariously liable, therefore, for the torts of police officers, or the employees of local authorities or other statutory or public corporations.

Liability for judicial actions and decisions

Section 2(5) retained the Crown's immunity in tort in respect of anything done or omitted to be done by those exercising responsibilities of a judicial nature or any responsibility 'in connection with the execution of judicial process'. Hence, were a judge to impose a sentence of imprisonment for an offence carrying a maximum penalty of a fine, no liability for false imprisonment could be imposed on the Crown.

The immunity was applied in *Quinland* v *Governor of Belmarsh Prison* [2002] EWCA Civ 174, where a Crown Court clerk mistakenly drew up an order of imprisonment for two years six months instead of two years three months. The Court of Appeal was satisfied that the clerk was acting in the execution of the judicial process and was thus immune from damages for false imprisonment.

Note also that judges in the superior courts (Crown Court in indictable cases, High Court and above) may not be made liable for anything said or done in the exercise of their judicial functions however malicious, corrupt or oppressive those actions or decisions might be (*Anderson* v *Gorrie* [1895] 1 QB 668). This remains the case even if the act or decision in question represented an excess of jurisdiction, provided this was an honest mistake. Liability may attach, however, to that done outside jurisdiction and in bad faith (*Re McC* [1985] AC 528).

Judges of inferior courts, e.g. county courts, also enjoy immunity for that done while acting judicially and in the honest belief that jurisdiction existed (*Sirros* v *Moore* [1975] QB 118).

Some uncertainty has surrounded the position of magistrates. Relatively recent authority suggested that a magistrate could be personally liable in respect of acts done in innocent excess of jurisdiction. Hence if a magistrate, acting bona fide, imprisoned a person where no power to impose a custodial sentence existed, liability for unlawful imprisonment could have been imposed. The position of magistrates is, however, now covered by the Justices of the Peace Act 1997, ss 51–57. These provide that a magistrate will not be liable for that done within jurisdiction or for that done without jurisdiction unless, in the latter case, the plaintiff can prove bad faith.

Liability for actions of members of the armed forces

Section 10 of the 1947 Act rendered the Crown immune from any legal proceedings in respect of death or injury suffered by any member of the armed forces while on active duty or on Crown property (provided the Secretary of State certified the injury was attributable to military service and, therefore, pensionable). This immunity was, however, removed by the Crown Proceedings (Armed Forces) Act 1987 which *suspended* s 10 of the 1947 Act. The section may be revived by the Secretary of State in case of imminent national danger, great emergency or warlike operations outside the United Kingdom.

It has been held that s 10 in its original form does not offend the right to a fair trial in Art 6 of the European Convention on Human Rights. This was so, according to the Court of Appeal, because s 10 intruded upon substantive rights in the law of tort and not the procedural guarantees protected by the Article (*Matthews* v *Ministry of Defence* [2002] EWCA Civ 773).

Providing s 10 has not been revived, it will be for the plaintiff serviceman in any action for negligence to establish the normal principles of liability – i.e. foresight, proximity and the existence of a duty of care.

In *Mulcahy v Minister of Defence* [1996] 2 WLR 474, the plaintiff sued for damages in respect of deafness caused by the alleged negligence of a fellow soldier when firing a howitzer during the Gulf War. The tests of foresight and proximity were satisfied but the Court of Appeal would not accept that it was just, fair and reasonable to impose a duty of care on one serviceman towards another while a battle was in progress or, in those circumstances, a duty on the Crown to maintain a safe system of work.

PRIVATE LAW LIABILITY FOR ABUSE OF STATUTORY POWERS

The overall consequences of the Crown Proceedings Act was to approximate the position of the Crown in tort to that of other public authorities. Both are now subject to the ordinary law as it applies between private citizens. Unlike private citizens, however, public authorities have been entrusted by Parliament with a wide range of legal powers and duties, the exercise of which may result in damage or interference with the rights of others. This has necessitated the development of additional tortious rules which are peculiar to those who exercise statutory functions.

Careless exercise of statutory powers and duties

The fact that a public body has been careless in the exercise of a statutory function will not, in itself, be sufficient to give a cause of action to any person who claims to have suffered damage as a result. Such action may only succeed if the plaintiff can show that the body owed him/her a legal duty of care in respect of the way that power/duty was exercised.

> In my judgement the correct view is that in order to found a cause of action flowing from the careless exercise of powers or duties, the plaintiff has to show that the circumstances are such as to raise a duty of care at common law (per Lord Browne-Wilkinson, *X (Minors) v Bedfordshire County Council* [1995] 3 WLR 152).

Such a duty of care may arise in respect of:

(a) the manner in which the body has exercised a statutory discretion, e.g. whether a child should be taken into care or not;
(b) the manner in which it has chosen to implement its decision, e.g. the way that child is cared for.

The cases show that the courts are extremely reluctant to impose liability for alleged careless exercise of discretion except where:

(a) the enabling statute displays a clear intent that, in addition to the public law remedies available, abuse of the power should be actionable in private law (*Murphy v Brentwood District Council* [1991] 1 AC 398);
(b) the decision was so unreasonable as to be beyond the decision-maker's lawful authority:

Most statutes which impose a statutory duty on local authorities confer on the authority a discretion as to the extent to which, and the methods by which, such duty is to be performed. It is clear both in principle and from the decided cases that the local authority cannot be liable in damages for doing that which Parliament has authorised. Therefore, if the decisions complained of fall within the ambit of such statutory discretion they cannot be actionable in common law. However, if the decision complained of is so unreasonable that it falls outside the ambit of the discretion conferred on the local authority, there is not a priori reason for excluding all common law liability (per Lord Browne-Wilkinson, *Bedfordshire* case).

Reasonableness and justiciability

The reasonableness of a particular exercise of discretion will not be subject to the above test, however, if it involved relevant policy considerations – e.g. the availability of resources.

> However, if the factors relevant to the exercise of the discretion include matters of policy, the court cannot adjudicate on such policy matters and therefore cannot reach the conclusion that the decision was outside the ambit of the statutory discretion. Therefore a common law duty of care in relation to the taking of decisions involving policy matters cannot exist (*ibid.*).

Hence, as a pre-condition to an action in tort for carelessness in the exercise of discretion, it must be shown that the decision-making power in issue was justiciable. The difference between justiciable and non-justiciable discretionary powers was explained by Lord Browne-Wilkinson in the *Bedfordshire* case. The case involved actions for damages relating to the way the local authority had used its child-care powers in relation to a number of children who appeared to have been seriously neglected by their parents.

> The first question is whether the determination by the court of the question whether there has been a breach of duty will involve unjusticiable policy questions. The alleged breaches of that duty relate for the most part to the failure to take reasonable practical steps, e.g. to remove the children, to allocate a suitable social worker or to make proper investigations. The assessment by the court of such allegations would not require the court to consider policy matters which are not justiciable. They do not necessarily involve any question of the allocation of resources or the determination of general policy. There are other allegations the investigation of which by a court might require the weighing of policy factors, e.g. allegations that the county council failed to provide a level of service appropriate to the plaintiff's needs (*ibid.*).

Intentions of Parliament and the public interest

Even though it may be decided that a particular decision-making power is justiciable, its careless exercise may still not be actionable if the court feels that the imposition of a common law duty of care would be inconsistent with the wishes of Parliament or the public interest. The question and impact of Parliament's intentions was considered in *Clunis v Camden and Islington Health Authority* [1998] QB 978. The plaintiff had been discharged from a mental hospital into the care of the defendants. He subsequently committed an unprovoked and fatal attack as a result of which he was convicted of manslaughter. He sued for negligence and alleged that had he been properly assessed by the defendants he would have been returned to hospital, either compulsorily or consensually, and would, therefore, have been unable to commit the offence. His action failed. The Court of Appeal felt that although the Mental Health Act 1983, s 117 imposed a duty on health authorities to provide after-care for mentally disordered persons discharged from hospital, there was nothing in the section to suggest that Parliament intended any alleged failures of the duty to be actionable in damages.

Similar reasoning lay behind the decision in *Philcox* v *Civil Aviation Authority, The Times*, 8 June 1995. The plaintiff sued for damages in respect of his aeroplane which had crashed just one month after being inspected and given a certificate of airworthiness by the defendants. The Court of Appeal held, however, that the Civil Aviation Authority's regulatory functions in this context had been cast upon it by Parliament primarily for the purposes of protecting the public. Hence it could not be just and reasonable to impose a duty of care on the Authority towards individual owners.

The law relating to the circumstances and extent to which policy considerations may exclude a public authority's liability in negligence is currently in a state of reappraisal and development and must be approached, therefore, with a degree of caution. In the *Bedfordshire* case, as already indicated, the court felt that for a variety of reasons it would not be appropriate to impose a duty of care in respect of the exercise of statutory child-care functions by local authorities. The principal reasons for this were:

(a)   that decisions in this context were multi-disciplinary involving police, educational bodies, doctors and others, and 'to impose such liability on all the participant bodies would lead to almost impossible problems of disentangling as between the respective bodies the liability...of each for reaching a decision found to be negligent';

(b)   that the spectre of litigation could lead to excessive caution and delay in decision-making to the detriment of children at risk.

The court went on to reach the more general conclusion that it had probably never been Parliament's intention that regulatory or welfare legislation passed for the benefit of society in general should be actionable in tort by individuals: 'In my judgement...the courts should hesitate long before imposing a common law duty of care in the exercise of common law powers or duties conferred by Parliament for social welfare purposes' (*ibid.*).

This aspect of the decision in the *Bedfordshire* case attracted a degree of comment and criticism and it was not long before the wisdom of granting local authorities such extensive legal immunity in social welfare matters was revisited.

In *Barrett* v *Enfield London Borough Council* [1999] 3 WLR 79, Lord Steyn expressed the view that while 'it was no doubt right for the courts to restrain within reasonable bounds claims against public authorities exercising statutory powers in the social welfare context' it was 'equally important to set reasonable bounds to the immunity such authorities may assert'. This, in turn, appeared to presage a move towards a more fact-based, and case-by-case approach, for determining the extent to which effective fulfilment of this genus of powers might be prejudiced by private legal proceedings. A similar process of judicial thought also appeared to influence the finding of the House of Lords in *Phelps* v *Hillingdon London Borough Council* [2000] 3 WLR 776, where the court concluded that public policy considerations did not operate as a complete barrier to actions for negligence against local authorities in respect of alleged failures by educational psychologists employed by them.

It would also appear to be the case that a rule of law which provides that the public interest in the effective performance of public law powers should, in all cases, prevail over the right of the individual to seek legal redress in cases of alleged negligence, may well be at odds with the right to a fair trial in Art 6 of the European Convention on Human Rights. In particular, denial of the right to legal process appears to preclude consideration of such matters as the gravity of the negligence and the seriousness of the injury sustained in particular cases (see *Osman* v *United Kingdom* (1998) 29 EHRR 245).

The implementation of the decision

As to the implementation of decisions after a statutory discretion has been exercised, the House of Lords in the *Bedfordshire* case felt that the ordinary principles of negligence should apply.

> If the plaintiff's complaint alleges carelessness, not in the taking of a discretionary decision to do some act, but in the practical manner in which that act has been performed (e.g. the running of a school), the question whether or not there was a common law duty of care falls to be decided by applying the usual principles, i.e. those laid down in *Caparo Industries plc* v *Dickman* [1990] 2 AC 605. Was the damage to the plaintiff reasonably foreseeable? Was the relationship between the plaintiff and the defendant sufficiently proximate? Is it just and reasonable to impose a duty of care?

This was subject to the proviso, however, that the imposition of a duty of care should not be 'inconsistent with, or have a tendency to discourage, the due performance by the local authority of its statutory duties'.

Negligence and police discretion

Operational decisions as to the most appropriate use of police powers and resources has been another context in which the judicial tendency has been to sublimate the individual right to sue for damages to the perceived needs of the public interest; in this instance, the effective and efficient prevention of crime. Hence it has been held that no action in negligence lies in respect of injury inflicted by a person who might previously have been arrested if police investigations had been conducted differently or more thoroughly (*Hill* v *Chief Constable of West Yorkshire* [1986] 2 All ER 238; *Osman* v *Ferguson* [1993] 4 All ER 344). There are also dicta to the effect that no common law liability attaches to the police in respect of injury or damage suffered as a result of public disorder (*R* v *Chief Constable of Sussex, ex parte International Traders' Ferry Ltd* [1997] 3 WLR 132).

The particular public policy reasons for these broad exemptions are as follows:

(a) The imposition of a duty of care in relation to the performance of police functions would limit police discretion and expertise as to the best use of personnel and resources and would lead inevitably to a greater concentration of police activity on those types of unlawful conduct which might lead to any type of actionable damage or loss.

(b) Such duty of care would also encourage 'defensive' policing – e.g. police might be reluctant to leave a suspect 'at large' so that he might lead the investigating officers to his accomplices if this tactic carried with it the risk of further actionable damage being caused.

(c) The recognition of a duty of care would operate to the detriment of police efficiency in dealing with crime as an inordinate amount of time and effort would have to be devoted to the probable resulting plethora of legal proceedings.

Failure to exercise a statutory power

One of the questions bedevilling English law over a considerable period has been whether a public authority may ever be liable in negligence where the damage suffered by the plaintiff resulted wholly or in part from the authority's failure to exercise a statutory power, i.e. where the damage is alleged to have been caused by omission rather than commission.

The type of situation in which this question may arise was illustrated by the facts of *Stovin v Wise (Norfolk County Council, third party)* [1996] 3 All ER 801. The plaintiff motorcyclist was injured when the defendant motorist pulled out of a side road into his path. The road junction where the accident occurred was known to be dangerous but the local highway authority had not used its powers under the Highways Act 1980 to make any improvements. It was argued that part of the blame and, therefore, liability for the plaintiff's injuries lay with the authority.

The decision of the House of Lords was that common law liability could result from the non-use of a power but only in very limited circumstances. To establish such liability it would have to be shown:

(a) that the failure to act was irrational in the public law sense; and
(b) that the imposition of liability would not be contrary to the policy of the Act in which the power was contained.

> I think that the minimum pre-conditions for basing a duty of care upon the existence of a statutory power, if it can be done at all, are, first, that it would in the circumstances have been irrational not to have exercised the power, so that there was, in effect, a public law duty to act, and secondly, that there are exceptional grounds for holding that the policy of the statute requires compensation to be paid to persons who suffer loss because the power was not exercised (per Lord Hoffman).

An evident judicial reluctance to impose liability except in these circumstances is based on the assumption that where Parliament gives an authority a discretion – i.e. a choice whether, when and how to act – it is not for the courts to transform that into a duty (from 'may' to 'ought') by exposing the authority to actions for damages by persons whose injuries can, in some way, be related to its inaction. Discretion, it must be assumed, was conferred for a purpose which must include allowing the authority to delay or not to act where this can be related to rational application of relevant factual and policy considerations, e.g. the availability of resources.

> The fact that Parliament has conferred a discretion must be some indication that the policy of the Act conferring the power was not to create a right to compensation. The need to have regard to the policy of the statute therefore means that exceptions will be rare (*ibid.*).

Applying the above to the particular facts, the decision in *Stovin* was:

(a) that as the road junction in question was not an accident 'black-spot' and was not as dangerous as other sites in its area, it could not be said that a decision not to put it at the top of the authority's priorities amounted to irrationality;

(b) that to have imposed a common law duty of care in these circumstances would probably have led to local authorities spending increased amounts of money in improving road safety at the possible expense of other public services and that it could not have been the policy of the Act to allow judges such direct involvement in essentially policy-orientated issues, i.e. how to make the best use of public funds.

> In my view the creation of a duty of care...even on grounds of irrationality in failing to exercise a power, would inevitably expose the authority's budgetary decisions to judicial inquiry. This would distort the priorities of local authorities which would be bound to try to play safe by increasing their spending on road improvements rather than risk enormous liabilities for personal injury accident. They will spend less on education or social services. I think that it is important, before extending the duty of care owed by public authorities, to consider the cost to the community of the defensive measures which they are likely to take in order to avoid liability (*ibid.*).

The principle that a failure to exercise a power was actionable only where this amounted to unreasonableness was applied by the Court of Appeal in *Larner* v *Solihull Metropolitan Borough Council*, 20 December 2000, Smith Bernal Casetrack. The case was not dissimilar to *Stovin* and arose from an allegation that a local highway authority had failed to use its powers under the Road Traffic Act 1988, s 39 to promote road safety and to take such measures as appeared appropriate to prevent road accidents. On this occasion Lord Woolf's view was that, if the only reasonable way an authority could exercise its discretion was to adopt a particular course of action but did not so act, this could create liability at common law. It was essential, however, that the authority's failure fell outside the ambit of its discretion in the sense that it was wholly unreasonable. As no such irrationality appeared on the facts, no question of liability arose.

Judicial awareness of the public policy implications of turning powers into duties, particularly in terms of the financing of public bodies was evident in the Court of Appeal's decision in *Capital and Counties plc* v *Hampshire County Council* [1997] 3 WLR 331, where it was held that, as a general rule, a fire brigade's power to answer a call for help could not be converted into a common law duty to exercise the power. Nor does a fire brigade owe any duty of care in respect of the way it deals with the fire or other dangerous situation except where its actions produce a risk which would otherwise not have existed (*Nelson Holdings Ltd* v *British Gas plc, The Times*, 7 March 1997).

In relation to the ambulance service, the position appears to be that it is not under any common law duty to answer a 999 call, but that once such call has been accepted the necessary degree of proximity is created and an actionable duty of care to provide assistance may arise if resources are available to provide an ambulance on which there were no overriding alternative demands (*Kent* v *Griffiths (No. 3)* [2000] 2 All ER 474).

Breach of statutory duty

This is a distinct tort with its own requirements. It is not simply a particular aspect of negligence or nuisance. In essence it requires the plaintiff to show:

(a) that a public body or statutory undertaking was under a statutory duty to take a certain course of action;
(b) that the duty to act was not fulfilled;
(c) that the failure caused damage to the plaintiff.

No carelessness or negligence need be established. Nor does the plaintiff have to prove any interference with a common law right: 'It is a general rule of law that, when a ministerial duty is imposed, an action lies for breach of it without malice or negligence' (per Bovill CJ, *Pickering* v *Jones* (1873) LR 8 CP).

This should not be understood, however, as a simplistic assertion that every breach of statutory duty is actionable in tort. Other factors must be established to the court's satisfaction. Of crucial importance will be the intention of the legislation in which the duty is contained. Some duties – such as the obligation lying on the Minister for Education 'to promote education in England and Wales' – may be regarded, primarily, as broad statements of political intent more suitable to parliamentary scrutiny and criticism than to judicial enforcement:

> Parliament has recently become fond of imposing duties of a kind which, since they are of a general and indefinite character, are perhaps to be considered as political duties rather than as legal duties which a court could enforce (Wade and Forsyth, *Administrative Law*).

In those cases where, given the nature of the duty and the resource constraints on the authority, exact or absolute compliance is probably impossible – e.g. the duty in the Highways Act 1980, s 41 to keep the roads clear of water, snow and ice – it is sufficient that the authority did all that it reasonably could under the circumstances (*Cross* v *Kirklees Metropolitan Borough Council* [1998] 1 All ER 564).

Thus in *R* v *Camden and Islington Health Authority, ex parte K* [2001] EWCA Civ 240, the Court of Appeal found the duty on health authorities to provide after-care services for patients discharged from mental hospitals was not an absolute obligation but a requirement to use their best endeavours to secure treatment in the community which was adequate for the needs of particular patients.

Other duties may be contained in statutory rules which are construed to be merely directory and, therefore, not intended to create legally enforceable rights. Hence, the prison rules made under the Prison Act 1952 (which regulate the government of prisons and the entitlement of inmates), have been held not to provide prisoners with any rights enforceable either in public or private law (*R* v *Deputy Governor of Parkhurst Prison, ex parte Hague* [1992] 1 AC 58). Also, even if it can be shown that the duty was intended to be legally enforceable, the court must be satisfied that this was meant to include private law actions for damages as well as public law proceedings for judicial review (*R* v *ILEA, ex parte Ali, The Times*, 21 February 1990).

If the statute which imposes the duty also provides a remedy for its enforcement, this may be understood as evincing a parliamentary intention that other remedies, including actions for damages, should be deemed to have been excluded. In

Atkinson v *Newcastle Waterworks Co* (1877) 2 Ex D 441, the defendants failed in their statutory duty to maintain a certain pressure in the water mains. As a result the local fire brigade were unable to extinguish a fire at the plaintiff's premises. The plaintiff's action for damages was, however, unsuccessful. This was because the statute in question (the Waterworks Clauses Act 1847) provided that, for breaches of the duties it imposed, a Waterworks Co could be prosecuted and fined to a maximum of £10. This was assumed to be an exclusive remedy precluding any right of action for damages. This is, however, not a rigid rule and there are examples of courts departing from it where it was felt that the degree and type of damage suffered was not that which the legislature could have had in mind when the statutory remedy was included. Thus the statutory remedy in the Waterworks Clauses Act, which operated against the plaintiff in the *Atkinson* case, was held not to be absolutely exclusive in *Read* v *Croydon Corporation* [1938] 4 All ER 631. On this occasion a water authority failed to fulfil its duty in the 1847 Act to provide a clean and wholesome water supply. This caused an outbreak of typhoid in Croydon which killed 38 people and affected hundreds of others. Stable J held that:

> While there is no doubt that for some of the statutory duties imposed...the penalty provided in the Act is exclusive, it is difficult to believe that the legislature intended that it should be exclusive in the case of each breach of every duty under the Act. I find it impossible to hold...that the legislature intended that there should be one remedy...equally applicable to so trivial a breach as the failure to maintain a certain pressure of water...and to a deliberate dereliction of duty resulting in the destruction of a large community by the supply of poisonous water.

Liability for breach of statutory duty will also not be imposed unless the plaintiff can show that he/she belongs to the particular category of persons that the statute was designed to protect (*Cutler* v *Wandsworth Stadium Ltd* [1949] AC 398) and, similarly, that the damage suffered was of a type which it was passed to guard against (*Gorris* v *Scott* (1874) LR 9 Ex 125).

It should also be remembered that, in the case of the Crown, liability under this head may only be imposed in respect of duties contained in statutes which bind the Crown expressly or by necessary implication.

Breach of European Community obligations

Government bodies are also subject to obligations laid on them by European Community law and a body of legal rules is currently being developed to determine the extent to which such obligations may be enforced by way of actions for damages.

The fundamental principle, now firmly established, is that the state may be made liable in damages for all executive, legislative and judicial acts in breach of Community law (*Brasserie du Pêcheur SA* v *Germany* [1996] 2 WLR 506). The conditions for successful enforcement of state liability are:

(a) there has been a sufficiently serious breach of Community law;
(b) the rule of law infringed was intended to confer legal rights on individuals;
(c) a causal link existed between the breach and the damage suffered by individuals.

State liability will usually arise in respect of directly effective obligations imposed by Treaty Articles or regulations – provided that, in both cases, the obligation was imposed in clear and unconditional terms.

In certain circumstances, however, a directly effective right of action against the state may also be found in a directive. This will be the case where, in addition to (a)–(c) above:

(i)   the directive imposes an obligation on the state (*Faccini Dori* v *Recreb Srl* [1995] 1 CMLR 665);

(ii)   the obligation contained therein has the necessary degree of specificity, i.e. it is possible to discern from it the exact nature of the directive's requirements;

(iii) the time allowed for implementation of the directive by national legislation has elapsed (*Marshall* v *Southampton and South West Hampshire Area Health Authority (No. 1)* [1986] QB 401).

A directive which seeks to create rights which are legally enforceable between individuals but not against the state would, by definition, not appear to give rise to any issue of state liability. A state may be made liable, however, in respect of its failure to give effect to such a directive. Here it would be the state's failure to ensure the directive's proper implementation in accordance with EC Art 249 which would be the basis of the cause of action and not its breach of any directly effective Community law (*Francovich* v *Italy* [1993] 2 CMLR 66).

The requisite conditions for this species of liability are:

(a)   there has been a sufficiently serious breach of Community law;

(b)   the result prescribed by the directive entails the granting of rights to individuals;

(c)   the content of those rights can be readily identified from the provisions of the directive;

(d)   there is a causal link between the breach of the obligation imposed on the state and the loss suffered by individuals.

These principles were applied in *Dillenkofer* v *Federal Republic of Germany* [1997] 2 WLR 253. The German government had failed to give effect to a directive which sought to impose on the suppliers of package holidays an obligation to ensure that funds were available to compensate those whose holiday plans might be disrupted by the insolvency of a holiday company. As a result the plaintiffs were unable to recover recompense after suffering the type of loss and inconvenience to which the directive related. On a reference under EC Art 234 by a German court, the European Court of Justice ruled that:

(a)   a failure to implement a European directive was, *ipso facto*, a sufficiently serious breach of Community law;

(b)   the directive had clearly been intended to confer legally enforceable rights on individuals;

(c)   the content of those rights was readily discernible;

(d)   there was an obvious causal link between the German government's failure and the loss suffered by the plaintiffs.

The right to damages for breach of Community law extends to compensatory damages only and does not include any right to claim punitive damages (*R* v *Secretary of State for Transport, ex parte Factortame (No. 5), The Times*, 28 April 1998).

It is for each member state to ensure that individuals obtain reparation for loss and damages caused to them by non-compliance with Community law whichever public authority may be liable for the breach and/or for the making of reparation (*Konle* v *Austria* [1999] ECR 1-3099). There is no absoute rule, however, that such reparation must be provided by the member state itself in order for its obligations under Community law to be fulfilled. Hence Community law does not preclude a public law body, in addition to the state itself, from incurring liability for loss or damage caused to individuals as a result of measures it took in breach of Community law. Where the criteria for state liability exist such claims should be determined on the basis of the relevant national legal rules for the award of reparation for such loss or damage (*Haim* v *Kassenzahnarztliche Vereinigung Nordrhein* [2000] All ER (D) 916).

Misfeasance in public office

A government official who causes injury through a deliberate misuse of power commits the tort of misfeasance in public office. Some conscious or malicious element of abuse must be present. Also, the perpetrator must have intended to inflict injury or have been aware that it would be the likely consequence of his/her actions. In *Three Rivers District Council* v *Bank of England (No. 3)* [1996] 3 All ER 558, the tort was said to be committed where a public officer:

(a) performed or omitted to perform an act with the object of injuring the plaintiff (i.e. where there was targeted malice);
(b) performed an act which he knew or ought to have known he had no power to perform and which he knew would or could injure the plaintiff.

That which was done *ultra vires* but innocently, or as a result of mere incompetence, is, therefore, not actionable (*Dunlop* v *Woollahra Municipal Council* [1982] AC 158). Damages would also appear to be available for deliberate government abuse of Community law (*Burgoin SA* v *Ministry of Agriculture, Fisheries and Food* [1986] QB 716).

The tort was found to have been committed in *Elliot* v *Chief Constable of Wiltshire, The Times*, 5 December 1996 where a police officer made false allegations to a newspaper editor. These were that one of the newspaper's reporters was guilty of various criminal offences. The officer's objective was to get the reporter 'sacked' so that he would be unable to continue investigating and reporting on corruption in the police.

Whether the employing authority would be vicariously liable for actions of this type is a matter of some uncertainty. One opinion is that vicarious liability should exist providing the act was done in pursuance of the authority's authorised functions. There is, however, *obiter* judicial opinion that a public authority should not be made liable for the deliberate excesses of its employees (*R* v *Deputy Governor of Parkhurst Prison, ex parte Hague* (above)).

The defence of statutory authority

Where the fulfilment of a statutory function is impossible without some level of interference with private rights, it is not actionable so long as the interference caused is inevitable and is the minimum necessary to secure the function's proper discharge. Hence, in *Allen* v *Gulf Oil Refining* [1981] AC 1001, those living in the vicinity of an oil refinery were unable to recover redress in respect of the smell, vibration and noise which was emitted. As the location and operation of the refinery were authorised by statute, no action could lie in respect of its inevitable consequences.

The requirement of inevitability is crucial if the defence is to be accepted. In *Manchester Corporation* v *Farnworth* [1930] AC 171, the existence of statutory authority did not exempt the Corporation from liability for the damage caused by noxious fumes and gases emitted by an electricity power station as the court was not satisfied that all due care had been taken to keep the emissions to a minimum. In *Metropolitan Asylum Board* v *Hill* (1891) 6 App Cas 193, the authority were liable in nuisance for building a smallpox hospital in a residential area. Although the authority had the statutory power to build hospitals, the siting of them was a matter for its discretion. Since the hospital could have been built in a place where less interference and nuisance would have been caused, the extent of transgression of private rights could not be said to be the inevitable minimum.

REMEDIES

The trial of an action against the Crown will be conducted according to the ordinary procedures of the High Court or county court. The action will normally be taken against the particular government department concerned or against the Attorney-General.

A judgment obtained against a public authority other than the Crown may be enforced in the normal way. By virtue of the Crown Proceedings Act 1947, however, the Crown retains a number of important immunities in this context. These would appear to be based on the premiss that the issuing of compulsory orders against the Crown could be prejudicial to its dignity and, in certain circumstances, to the public interest.

Section 25(3) of the 1947 Act provides that the Crown, through the appropriate department, shall make payment of damages and costs awarded against it in civil proceedings. Such awards may not be enforced, however, by the ordinary methods: '...no execution or attachment or process in the nature thereof shall be issued out of any court for enforcing payment by the Crown of any such money...' (s 25(4)). Since, however, the duty to make payment is contained in statute, it would appear that – in the extremely unlikely event of non-payment – it could be enforced by way of an order for *mandamus* against the responsible government department.

Section 21 of the 1947 Act has caused some problems of interpretation. Section 21(1) precludes a court from issuing any injunction, order for specific performance or order for the delivery up of property against the Crown. Section 21(2) contains the further prohibition against the granting of any injunction or order against an officer of the Crown 'if the effect of granting the injunction or making the order would be to give relief against the Crown which could not have been obtained in proceedings against the Crown'. After a period of some uncertainty this has now been interpreted to mean that an injunction may be issued against a minister in respect of powers conferred on him or her by name (e.g. 'the Secretary of State for Education'), but not where the powers or duties are conferred on the Crown itself (*M* v *Home Office* [1993] 3 WLR 433).

The prerogative orders of *mandamus certiorari* and prohibition (now mandatory, quashing old prohibitory orders) do not issue against the Crown. They may be used, however, against a minister of the Crown in respect of powers conferred on the minister by name.

CROWN PRIVILEGE

Background

Prior to the trial of a civil action the parties are required to exchange lists of relevant documents and materials and permit inspection of the same. Until the Crown Proceedings Act 1947, however, this duty did not apply to the Crown. It was also accepted that the Crown had the right to assert that documents should not be used in evidence if revelation of the contents would be damaging to the public interest. This was referred to as a plea of Crown privilege.

Section 28 of the 1947 Act removed the Crown's immunity from the duty of disclosure but reserved the Crown's right to plead privilege in appropriate circumstances:

> ...this section shall be without prejudice to any rule of law which authorises the withholding of any document or the refusal to answer any question on the ground that the disclosure of the document or the answering of the question would be injurious to the public interest (s 28(l)(b)).

As recent controversies have shown, the withholding of relevant evidence from legal proceedings can have significant consequences for the quality of justice dispensed to individuals and on public attitudes towards the fairness of the judicial system. It also raises concerns about the extent to which, in the absence of any freedom of information legislation, ministers and officials are able to 'cover up' their allegedly illegal or disreputable conduct when their actions and decisions are challenged in the courts.

The decision in *Duncan* v *Cammell Laird and Co Ltd* [1942] AC 624

The facts

In 1939 the submarine, *Thetis*, which had been built by the defendants, sank in the Irish Sea while undergoing sea trials. All 99 of the ship's company were lost. The widow of one of the victims sued the defendants for negligence and, in order to prove defects in the ship's design and construction, sought discovery of documents containing the plans and specifications used when the ship was built. On the ground that the revelation of such material might be useful to the enemy, the Crown entered a plea that disclosure of this material in evidence would prejudice the public interest.

The view of the House of Lords

In a wide-ranging and controversial decision, the House accepted the Crown's contentions in relation to the particular documents in issue and went on to explain the following general principles.

(a) The Crown could claim privilege – i.e. assert the need to withhold documents from legal proceedings – where it would be against the public interest to disclose the contents of the particular document(s) in question ('contents' claims) or the document(s) belonged to a class of documents which the public interest required should remain confidential whether or not the document in question contained anything of particular prejudice to such interest ('class' claims).

(b) Properly executed ministerial affidavits (sworn statements) to the effect that the production of documents would be prejudicial were to be regarded as final and conclusive – i.e. courts should accept and apply such assertions without question or inquiry as to the propriety of ministerial opinions.

Criticisms

It has been suggested that the decision should be understood in the context of the emergency conditions which prevailed at the time and that, under such circumstances, the sentiments expressed represented a perhaps understandable judicial reluctance to expose executive decisions to the type of detailed scrutiny which might otherwise have been appropriate. The decision remained in place, however, for a further 25 years, well beyond the needs and exigencies of wartime.

Mounting unease with the decision centred around the finding that conclusive privilege could be claimed for whole classes of documents. Hence, if in any proceedings the Crown claimed that the document or documents sought by a particular party belonged to a 'privileged' class, the court could neither inspect nor order production of same albeit that the material contained therein might be wholly innocuous. The decision created a situation in which the public interest in conducting government in an atmosphere of secrecy and confidentiality could always be given priority over the public interest in the proper administration of justice:

> The Minister who withholds production of a 'class' document has no duty to consider the degree of public interest involved in a particular case by frustrating in that way the due administration of justice. If it is in the public interest in his view to withhold documents of that class, then it matters not whether the result of withholding a document is merely to deprive a litigant of some evidence on a minor issue in a case of little importance or, on the other hand, is to make it impossible to do justice at all in a case of the greatest importance. I cannot think that it is satisfactory that there should be no means at all of weighing, in any civil case, the public interest involved in withholding the document against the public interest that it should be produced (per Lord Reid, *Conway v Rimmer* [1968] AC 910).

Academic analysis of the decision argued that the findings of the House of Lords were not entirely consistent with previous relevant case law. In *Robinson v South Australia (No. 2)* [1931] AC 704, privilege was claimed in respect of nearly two thousand documents relating to the way in which grain had been stored by the authorities in performance of the state's grain marketing scheme. Grain so stored belonging to the plaintiff and to many others had been damaged by water and mice. The Privy Council's opinion was that the law relating to privilege should be applied 'narrowly' and only rarely pleaded for documents relating to commercial transactions. It was also felt that the court should reserve the right to inspect the documents in issue if genuinely discontent with the state's case for non-production.

Their Lordships will accordingly humbly advise His Majesty to discharge the order appealed from and to remit the case to the Supreme Court of South Australia with a direction that it is a proper one for the exercise of the court's power of inspecting the documents for which privilege is claimed in order to determine whether the facts discoverable by their production would be prejudicial or detrimental to the public welfare in any justifiable case (per Lord Blakesburgh).

Critics of the *Duncan* case also referred to *Spiegelman* v *Hocker* (1933) 50 TLR 87, where the Home Office instructed the police to withhold documents (witness statements) from proceedings in which the plaintiff sought damages for injuries suffered in a road accident. These, it was argued, belonged to a class which the public interest required should not be disclosed. McNaughten J, however, felt that a plea of privilege should only be used in respect of particular documents and that the court should be able to inspect such documents to ensure that the plea was not being abused. He then inspected the documents in issue and, having found nothing harmful to the public interest, ordered their production.

Aftermath

Perhaps not surprisingly – safe in the knowledge that their decisions would not be subjected to judicial scrutiny – ministers began to claim privilege in relation to official documents almost as a matter of course; the justification often being that this was necessary to ensure frankness in exchanges between public servants or was required to protect sources of information.

> A favourite argument...was that official reports of many kinds would not be made fearlessly and candidly if there was any possibility that they might later be made public. Once this unsound argument gained currency, free rein was given to the tendency to secrecy which is inherent in the public service. It is not surprising that the Crown, having been given a blank cheque, yielded to the temptation to overdraw (Wade and Forsyth, *op. cit.*).

That the 'class' doctrine was being used to withhold relatively harmless information seemed apparent from a number of cases. In *Ellis* v *Home Office* [1953] 2 QB 135, privilege was used to deny the plaintiff access to prison medical records. The plaintiff had been attacked by another prison inmate while in the hospital wing of Winchester prison. He brought proceedings for negligence on the grounds that the attacker, although known to be dangerous – a fact recorded in medical reports – had been allowed to move around the wing without supervision. In response to the Crown's plea of privilege, all three judges in the Court of Appeal expressed regret at having to follow the decision in *Duncan* and were of the opinion that production of the documents sought would have been unlikely to have done any serious damage to the interests of the state. The executive penchant for secrecy was again evident in *Broome* v *Broome* [1955] P 190, where, in a divorce petition brought by a soldier's wife, the War Office successfully claimed privilege in respect of documents containing the details of attempts to secure reconciliation between the parties.

Discontent and criticism eventually produced administrative concessions. In 1956 the Lord Chancellor announced that privilege would no longer be claimed in respect of certain classes of documents including: witness statements of accidents on the road, or on government premises, or involving government employers; ordinary medical reports on the health of civilian employees; medical reports where the Crown was sued in negligence; papers needed for defence against a criminal charge; witnesses' ordinary statements to the police; and reports on matters of fact relating to liability in contract.

Increasing judicial dissatisfaction with *Duncan* v *Cammell Laird* also became apparent. The House of Lords held that the 'class' doctrine and the supposed conclusive nature of ministerial opinions were not part of the law of Scotland (*Glasgow Corporation* v *Central Land Board*, 1956 SC (HL) 1). The Court of Appeal also expressed its discontent and suggested that courts did have the power to inspect documents if merely contained in a class for which privilege had been claimed (*Re Grosvenor Hotel (No. 2)* [1965] Ch 210; *Wednesbury Corporation* v *Minister of Housing and Local Government* [1965] 1 WLR 261). In the latter case Lord Denning's typically strident view (*obiter*) on all of this was:

> If this be correct...the courts of this country are to be led through a kind of ritual dance, decorously receiving the Minister's certificate, and bowing to its authority...It is quite apparent to me that the government departments attach overweening importance to ensuring secrecy for their own documents. They think they cannot do their work properly if anyone outside should even be at liberty to see them. Even though the disclosure of the contents of any individual document may not be in the least harmful in itself nevertheless it must not be disclosed unless a gap be made in their treasured immunity. I cannot accept this contention. I repeat that, in a case where a Minister claims privilege for a class of documents, he must justify his objection with reasons...so that the court itself can see whether this claim is well taken or not. But...if a case should come before us where the interests of justice require it and that claim of privilege is not well taken, then this court will not hesitate to order production.

The decision in *Conway* v *Rimmer* [1968] AC 910

Duncan *v* Cammell Laird *revisited*

Given the discontent chronicled above, it was perhaps inevitable that the House of Lords would re-examine its controversial wartime decision. *Conway* v *Rimmer* was an action for malicious prosecution by Conway, an ex-probationary police constable, against his former superintendent, Rimmer. Conway had been accused of stealing a torch, but was acquitted of the charge of theft. In order to show Rimmer's malice in initiating the proceedings, Conway wanted the authorities to produce four reports he had made about Conway while the latter was a probationary constable, and a report made by Rimmer to his Chief Constable concerning the alleged theft. The Home Secretary claimed these documents belonged to a privileged class, viz. confidential reports about the conduct of police officers and the investigation of crime.

The House of Lords was unanimous that *Duncan* v *Cammell Laird* had been rightly decided on its facts. However, the finding that ministerial affidavits claiming immunity for documents were to be regarded as conclusive so far as the protection of the public interest was concerned, and that the documents could not be inspected by the courts, was rejected.

A new approach

The following principles related to the law of Crown privilege may be extrapolated from the case.

(a) Ministers were no longer to be regarded as the final arbiters between the competing public interests of government confidentiality and the needs of justice. Full weight should be given to ministerial opinions, but these should not be understood as absolutely conclusive or as precluding judicial inspection of the documents in issue:

> I would therefore propose that the House ought now to decide that courts have and are entitled to exercise a power and duty to hold a balance between the public interest, as expressed by a Minister to withhold certain documents or other evidence, and the public interest in ensuring the proper administration of justice. That does not mean that a court would reject a Minister's view: full weight must be given to it in every case, and if the Minister's reasons are of a character which judicial experience is competent to weigh, then the Minister's view must prevail (per Lord Reid).

(b) The judicial discretion to inspect documents should, however, be used particularly sparingly in relation to 'contents' claims:

> However wide the power of the court may be held to be, cases would be very rare in which it could be proper to question the view of the responsible Minister that it would be contrary to the public interest to make public the contents of a particular document (*ibid.*).

(c) In other cases, especially where privilege was claimed, not because of the contents of particular documents, but due to the class to which they belonged, and ministerial reasons for privilege appeared inadequate or unclear, courts should be prepared to exercise their power of inspection to decide whether the need to do justice was outweighed by the public interest in concealment:

> But in this field it is more than ever necessary that in a doubtful case the alleged public interest in concealment should be balanced against the public interest that the administration of justice, should not be frustrated. If the Minister, who has no duty to balance these conflicting public interests, says no more than that in his opinion the public interest requires concealment, and if that is to be accepted as conclusive...it seems to me not only that very serious injustice may be done to the parties, but also that the due administration of justice may be gravely impaired for quite inadequate reasons (*ibid.*).

(d) Judges should treat with caution the argument that classes of documents should be regarded as privileged for no better reason than this was necessary to secure 'freedom and candour of communication with and within the public service, so that government decisions can be taken on the best advice and the fullest information' (*ibid.*).

(e) Despite all of this, however, the House of Lords was still prepared to accept that certain specific classes of documents should still be regarded as unsuitable for use in judicial proceedings. These included Cabinet papers, Foreign Office dispatches, documents relating to national security, high level inter-departmental

minutes, and correspondence and documents pertaining to the general administration of the armed forces or high level personnel in the service of the Crown.

The justification for regarding the above as immune from production was
stated as follows:

> To my mind the most important reason is that such disclosure would create or fan ill-formed
> or captious public or political criticism. The business of government is difficult enough
> as it is, and no government could contemplate with equanimity the inner workings of the
> government machine being exposed to the gaze of those ready to criticise without adequate
> knowledge of the background and perhaps with some axe to grind (per Lord Reid).

Structuring the balancing process

As a result of *Conway* v *Rimmer*, courts have to make a series of contingent decisions
or choices if and when disputes arise relating to the discovery of documents. First, the
court has to examine the reasons given for non-disclosure to determine their quality
and adequacy and whether they relate to matters generally regarded as unsuitable for
judicial inquiry (e.g. natural security, defence, diplomatic exchanges). Second, if the
court has doubts about the case for non-disclosure and decides to inspect the documents in question, it will have to consider the evidential value of their contents for the
proceedings to which they relate. Hence, if on inspection the court is of the opinion
that the documents will be of little assistance to the party seeking discovery, its discretion to order production may be influenced accordingly. Third, having decided to
inspect and being of the opinion that documents may contain useful evidence, the
court has to weigh the competing public interests involved – i.e. the need for certain
types of information to remain confidential against the requirements of justice.

In *Conway* itself, having applied all these considerations to the facts, the House of
Lords decided to inspect the disputed documents and, having found that they would
benefit the plaintiff and that their disclosure would not damage the public interest,
ordered their production.

FROM CROWN PRIVILEGE TO PUBLIC
INTEREST IMMUNITY

Crown privilege a misnomer

In 1972 the House of Lords expressed disapproval of the term 'Crown privilege' and
said that the right to assert that documents should be withheld in order to protect the
public interest should not be confined to the Crown. This was in the case of *R* v
Lewes Justices, ex parte Home Secretary [1973] AC 388 (*sub nom Rogers v Home
Secretary*), which concerned the functions of the Gaming Board. Rogers applied for a
certificate of consent to apply to the magistrates for licences for certain bingo clubs.
The Board asked the police for information about Rogers. The police reply was prejudicial to his application and consent was refused. Rogers commenced proceedings for
criminal libel against the Chief Constable of Sussex and sought production of the
police report containing the information which had been submitted to the Board. The
Home Secretary and the Board claimed the document was privileged.

The House of Lords disposed of the case as follows.

(a) The term 'Crown privilege' is a misnomer and it should be open to any person or organisation, public or private, to question the benefit to be gained by allowing the production of particular documents.

> The ground put forward has been said to be Crown privilege. I think that expression is wrong and may be misleading. There is no question of any privilege in the ordinary sense of the word. The real question is whether the public interest requires that the letter should not be produced and whether that public interest is so strong as to override the ordinary right and interest of a litigant that he shall be able to lay before a court of justice all relevant evidence. A Minister of the Crown is always an appropriate and often the most appropriate person to assert this public interest, and the evidence or advice which he gives to the court is always valuable and may sometimes be indispensable. But in my view, it must always be open to any person interested to raise the question and there may be cases where the trial judge should himself raise the question if no-one else has done so (per Lord Reid).

(b) The dangers of disclosure outweighed the risk of injustice to Rogers, as a breach of confidentiality could have damaged the effectiveness of the Board. Hence, both the claims of the minister and that of the Board concerning the privileged nature of the documents were upheld. The court's view was that performance of the Board's statutory functions – i.e. the regulation and control of gaming establishments – could be seriously prejudiced if persons became reluctant or refused to supply the Board with relevant information out of fear that such might be revealed in legal proceedings. This, it was felt, outweighed the danger of individual applicants for licences feeling that they had been dealt with unfairly through not being made fully aware of the case against them.

Principal grounds for class claims after *Conway* v *Rimmer*

Candour

Notwithstanding Lord Reid's reservations, the argument that the frankness of views and advice tendered within organisations (both public and private) could be inhibited by the knowledge that such communications might be used as evidence has continued to be used as a ground for claims of immunity from production. This approach was relied on successfully in *Gaskin* v *Liverpool Corporation* [1980] 1 WLR 1549, where the plaintiff sought damages for negligence arising out of his treatment while in a children's home run by the defendants. His attempt to secure documents and files relating to the time spent in care failed. The court was of the opinion that these belonged to a class of documents – i.e. those concerned with the proper functioning of the child care service – which should remain confidential.

All three members of the Court of Appeal approved Boreham J's dicta in the court *a quo*.

> I am left in no doubt that it is necessary for the proper functioning of the child care service that the confidentiality of the relevant documents should be preserved. This is a very important service to which the interests – also very important – of the individual must bow. I have no doubt that the public interest will be better served by refusing discovery and this I do.

Claims based on the candour argument were, and are, of course, in no sense con-clusive and it remains for the court in each case to balance the public interest in con-cealment against the competing interests of justice. Hence the argument was rejected in both *Campbell* v *Tameside Metropolitan Borough Council* [1982] QB 1065, and *Williams* v *Home Office (No. 2)* [1981] 1 All ER 1151.

In *Campbell* a teacher sued for negligence arising out of injuries caused to her by a disruptive pupil, whom, she argued, the defendants had not taken reasonable steps to protect her against. The Court of Appeal's view was that any public interest in con-cealing psychiatric and other reports of evidential value to the plaintiff was not suffi-cient to justify a possible injustice. Some guidance was also given in terms of the considerations to be used in the balancing of interests. Hence, where documents are clearly of considerable significance for the success of a litigant's case, this casts a greater burden upon the party pleading immunity to establish a countervailing and overriding public interest in concealment. Conversely, where documents might appear to be of minimal evidential value, a court might be persuaded more easily of the pub-lic interest in concealment.

> In these cases the court should and can consider the significance of the documents in rela-tion to the decision of the case. If they are of such significance that they might well affect the very decision of the case, then justice may require them to be disclosed...But if they are of little significance, so that they are very unlikely to affect the decision...then the greater public interest may be to keep them confidential (per Lord Denning MR).

The *Williams* case involved a challenge by a prisoner to the legality of his detention in an experimental 'special control unit' at Wakefield prison. The Home Office again used the proper functioning of the public service argument to plead immunity for a whole variety of documents containing records of communications between civil ser-vants and between the latter and government ministers concerning the Wakefield experiment. After inspection of the documents in issue, six out of 23 were ordered to be produced. There was, said McNeill J, a 'reasonable probability that the documents were likely to contain material in support of the plaintiff's case'.

The merits of the candour argument were also considered by the House of Lords in *Burmah Oil* v *Bank of England* [1980] AC 1090. It was certainly not an argument which impressed Lord Keith:

> The notion that any conscientious public servant would be inhibited at all in the candour of his writings by consideration of the off-chance they might have to be produced in litiga-tion is, in my opinion, grotesque. To represent that the possibility of it might significantly impair the public service is even more so...[T]he candour argument is an utterly insub-stantial ground for denying access to relevant documents.

Lord Wilberforce, however, was more circumspect and was clearly still prepared to regard the need for candour as a matter to be considered in balancing the public interests involved:

> It seems now rather fashionable to decry this [candour] but if as a ground it may once have been exaggerated it has now, in my opinion, received an excessive dose of cold water. I am certainly not prepared – against the view of the minister – to discount the need, in the formation of such very controversial policy...for frank and uninhibited advice...from and between ministers.

Confidentiality

Closely related to the candour argument, this consists of the claim that organisations whose effectiveness depends on the receipt of information given in confidence should not be required to reveal that information or its sources as to do so might run the risk of these 'drying up', thus prejudicing future inquiries. As with the candour argument, the extent of the damage to the public interest resulting from a breach of confidentiality must be weighed against the public interest in the dispensation of justice.

Two of the most frequently cited cases in which confidentiality was accepted as a justification for public interest immunity are *Alfred Crompton Amusement Machines Ltd v Customs and Excise Commissioners (No. 2)* [1974] AC 405, and *D v NSPCC* [1978] AC 171. In the first case the Commissioners acquired information from customers and other sources concerning the value of machines supplied by an amusement company. This was done in the course of assessing the company's liability for purchase tax. In the opinion of the House of Lords, production of documents containing this information could have damaged the public interest in the effective execution of one of the Commissioners' principal functions, viz. the collection of revenue as authorised by Parliament.

> Here...one can well see that the third parties who have supplied this information to the commissioners because of the existence of their statutory powers would very much resent its disclosure by the commissioners...and it is not fanciful to say that the knowledge that the commissioners cannot keep such information secret may be harmful to the efficient working of the Act (per Lord Cross).

Similarly, in the *NSPCC* case it was felt that the Society should not be required to produce the source of an allegation of child abuse.

> I would extend to those who give information about neglect or ill-treatment of children to a local authority or the NSPCC a similar immunity from disclosure of their identity in legal proceedings to that which the law accords to police informers. The public interests served by preserving the anonymity of both classes of informants are analogous; they are of no less weight in the case of the former than in the latter class, and in my judgment are of greater weight than in the case of informers to the Gaming Board to whom immunity from disclosure of their identity has recently been extended by this House (per Lord Diplock).

Subsequently, in *Bookbinder v Tebbit* [1992] 1 WLR 217, public interest immunity was held to extend to information supplied to the Audit Commission in the course of investigating alleged irregularities in the financial affairs of a local authority. The court felt that the efficiency of the Commission – particularly its functions of inquiring into possible illegal usage of public finances – could be impaired if the identities of its informants were to be disclosed.

The case for confidentiality must, however, be convincing. In *Norwich Pharmaceutical Co Ltd v Customs and Excise Commissioners* [1974] AC 133, no public interest was found in permitting the Commissioners to conceal information received from traders concerning the identities of companies importing chemical compounds manufactured in breach of the plaintiff's patent. The House of Lords was not convinced that fear of disclosure would deter honest traders from supplying information exposing the activities of those seeking to obtain an unfair commercial advantage:

Any honest trader who was disturbed at the thought that a court could order the disclosure of importers' names in circumstances such as exist here would be a most unreasonable man and I cannot believe that there would be many such (per Lord Cross).

Contemporary attitudes to class immunity

Mounting judicial unease concerning extensive executive use of class claims was evident in *R v Chief Constable of West Midlands, ex parte Wiley* [1995] 1 AC 274. On that occasion the Master of the Rolls, Lord Woolf, said that 'the recognition of a new class based public interest immunity requires clear and compelling evidence that it is necessary'. The liberal use of class claims by ministers was also criticised by Sir Richard Scott in his report on the Matrix Churchill affair (Report of the Inquiry into the Export of Defence Equipment and Dual Use Goods to Iraq and Related Prosecutions, 1995–96 HC Deb 115).

In December 1996, by way of response to these expressions of concern, the Attorney-General made a statement to the House of Commons concerning the future use of public interest immunity (PII) certificates in both civil and criminal proceedings. The main principles of the statement were as follows:

Under the new approach, Ministers will focus directly on the damage that disclosure would cause. The former division into class and contents claims will no longer be applied. Ministers will claim public interest immunity only when it is believed that disclosure of a document would cause real damage or harm to the public interest... The new emphasis on the test of serious harm means that Ministers will not, for example, claim PII to protect either internal advice or national security material merely by pointing to the general nature of the document. The only basis for claiming PII will be a belief that disclosure will cause real harm.

This appeared to presage the end of class claims by central government. The statement was, however, not legally binding and could not affect the practice of other persons and bodies, whether public or private. It was inevitable, therefore, that class claims would continue to be asserted by bodies such as the police, local councils and health authorities. It would soon become apparent, however, that judicial unease with the entire concept of class immunities was hardening into the state of a general policy in whatever the context. This was consistent with the jurisprudence of the European Convention on Human Rights, which prefers concessions to the public interest to be considered on a case-by-case basis rather than applied as inflexible blanket immunities (see *Osman v United Kingdom* (2000) 29 EHRR 245). Hence in a number of cases claims to class or blanket immunities for information relating to police informers were rejected in favour of a balancing exercise by the court (see *Savage v Chief Constable of the Hampshire Constabulary* [1997] 1 WLR 1061; *Powell v Chief Constable of North Wales Constabulary*, The Times, 11 February 2002; *Whitmarsh v Chief Constable of Avon and Somerset*, unreported). The judicial reluctance to simply accept a class immunity in one of the most well established contexts was approved by the Court of Appeal in *Chief Constable of Greater Manchester Police v McNally* [2002] EWCA Civ 14. There Auld LJ spoke of the need to 'soften' the rigidity of the pre-existing class system:

so as to permit a balance of competing interest in a case specific manner [as] part of a wider jurisprudential move away from near absolute protection of various categories of public interest in non disclosure...Now with the advent of Human Rights to our law, this move has the force of European jurisprudence behind it.

A threshold test for inspection

The Air Canada *Decision*

The extent to which the public interest might be prejudiced by the use of high level government documents in legal proceedings was considered again by the House of Lords in *Air Canada* v *Secretary of State for Trade* [1983] 1 All ER 910. The case involved an allegation that the power in the Airports Authority Act 1975 to increase airport charges had been used for the purpose of reducing the public sector borrowing requirement rather than for the purpose intended by Parliament, viz. the efficient management, administration and maintenance of airports under the authority's control. The plaintiffs sought access to documents in the possession of the minister and the BAA which contained details of discussions at ministerial level which led to the decision in question.

In the High Court, Bingham J ordered production of the documents for inspection but directed that the order be stayed pending an appeal by the minister. Neither the Court of Appeal nor the House of Lords, however, were similarly persuaded of the need for inspection. The House of Lords felt that judges should not just 'take a peep' at any and all documents whenever immunity was claimed. An order for inspection should be made only where grave doubts about the dangers of disclosure existed and the party seeking disclosure was able to satisfy the court of a likelihood that the documents contained 'material of real importance' to the arguments to which they related – which the House felt the appellants had been unable to do.

Variations of opinion

Their Lordships expressed similar but not completely identical opinions concerning the exact nature of the burden of proof lying upon the party seeking disclosure.

> The most that can usefully be said is that, in order to persuade the court even to inspect documents for which public interest immunity is claimed, the party seeking disclosure ought at very least to satisfy the court that the documents are *very likely [author's emphasis]* to contain material which would give *substantial support [ibid.]* to his contention on an issue which arises in the case (per Lord Fraser).

Lord Edmund-Davies thought inspection should follow only when the party seeking production showed there was a 'likelihood' of the documents containing material evidence.
Lord Wilberforce's view was:

> The degree of likelihood (of providing support of the plaintiff's case) may be variously expressed: 'likely' was the word used by Lord Edmund-Davies in the *Burmah Oil* case; a 'reasonable probability' by Lord Keith...Both expressions must mean something beyond speculation, some concrete ground for belief which takes the case beyond a mere 'fishing' expedition.

Both Lords Scarman and Templeman, however, felt inclined to adopt a more liberal standard, taking the view that inspection should not be limited simply to cases where production would be likely to help the party seeking production but should also be permitted where the documents were 'likely to be necessary for fairly disposing of the case'. The main criterion, they felt, in deciding whether to inspect was whether this was necessary to ensure justice was done and not 'whether the party seeking production can establish the likelihood that the documents will assist his case or damage that of his opponent' (per Lord Scarman).

The objective of their Lordships was clearly to discourage litigants from embarking on mere 'fishing expeditions' into documents in possession of others. It has been said, however, that the case has created something of a 'Catch 22' in that, in order to persuade a court of the case for inspection, a pre-existing knowledge of the contents or relevance of the documents would appear to be required.

PLEADING PUBLIC INTEREST IMMUNITY: DUTY OR DISCRETION

The dilemma

In recent times one of the issues which has attracted particular attention in this area of legal development has been whether the pleading of public interest immunity should be regarded as a matter of obligation or merely of discretion. The argument has been advanced, for example, that there is a duty to claim immunity for all documents belonging, or believed to belong, to a class covered by public interest immunity. In other words, the repository in question does not have a choice: it is his/her legal duty to plead immunity and it is for the court, and the court alone, to balance the public interest in concealment against the public interest in the administration of justice. Thus, the balancing exercise is a purely judicial function and not something to be undertaken by government officials, domestic bodies or private citizens.

> Public interest immunity cannot be waived... it is the duty of a party to assert the immunity, even where it is to his disadvantage in the litigation... [A] party claiming immunity is not claiming a right but observing a duty... [A]lthough one can waive rights, one cannot waive duties (Keane (1994), *The Modern Law of Evidence* (3rd edn), p 440).

The duty to plead public interest immunity

Dicta favouring the existence of a general duty to plead immunity may be found in a number of cases, including the *Air Canada* decision.

> The Crown when it puts forward a public interest immunity objection is not claiming a privilege but discharging a duty. The duty arises whether the document assists or damages the Crown's case or if, as in a case to which the Crown is not a party, it neither helps nor injures the Crown. It is not for the Crown but the court to decide whether the documents should be produced (per Lord Scarman).

The principle was given more detailed expression by Bingham LJ in *Makanjuola v Metropolitan Police Commissioner* [1992] 3 All ER 617:

> [Where] a litigant asserts that documents are immune from production or disclosure on the grounds of public interest immunity he is not claiming a right...observing a duty. Public interest immunity is not a trump card vouchsafed to certain privileged players to play as and when they wish (at p 623).

Some qualifications to the above view were expressed when the issue was considered again by the House of Lords in *ex parte Wiley* [1995] 1 AC 274. The House expressed general approval of Bingham LJ's views but emphasised that any exclusive duty to plead public interest immunity should lie only on those not sufficiently qualified or competent to exercise the constitutional responsibility for deciding between competing public interests. The principle against waiver should not be understood, therefore, as applying to those such as ministers of the Crown who were accustomed and responsible to Parliament for the making of such decisions on a regular basis.

> If a Secretary of State on behalf of his department as opposed to any ordinary litigant concludes that any public interest in documents being withheld from production is outweighed by the public interest in the documents being available for the purpose of litigation, it is difficult to believe that unless the documents do not relate to an area for which the Secretary of State was responsible the court would feel it appropriate to come to any different conclusion...The position would be the same if the Attorney-General was of the opinion that the documents should be disclosed (per Lord Woolf).

This suggests an underlying judicial policy to develop principles designed to reduce the risk of prima facie immune documents being released by parties neither competent to undertake any valid weighing of the public interests involved nor politically answerable for the decisions made.

> Where, however, parties other than government departments are in possession of documents in respect of which public interest immunity could be claimed on a class basis, there are practical difficulties in allowing an individual to decide that the documents should be disclosed. The indiscriminate and, indeed, any disclosure of documents which are the subject of a class claim to immunity can undermine that class. If the reason for the existence of the class is that those who make the statement should be assured that the statement will not be disclosed, the fact that in some cases they are disclosed undermines the assurance (*ibid.* at p 297).

Note, however, that not all academic opinion would appear to be supportive of the *Wiley* approach.

> The problem here is that the exercise of such discretion would itself be likely to devalue the class claim. If the Minister were at liberty to determine the justification for non-disclosure in all the circumstances of the case, he would be free to manipulate the immunity to his own advantage. There would be a constant temptation to waive immunity when disclosure would serve the immediate interests of government, overlooking the less tangible or less quantifiable interests favoured by secrecy. And that temptation would itself engender judicial scepticism. How could the court attach any weight to a class claim when it is known that, despite its assertion of a general, strategic public interest in confidentiality, ministers may choose whether or not to invoke it in any particular case? (Allen, 'Public Interest Immunity and Ministers' Responsibilities' [1993] Crim LR 660).

The above principles do not appear to be applicable to contents claims since in this context there is no danger of an individual decision undermining a pre-existing case for class immunity.

PUBLIC INTEREST IMMUNITY AND CRIMINAL PROCEEDINGS

Disclosure of evidence: general principles

According to the Criminal Procedure and Investigations Act 1996, the prosecution in a trial on indictment or contested summary trial should disclose to the defence that which they intend to use as evidence in court and any other material which might tend to undermine the prosecution's case. Therefore, it is only in respect of a refusal to disclose such material that a court may be asked to rule on a plea of public interest immunity.

The application of public interest immunity

Notwithstanding that most of the law of Crown privilege and public interest immunity has been developed in the general context of civil litigation, it is now established that immunity may also be pleaded in criminal proceedings where disclosure of evidence could prejudice the public interest – particularly in relation to the investigation of crime or the protection of national security.

> The cases in regard to public interest immunity do not refer to criminal proceedings, but the principles are expressed in general terms. Asking myself why those general expositions should not apply to criminal proceedings, I can see no answer but that they do. It seems correct in principle that they should apply. The reasons for the development of the doctrine seem equally equivalent to criminal as to civil proceedings (per Mann LJ, R v Governor of Brixton Prison, ex parte Osman (No. 1) [1992] 1 All ER 108).

The balancing exercise

Where public interest immunity is raised in criminal proceedings additional weight should be given to the public interest in the administration of justice. Here, given the potentially grave consequences for the defendant, it is crucial that justice is both done and seen to be done.

> I acknowledge that the application of the public interest immunity doctrine in criminal proceedings will involve a different balancing exercise to that in civil proceedings... Suffice it to say for the moment that a judge is balancing on the one hand the desirability of preserving the public interest in the absence of disclosure against, on the other hand, the interests of justice. Where the interests of justice arise in a criminal case touching on or concerning liberty or conceivably on occasion life, the weight to be attached to the interests of justice is plainly very great indeed (ibid.).

The Air Canada test that the party seeking production is able to show that the information for which immunity is pleaded is likely to contain 'material of real importance', does not appear to apply to criminal proceedings. Hence, subject to a possible exception in relation to highly sensitive security material, it appears that inspection must follow automatically from any plea of immunity.

When and how public interest immunity should be claimed

If the prosecution believes that the public interest lies in not disclosing documents in their possession, this should be made known to the defence. It is not open to the prosecution to remain silent about the existence of possibly significant documents on the grounds of public interest immunity.

It is crucial in criminal cases – in relation to both class and contents claims – that the court should be the final arbiter of whether the public interest lies in concealment or disclosure. Hence, in every case in which the prosecution feels that material documents are covered by immunity they should, after giving notice to the defence and identifying the particular protected class to which the documents belong, apply to the court for an appropriate ruling. In general this should be dealt with *inter partes* with the defence being given the opportunity to make any related representations.

This is not, however, an absolute rule and a number of exceptions to it were identified by the Court of Criminal Appeal in *R v Davies, Johnson and Rowe* (1993) 97 Cr App R 110. Lord Taylor CJ said that where even to disclose the category of the material in question could cause damage to the public interest, the defence should still be notified that an application to the court was to be made (i.e. for a ruling whether public interest immunity applies) 'but the category of the material need not be specified and the application will be *ex parte*'. More controversially, it was also his opinion that in a 'highly exceptional case' where even to reveal an intention to apply for such a ruling would 'let the cat out of the bag' (i.e. indirectly put into the public domain information normally covered by immunity), 'the prosecution should apply to the court, *ex parte,* without notice to the defence'.

Should the prosecution be so concerned about the disclosure of documents that they are unwilling to entrust the balancing exercise to the court, they should – rather than risk injustice – abandon the prosecution.

In *Jasper v United Kingdom* (2000) 30 EHRR 441, the above procedure was found to be in general compliance with the requirements of Art 6 of the European Convention on Human Rights. The Court of Human Rights was, however, at pains to emphasise the need for *ex parte* applications to be subject to proper and adequate safeguards and, in particular, that the defence be kept informed and permitted both to make submissions and generally participate in the process so far as might be possible without revealing the material in question.

Denial of the existence of potentially public interest immunity material at the trial stage is a breach of Art 6 and is not cured by an *ex parte* application in respect of such material on appeal (*Atlan v United Kingdom* [2002] 34 EHRR 33).

Waiver

The general proscription against waiver of public interest immunity does not apply to the Crown Prosecution Service.

> Should then criminal cases on occasion be treated as 'exceptional' and should the court give its blessing to some measure of voluntary disclosure of class documents by the prosecution? I believe so, but provided always that proper procedures are established and safeguards observed (*Jasper*, above).

These safeguards are that, before voluntary disclosure, the CPS should submit to the Treasury Solicitor copies of the documents proposed to be disclosed. In turn, the Treasury Solicitor should consult any interested government departments to satisfy himself/herself that the balance of interests favours disclosure.

Some doubt appears to exist concerning whether voluntary disclosure by the CPS constitutes 'waiver' of public interest immunity in relation to the particular class or category of documents just for the purposes of the trial to which they relate or, more fundamentally, amounts to a general admission that the class immunity which, prima facie, excludes such documents from use in civil matters will not be asserted in criminal proceedings – i.e. to the extent that there is a public interest in keeping the class concealed – that interest is not sufficient to outweigh the need to ensure that everything is done to avoid conviction of the innocent.

This, of course, raises the question of the extent to which repeated disclosure of a particular class in criminal proceedings undermines any public interest there may hitherto have been for excluding that class from civil cases. Opinions here differ. In *R v Horseferry Road Magistrates, ex parte Bennett (No. 2)* [1994] 1 All ER 289, Simon Brown LJ suggested that a class claim might 'not necessarily be destroyed by repeated disclosure' (at p 298). TRS Allen, however, has argued, more restrictively, that the 'relevant class immunity may not be undermined by *occasional* [author's emphasis] disclosure' (*op. cit.*, at p 667) – which could be understood as implying that disclosure beyond the occasional would be inimical to maintenance of any case for a continued public interest in concealment in civil cases. The latter view would appear to be the more logical since, once repeated disclosure of a particular type of documents has occurred in criminal courts, it would seem almost absurd to argue that the repository of such remained under a duty to plead immunity for that same class in civil matters – particularly as this would increase the likelihood of the repository being obliged to plead public interest immunity in respect of information already in the public domain.

Public interest immunity in magistrates' courts

In *R v Bromley Magistrates Court, ex parte Smith and Wilkins* [1995] 1 WLR 944, the Divisional Court affirmed that magistrates have the power to rule on disputed issues of disclosure raised in summary proceedings and, in so doing, should be guided by the principles already developed for the disposal of such matters on indictment.

This did not appear to be entirely consistent with the same court's previous decision in *R v Crown Prosecution Service, ex parte Warby* (1994) 158 JP 190, where Watkins LJ said that it would be 'entirely inappropriate for decisions as to disclosure of unused material to be taken at a lower level of activity than the Crown Court'. The view taken in the *Bromley* case, however, was that *Warby* should be confined to its own facts and understood, therefore, as denying any magisterial power to consider these issues in the course of committal proceedings.

> The role of an examining Justice is to ensure that a defendant does not stand trial at the Crown Court unless there is a prima facie case against him. The decisions as to disclosure in these circumstances are, therefore, properly and solely made by the Crown Court (per Rose LJ, *R v South Worcester Justices, ex parte Lilley* [1995] 4 All ER 186).

The court in *Bromley* concluded that, as a general rule, a bench which had ruled on a matter relating to disclosure – normally as a preliminary issue – should not be disqualified from proceeding to deal with the actual trial. 'Ideally the same constitution of the magistrates should decide questions of disclosure as well as conduct the actual trial' (per Simon Brown LJ).

In *Lilley*, however, it was recognised that magistrates might not be so skilled at excluding from their minds material which they had previously decided should not be disclosed and which, therefore, should have no effect on the proceedings before them. It followed, felt Rose LJ, that in certain circumstances – as where an issue of public interest immunity had been dealt with *ex parte* – the need for justice to be seen to be done might require that the actual trial be heard by a differently constituted bench.

The facts in *Lilley* were that both the defendant and his legal representative had been excluded from the court while the bench considered documentary and oral testimony in support of the prosecution's claim for immunity. As a result, according to Rose LJ, 'a reasonable and fair-minded person sitting in the court would...have a reasonable suspicion that a fair trial for the defendant was not possible if the same bench of Justices continued with the hearing against him'.

Of these two approaches, subsequent cases have tended to favour that taken in *Bromley*. The court in *R v Norfolk Stipendiary Magistrate, ex parte Taylor* (1997) 161 JP 773 expressed its confidence in the intellectual capacity and integrity of magistrates to avoid being influenced by material which may have come to their attention by way of a public interest immunity hearing. As a result no unfairness was posed by allowing the same bench to deal with the public interest immunity application and the subsequent trial. The same confidence in the ability of magistrates both lay and stipendiary (district judges) to deal fairly with such proceedings was expressed by Lord Woolf in *R (on the application of DPP) v Acton Youth Court* [2001] EWCA (Admin) 402.

References

Allen (1993) 'Public Interest Immunity and Ministers' Responsibilities' [1993] Crim LR 660.

Calvert (1985) *An Introduction to British Constitutional Law*, London: Financial Training.

Hogg (1989) *The Liability of the Crown* (2nd edn), Town, Australia: Law Book Co Ltd.

Keane (1996) *The Modern Law of Evidence* (4th edn), London: Butterworths.

Wade and Forsyth (1994) *Administrative Law* (7th edn), Oxford: Clarendon Press.

Further reading

Craig (1994) *Administrative Law* (3rd edn), London: Sweet & Maxwell, Ch 20.

Cripps (1994) *The Legal Implications of Disclosure in the Public Interest* (2nd edn), London: Sweet & Maxwell, Ch 8.

Cross and Tapper (1994) *Cross and Tapper on Evidence* (8th edn), London: Butterworths, Ch 11.

Jones and Thompson (eds) (1996) *Garner's Administrative Law* (8th edn), London: Butterworths, Ch 10.

Mitchell (1984) *The Contracts of Public Authorities*, London: London School of Economics.

Turpin (1989) *Government Procurement and Contracts*, London: Longman.

Wade and Forsyth (1994) *Administrative Law* (8th edn), London: Butterworths.

Part 5

JUDICIAL REVIEW OF ADMINISTRATIVE ACTION

Chapter 14

THE NATURE OF JUDICIAL REVIEW

INTRODUCTION

Any person aggrieved by an alleged misuse of power by a public body and who feels that the body has acted *ultra vires* or in breach of the rules of natural justice may apply for judicial review of the action or decision in question. The application is made to the Divisional Court of the Queen's Bench Division of the High Court.

A public body acts *ultra vires* if it does that for which it had no legal authority either in statute or common law. It acts in breach of the rules of natural justice if, in making a decision, it contravenes any of the procedural rights the common law accords to a person affected by the exercise of a decision-making power. In either case such misuse of power will result in a finding that the body's actions were void *ab initio*, i.e. of no legal effect from the beginning.

The modern tendency is to deal with the specific rules contained within the doctrines of *ultra vires* and natural justice under the headings of illegality, irrationality, and procedural impropriety. This classification was first proposed by Lord Diplock in the *GCHQ* case and will be considered in more detail below.

Suffice it to say, at present, that a decision is void for illegality if the decision-making body stepped outside the legal limits of its authority or failed to exercise its discretion consistent with the intentions of Parliament or the underlying values of the legal system. A decision is irrational and of no legal effect if it is so extraordinary or perverse that no reasonable decision-maker could have arrived at it. Procedural impropriety occurs where the decision-maker fails to comply with any relevant procedural requirements imposed by the enabling statute (i.e. the one in which the decision-making power is contained) or the common law rules of natural justice (i.e. the right to a fair hearing and the rule against bias).

In applying these tests to determine the legality and validity of government action, the High Court is exercising its ancient supervisory jurisdiction over 'subordinate' government officials and bodies – in effect, all those vested by law with the authority of government. This jurisdiction is said to be inherent; in other words, it is derived from centuries of constitutional development and not from any formal grant of authority by Parliament. It is through the exercise of this jurisdiction that the British constitution gives practical effect to its most fundamental underlying values and to the imperatives contained in the doctrines of the sovereignty of Parliament, the rule of law and the separation of powers.

Judicial review and the sovereignty of Parliament

Acts of Parliament are the source of most of the powers exercised by administrative and judicial bodies. These are the commands of the sovereign body which lay down the nature and extent of the authority so granted. It is logical, therefore, for the courts to assume and insist that the repositories of such authority do that and only that which has been commissioned by Parliament. At its simplest level, therefore, a public body acts lawfully (*intra vires*) so long as it uses its powers within and according to the grant of authority given to it by Parliament. If not, it has exceeded its lawful authority and acted *ultra vires*.

Judicial review and the rule of law

Judicial review is given further justification and definition by the requirements of the rule of law. As already explained, the rule of law is a doctrine of political morality. It seeks to impose certain minimum standards of conduct on those responsible for the process of government. These are the standards which are perceived to be commensurate with the practice of good government in a liberal democracy. In the language of judicial review they are encapsulated in words such as legality, reasonableness, rationality, fairness and in the rejection of such concepts as arbitrary and unrestricted discretionary power (i.e. that without any legal foundation or discernable legal limits).

Judicial review is concerned with the enforcement of these standards and with the application of legal rules, enshrined in the doctrines of *ultra vires* and natural justice, which have been developed for this purpose. Thus, if a decision-maker makes a finding on the basis of wholly irrelevant considerations, this may be condemned as unreasonable in law and *ultra vires* the ambit of the power used. If the decision is one which may have a seriously detrimental effect on an individual's legal rights, and that individual has been given no opportunity to be heard orally or through written representations, the decision-maker may be said to have acted unfairly so that again the validity of the decision may be challenged in proceedings for judicial review.

Judicial review and the separation of powers

Judicial review may be further understood as an expression of, and as being underpinned by, the doctrine of the separation of powers. It is an expression of the doctrine in that it represents one of the principal 'checks and balances' developed by the constitution to guard against abuse of power. Judicial review is underpinned by the separation of powers in that its effectiveness and credibility depends on the existence of an independent and impartial judiciary. A judiciary subject to executive influence could not be relied upon to act as an impartial arbiter in disputes involving the individual and the state.

The legal and conventional rules which seek to guarantee judicial independence and impartiality have already been considered (see Chapter 2). These presume that, for meaningful legal control of power, judges must be able to find against government officials without fear of sanction or retribution and that they must be seen to be exercising their supervisory jurisdiction without political favour or bias.

THE SCOPE OF JUDICIAL REVIEW

Government bodies exercise both public and private law powers. It is in relation to the latter that an application for judicial review may be made. The distinction between the two is somewhat blurred and is considered in more detail below. For introductory purposes, however, a public law power may be described as one which will usually be authorised by statute or the royal prerogative and is concerned with the regulation or protection of some aspect of the public interest. The exercise of a public law power will often involve the restriction of private law rights where this is perceived to be for the public benefit – e.g. the compulsory purchase of land for the provision of public amenities.

Authority for the private law actions of a public body will be derived usually from the contract with, or from the consent of, those in relation to whom the function is exercised. It will be a function which is not integral to the usually understood meanings of the words 'government' or 'public administration'. An example would be the authority of a public body to dismiss an employee for incompetence or misconduct. This authority will be drawn from the contract of employment agreed between that body and the particular employee. It is a contractual right which will be claimed and exercised in the appropriate circumstances by all employers whether in the public or private sector. The exercise of the right is not directly related to any of the usually understood functions of government. It is a private legal arrangement between the public body in its role as an employer and the individual affected. It does not create any powers or obligations in which the public have a direct interest. If the body has done something not permitted by the contract, the individual's remedy is to sue in respect of the breach, not to apply for judicial review.

JURISDICTION AND POWER

These words appear frequently in the language of judicial review. They are generally used to demarcate the boundaries of decision-making authority within which a public body is free to act without judicial interference. Although the terms are often treated as synonymous, it is more accurate to confine the word 'power' to the administrative and secondary legislative authority conferred on executive bodies, both central and local. Thus the Home Secretary may be said to have the 'power' to deport from the United Kingdom any person whose presence here is not conducive to the public good (Immigration Act 1971). Where, however, it is the extent of the decision-making competence of a judicial body (e.g. an inferior court or administrative tribunal) which is in issue, the concept of 'jurisdiction' is generally to be preferred. Here, as a general rule, the word refers to the matters upon which the court or tribunal has been given the authority to make decisions and to the law which it has been empowered to apply for that purpose.

The existence of power or jurisdiction as so explained was once assumed to be discernable at the outset of the decision-maker's inquiry and could be determined by asking certain fundamental questions – principally, was the body properly constituted and was it dealing with a matter upon which it was legally entitled to decide. If such questions were answered in the affirmative then the decision-maker had power or jurisdiction to proceed safe from risk of judicial review. It was, therefore, not open to a court to question the sufficiency of evidence for a particular decision or its reasonableness (i.e. whether there were reasonable grounds for it or whether any irrelevant matter had been taken into account). Nor would a court say that a decision-maker had gone outside its lawful jurisdiction if it misinterpreted any of the legal rules which it had the authority to apply to the matters remitted to it. As a general principle, questions of fact, discretion and law were all assumed to lie within the decision-maker's jurisdiction or power. Errors relating thereto did not justify any finding that the decision-maker had acted *ultra vires*: 'Where a court has jurisdiction to entertain an application, it does not lose its jurisdiction by coming to a wrong conclusion, whether it was wrong in law or in fact' (per Lord Coleridge CJ, *R v Central Criminal Court JJ* (1886) 17 QBD 598).

As understood in this sense, the concepts of jurisdiction and power permitted only a limited role for judicial review.

> Although the courts would insist on compliance with statutory requirements as to form and procedure, it was extremely difficult to persuade them that a Minister had acted *ultra vires* by erring in law or fact, or that he was under an implied obligation to observe the rules of natural justice, or that in exercising a discretionary power he had been influenced by legally improper considerations (De Smith, *Judicial Review of Administrative Action*).

It is generally accepted that the position remained largely thus until the 1960s. By this time, however, pro-executive judicial tendencies – so evident during World War II and its immediate aftermath – had begun to diminish. A change in judicial policy became evident. Although not so articulated, this was no doubt in response to what was perceived to be the ever-increasing power of the state – particularly the wide discretionary powers being vested in ministers and other public officials. It became apparent from a number of key decisions that judicial understanding of the concepts of power and jurisdiction was being revised in order to permit more extensive and effective legal control of the powers of government. These were no longer to be questions determinable primarily at the outset of the inquiry. Henceforth, errors such as lack or insufficiency of evidence, abuse of discretion (e.g. irrelevancy) and mistake of law committed during the inquiry, were to be regarded as 'going to jurisdiction'. Lack or insufficiency of evidence was asserted as a jurisdictional matter in *Ashbridge Investments Ltd v Minister of Housing and Local Government* [1965] 1 WLR 1320: '...the court can interfere with the Minister's decision if he has acted on no evidence, or if he has come to a conclusion to which on the evidence he could not reasonably have come' (per Lord Denning MR).

The same was said of abuse of discretion by the House of Lords in *Padfield v Minister of Agriculture* [1968] AC 997:

> Parliament must have conferred the discretion with the intention that it should be used to promote the policy and objects of the Act.... [I]f the Minister...so uses his discretion as to thwart or run counter to the policy and objects of the Act...the law would be very defective if persons aggrieved were not entitled to the protection of the courts (per Lord Reid).

Perhaps the most important case in the 1960s in terms of extending the scope of judicial review was *Anisminic v Foreign Compensation Commission (No. 2)* [1969] 2 AC 147. On that occasion the House of Lords, in deciding that a tribunal could lose jurisdiction if it made a mistake of law, made it abundantly clear that jurisdictional errors could occur during, as well as at the beginning of, any inquiry.

> Lack of jurisdiction may arise in many ways. There may be an absence of those formalities or things which are conditions precedent to the tribunal having any jurisdiction to embark on an inquiry. Or at the end the tribunal may make an order that it has no jurisdiction to make. Or in the interviewing stage, while engaged on a proper inquiry, the tribunal may depart from the rules of natural justice; or may ask itself the wrong questions; or it may take into account matters which it was not directed to take into account. Thereby it would step outside its jurisdiction. It would turn its inquiry into something not directed by Parliament and fail to make the inquiry which Parliament did direct. Any of these things would cause its purported decision to be a nullity (per Lord Pearce).

All of this tends to suggest that the meaning of power or jurisdiction is a matter of judicial policy which may be adjusted from time to time in accordance with the judges' view of their relationship with the executive and the need to maintain the effectiveness of the constitutional balance inherent in the separation of powers.

REVIEW AND APPEAL CONTRASTED

In exercising the power of review the court's inquiry should be directed solely to the legality of the decision in issue – i.e. whether the decision-maker acted illegally, irrationally or improperly in a procedural sense. The merits of the decision are not in issue. It matters not, for example, that the body appears to have made the 'right' decision – i.e. one which, given the relevant factual and policy considerations, most objective observers would have agreed with. If it has acted unlawfully – e.g. the decision was not one that it was empowered to make – the matter is subject to judicial review. By the same token, if the body appears to have made the 'wrong' decision, but has done so without any abuse of power, its findings of fact are not a matter for judicial inquiry.

Where an individual feels that a decision made by a public body in relation to him/her was simply 'wrong', the appropriate remedy is to appeal. Whether a right of appeal exists will depend on the enabling Act (i.e. the statute which conferred the particular decision-making power). If such right has been granted, the person or body vested with the appellate jurisdiction may then reconsider the facts and either approve the original decision or superimpose its own. The issue of legality does not arise. The question for the appellate body is whether the original decision was right or wrong given the factual and, perhaps, policy considerations on which it was made.

This distinction between review and appeal is of fundamental constitutional importance and, as the following example will illustrate, is directly relevant to proper observance of the doctrines of the sovereignty of Parliament and the separation of powers.

R v Cambridge Health Authority, ex parte B [1995] 1 WLR 898, concerned a young girl who appeared to be terminally ill. The only treatment available which might have prolonged her life was extremely expensive and had only a remote chance of success. It was decided, therefore, that as this would not represent a prudent use of scarce public resources, the treatment would not be given.

This caused considerable public outcry. Many thought the decision not only 'wrong' but morally indefensible. This may have weighed heavily on members of the judiciary for, although the Health Authority did not appear to have acted beyond the ambit of its powers, the High Court granted an application for judicial review. *Certiorari* was issued to quash the decision and the Health Authority was ordered to reconsider the issue.

An appeal against the grant of review was then made to the Court of Appeal. Its members were also clearly in great sympathy with the girl's plight. Sir Thomas Bingham MR said that 'in a perfect world any treatment which a patient…sought would be provided if doctors were willing to give it'. He also recognised, however, that judicial review should not be granted simply because a court had misgivings about an administrative body's findings on a particular matter which fell within the jurisdictional limits given to it. It would be an abuse of the court's proper constitutional function to exercise a power of appeal in the guise of judicial review:

> …the courts are not, contrary to what is sometimes believed, arbiters as to the merits of cases of this kind. Were we to express opinions as to the likelihood of the effectiveness of medical treatment, or as to the merits of medical judgement, then we would be straying far from the sphere which, under our constitution, is accorded to us. We have one function only which is to rule upon the lawfulness of decisions. That is a function to which we should strictly confine ourselves.

Thus the Court of Appeal was emphasising that it was not for a court to question decisions on matters of fact and policy which Parliament has entrusted to a particular administrative authority. So to do would subvert the will of Parliament and transgress the separation of powers by taking the court into the realms of public policy. In this case the question of how best to use the limited resources made available to the Health Service was a matter which clearly fell within the domain of the executive branch of government.

Review and appeal may also be contrasted by reference to their legal origins. The right to judicial review emanates from the common law. It is the fundamental right of any person aggrieved by an act of government. It is not something which is derived from, or dependent on, an Act of Parliament.

As already indicated, however, there is no inherent common law right to appeal against the merits of a public body's decision. In some instances, where Parliament confers a power to decide, that power will be made subject to a right of appeal. In others it may not. All will depend on the enabling legislation and whether those responsible for its enactment felt that a right of appeal would be detrimental to administrative efficiency or any other public interest (e.g. national security). This has produced a somewhat haphazard system of appeals in which some powers to decide are appealable and others are not.

SOURCES OF PUBLIC LAW POWER

The principal source of public law decision-making authority for central and local government bodies is statute. However, the Crown or central government also draws other important public law powers from the royal prerogative. The nature and subject matter of these common law or prerogative powers has already been explained. Other bodies which perform significant administrative and regulatory functions in certain contexts may have no legal origins or powers whatsoever (e.g. the City Panel on Take-Overs and Mergers). The undoubted authority of such bodies will usually be derived from contractual arrangements with, or the consent of, those engaged in the activities for which such bodies are responsible.

Whether such powers may be regarded as 'public' in nature and subject, therefore, to judicial review, is a matter of some uncertainty (see Chapter 17: Exclusivity). As a general rule, however, it may be said that if such powers are of major significance for the protection of a particular public interest, and would otherwise have to be cast into statutory form and exercised by a government body, they may be regarded as falling within the realms of public law and the supervisory jurisdiction of the High Court.

Reference

De Smith (1995) *Judicial Review of Administrative Action* (5th edn), London: Stevens.

Further reading

Cane (1996) *An Introduction to Administrative Law* (3rd edn), Oxford: Clarendon Press, Ch 1.

Fenwick and Phillipson (1997) *Sourcebook on Public Law*, London: Cavendish, Pt V, Ch 1.

Jones and Thompson (eds) (1996) Garner's *Administrative Law* (8th edn), London: Butterworths, Ch 8.

Chapter 15

GROUNDS FOR JUDICIAL REVIEW: ILLEGALITY, IRRATIONALITY AND PROCEDURAL IMPROPRIETY

ILLEGALITY: INTRODUCTION

This head of judicial review is concerned with the control of:

(a) power and jurisdiction, i.e. ensuring that the body acts within the legal authority remitted to it;
(b) discretion, i.e. ensuring that when dealing with a matter within its jurisdiction the body exercises the full ambit of the discretionary power entrusted to it and in a way which Parliament is entitled to expect of a responsible and prudent decision-maker.

ILLEGALITY AND JURISDICTIONAL CONTROL

A body acts outside its power or jurisdiction if it:

(a) takes any decision or action which was beyond its legal authority or fails to do something which it was obliged to do ('simple' *ultra vires*);
(b) takes any decision or action for which it had legal authority but in relation to the wrong subject matter (error of jurisdictional fact);
(c) misinterprets the law applicable to the issue to be decided (error of law).

Simple ultra vires

Lack of power

The case traditionally cited to illustrate this type of error is *Attorney-General v Fulham Corporation* [1921] 1 Ch 440. The Corporation had a statutory power to provide washhouses. These were to be places with facilities for people to come and wash their clothes. Instead the Corporation provided a laundry, i.e. a place to which people could bring their clothes to be washed by local government employees in return for a small payment. This clearly was something which the Corporation had not been empowered to do.

The principle may also be seen from the decision in *Attorney-General v Wilts United Dairies* (1921) TLR 884. On this occasion the House of Lords enforced the basic constitutional principle that a public authority should not impose any tax or financial charge without clear statutory authorisation. The facts were that under emergency wartime legislation the government had been given the power to control the production and supply of food. In a purported exercise of this power the Minister of Food granted the Dairy Company a licence to buy and distribute milk in the south-west of England. This was subject to a condition that the company pay a 2d charge to the government for every gallon of milk purchased. When the government brought proceedings for arrears of such payments, the court found that the imposition of the charge offended the ancient rule, embodied in the Bill of Rights 1689, that no tax should be levied without the approval and authority of Parliament. No such express or implied authority could be construed from the enabling legislation:

> ...if an officer of the executive seeks to justify a charge upon the subject made for the use of the Crown he must show in clear terms that Parliament has authorised the particular charge. I am clearly of the opinion that no such powers...are given to the Minister of Food by the statutory provisions on which he relies (per Atkin LJ).

It should not be assumed from the above that there is any rigid principle confining a body solely to that which has been expressly authorised by statute. A body may also do that which is reasonably incidental to the fulfilment of specific express powers:

> ...whatever may be fairly regarded as incidental to, or consequential upon, those things which the legislative has authorised, ought not...to be held, by judicial construction, to be *ultra vires* (per Lord Selborne, *Attorney-General* v *Great Eastern Railway Co* (1880) 4 App Cas 473).

Failure to fulfil a statutory duty

The difficulties associated with the legal enforcement of statutory duties have already been considered in the context of private actions for damages for breaches of the same. Where, however, such duty is sufficiently specific as to enable a court to identify its requirements with reasonable precision, it will be *ultra vires* and illegal for a public body to fail to give effect to it.

In most cases, however, a statutory duty will be couched in language which allows some flexibility and discretion in terms of what is required to fulfil it. Hence, if a local authority is under a statutory duty to ensure that its streets are lit adequately, this does not impose any exact obligation as the word 'adequately' permits different interpretations. Clearly, if an authority failed to provide any lighting whatsoever, it would act *ultra vires*. If it were to provide some lighting but less than that which could reasonably be regarded as adequate, this also would not be sufficient to bring its actions within the boundaries of legality. In *R* v *Camden London Borough Council, ex parte Gillan* (1988) 21 HLR 114, the Council was under a duty in the Housing Act 1985 to hear and decide whether persons were homeless intentionally or unintentionally and to secure the provision of accommodation as appropriate. Due to a lack of resources, however, the authority's homeless persons unit was open between 9.30 am and 12.30 pm on weekdays only, during which time its staff were available to deal with applications and enquiries made by telephone but not in person. This was held to be less than the acceptable minimum in terms of fulfilment of the duty and, therefore, *ultra vires*.

Error of jurisdictional fact

It is not uncommon for enabling legislation to provide that a power or jurisdiction to decide may be exercised only when a particular fact or state of fact is in existence. Hence if a local council has the statutory authority to seize and destroy all black dogs the lawful use of the power to seize and destroy is dependent on the existence of two questions of fact, viz. is the animal in question (a) black, and (b) a dog. Use of the power to seize and destroy a brown dog or a black cat would therefore be *ultra vires*.

Such facts have been variously defined as jurisdictional facts, precedent facts, preconditional facts and collateral facts. The particular terminology favoured is not of great significance providing it is understood that their function is to delineate the subject matter or factual context in relation to which the power should be exercised.

The principle is sometimes traced to the decision in *White and Collins* v *Minister of Health* [1939] 2 KB 838. The case concerned the validity of a compulsory purchase order. This was made in the course of a local authority's statutory power to acquire land compulsorily for the purpose of building houses providing that the land in question did not form part of any 'park, garden or pleasure ground'. According to the Court of Appeal this made the *vires* of any such order dependent on the existence of a certain state of fact, i.e. that the land to be acquired did not fall into any of the proscribed categories.

> The first and most important matter to bear in mind is that the jurisdiction to make the order is dependent on a finding of fact; for, unless the land can be held not to be part of a park...there is no jurisdiction in the borough council to make, or in the Minister to confirm, the order (per Luxmoore LJ).

The principle was also articulated in *R* v *Home Secretary, ex parte Khawaja* [1984] AC 74, where it was held that the statutory power to arrest, detain and exclude illegal entrants from the United Kingdom could be exercised only against those who were, in fact, illegal entrants. It could not be used, therefore, against persons whom the Home Office simply believed to be illegal entrants, no matter how reasonable that belief may have been: 'That is a "precedent fact" which has to be established. It is not enough that the immigration officer reasonably believes him to be an illegal entrant if the evidence does not justify his belief' (per Lord Fraser).

Similarly, in *Tan Te Lam* v *Superintendent of Tai a Chau Detention Centre* [1996] 4 All ER 256, the Privy Council held that a power to detain an illegal migrant to Hong Kong 'pending' that person's removal and return to Vietnam could be exercised lawfully only where such removal was actually pending, i.e. as a matter of fact was likely to occur within a reasonable time.

The no-evidence rule

Where the necessary jurisdictional facts are in existence so that a body enters upon its jurisdiction lawfully, its findings of fact therein are not subject to review. Findings of fact within jurisdiction are, as a general rule, a matter for appeal and not judicial review.

However, this is subject to one major qualification, usually referred to as the 'no-evidence rule'. According to this a decision may be *ultra vires* if:

(a) it was based on no evidence whatsoever;
(b) the evidence available was so minimal that no reasonable decision-maker could have based a decision of any kind upon it.

In *Coleen Properties Ltd* v *Minister of Housing and Local Government* [1971] 1 WLR 433, a local authority had power to compulsorily acquire slum properties for the purpose of redevelopment and, as part of such scheme, to acquire other properties (i.e. those which were not slums) where this was 'reasonably necessary for the satisfactory development' of the area in question (Housing Act 1957, s 43). A compulsory purchase order was served on a property of this type belonging to Coleen Properties Ltd. They appealed against it. A local public inquiry was convened. At the inquiry the local housing authority offered no evidence relating to the need to acquire the property in question. The compulsory purchase order was later confirmed by the minister after he had considered the report of the inspector who had presided over the inquiry.

In the instant proceedings the Court of Appeal held that the minister could not have reached any valid conclusion that it was 'reasonably necessary' to acquire the property for the proper development of the area concerned. In the absence of evidence to this effect having been put to the local inquiry, no such evidence was contained in the inspector's report. Therefore, there was no factual material before the minister on which he could have based his decision.

Error of law

This occurs where a public body (e.g. a tribunal) misconstrues or gives an incorrect meaning to legal rules which it has been empowered to apply to the facts of cases coming before it for decision.

The traditional view was that where a decision-maker erred in law this did not 'go to jurisdiction'; that is, the decision-maker did not act *ultra vires*. Mistakes of law within jurisdiction could only be remedied through an appeal (where such right existed) or by applying for review for what was known as 'error of law on the face of the record'. The latter was an ancient ground of relief, popular until the mid-nineteenth century, and was used to challenge the validity of decisions where a mistake of law or procedure could be found in the record of the particular proceedings. It was a useful remedy in the days before the present hierarchy of courts was established (Judicature Acts 1873–5) when rights of appeal from inferior courts and tribunals did not always exist, and was typical of an age in which procedural correctness and the keeping of accurate records was sometimes accorded a higher priority than justice itself. As a result, however, of the Summary Jurisdiction Act 1848, after which petty sessions or magistrates' courts were no longer required to keep detailed records of decisions, and the Judicature Acts (above) which provided for appeals on matters of fact and law from inferior courts, the remedy lost much of its significance.

Where an official or body committed this type of abuse the resulting decision was 'voidable' (i.e. valid unless and until challenged), and not *ultra vires* and void *ab initio* (i.e. of no legal effect from the beginning).

The remedy of error of law on the face of the record staged something of a revival as a result of the decision in *R v Northumberland Compensation Appeal Tribunal, ex parte Shaw* [1952] 1 KB 338, where the Appeal Tribunal misapplied a regulation which determined the amount of compensation payable to persons who became redundant as a result of the health service reorganisation in 1946. The complainant had no right of appeal from the tribunal's decision and resort to this ancient remedy was the only means by which the court could relieve an obvious injustice:

> ...the court of King's Bench has an inherent jurisdiction to control all inferior tribunals, not in an appellate capacity, but in a supervisory capacity. This control extends not only to seeing that the inferior tribunals keep within their jurisdiction, but also to seeing that they observe the law...the Lord Chief Justice has, in the present case, restored *certiorari* to its rightful place and shown that it can be used to correct errors of law which appear on the fact of the record, even though they do not go to jurisdiction...With the advent of many new tribunals, and the plain need for supervision over them, recourse must once again be had to this well-tried means of control (per Lord Denning).

The law remained thus until the landmark decision in *Anisminic v Foreign Compensation Commission (No. 2)* [1969] 2 AC 47, wherein the House of Lords expressed the view that henceforth an error of law which affected the decision of a tribunal or official should be regarded as 'going to jurisdiction', i.e. as rendering the decision *ultra vires* and void.

> The breakthrough that *Anisminic* made was the recognition...that if a tribunal whose jurisdiction was limited by statute or subordinate legislation mistook the law applicable to the facts as it had found them, it must have asked itself the wrong question, i.e. one into which it was not empowered to inquire and so had no jurisdiction to determine (per Lord Diplock, *O'Reilly v Mackman* [1983] 2 AC 237).

The facts of the *Anisminic* case were as follows. After the Suez War 1956–7, the United Kingdom received a payment of £27.5 million from Egypt to be distributed among British nationals and companies whose property had been seized or destroyed by the Egyptian authorities during the crisis. The task of determining which persons and companies so qualified was given to the Foreign Compensation Commission (established under the Foreign Compensation Act 1950). The Commission was to decide individual claims according to the terms of eligibility set out in the Foreign Compensation (Egypt) (Determination) Order 1959. These provided, *inter alia*, that any claimant or 'successor in title' to the same had to be of British nationality.

Anisminic was a British company whose claim appeared to fall within the necessary criteria. The company claimed compensation in respect of one of their subsidiaries (Sinai Mining) which had been seized during the hostilities and subsequently given over to an Egyptian company, which operated under the name TEDO. Anisminic's claim was, however, rejected. The Foreign Compensation Commission based its decision on the ground that although Anisminic had British nationality, its successor in title, TEDO, did not.

When Anisminic challenged the validity of this conclusion, the House of Lords held that the Foreign Compensation Commission had misconstrued the Order in Council. In particular, the Commission had been wrong to concern itself with the nationality of Anisminic's successor in title. This only became a relevant issue where a successor in title was making the claim. Where a claim was made by the original owner, as in this case, the question of any successor's nationality did not arise and was not something that the Commission was empowered to consider. The Commission had, therefore, 'asked itself the wrong question' or, put another way, had applied an element of the Order in Council which did not relate to the facts before it.

The judgment appeared to suggest, however, that it remained possible for an error of law to be made which did not affect a tribunal's findings and that, if and when this lesser type of error occurred, the mistake would not render the decision to be *ultra vires* and void. In later cases, however, both the Court of Appeal and the House of Lords cast doubt upon the view that it was possible to draw any rational or workable distinction between jurisdictional and non-jurisdictional errors in the sense explained above (see Lord Denning MR, *Pearlman v Keepers and Governors of Harrow School* [1979] QB 56; *Re Racal Communications Ltd* [1981] AC 374). Gradually the view began to emerge that any error of law made by administrative tribunals, officials or inferior courts (e.g. magistrates' and county courts) should be regarded as jurisdictional. The rationale for this was that Parliament could not have intended such bodies to possess the authority to make conclusive findings as to the correct meaning of the law (i.e. the rules and regulations such bodies had been empowered to apply to cases coming before them). Hence, where it was claimed that an administrative tribunal, etc. had 'erred in law', this was a proper matter to be brought before the High Court by way of judicial review.

The present attitude of the courts in this matter has been summarised as follows:

> The concept of error of law within jurisdiction is rapidly becoming obsolete. As a result of a series of judgements the courts now assume that Parliament does not intend to confer jurisdiction or power on inferior courts or public authorities to determine questions of law. All errors of law by public authorities except superior courts are now regarded (or may easily be turned into) jurisdictional errors (Lewis, *Judicial Remedies in Public Law*).

This approach was confirmed by the House of Lords in *Page v Hull University Visitor* [1993] 1 All ER 97, and in *Williams v Bedwellty Justices* [1996] 3 All ER 737. In the latter case Lord Cooke said that 'the authorities now establish that the Queen's Bench Division of the High Court has now in judicial review proceedings jurisdiction to quash a decision of an inferior court, tribunal or other statutory body for error of law'.

ILLEGALITY AND CONTROL OF DISCRETION

Introduction

A body acts *ultra vires* in this context if it fails to exercise or abuses a discretionary power. A failure to exercise discretion occurs where a body:

* delegates its power to decide to a subordinate without statutory authority so to do (unlawful delegation);
* allows its power to decide to be exercised by another and unauthorised body (surrender or abdication of discretion);

- limits its freedom of action by rigid rules of policy (fettering discretion by policy);
- restricts its power to decide by contractual obligations or other undertakings (fettering of discretion by contract);
- decides under the dictation of another body or as a result of improper pressure.

A body abuses its discretion (i.e. uses it unlawfully) if it:

- takes into account wholly irrelevant or extraneous considerations or, conversely, fails to take into account that which was relevant (irrelevancy);
- uses its power to achieve a purpose or objective which is not that for which the power was given (improper purpose).

Unlawful delegation

This occurs where a statute has given power or jurisdiction to body A and body A, without express or implied authority, delegates the exercise of that power or jurisdiction to body B. This is unlawful delegation. Any decision or action by body B is *ultra vires* and unlawful.

In *Barnard* v *National Dock Labour Board* [1953] 2 QB 18, the Dock Workers (Regulation of Employment) Order 1947 had conferred disciplinary powers over dock workers onto the National Dock Labour Board with authority to delegate the exercise of the same to Local Dock Labour Boards. No authority for further delegation of the power could be construed from the legislation. The delegation to, and the exercise of, the disciplinary power by a Port Manager was, therefore, *ultra vires* and unlawful.

The principle was also applied in *R* v *Liverpool City Council, ex parte Professional Association of Teachers*, *The Times*, 22 March 1984. The Education Act 1944 stipulated that a local education authority should consider a report from its education committee before exercising any of its powers. This made it clear that any report was to be formulated by the education committee collectively and not by any other person or body. It was unlawful, therefore, both for an education committee (as in this case) to delegate the formulation of such report to its chairman and for the education authority to act on the basis of the same.

In the interests of administrative efficiency the rule is applied with a degree of flexibility to those exercising administrative powers. A more strict approach is adopted, however, in relation to judicial functions. Thus, where an administrative body is empowered to decide, its decision remains valid albeit that the body has relied upon the recommendations or advice of a committee or an executive official. Where, however, the function is judicial in nature, it would appear that the decision-maker may not rely on reports or recommendations and must consider all the relevant materials before reaching a decision.

> Every member of a judicial body must have access to all the evidence and papers in the case, he must have heard all the arguments and he must come to his own conclusion. The maxim *delegatus non potest delegare* applies strictly to judicial functions (per Denning MR, *R* v *Race Relations Board, ex parte Selvarajaran* [1975] 1 WLR 1686).

Even an administrative body must, however, have something before it more than a mere recommendation. There must be some sort of report, albeit brief, which explains the reasons for the recommendation (see *R v Chester Borough Council, ex parte Quietlynn Ltd* (1985) 83 LGR 308).

The rule against delegation does not mean that all the decision-making powers conferred by statute on specific government ministers have to be exercised by those ministers personally. If it were so the efficient disposal of administrative business would become impossible. Hence it is permissible for such powers to be exercised by a civil servant on the minister's behalf. This is consistent with the constitutional convention that the minister is politically answerable for all the actions and decisions of his/her civil servants. 'Constitutionally, the decision of such an official is, of course, the decision of the Minister. The Minister is responsible. It is he who must answer before Parliament' (per Lord Greene MR, *Carltona Ltd v Commissioners of Works* [1943] 2 All ER 560).

In *R v Skinner* [1967] 2 QB 700, S appealed against a conviction for drink-driving. The Road Traffic Act 1967, s 7 required the Home Secretary's consent for the use of any particular breathalyser device. S argued that the device used in his case had been approved by a senior civil servant but not by the minister personally. His appeal was rejected. Widgery LJ explained that: 'It is not strictly a matter of delegation, it is that the official acts as the Minister himself and the official's decision is the Minister's decision.'

Surrender or abdication of discretion

This occurs where a public body without any formal or conscious act of delegation to a subordinate, allows, or agrees to, the exercise of its power by another body or official or, without due consideration, simply applies the views or recommendations of another body or official to the issues before it. The principle may be illustrated by reference to two well-known cases.

In *Ellis v Dubowski* [1921] 3 KB 621, a local authority had statutory power to license premises to be used as cinemas and to attach to such licence conditions regulating the types of material which could be shown, i.e. as to good taste, public decency, etc. (Cinematograph Act 1909). This was, in effect, a power of censorship. In purported exercise of the power an authority granted a licence subject to the condition that no film be shown which had not been granted a certificate by the British Board of Film Censors. This condition was held to be invalid. It was clear that the authority, instead of exercising and retaining the discretion entrusted to it, had decided to defer, in all cases, to the views of the Board of Film Censors. The Board was, however, a domestic body without any statutory powers whatsoever. Its certificates were intended to be regarded as advisory only. In each case, therefore, the final decision as to the fitness of a particular film for public exhibition was to be taken by the local authority to which Parliament had given the appropriate statutory power (cf. *Mills v London County Council* [1925] 1 KB 213).

The second case, *Lavender v Minister of Housing and Local Government* [1970] 1 WLR 1231, concerned the minister's power to determine appeals against refusals of planning permission by local planning authorities. Lavender appealed against a refusal to allow him to mine gravel deposits in an area of prime agricultural land. It was the minister's policy not to grant appeals in such cases unless so advised by the Minister of Agriculture. In effect, therefore, the discretion to grant or refuse an appeal in this context was being exercised by the Minister of Agriculture and not by the minister to whom the power had been given: 'by applying and acting on his stated policy I think the Minister had fettered himself in such a way that in this case it was not he who made the decision for which Parliament had made him responsible' (per Willis J).

Fettering of discretion by policy

This occurs where a public body, perhaps a local council, adopts a particular policy – e.g. not to give any discretionary grants to students – and then applies that policy so rigidly and dogmatically that the merits of individual cases are not considered. A body may adopt a general policy to guide and give consistency to the exercise of its decision-making powers. It is still bound, however, to apply its mind to each case or application which comes before it and must be prepared to make exceptions where this would appear to be deserved or appropriate.

The rule is sometimes traced to the decision in *R v Port of London Authority, ex parte Kynoch Ltd* [1919] 1 KB 176 and, in particular, to the dictum of Bankes LJ:

> There are on the one hand, cases in which a tribunal in the honest exercise of its discretion has adopted a policy, and, without refusing to hear an applicant, indicates to him what its policy is, and that after hearing him it will in accordance with its policy decide against him, unless there is something exceptional in his case.

The principle was applied in *British Oxygen Co Ltd v Minister of Technology* [1971] AC 610. The Industrial Development Act 1966 had given the Minister a power to give grants to companies investing in new plant and machinery. The Minister's policy was, however, not to award such grants for items costing less than £25. British Oxygen applied for a grant to assist in the purchase of new gas cylinders each costing about £20. Their application was refused. They then challenged the Minister's decision claiming that his policy had precluded proper consideration of their application. It was held that the policy was perfectly lawful providing that the Minister, through his officials, considered each application with a genuine readiness to make exceptions to it. The rule was articulated with eminent clarity by Lord Reid:

> The general rule is that anyone who has to exercise a statutory discretion must not 'shut his ears to an application'…[A] ministry or large authority may have had already to deal with a multitude of similar applications and they will almost certainly have evolved a policy…There can be no objection to that providing the authority is always willing to listen to anyone with something new to say.

On the facts it was held that Ministry officials had 'listened to all that the applicant…had to say'. Thus there had been a valid exercise of discretion and there was no ground for regarding the refusal of British Oxygen's application as being unlawful.

Changing policies

A change of policy may sometimes operate to an individual's detriment and may mean, for example, that a person may no longer qualify for some benefit or advantage that he/she might otherwise have expected to receive. This might occur, for example, if lack of funds caused a local education authority to reduce the number of discretionary awards it had hitherto decided to make available to persons seeking to pursue postgraduate studies.

The cases show that a public body cannot be prevented from changing its policies and must be free to do so as is required by the public interest. Judicial review may only be granted in the context of policy changes in two circumstances:

(a) where the policy adopted or the decision to depart from a particular policy or policy rule(s) is wholly irrational (*R v Secretary of State for Health, ex parte US Tobacco International Inc* [1992] QB 353; *R v Home Secretary, ex parte Gangadeen; R v Home Secretary, ex parte Khan, The Times,* 12 December 1997);

(b) where a refusal to exempt an individual from the new policy can be shown to be unreasonable in the *Wednesbury* sense (*Associated Picture Houses v Wednesbury Corporation*, above), i.e. the policy-maker 'took into account matters he ought not to have taken into account or neglected to take matters into account which he ought to have taken into account' and 'has come to a conclusion so unreasonable that no reasonable Secretary of State could have come to it' (per Pill LJ, *R v Home Secretary, ex parte Hargreaves* [1997] 1 All ER 397).

Fettering of discretion by contract or agreement

A public body abuses its discretion if by contract or agreement it undertakes not to exercise a power to decide or to limit the range of decisions otherwise available to it. As stated, Parliament intends the discretionary powers it confers on public bodies to be exercised in accordance with the public interest. Hence those entrusted with this task should avoid private arrangements which inhibit the fulfilment of such intention.

> If a person or body is entrusted by the legislature with certain powers or duties expressly or impliedly for public purposes, those persons cannot divest themselves of those powers or duties. They cannot enter into any contracts or take any action incompatible with the due exercise of their powers or duties (per Earl of Birkenhead, *Birkdale District Supply Co v Southport Corporation* [1926] AC 355).

In *Stringer v Minister of Housing and Local Government* [1970] 1 WLR 1281, S applied for planning permission to build houses near the Jodrell Bank telescope in Cheshire. His application was, however, refused pursuant to an agreement between the University of Manchester (the owners of the telescope) and the local planning authority to the effect that no development would be permitted in the telescope's immediate environs. This agreement, and the refusal of planning permission in execution of it, was held to be *ultra vires* and void. The local planning authority had been entrusted with a statutory power to grant or refuse applications for planning permission (Town and Country Planning Act 1971). It was obliged, therefore, to consider each and every application on its merits and not to disable itself from doing so by inconsistent undertakings.

The rule is sometimes attributed to the decision in *Ayr Harbour Trustees* v *Oswald* (1883) 8 App Cas 623. In this case the Harbour Trustees had a statutory power to acquire land compulsorily for the purpose of developing the harbour. A piece of land was acquired from Oswald for this purpose. In order to reduce the cost of compensation by way of severance payments to him in respect of that part of his land which had not been acquired, the Harbour Trustees agreed to a perpetual covenant in which they promised not to use the land acquired in any way which would restrict Oswald's access to the harbour. This agreement was held to be *ultra vires* and illegal. It was clearly inconsistent with the objectives of the enabling Act, i.e. that land acquired under it would be used as the public interest in the proper development of the harbour might from time to time require.

This principle should not be understood as giving a public body the freedom to avoid any contract which, at some later stage, may be found to be incompatible with the unfettered use of a statutory power. Hence, in *R* v *Hammersmith and Fulham Borough Council, ex parte Beddowes* [1987] 1 WLR 1050, the Conservative-controlled council decided to sell a number of blocks of flats which were in need of refurbishment. They did this so that the cost of making the flats habitable and returning them to the local housing stock could be borne by the private sector. Concerned, however, by the imminence of local elections, a scheme was devised to try and prevent the decision being reversed should the council 'change hands'. The device used was the inclusion of a restrictive covenant in the contract of sale for the first block which prevented the council from reletting any of the flats in the remaining blocks if and when these (the flats) became vacant. This, it was hoped, would make the sale of the other blocks unavoidable since their utility for public sector housing would be increasingly diminished. It was accepted that the council had both the statutory power to sell the flats and to include restrictive covenants in the contracts of sale.

It was clear, however, that this particular covenant operated as a major restriction on the ways in which any subsequent council might wish to use its housing powers in relation to these properties. According to the Court of Appeal, however, this did not render the covenant to be unlawful *per se*. What mattered was whether the insertion of the covenant could be regarded as a reasonable method of achieving the authority's 'primary purpose' in the use of its housing powers, viz. 'the provision of housing accommodation in the district' – which the court felt it could:

> if the purpose for which the power to create restrictive covenants is being exercised can reasonably be regarded as the furtherance of the statutory object, then the creation of the covenant is not an unlawful fetter. All the powers are exercisable for the achieving of the statutory objects in relation to the land, and the honest and reasonable exercise of a power for that purpose cannot properly be regarded as a fetter upon another power given for that same purpose.

Therefore, not every contract which fetters discretion will be unlawful. All will depend on whether the contract in issue may be seen as a reasonable way of achieving the objectives of the statute in which the particular contractual power was contained. If it may, then the contract is *intra vires* and effective notwithstanding that the use of other powers to achieve that same objective have thereby been inhibited (per Fox LJ).

Acting under dictation

If a public body allows its decision to be dictated or influenced unduly by an unauthorised person or body it cannot be said that its discretion has been exercised lawfully. Subject to what has been said already, a public body must remain free to exercise its discretion on both the merits of the particular issue to be decided and the requirements of any relevant public interests. The body acts *ultra vires*, therefore, if, for example, it decides on the basis of instructions of some unauthorised superior in the constitutional hierarchy. Nor must it allow itself to be inf￵ ￵nced by threats of what may occur (e.g. public disorder), unless it reaches a particular decision.

For many years there were few proven examples of this type of abuse in Englis￵ ￵ and it was generally illustrated by reference to the Canadian case of *Roncarelli v Duplessis* (1959) 16 DLR (2d) 689. This concerned a decision of a statutory body (the Quebec Licensing Commission) to revoke R's liquor licence after being instructed to do so by the state's Prime Minister and its Attorney-General. R had apparently incurred the state government's displeasure by standing as surety for certain Jehovah's Witnesses charged with distributing literature – some of which was believed to be seditious – without a licence. The licensing commission's decision was quashed. It had not applied itself objectively to the case against R. It had simply done as it was told.

In more recent times, however, allegations of such flawed decision-making have been raised in English courts. In *R v Waltham Forest LBC, ex parte Baxter* [1988] QB 419, the Court of Appeal was asked to consider whether the practice of local councillors to vote in accordance with party policy as determined by a local party caucus could be regarded as a failure by them to exercise their individual discretion according to the particular merits of questions put before them. The Court's view was that, while councillors were entitled to be influenced and guided by party policy, it would be unlawful for them to behave as if bound by it so absolutely and rigidly as to disable them from making up their own minds.

The exercise of discretion on the basis of a threat of public disorder was in issue in *R v Coventry City Council, ex parte Phoenix Aviation* [1995] 3 All ER 37. On this occasion, to avoid the danger of further disorder and disruption by animal rights protestors, the council decided to suspend the permission, previously granted to applicants, to export livestock from Coventry City Airport. The Divisional Court's view was that the rule of law did not allow a public body to act as directed by unlawful protests and threats from a particular pressure group. According to the legislative scheme under which the authority had acted, it was not empowered to discriminate between lawful traders except in emergency circumstances. In the absence of such emergency the authority was bound, with the assistance of the police, to keep the airport open to all lawful users.

Fettering of discretion by estoppel

In private law the equitable doctrine of estoppel holds a person to a promise or assurance which has been relied and acted upon to his/her detriment by the person to whom it was made (*Central London Property Trust Ltd v High Trees House Ltd* [1947] KB 130).

Attempts have been made to utilise the doctrine in public law. In particular it has been argued that if an official or employee of a public body gives an assurance that the body will exercise a power to decide in a person's favour or misleads a person into believing that something may be done without the body's consent (e.g. that a proposed building development may be commenced without planning permission), the body is then bound by that assurance – providing, of course, that it has been relied and acted upon.

The use of the doctrine in public law has its attractions as it would give protection to an individual who had acted in good faith on the basis of what had been said by a public official. On the other hand, this might often result in a public body being bound to exercise a power in a way which did not best serve the requirements of the public interest (as in the above example, if the proposed building development had injurious consequences for the local community).

For some time judicial comment on the relevance of estoppel in public law was marked by a lack of clarity and uniformity. It now appears to be established, however, that estoppel cannot be pleaded if this would result in a public body being unable to use its discretion or decision-making power as the public interest demands.

This basic principle may be attributed to two cases in both of which a local government officer gave an unauthorised assurance that a particular development or use of land could be commenced without a grant of planning permission by the local planning authority (i.e. the local council).

In *Southend Corporation v Hodgson (Wickford) Ltd* [1962] 1 QB 416, H was considering buying a piece of land for use as a builder's yard. He contacted the authority's borough engineer and asked whether planning permission was required. The borough engineer, without any authorisation or reference to the local council, told H that it was not. H bought the land and began to use it for the purpose stated. Complaints were then received from nearby residents. As a result, the local planning authority served H with an enforcement notice under the Town and Country Planning Act 1947 (i.e. an order to discontinue a use of land for which planning permission has not been granted). H claimed that the assurance he had received disabled the council from using its enforcement power in respect of the land in issue.

This was not something the court was prepared to accept. In its view power to issue enforcement notices had been conferred on local planning authorities to enable them to protect their local communities against unauthorised development, particularly where such might cause unwarranted interference with the rights or interests of others. An unauthorised and erroneous statement of a local official could not prevent the authority from using its discretion as intended by Parliament.

> After all, in a case of discretion there is a duty under the statute to exercise a free and unhindered discretion. There is a long line of cases...which lay down that a public authority cannot by contract fetter the exercise of its discretion. Similarly...an estoppel cannot be raised to prevent or hinder the exercise of the discretion (per Lord Parker CJ).

A similar decision was reached in *Western Fish Products Ltd v Penwith District Council* [1981] 2 All ER 204. On this occasion conversations with local planning officers misled the complainants into believing that they could use premises as a fish processing factory without applying for planning permission. When an enforcement notice was served by the local planning authority they argued that the authority was bound by its officers' statements. The Court of Appeal's decision was summarised in the following comment by Megaw LJ:

> The defendant council's officers, even when acting within the apparent scope of their authority, could not do what the 1971 Act [Town and Country Planning Act] required the...council to do and if their officers did or said anything which purported to determine in advance what the...council would have to determine in pursuance of their statutory duties, they would not be inhibited from doing what they had to do.

Also see *R v East Sussex County Council, ex parte Reprotech (Pebsham) Ltd* [2002] UKHL 8, where, once again, the court refused to accept that a misleading statement by a planning officer that planning permission was not needed was binding on the authority.

In addition to the above, it has long been established that estoppel cannot be used:

(a) to prevent a public body performing a statutory duty (*Maritime Electric Co Ltd v General Dairies Ltd* [1937] 1 All ER 248);
(b) to bind a public body to a decision or course of action which is beyond its powers (*Rhyl UDC v Rhyl Amusements Ltd* [1959] 1 All ER 257).

However, there appear to be just two circumstances in which an estoppel may hold a public body to a statement or decision it wishes to avoid. The first of these is where the decision or statement is made by an official in the exercise of a power to decide validly delegated to him/her (*Lever Finance Ltd v Westminster Corporation* [1971] 1 QB 222). The second occurs where the public body claims that a decision or action is not valid due to minor procedural irregularities (*Wells v Minister of Housing and Local Government* [1967] 2 All ER 104).

Before leaving this topic, it should be pointed out that attempts to use estoppel in public law, such as the above, were made at a time when the concept of legitimate expectation and abuse of power had not been fully developed. It may be, therefore, that now the concept is recognised, such claims would be dealt with within its terms. If so, there is probably 'no longer a place for the private law doctrine of estoppel in public law or for the attendant difficulties which it brings with it' (*Flanagan v South Buckinghamshire District Council* [2002] EWCA Civ 690).

It should be noted also that bad or misleading advice by public servants may give cause for an action in negligence where it falls within the principles set out in *Hedley Byrne and Co v Heller* [1964] AC 465. Hence in *Lambert v West Devon BC, The Times*, 27 March 1997, damages were awarded to the plaintiff after he had been wrongly informed by a senior local government officer that he could commence building work pending a related application for a variation in planning permission.

ABUSE OF DISCRETION

Irrelevancy

The above discussion of judicial supervision of discretionary power has concentrated on the various ways in which a public body may be said to have failed to exercise the decision-making power conferred upon it. Under the head of irrelevancy and the one that follows (improper purpose) the concentration changes to those situations in which the discretion is exercised but in ways which contravene the intentions of Parliament.

Except where the enabling power has specified the matters to be considered when a power to decide is used, or a legitimate expectation has been created that some matters will or will not be taken into account (see *R v Home Secretary, ex parte Findlay* [1985] AC 318), the repository of the power has a wide discretion in terms of the factors which may be relied upon. The court will intervene, however, if it feels that matters clearly pertinent to a particular inquiry have been ignored or that other factors which had no relevance were considered.

Hence, in the famous case of *Roberts v Hopwood* (above), a local council (Poplar) had statutory authority to pay its employees such wages as it thought fit. The council decided to pay its employees a minimum wage of £4 per week. This was to apply to both men and women. When the reasonableness and legality of the council's actions was challenged the House of Lords held that the council had been influenced by such irrelevances as 'eccentric principles of socialist philanthropy' and a 'feminist ambition to secure the equality of the sexes in the matter of wages' (per Lord Atkinson), and that it had failed to take into account the falling cost of living and the level of wages nationally.

It would appear that if a judge wishes to interfere with a particular decision it will seldom be beyond their powers of intellect to identify some matter which should or should not have been considered and to use this as a justification for judicial review. Hence, this is a ground of review which gives the judges themselves a considerable degree of discretion in terms of whether to invalidate a particular action or decision. It has even been alleged that a judge's view of what is or is not relevant to the making of a decision may sometimes be influenced by political or other values. Clearly, for example, in *Roberts* (above), the court was uneasy about the council allowing itself to be influenced by egalitarian concepts of social engineering and the equality of men and women in the labour market. Also, in *Bromley Borough Council v Greater London Council* [1982] AC 768, where the council in Bromley decided to provide cheap and subsidised public transport in the metropolis, their Lordships felt that the statutory requirement to run London Transport 'economically and efficiently' (London Transport Act 1969) meant that fares should be fixed 'in accordance with ordinary business principles' (per Lord Keith). This appeared to exclude the wider social and environmental considerations which had influenced the council. In both this and the *Roberts* case – in what were, arguably, as much political as legal opinions – their Lordships felt that the councils involved should have given greater attention to their fiduciary duty to their ratepayers (i.e. to control public spending) and rather less to the political mandates which the councils claimed they were fulfilling. (The relevance of a political mandate to the exercise of discretion was also discounted in *Secretary of State for Education and Science v Metropolitan Borough of Tameside* [1977] AC 1014.)

The cases suggest that judges are particularly concerned to see that authorities give careful attention to the financial consequences of their actions. In other words, at least from the judicial perspective, financial considerations would appear to be of a higher priority than other factors which may have influenced a decision, e.g. social policy or an electoral mandate. The judicial prioritisation of financial considerations obvious in the *Roberts* and *Bromley* cases was also evident in *Prescott v Birmingham Corporation* [1955] Ch 210, where it was felt that a decision to grant concessionary public transport to old-age pensioners had also been affected by a failure to give sufficient consideration to the extra costs that this might impose upon ratepayers (see also earlier cases such as *Price v Rhondda UDC* [1923] 2 Ch 372; *Short v Poole Corporation* [1926] Ch 66).

Where an allegation of irrelevancy is made, it is for the applicant to identify the issues which should or should not have been considered. It is not open to the applicant to suggest that a decision appears to be so illogical that it could not have been reached without consideration of some unspecified irrelevant material. In *R v Lancashire County Council, ex parte Huddleston* [1986] 2 All ER 941, an unsuccessful allegation of irrelevancy was made by a prospective student who was refused a discretionary maintenance award. As she had an excellent academic and personal record she could not understand why her application had been unsuccessful. However, although she suspected something extraneous may have influenced the authority's thinking, she was unable to specify what this might have been (see also *Kelly v Cannock Chase UDC* [1978] 1 WLR 1).

Improper purpose

Statutory powers must be used for the express or implied purposes for which they were given. If a power is used for some ulterior purpose, or in a way which is clearly inconsistent with the objectives of the enabling Act, then it has been used illegally. Where a power is used to achieve more than one purpose – e.g. as in *Webb v Minister of Housing and Local Government* [1965] 2 WLR 755, where a power to build sea defences was used to build both a sea wall and a promenade – the court has to identify the authority's main purpose or objective and determine whether this was consistent with the dominant purpose for which the power was given:

> If Parliament grants power to a government department to be used for an authorised purpose, then the power is only validly exercised when it is used by the department genuinely for that purpose as its dominant purpose. If that purpose is not the main purpose but is subordinated to some other purpose which is not authorised by law, then the department exceeds its powers and the action is invalid (per Lord Denning LJ, *Earl Fitzwilliams Wentworth Estates Co Ltd v Minister of Town and Country Planning* [1951] 2 KB 284).

The fact that other purposes are achieved is not fatal so long as these are reasonably incidental to the main and authorised purpose. Hence, in *Hanks v Minister of Housing and Local Government* [1963] 1 QB 999, alterations to the pattern of roads in an area compulsorily acquired for housing redevelopment, being secondary and reasonably consistent with the development process, were found to be permissible. Also, in *Westminster Corporation v London and North Western Railway Co Ltd* [1905] AC 426, the court took no objection to a power to provide public conveniences being used to build the same under a road with accesses on either side thereby creating a subway. Again it was felt that the authorised purpose – the provision of a public convenience – had been the authority's main concern and that the creation of a subway was merely secondary and reasonably incidental to this purpose.

What is an authorised purpose may not always be easily discernible from the statutory language used. In these circumstances, as with irrelevancy, the decision as to whether to intervene or not is largely a matter of judicial discretion which, it has been alleged, may occasionally be influenced by values rather than law. In *R v Inner London Education Authority, ex parte Westminster City Council* [1986] 1 WLR 28, for example, a power to use public moneys to provide information about the services provided by local authorities was found to have been used for an unauthorised purpose when moneys were spent on a campaign explaining how those services were being adversely affected by reductions in central government funding.

> I have already said that I find that one of...[the] purposes was the giving of information. But I also find that it had the purpose of seeking to persuade members of the public to a view identical with that of the authority itself, and indeed I believe that this was a, if not the, major purpose of the decision (per Glidewell J).

It has also been held that local councils should not use their powers for the purpose of penalising those of opposing political opinions (see *Wheeler v Leicester City Council* [1985] AC 1054; *R v Lewisham Borough Council, ex parte Shell UK Ltd* [1988] 1 All ER 938; *R v Derbyshire County Council, ex parte Times Supplements Ltd* (1990) 3 Admin LR 241; *R v Somerset County Council, ex parte Fewings* [1995] 3 All ER 20).

Similarly, powers should not be used for purely party-political gains without any reference to public interest which the power was designed to serve. This was the essence of the decision in *Porter v Magill* [2002] UKHL 67, where a local Conservative controlled authority adopted a policy of increasing the numbers of council houses made available for sale in the marginal wards of its district. This was not primarily done for the house objectives of the enabling Act but to increase the number of owner-occupiers and, therefore, potential Conservative voters in the wards affected.

For the sake of convenience and similarity, using power in ways which frustrate the objectives of the enabling Act may also be dealt with in the general context of improper purpose. The two leading cases on this point are *Padfield v Minister of Agriculture* [1968] AC 997, and *Laker Airways v Department of Trade* [1977] QB 643. In *Padfield* the minister acted illegally when, without good reason, he refused to refer a complaint made by a milk producer to a complaints procedure which had been set up to deal with problems arising out of the national milk marketing scheme. According to the House of Lords, the complaints procedure had been included in the Act (the Agricultural Marketing Act 1958) as a means of dealing with all reasonable and relevant concerns raised by producers and, absent good reasons, it was not open to the minister to use his power of referral in a way which thwarted this objective. In the *Laker* case it was held that the minister could not seek to protect British Airways' dominant position on the transatlantic route by using powers contained in an Act designed, *inter alia*, to ensure competition on all long-distance passenger routes.

THE CONCEPT OF REASONABLENESS

In *Associated Picture Houses v Wednesbury Corporation* [1948] 1 KB 223, the Court of Appeal explained that unreasonableness as a species of *ultra vires* could be understood in two senses. First, the term could be used as a general heading for those types of error usually dealt with under the heading of abuse of discretion.

Lawyers familiar with the phraseology commonly used in relation to the exercise of statutory discretion often use the word unreasonable in a rather comprehensive sense. It has frequently been used and is frequently used as a general description of things that must not be done. For instance, a person entrusted with discretion must...direct himself properly in law. He must call his attention to matters he is bound to consider. If he does not obey these rules he may truly be said...to be acting unreasonably (per Lord Greene MR).

Second, it was said that unreasonableness could be used as a separate and distinct head of review. In this sense it would apply to that type of decision which it might not be possible to impugn for the more usual causes of abuse of discretion, e.g. irrelevancy, improper purpose, etc., but which might appear to be 'so unreasonable that no reasonable authority could even have come to it' (*ibid.*). As Lord Greene admitted, however, 'to prove a case of that kind would require something overwhelming'.

FROM REASONABLENESS TO IRRATIONALITY

Irrationality is generally regarded as a reformulation of the *Wednesbury* principle. It is usually attributed to Lord Diplock in the *GCHQ* case, where he said:

By irrationality I mean what can now be succinctly referred to as 'Wednesbury unreasonableness'...It applies to a decision which is so outrageous in its defiance of logic or of accepted moral standards that no sensible person who had applied his mind to the question to be decided could have arrived at it.

It is clear from the statements of both Lord Greene and Lord Diplock that this ground of review may only be used to attack that which is completely perverse or extraordinary. Hence, it would be unconstitutional for a judge to intervene for unreasonableness or irrationality merely because he/she might not agree with, or approve of, a particular decision. The test is therefore pitched at a particularly high level to avoid any danger or accusations of judges using the unreasonableness/irrationality test as a means of substituting their own opinions for those vested with the power of government.

This standard of unreasonableness, often referred to as the irrationality test, has been criticised as being too high. But it has to be expressed in terms which confine the jurisdiction exercised by the judiciary to a supervisory as opposed to an appellate jurisdiction (Lord Ackner, *R v Home Secretary, ex parte Brind* [1991] 1 AC 696).

There are very few examples of decisions being struck down solely on the grounds of their unreasonableness or irrationality in the sense just explained. It may well be that where a power has been used in such an extraordinary way it will be likely – some would say inevitable – that one of the more specific types of abuse (e.g. irrelevancy or improper purpose), will have occurred and will therefore constitute the main ground of challenge.

PROPORTIONALITY

According to the jurisprudence of the European Convention on Human Rights, European Community law and the domestic law both of Germany and France, the use of discretionary powers by a public body should not result in actions or decisions which cause a greater degree of interference with the rights or interests of individuals than is required to deal with the state's objectives. In other words, a public body should only do that which, within a reasonable margin of appreciation, is proportionate to the end to be achieved.

Proportionality was mentioned in the *GCHQ* case as an additional ground of judicial review which courts in this country might wish to incorporate into English law at some future date. Since then, however, there has been an evident reluctance to do so as the test involves more than a simple application of the rules already evolved for the regulation of the use of power and discretion. Used in its proper sense, proportionality must involve some consideration of whether, given the circumstances, the public body chose the most appropriate course of action available to it – which comes perilously close to the court putting itself in the position of the decision-maker.

> The decision-makers, very often elected, are those to whom Parliament has entrusted the discretion and to interfere with that discretion beyond the limits hitherto defined would itself be an abuse of the judges' supervisory jurisdiction...The judges are not generally speaking, equipped by training or experience, or furnished with the requisite knowledge and advice, to decide the answer to an administrative problem where the scales are evenly balanced...(per Lord Lowry, *R v Home Secretary, ex parte Brind* [1991] 1 AC 696).

In some cases the tendency has been to treat proportionality as little more than another species of reasonableness or irrationality (see Lord Donaldson MR in *R v Home Secretary, ex parte Brind*, above) – i.e. if the chosen course of action is unreasonable in the *Wednesbury* sense it must, *per se*, be disproportionate to the solution of the perceived problem. The two tests cannot, however, be equated with any genuine exactitude for, as Wade and Forsyth have pointed out, 'proportionality requires the court to judge the necessity of the action taken as well as whether it was within the range of courses of action that could reasonably be adopted' (*Administrative Law* (7th edn), p 403).

Domestic judicial unease with the proportionality test is derived from the fact that it would appear to import a more rigorous standard of judicial review than that permitted by the test of reasonableness or irrationality and thus to permit some degree of judicial scrutiny of the factual basis and merits of particular decisions, thereby confusing the roles of the judicial and executive branches of government. The traditional English constitutional basis for the test of reasonableness, which limits judicial interference with executive action to extreme cases of abuse, was explained by Lord Irvine LC in 1999:

> There are three good reasons why this is so. First, there exists a constitutional imperative: if Parliament confers decision-making power on a particular agency, the courts would frustrate Parliament's sovereign will if they arrogated that power to themselves. Secondly, there is the pragmatic imperative: the courts, particularly on substantive matters of policy, have considerably less expertise than the designated authority...And, thirdly, there exists a democratic imperative: the electoral system operates as an important safeguard against abuse of public power by requiring many public authorities to submit themselves to the verdict of the electorate at periodic intervals. If this system of political accountability is to function, it is important that the decision-making role of these agencies is not usurped by the courts (Sixth Annual Lecture to the Singapore Academy of Law, 1999).

Notwithstanding these sentiments, however, it is now generally accepted that proportionality is the test to be applied in English courts when determining the legality of the actions of public authorities where these relate to:

(a)   the carrying out of functions regulated by European Community law;
(b)   since the coming into effect of the Human Rights Act 1998, functions which
      touch on the rights protected by the European Convention on Human Rights.

Based on this minimalist analysis, it would appear that the tests of reasonableness
and proportionality will henceforth operate side by side in their particular spheres of
reference, i.e. proportionality being the test of legality to be applied in contexts (a)
and (b) above with the test of reasonableness to remain applicable in areas of public
law not affected by the two European legal systems.

For two principal reasons this was the approach favoured by the Lord Chancellor
in his 1999 lecture referred to above. In the first case, according to Lord Irvine, the
Human Rights Act clearly intended the use of the more stringent standards of review
permitted by proportionality to be restricted to the particular context of fundamental
human rights.

> The effect of the Act, therefore, is not to change the implications of proportionality-based
> review but rather, to ordain that the use of proportionality is constitutionally acceptable
> notwithstanding that it carries such implications. In this sense, the Act will form a warrant
> which will confer constitutional legitimacy on proportionality-based review. It is, however,
> perfectly clear from the Human Rights Act that this warrant extends only to cases which,
> in the first place engage fundamental human rights. It follows that the considerations
> based on constitutional propriety which have, to date, rightly deterred English courts from
> embracing proportionality will, in the future, continue to apply to cases which do not fall
> under the new human rights legislation.

Beyond these constitutional considerations there was further legal logic for retaining a flexible test of reasonableness which allowed the rigour of judicial review to be
related to the subject matter of the decision or exercise of public law power in issue:

> it is already a well-established principle in English public law that judicial review does not
> constitute a monolithic standard of supervision. Rather, the intensity of review in any
> particular case is determined by its facts and context. For example, the courts accept that
> it is appropriate to adopt a relatively deferential attitude to decisions concerning national
> economic policy. In contrast...the courts certainly subject executive action of what
> engages human rights to much more thoroughgoing scrutiny.

Clearly this is another area of English public law which, at best, can be said to be in a
state of development and change. That this is so was evidenced by the rather different
sentiments of Lord Slynn in R v *Secretary of State for the Environment, Transport and
the Regions, ex parte Holding and Barnes* [2001] 2 All ER 929, in which he expressed
clear preference for a single test of public law legality based on proportionality.

> I consider that even without reference to the Human Rights Act the time has come to
> recognise that this principle [proportionality] is part of English law, not only when judges
> are dealing with Community acts, but also when they are dealing with acts subject to
> domestic law. Trying to keep the Wednesbury principle and proportionality in separate
> compartments seems to me to be unnecessary and confusing.

Were this to be the chosen path of development, the likelihood would probably
be the emergence of a flexible test of proportionality with the intensity of review varying with the nature of the subject matter in issue and, therefore, not radically different

from the modern understanding of reasonableness explained above by Lord Irvine. If so, this might encompass, at one end of the spectrum, a rather demanding fact-based standard applicable to actions or decisions affecting fundamental human rights, e.g. the right to life, where the test might be based on the question 'did the action taken by the authority do more damage to the right than was required to achieve its objective'. At the other end of the spectrum, where an authority's actions might have affected less heavily weighted rights or interests, or have been related to aspects of government activity thought unsuited for intense judicial scrutiny, a more objective, discretion-based test may be preferred. Here the question might be 'did the decision or action taken represent a reasonable assessment of how the authority's objectives might be achieved without doing undue damage to the rights or interests affected'.

PROCEDURAL IMPROPRIETY: INTRODUCTION

Albeit a public body acts within its powers or jurisdiction and uses its discretion according to law, the validity of its decisions may still be questioned on procedural grounds. The complaint may allege procedural *ultra vires* or a breach of the rules of natural justice.

PROCEDURAL *ULTRA VIRES*

It is commonplace for enabling statutes to require the powers they confer to be exercised in accordance with specified procedural requirements. Thus, where an Act gives a minister the power to legislate by way of statutory instrument, it will often stipulate that the minister should consult with interests affected and that the instrument should be laid before Parliament according to one of the procedures set out in the Statutory Instruments Act 1946.

Mandatory and directory requirements

As a matter of statutory construction, the courts draw a distinction between procedural requirements which should be treated as mandatory and those which may be regarded as directory.

A mandatory procedural requirement must be complied with if the action or decision taken is to be valid in law. As a general principle such a requirement will be regarded as mandatory if non-compliance with it might cause substantial prejudice to the person or persons affected by the exercise of the power. The requirement will usually have been imposed to improve the quality of the decision-making process, i.e. by providing for greater public participation and more openness than might otherwise have been the case. Hence a requirement to consult those likely to be affected by administrative or legislative action will usually be treated as mandatory, as will a requirement to hear objections from those who may be affected detrimentally. Thus, in *Bradbury v Enfield Borough Council* [1967] 1 WLR 1311, a local education authority acted procedurally *ultra vires* when it failed, as required by the Education Act 1944, to give adequate public notice of and opportunity to object to its plan to change the status of a number of its secondary schools from selective to comprehensive. In *R v Camden London Borough Council, ex parte Cran* [1995] RTR 346, a local council failed to comply with a statutory obligation to consult with local residents before making an order designating an area as a controlled traffic zone. This was held to be fatal to the validity of its scheme.

Failure to comply with a directory requirement does not have such drastic consequences. A public body is expected to act in accordance with the same but should it fail to do so this does not affect the validity of the action or decision in question. By definition, therefore, directory requirements tend to be concerned with matters of procedural detail rather than substance. Non-compliance is, therefore, unlikely to result in any serious prejudice or disadvantage. *Coney v Choice* [1975] 1 All ER 979, was another case in which a local education authority had decided to change from a selective to a comprehensive system of education. In accordance with the 1944 Education Act, the authority gave public notice of its intentions in local newspapers and public buildings. It failed, however, to post the required notices outside all the schools affected. It was held that the principal objective of the relevant provisions in the 1944 Act was that adequate publicity should be given to such intended changes and that those affected should be notified both of the right to object and how that right should be exercised. The court felt that, in substance, this had been done. The requirement to put up notices outside the particular schools was treated, therefore, as directory only.

A procedural requirement may also be regarded as being merely directory for reasons of public policy. In *Williams v Home Office (No. 2)* [1981] 1 All ER 1151, W was serving a long term of imprisonment. He was believed to be a difficult prisoner and was put in solitary confinement for six months. This decision was not reviewed every 28 days as required by Prison Rule 43 (made under the Prison Act 1952). Accordingly, W challenged the validity of his treatment. The court conceded that the prison authorities had not acted as required but felt that the system of prison government would be undermined if prisoners were allowed to mount legal challenges to the implementation of the prison rules.

THE RULES OF NATURAL JUSTICE

Introduction

These are the common law's procedural requirements for the valid exercise of decision-making powers. Hence, even in the absence of procedural rules imposed by statute, the rules of natural justice enable the courts to insist that public bodies make decisions in accordance with certain minimum standards of procedural fairness. These are encapsulated in two general principles:

* the right to a fair hearing (*audi alteram partem*);
* the rule against bias (*nemo judex in causa sua*).

In general it may be said that the rules apply to the exercise of a decision-making power by a public body where this may have detrimental consequences for the person or persons affected. In a sense the rules perform a similar function to the due process clause in the constitution of the United States of America. They have been described as the 'principles of fair play' (per Maughan J, *Maclean v The Workers' Union* [1929] 1 Ch 602). Their contribution to the wider process of government has been said to be that 'severe substantive laws can be better endured if they are fairly and impartially applied' (per Jackson J, *Shaughnessy v United States* (1953) 345 US 206).

Origins

It was once believed that there existed a metaphysical body of ideal rules against which the validity of man-made laws, including parliamentary enactments and decisions, could be tested. This was variously referred to as natural law, natural justice or equity, and was often believed to be of divine origins. The rights of an individual to be tried by an impartial judge and to be heard in his defence were perceived as fundamental elements of this immutable order. Coke CJ in *Dr Bonham's Case* (1610) 8 Co Rep 1146, asserted that even an Act of Parliament could be declared invalid by the courts if it offended 'common right and reason' by making a man judge in his own cause; and a century later, in *Dr Bentley's Case* (1723) 1 Stra 557, the court made the point that 'even God himself did not pass sentence upon Adam before he was called to make his defence' (per Fortescue J).

The eighteenth century saw the dawning of a more secular age. The notion that natural justice had divine origins and was superior to the will of Parliament began to lose credibility. However, the notion of procedural fairness was by this time firmly rooted in the common law. Natural justice might no longer be a measure against which the validity of parliamentary enactments could be tested, but its procedural requirements remained something which the superior courts assumed should be complied with by inferior bodies entrusted with judicial functions.

The scope and development of natural justice

Consequentialism

The foundations of the modern regulatory state were laid in the nineteenth century. This was evident in the creation of administrative bodies equipped with statutory powers to restrict and extinguish private legal rights in the interests of the wider community – e.g. the Artisans and Labourers Dwellings Improvement Acts 1875–9 which gave local authorities powers of slum clearance and redevelopment.

Initially the judges responded to these developments in an essentially pragmatic way. Such powers might not be 'judicial' in the traditional sense of that done by a judge or justice of the peace in a court of law, but their exercise might still have serious consequences for the legal rights of those affected. Such powers were, therefore, to be regarded as 'judicial' for the purposes of the application of the rules of natural justice. It was made clear, however, that such administrative bodies would not be expected to observe the procedural standards of courts of law. This, it was realised, would have made the decision-making process so slow and protracted as to have undermined the public interest in administrative efficiency.

> Comparatively recent statutes have extended, if not originated, the practice of imposing upon departments or officers of state the duty of deciding or determining questions of

various kinds. In such cases they must act in good faith and fairly listen to both sides, for that is a duty lying upon anyone who decides anything. But I do not think they are bound to treat such questions as though it were a trial (per Lord Loreburn, *Board of Education v Rice* [1911] AC 179).

Hence, by concentrating on the consequences of the exercise of decision-making powers, rather than on the form of particular decision-making processes, the supervisory jurisdiction of the superior courts was extended to the decisions of administrative bodies affecting the rights of individuals.

Cooper v Wandsworth Board of Works (1863) 14 CB (NS) 180, provides a classic illustration of the above. The Board of Works had a statutory power to enter upon land and demolish any property in relation to which it had not been given seven days' notice of the intention to build. The plaintiff, whose property had been demolished pursuant to this power, sued for trespass on the ground that 'no man [was] to be deprived of his property without his having an opportunity to be heard'. The court felt that the power in issue could properly be classified as judicial. It involved interference with rights over property and the imposition of a penalty. In these circumstances it had to be exercised in accordance with natural justice: '...a long course of decisions...establish that although there are no positive words in a statute requiring that the party shall be heard, yet the justice of the common law will supply the omission of the legislature' (per Byles J). The plaintiff's action was thus successful.

Later, in *Hopkins v Smethwick Local Board* (1890) 24 QBD 713, Willes J said that 'in condemning a man to have his house pulled down, a judicial act is as much implied as in fining him £5; and as the local board is the only tribunal that can make such an order its act must be a judicial act and the party to be affected should have a notice given to him'.

Conceptualism

This pragmatic attitude to definition of a judicial function did not last long into the twentieth century. From the 1920s onwards it became apparent that a more restrictive and conceptual test was being applied. According to this approach, a power to decide was to be classified as judicial only if it required the decision-maker to determine a dispute affecting the rights of the parties to it (a '*lis inter partes*'). Hence, where a person appealed against a slum clearance order made by a local authority, the minister empowered to decide the appeal was said to be acting in a 'quasi-judicial' capacity and bound, therefore, to act in accordance with natural justice, i.e. to ensure the appellant was given a fair hearing (*Errington v Minister of Health* [1935] 1 KB 249). Where, however, a chief constable revoked a taxi-driver's licence on the ground that he was using his taxi to help prostitutes to ply their trade, this was held to be in the exercise of an administrative power. The chief constable was not deciding a *lis inter partes* and it mattered not that the effect of the decision was to deprive the taxi-driver of his livelihood. The power was administrative only and not subject to natural justice. There was no obligation, therefore, on the chief constable to give the taxi-driver a hearing before making the decision (*R v Metropolitan Police Commissioner, ex parte Parker* [1953] 1 WLR 1150).

As a result, and as long as this restrictive approach remained in the ascendancy, the procedural protection of the rules of natural justice was denied to those affected by the exercise of decision-making powers not falling within this narrow perception of a judicial function.

Consequentialism restored

The retreat from the older authorities such as *Cooper* and *Hopkins* was ended by the decision of the House of Lords in *Ridge* v *Baldwin (No. 1)* [1964] AC 40, where the older meaning of acting judicially was reinstated and held to extend to the exercise of any power to decide which resulted (for the person affected) in the deprivation of any right, status or livelihood. Once again, therefore, for the purpose of the application of the rules of natural justice, the consequences of the exercise of the power were to be the determining factor and not the nature of the decision-making process itself. *Ridge* v *Baldwin* presaged the development of a much more sophisticated doctrine of procedural justice – one which was based on the assumption that the individual affected by a decision of a public body was entitled to the highest standard of procedural justice which was compatible with the efficient performance of the statutory function in issue.

The duty to act fairly

Although *Ridge* v *Baldwin* restored the meaning of acting judicially to that favoured in earlier times, it left in place the principle that natural justice applied to judicial functions only, however liberally these might be defined. Shortly afterwards, however, it was suggested that any power to decide – whether judicial, administrative or howsoever described – which affected an individual's rights or other interests, should be exercised in a way that was procedurally 'fair' ('the duty to act fairly': *Re HK, an infant* [1967] 2 QB 617). In effect this meant that all decision-makers were bound to exercise their powers in ways which represented a reasonable balance between the competing needs of efficient administration and that of not leaving the individual feeling aggrieved and disadvantaged by the decision-making process.

The development of the duty to act fairly inevitably begged the question as to the exact demarcation, if any, between this and the rules of natural justice. Two approaches have been adopted. One has been to argue that attempts to draw any distinction are largely artificial and that both concepts may be subsumed within the terminology and requirements of a new and flexible concept of procedural justice or fairness. Alternatively, it has been proposed that that the term 'natural justice' should be understood as referring to a higher standard of procedural correctness applicable to those exercising judicial powers. The duty to act fairly would then be applicable to those exercising administrative functions and would import a less demanding standard of procedural propriety.

> If one accepts that natural justice is a flexible term which imposes different requirements in different cases, it is capable of applying appropriately to the whole range of situations indicated by such terms as 'judicial', 'quasi-judicial' and 'administrative'. Nevertheless the further the situation is away from anything that resembles a judicial or quasi-judicial situation and the further the question is removed from what may reasonably be called a

justiciable question, the more appropriate it is to reject an expression which includes the word 'justice' and to use instead such terms as 'fairness or the duty to act fairly' (per Megarry VC, *McInnes* v *Onslow-Fane* [1978] 1 WLR 1520).

A brief resumé of some of the leading cases dealing with the duty to act fairly will serve to illustrate how this has been applied to improve the procedural quality of administrative decision-making. The cases also show the extent to which the require- ments of procedural fairness now apply in contexts far removed from those falling within the qualifying terminology of acting judicially as understood prior to *Ridge* v *Baldwin*.

In *Re HK* itself it was held that, before deciding whether a prospective immigrant satisfied the statutory criteria for entry to the United Kingdom, an immigration officer was 'bound to let the immigrant know what his immediate impression [was] so that the immigrant [could] disabuse him of it' (per Lord Parker CJ). *Re Pergamon Press* [1971] Ch 388, was concerned with the conduct of a Board of Trade inquiry into the affairs of a company. In the Court of Appeal Lord Denning MR said:

> the inspectors must act fairly. This is a duty which rests on them, as on many other bodies, even though they are not judicial or quasi-judicial but only administrative. The inspectors can obtain information in any way they think best, but before they condemn or criticise a man they must give him a fair opportunity for correcting or contradicting what is said against him. They need not quote chapter and verse, an outline of the charge will suffice.

In *R* v *Liverpool Corporation, ex parte Liverpool Taxi Fleet Operators' Association* [1972] 2 QB 299, the authority was held to have acted unfairly when it failed to hon- our an express undertaking to consult those affected before any decision was taken to increase the number of Hackney cab licences and thereby increase the number of licensed taxicabs operating in the city. Here was the classic example of the scope of the duty to act fairly. The decision in issue had no judicial element and affected the financial interests of taxi owners rather than their legal rights. The court was still pre- pared to intervene, however, for procedural unfairness. In a more recent case, the duty to act fairly was held to apply to local authority decisions closing residential homes for the elderly (*R* v *Devon County Council, ex parte Baker*; *R* v *Durham County Council, ex parte Curtis* [1995] 1 All ER 73). In such cases, acting fairly required that the residents of the homes affected be given adequate advance notice of the closure decisions, reasonable time to formulate and submit their representations to the authority, and that those representations be duly considered by the same.

The right to a fair hearing: general principles

Introduction

Depending on the circumstances, and as indicated by the above cases, a fair hearing may involve any or all of the following elements:

- the right to be informed in advance of the case to be met – i.e. the factual basis on which the decision-maker may act;
- the right to a reasonable time in which to prepare a response;
- the right to be heard verbally or in writing;

- the right to cross-examine persons who may have made prejudicial statements to the decision-maker;
- the right to be legally represented;
- the right to reasons for the decision.

As has been indicated, however, the right to a fair hearing is a flexible concept. This means that its requirements are not fixed or constant – i.e. it is not possible to state that whenever the rule applies its content must always consist of all the elements listed above. The case law illustrates that the requirements of a fair hearing will vary from case to case depending on the circumstances:

> it is important to bear in mind that the recognition of an obligation to observe procedural fairness does not call into play a body of rigid procedural rules which must be observed regardless of circumstances. Where the obligation exists its precise content varies to reflect the common law's perception of what is necessary for procedural fairness in the circumstances of the particular case (per Deane J, *Haoucher v Minister of State for Immigration and Ethnic Affairs* (1990) 93 ALR 51).

To determine the precise procedural obligations resting on the decision-maker in any given case the courts apply a number of criteria. Paramount amongst these are:

- the nature of the decision-making power;
- the consequences of its exercise for the person affected;
- the demands of the wider public interest;
- the intentions of Parliament.

Hence if it is concluded that the power in issue has the tripartite structure so typical of the judicial process and requires the decision-maker to determine a dispute between two parties, it will generally be assumed that this imposes an obligation to act in accordance with a high standard of procedural fairness which might, for example, include the right to be heard personally. If, added to this, it is clear that the decision may have very serious consequences for the person affected then the procedural expectations may be further increased so as to extend perhaps to rights of cross-examination and legal representation.

Applying the same rationale, if the power to decide is classified as being purely administrative or bureaucratic – e.g. a bipartite decision by a local authority to refuse an application for a discretionary student grant – the decision-maker will still be expected to act fairly but the requirements of fairness in this situation will be less demanding. Proper consideration of the individual's written application would probably suffice.

In effect, therefore, the court will place the power in issue on a notional decision-making spectrum which extends from that which is wholly administrative to that which is purely judicial as would occur in a court of law. If a power is placed towards the judicial end of the spectrum, the procedural obligations on the decision-maker are increased. If the power is placed towards the administrative end of the spectrum, less will be expected to satisfy the demands of acting fairly.

This type of approach was evident in *R v Hull Prison Board of Visitors, ex parte St Germain (No. 2)* [1979] 3 All ER 545. The applicant, a prisoner, was accused of breaches of the prison code of discipline arising out of a riot in Hull prison in 1976.

The prison rules provided that prisoners charged with less serious offences against the code should be dealt with by prison governors. The cases of those charged with more serious matters were to be referred to the prison's board of visitors. The allegations against St Germain fell into the latter category.

Each prison has a board of visitors. These perform a variety of functions including acting as disciplinary tribunals. By way of punishment a board of visitors could award loss of remission for up to six months or loss of privileges for each charge proved. When the applicant appeared before the board the evidence against him was presented by the prison governor. Much of this consisted of statements which had been collected from prison officers who had been on duty at the material times. None of these officers was present at the hearing. The charges against the applicant were found proved and, by way of punishment, he suffered a substantial loss of remission. He applied for judicial review on the ground that he had not been given a fair hearing, i.e. he had not been given an opportunity to cross-examine those officers whose prejudicial statements had been put to the board.

It was held that the facility to cross-examine was not an inevitable element of the right to a fair hearing. The proceedings were, however, clearly judicial in nature and had resulted in further loss of liberty for the applicant – the most serious penalty of all under English law. Also, some of the evidence in question had included eyewitness accounts of the applicant's alleged wrongdoing. It followed from all this that the board was bound to observe a fairly rigorous standard of procedural fairness which, in the circumstances, extended to a right of cross-examination. The board's refusal to permit this meant that the applicant had been treated unfairly.

Note that in April 1992 the disciplinary powers of prison visitors were removed under powers contained in the Criminal Justice Act 1991.

This may be contrasted with the decision in *R* v *Manchester Metropolitan University, ex parte Nolan*, 1993, unreported. The applicant was a law student who was alleged to have committed a serious breach of the University's examination regulations (by having lecture notes on his desk during two examinations). The examination board which considered his case resolved that he should be deemed to have failed his examinations and should not be given an opportunity to resit them. The board took into account the applicant's written submissions but did not permit him to appear in person.

The applicant applied for judicial review on the ground, *inter alia*, that he had not been given a fair hearing. In the circumstances, however, it was held that the board had done enough to satisfy the requirement of procedural fairness. It had not exercised a judicial power and the consequences of its decision were not so serious as to warrant observance of the type of procedural rights claimed by the applicant. In particular, the court pointed out, the exam board's decision did not preclude the applicant from pursuing the same qualification at an alternative institution of higher education.

In determining the appropriate standard of procedural fairness in any given situation a court will also be aware that the decision-making power in issue will have been entrusted to the body for a particular statutory purpose, usually related to the protection of some aspect of the public interest. While it is important that the individual is treated fairly, it is not the function of the court to impose procedural requirements on the decision-maker which would inhibit the proper exercise of the power as intended by Parliament.

Where a power has been given to a public body to deal with matters of urgency or it is necessary to use a power immediately to avoid public danger, insistence on procedural exactitude – i.e. the need to give advance notice, hearings, etc. before taking action – would clearly not accord with either the wishes of Parliament or the obvious and overriding demands of the public interest. In *R v Secretary of State for Transport, ex parte Pegasus Holdings Ltd* [1988] 1 WLR 990, the minister did not act unfairly when he summarily suspended permits to fly aircraft in and out of the United Kingdom previously granted to certain Romanian pilots. This was after they had failed flying tests conducted by the Civil Aviation Authority. Schiemann J's comment was that 'the rules of natural justice do apply but…in such an emergency as the present, with a provisional suspension being all that one is concerned with, one is at the low end of the duties of fairness'.

Application of the rules of natural justice may also have potentially negative implications for a variety of other key public interests including those relating to the efficient expedition of public administration (e.g. by causing delays in decision-making) and the need for confidentiality in relation to certain types of information (e.g. that relating to national security and the investigation of crime).

All of these are matters which the court must be cognisant of when determining the procedural demands appropriate to the circumstances of any particular case.

Potential elements of a fair hearing

The right to be informed of the case to be met

In most circumstances a person who may be affected prejudicially by the decision of a public body will be entitled in advance to know at least the substance of the case on which that decision will be based: 'If the right to be heard is to be a real right which is worth anything it must carry with it a right in the accused man to know the case which is made against him' (per Lord Denning, *Kanda v Government of Malaya* [1962] AC 322).

The rule was applied in *R v Hampshire County Council, ex parte K* [1990] 2 All ER 129. The local authority had reason to suspect that the applicant had been sexually abusing his daughter. These suspicions were given added credence by certain medical examinations and reports commissioned by the authority to which the applicant was not given access. In the ensuing application for judicial review, the Divisional Court ordered the suspension of care proceedings initiated by the authority. The applicant had been treated unfairly. Prior to the commencement of such proceedings he should have been allowed access to the medical reports so that he might have had a realistic opportunity to contest their contents.

Disclosure of the public body's information in detail and its precise sources may be required in the exercise of judicial or disciplinary powers, particularly where these may intrude upon a legal right or other substantial interest (*R v Army Board of the Defence Council, ex parte Anderson* [1992] 1 QB 169). Otherwise, in the interests of administrative efficiency, 'chapter and verse' may not be required and, as indicated, the general 'gist' of the case to be answered may be sufficient. Other public interests may also limit the extent of the right. Thus it has been held that natural justice does not require disclosure of information which would be injurious to national security (*R v Home Secretary, ex parte Agee and Hosenball* [1977] 1 WLR 766), or prejudicial to the fight against crime (*R v Gaming Board for Great Britain, ex parte Benaim and Khaida* [1970] 2 QB 417).

The right to reasonable time to prepare a response

Giving a person the substance of the case to be answered will provide only minimal procedural benefit if that occurs only a short time before the actual decision is to be made. Save what has been said above about the possible effects of any countervailing public interests, the person affected will usually be entitled to sufficient time in which to digest that information and formulate a response.

In *R v Thames Magistrates, ex parte Polemis* [1974] 1 WLR 1371, a cargo ship docked in the Thames and shortly afterwards an oil slick appeared beside it. A summons to answer a charge under the Control of Pollution Act 1971 was served on the ship's master. This required him to appear in the local magistrates' court in the afternoon of the same day on which the summons was served. His subsequent conviction was quashed for unfairness. Lord Widgery CJ concluded that 'any suggestion that he had been given a reasonable chance to prepare his defence [was] completely unarguable'.

See also *R (on the application of Clark-Darby) v Highbury Corner Magistrates' Court* [2001] EWHC Admin 959, where a magistrates' order in respect of unpaid council tax was quashed due to failure to give the applicant adequate notice of the proceedings.

The right to be heard

Due to the wording of this central element of the fair hearing rule, it is often assumed that it implies a right to be heard orally before the decision-maker. This is not the case. The essence of the rule is that the individual must be given a reasonable opportunity of conveying his/her views to the decision-maker whether this be orally or by written representations. The giving of oral hearings may often cause serious delays in administrative decision-making generally. The recognition of such a right will occur, therefore, only in the context of the exercise of powers which, according to the criteria already considered, attract the highest standards of procedural fairness. Hence, in *R v Army Board of the Defence Council, ex parte Anderson*, above, notwithstanding the court's view that in dealing with the applicant's allegations of racial abuse by his fellow soldiers the Board was bound to act judicially, this did not mean that the applicant should have been given an oral hearing. The flexible nature of the right was summarised by Taylor LJ:

> Whether an oral hearing is necessary will depend upon the circumstances of the particular case and upon the nature of the decision to be made. It will also depend upon whether there are substantial issues of fact which cannot be satisfactorily resolved on the available written evidence. This does not mean that whenever there is a conflict of evidence in the statements taken, an oral hearing must be held to resolve it. Sometimes such a conflict can be resolved merely by the inherent unlikelihood of one version or the other. Sometimes the issue is not central to the issue for determination and would not justify an oral hearing.

Cross-examination

Inevitably, the question whether procedural fairness requires cross-examination will only arise in those circumstances where the individual is entitled to an oral hearing. Where this is required it has been suggested that it carries with it an automatic right to question those who give evidence to the decision-maker (*R v Deputy Industrial Injuries Commissioner, ex parte Moore* [1965] 1 QB 456). This is, however, probably too great a generalisation. In *Bushell v Secretary of State for the Environment* [1981] AC 75, the House of Lords was not prepared to conclude that objectors to a new road scheme had any absolute right to question government experts when these appeared before the ensuing public inquiry. The House was mindful of the need not to 'over-judicialize' the procedure and was not convinced that, even in judicial proceedings, cross-examination was the only fair way of ascertaining relevant factual material. All depended on the circumstances of the particular case and whether, in that specific context, a fair hearing could be provided without 'insisting on observance of the procedures of a court of justice which professional lawyers alone are competent to operate effectively' (per Lord Diplock). The House concluded, therefore, that 'refusal by an inspector to allow a party to cross-examine orally at a local inquiry a person who had made statements of fact or expressed expert opinions is not unfair *per se*' (*ibid.*).

Legal representation

The existence of a right to be legally represented before the decision-maker will be recognised only where the individual has a right to be heard orally and all the surrounding circumstances indicate that the hearing cannot be conducted fairly unless legal representation is allowed.

In *R v Maze Prison Board of Visitors, ex parte Hone and McCartan* [1988] 1 AC 379, it was argued that the right should extend to all prisoners appearing before boards of prison visitors. The House of Lords rejected any such rigid rule. In its view the matter lay within the discretion of the decision-maker. The criteria to be taken into account in exercising this discretion had been explained previously in *R v Home Secretary, ex parte Tarrant* [1985] QB 251. These were as follows:

(a) the seriousness of the charge and the potential penalty;
(b) where any points of law were likely to arise;
(c) the capacity of the prisoner to present his/her own case;
(d) the complexity of the procedure;
(e) the need for reasonable speed in decision-making;
(f) the need for fairness between prisoners and between prisoners and prison officers.

With the exception of (f), these criteria would appear to be of relevance to decision-makers generally when the question of allowing legal representation or not falls to be decided. Hence, in those circumstances where a severe penalty may be imposed and difficult questions of law or procedure may be involved, the decision-maker should ponder carefully before refusing a request for representation. Any refusal must be based on careful consideration of the above criteria and their proper application to the facts of the case.

Reasons

A duty to give reasons may be imposed by statute. Such duty is imposed by the Tribunals and Inquiries Act 1992, s 10 on all those tribunals listed in Sched 1 to the Act. Where this is the case the reasons given should be 'proper, intelligible and adequate' (per Megaw J, *Re Poyser and Mills' Arbitration* [1964] 2 QB 467). If the reasons given are 'improper' they will 'reveal some flaw in the decision-making process which will be open to challenge on some ground other than the failure to give reasons' (e.g. irrelevancy) (per Lord Bridge, *Save Britain's Heritage* v *No 1 Poultry Ltd* [1991] 1 WLR 153). If they are unintelligible 'this will be equivalent to giving no reasons at all' (*ibid.*). Where the function is purely administrative, a relatively brief outline of the basis for the decision may suffice. Thus an immigration officer satisfied the obligation with the words 'I am not satisfied that you are genuinely seeking entry only for this limited period' (*R* v *Home Secretary, ex parte Swati* [1986] 1 WLR 477). Tribunals exercising judicial functions may be expected to give greater detail. Hence, in *R* v *Immigration Appeal Tribunal, ex parte Khan* [1983] QB 790, the view was that the tribunal should provide parties with sufficient information to show that the matter remitted to it had been duly considered and that this should be accompanied by the evidence for its conclusions.

Deficiency of reasons may not be a ground for judicial review *per se*. In the context of refusals of planning permission it has been held that such deficiency 'will only afford a ground for quashing the decision if the court is satisfied that the interests of the applicant have been substantially prejudiced by it' (*Save Britain's Heritage*, above).

Where there is no statutory obligation, the giving of reasons may be required by the duty to act fairly. The following cases provide some indication of the circumstances in which this may apply.

In *R* v *Civil Service Appeals Board, ex parte Cunningham* [1991] 4 All ER 310, the Board awarded the applicant £6,500 by way of compensation for his dismissal from the prison service. On the facts this was some £9,000 less than he might have expected from an industrial tribunal. No reasons for awarding the lower amount were given. All three members of the Court of Appeal felt that the Board had acted unfairly but reached this conclusion by different 'routes'. Lord Donaldson MR felt that the failure to give reasons contravened the applicant's legitimate expectation that, in a procedural sense, he would not be treated less fairly than those whose employment disputes would be dealt with before an industrial tribunal to which the statutory duty to give reasons in the Tribunals and Inquiries Act 1992 applied. McCowan LJ's view was that an obligation to give reasons followed from the fact that the Board had exercised a judicial function which was not subject to appeal. Leggett LJ also emphasised that the Board had made a judicial decision which affected the applicant's livelihood but which, in the absence of reasons, could not be subjected to judicial review: 'For it is only by judicial review that the board's award can be challenged; and without reasons neither the person dismissed nor the court can tell whether to apply for or to grant judicial review'. He further pointed out that the 'unexplained meagreness' of the award compelled an inference that the decision was irrational.

The issue of the right to reasons was considered subsequently by the House of Lords in *R* v *Home Secretary, ex parte Doody* [1993] 3 WLR 154, where it was decided that a mandatory life prisoner was entitled to reasons if the minister decided to depart from the 'tariff' (the minimum term to be served) recommended by the trial judge. It was felt to be unfair that a prisoner given a mandatory life term should be treated any less favourably than a person sentenced to a specific term for which reasons would be given by the trial judge when the sentence was imposed. Other considerations which appeared to influence the decision in Doody were that 'tariff' decisions affected a fundamental freedom and that the giving of reasons would have no major adverse consequences on the functioning of the penal system or other public interest. It was also pointed out that the giving of reasons would provide the only 'means of detecting the kind of error which would entitle the court to intervene' (per Lord Mustill).

An attempt to extract some broader principles from *Cunningham* and *Doody* was made by the Divisional Court in *R v Higher Education Funding Council, ex parte Institute of Dental Surgery* [1994] 1 WLR 242. The applicants were aggrieved by the research rating given to them by the Council. This was lower than they had expected and, it was estimated, would result in a loss of research funding in the region of £270,000. No reasons had been given for the decision.

Sedley J felt that *Cunningham* and *Doody* could be used as authorities for the following two principal categories of cases in which fairness required the giving of reasons:

(a)   where this was an obvious consequence of 'the nature of the process' and its effect on the person concerned – e.g. as in *Doody*, where the subject matter was 'an interest so highly regarded by the law (for example, personal liberty) that fairness requires that reasons be given as of right';

(b)   where there was 'something peculiar' or 'aberrant' about the decision which operated as a 'trigger factor' for the giving of reasons – e.g. as in *Cunningham* where the amount of compensation awarded appeared to be excessively low.

It was not felt, however, that the Funding Council's decision fell into either of these categories. Academic judgements were not such that their very 'nature and impact' called for reasons 'as a routine aspect of procedural fairness'.

The court felt it could not intervene simply because the decision had serious consequences for the applicants as this would have been tantamount to imposing a general duty to give reasons on all administrators ('a point to which the court...cannot go'). Nor was there anything so peculiar or aberrant about the decision so as to 'trigger' the reasons requirement.

In accordance with the principles laid down in the *Dental Surgery* case, the right to reasons has been held to apply to:

(a)   a decision of the Home Secretary as to the tariff period to be served by a person sentenced to indeterminate periods of imprisonment – i.e. the period to be served by way of retribution and deterrence (*R v Home Secretary, ex parte Hindley* [1998] 2 WLR 505);

(b)   decisions of courts martial (*R v Ministry of Defence, ex parte Murray, The Times*, 17 December 1997).

(c)   a decision of the General Medical Council relating to a doctor's fitness to practise (*Stefan v General Medical Council (No. 1)* [1999] 1 WLR 1293 (Privy Council);

(d)   a decision of the Director of Public Prosecutions not to prosecute where this had implications for rights protected by the European Convention on Human Rights;

in this case the right to life after the DPP decided not to prosecute in respect of the death of a prisoner following physical confrontation with prison officers (*R v Home Secretary, ex parte Manning* [2000] 2 WLR 463).

(e) reclassifying a post tariff discretionary life prison from category C to category B (*Hirst v Home Secretary* [2001] EWCA Civ 378);

(f) a decision to administer medical treatment to a non-consenting adult (*R (on the application of Wooder) v Feggetter* [2002] EWCA Civ 554).

The doctrine of legitimate expectation

As already indicated, it is now well established that the rules of natural justice should be observed in the exercise of a decision-making power which could have serious detrimental consequences for the rights or interests of the person affected. In more recent times the courts have refined this to mean that natural justice should be observed in circumstances where the individual has a legitimate expectation that this will be so. A legitimate expectation in this context may be defined, therefore, as a legally enforceable procedural right. Such legitimate expectations or right may arise in a variety of ways.

First, this may result from an assurance given by the decision-maker that no decision will be made without prior consultation with, or hearing the representations of, the person affected. This element of the doctrine was applied in *Attorney-General for Hong Kong v Ng Yuen Shiu* [1983] 2 AC 629. The complainant had entered Hong Kong illegally. Prior to being served with a deportation order he had been questioned by the authorities but had been given no proper opportunity to present his case in full. Previously, however, the Hong Kong authorities had given an undertaking that such persons would be 'interviewed' personally and that 'each case will be treated on its merits'. The Privy Council quashed the deportation order on the ground that the complainant had been given a legitimate expectation of a fair hearing and that this had not been honoured:

> when a public authority has promised to follow a certain procedure, it is in the interests of good administration that it should act fairly and should implement its promise, so long as implementation does not interfere with its statutory duty.

Second, a legitimate expectation may arise from the previous practice of the decision-maker. Thus, if it has been usual practice to give the person affected a hearing before exercising a particular power to decide, this may give an individual a legally enforceable expectation that they will be treated in the same way. Hence in *R v British Coal Corporation, ex parte Vardy* [1993] ICR 720, a decision to close several coal mines was quashed due to the corporation's failure to consult with miners and trade unions affected in accordance with established practice.

The above two methods of creating procedural legitimate expectations were recognised by the House of Lords in the *GCHQ* case: 'Legitimate, or reasonable, expectation may arise either from an express promise given on behalf of a public authority or from the existence of a regular practice which the claimant can reasonably expect to continue' (per Lord Fraser).

Third, there are plentiful dicta to the effect that an expectation of being treated in accordance with natural justice may flow from the nature of the interest or benefit enjoyed by the individual. Thus, for example, in *GCHQ* Lord Diplock spoke of:

the prima facie rule of procedural propriety in public law applicable to a case of legitimate expectations that a benefit ought not to be withdrawn until the reason for its proposed withdrawal has been communicated to the person who has theretofore enjoyed that benefit and that person has been given an opportunity to comment on the reason.

The benefit or interest enjoyed must be one of substance so that it would be unfair to remove it without a hearing. Thus the holder of a licence on which a livelihood depends has a legitimate expectation of a hearing before any decision may be made not to renew or to revoke it (*McInnes v Onslow-Fane*, above). In *R v Brent London Borough Council, ex parte Gunning* (1985) 84 LGR 168, it was held that the interest of parents in the provision of local education was sufficient to create a legitimate expectation that they would be consulted by the local education authority before it made any recommendations for the closure and amalgamation of any of its schools.

It should be noted also that a legitimate expectation may be lost because of the behaviour of the person on whom the benefit has been bestowed. In *Cinnamond v British Airports Authority* [1980] 1 WLR 582, the Court of Appeal held that a number of private hire car drivers had no right to a hearing prior to a decision by the authority denying them access to Heathrow airport. They had repeatedly ignored airport by-laws by 'jumping' the queue of licensed hackney cabs to pick up passengers at the arrivals terminus and had charged such passengers exorbitant fares. Repeated warnings and prosecutions had failed to achieve any change of conduct. Shaw LJ concluded that 'the drivers had put themselves so far outside the limits of tolerable conduct as to disentitle themselves to expect any further representations on their part could have any influence or relevance'.

It is now also well established that assurances or the past practice of a public authority may create substantive as well as procedural legitimate expectations. Such substantive legitimate expectations may arise in the following circumstances:

(a) where a public body gives an assurance that it will act in a certain way but then seeks to resile on the assurance after it has been relied upon;

(b) where a public body seeks to depart from an existing policy which has guided its actions and decisions in a certain context.

A leading example of circumstances falling within category (a) was provided by *R v North and East Devon Health Authority, ex parte Coughlan* [1999] LGR 703. The case centred around an assurance given to a group of disabled persons living in local authority accommodation that they would not be moved from that accommodation and would be allowed to remain there 'for as long as they chose'. The Court of Appeal held that the assurance bound the authority. It was, however, at pains to point out that this did not set aside the general rule that an authority must be free to change a decision where it is in the public interest to do so. Rather, it represented the recognition of an exception where, on the facts of a particular case, the requirements of fairness clearly overrode the authority's public policy concerns. The crucial facts in the case before them which persuaded the Court of Appeal that the authority should honour its assurance were:

(i) the promise had been given on a number of occasions and in precise terms to a group of severely disabled people and related to what would be their home for the rest of their lives;

(ii) the representation was unqualified and had been relied on by those to whom it had been made;

(iii) a decision not to honour the promise would be equivalent to a breach of promise in private law;

(iv) no overriding public policy reasons for departing from the promise had been provided by the authority;

(v) requiring the authority to honour its promise would not place it in breach of other statutory or common law duties.

On similar facts, *Coughlan* was followed in *R v Merton, Sutton and Wandsworth Health Authority, ex parte Perry* [2001] Lloyd's Rep Med 73. Note, however, the decision in *R (on the application of Collins) v Lincolnshire Health Authority* [2001] EWHC Admin 685, where the court's view was that there was no overriding unfairness in not holding an authority to a 'home for life' promise where it was generally agreed that moving the patients into the community would be to their benefit.

The extent of the protection offered by the doctrine of legitimate expectation was further developed by the decision in *R (Bibi and Nash) v Newham London Borough Council* [2001] EWCA Civ 240, where it was stated that, although detrimental reliance on a promise would normally be required for legal enforcement of a substantive expectation, this was not an absolute rule. In appropriate circumstances fairness could render an assurance binding on an authority despite the absence of such reliance.

The rule against bias

Introduction

A person empowered by law to make decisions having potentially detrimental consequences for the rights, interests or legitimate expectations of others, should not act if he or she has any actual, financial or apparent interest in the subject matter of the issue to be determined. Should this occur the decision will be tainted by bias and may be held to be void or of no legal effect. The law in this context is presaged on the maxims that 'no man should be judge in his own cause' (*Dr Bonham's* case, above) and that 'justice should not only be done but should manifestly and undoubtedly be seen to be done' (*R v Sussex Justices, ex parte McCarthy* [1924] 1 KB 256).

Actual bias

If the decision-maker has a preconceived personal bias in the outcome of the decision or consciously favours or disfavours one of the parties who may be affected by it, this may well amount to bad faith in addition to representing a blatant contravention of natural justice. Examples of this type of abuse are rare. 'It is necessary...to put on one side the very rare case where actual bias is shown to exist. Of course, if actual bias is proved, that is an end of the case; the person concerned must be disqualified' (per Lord Goff, *R v Gough* [1993] AC 646).

Financial bias

A decision-maker with a direct financial interest is disqualified and decisions made by the same are thereby rendered void. Actual bias need not be shown. The existence of the financial interest is sufficient. In *Dimes v Grand Junction Canal Proprietors*

(1852) 3 HL Cas 759, a decision of the Lord Chancellor was set aside for bias because he had a financial shareholding in the canal company. It was emphasised that the finding of bias contained no inference that the Lord Chancellor had been 'in the remotest degree influenced by the interest that he had in this concern'. It was, however, 'of the last importance that the maxim no man is to be judge in his own cause should be held sacred' (per Lord Campbell).

The vitiating financial interest need not be substantial but it must be direct. In *R v Hendon Rural District Council, ex parte Chorley* [1933] 2 KB 696, a council granted planning permission for the development of a certain piece of land. Their decision was held to be invalid on the ground that one of the councillors who voted for the resolution was also an estate agent acting for the owners of the land in a prospective sale which was contingent on planning permission being granted.

A financial interest will not operate as a vitiating factor, therefore, if it is too remote. Hence two justices who were trustees of institutions (a hospital and a friendly society) which held bonds in Bradford Corporation were not disqualified from acting in a case in which the Corporation was involved (*R v Rand* (1866) LR 1 WB 230). In these circumstances a finding in favour of the Corporation could not have resulted in any discernible or tangible benefit for the justices.

The decision of the House of Lords in *R v Bow Street Stipendiary Magistrate, ex parte Pinochet Ugarte (No. 2)* [1999] 1 All ER 577, illustrated that a decision might also be quashed for bias where a decision-maker, although not shown to be actually biased or to have a direct stake in the decision, has some other direct interest in its outcome.

In November 1998, a five-member appellate committee of the House of Lords, including Lord Hoffman, ruled that General Pinochet enjoyed no continuing immunity in respect of alleged crimes against humanity committed while Head of State of Chile and that it was open to the Home Secretary, therefore, to decide whether the General should be extradited to Spain under the Extradition Act 1989 for alleged offences against Spanish nationals during the period he was in office. During the proceedings leading to this decision, Amnesty International was given leave to put written and oral testimony to the House which was of significant prejudice to the General's case.

Within a matter of days, however, it emerged that Amnesty had close and longstanding links with both Lord and Lady Hoffman. Lady Hoffman had been in Amnesty's employ in an administrative capacity for over twenty years while Lord Hoffman was currently a director of Amnesty International Charity Ltd. General Pinochet's lawyers responded by petitioning the House of Lords that the decision should be set aside or Lord Hoffman's judgment be discounted.

Held

(a) The House had jurisdiction to rescind or vary any of its earlier decisions where a party had been dealt with unfairly. A decision could not be reopened, however, simply because it was alleged to be wrong:

> In principle it must be that your Lordships, as the ultimate court of appeal, have power to correct any injustice caused by an earlier order of this House. There is no relevant statutory limitation on the jurisdiction of the House in this regard and therefore its inherent jurisdiction remains unfettered...However, it should be made clear that the

House will not reopen any appeal save in circumstances where, through no fault of a party, he or she has been subjected to an unfair procedure...[T]here can be no question of [a] decision being varied or rescinded...just because it is thought that [it] is wrong (per Lord Browne-Wilkinson).

(b) A judge, including a member of the House of Lords, who had a direct interest, albeit non-pecuniary, in the outcome of a case was disqualified for bias:

> ...although the cases have all dealt with automatic disqualification on grounds of pecuniary bias, there is no good reason in principle for so limiting automatic disqualification. The rationale of the whole rule is that a man cannot be a judge in his own cause. [I]f, as in the present case, the matter at issue does not relate to money or economic advantage but is concerned with the promotion of the cause, the rationale of disqualifying a judge applies just as much if the judge's decision will lead to the promotion of a cause in which the judge is involved together with one of the parties (*ibid*.)

(c) The decision of November 1999 should, therefore, be set aside and the issue reheard before a differently constituted House.

Apparent bias

The test of bias generally accepted as applicable in English law prior to the coming into effect of the Human Rights Act 1988 was that laid down by Lord Goff in *R v Gough* (above).

> [H]aving ascertained the relevant circumstances the court should ask itself whether...there was a real danger of bias on the part of the relevant member of the tribunal in question, in the sense that he might unfairly regard (or have unfairly regarded) with favour, or disfavour, the case of a party to the issue under consideration by him (per Lord Goff).

This was the test used to invalidate the controversial decision not to resume the inquest into the *Marchioness* disaster (*R v Inner West London Coroner, ex parte Dallaglio* [1994] 4 All ER 139). The coroner had described some of the relatives seeking the resumption as 'mentally unwell' and 'unhinged'. This led the Court of Appeal to conclude that 'there was a real danger that the coroner might have unfairly regarded with disfavour' the cases of those towards whom he had expressed these negative sentiments.

A real danger of bias required 'more than a minimal risk' but 'less than a probability'. To 'unfairly regard with disfavour' required that the decision-maker 'was predisposed or prejudiced against one party's case for reasons unconnected with the merits of the issue' (per Simon Brown LJ, *ex parte Dallaglio*).

The real danger test was said to be applicable to the exercise of administrative as well as judicial powers (*R v Secretary of State for the Environment, ex parte Kirkstall Valley Campaign Ltd* [1996] 3 All ER 304). The test was, however, applied more or less rigorously depending on the circumstances: 'what amounts to bias is not a fixed quantity but a function of the procedure under scrutiny and the events occurring in the course of it' (per Sedley J, *R v Manchester Metropolitan University, ex parte Nolan*, above). Hence it was held that the decision of a local council could not be impugned for bias simply because a majority of councillors were predisposed to take a particular view by virtue of their party-political affiliations. It was inevitable in a pluralist democracy that party policy will influence the decisions of those elected to positions of authority. Parliament must have had this in its contemplation, therefore, when it conferred the powers in issue. Judicial intervention for bias in these circumstances would thus be incompatible with the intentions of the sovereign body and inimical to the process of decision-making in a democratic system of government (*R* v *Amber Valley District Council, ex parte Jackson* [1985] 1 WLR 298).

With the advent of the Human Rights Act 1998, and the requirement that domestic public authorities, including courts, should exercise their functions in accordance with the European Convention on Human Rights, the test of bias as explained in *Gough* has been subjected to a degree of linguistic modification. Domestic courts have sought to stress its strictly objective nature and compatibility with the test preferred by the Court of Human Rights in its jurisprudence relating to Art 6 (right to a fair trial), i.e. was there an objectively justified and legitimate reason for fearing a lack of partiality in the decision-maker (*McGonnell* v *United Kingdom* (2000) 30 EHRR 289).

The reconstructed 'real danger' test was set out by Chadwick LJ in *Taylor* v *Lawrence* [2001] EWCA Civ 119:

> Where actual bias has not been established the personal impartiality of the judge is to be presumed. The court then has to decide whether, on an objective appraisal, the material facts give rise to a legitimate fear that the judge might not have been impartial. If they do, the decision must be set aside. The court must ask itself whether the circumstances – and that includes all the circumstances which a fair minded and impartial observer would have properly regarded as material, whether known to the appellants or not – would leave a fair minded and informed observer to conclude that there was a real danger that the judge was biased.

The *Gough* test as so modified was approved by the House of Lords in *Porter* v *Magill* [2002] UKHL 67.

References

Lewis (1993) *Judicial Remedies in Public Law*, London: Sweet & Maxwell.

Wade and Forsyth (1994) *Administrative Law* (7th edn), Oxford: Clarendon Press.

Further reading

Allen and Thompson (1996) *Cases and Materials on Constitutional and Administrative Law* (3rd edn), London: Blackstone, Chs 7–8.

Fenwick and Phillipson (1997) *Sourcebook on Public Law*, London: Cavendish, Pt V, Ch 2.

Fordham (1994) *Judicial Review Handbook*, London: Wiley/Chancery Lane Publishing, Ch 5, pp. 319–56.

Jones and Thompson (eds) (1996) *Garner's Administrative Law* (8th edn), London: Butterworths, Ch 8.

Jowell and Oliver (1988) *New Directions in Judicial Review*, London: Stevens, pp. 51–72.

Marston and Ward (1997) *Cases and Commentary on Constitutional and Administrative Law* (4th edn), London: Pitman Publishing, Chs 14–15.

Supperstone and Goudie (1992) *Judicial Review*, London: Butterworths, Ch 6.

Wade and Forsyth (1994) *Administrative Law* (7th edn), Oxford: Clarendon Press, Chs 13–15.

Chapter 16

EXCLUSION OF AND APPLICATIONS FOR JUDICIAL REVIEW

EXCLUSION OF JUDICIAL REVIEW: INTRODUCTION

Just as Parliament may use its sovereign legislative authority to confer legislative, executive and judicial powers on its subordinates, it may also exert that same authority to protect the exercise of such powers from judicial interference. This may be done as follows:

(a) by inserting an exclusion or 'ouster' clause in the enabling Act which seeks, in express terms, to exclude or 'oust' the power of judicial review;

(b) by phrasing the powers so conferred in such wide subjective terms as to minimise the grounds on which the exercise of the power may be questioned;

(c) by providing a statutory remedy to deal with any alleged abuses of powers or duties in the enabling Act.

The courts also assume that Parliament intends certain powers to be regarded as 'non-justiciable', i.e. as matters beyond the scope of judicial review. These tend to be discretionary powers which relate to sensitive political or security issues. The view here is that judicial intervention would be inimical to the public interests which such powers seek to protect.

This illustrates that the effectiveness of judicial review and of the functioning of the separation of powers in the British constitution are, at all times, subject to the sovereignty of Parliament. In a strictly legal sense, there is nothing inevitable about the 'balanced' relationship between the legislative, executive and judicial powers of government. Parliament's sovereign legislative will is, after all, little more than a constitutional euphemism for the wishes of the executive or those who control the House of Commons. Moreover, it is probably naive to believe that those in power gain any great satisfaction or comfort from the knowledge that their excesses may be corrected by judicial intervention.

There is a danger, therefore, that judicial review could be rendered nugatory by the executive control of the drafting of enabling legislation. Wholesale use of this tactic would, however, be regarded as a flagrant breach of British constitutional traditions and would no doubt attract considerable political opprobrium. The courts have also made it clear that the citizen's access to the courts to challenge alleged abuses of power is to be regarded as a crucial and fundamental constitutional right. As such, legislative restriction of it will only be given judicial recognition if couched in the clearest of express terms without any uncertainty or ambiguity. Thus, where the Lord Chancellor sought to radically increase the fee for issuing a writ (i.e. for commencing civil proceedings), the order purporting to implement his decision was declared to be *ultra vires* the powers conferred on him by the Supreme Court Act 1981 (*R v Lord Chancellor, ex parte Witham* [1997] 2 All ER 779). Laws J said that access to the courts was 'as near to an absolute right as any which could be envisaged' and that he would find 'great difficulty in conceiving a form of words capable of making it plain beyond doubt to the reader of a statute that the provision in question prevented him from going to court'. Therefore, since the radically increased fee would have seriously prejudiced the right for the less affluent, it could not be allowed to stand.

Given these restraining factors, legislative attempts to render the use of powers 'judge proof' have generally been restricted to those circumstances where this appears to be justified by what is perceived to be an overriding public interest.

OUSTER CLAUSES

'Shall not be questioned in any legal proceedings whatsoever'

In *Smith* v *East Elloe RDC* [1956] AC 736, Mrs Smith sought to challenge the validity of a compulsory purchase order by virtue of which 8½ acres of her property had been acquired by the local authority. The order had been made in 1948 and confirmed in the same year by the Minister of Health after a local public inquiry. The procedure for making compulsory purchase orders was contained in the Acquisition of Land (Authorisation Procedure) Act 1946. This provided that 'if any person aggrieved by a compulsory purchase order desires to question the validity thereof…he may within six weeks from the date on which notice of the confirmation or making of the order…is first published…make an application to the High Court'. The Act went on to provide that once this period had elapsed 'a compulsory purchase order…shall not…be questioned in any legal proceedings whatsoever'.

Mrs Smith commenced her proceedings in 1954 alleging, *inter alia*, that the order had been 'wrongfully made and in bad faith'. The court felt that the action could not be entertained and that it was bound to accept and apply the will of Parliament as clearly expressed in the ouster clause. It was cognisant of both the deep-rooted principle that the legislature cannot be assumed to oust the jurisdiction of the court – particularly where fraud is alleged – except by clear words and the view that 'a statute is, if possible,…to be construed as to avoid injustice'. Nevertheless, as there was nothing ambiguous about the language or the intent of the ouster, the court felt bound to apply the 'first of all principles of construction that plain words must be given their plain meaning'. Thus the court accepted that once the six-week period had elapsed no judicial redress was available in respect of a compulsory purchase order, no matter that it was made in bad faith or in blatant abuse of the prescribed procedures.

The effectiveness of such 'partial' ousters – i.e. those which restrict legal proceedings to a prescribed period – was later confirmed in *R v Secretary of State for the Environment, ex parte Ostler* [1976] 3 WLR 288. Such clauses are found typically in Acts which permit the compulsory acquisition of land for public works, housing, highways, etc. The policy behind them is to protect public bodies against the complications, particularly the financial costs, which might accrue if, after such works had been completed, the legal process for acquiring the land necessary was found to have been defective.

The meaning of a similarly worded clause was considered by the House of Lords in *Anisminic v Foreign Compensation Commission*, above. On this occasion the ouster clause in question provided that any 'determination by the Commission…shall not be questioned in any court of law' (Foreign Compensation Act 1950, s 4). Unlike the clause in issue in the *Smith v East Elloe* case, this was an absolute ouster – i.e. no limited period was provided in which a legal challenge to the Commission's decisions could be made.

In its judgment the House of Lords displayed a clear reluctance to accept that a decision-making power could be put completely beyond the scope of judicial scrutiny so that not even blatant abuses of power could be rendered *ultra vires* and of no effect. Hence the conclusion that if the Commission made a decision which was outside its jurisdiction, so as to be null and void, this could not in law be regarded as any sort of determination at all. Therefore, since the express language of the ouster limited its application to 'determinations' of the Commission, it could not give any protection to that which did not qualify to be so described.

Any apparent inconsistency between this and the approach taken in the *Smith* case was explained in *Ostler* on the grounds that in the *Anisminic* case:

(a)   there was a complete or absolute ouster which 'precluded the court from entertaining a complaint at any time about the determination';
(b)   'the House was considering a determination by a truly judicial body';
(c)   'the House had to consider the actual determination of the tribunal, whereas in the *Smith v East Elloe* case the House had to consider the validity of the process by which the decision was reached' (per Denning MR).

However convincing this attempt to distinguish the two cases may be, it leaves the conclusion that a court will give full effect to the intended meaning of a partial ouster clause but may resort to the *Anisminic* approach to avoid compliance with an absolute or complete ouster. This was confirmed by the Court of Appeal in *R v Cornwall County Council, ex parte Huntington* [1994] 1 All ER 694, where Simon Brown LJ quoted with approval the following statement made when the case was before the Divisional Court:

> The intention of Parliament when it uses an Anisminic clause is that questions as to validity are not excluded…When paragraphs such as those considered in *Ex parte Ostler* are used, then the legislative intention is that the question as to validity may be raised…in the prescribed time…but that otherwise the jurisdiction of the court is excluded in the interest of certainty (per Mann LJ).

The *Anisminic* decision was followed and applied by the Court of Appeal in *R v Home Secretary, ex parte Fayed* [1997] 1 All ER 228, where the applicant was allowed to apply for judicial review of the minister's decision to refuse him British nationality despite the existence in the enabling Act (British Nationality Act 1981, s 44) of a clause stating that the 'the decision of the Secretary of State…shall not be subject to appeal…or review in any court of law'. Lord Woolf quoted from the Privy Council decision in *Attorney-General v Ryan* [1980] AC 718, to the effect that 'to come within the prohibition of appeal or review by an ouster clause of this type, the decision must be one which the decision-making authority . . . had jurisdiction to make'.

'Shall be final'

The effect of clauses which state that exercise of a particular decision-making power shall be regarded as 'final' was summed up with eminent clarity by Denning LJ, *R v Medical Appeal Tribunal, ex parte Gilmore* [1975] 1 QB 574:

> I find it very well settled that the remedy by *certiorari* is never to be taken away except by the most clear and explicit words. The word final is not enough. That only means 'without appeal'. It does not mean 'without recourse to *certiorari*' [i.e. judicial review]. It makes the decision final on the facts but not final on the law.

Such clauses do not, therefore, exclude judicial review. They merely protect exercises of the decision-making power from any statutory right of appeal that might otherwise have been available. Whether such clauses are effective to exclude a right of appeal on a point of law is a matter of uncertainty. Lord Denning MR in *Pearlman v Keepers and Governors of Harrow School*, above, thought they did not. His view was not supported, however, by the House of Lords in *Re Racal Communications*, above, where the House felt that if a power was to be treated as not subject to appeal this rendered it non-appealable on any ground.

It has also been held that, if the effect of a finality clause is to prevent any challenge to the factual merits of a decision, this also precludes any right of action in negligence against the decision-maker since such action would inevitably bring into question the quality of the decision-maker's conclusions (*Jones v Department of Employment* [1989] QB 1).

'As if enacted in this Act'

This form of words has been used in enabling Acts which have conferred subordinate law-making powers on ministers and other public bodies. The apparent objective of the formula is to give the subordinate legislation so made the sovereign legal status of the enabling Act itself, thus rendering it immune from judicial review.

Once again, however, the exclusive effect of such attempted ouster has been minimised by judicial interpretation. Thus it has been held that as Parliament could not have intended subordinate law-makers to act unlawfully it must be assumed that the clause could relate only to that which had been made according to and, therefore, *intra vires* the Act containing the law-making power (*R v Minister of Health, ex parte Yaffe* [1930] 2 KB 98).

SUBJECTIVELY WORDED POWERS

It is not uncommon for an Act to provide that a power may be exercised where the repository is 'satisfied' or 'of the opinion' that certain facts or conditions exist. Alternatively the Act may provide that the repository may do whatever is thought 'fit' or 'necessary and expedient' to deal with particular circumstances.

Such terminology was presumably intended, and in the past has been held to mean, that any honest, albeit subjective, belief in the existence of the prerequisite facts or circumstances, or the need for a certain course of action, must be accepted as sufficient for a valid exercise of the power. Hence, in *Robinson v Minister of Town and Country Planning* [1947] KB 702, the minister had a statutory power to compulsorily acquire bomb-damaged property 'where...satisfied that it is requisite for...dealing satisfactorily with extensive war damage' that an area should be 'laid out afresh and developed as a whole'. In answer to a challenge to the validity of a particular compulsory purchase order the response of the Court of Appeal was:

> How can this Minister, who is entrusted by Parliament to make or not to make an executive order according to his judgement and acts bona fide (as he must be assumed to do in the absence of evidence to the contrary) be called upon to justify his decision by proving that he had before him materials sufficient to support it (per Lord Greene MR).

Consistent with the approach already explained towards express ousters, the modern judicial attitude towards such subjectively worded powers is to insist that, in so far as the subject matter of a particular decision is justiciable – e.g. is not a matter of political opinion or judgement – it is reviewable for *Wednesbury* unreasonableness. Thus, in *Secretary of State for Education and Science v Metropolitan Borough of Tameside* [1977] AC 1014, the House of Lords refused to accept that the minister's power to issue directives to a local education authority 'if satisfied' that such authority had acted unreasonably in the exercise of its statutory functions was beyond the scope of judicial scrutiny.

> The section is framed in subjective form – if the Secretary of State 'is satisfied'. This form of section is quite well known, and at first sight might seem to exclude judicial review. Sections in this form may, no doubt, exclude judicial review on what is...a matter of pure judgement. But I do not think that they go further than that. If a judgement requires, before it can be made, the existence of some facts, then, although the evaluation of those facts is for the Secretary of State alone, the court must inquire whether those facts exist, and have been taken into account, whether the judgement has been made upon a proper self-direction as to those facts, whether the judgement has not been made upon other facts which ought not to have been taken into account (per Lord Wilberforce).

ALTERNATIVE REMEDIES

A statute which confers a power on a public authority may, at the same time, provide a remedy for dealing with alleged abuses of that power. Hence, as already explained, statutes which authorise the compulsory acquisition of land and property will normally provide a right of appeal on a point of law (to the High Court) against a compulsory purchase order, which right should be exercised within six weeks of the order's confirmation by the Secretary of State (usually the Minister for the Environment).

Such statutory remedy may be regarded as exclusive by the courts if this appears to have been the intention of Parliament. If the statutory remedy is so regarded this means that the validity of the administrative action or decision in question cannot be challenged by judicial review or any other procedure.

Where the statutory remedy provided is a right of appeal to a court of law – frequently the High Court – this will usually be assumed to exclude resort to judicial review 'save in exceptional circumstances' (per Sir John Donaldson MR, *R v Home Secretary, ex parte Swati*, above). In *R v Cornwall County Council, ex parte Huntington*, above, the applicants sought judicial review of an order made by the local authority under the Wildlife and Countryside Act 1981 recognising a newly established right of way. The Act provided a right of appeal to the High Court against any such order to be exercised within six weeks of its confirmation by the minister. In this case, however, the application for judicial review was made prior to the order being confirmed. Thus, the applicants argued, as they were not challenging a confirmed order, they were not bound by the statutory procedure and remained free to commence proceedings for judicial review.

This argument was firmly rejected. Parliament had provided a scheme for making, confirming and challenging the order in question and it was clearly Parliament's intention that all related legal proceedings should be conducted thereby. All other methods of challenge either before, during, or after the six-week period allowed – had therefore been excluded:

> it seems clear as a matter of construction that Parliament intended – and, indeed, to my mind intended for good reason – that the remedy by way of statutory application...should be the exclusive avenue of address available to those aggrieved by...orders of this kind if and when such orders come to be confirmed (per Simon Brown LJ).

Note, however, the decision in *R v Wiltshire County Council, ex parte Lizard Brothers and Co Ltd, The Times*, 13 January 1998, which held that, where a local council had resolved to make an order under the Wildlife and Countryside Act 1981 (in this case designating a road through a village as a byway open to all traffic), the decision remained open to review until the consequent order had actually been made. In the opinion of the court, judicial review was not excluded by the existence of the statutory remedy mentioned above, i.e. appeal to the High Court against a confirmed order. Rather, this was just one of the many matters which a court could take into account in exercising its discretion whether or not to grant review.

Where a statute provides an administrative remedy only – e.g. by way of complaint to the relevant minister – the courts are less likely to accept that this is intended to exclude judicial review where it is alleged that the body invested with the power or duty has acted *ultra vires*. This would appear to be the ratio of the Court of Appeal decision in *Meade v Haringey London Borough Council* [1979] 1 WLR 637. The authority had closed a number of schools after their caretakers had taken strike action. The Education Act 1944, s 99 provided that if the minister was satisfied 'upon complaint by any person...that any local authority...have failed to discharge any duty imposed on them by...this Act, the Minister may make an order declaring the authority...to be in default...and giving such directions for enforcing the execution thereof as appear...to be expedient...'. Despite the existence of such statutory remedy, legal proceedings were brought for, *inter alia*, a declaration that the authority was in breach of its statutory duty in s 8 of the 1944 Act to provide adequate schools and education for the needs of the community. To the argument that any such proceedings were excluded by the statutory remedy, Lord Denning MR replied:

Now although that section does give a remedy – by complaint to a Minister – it does not exclude any other remedy. To my mind it leaves open all the established remedies which the law provides in cases where a public authority fails to perform its statutory duty either by an act of commission or omission.

JUSTICIABILITY

The courts regard certain types of decision-making powers as being unsuitable for judicial review. These are generally matters relating to sensitive issues of public policy and the allocation of financial resources. The general judicial opinion appears to be that the scrutiny and control of decision-making in these contexts is essentially a matter for the parliamentary and political processes. Hence, although not excluded from questioning the exercise of such powers, the courts tend to treat such subjects as being 'non-justiciable'. The following represent some of the most significant of these areas of government activity.

The formation of legislation

Primary legislation is, of course, not subject to judicial scrutiny except in so far as it contravenes the law of the European Community. Subordinate legislation, however, may be reviewed for both simple and procedural *ultra vires*. The formulation of both types of legislation is, however, regarded as part of the political process which may be questioned and debated in Parliament but not in the courts. Hence it is extremely unlikely that a court would entertain an application for judicial review which alleged abuse of discretion by a minister in the formulation of a regulation – e.g. failure to consider relevant considerations. Also, it has been held that a person likely to be affected by a piece of subordinate legislation has no right to be heard as its content is being determined unless it is so provided in the enabling Act (*Bates v Lord Hailsham* [1972] 1 WLR 1373).

Policy and finance

The judiciary have displayed a marked reluctance to entertain disputes dealing with the reasonableness or rationality of government policy or decisions relating to the allocation of public finances.

R v Secretary of State for the Environment, ex parte Hammersmith and Fulham London Borough Councils [1991] 1 AC 521, concerned the minister's power in the Local Government Act 1988, s 100 to 'cap' the spending plans of any local council if these were 'in his opinion…excessive'. The applicants argued that a local council should be free to spend what a 'sensible' authority in the particular circumstances obtaining in its area might reasonably decide was appropriate and that the minister was entitled to form the opinion that projected expenditure was 'excessive' only where it was so 'profligate and extravagant that no sensible authority could have approved it'.

In rejecting this argument the House of Lords held that there were no 'objective criteria' by which spending decisions could be judged to be excessive or unreasonable.

This was entirely a matter of political opinion to be determined on the basis of what would best serve the public interest. The minister's discretion in this matter was, therefore, non-justiciable.

> The formulation and implementation of national economic policy are matters depending essentially on political judgement. The decisions which shape them are for politicians to take and it is in the political forum of the House of Commons that these are to be properly debated and approved or disapproved on their merits (per Lord Bridge).

National security

English judges have long been reticent about upsetting executive decisions relating to the defence of the realm or the protection of national security. An impressive litany of cases attests to this judicial preference and sympathy for the maxim *salus populi suprema lex* (the safety of the people is the highest law).

Two wartime decisions provide classic illustration of this tendency. In *R v Halliday, ex parte Zadig* [1917] AC 260, the House of Lords refused to quash a regulation authorising internment without trial. No specific authority for this ultimate restriction on personal freedom could be found in the enabling Act (Defence of the Realm Act 1914). Their Lordships felt, however, that the traditional canon of interpretation forbidding denial of basic freedoms except with express parliamentary authority, i.e. unrestricted access to the courts, should not be applied during wartime.

> It appears to me to be sufficient answer to this argument that it may be necessary in time of great public danger to entrust great powers to His Majesty in Council and Parliament may do so feeling certain that such powers will be reasonably exercised (per Lord Finlay LC).

Similarly, in *Liversidge v Anderson* [1942] AC 206, during the Second World War, the Home Secretary's power to intern without trial any person he had 'reasonable cause to believe...to be of hostile origins or associations' was construed by the House of Lords to mean that he could intern any person he *honestly* believed to be of such origins or associations whether such belief was reasonable or not.

Other more recent cases attest to the continuing judicial reluctance to question either the use of discretion or the procedure employed when executive officials make decisions in this context. The non-justiciable nature of discretionary powers in the sphere of national security was restated by the Court of Appeal in *R v Home Secretary, ex parte Chahal* [1995] 1 All ER 658. The applicant challenged a deportation order served on him under the power contained in the Immigration Act 1971 to remove from this country any person whose presence in the United Kingdom is deemed 'not to be conducive to the public good'. The particular reason for the Home Secretary's decision was that the applicant was believed to be involved in Sikh terrorism. In response to the applicant's argument that the decision was irrational because any such involvement would be no threat to the United Kingdom, the court concluded that in matters of national security it was not competent to review or question the evidence on which the minister had based his decision.

Most of the other modern cases concerning the justiciability of issues relating to national security have involved alleged breaches of the rules of natural justice – particularly the right to a fair hearing. In the most famous of these, the *GCHQ* case, the House of Lords conceded that for the effective protection of the public interest in national security, it was for the executive and not the courts to determine the degree of procedural justice which could properly or safely be afforded to those detrimentally affected by related decisions.

> The decision on whether the requirements of national security outweigh the duty of fairness in any particular case is for the Government and not for the courts. The Government alone has access to the necessary information, and in any event, the judicial process is unsuitable for reaching decisions on national security (per Lord Fraser).

A number of the cases have concerned the making of deportation orders and exclusion orders under the Immigration Act 1971 and the Prevention of Terrorism Act 1989 respectively. Contravention of the right to a fair hearing and the failure to give reasons for decisions have been the principal complaints. On each occasion, however, the courts have refused to intervene and have preferred the public interest in national security to that of procedural fairness: 'Great as is the public interest in the freedom of the individual and the doing of justice to him, nevertheless, in the last resort, it must take second place to the security of the country itself' (per Lord Denning MR, *R v Home Secretary, ex parte Agee and Hosenball* [1977] 1 WLR 766).

It would appear, therefore, that the making of such orders is non-justiciable for either abuse of discretion or procedural unfairness (see *R v Home Secretary, ex parte Cheblak* [1991] 2 All ER 319: judicial review of deportation order refused; *R v Home Secretary, ex parte Stitt, The Times*, 3 February 1987: judicial review of prevention of terrorism exclusion order refused). A court is, however, unlikely to submit to ministerial claims to be acting in the interests of national security unless it can be shown that there is some plausible connection between the action taken and the alleged security demands. 'Once the factual basis is established by evidence so that the court is satisfied that the interest of national security is a relevant factor, the court will accept the opinion of the Crown...as to what is required to meet it' (per Lord Scarman, the *GCHQ* case). In *R v Home Secretary, ex parte Ruddock* [1987] 1 WLR 1482, Taylor J's opinion was that 'cogent evidence' was required to justify a plea of national security for the purpose of excluding judicial review. In *R v Home Secretary, ex parte Stitt*, above, Watkins LJ felt that the minister's decision could not be questioned 'once there was bona fide evidence that national security was involved'.

Also, more recently, there have been suggestions that judges should attempt to distinguish between 'high' and 'low level' national security issues and regard only the former as non-justiciable (*Doherty v Ministry of Defence* [1991] NIJB (No. 1) 86).

APPLYING FOR JUDICIAL REVIEW: INTRODUCTION

The process of judicial review is a distinct and discrete public law remedy with its own procedure and related terminology. Words such as 'plaintiff', 'defendant', 'sue' and 'action' are generally appropriate in this context. These are more usually part of the language of 'ordinary' private law proceedings in, for example, contract and tort. Nor, in describing judicial review, is it acceptable to speak of the aggrieved person 'appealing' against the decision in question. An appeal is an entirely different legal process which, as already explained, may be concerned with the merits or factual quality of a decision rather than with its substantive or procedural legality which is the purpose of judicial review.

THE PROCEDURE

Until very recent times this was contained in the Supreme Court Act 1981, s 31 and in RSC Ord 53. In 2000, however, Ord 53 was replaced by Part 54 to the new Civil Procedure Rules made pursuant to the Civil Procedure Act 1997. This followed the recommendations of the Bowman Committee charged by the Lord Chancellor in 1999 with making proposals for modernising and giving greater expedition to the judical review process.

Applying for leave

The applicant begins by applying for 'permission' (previously referred to as 'leave') to apply for judicial review (r 54(1)) to a single High Court judge. Prior to the recent procedural modifications, an application for leave was made *ex parte* (i.e., in the absence of the respondent). According to the new procedure, the decision is taken on the basis of written submissions from both parties. Where permission is refused, the applicant may request that the decision be reconsidered at a later oral hearing of which the respondent should be given notice and opportunity to appear. An application must be made 'promptly' and within three months from the date when the grounds for the application first arose (s 31(7)). The court has a discretion to accept out-of-time applications where there is 'good reason' for doing so (per Lord Goff, *R v Dairy Produce Quotas Tribunal, ex parte Caswell* [1990] 2 AC 738). Applications made within three months but not promptly may also be rejected (*R v Independent Television Commission, ex parte TVNI, The Times*, 30 December 1991). An appeal against a refusal of an application for leave may be made to the Court of Appeal.

Standing or sufficient interest

Leave will not be granted unless the applicant can show that he/she has 'sufficient interest' in the subject matter of the complaint (s 31(3)). The test appears to have two elements.

First the applicant must establish that he/she has an 'arguable case', i.e. that an abuse of power is a 'real as opposed to theoretical possibility' (per Lord Donaldson MR, *R v Home Secretary, ex parte, Swati*, above). This excludes 'obviously hopeless cases' but does not impose a particularly demanding evidential threshold. Thus it is not necessary that a prima facie case of abuse must be established: 'The threshold, if one excludes hopeless cases, is fairly low' (per Nolan J, *R v Inspector of Taxes, ex parte Kissane* [1986] 2 All ER 37).

Second, the applicant must be able to show that he/she has 'standing' or *locus standi* in relation to the alleged abuse of power, i.e. that some right, interest or legitimate expectation deserving of legal protection has been detrimentally affected or that the alleged abuse of power appears to be of such severity or substance that any member of the public or community served by the public body in question is justified in bringing it before the courts.

If leave is granted, the sufficiency of the applicant's interest may be considered again when the full application for judicial review goes for trial. At this stage the proceedings are *inter partes* (literally 'between the parties') with the result that the court is in possession of all the relevant facts and submissions of law. It thus has a fuller and clearer perspective of the nature and extent both of the alleged abuse and the extent of the applicant's interest in it.

> There may be simple cases in which it can be seen at the earliest stage that the person applying for judicial review has no interest at all or no sufficient interest to support the application...But in other cases this will not be so. In these it will be necessary to consider the powers or duties in law of those against whom the relief is asked, the position of the applicants in relation to those powers and duties and to the breach of those said to have been committed. In other words, the question of sufficient interest, in such cases, cannot be considered in the abstract...it must be taken together with the legal and factual context (per Lord Wilberforce, *R v Inland Revenue Commissioners, ex parte National Federation of Self-Employed and Small Businesses Ltd* [1982] AC 617).

Thus an applicant who has been accorded standing at the *ex parte* leave stage may find that recognition withdrawn when the substantive application for review is made.

Clearly, where an application shows that a party's interests have been particularly affected (i.e. more than the interest of others), this will probably be sufficient to satisfy the standing requirement. The test is, however, not so strict. Hence, there are many examples of ratepayers and community charge payers being held to have standing to challenge spending decisions which affected entire communities (*R v Waltham Forest London Borough Council, ex parte Baxter* [1988] QB 419: decision to impose general rate increase; *Prescott v Birmingham Corporation* [1955] Ch 210: decision to grant old-age pension concessionary travel on local public transport).

There are also numerous dicta to the effect that a person no more affected by an abuse than any other member of the general public 'may be allowed to seek judicial review where there is a serious issue of public importance which the court should examine' (Lewis, *Judicial Remedies in Public Law*). Were it not so, then an individual would be unable to challenge an abuse of power with national rather than purely individual or local implications.

> I regard it as a matter of high constitutional principle that if there is good grounds for supposing that a government department or public authority is transgressing the law...in a way which offends or injures thousands of her Majesty's subjects, then any one of those offended or injured can draw to it the attention of the courts of law and seek to have the law enforced (per Lord Denning MR, *R v Greater London Council, ex parte Blackburn* [1976] 1 WLR 550).

Thus, in *R v HM Treasury, ex parte Smedley* [1985] QB 657, a taxpayer had standing to challenge the validity of an Order in Council approving a supplementary budget for the European Community.

In line with this flexible and liberal approach towards standing, it is now clear that interest or cause groups have standing to represent or protect their particular sectional concern. This remains the case notwithstanding that the group is an unincorporated association which cannot sue or be sued in private law as it has no private rights to defend (*R v North West Traffic Commissioners, ex parte Brake*

[1995] NPC 167). Both the Child Poverty Action Group and the National Association of Citizens Advice Bureaux have been held to have standing to challenge social security regulations (R v *Secretary of State for Social Services, ex parte Child Poverty Action Group* [1989] 3 WLR 1116). In another case a public sector union was held to have sufficient interest to challenge a decision of a local authority not to pay those employees who had taken part in a 'day of action' (R v *Liverpool City Corporation, ex parte Ferguson* [1985] IRLR 501).

The approach of the courts appears to be that if a substantial issue of public law is raised by an established, genuine and respected interest group, it should be accorded standing. This was the view expressed in R v *Inspectorate of Pollution, ex parte Greenpeace Ltd (No. 2)* [1994] 4 All ER 329, where Greenpeace was given standing to challenge a decision authorising British Nuclear Fuels to discharge radioactive waste from its plant at Sellafield in order to test its new thermal oxide processing plant (THORP). In recognising the sufficiency of Greenpeace's interest, Otton J said:

> I have not the slightest reservation that Greenpeace is an entirely responsible and respected body with a genuine concern for the environment...It seems to me that if I were to deny standing to Greenpeace, those it represents would not have an effective way to bring issues before the court.

A similar rationale for according standing to an interest group was given by Rose LJ in R v *Foreign Secretary, ex parte World Development Movement Ltd* [1995] 1 All ER 611. The court felt that the applicants were an internationally recognised and widely supported group which for over twenty years had been campaigning 'by democratic means to improve the quantity and quality of British Aid to other countries'. As such they had sufficient interest to seek review of a government decision to fund the Pergau dam project in Malaysia.

> It cannot be said that the applicants are 'busybodies', 'cranks' or 'mischief-makers'. They are a non-partisan pressure group concerned with misuse of aid money. If there is a public law error, it is difficult to see how else it could be challenged and corrected except by such an applicant.

Discovery of documents

An applicant for judicial review may apply for, but has no right to, discovery of documents. Where an application for discovery is made the matter lies within the discretion of the court:

> ...discovery should not be ordered unless and until the court is satisfied that the evidence reveals reasonable grounds for believing that there has been a breach of public duty: and it should be limited to documents strictly relevant to the issue which emerges from the affidavits (per Lord Scarman, the *IRC* case).

Discovery will not be ordered to test the accuracy of an affidavit unless there is evidence before the court to suggest that the affidavit is unreliable or misleading (R v *Secretary of State for the Environment, ex parte Doncaster Borough Council* [1990] COD 441). Nor will it be ordered merely 'in the hope that something might turn up' (*ibid.*).

Cross-examination

Most of the evidence in review proceedings is submitted to the court in the form of affi-davits (sworn written statements) and not through oral testimony. Cross-examination may be permitted, however, for the purpose of clarification or for disposing of factual inconsistencies between the parties. This will be the exception rather than the rule and should only occur 'where the justice of the particular case so requires' (per Lord Diplock, *O'Reilly* v *Mackman* [1983] 2 AC 237).

Changes of terminology

A Practice Direction given by Lord Woolf CJ in July 2000, made pursuant to Part 54 of the new civil procedure rules, effected the following changes to the traditional terminology used in the context of proceedings for judicial review:

(a) that element of the Divisional Court of the High Court dealing with applications for judicial review to be referred to as the Administrative Court;
(b) the orders of *certiorari*, *mandamus* and prohibition hitherto to be known as quashing, mandatory and prohibiting orders respectively;
(c) parties to an application for judicial review henceforth to be cited as:

> The Queen (R), on the application of (name of applicant), versus, the public body against which the proceedings are brought, i.e. *R (Black)* v *Blankshire District Council*.

REMEDIES

Introduction

A successful applicant for judicial review may be awarded any one or a combination of the following remedies: a quashing order (*certiorari*), a mandatory order (*mandamus*) or a prohibiting order (prohibition) (the prerogative orders), or an injunction or dec-laration. An award of damages may be made in conjunction with one of the above in appropriate circumstances (see below). The prerogative orders are entirely public law remedies and may only be awarded through an application for judicial review. Both the injunction and the declaration are, however, also private law remedies and may be awarded in ordinary civil proceedings (i.e. other than applications for judicial review).

In review proceedings the award of a remedy is entirely at the discretion of the court. This means that even though a ground for judicial review may be established, the applicant may still not be awarded a remedy. Thus relief may be refused because of, *inter alia*, the applicant's unmeritorious or unreasonable behaviour (*Cinnamond* v *British Airports Authority*, above), their delay in commencing proceedings (*R* v *Aston University, ex parte Roffey* [1969] 2 QB 538) or because of the damage that might be done to the public interest in administrative efficiency. Hence, in *R* v *Secretary of State for Social Services, ex parte Association of Metropolitan Authorities* [1986] 1 All ER 164, the court refused to quash social security regulations which were proced-urally *ultra vires* due to the minister's failure to consult with certain prescribed organisations (i.e. those representative of local authorities). To have granted relief, it was felt, would have caused serious administrative problems for the majority of authorities which had already implemented the regulations, not least because all applications for benefit decided under them would have had to be reconsidered.

Quashing and prohibiting orders

A quashing order (*certiorari*) quashes a decision which was *ultra vires* the power of the decision-making body or made in breach of the rules of natural justice. A prohibiting order prevents a public body or official from taking any *ultra vires* action or decision.

Although authority exists for the view that both *certiorari* and prohibition were restricted to judicial decisions affecting the 'rights of subjects' (*R v Electricity Commissioners, ex parte London Electricity Joint Committee* [1924] 1 KB 171), it is now generally accepted that the remedies go to both administrative and judicial decisions having detrimental consequences for an individual's rights, interests or legitimate expectations (*R v Hillingdon Borough Council, ex parte Royce Homes* [1974] 1 QB 720).

The remedies will not issue against the Crown specifically but are available against ministers of the Crown. This is not a serious limitation since most statutory powers of government are conferred on secretaries of state rather than on the Crown by name. It was generally believed that *certiorari* did not lie in relation to *ultra vires* subordinate legislation (*R v Hastings Board of Health* (1865) 6 B & S 401). There is, however, some uncertainty on this point as the remedy was used to quash regulations in *R v Secretary of State for Health, ex parte United States Tobacco International Inc* [1992] QB 353.

Mandatory order

A mandatory order (*mandamus*) lies to compel a body to perform or fulfil a public law duty which has been imposed upon it by statute or common law. The remedy will issue where there has been a refusal or unreasonable delay in performing the duty in question (*R v Home Secretary, ex parte Phansopkar* [1976] QB 606). As a general rule the applicant should have requested performance before the order is applied. However, both the request and refusal may be construed from the circumstances.

The duty in question must be reasonably specific. Hence, where the extent and mode of compliance with a duty is a matter of policy and the availability of resources, a mandatory order would appear to be inappropriate. Alleged failures in such cases may be remedied at the political level, e.g. criticism in Parliament and media, etc. Such 'political' duties would include that laid on the Secretary of State for Education by the Education Act 1944, s 1:

> to promote the education of the people of England and Wales and to progressive development of institutions devoted to that purpose and to secure the effective execution by local authorities... of the national policy for providing a varied and comprehensive educational service in each area.

The need for specificity does not mean that the duty must be express. Hence, while the mandatory order does not lie to order the performance of a power, it may issue to require that the discretionary element of a decision-making power be exercised according to law (e.g. on the basis of relevant considerations and for authorised purposes). This may be seen from the facts of *R v Hounslow London Borough*

Council, ex parte Pizzey [1977] 1 WLR 58. The applicant had applied to the Borough Council to have premises registered under the Public Health Act 1936 as a common lodging house. The authority, however, refused to consider her application. *Mandamus* then issued on the basis that it was implicit in the grant of a power to decide that the body would apply its discretion to the facts of each case.

A mandatory order does not lie against the Crown but, as with the other prerogative orders, may be used where the duty is cast upon a named minister or official. In its discretion the court may also refuse the order where the 'authority is doing all that it honestly and honourably can to meet the statutory obligation, and that its failure…arises really out of circumstances over which it has no control' (*R v Bristol Corporation, ex parte Hendry* [1974] 1 WLR 498). Albeit that a breach of duty is established, *mandamus* may also be refused if the court feels that a more appropriate alternative remedy is available – e.g. a default power whereby the enabling statute enables the appropriate minister to give 'such directions as to the exercise…of the duty as appear to him to be expedient' (Education Act 1944, s 68).

Failure to comply with a mandatory order amounts to a contempt of court for which the offending body, e.g. local authority, may be fined (*Re Cook's Application* (1986) 2 NIJB 64) or its members imprisoned (*R v Poplar Borough Council (No. 2)* [1922] 1 KB 95).

Injunction

Injunctions may be mandatory or prohibitory. A mandatory injunction requires the party to whom it is addressed to take some action to redress an unlawful act. In *Attorney-General v Bastow* [1957] 1 QB 514, a mandatory injunction issued to remove caravans from land which had been put there without planning permission. A prohibitory injunction may issue to:

*   restrain *ultra vires* actions;
*   restrain breaches of statutory duties;
*   restrain repeated breaches of the criminal law (*Attorney-General v Sharpe*, see below);
*   restrain a public nuisance, e.g. repeated obstruction of the highway.

Where a party seeks an injunction against a public body other than in an application for judicial review, it must be shown that there has been interference with a public right 'such that some private right of his is at the same time interfered with' or 'where no private right is interfered with…the plaintiff, in respect of his public right, suffers special damage peculiar to himself from the interference with the public right' (per Buckley J, *Boyce v Paddington Borough Council* [1903] 1 Ch 109). A party seeking an injunction in an application for judicial review must satisfy the test of sufficient interest.

An injunction may not issue against the Crown in civil proceedings or against an officer of the Crown 'if the effect…would be to give any relief against the Crown which could not have been obtained in proceedings against the Crown' (Crown Proceedings Act 1947, s 21(2)). This does not impose any barrier to the use of injunctions against a minister where the power, usually in statutory form, is conferred on them by name (*M v Home Office* [1993] 3 WLR 433).

Declaration

In its present form the declaration is a statutory remedy introduced by the Rules of Court of 1883 made under the Judicature Acts 1873–5. Like the injunction, it is not a purely public law remedy and is used extensively in some areas of private law.

The perhaps peculiar feature of the declaration is that it has no coercive force but simply defines and states the legal rights and obligations of the parties to the proceedings. This, however, has proved to be a great advantage as it means that the remedy is available not just against ministers named in empowering statutes but against the Crown itself. As a result of the Crown's traditional legal immunity, the coercive remedies already mentioned do not issue. Hence, in review proceedings against the Crown, the declaration is the appropriate remedy.

The declaration's lack of coercive force has not had detrimental consequences for its effectiveness. If an action or decision of a public body is declared to be unlawful this is normally sufficient to ensure that the offending act is rectified. There is only one modern example of a public body refusing to comply with terms of a declaratory judgment (*Webster* v *Southwark Borough Council* [1983] QB 698).

The declaration is available for review of all types of decision and action, whether taken in the exercise of administrative, judicial or legislative powers.

As a general rule, a court (in its discretion) will refuse to make a declaration where the complaint raises a purely hypothetical issue. Hence, it was refused in *Blackburn* v *Attorney-General* [1971] 1 WLR 1037, where it was alleged that it would be unlawful for the government to sign the Treaty of Rome as this would involve an irreversible surrender of the sovereignty of the Westminster Parliament.

Damages

An award of damages may be made to an applicant for judicial review but only in conjunction with one of the other remedies. Also, the applicant must be able to show that 'such damages could have been awarded to him in an action begun by him by writ at the time of the making of the application' (Supreme Court Act 1981, s 4) – i.e. where the abuse of power by the authority interfered with a private or actionable public law right of the applicant.

Also, where an application for judicial review is misconceived because it is concerned with the enforcement of private rather than public law rights, the court has a discretion to allow the proceedings to continue as if they had been begun by writ. For the applicant, who then becomes the plaintiff, this avoids the expense and delay which would be occasioned if the review proceedings were struck out and had to be recommenced by ordinary private law procedure.

Habeas corpus

The prerogative writ of habeas corpus issues to secure the release of a person who has been detained unlawfully. The writ was not affected by the procedural reforms of 1978. It has its own special procedure and is not sought, therefore, through an application for judicial review.

An application for the writ may be made by the detainee or, if this is not possible, by some other person on his/her behalf. The application is made to the Divisional Court *ex parte* (i.e. without notice to the other side) supported by the grounds in the form of an affidavit. If a prima facie case is shown notice will be served on the 'gaoler' (in modern times usually the Home Secretary or a prison governor) specifying the date and place where the merits of the case will be heard. It is for the gaoler to prove the lawfulness of the detention. If this is not done the writ issues *ex debito justiciae*, i.e. as of right and not as a matter of judicial discretion.

Habeas corpus will issue for jurisdictional errors only – in particular:

- simple *ultra vires* (see *ex parte Hopkins* (1891) 61 LJ QB 640);
- non-existence of a jurisdictional fact or preconditional circumstances (see *R v Home Secretary, ex parte Khawaja*, above);
- no evidence;
- error of law.

It will not issue, therefore, for alleged procedural unfairness, abuse of discretion (e.g. irrelevancy) or unreasonableness. The sole concern of the court is the existence of a power to detain.

It follows from this that habeas corpus may not be used to question the validity of a decision which preceded the exercise of the power to detain. Hence, if a prospective immigrant is refused leave to enter the United Kingdom and is then detained pending deportation, the validity of the refusal of leave may be tested in an application for judicial review but not by way of habeas corpus (*R v Home Secretary, ex parte Muboyayi* [1991] 3 WLR 442).

In relatively modern times the writ has been used to determine the validity of detention:

- pending extradition (*Oskar* v *Government of Australia* [1988] AC 366);
- pending the removal of illegal immigrants (*Azam* v *Home Secretary* [1974] AC 18);
- pending deportation (*R v Governor of Brixton Prison, ex parte Soblen* [1963] 2 QB 243);
- pending the return of fugitive offenders (*R v Governor of Pentonville Prison, ex parte Osman* [1990] 1 WLR 277);
- on remand in custody (*R v Governor of Armly Prison, ex parte Ward, The Times*, 23 November 1990);
- by the police for questioning (*R v Holmes, ex parte Sherman* [1981] 2 All ER 612);
- under the mental health legislation (*R v Board of Control, ex parte Rutty* [1956] 2 QB 109).

RELATOR PROCEEDINGS

The Attorney-General has the prerogative power to commence private or public law proceedings against any person or body whose unlawful activities would appear to be injurious to the public interest. Since the Crown is responsible for ensuring that the law is obeyed and that power is not abused the question of standing does not arise. The Attorney always has standing to litigate for the general public benefit.

An example of the Attorney-General enforcing the public interest occurred in *Attorney-General* v *Sharpe* [1931] 1 Ch 121. The defendant had been prosecuted 48 times for operating bus services without a licence. The business was so profitable he had carried on regardless in flagrant breach of the relevant regulations which sought to impose certain minimum standards for the protection of the public. Eventually proceedings for an injunction were brought by the Attorney-General to enforce compliance with the law on pain of imprisonment for contempt of court.

The Attorney-General may also give leave for his name to be joined in proceedings instigated by an individual. This will tend to occur where the individual's personal standing may be insufficient to bring the alleged abuse before the court. In theory the proceedings are then brought by the Attorney-General 'at the relation' or request of the individual. The Attorney has a discretion whether to give such leave. There is authority for the view that his decisions in this context are non-justiciable (*Gouriet* v *Union of Post Office Workers* [1978] AC 435). The use of the Attorney's name avoids all problems of standing albeit that for all practical purposes 'the actual conduct of proceedings is entirely in the hands of the relator who is responsible for the costs of the action' (per Lord Denning MR, *Attorney-General, ex relator McWhirter* v *IBA* [1973] QB 629).

The remedies sought in a relator action will be the injunction or the declaration. Where such proceedings are brought to enforce a public right or duty, it remains to be decided whether the rule in *O'Reilly* v *Mackman* applies (see Chapter 17). According to Lewis in *Judicial Remedies in Public Law*, it 'is likely that the courts will allow the Attorney-General to proceed by ordinary action'.

Although the facility to commence relator actions remains, it may be that the current willingness of the courts to grant standing both to individuals and interest groups where the public rather than an individual interest may be at stake will reduce the need for the Attorney-General's involvement.

Reference

Lewis (1993) *Judicial Remedies in Public Law*, London: Sweet & Maxwell.

Further reading

Bailey, Jones and Mowbray (1997) *Cases and Materials on Administrative Law* (3rd edn), London: Sweet & Maxwell, Ch 15.

Jones and Thompson (eds) (1996) *Garner's Administrative Law* (8th edn), London: Butterworths, Ch 9.

Supperstone and Goudie (1992) *Judicial Review*, London: Butterworths, Ch 16.

Wade and Forsyth (1994) *Administrative Law* (7th edn), Oxford: Clarendon Press, Chs 18 and 19.

Chapter 17

EXCLUSIVITY

BACKGROUND

In 1978 a new procedure for challenging the actions and decisions of government bodies was introduced. This was effected by amending Ord 53 of the Rules of the Supreme Court. To settle any uncertainty concerning the extent to which procedural rules could affect substantive legal rules – e.g. those relating to standing – the main elements of the Order were given statutory force by the Supreme Court Act 1981, s 31.

The effect of the new procedure was that persons seeking relief by way of *certiorari*, prohibition or *mandamus* were required to make an application for judicial review to the Divisional Court. These remedies were not to be available by any other procedure. Relief by way of declaration and injunction could also be sought through an application for review, but these essentially private law remedies could still be granted independently of the Ord 53 procedure. Neither Ord 53 nor s 31 made it absolutely clear whether a person with a grievance of a public law nature and seeking relief by declaration or injunction, perhaps with damages, had a free choice either to apply for judicial review in the Divisional Court or simply to pursue relief by ordinary procedure in any other court of competent jurisdiction.

In the immediate aftermath of these reforms there was some judicial reluctance to regard the new procedure as the sole method for challenging alleged abuses of public law. Initially choice of procedure was apparently permissible; so, in *De Falco v Crawley Borough Council* [1980] QB 460, the court permitted a challenge to a local authority's interpretation of its obligations under the Housing (Homeless Persons) Act 1977 by writ rather than by judicial review.

Gradually, however, the mosaic of judicial opinion began to form a pattern showing general preference for confining public law disputes to the Ord 53 procedure. In *Uppal v Home Office* (1978) *Times*, 11 November, the Court of Appeal said that application for judicial review was the appropriate method for challenging the *vires* of a deportation order rather than action by writ for a declaratory judgment in the Chancery Division. Similarly, in *Heywood v Hull Prison Board of Visitors* [1980] 3 All ER 394, action by ordinary procedure for a declaration that the Board had conducted disciplinary proceedings in breach of the rules of natural justice was held to be an abuse of process.

THE RULE IN *O'REILLY* v *MACKMAN*

This trend of authority was finally confirmed by the House of Lords in *O'Reilly* v *Mackman* [1983] AC 237. The case concerned an attempt by a group of prisoners to use ordinary procedure (by writ and, in one case, originating summons) to challenge decisions of a prison board of visitors some six years after the event. This was held to be a blatant abuse of process. Naturally, the prisoners had sought to avoid proceedings by way of judicial review as, according to RSC Ord 53, r 4, such applications should be commenced within three months of the alleged abuse. Lord Diplock – in what has subsequently become known as the rule in *O'Reilly* v *Mackman* – explained that henceforth, and as a general rule, it would be 'contrary to public policy, and as such an abuse of the court, to permit a person seeking to establish that a decision of a public authority infringed rights to which he was entitled to protection under public law to proceed by ordinary action'. He added that exceptions to this rule might be permitted where a question of *vires* arose only as a collateral or ancillary issue in the enforcement of a private right (see *Davy* v *Spelthorne BC* [1948] AC 262, below) or 'where none of the parties objects to the procedure by writ or originating summons'. Other exceptions, he said, could be developed on a case-to-case basis.

The public policy justification for regarding the application for judicial review as the exclusive procedure for dealing with alleged abuse of public law powers was closely related to the requirement that such applications should be made within three months of the alleged abuse. This was inserted to prevent the progress of good government being imperilled by legal uncertainty. Efficient public administration and the sedate pace of ordinary civil procedure are often incompatible. Access to review was restricted, therefore, to avoid governmental actions and decisions being found to be legally invalid years after these had been implemented.

Delay can also amount to an abuse of process under the civil procedure rules introduced under the Civil Procedure Act 1997. This being the case, it may not be so important in the future to insist that proceedings affecting the public interest be brought by way of judicial review only where the three-month rule provided the crucial safeguard (*Clarke* v *University of Lincolnshire and Humberside* [2000] 3 All ER 752).

In its own time, the decision in *O'Reilly* v *Mackman* precipitated a proliferation of litigation in which courts attempted to draw distinctions between matters of private and public law and thus to determine which types of disputes should be dealt with by way of judicial review and which should remain within the domain of private law and its related procedures, e.g. action by writ or originating summons. Although this area of law is still uncertain, the case law suggests the existence of a number of general principles.

ABUSE OF POWER AS A COLLATERAL ISSUE

It is not uncommon for both public and private law questions to be raised in the same case. Where this occurs it presents an obvious problem in terms of the procedure through which the dispute should be resolved.

The general rule applicable in these circumstances would now appear to be that contained in *Roy v Kensington, Chelsea and Westminster Family Practitioner Committee* [1992] 2 WLR 239. On this occasion the House of Lords took the view that the questioning of a public law decision in private law proceedings does not amount to an abuse of process where the primary purpose of the proceedings is to establish and enforce a private law right. Lord Lowry expressed a preference for a 'broad approach' to the meaning of *O'Reilly v Mackman* according to which the aggrieved person should be required to 'proceed by judicial review only when private law rights were not at stake'. From this it follows that the *vires* of a public law decision may be questioned in proceedings other than judicial review where this is merely 'collateral' or incidental to the pursuit of a private law right.

> But where a litigant asserts his entitlement to a subsisting right in private law...the circumstance that the existence and extent of the private law right asserted may incidentally involve the examination of a public law issue cannot prevent the litigant from seeking to establish his right by action commenced by writ or originating summons (per Lord Bridge).

Hence it was held that Roy, a doctor, could sue a Family Practitioner Committee in respect of payment withheld from him pursuant to a decision by the Committee that he had devoted insufficient time to general practice. This remained the case notwithstanding that the Committee had exercised a discretionary power derived from statutory rules made for the effective provision of a public service.

A similar approach was adopted in *British Steel plc v Customs and Excise Commissioners* [1997] 2 All ER 266. Here the Court of Appeal found that no abuse of process was committed by seeking repayment of taxes through a common law action for restitution notwithstanding that the success of the proceedings depended on a finding that the original tax demand had been *ultra vires* and unlawful. Also see *Mercury Communications v Director-General of Telecommunications* [1996] 1 WLR 48, where the House of Lords permitted a private law action for a declaration that the Director-General, in resolving a dispute arising from an agreement between two licensed operators (Mercury and British Telecom) as to the amount to be charged for the connection and conveyance of telephone calls, had misconstrued the provisions of a licence granted to British Telecom under the Telecommunications Act 1984.

ABUSE OF POWER AS A DEFENCE

It has been accepted that the alleged invalidity of official action may be used as a defence in ordinary criminal and civil proceedings to protect pre-existing rights. Hence, in *R v Jenner* [1983] 1 WLR 873, the Court of Appeal (Criminal Division) quashed J's conviction for contravention of a stop notice (served in respect of a breach of planning laws) on the ground that he had not been allowed to raise issues relating to the *vires* of the stop notice in his defence. The court did not accept the view that the only way to challenge the validity of the notice was by judicial review.

Abuse of public law power was also relied on as a defence in *Wandsworth London Borough Council v Winder* [1985] AC 461. A council tenant, when sued for arrears of rent, was allowed to plead that the rent charged by the authority amounted to an unreasonable and *ultra vires* use of its powers. Lord Fraser said that despite the inconvenience which might be caused to public authorities by the avoidance of the rules relating to applications for judicial review – particularly that applications should be made promptly – the substantive right of every individual to raise public or private law principles in their defence could not be relegated by an essentially procedural rule to a matter of judicial discretion (i.e. confined to review procedure which commences not as of right by a judicial leave). Only clear words in an Act of Parliament could so proscribe this right. Note, however, *Avon County Council* v *Buscott* [1988] QB 656, where it was held that trespassers could not plead the invalidity of an eviction decision in subsequent eviction proceedings. They did not have any existing or pre-existing legal rights to protect.

The validity of by-laws may also be questioned in prosecutions for alleged contravention of the same (see *R* v *Reading Crown Court, ex parte Hutchinson* [1988] QB 384; *Boddington* v *British Transport Police, The Times*, 3 April 1998).

ABUSE OF POWER WHERE STATUTORY REMEDY PROVIDED

Public law issues may also be argued outwith review proceedings where a statute provides its own alternative remedy for dealing with abuses of the powers contained therein. Thus, in *Buckley* v *The Law Society* [1983] 2 All ER 1039, the defendants, acting under the Solicitors Act 1957, took control of the plaintiff's business finance pending inquiry into allegations of dishonesty. According to the same Act, solicitors so affected could contest the Law Society's decisions in the Chancery Division, proceeding by way of originating summons. The plaintiff solicitor abided by these procedural dictates. The Law Society, however – apparently in an attempt to avoid his subsequent requests for discovery – argued that, since their disciplinary and supervisory powers over the legal profession emanated from statute, they were in nature and origin manifestly public law powers so that the plaintiff should have proceeded by way of judicial review. According to this procedure, it was argued, he would have been unlikely to secure discovery since this is seldom awarded against bodies exercising judicial or disciplinary functions. Sir Robert McGarry VC, in the Chancery Division, said it would be 'remarkable indeed' if the Law Society could resort to a specific statutory power to discipline a solicitor but the solicitor could not rely on the remedies in that same statute to seek redress. Hence, although the power used by the Law Society was of a public nature, the complainant was not disqualified from using the statutory remedy. Discovery was ordered against the Law Society to establish whether or not they had adequate information in their possession on which to base a finding of dishonesty against the plaintiff.

JUDICIAL REVIEW AND CONTRACTUAL POWERS

Public law procedure is not the appropriate method for challenging the decisions of government agencies when exercising contractual powers. In *R* v *British Broadcasting Corporation, ex parte Lavelle* [1983] 1 WLR 23, the applicant was suspected of theft from her employers. She was given only one hour's notice of the disciplinary hearing to which she was entitled according to the BBC's disciplinary code, after which she was dismissed from their employ. She applied for judicial review on the ground that she had not been given a fair hearing. Woolf J in the High Court said that Ord 53 made it clear that applications for judicial review should be confined 'to reviewing activities of a public nature as opposed to those of purely private or domestic character'. Since the BBC's disciplinary appeals procedure derived its authority from the contract of employment, and was not underpinned or regulated by statute in any way, it should be classified as essentially domestic. *A fortiori*, the correct procedure was by writ and not by application for review.

In *McClaren* v *Home Office* [1990] ICR 824, Lord Woolf explained:

> an employee of a public body is normally in exactly the same situation as other employees. If he has a cause of action and he wishes to assert or establish his rights in relation to his employment he can bring proceedings for damages, a declaration or an injunction...in the High Court or County Court in the ordinary way. The fact that a person is employed by the Crown may limit his rights against the Crown but otherwise his position is very much the same as any other employee. However, he may, instead of having an ordinary master and servant relationship with the Crown, hold office under the Crown and may have been appointed to that office as a result of the Crown exercising a prerogative or...a statutory power. If he holds such an appointment then it will almost invariably be terminable at will...but whatever rights the employee has will be enforceable normally by an ordinary action.

Disputes between a public sector employer and an employee may, however, be susceptible to judicial review where:

(a) the decision in question (i.e. to dismiss or otherwise), was made for reasons of public policy – e.g. 'the public interest that the civil service should be administered in a way which is free from political bias and other improper motive' (per Roche J, *R* v *Civil Service Appeal Board, ex parte Bruce* [1988] 3 All ER 686);

(b) the power to dismiss or otherwise is regulated by statute (*McClaren* v *Home Office*, above);

(c) the power to dismiss or otherwise is subject to a right of appeal to a body created under statute or the prerogative (*ex parte Bruce*, above).

JUDICIAL REVIEW BEYOND STATUTORY OR PREROGATIVE POWERS

Although judicial review is normally concerned with the abuse of power by bodies established by, and deriving their authority from, statute or the prerogative, it is now firmly established that it is also the appropriate remedy for the abuse of power by bodies having no such origins but which perform monopolistic regulatory functions which would otherwise – for the better protection of the public interest – have to be exercised by a government agency. This was decided by the Court of Appeal in *R* v *Panel on Takeovers and Mergers, ex parte Datafin plc* [1987] QB 815. Neither the facts of the case nor the eventual decision that no abuse of power had been committed by the Panel are of any great significance. Of crucial importance, however, was the Court of Appeal's view that the Panel fell within the scope of judicial review notwithstanding that it possessed no formal legal foundations or powers, whether from statute, the prerogative or otherwise. The reasons given for this finding were as follows.

(a) There is no absolute rule restricting judicial review to powers emanating from statute or the prerogative only (see R v *Criminal Injuries Compensation Board, ex parte Lain* [1967] 2 QB 864).

(b) The Panel performed functions of national importance as the body through which self-regulation of the City was effected.

(c) Although possessing no legal power *de jure*, it exercised 'immense power' *de facto* by:

- 'devising, promulgating, amending and interpreting the City Code on Take-overs and Mergers';
- investigating and determining through quasi-judicial procedures whether breaches of the Code had been committed;
- the imposition or threat of sanctions relating thereto.

(d) The government had accepted that the City should be subject to effective regulation and control. As a matter of policy, however, it had been decided that this regulatory function should not, at least for the time being, be undertaken by a government agency armed with legislative powers. The favoured approach was for self-regulation through application by the Panel of the aforementioned Code. Therefore, although not backed by legislation, the Panel could be said to be fulfilling government policy in this context. Were these functions not performed by the Panel, it was highly likely that an alternative body would have to be created either by statute or under the royal prerogative.

> The picture which emerges is clear. As an act of government it was decided that, in relation to take-overs, there would be a central self-regulatory body...No one could have been in the least surprised if the panel had been instituted and operated under the direct authority of statute law, since it operates wholly in the public domain. Its jurisdiction extends throughout the United Kingdom. Its code and rulings apply equally to all who wish to make take-over bids or promote mergers...Its lack of a direct statutory base is a complete anomaly, judged by the experience of other comparable markets world-wide (Sir John Donaldson MR).

Subsequently, in R v *Insurance Ombudsman, ex parte Aegeon Life Assurance Ltd* [1994] COD 426, the principle established by the Datafin decision was summarised as follows:

> ...a body whose birth and constitution owed nothing to any exercise of governmental power may be subject to judicial review if it had been woven into a system of governmental control or was integrated into a system of statutory regulation or was a surrogate organ of government or, but for its existence, a government body would assume control.

To date there would appear to be a judicial preference for confining the legal supervision of other such regulatory bodies – i.e. those without *de jure* legal powers or origins – to those concerned with the maintenance of ethical standards in the commercial and professional spheres. Hence the following have been held to fall within the scope of judicial review:

- the Advertising Standards Authority Ltd (*R* v *Advertising Standards Authority, ex parte Insurance Service plc* (1990) 2 Admin LR 77): 'a body clearly exercising a public function which, if the Authority did not exist, would no doubt be exercised by the Director-General of Fair Trading';
- the Code of Practice Committee of the British Pharmaceutical Industry (*R* v *Code of Practice Committee of the British Pharmaceutical Industry, ex parte Professional Counselling Aids Committee* (1991) 3 Admin LR 697);
- LAUTRO (*R* v *Life Assurance and Unit Trusts Regulatory Organisation, ex parte Ross* [1993] QB 17);
- FIMBRA (*R* v *Financial Intermediaries Managers and Brokers Regulatory Organisation, ex parte Cochrane* [1990] COD 33);
- hospital ethics committee (*R* v *Ethical Committee of St Mary's Hospital* [1988] 1 FLR 512);
- the professional conduct committee for barristers (*R* v *General Council of the Bar, ex parte Percival* [1991] 1 QB 212);
- the disciplinary process of the London Metal Exchange (*R* v *London Metal Exchange Ltd, ex parte Albatros Warehousing BV* (unreported, 30 March 2000).

For the present, however, this is as far as the courts have been prepared to go in the development of this new dimension of judicial review. Thus there have been repeated refusals to extend judicial review to bodies responsible for the administration and conduct of various sporting activities (see *R* v *Jockey Club, ex parte Ram Racecourses Ltd* [1993] 2 All ER 225; *R* v *Jockey Club, ex parte Massingberd-Mundy* [1993] 2 All ER 207; *R* v *Football Association of Wales, ex parte Flint Town United Football Club* [1991] COD 44). Attempts to seek judicial review of the decisions of those responsible for the 'government' of religious communities have also been held to be an abuse of process (see *R* v *Chief Rabbi, ex parte Wachmann* [1991] COD 309; *R* v *Imam of Bury Park Mosque, Luton, ex parte Sulaiman Ali, The Independent*, 13 September 1991).

Further reading

Craig (1994) *Administrative Law* (3rd edn), London: Sweet & Maxwell, Ch 15.

Fordham (1994) *Judicial Review Handbook*, London: Wiley/Chancery Lane Publishing, Ch 4, pp. 216–26.

Lewis (1993) *Judicial Remedies in Public Law*, London: Sweet & Maxwell, Ch 3.

Part 6

HUMAN RIGHTS

Chapter 18

THE EUROPEAN CONVENTION ON HUMAN RIGHTS

INTRODUCTION

By virtue of the Human Rights Act 1998, the principal provisions of the Convention are now enforceable directly in the English legal system to the extent that these are compatible with the unambiguous requirements of domestic legislation. The Convention and its jurisprudence has thus become the basis of any detailed analysis of the source and extent of civil and human rights within the United Kingdom and of the reciprocal duties of the state in ensuring the necessary conditions in which such rights may be enjoyed. This is widely regarded as the most significant development in English law since the passing of the European Economic Communities Act in 1972 and gives citizens of the United Kingdom the direct protection of a range of rights hitherto either not recognised by, or developed fully within, the English common law.

The European Convention on Human Rights has now been given in effect in the domestic systems of nearly all of its contracting members thus providing a common basis to the human rights law of over forty European states.

FORMULATION

The Convention was formulated in 1949 by the Council of Europe. It was signed in Rome by the Council's original members in November 1950 and took effect in September 1953. Its objective was to avoid the sort of atrocities and abuses of human rights witnessed in Europe in World War II.

The Council of Europe pre-dates the European Community and is a separate organisation. It was established to secure greater understanding and cooperation between European states and, in particular, to promote the ideals of parliamentary government, social and economic development, and to advance the cause and protection of human rights. The Council is the widest association of European states. It acts through a Committee of Ministers (usually foreign secretaries) advised by a Parliamentary Assembly consisting of members from national legislatures.

At its inception the Council consisted of representatives from the United Kingdom, the Republic of Ireland, France, Italy, Holland, Belgium, Sweden, Denmark, Luxembourg, Greece and Turkey. Most other European states have since become members including some from the former 'communist bloc'.

The European Convention on Human Rights is not part of the law of the European Community. As indicated above, it was instituted and developed as a separate system of jurisprudence with its own institutions and procedures. However, as European Community law begins to develop its own conception of human rights, it is increasingly apparent that this will be influenced by the standards and ideals to which the Convention is directed. Thus, in a number of cases in which the interpretation and application of Community law has touched on issues of human rights, the Court of Justice has indicated its willingness to be guided by the jurisprudence of the Convention and to give recognition to the rights protected thereby: 'international treaties for the protection of human rights on which the member states have collaborated or of which they are signatories, can supply guidelines which should be followed within the framework of community law' (*Nold* v *Commission* [1974] ECR 491). In addition the EC Treaty does provide a degree of protection to those aspects of human rights related to its central economic and social objectives including equal treatment of women and freedom from discrimination generally in the workplace and the freedoms attaching to EU citizenship, particularly the freedoms of movement and labour between member states.

As a result, although the Convention did not have direct legal force in the United Kingdom, elements of its jurisprudence had already begun to be assimilated into the domestic legal system to the extent that these have influenced the law of the European Community: 'Through the jurisprudence of the Court of Justice the principles, though not the text, of the Convention now inform the law of the European Union' (per Sedley J, *R* v *Home Secretary, ex parte McQuillan* [1995] 4 All ER 400).

The close relationship between Community law and the Convention on Human Rights was given formal recognition in the Treaty of European Union 1992 which provided that the Union 'shall respect fundamental rights as guaranteed by the European Convention' (EC Art 6). This did not amount, however, to a formal incorporation of the Convention into European Community law. The Community's commitment to human rights was, however, taken a step futher by the Treaty of Amsterdam 1997 which conferred powers on the Council of Ministers, acting with the consent of the European Parliament, to suspend the voting and other rights of member states found to be guilty of 'serious and persistent breaches' of Convention rights.

The European Court of Justice has emphasised that its jurisdiction in matters of human rights, and its competence to be guided by the jurisprudence of the European Convention on Human Rights, applies only where it is seized of a question relating to the meaning of Community law. It is not the appropriate forum, therefore, for raising issues of compatibility between the Convention on Human Rights and national law if no question of Community law is directly involved (*Kremzow* v *Austria* [1997] ECR I-2629).

The competence of the European Community to ratify the Convention was given detailed consideration by the European Court of Justice in *Opinion 2/94, The Times*, 16 April 1996. It was felt that such a radical extension of the scope and content of Community law could not be effected without substantial amendment of the EC Treaty itself. No provision could be found in the existing Treaty which conferred on Community institutions any general power to enact rules on human rights or to conclude international conventions in that context.

The formulation of a charter of basic human rights, if only of the status of a political declaration, was one of the major priorities of the German presidency of 1999 and led to the commissioning of a Draft Charter of Fundamental Human Rights of the European Union by the Cologne European Council in June of that year. The Charter was formulated by a specially appointed convention consisting of the European Commission, representatives of the fifteen national governments, 30 representatives from national legislatures, and sixteen MEPs. It was completed in October 2000 and 'welcomed' by the Nice European Council in the following December. Implementation of the Charter, i.e. its transformation into Community law, will depend on a political decision to this effect followed by its incorporation into a future treaty and approval by all member states. No such agreement or timetable for implementation of same exists at present.

The Charter represents a more ambitious and wide-ranging statement of human rights than that currently provided by the 1953 Convention. In the event of implementation and in an attempt to avoid incompatibility between the two, Art 52(3) of the Charter states that to the extent that it 'contains rights which correspond to rights guaranteed by the Convention for the Protection of Human Rights and Fundamental Freedoms, the meaning and scope of those rights shall be the same as those laid down by the said Convention...'. The Charter is intended, therefore, to complement rather than to compete with Europe's existing human rights legal system.

THE CONVENTION IN ENGLISH LAW PRIOR TO THE HUMAN RIGHTS ACT

Prior to 2 October 2000, the status of the European Convention in the domestic legal system was that of an international treaty to which the UK was a contracting party. As with other such treaties, signed by the UK but not ratified by Act of Parliament, the Convention imposed obligations binding in international law on the UK government but did not confer rights directly enforceable by individuals. Hence, where an individual asserted a 'right' guaranteed by the Convention, but not hitherto recognised by statute or common law, English courts tended to decline any authority to enforce the right in question and merely repeated the rule that international treaties are not part of the law of England: 'I would dispute altogether that the Convention is part of our law. Treaties and declarations do not become part of our law until they are made by Parliament' (per Lord Ackner, *R v Home Secretary, ex parte Brind* [1991] AC 696).

In *Malone v Metropolitan Police Commissioner* [1979] Ch 344, the plaintiff sued for trespass in respect of an interference with his alleged right to privacy caused by the police 'bugging' his telephone. It was held that no right to privacy was recognised by English law and none could be imported by way of reference to Art 8 of the Convention. McGarry VC's view was that English courts should not be deterred from developing a new right where this was possible from 'analogies with the existing rules, together with the requirements of justice and common sense'. It was not the function of the courts, however, to 'legislate in a new field'. Judicial law-making, he felt, should be done 'interstitially' and should be concerned with 'molecular rather than molar motions'.

On the other hand, there had long been a clear expectation that Parliament should try to avoid legislating contrary to the Convention's requirements and that the Convention should be used by the courts as a primary aid to the construction of domestic statutes where these may be unclear or ambiguous:

> The position as I understand it is that if there is any ambiguity in our statutes, or uncertainty in our law, then these courts can look to the convention as an aid to clear up any ambiguity or uncertainty, seeking always to bring them into harmony with it (per Lord Denning, *R v Chief Immigration Officer, Heathrow Airport, ex parte Salamat Bibi* [1976] 3 All ER 843).

By definition therefore, where a statutory provision was found to be in conflict with the Convention, and no such ambiguity or uncertainty was present, the courts generally felt obliged to give effect to the statute.

> While English courts may strive where they can to interpret statutes as conforming with the obligations of the UK under the Convention, they are nevertheless bound to give effect to statutes which are free from ambiguity even if those statutes may be in conflict with the Convention (per Lord Brandon, *Re M and H (Minors)* [1988] 3 WLR 485).

There were also judicial dicta supportive of the view that the Convention should be taken into account in resolving uncertainties in the common law. It was not clear, however, whether this was merely a matter of judicial discretion or one of obligation.

THE EUROPEAN COURT OF HUMAN RIGHTS

Restructuring and reform

The current provisions relating to the composition and workings of the Court are contained in Arts 19–51 of the Convention. These are amendments to the original text and came into effect on 1 November 1998. They were instituted by Protocol 11 as part of the general process of improving the Convention's decision-making processes, particularly in terms of the time taken to dispose of applications and the resulting costs to litigants (by the mid-1990s estimated, on average, to be five years and £30,000 respectively).

The principal changes made by Protocol 11 were the creation of a restructured Court, as described below, capable of dealing more expeditiously with all issues relating to the admissibility and merits of particular applications. The European Commission on Human Rights, consisting of one member from each contracting state and which had previously been responsible for questions of admissibility, was, therefore, abolished and ceased to operate on 20 October 1999, after disposing of its remaining caseload. Protocol 11 also removed the jurisdiction of the Committee of Ministers (also one member from each contracting state) to decide the merits of applications not referred to the Court within three months of being found admissible and the submission of recommendations by the Commission. The Committee remains responsible for the supervision and execution of the Court's judgments (Art 54).

Composition

Judges of the Court are elected by the Parliamentary Assembly from lists of three nominees proposed by each member state (Art 22). The number of judges elected is equivalent to the number of contracting states at any one time (Art 20). They are appointed for six years but may be re-elected (Art 23). The age of retirement is 70 (*ibid.*). Those appointed are required to be persons of high moral character and of recognised juristic competence (Art 21). Judges sit in their individual capacity. They do not represent any state and must not engage in any activity which is incompatible with their independence or with the demands of full-time office (Art 23). A judge may not be removed from office unless the other judges decide by a two-thirds majority that he/she has ceased to fulfil the required obligations (Art 24).

Organisation and operation

The Court functions through Committees, Chambers and a Grand Chamber (Art 27). Committees consist of three judges and deal primarily with questions of admissibility relating to individual applications under Art 34. The principal grounds for admission are that:

(a)   all domestic remedies whether judicial or administrative have been exhausted;
(b)   the complaint was made within six months of such exhaustion;
(c)   the complaint does not amount to an abuse of the right to complain, i.e. it raises a genuine rather than frivolous or vexatious grievance and is not made for any improper purpose, e.g. political propaganda;
(d)   it relates to a right protected by the Convention;
(e)   it does not attempt to assert a right in a way which extinguishes another, e.g. by assertion of the right of assembly to an extent incompatible with the freedom of expression;
(f)   it is substantially the same as a matter already examined by the Court or by another procedure of international investigation.

Where a Committee concludes that an application 'is not considered inadmissible', the application will be transferred to a Chamber (Art 29). Chambers consist of seven judges and are empowered to decide on both the admissibility and merits of individual and inter-state applications (*ibid.*). Chamber decisions will normally be final save for any case which raises 'a serious question affecting the interpretation of the Convention in or where the resolution of the questions...might have a result inconsistent with a judgment previously delivered by the Court' (Art 30). In these circumstances a Chamber may 'relinquish jurisdiction in favour of the Grand Chamber unless one of the parties objects' (*ibid.*). The Grand Chamber consists of seventeen judges. In addition to that just described, its jurisdiction extends at the request of one of the parties and 'in exceptional circumstances' to the re-examination of a Chamber decision where this 'raises a serious question affecting the interpretation or application of the Convention...on a serious issue of general importance' (Art 43). Such application for re-examination should be made within three months of the

Chamber decision complained of (Art 44). Except in these circumstances, i.e. those provided for in Art 30 and 43, Chamber decisions are to be regarded as final.

Procedure

Applications may be made by one contracting state against another (state application, Art 33) or by an individual against any such state (individual application, Art 34). The procedure before the Court is adversarial and in public unless, 'in exceptional circumstances' it decides otherwise (Art 40). Much of the Court's work, however, is based on consideration of written submissions which are also accessible to the public (*ibid.*). Oral proceedings are conducted through legal representation for which legal aid is available.

Once a case has been admitted and before proceeding to a decision on the merits, the Court will attempt to achieve a 'friendly settlement' between the parties (Art 38). Negotiations to this end are confidential and may result, for example, in the payment of compensation, the changing of an offending government decision or a commitment to a change of law or administrative practice. In *Faulkner v United Kingdom*, 11 January 2000, The Times, the applicant complained that legal aid was not available in Guernsey to enable him to sue the authorities there for false imprisonment – an alleged breach of Art 6 (right to a fair trial). The matter was resolved by friendly settlement involving an undertaking by the United Kingdom to reform the legal aid system in Guernsey to bring it into compliance with Convention requirements and by payment to the applicant of £6,000 compensation and £14,000 costs. A friendly settlement also disposed of the application in *Tsavachidis v Greece*, 21 January 1999, Hudoc, alleging breaches of Arts 8, 9 and 10 as a result of government interference with the activities of Jehovah's Witnesses. The Greek government undertook to pay compensation to the applicant and, more significantly, to discontinue the practices complained of, in particular that of secret surveillance.

If no such settlement can be reached, the Court will proceed to judgment. Findings on the merits are by majority vote (Art 44) and are binding on contracting states in international law (Art 46).

GENERAL PRINCIPLES OF EUROPEAN HUMAN RIGHTS LAW

Matters of interpretation

As the Convention was originally conceived as a treaty between its signatory or contracting states, it is to be interpreted in accordance with the international rules governing such matters contained in the Vienna Convention on the Law of Treaties 1969.

In particular, this requires that a treaty 'be interpreted in good faith in accordance with the ordinary meaning to be given to the terms of the treaty in their context and in the light of its object and purpose' (Art 31).

This may be seen as the foundation of the Court's assertion that pursuit of the Convention's objectives should not be hindered by pedantic literalism or rigid adherence to out-dated precedent. Rather, the Convention should be understood as a 'living instrument' to be given a meaning consistent with prevailing social, cultural and political tendencies in a contracting state (*Tyrer* v *United Kingdom* (1978–80) 2 EHRR 1, see below).

The general objectives of the Convention have been defined as the 'protection of individual rights' (*Soering* v *United Kingdom* (1989) 11 EHRR 439) and the 'promotion of the ideals and values of a democratic society', to wit, 'pluralism, tolerance and broadmindedness' (*Kjeldsen, Busk Madsen and Pedersen* v *Denmark* (1979–80) 1 EHRR 711); *Handyside* v *United Kingdom* (1979–80) 1 EHRR 737). Hence the Court's continued emphasis on the importance of Art 10 (freedom of expression), as underpinned by Art 11 (association and assembly), as one of the 'basic conditions for the foundation and progress of a democratic society' (*Piermont* v *France* (1995) 20 EHRR 301).

Consistent with the above, the Court does not recognise the doctrine of precedent beyond that necessary to ensure a reasonable degree of 'legal certainty and the orderly development of the Convention's case-law' (*Cossey* v *United Kingdom* (1990) 13 EHRR 622). The Court therefore preserves the right to depart from previous decisions where there are 'cogent reasons for doing so' (*ibid.*).

Negative and positive obligations

When first instigated the Convention seems generally to have been understood as imposing a series of negative obligations on states by identifying those human rights with which they should not interfere. According to this approach, the state was not under any clear duty to act as guarantor of such rights by seeking to ensure that the activities of one individual did not impinge on the rights of another. It was enough that the state simply 'stood back' and refrained from any unwarranted transgression by itself and those under its direction.

In more recent times, however, the Court has begun to develop a theory of state obligation which requires more than mere negative compliance. This has been premised to a considerable extent on the general but positive duty in Art 1 which requires contracting states 'to secure to everyone within that jurisdiction the rights and freedoms defined in ... this Convention'.

Making the requirement effective and meaningful, it has been argued, requires the state to go beyond negative compliance and to do so by providing a system of laws, law enforcement and public administration which enable the individual to enjoy Convention rights free from interference whatever the source, i.e. whether from a state or the individual citizens.

This was the approach adopted by the Court in *Plattform 'Ärtze für das Leben'* v *Austria* (1988) 13 EHRR 204, where it found that the state's obligation in relation to the right of assembly (Art 11) was not discharged simply by allowing marches and demonstrations to take place within its jurisdiction. The state was obliged to go further by taking reasonable steps to ensure that any person or group wishing to exercise the right peacefully was able to do so notwithstanding the opposition of others. This, and cases like it, form the basis of the emerging principle that although the Convention was not designed to have 'horizontal effect' i.e. to be enforceable by one individual against another, an individual whose right is infringed by another private person may have a cause of action, albeit against the state, if the breach of the Convention right can be attributed to the state's failure to guarantee adequately the right in question.

This principle was applied in *Z v United Kingdom* [2002] 34 EHRR 310, where it was held that serious parental neglect could amount to inhuman and degrading treatment and that a failure by a local authority to use its powers to protect a child from being treated in this way constituted an actionable breach of its rights in Art 3.

The margin of appreciation

In securing the rights articulated by the Convention, each state is permitted a 'margin of appreciation'. The Convention thus concedes a degree of flexibility and discretion in the way it is interpreted and applied in the national context. No attempt is made, therefore, to set rigid and absolute standards. Were it otherwise the potential for political tensions between member states, and between such states and the court, would be greatly increased to the detriment of the consensual basis on which the effective operation of the Convention depends. What is required, therefore, is that member states achieve the maximum degree of compliance with the Convention's general standards as is compatible with particular national interests, circumstances and traditions. The doctrine of the margin of appreciation reflects the conception on which the Convention was originally based, i.e. that the primary obligation for the protection of human rights lies with the state. According to this view, the Convention should be seen as imposing general standards of official conduct and a right to challenge state action where there has been less than substantial compliance.

It is apparent that the extent of the margin of appreciation permitted to states varies depending on the particular legitimate aim pursued and the nature of the right alleged to have been infringed. A considerable margin appears to be permitted to states, for example, in relation to measures dealing with public morality. Hence the Court's view in *Handyside v United Kingdom* (1976) 1 EHRR 737, that 'the view taken…of the requirements of morals varies from time to time and from place to place, especially in our era' and that 'by reason of their direct and continuous contract with the vital forces of their countries, state authorities are in principle in a better position than the international judge to give an opinion on the exact content of those requirements'. A similar tendency to give considerable deference to the judgment of state authorities also appears to apply to measures dealing with national security and with social and economic policies.

The nature and subject matter of the right in issue are further factors to be considered. Thus, for example, greater flexibility appears to be afforded to states in matters affecting Arts 8 and 9 (respect for family life and the freedom of religion, than is permitted in relation to Art 10 (freedom of expression) which the Court has repeatedly stressed has an irreducible minimum if the standards of liberal democracy on which the Convention is founded are to be maintained.

Unqualified, limited and qualified rights

The Convention contains what has been referred to as a hierarchy of rights which fall into three broad categories distinguished by the grounds and the extent to which the rights therein may be restricted by the state.

The first category contains the unqualified or absolute rights. It encompasses Arts 3 (prohibition of torture), 4 (prohibition of slavery), and 7 (no punishment without law) and elements of Art 9 (thought, conscience and religion). These rights may not be restricted or interfered with by the state whatever the circumstances or however pressing the state may perceive the public or social interest to be.

Articles 2, 5 and 6 fall into the second category, the limited rights. These deal with the right to life, the right to liberty and security of the person and the right to a fair trial. Such rights may be subject to restrictions but only in accordance with the specific and strictly limited circumstances as prescribed by the Articles.

The third category is comprised of the Convention's qualified rights. The exact circumstances in which these may be subject to state interference are not so precisely defined as with the limited rights, but any restriction must be based on clear legal authority ('according to' or 'prescribed by law') and must be proportionate ('reasonably necessary in a democratic society') to the achievement of any of the Convention's legitimate aims, e.g. the prevention of crime or the protection of public order or health. The principal rights in this category are those contained in Arts 8 (private and family life), 9 (freedom to manifest one's religion), 10 (expression) and 11 (assembly and association).

The principle of certainty (according to or prescribed by law)

The requirement that restrictions imposed on Convention rights should be according to or prescribed by law (see in particular, Arts 8, 9, 10 and 11) has three principal, related elements all inherent in the doctrine of the Rule of Law and its insistence that that which is to qualify as law must have a certain minimum form and quality. Hence, according to the case law of the European Court of Human Rights, any attempted restriction of a Convention right will be legally valid and effective only if it is:

(a) founded on and in full compliance with an established form of law, i.e. in the United Kingdom context, legislation or common law, rather than mere policy rules or administrative guidelines;
(b) readily accessible and available to members of the general public;
(c) phrased in sufficiently clear terms to enable individuals affected to adjust their conduct as required.

The principle is well illustrated in the domestic context by the recent decisions in *Steel and Others* v *United Kingdom* (1999) 28 EHRR 603, and *Hashman and Harrup* v *United Kingdom* (2000) 30 EHRR 241. Both were concerned with the common law powers of police and magistrates in the United Kingdom to deal with alleged breaches of the peace at public demonstrations and the compatibility of such powers with the requirement in Art 10(2) that any interference with the right of assembly (Art 10(1)) should be 'prescribed by law'.

In *Steel* exception was taken to the common law power of police officers to arrest and detain any person behaving in a way likely to cause such breach of the peace. This, it was argued, did not achieve the necessary degree of legal certainty since neither the meaning of what constituted a breach of the peace or amounted to behaviour likely to cause the same had ever been adequately defined. After careful consideration of the common law in issue, the Court came to the conclusion that this hitherto rather vague aspect of English police powers had been addressed to its satisfaction by the English courts in a number of decisions during the 1980s and 1990s. It was thereby 'sufficiently established that a breach of the peace is only committed when an individual causes harm, or appears likely to cause harm, to persons or property or acts in a manner the natural consequence of which would be to provoke others to violence'.

The application in the *Hashman* case was rather more successful. The case arose out of a demonstration against fox hunting and was concerned with the power of magistrates to bind persons over to keep the peace and to be of good behaviour as entrusted to them as long ago as the Justice of the Peace Act 1361. In this instance the court accepted the complaint that the prescription 'to be of good behaviour' did not make clear exactly what it was 'that the subject of the order may or may not lawfully do'. Nor could the court, as in the *Steel* case, find any previous judicial decisions in which the exact meaning of the phrase had been adequately defined. It amounted, therefore, to the very type of vague and imprecise restriction on the right of assembly which Art 10(2) sought to proscribe.

Proportionality

The concept of proportionality as a means of testing whether municipal action is compatible with Convention standards is well established in the jurisprudence of the Court of Human Rights. Hence where a state claims that a particular action represented an exercise of a lawful power to protect a legitimate public interest, the test applied will be whether the action taken was proportionate to the aims pursued and whether the reasons for it given by the state were both relevant and sufficient. In *Bowman* v *United Kingdom, The Times*, 23 February 1998, the applicant distributed literature in a parliamentary constituency (Halifax) during the 1997 General Election which contained information explaining the views of the main candidates concerning abortion. This was alleged to be an offence under the Representation of the People Act 1983, s 75, which prohibited expenditure of over £5 in a particular constituency during an election campaign by any unauthorised person (i.e. a person not authorised by an election agent) for the purpose of promoting or disparaging a specific candidate or candidates.

The applicant argued that the offence represented a constraint on her freedom of expression contrary to Art 10 of the Convention. Article 10 permits restrictions on the right only to the extent that these are 'necessary in the interests of a democratic society' for the protection of certain public interests. The court recognised that some limits on election expenditure during general election campaigns might be legitimate for the purpose of preserving equality between candidates and, therefore, ensuring fair elections as required by Protocol 1, Art 3. The provision of the 1983 Act, s 75, however, operated as an unnecessarily severe restriction on the dissemination of opinions during such elections. The court found difficulty in understanding how, in a society which imposed no limits on the amount of money political parties could spend on their national publicity campaigns, it could be thought 'necessary' to restrict the expenditure of individuals seeking to disseminate views in particular constituencies to just £5.

The concept was also applied in *Steel v United Kingdom* which, as already explained, dealt with the power of police in the United Kingdom to arrest and detain demonstrators for behaviour likely to cause a breach of the peace.

The case was a composite of three separate applications under Art 10, all raising similar issues. In the first a demonstrator had walked in front of a member of a grouse shoot to prevent him discharging his gun. The applicant in the second case had placed herself in front of construction machinery to prevent it from being used to clear the ground for the construction of a motorway. In both instances the court felt the behaviour in issue posed a real danger to public order to the extent that the arrest and detention of the applicants could not be regarded as disproportionate to the legitimate aim pursued by the police, viz. 'the prevention of disorder' (Art 10(2)).

The third application was made by a group of demonstrators who had assembled outside a conference centre where a meeting of the arms industry was taking place. The demonstrators carried placards and distributed leaflets. No disruption was caused nor was anything said or done which was particularly an offence to those entering the building. In these very different circumstances the court was unable to discern any acceptable degree of proportionality between the actions of the police and the needs of public order.

Legitimate aims

Restrictions placed on the Convention's qualified rights must be directed towards the promotion of one or more of the public interests or 'legitimate aims' recognised by the Article in question. The legitimate aims common to Arts 8–11 are public safety, the protection of public order, health or morals and the rights of others. Other legitimate aims include the protection of national security and the prevention of crime (Arts 8(2), 10(2) and 11(2)), the economic well-being of the country (Art 8(2)), territorial integrity, confidentiality and the reputation of the judiciary (Art 10(2)).

Imposition of a restriction for any other purpose or public concern, however laudable this may appear to be, would breach the Convention article to which it related. In *Piermont v France* (above) the applicant, a German 'green' MEP went to a French administered island in the South Pacific where a general election was about to be held. The applicant spoke at a number of political rallies and was extremely critical of the French government's reluctance to discontinue nuclear tests in that part of the world. Despite the fact that no recorded incidents of violence had occurred on such occasions and that she had not advocated any such violence or disorder, the applicant was ordered to be deported for what was described as 'an attack on French policy'. The court found a breach of Art 10(1) on the ground that the action taken against her had been taken for largely political reasons none of which fell within the legitimate aims for which restrictions of freedom of expression could be imposed according to Art 10(2).

THE RIGHTS PROTECTED BY THE CONVENTION

Article 1 requires the contracting states to secure adequate protection for the following rights and freedoms.

Right to life (Art 2)

Article 2 provides that everyone's right to life shall be protected by law. The obligation cannot be derogated from in times of war or national emergency. The Strasbourg Court's interpretation of the Articles shows that it imposes both negative and positive obligations on the state. The negative obligation is to refrain from taking life except where this results from the use of force which is no more than is absolutely necessary:

- to defend a person from unlawful violence;
- to effect an arrest or prevent the escape of a person lawfully detained;
- to quell a riot or insurrection by lawful means (Art 2(2)).

The second and positive duty imposed is to have in place a system of policing and law enforcement sufficient to ensure a reasonable level of protection from life-threatening actions or situations (*X* v *United Kingdom* (1978) 14 DR 31). This, in turn, may involve taking specific steps to protect the life of a particular individual where this is threatened by a 'real and immediate risk...from the criminal acts of a third party' of which the authorities had a right to have knowledge (*Osman* v *United Kingdom* (2000) 29 EHRR 245).

In *Edwards* v *United Kingdom* (2002) 12 BHRC 190 the duty was violated when a prisoner was killed after being placed in a cell with another prisoner who was known to be highly dangerous and unstable. This had exposed the deceased to a 'real and serious risk' of loss of life.

The Convention concedes expressly to contracting states the right to administer capital punishment (Art 2(1)). This is, however, now subject to Protocol 6 (see below). It also appears to permit both withdrawal of medical treatment (*Widner* v *Switzerland* 1993, unreported) and the termination of pregnancy for legitimate medical or social reasons (*H* v *Norway* 73 DR 155).

The positive duty to protect life has been held to be infringed where no 'thorough and adequate investigation' has been conducted into deaths in police custody or as a result of the operations of security forces (*Aksoy* v *Turkey* (1997) 27 EHRR 553). Failure to investigate properly the lethal shooting of IRA suspects at a time when it was alleged that the security forces in Northern Ireland were engaged in a shoot-to-kill policy was, according to this principle, held to be a breach of Art 2 in *Jordan and Others* v *United Kingdom* (2001) 11 BHRC 1.

The legitimacy of the use of lethal force by the United Kingdom's security forces was also considered in *McCann, Farrell and Savage* v *United Kingdom* (1995) 21 EHRR 97. The case concerned the attempted arrest and shooting dead of three IRA suspects in Gibraltar. It was held that, although it might not be a breach of the Convention to take the lives of terrorists believed to be about to detonate a bomb, the lack of proper planning or exercise of effective control over the arrest operation itself precluded those in charge of it from ensuring that lethal force was resorted to only in those circumstances permitted by Art 2(2), viz. that which was absolutely necessary to effect a lawful arrest.

The right to life in Art 2, as interpreted by the Court of Human Rights, does not give a person the right to end their life at the time of their own choosing. This remains the case notwithstanding that the person is terminally ill or that, through illness, their life has become intolerable (*Pretty* v *United Kingdom* [2002] 35 EHRR 1).

Prohibition of torture, inhuman and degrading treatment (Art 3)

Article 3 permits of no exceptions and is non-derogable (see below, Art 15). Thus, however pressing a particular public interest may be, departure from the Article's requirements is not permitted. Such treatment or punishment is not justified, therefore, in the fight against terrorism (*Ireland* v *United Kingdom*, below).

Torture constitutes 'deliberate inhuman treatment causing very serious and cruel suffering' (*ibid.*). The case law indicates that inhuman treatment may be committed by the threat of torture, physical assault, detention in oppressive conditions, deportation or extradition to a state where the individual may be at risk of serious ill-treatment, and by the use of psychological interrogation techniques.

Degrading punishment or treatment is that which grossly humiliates or debases. A degrading punishment was held to have been inflicted in *Tyrer* v *United Kingdom* (1978) 2 EHRR 1, where an Isle of Man court sentenced a fifteen-year-old boy to three strokes of the birch after he had been found guilty of an assault. On the same basis, a decision to deport a woman to her country of origin where she was accused of adultery and where stoning remained one of the penalties which could be imposed, was found to be potentially offensive to Art 3 in *Jabari* v *Turkey* (2001) 29 EHRR CD 178.

Allegations of breach of Art 3 have often related to the treatment of persons in detention. The inevitable and usual degree of degradation and humiliations resulting from detention or imprisonment does not, of itself, amount to a breach (*AM* v *Italy*, 14 December 1999, Hudoc). This would be occasioned, however, by any recourse to physical force against a detainee not made 'strictly necessary' by his own conduct (*Thomasi* v *France* (1993) 15 EHRR 1). Even the use of handcuffs may offend Art 3 if not reasonably necessary in the prevailing circumstances (*Raninen* v *Finland* (1998) 26 EHRR 563).

Poor conditions, e.g. over-crowding, inadequate food, toilet facilities, heating, etc., may amount to degrading treatment (*Nazarenko* v *Ukraine* (1999) 28 EHRR CD 246) as may the denial of medical treatment (*Hurtado* v *Switzerland*, 28 January 1994, Hudoc). Detention of a severely disabled person in physical conditions completely unsuitable to their needs was found to amount to degrading treatment in *Price* v *United Kingdom* [2002] 34 EHRR 53. The state is not liable under Art 3, however, where a prisoner is kept in poor conditions of their own making. Hence the failure of the application in *McFeeley* v *United Kingdom* (1981) 3 EHRR 161, a case arising out of the 'dirty protest' in the Maze Prison, Belfast, where prisoners daubed their cells with excrement and refused to wear prison clothes as a protest against the withdrawal of their status as political prisoners.

Solitary confinement of a prisoner without good cause or in unacceptable conditions has been held to be within the margin of appreciation applicable to Art 3 even to the extent of rigorous programmes of isolation devised for terrorist suspects (*Krocher and Muller* v *Switzerland* 34 DR 25). The line of acceptability is crossed, however, by 'complete sensory isolation coupled with complete social isolation' such as could 'destroy the personality' (*Ennslin, Baader and Raspe* v *FRG* 14 DR 64).

Ireland v *United Kingdom* (1978) 2 EHRR 25, represents the most controversial and well-known case brought under Art 3 involving the domestic government. The case arose out of the interrogation techniques and general treatment used against suspected republican activists and sympathisers arrested in the internment operation of August 1971. The principal allegation was that suspects had been hooded and forced to lean against a wall supported only by their fingertips and on tip-toe while being subjected to white noise and continuous questioning for long periods. Those who collapsed were subject to beatings and all were deprived of food, drink and sleep. The court's conclusion was that this constituted inhuman and degrading treatment but not torture. This illustrates that the threshold for torture is high. Deliberately inhuman treatment causing serious and cruel suffering appears to be required as in *Cakici* v *Turkey* (2001) 31 EHRR 133, in which the applicant's brother was beaten, one of his ribs broken, his head split open, and he was subjected to electric shock treatment while in police custody.

The United Kingdom was also found to be at fault under Art 3 in *A* v *United Kingdom* (1999) 27 EHRR 611, a case involving the physical chastisement (beating with a stick) of a nine-year-old boy by his stepfather. The court found that the obligation on contracting states imposed by the Convention in Art 1 to secure to everyone within their jurisdiction the rights and freedoms defined therein, taken together with Art 3, required states to adopt measures sufficient to protect individuals against abuse by other private citizens.

The positive obligations imposed on states by Art 3 were also illustrated by the decision *Z* v *United Kingdom* [2002] 34 EHRR 310. On this occasion a local authority was found to be in breach through its failure to take adequate measures to prevent the abuse and neglect of two young children.

Albeit that a contracting state has not itself been guilty of the type of treatment forbidden by Art 3, it may still act in breach of the Article if it expels a person to another state where that individual could face a real risk of being subjected to such treatment. This remains the case notwithstanding that the person's presence is believed to be prejudicial to national security (*Chahal* v *United Kingdom* [1997] 23 EHRR 413). In *D* v *United Kingdom* (1997) 24 EHRR 423, it was held that a decision to remove from the United Kingdom a seriously ill alien who had been convicted of drug trafficking could amount to a breach of Art 3 if it increased the risk that the person might die in distressing circumstances.

Freedom from slavery, servitude and forced or compulsory labour (Art 4)

This prohibition does not extend to work done in the ordinary course of detention, to military service or to any service exacted in time of emergency or calamity threatening the life or well-being of the community.

Slavery has been defined as 'the status or condition of a person over whom any or all of the powers attaching to the right of ownership are exercised' (1926 Slavery Convention).

It has been held that forced or compulsory labour does not extend to: a requirement that a lawyer give his services free to impecunious defendants (*Van der Mussele* v *Belgium* (1984) 6 EHRR 163); a requirement that a notary charge less for work done for non-profit-making organisations (*X* v *Federal Republic of Germany* (1979) 18 DR 216); or to a rule that unemployed persons who refuse to accept work could be denied unemployment benefit (*X* v *Netherlands* (1976) 7 DR 161).

The right is non-derogable. To date it has generated little case law, nor have any breaches of Art 4 yet been found to have been committed.

Right to liberty and security of the person (Art 5)

The right, as articulated by the Convention, is subject to various exceptions. These permit that a person's liberty may be denied:

- following a sentence of imprisonment imposed by a competent court;
- for non-compliance with a court order or an obligation imposed by law;
- following a lawful arrest and preparatory to being brought before a competent legal authority;
- in the case of a minor, for the purpose of educational supervision or bringing him/her before a competent legal authority;
- in the case of persons of unsound mind, alcoholics, drug addicts or vagrants, for preventing the spread of infectious diseases;
- to prevent a person entering a state unlawfully or prior to extradition or deportation.

  Article 5 also provides that everyone who has been arrested has the right:

- to be informed promptly of the reasons for the arrest and any charge(s) to be made;
- to be brought promptly before a court and to release on bail or trial within a reasonable time;
- to challenge the legality of the detention before a competent legal authority.

Detention following conviction by a competent court

The Convention may not be used to challenge a conviction (*Krzycki v Federal Republic of Germany* (1978) 13 DR 57 or sentence (*Weeks v United Kingdom* (1988) 10 EHRR 293) imposed in accordance with municipal law. The Court of Human Rights might, however, be prepared to consider the legality of a period of detention resulting from a purely administrative decision, i.e. a decision to recall a prisoner who had been released on licence. In *Weeks v United Kingdom*, the applicant had been released on licence after serving ten years of a life sentence. He was then recalled to prison a year later. The court's opinion was that there was sufficient causal link between the Home Office's recall decision and the municipal court's original sentence. Both the original sentence and the recall decision had been made in the interests of social protection and the rehabilitation of the applicant based on his record. Also, the trial court had imposed a life sentence in the full knowledge that it lay within the discretion of the Home Secretary to release and recall life prisoners.

This may be contrasted with the decision in *Stafford v United Kingdom* (2002) *Times*, 31 May. On this occasion, Art 5 was found to have been violated by the continuing to hold a life prisoner after the tariff element (deterrence and retribution) had been served on the ground that, if released, he might commit other non-violent offences unconnected with the original reason for his imprisonment. This, in effect, amounted to imprisonment by executive decree.

Non-compliance with a court order or an obligation imposed by law

This exception recognises the legality of imprisonment for matters such as civil contempt, refusal to pay a fine or maintenance order, or failure to comply with specific legal obligations, e.g. refusal to do military service (*Johansen* v *Norway* (1985) 44 DR 155). In this type of case the imprisonment usually follows the act of non-compliance. It has also been held, however, that this provision gives the state the right to detain a person where there is an immediate and pressing need to ensure that a significant legal obligation *is* actually complied with. Hence, no breach of the Convention was committed where three persons entering Great Britain from Ireland were detained for 45 hours to ensure compliance with the obligation in the Prevention of Terrorism Order 1976 that such persons submit themselves to 'further interrogation' if required (*McVeigh, O'Neill and Evans* v *United Kingdom* (1983) 5 EHRR 71).

Detention on suspicion of commission of a criminal offence

It appears to be sufficient that the suspect is arrested on suspicion of the type of activity which presupposes or necessarily involves the commission of a specific offence albeit that the particular offence or offences with which the suspect may be charged have not yet been identified. In *Brogan* v *United Kingdom* (1988) 11 EHRR 117, the applicant had been arrested on suspicion of being 'concerned in the commission...of acts of terrorism' (viz. the use of violence for political ends). This does not constitute a specific offence. The court was satisfied, however, that the above statutory definition of terrorism was sufficiently clear and 'in keeping with the idea of an offence' as to satisfy the Convention's requirements.

The initial arrest must be for the purpose of enforcing the criminal law. It matters not that no charges are eventually brought or that, at the time of arrest, the police do not have sufficient evidence for that purpose (*Brogan*, above). There must be, however, reasonable suspicion that an offence has been committed which supposes 'the existence of facts or information which would satisfy an objective observer that the person concerned may have committed the offence' (*Fox, Campbell and Hartley* v *United Kingdom* (1990) 13 EHRR 157).

Article 5(2) requires that the suspect shall be 'informed promptly...of the reasons for his arrest and any charge against him'. 'Promptly' need not necessarily be at the time of the arrest and it appears to be sufficient that reasons are revealed or may be deduced during the subsequent interrogation (*Fox,* above). The reasons must be given in language which the suspect can understand and must be sufficient to enable the legality of the arrest to be challenged in a municipal court (Art 5(4)).

After arrest the suspect should be brought 'promptly' before a judge or competent legal authority (Art 5(3)) for review of 'the circumstances for and against detention and of ordering release if there are no such reasons' (*Schiesser* v *Switzerland* A34 para 31 (1979). Such judge or legal authority must not be a person or body having any connection with the bringing, defending or determining any charges which may be brought against the person detained.

In *Hood* v *United Kingdom* (2000) 29 EHRR 365, Art 5(3) was found to have been violated by domestic courts martial procedures particularly in terms of the role of commanding officers and their involvement in decisions relating both to the need for continued detention of particular suspects and the charges to be brought against them. In *Brogan* v *United Kingdom* (above) the requirement that review of the need for detention take place promptly was held to have been offended by the applicant's detention for four days pursuant to the Prevention of Terrorism Act 1984, s 12. This remained the case notwithstanding the particular conditions prevailing in Northern Ireland. Rather than amend the 1984 Act, the United Kingdom government opted to enter a derogation from Art 5 according to the terms of Art 15 (see below). The circumstances applying in Northern Ireland were later found to be within the permitted grounds for such departure from normal Convention standards (*Brannigan and McBride* v *United Kingdom* (1993) 17 EHRR 539).

The suspect has a right to be tried within a reasonable time. What is reasonable will depend on the circumstances and the complexity of each case. This does mean, however, that preparation of the case against the suspect must be conducted with all due expedition. The suspect may be kept in detention during this period providing there are 'relevant and sufficient reasons' (*Wemhoff* v *Federal Republic of Germany* (1980) 1 EHRR 55). These have been held to include the dangers of flight and interference with the course of justice, the prevention of crime, and the maintenance of public order. Strong suspicion of guilt, in the absence of one of the above dangers, is not sufficient for continued pre-trial detention (*Morganti* v *France* (1996) 21 EHRR 34). Periods of pre-trial detention for seven years (*Mansur* v *Turkey* (1995) 20 EHRR 535), and four years (*Yagie and Sargin* v *Turkey* (1995) 20 EHRR 505) have both been held to contravene Art 5.

The automatic refusal of bail pursuant to the Criminal Justice and Public Order Act 1994, s 25, without reference to the defendant's particular circumstances, was condemned in *Caballero* v *United Kingdom* (2000) 30 EHRR 643. In its original form the section stipulated that bail could not be granted to defendants charged with homicide or rape having previously been convicted for such offences.

A person deprived of their liberty should also be allowed access to a court or competent tribunal at reasonable intervals to test the legality of their detention. The court or tribunal should be possessed of the power to order the person's release if such legality is lacking and should make such decisions 'speedily' (Art 54). This has been the basis of successful challenges to the length of time between Parole Board reviews of the need for further detention of a person recalled from parole after serving a life sentence (*Oldham* v *United Kingdom* (2001) 31 EHRR 34) and of a young offender detained 'at her Majesty's pleasure' (*Hussain* v *United Kingdom* (1996) 21 EHRR 1). The Parole Board's powers and procedures were also found to be at fault under Art 5(4) in *Curley* v *United Kingdom* (2001) 31 EHRR 14. The breach on this occasion was the Board's inability to order the release of a life prisoner once the tariff period of his sentence, i.e. that for deterrence and punishment, had been served; the Board's powers at that time being limited to the making of recommendations subject to the approval of the Home Secretary.

Detention of minors

For the purposes of the Convention a minor is a person under eighteen years of age. A minor may be detained for educational supervision, e.g. to ensure attendance at school, or in order to be brought before a court so that he/she may be removed from harmful surroundings. Detention for educational supervision should be in an institution designed for that purpose and not in a remand or other prison except for a short period as a preliminary to allocation to the former (*Bouamer* v *Belgium* (1988) 11 EHRR 1).

Detention of a minor prior to a court appearance is permitted if this is in the child's interests, e.g. for the preparation of psychiatric reports or pending a judicial order placing him/her in care.

Detention to prevent the spread of infectious diseases

This is permitted in relation to persons of unsound mind, alcoholics, drug addicts and vagrants for their own protection and in the interests of public safety. The terms 'alcoholics', 'drug addicts' and 'infectious diseases' have not yet been interpreted by either the Commission or the Court of Human Rights. Persons of unsound mind are those who, according to reliable and objective medical expertise, are suffering from the kind or degree of mental disorder warranting confinement (*Winterwerp* v *Netherlands* (1980) 2 EHRR 387). Vagrants have been defined as persons 'who have no fixed abode, no means of subsistence and no regular trade or profession' (*De Wilde, Ooms and Versyp* v *Belgium* (1979–80) 1 EHRR 373).

Detention of an illegal entrant pending deportation or extradition

Such detention is lawful providing it occurs in relation to the exercise of a valid power to exclude, deport or extradite according to the municipal law of the state concerned (*Bozano* v *France* (1987) 9 EHRR 297). The subsequent deportation in extradition proceedings must be expedited with 'requisite diligence' (*Lynas* v *Switzerland* (1976) 6 DR 141).

Right to a fair trial (Art 6)

Article 6 gives every person the right to a fair and public hearing within a reasonable time by an independent and impartial tribunal 'in the determination of his civil rights and obligation or any criminal charge'. It further provides that each person charged with a criminal offence shall be presumed innocent until proven guilty and shall have the right to:

(a) be informed promptly of the nature of the charge against him in language he understands;
(b) adequate time and facilities to prepare a defence including the right to appoint and communicate with a legal adviser;
(c) defend the case personally or through legal representation;
(d) obtain the attendance and examine witnesses on his behalf;
(e) be assisted by an interpreter if he cannot understand the language used in the court.

Since the fair trial guarantees in the Article extend to the 'determination of civil rights and obligations' generally, their application is not confined solely to the proceedings of courts of law in the traditionally understood sense. The decision-making powers of administrative tribunals are clearly covered as is the exercise of powers to decide by public authorities and officials providing civil rights and obligations are affected.

What amounts to a civil right or obligation has not been precisely defined. In general, however, the term encompasses the rights and obligations of private persons in their relationship with each other and with the state other than the exercise of its public law functions. As a result, Art 6 has been found to apply to decisions relating to individual rights protected by commercial law, tort, family law, the law of succession and land law. In addition, in recent years, the Article has been applied to disputes between states and civil servants relating to the termination of employment (*Satonnet v France*, 25 September 1998, Hudoc), and to pensions (*Lambourdiere v France*, 2 August 2000, Hudoc). Note, however, that civil servants are not protected by Art 6 if engaged in the exercise of public law powers directly affecting the 'state's sovereign functions', i.e. those designed to protect its general interest in matters of defence, national security, the formation of public policy, etc. (*Pellegrin v France* (2001) 31 EHRR 26; *Castanheira Barros v Portugal*, 26 October 2000, Hudoc).

In relation to criminal charges the Court of Human Rights has taken the view that Art 6 is engaged where a person has been informed by a competent legal authority that an allegation of a criminal act has been made against him (*Corigliano v Italy (A/57)* (1983) 5 EHRR 334). It is applicable, therefore, before any charge is made in the formal and official sense and, therefore, at least from the time of arrest on suspicion (*Wemhoff v Federal Republic of Germany* (1968) 1 EHRR 55).

Key factors in determining what amounts to a criminal charge are the nature of the act itself (see *Steel v United Kingdom* (above), where a breach of the peace was found to constitute a criminal offence for the purposes of Art 5(1)); its classification in the domestic law of the state involved; and the severity of the penalty which could be imposed. Hence disciplinary charges have been held to be 'criminal' for the purposes of Art 6 where these may result in loss of liberty (*Campbell and Fell v United Kingdom* (1984) 7 EHRR 165, Art 6 applicable to serious charges under code of prison discipline).

Where a body exercising powers which engage Art 6 fails to act fairly, no breach will be committed if its decisions are subject to an effective process of review, i.e. one which enables the complainant to have the defective decision set aside and remade subject to the Article's requirements (*Bryan v United Kingdom* (1996) 21 EHRR 342).

The decision in *Kingsley v United Kingdom* (2001) 33 EHRR 13, illustrates that the domestic process of judicial review may sometimes be inadequate to ensure that such redress is available in domestic courts. The applicant had applied for judicial review of a decision of the Gaming Board to revoke his Certificate of Approval as a person fit to hold a management position in the gaming industry (Gaming Act 1968, s 19). Despite the Court of Appeal's acceptance that the applicant had shown an arguable case of bias, it was felt that the Gaming Board's decision could not be set aside. This was premised on the 'doctrine of necessity', i.e. that since the allegation of bias affected all of the Board's members it was not possible for the matter to be remitted to it for a fresh decision. Moreover, since, according to English law, issues relating to the merits of a decision could not be considered in an application for judicial review, the Court was also precluded from making any findings or superimposing its views concerning the applicant's fitness to manage gaming clubs or businesses. In these circumstances, therefore, English judicial review offered no process through which the offending decision could be corrected and remade in accordance with the Convention's procedural standards.

Right of access to a court

In *Golder* v *United Kingdom* (1975) 1 EHRR 524, it was held that the right to a fair trial presupposed an individual's unimpeded right of access to the appropriate court. Golder was a prisoner who wished to commence proceedings for defamation against a prison officer. According to the Prison Rules then in force he could not be prevented from bringing such action to trial but could be denied access to a solicitor in the preparation of his case. This was held to be sufficient impediment to contravene Art 6. The refusal to grant legal aid to an impecunious indigent was also found to amount to an unlawful impediment in *Airey* v *Ireland (No. 2)* (1981) 3 EHRR 592.

Right to a fair hearing

This has been interpreted to include the following.

(a) The right to know the case to be answered and the evidence relating thereto (*McMichael* v *United Kingdom* (1995) 20 EHRR 205). The withholding of evidence to protect the public interest is permissible only after careful weighing of the public interests involved by a competent judicial authority (*Rowe* v *United Kingdom* (2000) 30 EHRR 1).

(b) In criminal cases and in civil cases involving an assessment of the person's conduct, character or lifestyle, the right to an oral hearing before the court or tribunal. Trial *in absentia* may be permitted where the right to a hearing has been waived or where every effort has been made to secure the person's presence (*Colozza* v *Italy* (1985) 7 EHRR 516).

(c) The right to 'equality of arms'. This has been held to mean that everyone who is a party to proceedings subject to Art 6 shall have a reasonable opportunity of presenting his/her case under conditions which do not cause any substantial disadvantage *vis-à-vis* his/her opponent (*Kaufman* v *Belgium* (1986) 50 DR 98). The principle was offended by conducting the trial of the two juvenile defendants in the Jamie Bulger case in a crown court before a judge and jury with all the formality of adult proceedings 'which must at times have seemed incomprehensible and intimidating for a child of 11' (*T and V* v *United Kingdom* (2000) 30 EHRR 121).

(d) The existence of rules of evidence regulating the use of unfairly or illegally obtained evidence, hearsay testimony and providing for adequate pre-trial disclosure of relevant materials (*Schenk* v *Switzerland* (1988) 13 EHRR 242).

(e) The freedom from self-incrimination. This right was held to have been infringed in *Saunders* v *United Kingdom* (1996) 23 EHRR 313, where, in the course of a

Department of Trade and Industry investigation into a company takeover, the applicant was obliged to answer questions on pain of criminal sanctions, including imprisonment, according to powers given to DTI inspectors by the Companies Act 1985, ss 434–36. A further violation was found to be apparent in the requirement in the Irish Republic's anti-terrorist legislation that a person in custody who failed to provide a full account of their movements during any specified period was liable to summary conviction and imprisonment for up to six months (*Heaney and McGuinness* v *Ireland* (2001) 33 EHRR 12).

(f) Reasons for the decision. These must be given with sufficient clarity to enable the individual to 'usefully exercise the right of appeal available to him' (*Hadjianastassiou* v *Greece* (1993) 16 EHRR 219).

(g) The right to legal representation and to legal aid where necessary for the administration of justice. These are express rights in criminal cases and extend to pre-trial proceedings including questioning in police custody (*Magee* v *United Kingdom* (2001) 31 EHRR 35; *Averill* v *United Kingdom* (2001) 31 EHRR 36). In *Benham* v *United Kingdom* (1996) 22 EHRR 293, the applicant had been tried without legal representation and committed to prison for three months for non-payment of the community charge. The Court of Human Rights held that although the proceedings were civil, the potential severity of the sentence meant that he should have been allowed access to legal aid and thus enabled to be legally represented at his trial.

Right to a public hearing

This right exists to protect litigants from the dangers of 'justice in secret with no public scrutiny' (*Pretto* v *Italy* A 71 (1984) 6 EHRR 182). The press and public may, however, be excluded from all or part of a trial where this is in the interests of 'morals, public order or national security...where the interests of juveniles or the private life of the parties so require, or...where publicity would prejudice the interests of justice' (Art 6(1)). This proviso was held to justify excluding the press and public from prison disciplinary proceedings in *Campbell and Fell* v *United Kingdom* (1984) 7 EHRR 165. The court felt that such proceedings could be conducted *in camera* for reasons of 'public order and security' and that public hearings would impose a disproportionate burden on the state in terms of the risks to security which would have to be guarded against.

The giving of evidence *in camera* or out of view of the court and public in legal proceedings generally may be permissible if this is necessary to ensure a witness's safety (*X* v *United Kingdom* 2 Digests 456 (1980)).

Right to trial within a reasonable time

In criminal cases 'time' for this requirement starts to run from the time a person has been notified that they have been accused of an offence. In civil cases time begins to run from the initiation of legal proceedings.

What is a reasonable time will depend on the circumstances of each case. The case should be prepared as expeditiously as is permitted by the complexity of the issues involved and any difficulties in gathering evidence or securing the attendance of witnesses. Greater expedition is expected in criminal cases so that the suspect should not 'remain too long in a state of uncertainty about his fate' (*Stogmuller* v *Austria* (1980) 1 EHRR 155). This requirement was breached in *Zimmerman and Steiner* v *Switzerland* (1984) 6 EHRR 17, where, because of a backlog of cases, an appeal was pending before the Swiss Supreme Court for three and a half years. The obligation applies also to the determination of matters arising out of the litigation in question. Thus, a breach of Art 6 was committed where it took over four years to determine a particular litigant's liability for costs (*Robins* v *United Kingdom, The Times*, 24 October 1997).

Right to an independent and impartial tribunal

An independent tribunal is one which is free from any outside influences, particularly from the executive branch of government. The crucial requirement here is that those exercising judicial functions must have genuine security of tenure. This need not be protected by law but must exist in fact (*Eccles, McPhillips and McShane* v *Ireland* (1988) 59 DR 212).

An impartial tribunal is one which is free of prejudice or bias. Impartiality may result from actual personal bias or a sufficient appearance of bias to cast 'legitimate doubt' on a particular judicial officer's fitness to dispose of the proceedings (*Hauschildt* v *Denmark* (1990) 12 EHRR 266). In criminal cases the need for impartiality extends to members of the jury where one is used (*Sander* v *United Kingdom* (2001) 31 EHRR 44, breach of Art 6 where juror made racist remarks in considering case against Asian defendant).

The United Kingdom's courts martial procedures were held to be inadequate to satisfy this element of Art 6 in a series of cases decided during the 1990s. This was in addition to their deficiencies under Art 5(4) as explained above. The court took particular exception to the overriding powers exercised by the 'convening officer' (often the relevant commanding officer) according to the terms of the Army and Air Force Acts 1955. Such powers extended to determining the charges to be brought, appointing members of the court, its prosecuting officer, and confirming its findings before these could be given effect – all of which fell far short of the requirements of independence and impartiality (see *Findlay* v *United Kingdom*, 6 June 2000, Hudoc; *McDaid* v *United Kingdom*, 10 October 2000, Hudoc; *Cable* v *United Kingdom* (2000) 30 EHRR 1032). The procedures for domestic courts martial were amended by the Armed Forces Act 1996 which, *inter alia,* abolished the position of convening officer. The changes effected by the 1996 Act were found to be Convention compatible in *R* v *Spear*; *R* v *Hastie*; *R* v *Boyd* [2001] 2 WLR 1692.

Executive involvement in the sentencing process by the fixing of tariffs for persons sentenced to indeterminate terms of imprisonment (i.e. the period for punishment and deterrence) was condemned in *T* v *United Kingdom*, 14 December 1998, Hudoc. Although a long-standing procedure in the United Kingdom, its effect was to minimise judicial involvement in determining the actual form to be served.

Amongst the rights guaranteed specifically for the conduct of criminal cases, the right to an independent and impartial tribunal is perhaps the most significant.

Presumption of innocence

The requirement is that 'when carrying out their duties, the members of a court should not start with the preconceived idea that the accused has committed the offence charged; the burden of proof is on the prosecution, and any doubt should benefit the accused' (*Barberà, Messegué and Jabardo* v *Spain* (1989) 11 EHRR 360).

To avoid such misconceptions it has been held that public officials should not make statements to the effect that they believe a suspect to be guilty of a particular offence before that person has been tried by a competent court. 'Article 6(2)…may be violated by public officials if they declare that somebody is responsible for criminal acts without a court having found so' (*Krause* v *Switzerland* (1978) 13 DR 73).

Violation was held to have occurred in *Allenet de Ribemont* v *France* (1995) 20 EHRR 557, where, during a press conference, the French Minister of the Interior and other high-ranking police officials made clear their belief that the applicant had been involved in the murder of a French MP. It was held that the French authorities had encouraged the public to believe that the applicant was guilty and had thus prejudiced the outcome of any subsequent judicial proceedings. In the event the applicant was never brought to trial.

The presumption of innocence does not imply any absolute right to silence. It is, therefore, permissible for a court to place reasonable adverse inferences on a suspect's refusal to answer police questions so long as this is done in the context of all the evidence (*Murray* v *United Kingdom* (1996) 22 EHRR 29).

A court should not convict a person on the basis of his or her silence alone (*Averill* v *United Kingdom* (above)) and should hesitate to use such silence against a suspect where a plausible excuse for it has been offered, e.g. where the suspect was advised to remain silent by his solicitor who believed him to be suffering from the symptoms of heroin withdrawal (*Condron* v *United Kingdom* (2001) 31 EHRR 1).

The right of the defendant in criminal proceedings to be informed promptly of the case to be answered does not duplicate the requirement relating to the giving of reasons for arrest in Art 5(2). The obligation in Art 6 is to provide sufficient information to enable a suspect to prepare an adequate defence. The suspect is also entitled to sufficient time and means, particularly through access to legal advice, for that purpose. This is a particularly important guarantee for those in custody on remand. If the suspect does not wish to conduct his/her own defence, he/she has the right to be legally represented. There is also a right for this to be paid for by legal aid where the suspect does not have sufficient means and where the interests of justice so require.

Freedom from retrospective penal legislation (Art 7)

This article provides that no one should be convicted of an offence or subjected to a penalty which did not exist at the time the allegedly criminal act was committed. This prohibition applies both to the creation of new offences having retrospective effect and to the reinterpretation of pre-existing laws 'to cover facts which previously clearly did not constitute a criminal offence' (*X Ltd and Y* v *United Kingdom* (1982) 28 DR 77).

It is permissible, however, for an existing offence to be given judicial clarification and 'adapted to new circumstances which can reasonably be brought under the original conception of the offence' (*ibid.*). Hence, no breach of Art 7 was committed by two decisions in the United Kingdom courts that a husband could be guilty of raping his wife. It was held that this development in the common law was reasonably foreseeable given changing social attitudes and the contingent dismantling by the courts of the husband's legal immunity (*SW v United Kingdom; CR v United Kingdom* (1996) 21 EHRR 363).

The rule against retrospective penalties was held to have been contravened in *Welch v United Kingdom, The Times*, 15 February 1995. In 1988 the applicant was convicted of drugs offences committed in 1986. The judge made a confiscation order against him (for £59,000) under the Drug Trafficking Offences Act 1986. The provisions of the Act did not become effective, however, until 1987, well after the offences had been committed.

Right to respect for private, family life, home and correspondence (Art 8)

Private life

Respect for private life has been held to extend to such matters as personal and sexual identity, i.e. personal preferences in terms of name or gender, to matters of sexual orientation and lifestyle and to the safeguarding of physical and moral identity.

The right of personal identity may be pleaded, for example, to secure access to official records for such purposes as determining parentage (*Rasmussen v Denmark* (1984) 7 EHRR 371) or in relation to a person's upbringing in care (*Gaskin v United Kingdom* (1989) 12 EHRR 36). It does not give an individual an absolute right to the name of his or her choosing. States have a wide margin of appreciation in such matters and may impose restrictions 'in the public interest, for example, to ensure accurate population registration or to safeguard means of personal identification and of linking the bearers of a given name to a family' (*Stjerna v Finland*, 25 November 1994, Hudoc).

The issue of gender is particularly relevant to those who have undergone gender reassignment therapy. Until recent times the Court had refused to interpret the Convention as guaranteeing full legal recognition to post-operative gender and had not been prepared to accept that Art 8 gives any absolute right to alteration of birth certificates (*Sheffied and Horsham v United Kingdom* (1998) 27 EHRR 163). The position appeared to be that a refusal to allow birth certificates and other personal documents to be altered could constitute a breach where the use and need for such documentation was a regular feature of daily life (*B v France* (1993) 16 EHRR 1). Otherwise, however, in states where this did not appertain and where, accordingly, the administrative burden imposed on the state would be out of proportion to the advantages to be gained by the individual, no breach of Art 8 was committed.

Whatever the contemporary validity of this distinction, and in a classic manifestation of the 'living' nature of the Convention, the Grand Chamber in *Goodwin v United Kingdom* [2002] IRLR 664, decided that the time had come to give full legal recognition to post-operative transsexuals:

In the twentyfirst century the right of transsexuals to personal development and to physical and moral security in the full sense enjoyed by others in society cannot be regarded as a matter of controversy requiring the lapse of time to cast clearer light on the issues involved.

The court's principal reasons for this major development were:

- the conflict between social reality and law which exposed transsexuals to feelings of vulnerability, humiliation and anxiety was a serious interference with private life;
- it was anomalous that the state authorised gender reassignment treatment but did not recognise its full legal implications;
- there was clear evidence of a continuing international trend in favour of full legal recognition of the new sexual identity of post-operative transsexuals;
- while the court did not underestimate the important repercussions any major change would have both in the sphere of birth registration and other official documentation, it did not regard these as insuperable;
- it had not been shown that any such change would cause disproportionate damage to any related public interest.

In the matter of sexual orientation and the practice of same between consenting adults, the Convention gives each individual the freedom to follow his/her personal inclinations and to protection from discrimination relating thereto. An individual's sexuality had been described as a most 'intimate aspect' of private life which should not be restricted except for 'serious reasons having to do with the preservation of public order and decency and the need to protect the citizen from what is offensive and injurious' (see *Dudgeon* v *United Kingdom* (1981) 4 EHRR 149; Art 8 violated by legal rules in Northern Ireland which made intercourse between men a criminal offence). The Article has been used successfully to challenge the ban on gays in the British armed forces (*Lustig-Prean* v *United Kingdom*; *Smith and O'Grady* v *United Kingdom* (2000) 29 EHRR 548) and the conviction for gross indecency of a group of males who engaged in group sex which was wholly consensual and non-violent (*ADT* v *United Kingdom* (2001) 31 EHRR 33). No breach of Art 8 was committed, therefore, by the criminalisation of sadomasochistic sexual activity where this was violent and caused injury (*Laskey* v *United Kingdom* (1997) 24 EHRR 39).

The right to private life guarantees respect for each person's personal and physical integrity (*X and Y* v *Netherlands* 8 EHRR 235). In this sense Art 8 may be engaged by such matters as the taking of compulsory blood tests in paternity proceedings (*X* v *Austria* (1979) 18 DR 154) or by compulsory testing for various medical purposes (*Acmanne* v *Belgium* (1984) 40 DR 252). In both cases the interference in question was found to be legitimate under Art 8(2) as being in the interests of the protection of health generally and the rights and freedoms of others. See also *Association X* v *United Kingdom* (1978) 14 DR 31, where the Commission again accepted the same Art 8(2) justification for a national vaccination programme.

Other physical integrity issues engaged by Art 8 have included compulsory urine tests for road traffic purposes (*Peters* v *Netherlands* (1994) 77-A DR 75); persistent loud noise caused by aeroplanes (*Rayner* v *United Kingdom* (1986) 47 DR 5); offensive smells (*Lopez-Ostra* v *Italy* (1994) 20 EHRR 277); the use of corporal punishment in schools (*Costello-Roberts* v *United Kingdom* (1993) 19 EHRR 112); and the failure to protect against chemical pollution (*Guerra* v *Italy* (1998) 26 EHRR 357).

Article 8 also has relevance for the protection of personal data and information. It may be engaged, therefore, by refusals of access to such information (*Gaskin* v *United Kingdom*, above) and by keeping and storing such materials without consent (*Harman* and *Hewitt* v *United Kingdom* (1989) 14 EHRR 657). To date, however, assertions of a right of access under Art 8 have not met with great success where these have related to information withheld for national security or other sensitive public interest concerns.

No breach of Art 8 is committed by the collection of personal information for the purpose of a criminal investigation (*Murray* v *United Kingdom* (1995) 19 EHRR 193). The retention of such information would also appear to be justified by the needs of national security and the prevention of crime and disorder (*McVeigh* v *United Kingdom* (1984) 25 DR 15).

Family life

For the Convention's purposes, the concept of family life extends considerably beyond the formal relationships created by marriage or cohabitation and any offspring created thereby. In this wider sense the concept has been held to extend to the relationship between a child and its grandparents with whom she had lived in her early years (*Bronda* v *Italy*, 9 June 1998, Hudoc) and that between a child in care and his uncle following allegations of sexual abuse against the child's mother (*Boyle* v *United Kingdom* (1994) 19 EHRR 179). It has also proved of considerable utility for those affected by relationships created outside wedlock and those which have become dysfunctional. Thus Art 8 was violated by the failure to consult a child's natural father before its adoption was arranged (*Keegan* v *Ireland* (1994) 18 EHRR 342). Other violations have resulted from denials of parental access to a child in care (*Johansen* v *Norway* (1996) 26 EHRR 33; *Glaser* v *United Kingdom*, 19 September 2000, Hudoc) and by an authority's failure to consult the natural parents when making decisions affecting the well-being of a child also in care (*W* v *United Kingdom* (1983) 10 EHRR 29).

If family life has been disrupted by a sentence of imprisonment the state is under an obligation to seek to maintain the prisoner's family ties although it is unlikely that this gives the prisoner any right to be incarcerated in the prison nearest to his family's place of abode (*McCotter* v *United Kingdom* (1993) 15 EHRR CD 98).

Family life may also be affected prejudicially by deportation. Hence it was a breach of Art 8 for the Dutch government to deport an alien male after his marriage to a person with the right of abode in Holland had come to an end. In particular, this severed his links with his son in circumstances where the deportee had committed no offence and posed no obvious threat to any of the legitimate interests for which, according to Art 8(2), restrictions on family life may be imposed (*Clitz* v *Netherlands* (1988) 11 EHRR 360). Even where deportation is for a legitimate aim, e.g. prevention of disorder or crime, it may still be disproportionate to the aim's achievement if its effect is the potential destruction of a family (*Beldjoudi* v *France* (1992) 14 EHRR 801; breach of Art 8 to deport Algerian male married to a French female albeit he had a criminal record and had served over ten years in prison).

In a quite different context, an interesting extension to the rights of family life occurred in *Foxley* v *United Kingdom* (2001) 31 EHRR 25. Here, it was held to be a breach of Art 8 to withhold from a 'widowed' father a state benefit (i.e. widowed mother's allowance) which would have accrued to him had be been a widowed mother.

Home

The right to respect for an individual's home does not imply a right to a place of abode. Providing the individual has a home, however, it gives a right to peaceful enjoyment of the same free from unwarranted expulsion or eviction. No breach of Art 8 was committed, therefore, by refusing planning permission to a group of gypsies wishing to keep caravans on a piece of land for domestic purposes. The refusal was in accordance with planning legislation and for the legitimate aim of protecting the rights of others through preservation of the environment (*Buckley* v *United Kingdom* (1997) 23 EHRR 101; *Chapman* v *United Kingdom* [2001] 33 EHRR 18).

This aspect of Art 8 is clearly engaged by an unjustified entry into an individual's premises (see *McLeod* v *United Kingdom* (1999) 27 EHRR 493) or by the use of covert surveillance techniques other than in accordance with Art 8(2) (*Govell* v *United Kingdom*, 14 January 1998, Hudoc; *Khan* v *United Kingdom* (2001) 31 EHRR 45).

The right to peaceful enjoyment was at issue in two cases, one decided at Strasbourg and one domestically, both of which illustrated the positive environmental implications inherent in the Article.

Hatton v *United Kingdom* [2002] 34 EHRR 1, was concerned with the noise made by aeroplanes taking off and landing at Heathrow Airport during the night and the consequent sleep disturbance caused to nearby residents. It was held that, although the state had not actually caused the noise, it remained in breach of Art 8 in not ensuring that adequate research was carried out into the merits of the competing interests to enable a fair and proportionate balance to be drawn in terms of the amount of night-time use of the airport. In *Marcic* v *Thames Water Utilities Ltd* [2002] EWCA Civ 64, the breach of Art 8 was caused by the water authority's failure to act effectively in respect of regular and serious flooding at the claimant's home.

Correspondence

To the extent that secret surveillance activities involve interference with an individual's correspondence or electronic communications, this further element of Art 8 may also be affected. Breaches may result, therefore from telephone-tapping of domestic phone calls (*Malone* v *United Kingdom* (1985) 7 EHRR 14) and those made and received at the workplace (*Halford* v *United Kingdom* (1997) 24 EHRR 523).

Correspondence in the traditional sense, i.e. letters etc., is, of course, also protected. Breaches here have included interceptions of a bankrupt's mail pursuant to a court order redirecting this to a trustee in bankruptcy (Insolvency Act 1986, s 371) after the order had expired (*Foxley* v *United Kingdom*, 20 June 2000, Hudoc) and official interference with prisoners' correspondence where this was not based on any significant public interest justification (*Campbell* v *United Kingdom* (1993) 15 EHRR 137).

Other related breaches of Art 8 have included collecting personal information without consent (*Harman and Hewitt* v *United Kingdom* (1989) 14 EHRR 657) and the failure to destroy the fingerprints of a person no longer suspected of criminal activity (*McVeigh* v *United Kingdom* (1984) 25 DR 15).

Interference with privacy and family life

The state may not interfere with the rights in Art 8 except where any restriction imposed is 'in accordance with the law and is necessary in a democratic society in the interests of national security, public safety or the economic well-being of the country, for the prevention of disorder or crime, for the protection of health or morals, or for the protection of the rights and freedoms of others'.

As explained above, to be 'in accordance with the law' a restriction must be founded on and regulated by clearly expressed and accessible legal rules. Mere administrative guidelines are not enough (*Malone* v *United Kingdom* (above), authority and criteria for telephone-tapping Home Office guidelines only; *Khan* v *United Kingdom* (above), similarly for use of covert listening devices).

In order to be 'necessary' a restraint must relate to a 'pressing social need' and be proportionate to the aims pursued (*Olsson* v *Sweden* (1989) 11 EHRR 259). In *Dudgeon* v *United Kingdom* (above) it was held that interference with private life and privacy could be justified only for 'particularly serious reasons'. Such reasons were found to exist in *Klass* v *Federal Republic of Germany* (1980) 2 EHRR 214, where the tapping of telephones was done in the interests of counter-terrorism operations. Also in *Leander* v *Sweden* (1981) 9 EHRR 443, the national security interest was held to be sufficient to justify the collection of information and the keeping of secret police files on candidates for sensitive postings within the armed services.

To be proportionate the restriction should be no more than is necessary to deal effectively with the issue in question. Entry into private premises to prevent a breach of the peace was, therefore, not 'necessary' in this sense where the apprehended breach was not imminent (*McLeod* v *United Kingdom* (above)).

Freedom of religion (Art 9)

Each individual has the right to freedom of thought, conscience and religion, alone or in community with others, in private or in public and the right to manifest that religion or belief in worship, teaching, practice and observance (Art 9(1)). The state is under a positive duty to ensure that the holders of a particular belief can enjoy it safe from interference, impediment or discrimination (*Otto Preminger Institut* v *Austria* (1994) 19 EHRR 34). This does not extend, however, to guaranteeing a right of absence from employment on particular religious holy days or days of worship (*X* v *United Kingdom* (1981) 22 DR 27). The right protects both religious and non-religious beliefs.

> It is in its religious dimensions, one of the most vital elements that go to make up the identity of believers and their conception of life, but it is also a precious asset for atheists, agnostics, sceptics and the unconcerned (*Kokkinakis* v *Greece* (1994) 17 EHRR 397).

In *Arrowsmith* v *United Kingdom* (1978) 19 DR 5, the Commission of Human Rights felt that the Article extended to pacificism but did not accept that this gave the applicant the right to attempt to subvert others from their legal and military duty (the applicant had been convicted under the Incitement to Disaffection Act 1934 after she had distributed leaflets at an army barracks urging soldiers not to serve in Northern Ireland).

The state is not entitled to prevent the practice of a religion or other belief, nor must it attempt to enforce the same on those within its jurisdiction (*Angelini* v *Sweden* (1986) 51 DR 41). The Article is, therefore, a protection against state discrimination or indoctrination, whether for religious or atheistic purposes.

While the Article seeks to protect the individual's right of belief, it does not preclude the existence of laws which have been influenced by the state's dominant religion. Hence the now repealed prohibition of divorce in the Irish Constitution did not offend the Convention (*Johnston* v *Ireland* (1987) 9 EHRR 203).

Breaches of Art 9 have been committed by the imposition of criminal penalties on evangelical Christian sects in respect of their proselytising activities (*Kokkinakis* v *Greece*, 25 May 1993, Hudoc); by dismissal from military service due to sympathies with Muslim fundamentalists (*Kalac* v *Turkey* (1999) 27 EHRR 552); by requiring incoming members of a national legislative assembly to take a religious oath of allegiance (*Buscarini* v *St Marino* (2000) 30 EHRR 208); and by state refusal to recognise and allow a church to practise its faith where this posed no realistic danger to the public interest (*Church of Bessarabia* v *Moldova*, 13 December 2001, Hudoc).

Interference with the freedom of thought and religion

The first element of Art 9(1), the right to freedom of thought, conscience and religion, is an absolute right and is not subject to the types of restrictions permitted by Art 9(2). Article 9(2) applies to the right to manifest one's religion or belief only. Restrictions may be imposed such as are 'prescribed by law and are necessary in a democratic society in the interests of public safety, for the protection of public order, health or morals, or for the protection of the rights and freedoms of others'.

Interference with the right to manifest one's religion or beliefs which have fallen within that permitted by Art 9(2) have included requiring conscientious objectors to undertake alternative public duties extending beyond the standard period of compulsory military service (*Autio* v *Finland* (1991) 72 DR 245: necessary for the protection of public safety) and refusal to grant religious exemptions from legislation requiring the wearing of crash-helmets by motorcyclists (*X* v *United Kingdom* (1978) 14 DR 243: necessary in the interests of public safety).

Freedom of expression (Art 10)

This includes the freedom 'to hold opinions and to receive and impart information and ideas without interference by public authority and regardless of frontiers'. The jurisprudence of the Convention recognises this as one of the most important freedoms protected thereby – particularly so because it underpins and is essential for the realisation of many of the Convention's other guarantees. Feldman, *Civil Liberties and Human Rights in England and Wales* (1993) gives four principal reasons for the special position of this right:

(a)   it is a 'significant instrument of freedom of conscience and self-fulfilment';
(b)   it enables peoples 'to contribute to debates about social and moral issues';
(c)   it allows the 'political discourse which is necessary in any country which aspires to democracy';
(d)   it 'facilitates artistic and scholastic endeavour of all sorts'.

It is also clear that the freedom of expression is at constant and considerable risk of political interference. This is because those who pursue power may, having achieved it, find difficulty in resisting the temptation to use it against critics and opponents.

The Article, in essence, contains two related but distinct rights. These are the rights to impart and disseminate information and the right to receive it. Article 10 does not create a general right of freedom of, and access to, information albeit that this may relate to an individual or to a matter of public concern (*Guerra v Italy*, above). It does, however, prohibit a government from restricting the flow of information to a person from those willing to impart it (*Open Door Counselling and Dublin Well Woman Clinic v Ireland* (1992) 15 EHRR 244; breach by court injunction prohibiting dissemination of information concerning access to abortion).

The freedom extends to the spoken word and to radio and television broadcasting, pictures, images, print, films, plays, works of art and to computer information systems. It also implies the negative freedom not to speak (*Goodwin v United Kingdom* (1996) 20 EHRR 123).

While the Article would appear to be directed principally at the activities of the state, it would also appear to contain an obligation requiring the state to provide conditions in which the individual may exercise the right free from oppressive interference by others, e.g. groups opposed to the view in issue (*Plattform 'Ärtze für das Leben' v Austria* (above).

The protection of the Article extends to that which shocks, offends or which is regarded as distasteful as well as that which may be received with equanimity (*Sunday Times v United Kingdom* (1979) 2 EHRR 245). It is unlikely, however, that it protects that which is racist in content (*Glimmerveen and Hagenbeck v Netherlands* (1979) 18 DR 187), or which is openly sympathetic to terrorism activities (*Purcell v Ireland* (1991) 70 DR 262). The principle is also well established that no breach is committed by the public espousal of controversial views at a demonstration or protest meeting albeit that such views may be profoundly disturbing to others (*Plattform Ärtze* (above); *Steel v United Kingdom* (above)). The Convention does not seek to protect, however, that which is merely abusive and which does not contribute in any meaningful way to the open discussion of matters of public concern or legitimate interest (*Janowski v Poland* (2000) 29 EHRR 75). It follows that the positive duty on the state to guarantee freedom of expression obliges it to give protection to those elements of the media which may be critical of, or even ideologically opposed to, the government itself (*Ozgur v Turkey*, 16 March 2000, Hudoc).

Although the court has, on occasions, stressed that it does not attribute greater or lesser importance to freedom of speech in particular contexts (*Muller v Switzerland* (1988) 13 EHRR 212), the case law does suggest a recognition of the democratic

advantages in allowing a considerable degree of latitude to the press and media generally in relation to matters of public interest and the activities of those in political and
public life. Article 10 was breached, therefore, by a finding of criminal defamation
against the editor of a magazine after the publication of an article attributing neo-nazi
views to a prominent politician (*Oberschlick v Austria* (1991) 19 EHRR 389). The
court was clearly of the opinion that those engaged in the hurley burley of political
life must expect to be subjected to a more rigorous degree of criticism than is appropriate in comment on the activities and integrity of private citizens.

> The limits of acceptable criticism are accordingly wider in regard to the politician acting in
> his public capacity than in relation to a private individual. The former inevitably and
> knowingly lays himself open to close scrutiny of his every word and deed by both journal-
> ists and the public at large and he must display a greater degree of tolerance, especially
> when he himself makes statements that are susceptible to criticism. A politician is certainly
> entitled to have his reputation protected even when he is not acting in his private capacity,
> but the requirements of that protection have to be weighed against the interests of open
> discussion of political issues.

Other cases in which judicial restrictions on material critical of those in public life
were held to offend Art 10 would include *Krone Verlag GmbH v Austria*, 26
February 2002, Hudoc; and *Feldek v Slovakia*, 12 August 2001, Hudoc. In the latter
case, a breach of Art 10 was committed by a court's decision that it was defamatory
to refer to a politician's 'fascist past'.

Judicial sanctions for defamation were also found to violate Art 10 following allegations in a Norwegian newspaper of the use of cruel and illegal methods by some of
those engaged in seal hunting. On this occasion the court's view was that the private
interest in the protection of reputations was 'outweighed by the vital public interest' in
ensuring an informed public debate over a matter of local and national as well as international interest (*Bladet Tromso v Norway* (1999) 29 EHRR 125). The court added,
however, that journalistic freedom in relation to matters of public concern generally
was 'subject to the provison that they are acting in good faith in order to provide
accurate and reliable information in accordance with the ethics of journalism'.

One of the most well-known cases in which the law of the United Kingdom was
measured against the requirements of Art 10 was *Sunday Times v United Kingdom*
(1979) 2 EHRR 245. The case concerned a series of articles which the newspaper
wished to publish about the drug thalidomide. This had been prescribed for pregnant
mothers and had resulted in numbers of children being born with various degrees of
deformity. A writ had been issued alleging negligence against Distillers Ltd, the
company responsible for manufacturing the drug. The proceedings had, however, been
dormant for some time while the parties negotiated a possible settlement. This
notwithstanding, an injunction was granted to prevent the *Sunday Times* articles being
published. The court felt that the information contained therein could be contemptuous
in that it might prejudice the trial of the action if and when it took place.

The view of the Court of Human Rights was that the English law of contempt did
not achieve an acceptable balance between the freedom of expression and the proper
administration of justice and was weighted too heavily in favour of the latter. This
was so because it prevented the publication of information concerning an issue of

public concern once a writ had been issued albeit that, in the particular circumstances, it was unlikely that the matter would come to trial for some considerable time, if at all.

This decision resulted in the enactment of the Contempt of Court Act 1981. The Act permits the publication of material relating to legal proceedings up and until the time those proceedings have become 'active', viz. when the case has been set down for a hearing.

English law was also found to be incompatible with Art 10 in *Tolstoy Miloslavsky v United Kingdom* (1995) 20 EHRR 442. The applicant complained about an award of damages of £1.5 million which had been made against him by a jury in a libel action. The Court of Human Rights felt this to be excessive and not proportionate to the damage suffered by the person who had been defamed. It was also of opinion that the rule in English law which restricted judicial interference with such awards to circumstances where the jury's decision could be said to be capricious, unconscionable or irrational prevented appellate courts from ensuring that damages were reasonably commensurate with the loss which they were designed to compensate.

Interference with the freedom of expression

As with the preceding two Articles, Art 10 may be departed from for a variety of public concerns. These include national security, territorial integrity, public safety, the prevention of disorder or crime, the protection of health or morals, the reputation or rights of others, the impartiality of the judiciary and the safeguarding of information received in confidence (Art 10(2)). Any interference must be proportionate to the aim pursued and 'be prescribed by law'. In *Prager and Oberschlick v Austria* (1996) 21 EHRR 1, it was held that law which restricted criticism of the judiciary did not amount to a breach of the right to freedom of expression. It was necessary in a democratic society to maintain confidence in the judicial system. Reasonable restrictions proportionate to this objective were, therefore, consistent with the public interest exceptions in Art 10(2).

It is clear that the Court of Human Rights will only accept interference with the freedom of press where, in the circumstances, the needs of a competing public interest appear to be particularly pressing. Thus, in *Goodwin v United Kingdom* (1996) 22 EHRR 123, a court order requiring a journalist to reveal his sources, in order to prevent further disclosures of confidential information concerning a company's financial difficulties, was found to be incompatible with Art 10. The journalist was already subject to an interim injunction in respect of the publication of information believed to have been extracted from a stolen copy of the company's business plan. This, it was felt, was sufficient to protect the legitimate interests of the company concerned. The further order relating to the production of sources amounted, therefore, to an unnecessary and disproportionate response to the needs of the situation.

Other disproportionate interferences with the right have been committed by the total prohibition of comment on matters pending before the courts (not 'necessary' for maintaining the authority and impartiality of the judiciary (*Worm v Austria*

(1998) 25 EHRR 454)); refusing to lift interlocutory injunctions restraining the publication of information relating to the security services after such information had become otherwise widely available (not 'necessary' in the interests of national security (*Observer and Guardian Newspapers v United Kingdom* (1991) 14 EHRR 153)); and the arrest and detention of demonstrators not using or provoking violence (not 'necessary' for the prevention of disorder (*Steel v United Kingdom*, above)).

Restrictions held to be compatible with Art 10(2) as proportionate responses in the circumstances to legitimate public concerns have included prohibiting children's literature due to its sexual content ('necessary' for the protection of morals (*Handyside v United Kingdom*, above)) and the seizure of an allegedly blasphemous film to prevent its exhibition in a predominantly Roman Catholic community ('necessary' for the protection of rights of others (*Otto Preminger Institut v Austria*, above)).

Freedom of assembly and association (Art 11)

Article 11 protects the right of the individual to organise and meet peacefully with others for the propagation of ideas and the furtherance of political, social, cultural or economic interests. It expressly guarantees the right to join a trade union.

Freedom of assembly

The individual is given the right to meet with others in public or in private and to engage in peaceful marches and demonstrations. The right extends to peaceful assemblies only. It does not apply to 'a demonstration where the organisers and participants have violent intentions which result in public disorder' (*G v Federal Republic of Germany* (1989) 60 DR 256). The danger that an otherwise peaceful demonstration may meet with opposition is not, therefore, of itself, a sufficient reason for imposing restrictions or refusing to allow it to proceed (*Christians Against Fascism and Racism v United Kingdom* (1980) 21 DR 138). If it were, the freedom could be completely negated by the aggressive tactics of those prepared to take direct action to obstruct the promotion of causes to which they were opposed. In these circumstances, therefore, the state is under a positive obligation to do that which is reasonable to ensure that the right to assemble peacefully can be exercised free from disruption and intimidation (*Plattform Ärtze* (above)).

It is unlikely that Art 11(1) guarantees the freedom to assemble for purely social purposes. No breach was committed, therefore, by the owners of a shopping centre who, after a series of incidents of vandalism, excluded a group of young adult males from the centre's common areas. According to the European Commission on Human Rights there was no indication in existing European human rights case law 'that freedom of assembly is intended to guarantee a right...to assemble for purely social purposes anywhere one wishes' (*Anderson v United Kingdom*, 27 October 1997, Hudoc).

An assembly which is peaceful but not lawful, e.g. is trespassory, would appear to fall within the protective compass of the right with the result that any interference must be in accordance with the criteria prescribed in Art 11(2), i.e. be prescribed by law and be proportionate to the securing of a legitimate aim (*G* v *Federal Republic of Germany* (above)).

State legislation requiring a grant of permission before an assembly may be held does not constitute a violation of the right providing again the discretion is exercised in accordance with the requirements of Art 11(2) (*Rassemblement Jurasien Unité* (1978) 17 DR 93). The ultimate state power is, of course, that which could be used to prevent an assembly from taking place at all, thus extinguishing the right entirely for those affected. Such drastic action may be justified, therefore, only if its object, e.g. the prevention of disorder, cannot be achieved by other means (*Christians Against Racism and Fascism* (above)). The banning of a march may also be legitimate, albeit that no immediate violence may result from it, if this is done in the overall context of seeking to diffuse a politically tense or volatile situation (*Milan Rai* v *United Kingdom*, 6 April 1995, Hudoc).

An assembly should not be banned merely because it is feared that it may be used to express controversial views unless, of course, it can be shown that this could lead to disorder or other undue damage to a legitimate public interest (*Stankov* v *Bulgaria*, 2 October 2001, Hudoc).

Although the restrictions on the right of assembly may often be imposed prior to or during the march or demonstration concerned, Art 11 may also be infringed by resort to post-demonstration penalties or sanctions. In *Ezelin* v *France* (1991) 14 EHRR 362, the applicant, a French lawyer, suffered a violation of his Art 11 rights when he was subjected to the disciplinary processes of the French legal profession after participating in a public protest against the imprisonment of members of the Guadeloupe independence movement.

In recent years, as already explained, police regulation of public protest in the United Kingdom by use of the ancient common law power to prevent breaches of the peace has been referred to the Court of Human Rights on a number of occasions. The overall result of these applications appears to be that although the meaning of the breach of the peace power is now sufficiently well defined in case law to be 'according to law', this level of certainty and legitimacy does not extend to the related judicial power to bind over persons to keep the peace and to be of good behaviour (*Steel* v *United Kingdom* (above); *Hashman* v *Harrup* (above)).

Freedom of association

This element of the Article guarantees the right of the individual to form and join organisations for the purpose of advancing a particular cause or interest. In *Vogt* v *Germany* (1996) 2 EHRR 205, it was applied to the dismissal of a teacher because she was a member of the Communist party. The individual is given a degree of choice in terms of whether he/she joins or refuses to join an interest group or other collective entity. The Article does not guarantee the right to membership of any organisation of a person's choosing nor does it contain a right not to be expelled from the same. In the case of trade union membership, however, it has been suggested that expulsion might be contrary to Art 11 if it was not done 'in accordance with union rules or where the results were wholly arbitrary or where the consequences of exclusion...resulted in exceptional hardship such as job loss because of a closed shop' (*Cheall v United Kingdom* (1985) 42 DR 178).

Closed shop agreements were considered in *Young, James and Webster v United Kingdom* (1982) 4 EHRR 38. Such agreements were prohibited if they struck 'at the very substance of the freedom guaranteed by Article 11' as would be the case if they required the dismissal of persons already in employment. The substance of Art 11 was found to have been infringed in *Sigurjonssen v Iceland* (1993) 16 EHRR 462. The offending provision was a legal requirement that licensed taxi-drivers be members of a particular drivers' association. Persons who felt unable to join would not be given a licence and would thus be denied the opportunity to earn a living as a taxi-driver.

The positive duty on the state to ensure that persons are able to enjoy the right and protection offered by Art 11 was in issue in *Wilson v United Kingdom* (2002) *Times*, 5 July. The duty was not fulfilled, the court found, in circumstances, as in the United Kingdom, where it was possible for an employer to offer employees financial incentives to give up trade union membership.

Public bodies and organisations are not regarded as 'associations' for the purposes of Art 11(1). Hence, no right to membership or to participate in their activities is given. The Article is not infringed, therefore, by rules requiring compulsory membership of professional regulatory bodies providing these qualify as 'public bodies' according to the applicable legal criteria (*Le Compte, Van Leuven and De Meyere v Belgium* (1981) 4 EHRR 1).

Interference with the right of assembly and association (Art 11(2))

Interference with the rights in Art 11 is permitted for reasons of national security, public order, the prevention of crime, the protection of health, morals or for the protection of the rights and freedoms of others (Art 11(2)). The rights may also be restricted in terms of the extent to which they may be relied upon by members of the armed forces, the police and government employees (*ibid.*). In *Council of Civil Service Unions v United Kingdom* (1988) 10 EHRR 269, the European Commission considered the extent to which the government could invoke Art 11(2) to interfere with the right of its employees to enjoy trade union membership. The view was that the Prime Minister's order excluding trade union members from employment at the General Communications Headquarters at Cheltenham fell within the permitted restrictions. This was so because the institution (GCHQ) dealt with highly sensitive information having to do with national security and which could be related to the activities of the police and armed forces.

As with the Convention's other qualified rights, any such interference must be 'prescribed by law' and 'necessary in a democratic society'. These requirements were not breached by an order preventing Druids from holding a service at Stonehenge to celebrate the summer solstice (*Pendragon v United Kingdom*, 19 October 1998, Hudoc). The order was made under the Public Order Act 1986, s 14A (power to ban trespassory assemblies) which was phrased with sufficient precision and clarity to be 'prescribed by law'. The Commission was also satisfied that the action was 'necessary in a democratic society', as proportionate to the legitimate aim of preventing disorder 'as there had been considerable disorder at Stonehenge in previous years and more recently'. Other factors noted by the Commission were that the ban was limited to four days only, did not apply to gatherings of twenty or fewer and did not prevent the applicants from conducting their service somewhere else.

Right to marry and found a family (Art 12)

Marriage

The Article confers the right on 'men and women of marriageable age'. It is generally assumed that the guarantee was originally intended to protect marriage between heterosexual partners. The Article was infringed in *F v Switzerland* (1988) 10 EHRR 411, where a Swiss court ordered that a person who had been solely responsible for the breakdown of his first marriage should not marry again for three years. The European Commission has also expressed the view that Art 12 gives the right to marry to persons in prison (*Howes v United Kingdom* (1979) 24 DR 5; *Draper v United Kingdom* (1980) 24 DR 72). Following these decisions the right was recognised in the United Kingdom by the Marriage Act 1983.

The right to marry has been held not to include any implicit right to divorce (*Johnston v Ireland* (1987) 9 EHRR 56). It has also been held not to apply to transsexuals (*Rees v United Kingdom*, above; *Cossey v United Kingdom*, above). This interpretation appears to be based on the assumption that marriage as defined by the Convention exists for the purpose of procreation. By the same reasoning, therefore, it would appear that the right does not extend to homosexuals (*W v United Kingdom* (1989) 63 DR 34).

Founding a family

This limb of the Article precludes compulsory but not voluntary sterilisation or abortion. The right to family life would also appear to be incompatible with the imposition of excessive restrictions on the opportunity available for adoption. It is unlikely that Art 12 imposes any obligations on the state in terms of providing the social and economic conditions which could be said to reinforce the stability of marriage.

The Protocols

These represent further agreements between the contracting states which have supplemented the rights originally guaranteed. The protocols seek to require or guarantee:

* the right to peaceful enjoyment of property (Protocol 1, Art 1);
* the right to education in conformity with religious or philosophical convictions (Protocol 1, Art 2);
* the right to free elections at reasonable intervals by secret ballot (Protocol 1, Art 3);

- the right not to be imprisoned for breach of a contractual obligation (Protocol 4, Art 1);
- freedom of movement and residence (Protocol 4, Art 2);
- the right not to be expelled or refused entry to the contracting state of which an individual is a citizen (Protocol 4, Art 3);
- the prohibition of the collective expulsions of aliens and stateless persons (Protocol 4, Art 4);
- the abolition of the death penalty (Protocol 6);
- the right of aliens not to be expelled from a contracting state except in accordance with legal procedures which require the giving of reasons accompanied by the right to have the decision reviewed and to be legally represented at such review (Protocol 7, Art 1);
- the right to a review of criminal convictions and sentences (Protocol 7, Art 2);
- the right to compensation for miscarriages of justice (Protocol 7, Art 3);
- the right not to be tried twice for the same offence (Protocol 7, Art 4);
- the right of spouses to equal legal treatment (Protocol 7, Art 5).

To date the United Kingdom is not a party to Protocols 4, 6 or 7. The Human Rights Act 1998 gives legal effect in the United Kingdom to the right to peaceful enjoyment of property (Protocol 1, Art 1), the right to education (Protocol 1, Art 2), and the abolition of the death penalty (Protocol 6).

The right to property (Protocol 1, Art 1)

The right is conferred on both natural and legal persons. A person has the right to 'peaceful enjoyment of his possessions' and should not be deprived of these 'except in the public interest and subject to the conditions provided for by law and by the general principles of international law'. The Convention recognises, however, that the state has the right 'to enforce such laws as it deems necessary to control the use of property in accordance with the general interest or to secure the payment of taxes or other contributions or penalties'.

The case law to date demonstrates a preference for the term 'possessions' to be given a liberal interpretation thus allowing the protocol an extensive sphere of application. Accordingly its protection covers both tangible and intangible assets and has been held to encompass, *inter alia*, contractual rights, shares, leases, licences, business goodwill, patents, debts, entitlements to rents and rights under contributory pensions.

The state's judgment as to what is in the public interest will be respected unless that judgment is 'manifestly without reasonable foundation' (*Handyside v United Kingdom* (above)). This is particularly so in social and economic matters where a wide margin of appreciation is allowed (*James v United Kingdom* (1986) 8 EHRR 123). In this case the aim of social justice in housing was accepted as a legitimate public interest for legislation permitting the compulsory transfer of ownership of property from one individual to another. Protocol 1, Art 1 was, therefore, no impediment to the implementation of the Leasehold Reform Act 1967 which allowed the tenants of residential properties in central London held on long leases to acquire the ownership of those properties notwithstanding the claims of the original lessors.

Social justice in housing and the need to prevent a large number of persons becoming homeless at the same time has also been accepted as a legitimate public interest for laws suspending tenant eviction orders (*Spadea v Italy* (1995) 21 EHRR 482) provided such suspensions were not continued for such long periods as effectively to deprive the landlord of his/her property (*Palumbo v Italy*, 4 September 1996, Hudoc).

An obvious public interest justifying proportionate interference with property rights is the investigation and prevention of crime. No breach of the protocol was committed, therefore, by the seizure and destruction of property found to be obscene under the Obscene Publications Act 1959, s 3 (*Handyside v United Kingdom* (above)).

Any interference with property or possessions must be 'provided for by law'. This imports the test of certainty as considered above. It was satisfied in *James v United Kingdom* (above), as the authority for the interference complained of was the Leasehold Reform Act 1967.

In order to prove a violation it must be shown that the state has interfered with the applicant's peaceful possession of his/her property or has deprived the applicant of his/her possessions or has subjected those possessions to some unacceptable degree of control (*Sporrong v Sweden* (1982) 5 EHRR 35).

Any act of interference should be proportionate to the aim pursued and must secure a fair balance between the competing public and private interests involved (*ibid.*). This balance was not achieved in the *Sporrong* case where the applicant's property was subjected to lengthy 'expropriation permits' and prohibitions on construction pending the redevelopment of the centre of Stockholm. No domestic procedure existed through which these restrictions could be challenged and their length of application possibly reduced. The result was that the applicant's property was effectively placed under planning 'blight' for the considerable period of years during which the restrictions applied.

Although the protocol does not give an express right to compensation for invasion of property rights, whether and to what extent compensation is paid is relevant to the question of the proportionality of the action in question. It is probable that the taking of property without compensation would satisfy the proportionality test only where this was done for the purposes of the most urgent and weighty of public interest needs:

> ...the taking of property without payment of an amount reasonably related to its value will normally constitute a disproportionate interference and a total lack of compensation can be considered justifiable...only in exceptional circumstances. Article 1 does not, however, guarantee a right to full compensation in all circumstances, since legitimate objectives of public interest may call for reimbursement of less than the full market value (*Holy Monasteries v Greece* (1994) 20 EHRR 1).

These principles were recognised and applied in *Lithgow v United Kingdom* (1986) 8 EHRR 239, where the court found no violation in the United Kingdom government's method of assessing compensation for the purposes of nationalising the aircraft and shipbuilding industries. The method was based on a valuation of individual share-holdings at the particular date prior to the decision to nationalise and not on the market value of the assets affected. It was permissible, the court said, in determining compensation, to take into account 'the nature of the property taken and the circumstances of the taking', i.e. the political and economic background for the state's actions.

> The standard of compensation for a whole industry may differ, therefore, from the standard required in other cases (*ibid.*).

The protocol concludes by preserving expressly the right of the state to resort to seizure and other measures against an individual's property in order to enforce liabilities for non-payment of taxes or 'other contributions and penalties', e.g. national insurance payments, judgment debts, etc. As a general rule state laws for these purposes will be accepted by the court unless they are devoid of reasonable foundation (*Gasus Dasier-und Fordertechnik GmbH v Netherlands* (1995) 20 EHRR 403).

The right to education (Protocol 1, Art 2)

The protocol is phrased in the negative and provides that no one 'shall be denied the right to education'. The state is also enjoined to 'respect the rights of parents to ensure such education and teaching in conformity with their own religious and philosophical convictions'.

The duty on the state, therefore, is not to finance and provide a universally available educational system, but to the extent that educational facilities are available, whether publicly or privately funded, to avoid restriction and regulation of them to a degree which undermines the substance of the right (*Belgium Linguistics Case* (1979–80) 1 EHRR 241). If state funded education is available, but the parents wish their child to be educated outside that system, no obligation lies on the state to finance their choice (*Family H v United Kingdom* (1984) 37 DR 10J). The protocol does not provide an absolute guarantee of access to the school of the parents' choosing (*X v United Kingdom*, Application 11644/8J, unreported) nor does it prevent the suspension and possible expulsion of a disruptive child if that is a proportionate response to the difficulties caused (*X v United Kingdom*, Application 13477/87, unreported).

The right is generally accepted as being concerned mainly with primary and secondary education. The state is permitted to restrict access to third level education to those with appropriate academic qualifications (*Patel v United Kingdom* (1980) 4 EHRR 256).

The need to show respect for the rights of parents requires the state to consider whether and to what extent those wishes may be accommodated. It is not enough that these are simply 'noted' or 'taken into account' (*Campbell and Cozens v United Kingdom* (1982) 4 EHRR 293). It was a breach of this requirement to suspend a pupil for almost a year because his parents disagreed with the school's policy towards corporal punishment. This made the pupil's access to education conditional on agreeing to accept the risk of that which was contrary to their philosophical convictions.

Including studies of religious, philosophical or ethical nature in a school's curriculum does not offend the requirement to respect parents' wishes providing the material is delivered in an objective fashion and is not employed for the purposes of indoctrination (*Kjeldsen, Busk Madsen and Pedersen* v *Denmark* (above)).

If a child is adopted, the rights conferred by the protocol pass from the natural to the adoptive parents (*X* v *United Kingdom* (1977) 11 DR 160). Where one parent is granted custody of a child, the other parent's Convention's education rights cease to exist (*X* v *Sweden* (1977) 12 DR 192).

That element of Protocol 1, Art 2 dealing with the wishes of parents is subject to a reservation by the United Kingdom to the effect that it is accepted 'only as far as is compatible with the provision of efficient instruction and training and the avoidance of unreasonable public expenditure'.

The right to free elections (Protocol 1, Art 3)

States which have signed the European Convention on Human Rights 'undertake to hold free elections at reasonable intervals by secret ballot under conditions which will ensure the free expression of the will of the people in the choice of legislation'. This confers an individual right of action as exercised in *Matthews* v *United Kingdom* (1999) 28 EHRR 361, where an EU citizen resident in Gibraltar challenged successfully his exclusion from the franchise for the European Parliament. The Court of Human Rights felt it was axiomatic that as Gibraltar was subject to EU law, EU citizens resident there should be able to participate in elections for the European Parliament.

Implicit in the obligation to hold free elections are the rights to vote and stand as a candidate in elections for national legislatures (*Mathieu-Mohin* v *Belgium* (1987) 10 EHRR 1), but not according to a particular electoral system (*Liberal Party* v *United Kingdom* (1980) 21 DR 211).

The state is not precluded from imposing conditions on candidature, e.g. requirements for nomination papers to be endorsed by a minimum number of signatures (*Association X, Y and Z* v *Federal Republic of Germany* (1986) 5 DR 90) or from excluding with good cause certain categories of persons from the electoral register, e.g. convicted prisoners (*X* v *Federal Republic of Germany* (1960) 3 YB 184).

Abolition of the death penalty (Protocol 6)

Protocol 1, Art 6 states that 'the death penalty shall be abolished' and that 'no person shall be condemned to such penalty or executed'. The requirement is, therefore, for the repeal of any legal provisions authorising judicial execution. It is not enough that the authority is available but is not used.

While phrased in the form of a prohibition, the protocol gives the individual the positive right not to be subjected to the ultimate sanction. The absolute nature of the prohibition is, however, limited to peacetime; Art 2 permitting provisions authorising the death penalty to be introduced in time of war.

The state may not derogue from or enter a reservation in respect of its obligations under Protocol 6.

In the United Kingdom use of the death penalty was suspended in 1959. The legal authority for it was removed by the Abolition of the Death Penalty Act 1965.

Collateral rights

The substantive rights and guarantees in Arts 2–12 and the subsequent protocols are underpinned by Arts 13 and 14. Article 13 provides that each contracting state must have systems or procedures in place through which these rights may be pursued by the individual. This should not be interpreted as meaning that national remedies must exist for enforcement of the guarantees contained in the Convention. It does require, however, that procedures should be available to allow arguments related to the Convention to be raised. In the context of the United Kingdom, judicial review on grounds of irrationality and abuse of discretion have been held to provide an effective remedy where executive power is exercised in ways which appear substantially at odds with the standards required by the Convention (*Soering v United Kingdom* (1989) 11 EHRR 439).

The European Court of Human Rights has, however, passed adverse comment on the reluctance of English courts to question executive decisions made in the alleged interests of national security. In *Chahal v United Kingdom* (1997) 23 EHRR 413, the applicant had been ordered to be deported from the United Kingdom for reasons of national security. Deportation decisions made on this ground were, at the time, not subject to a right of appeal to the Immigration Appeals Tribunal (Immigration Act 1971, s 15(3)). Nor did the applicant achieve any satisfaction from an application for judicial review, as the court felt unable to question the minister's reasons due to the national security implications (*R v Home Secretary, ex parte Chahal*, above). In effect, therefore, English law provided no competent procedure through which the applicant could pursue rights protected by the Convention.

The state is under an obligation to ensure that Convention rights are secured 'without discrimination on any ground such as sex, race, colour, language, religion, political or other opinion, national or social origin, association with a national minority, property, birth or other status' (Art 14). Thus the proscription of discrimination is limited to the rendering of the Convention's guarantees and is not, therefore, a discrete and exhaustive prohibition. It follows that Art 14 does not apply to government practice in relation to social and economic rights, e.g. access to welfare benefits, housing, etc. The Article was found to have been breached in *Abulaziz, Cabalos and Balkandali v United Kingdom* (1985) 7 EHRR 471. At the time the United Kingdom's immigration rules permitted the wives of resident non-national males to enter the country in order to live with their husbands. The same facility did not extend, however, to the husbands of resident non-national women. The Court felt that there had been no breach of Art 8 (the right to family life) as this did not give or confer a right to establish a home in a country of a couple's choosing. It was clear, however, that the immigration rules in issue gave greater protection to the family life of non-national men than that accorded to their female counterparts. The case illustrates that breach of one of the substantive guarantees in Arts 2–12 is not a prerequisite to a finding that a particular right has been recognised or observed in a way which manifests a degree of discrimination (*Inze* v *Austria* (1988) 10 EHRR 394).

Derogation in times of national emergency (Art 15)

Article 15 permits contracting states to take measures which interfere with the rights protected by the Convention 'in time of war or other public emergency threatening the life of the nation'. These measures should be no more than that which is 'strictly required by the exigencies of the situation'. The right of derogation does not apply to Arts 2 (except for death resulting from lawful acts of war), 3, 4 or 7. A state wishing to take advantage of this facility should inform the Secretary-General of the Council of Europe of the measures it has taken and the reasons for them. The fact that a derogation has been made does not prevent an individual petition in respect of the Article to which the derogation relates. It would be necessary, however, for the applicant to show that the derogation was not justified by the circumstances or that the action taken went beyond that which was necessary to deal with the danger to the public.

In 1988 the United Kingdom entered a derogation from the requirements of Art 5(3) (arrested or detained persons to be brought promptly before a judge) in respect of the special powers of arrest and detention in the Prevention of Terrorism Acts 1974–89. The European Commission later recognised the derogation as falling within the criteria laid down by Art 15 (*Brannigan and McBride* v *United Kingdom* (above)).

Reservations (Art 57)

Article 57 allows that at the time of signing the Convention or any of its protocols a contracting state may 'make a reservation in respect of any particular provision of the Convention to the extent that any particular law then in force in its territory is not in conformity with the provision'.

The United Kingdom took advantage of Art 57 when signing Protocol 1, Art 2 (right to education) by declaring 'in view of certain provisions in the Education Acts...the principle affirmed in the second sentence in Article 2 [requirement to respect the wishes of parents] is accepted by the United Kingdom only so far as it is compatible with the provision of efficient instruction and training, and the avoidance of unreasonable public expenditure'.

References

Feldman (1993) *Civil Liberties and Human Rights in England and Wales*, Oxford: Clarendon Press.

Fenwick (1998) *Civil Liberties* (2nd edn), London: Cavendish.

Harris, O'Boyle and Warbrick (1995) *Law of the European Convention on Human Rights*, London: Butterworths.

Stone (1997) *Textbook on Civil Liberties* (2nd edn), London: Blackstone.

Further reading

Jacobs and White (1996) *The European Convention on Human Rights* (2nd edn), London: Clarendon Press.

Janis, Kay and Bradley (1995) *European Human Rights Law: Text and Materials*, Oxford: Clarendon Press.

Marston and Ward (1997) *Cases and Commentary on Constitutional and Administrative Law* (4th edn), London: Pitman Publishing, Ch 8.

Chapter 19

THE HUMAN RIGHTS ACT 1998

FREEDOM VERSUS RIGHTS

Introduction

Prior to 1998, the British Constitution contained no positive statement of basic human rights similar to those found in the constitutional provisions of many other liberal democracies. According to the traditional domestic approach, the citizen was possessed of a range of 'freedoms' or civil liberties, the principal of these being the freedom of expression, association and assembly and of the person. In these contexts, and beyond certain minimal legal restrictions, the belief was that the individual should be free to do or say as he/she wished without fear of interference by officialdom or the forces of law and order. Freedom in this negative sense was founded on certain generally held assumptions concerning the proper distribution of power and liberty in the relationship between the state and the individual and on the contingent expectation that in a free society certain aspects of human conduct should be restricted only to the extent strictly necessary for the effective protection of certain essential public interests, viz. the prevention of crime and disorder; defence and national security; and the maintenance of public morality. In domestic terms, therefore, freedom was understood as a natural and residual attribute of citizenship which, for many, was so ingrained in the nation's political culture as to obviate the need for any express articulation of 'fundamental rights' or the need to protect the same through legislative entrenchment or other procedures.

The role of Parliament and the courts

Throughout the greater part of the twentieth century it was widely assumed that the maintenance of these individual freedoms could be safely entrusted to Parliament and the judiciary. Parliament, it was widely believed, with its representative credentials and history of resistance to the untrammelled expansion of executive power, could be relied upon to resist pressure from governments to enact legislation which violated unduly generally held expectations concerning the proper boundaries of executive authority.

Similar assumptions tended to pervade popular views and rhetoric concerning the role and responsibilities of the judiciary in its related tasks of interpreting Parliament's will and the development of the common law. Generations of judicial independence and the judiciary's oft-stated preference for effective legal control of executive discretion were, in many quarters, accepted as providing a sufficient structural and ideological basis for a sustained and reliable judicial policy of identifying and insisting upon a sacrosanct and irreducible minimum of individual freedoms which the judges would be vigilant to protect.

As the century progressed, however, developments within and external to the United Kingdom began to cast doubt on some of these old certainties and on the continuing viability of the traditional model for securing individual freedom in modern political circumstances.

In particular, the role of Parliament began to be questioned as increasingly effective party-political control of the House of Commons made it possible for governments to use compliant parliamentary majorities to support illiberal legislature provisions for short-term political gain. This led to the expressions of unease concerning the ability of Parliament in this political sense to defend the citizen's traditional freedoms against the cumulative effects of such incremental infringement and the apparently entirely piecemeal and *ad hoc* process of subjecting established freedoms to minor legislative 'modifications' in order to respond to what, at any particular time, was perceived to be a justified public need.

All too often this proved too tempting for governments to resist as it enabled those in power to assuage media and public criticism by being seen to have acted decisively to deal with the political or social issue of the moment. In the last quarter of the twentieth century legislation of this type encompassed a range of anti-terrorist provisions authorising extended periods of detention, restrictions on movement within the United Kingdom (exclusion orders) and stop and search without reasonable suspicion (Prevention of Terrorism Acts); measures increasing the powers of the police to detain and question suspects in 'ordinary' criminal investigations (Police and Criminal Evidence Act), to regulate the conduct of public protest (Public Order Acts) and to intercept communications (Interception of Communications Act 1985); and those effecting changes to criminal procedure including the reduction of the right to silence (Criminal Justice and Public Order Act 1994) and restriction of the accused's right of access to material collected by the prosecution in the course of formulating the case to be answered (Criminal Procedure and Investigations Act 1996).

For each measure of this type a rational justification could be advanced. Those not so concerned with the immediate politics of such matters began, however, to draw attention to the long-term consequences of such continuing one-off acts of political expediency and to the danger that, perhaps almost imperceptibly, the substance of civil liberties in the United Kingdom might be reduced to a level below that necessary for the maintenance of a genuinely free and democratic society.

Also, despite the confidence often reposed in the judiciary in these matters, it became increasingly apparent that while judges might usually attempt to interpret legislation in ways which minimised its impact on individual freedoms, they could not resist provisions enacted for the unambiguous purpose of increasing executive power to the cost of such freedoms. Hence, despite judicial assertions that certain 'fundamental values are part of the common law's priorities' (per Sedley J, *R v Home Secretary, ex parte McQuillan* [1995] 4 All ER 400), judges have long been powerless to defend these against the clear intent of the sovereign body.

Within the British Constitution, it has traditionally been assumed that every social value is constantly prey to the vicissitudes of political controversy; that no moral principles are beyond the reach of majorities; that no constituent concept enjoys protection from the outcome of parliamentary elections (Loveland, *Constitutional Law: A Critical Introduction*).

At the same time as concerns were being expressed about the domestic state of affairs in these matters, extensive liberal statements of human rights, often modelled or based directly on the International Declaration of Human Rights 1948 and the European Convention on Human Rights 1953, were becoming the norm in the constitutions of other European states, a trend which extended to those states in the eastern part of the continent just emerging from the Soviet era. Against this background, the rather narrow and negative conception of individual freedoms still pertaining in the United Kingdom appeared increasingly out-dated and inadequate particularly in terms of the lack of any developed jurisprudence in relation to such matters as rights to privacy, thought, conscience, religion and family life.

All of this had been part of the debate in English legal and political circles concerning the case for a Bill of Rights in the United Kingdom which had been going on for nearly three decades prior to the passing of the 1998 Act. The issue was placed firmly on the political agenda by the promotion of a series of private members' Bills seeking to give domestic effect to the European Convention and its protocols. The first of these was put before the House of Lords in 1977 (Lord Wade) and was followed by further similar Bills in the House of Commons in 1987 (Sir Edward Gardiner) and in the House of Lords again in 1994 and 1996 (Lord Lester of Herne Hill).

As the twentieth century drew to a close, and after nearly twenty uninterrupted years of Conservative administrations, the public mood in the United Kingdom appeared to be ready for change in a variety of contexts including matters relating to the constitution. In the run-up to the 1997 General Election the Labour party sought to take advantage of this by promising reform of the House of Lords, the creation of regional parliaments and, most significantly in the present context, the enactment of legislation to enable citizens of the UK to rely on the European Convention on Human Rights for the purpose of initiating and defending legal proceedings involving the state in domestic courts and tribunals.

Labour's resounding victory in the election of May 1997 is now a matter of political history. Having gained power with a massive parliamentary majority, legislation to give effect to the above manifesto proposals was duly enacted.

OBJECTIVES OF THE 1998 ACT

Enactment and constitutional implications

The Act received the Royal Assent on 9 November 1998. It came into effect in England and Wales on 2 October 2000. From that date the rights and freedoms guaranteed by the European Convention on Human Rights (ECHR) became directly enforceable in the courts of the United Kingdom to the extent that is compatible with primary legislation and the ultimate sovereignty of Parliament. The Act imposes a duty on all public bodies to act in accordance with Convention rights in all their doings and requires courts and tribunals to take into account the jurisprudence of both the European Court and

Commission on Human Rights where these touch on a case before them. It is also required that all legislation should be interpreted in accordance with the Convention in so far as this is possible.

The Act is a legislative instrument of great significance and has been described as the most important domestic legal development for a generation. For the first time in the history of English law, individuals were provided with a charter of positive human rights which the state is obliged to respect and observe. Some of these rights, particularly the rights to life, religion and privacy, had not hitherto enjoyed direct legal protection in the United Kingdom.

The Act inevitably enhances the role of the judiciary as guardian of individual rights and gives judges a more specific and firm legal basis on which to measure the correct balance of power and rights between individual and the state. Some critical voices have argued that, because of the rather general terms in which the rights in the European Convention are expressed, the Act opens the way for increased judicial law-making in the most sensitive of contexts with minimal political and democratic supervision. Whatever the truth of these sentiments, they would appear to understate, whether consciously or not, the role which English judges have already played in the formation of English law, particularly the common law, where, in the absence of immediate legislative parameters, the judges' perceptions of underlying social and moral values have long exercised a powerful influence.

In the English legal system, the Act's effects will be felt far beyond the narrow confines of those matters traditionally regarded as falling within the compass of public law. The Human Rights Act will impact on all legal disciplines where the interpretation and application of the rules therein may have any direct or indirect consequences for any of the rights guaranteed by the Convention.

Particular objectives

Amongst the many reasons advanced for the 1998 Act and the advantages to be gained from it, the following have been prominent:

- It will enable individuals to enforce and benefit from the protection of the European Convention in the United Kingdom's domestic courts rather than having to endure the added costs and inconvenience of taking proceedings in Strasbourg. Prior to the Act, the United Kingdom and the Irish Republic were the only two signatory states which did permit direct domestic enforcement. The White Paper which preceded the Human Rights Bill stated that the time had come 'to enable people to enforce their Convention Rights against the state in the British courts, rather than having to incur the delays and expense which are involved in taking a case to the European Human Rights Commission and Court...and which may altogether deter some people from pursuing their rights' (*Rights Brought Home: The Human Rights Bill*, Cmd 3782, 1997).
- The Act will respond to the complaint that, although the United Kingdom was found to be in breach of Convention rights in a significant number of serious and controversial cases, lack of effective redress available in domestic courts continued to force complainants to seek redress in Strasbourg.

- The retention and positive articulation of the individual's rights will supply the omissions of the negative concept of freedom hitherto recognised by English law.

  The traditional freedom of the individual under a written constitution to do himself that which is not prohibited by law gives no protection from misuse of power by the state, nor any protection from the acts of public bodies...incompatible with...human rights under the Convention (Lord Irvine LC, Hansard, HL, 3 November 1997, col 1228).

- Given the margin of appreciation permitted to states, domestic enforcement will enable judges in the United Kingdom to interpret the Convention in ways which reflect and complement British legal, cultural and social traditions. The Convention may no longer be perceived, therefore, as an alien system of jurisprudence devised and administered by those not entirely sensitive to the United Kingdom's circumstances and predilections.
- The Act will help to 'redress the dilution of individual rights by an over-centralising government that has taken place over the past two decades' (*Bringing Rights Home: Labour Party Consultation Paper*, December 1996).
- By insisting on greater human rights awareness in the public services, the Act will enhance the quality of decision-making at all levels of the administrative process.
- Enforcement of the European Convention on Human Rights will provide the legal basis for a modern, stable civic society in which the rights are responsibilities of both the individual and the state and are clearly defined and understood. Enhancing the legal standing and value of the individual in relation to the state increases the individual's stake in the body politic generally thereby underpinning a greater sense of social and political responsibility.

  By increasing the stake which citizens have in society through a stronger constitutional framework of civil and political rights, we also encourage them to better fulfil their responsibilities. This is an essential part of our strategy to establish a balanced relationship between rights and responsibilities (*Bringing Rights Home*, above).

PRINCIPAL PROVISIONS

Application of ECHR jurisprudence (s 2)

In deciding any matter to which the Convention relates, courts and tribunals in the United Kingdom 'must take into account' any relevant decisions of the European Court of Human Rights, the European Commission of Human Rights or the European Committee of Ministers (s 2(1)).

The obligation is, therefore, to take into account rather than to follow and apply. Hence the only decisions of the court which are binding in the United Kingdom are those to which the United Kingdom was a party. This does not, however, leave it entirely up to the United Kingdom's courts to interpret the meaning of the Convention as they think fit. From the supervisory perspective of the Strasbourg court, domestic courts may do so only to the extent compatible with the margin of appreciation permitted to contracting states. Beyond this the United Kingdom remains under an international legal obligation to abide by the Convention – an obligation which would be violated by domestic decisions, judicial or otherwise, significantly at odds with those decided at Strasbourg.

Interpretation of domestic legislation

Primary and secondary legislation, passed or to be passed, is to be interpreted in accordance with Convention rights 'in so far as it is possible to do so' (s 3(1)). Legislation, therefore, is to be given a purposive meaning but to an extent which falls short of that which would 'contort the meaning of words to produce implausible or incredible meanings' (the Home Secretary, Jack Straw, *Hansard* HC, 3 June 1998, col 422).

This will mean that the interpretative function of the domestic courts will be increasingly concerned, not with the intentions of Parliament, as has traditionally been the case, but with the meaning of the Convention – at least, that is, in those many cases to which the Convention will no doubt have some relevance. To this extent, therefore, reference to *Hansard* for purposes of statutory interpretations as permitted by *Pepper v Hart* (above) would appear to be otiose for the purpose of rendering statute to be Convention compatible.

No attempt is made to repeal or amend expressly or by necessary implication the provisions of previous primary legislation which are inconsistent with the Convention. Where the meaning of a statute is sufficiently clear that it is not possible for it to be given an interpretation which complies with the Convention, the court remains under a duty to abide by and to apply that clear intent. Nor does the 1998 Act attempt to diminish the legal competence of future parliaments to legislate in ways which may offend the Convention. It does, however, as will be explained below, introduce a procedural device into the legislative process which is designed to limit the tendency of governments to promote such incompatible legislation to circumstances where public needs would appear to be compulsive.

The extent of the interpretive obligation imposed by s 3 was considered by the House of Lords in *R v A* [2001] UKHL 25. Lord Steyn was of the opinion that to carry out 'the will of Parliament as reflected in section 3 it might sometimes be necessary to adopt an interpretation which linguistically may appear strained' and that 'the techniques to be used will not only involve the reading down of express language... but also the implication of provisions'. Lord Hope was similarly robust. His view was that where words in a statute were incapable of standing up to the test of compatibility, s 3 permitted a court to 'modify, alter or supplement' the words used to achieve the desired result.

Secondary legislation which is incompatible with the Convention may be regarded as invalid unless 'primary legislation prevents the removal of the incompatibility' (s 3(2)(c)), e.g. where the enabling Act ousts any judicial jurisdiction to quash any secondary legislation made under it.

Although the obligation to read and give effect to legislation in ways which are compatible with the Convention would appear to be directed primarily at courts and tribunals, it is not so expressly restricted and would appear to apply, therefore, to any person or body in whatever capacity charged with interpretation and application of the Act.

Declarations of incompatibility (ss 4 and 5)

When it is not possible to interpret a provision in primary legislation in accordance with the Convention, or where a piece of incompatible subordinate legislation cannot be quashed due to the wording of its enabling Act, a court at the level of the High Court and above may make a 'declaration of incompatibility' (s 4(1)–(4)). Such declaration will not affect the validity, continued operation or enforcement of the legislation in question.

On those occasions where the making of such declaration is contemplated by a court, notice should be given to the Crown in order that it may be able to exercise its entitlement to be joined in the proceedings (s 5). This will enable the Crown, usually through the Attorney-General, to plead the legislation's compatibility with the Convention should it so wish and, in any case, prepare itself for the possibility of a declaration of incompatibility being made.

While no power to make such declarations of incompatibility is given to lower courts and tribunals, it should be remembered that such bodies, in addition to being obliged to give effect to the Convention so far as domestic legislation permits, are subject to a further duty to give reasons for their decisions. Hence, where such inferior court or tribunal is unable to arrive at a Convention compatible decision because of the clear and contrary intent of a legislative provision applicable to the case before it, this will inevitably appear in, and form an important element of, its statement of reasons. In effect, therefore, where this occurs, the inferior body in question will be making what amounts to a statement of incompatibility albeit not of the type, or with the consequences, of those falling within the express terms of the Act.

Following the making of a declaration of incompatibility under s 4, and upon determination of any right of appeal, a minister of the Crown, to be determined presumably by the subject matter of the legislation, may 'by order make such amendment to the legislation as he considers necessary to remove the incompatibility' (s 10), Such remedial orders may also be made following a finding of incompatibility by the European Court of Human Rights in a case in which the United Kingdom is involved (s 10(1)(4)) or where, also for reasons of incompatibility, a provision of domestic legislation has been quashed by a domestic court and such remedial action is deemed to be a matter of urgency (s 10(4) and Sched 2(2)(b)).

Use of this 'fast-track' procedure should not be resorted to as a matter of course but should be confined to circumstances where there are compelling reasons for proceeding in this way (s 10(2)). In the normal course of events, therefore, remedial action should be by way of primary legislation.

Remedial orders made under s 10 must be laid before Parliament for 60 days and approved by resolutions of both Houses (Sched 2, para 2). The draft orders should be accompanied by an explanation of the incompatibility and the reasons for proceeding by way of remedial order rather than by primary legislation (Sched 2, para 3). An order may come into effect before being laid before Parliament 'because of the urgency of the matter' (Sched 2, para 2). The order should then be laid before Parliament in the normal way and will cease to have effect unless approved by resolutions of both Houses within 120 days (Sched 2, para 4).

The first declaration of incompatibility to be confirmed by the Court of Appeal occurred in *Wilson v First County Trust Ltd (No. 2)* [2001] 3 WLR 42. The case concerned the provision in the Consumer Credit Act 1974 that a contract for the loan of money was not enforceable by the money-lender unless made in a certain prescribed form and, in particular, included a term correctly stating the amount of credit involved (s 127(3)). The effect of the provision was to deny a money-lender access to the courts to enforce such agreement regardless of the circumstances including those in which the contract may have been made in good faith and have genuinely reflected the agreement made. The court accepted that the impugned provision could be said to have been enacted for a legitimate policy aim, i.e. protection against unscrupulous lenders, but felt that the blanket exclusion of all rights of action by money-lenders, other than in the circumstances permitted by s 127(3), and regardless of the facts of particular cases, was disproportionate to its achievement and incompatible, therefore, with the fair trial requirements in Art 6.

New legislation and statements of compatibility (s 19)

A minister introducing new legislation into either House of Parliament is required to make a statement of compatibility declaring that 'in his view' the bill is compatible with the Convention rights (s 19(1)(a)). Where any doubt exists, a statement should be made declaring that, although the minister is not able to make a statement of compatibility, it remains the government's intention to proceed with the Bill in question (s 19(1)(b)). Such statement should be in writing and should be submitted to whichever House is appropriate prior to the Bill's second reading (s 19(2)).

The purpose of this requirement is to ensure that a government wishing to legislate inconsistently with the Convention does so openly making it plain that this is its conscious objective, thereby subjecting its intention to debate in Parliament and to wider scrutiny and analysis by the media and public at large.

> Parliament would expect the Minister to explain his or her reasons during the normal course of the proceedings on the bill. This would ensure that the human rights implications are debated at the earliest opportunity (Cmd 3782, above, para 3.3).

Section 19 does not apply to private members' Bills or to secondary legislation. The government has said, however, that 'as a matter of good practice, a Minister inviting Parliament to approve a draft statutory instrument or statutory instrument subject to affirmative resolutions should volunteer his or her view concerning its compatibility with the Convention rights' and that 'such a statement should always be made regarding secondary legislation which amends primary legislation' (*The Human Rights Act 1998: Guidance for Departments*, 2nd edn, February 2000).

The duty on public authorities

The Act requires public authorities to act in accordance with Convention rights in the discharge of any of their functions or powers. The obligation is contained in the negative pronouncement that 'it is unlawful for a public authority to act in a way which is incompatible with a Convention right' (s 6(1)). The obligation does not apply where the authority could not have acted differently because of the requirements of relevant primary legislation (s 6(2)).

The definition of public authority preferred by the Act is wide and extends to:

(a) government bodies in the usually understood or 'obvious' sense, e.g. ministers, government departments, local and health authorities, the police, prison and immigration authorities and the armed forces but not Parliament itself or those executing its functions (s 6(3));
(b) courts and tribunals;
(c) any other person or body to the extent that it has been entrusted with public law functions, i.e. those which contribute to the fulfilment of government powers, functions or responsibilities.

The third element of the above definition is intended to put within the ambit of the Act's requirements those many private utilities and companies now responsible for areas of activity which were previously performed by nationalised industries or by government departments. Hence, for example, to the extent that organisations such as private security companies involved in the running of prisons have responsibilities for the provision of statute regulated public services, they must act in accordance with Convention rights.

Enforcing Convention rights (ss 7–9)

An individual may use a breach of a Convention right as a sword or a shield. Hence such breach may be relied upon to found an action for damages, as a ground for judicial review, or may be used by way of defence in any civil or criminal proceedings (s 7(1)). Subject to any pre-existing and more restrictive limitation period, proceedings against an authority should be commenced within twelve months of the act complained of or such longer period as the court may consider equitable having regard to all the circumstances (s 7(5)).

A person who relies on a breach of Convention rights in legal proceedings must be a 'victim' of the unlawful act for the purposes of the Convention in Art 34. The victim may be an individual, a company (*Pine Valley Developments* v *Ireland (A/222)* (1991) 14 EHRR 319), or the relative of a victim who is dead providing the complaint relates to the cause of death or the relative has sufficient legitimate moral or pecuniary interest in pursuing the deceased person's claim (*Sadik* v *Greece* (1997) 24 EHRR 323). A person who has not yet been affected by a breach of a Convention right may also be a victim within the meaning of Art 34 if there is a reasonable likelihood that they may be at imminent risk of such a breach, i.e. the application of Convention intrusive legislation (*Norris* v *Ireland* (1991) 13 EHRR 186).

Where the victim is a member of a trade union or interest group, such organisation has no standing to bring the proceedings on the person's behalf (*Greenpeace* v *Switzerland* (1996) 23 EHRR 116). It may bring a case, however, if a breach of a Convention right has affected its collective interests, e.g. its right to act on behalf of its members or to demonstrate in favour of its cause (*Plattform Ärtze*, above). Similarly, churches (*Church of Scientology* v *Sweden* (1980) 21 DR 109), professional associations (*Hodgson* v *United Kingdom* (1988) 10 EHRR 503) and political parties (*Liberal Party* v *United Kingdom* (1982) 4 EHRR 106) have all qualified as victims in respect of prejudicial government decisions.

The Convention's victim test would appear to be narrower than that developed domestically for the purposes of judicial review and would appear to exclude an applicant having no greater interest than any other member of the community. Such *actio popularis* have been permitted in review proceedings generally in respect of serious abuses of power or where no other means existed of testing the legality of the allegedly unlawful act (see above, pp. 329–30).

To enforce a Convention right a court or tribunal may grant any remedy within its jurisdiction as appears to be 'just and appropriate' (s 8(1)). Where the complaint relates to a judicial act, it should proceed by way of:

(a) a right of appeal;
(b) an application for judicial review;
(c) in any other forum as may be prescribed (s 9(1)).

In order to preserve the principle of judicial immunity, the right to damages for judicial acts done in good faith 'may not be awarded otherwise than to compensate a person to the extent required by Article 5(5) of the Convention', i.e. for arrest and detention in contravention of any of Art 5's provisions (s 9(3)). Judicial acts not in good faith and in breach of Convention rights will be actionable under s 8(1). Awards of damages under s 9(3) should be against the Crown and not the judicial officer responsible (s 9(4)).

RETROSPECTIVE EFFECT

Given the overall significance of the Act and the range of rights protected by it, it was perhaps not surprising that, in the immediate aftermath of its taking effect, attempts would be made to test the extent to which it might be applied retrospectively. The judicial response to this was that the Act could be used retrospectively only to the extent permitted by s 22(4), including, viz.:

(a) to defend proceedings brought by a public authority in respect of a decision made before 2 October 2000;
(b) to appeal against the fairness of a decision made in legal proceedings prior to 2 October 2000, albeit that the proceedings were initiated by a public authority (*R* v *Lambert* [2001] UKHL 37; *R* v *Kansal (No. 2)* [2001] UKHL 62);
(c) to defend an appeal by a public authority also in respect of a decision in legal proceedings made prior to 2 October 2000 (*R* v *Benjafield* [2001] 3 WLR 75).

Otherwise, it has been made clear, the Act may not be relied on to initiate a challenge either to:

(i) the legality of a decision made before 2 October 2000 (*Biggin Hill Airport Ltd* v *Bromley Borough Council* [2001] EWCA Civ 1089); or,
(ii) the implementation of such decision at some future date after 2 October 2000 particularly where this might inevitably involve impugning the legality of the decision itself (*R* v *Home Secretary, ex parte Mahmood* [2001] 1 WLR 840).

Note too the decision in *R v Director of Public Prosecutions, ex parte Kibilene* [2000] 2 AC 326, that the enactment of the 1998 Act did not raise any legitimate expectation that, during the period prior to its coming into effect, a person would not be charged with an offence under legislative provisions potentially inconsistent with Convention rights.

HUMAN RIGHTS AND JUDICIAL REVIEW

Amongst the more general developments pursuant to the Act taking effect, one of the most significant has been presaged in judicial dicta concerning the extent to which the existing English model of judicial review, based on the test of *Wednesbury* reasonableness, is sufficient to ensure adequate protection of Convention rights from the exercise of executive discretion.

In the last five years of the twentieth century, and pursuant to the Court of Appeal's decision in *R v Ministry of Defence, ex parte Smith* (above), judicial review had already developed to the point that where an executive decision affected a fundamental right recognised by the common law that decision was to be subjected to 'anxious scrutiny' and 'rigorous examination' (per Simon Brown LJ, *R v Home Secretary, ex parte Turgut* [2001] 1 All ER 719) sufficient to ensure that there existed considerations which might 'reasonably be accepted as amounting to a substantial objective justification for the interference' (*R v Home Secretary, ex parte Farooq* [2001] EWCA Civ 100). According to this approach, therefore, a court could interfere with a decision which did not represent a reasonable finding on the facts before the decision-maker; the demands of what amounted to 'substantial objective justification' being determined by reference to the extent to which fundamental rights were engaged and affected by the decision.

> Where the decision interfered with human rights, the court would require substantial justification for the interference in order to be satisfied that the response fell within the range of responses open to a reasonable decision-maker. The more substantial the interference, the more was required to justify it (Lord Bingham MR, *R v Home Secretary, ex parte Mahmood* (above)).

This clearly represented a modification of the *Wednesbury* test which, in its original formulation, permitted judicial interference only on the grounds of irrelevancy, improper purpose or irrationality in the extreme of a decision which defies the bounds of logic.

After 2 October 2000 judicial comment made it clear that a similarly rigorous standard of review would also be the basis for determining the test applicable to the review of decisions affecting rights protected directly by the Convention. In *ex parte Mahmood* (above) the Court of Appeal attempted to lay down some general guidelines for further developments 'in the search for a principled measure of scrutiny which will be loyal to the Convention rights, but also to the legitimate claims of democratic power' (per Laws LJ). These were:

(a) the role of courts was to remain supervisory with the result that judicial review of executive discretion in this context should be limited to circumstances 'where the decision fell outside the range of responses open to a reasonable decision-maker';

(b) that, as with fundamental rights protected by the common law, executive decisions engaging directly effective Convention rights should be subjected to the 'most anxious scrutiny';

(c) that the tests of legality to be applied were those articulated by the Convention itself, viz., in relation to the Convention's qualified rights, was the action taken necessary in a democratic society (i.e. proportionate to its objective) and was it taken in the interests of a legitimate aim.

> When anxiously scrutinising an executive decision that interferes with human rights the Court will ask the question, applying an objective test, whether the decision-maker could reasonably have concluded that the interference was necessary to the achievement of one or more of the legitimate aims recognised by the Convention. When considering the test of necessity in the relevant context, the court must take into account the European jurisprudence in accordance with section 2 of the 1998 Act (Lord Bingham MR).

Similarly, in *R (on the application of Samaroo)* v *Home Secretary* [2001] EWCA Civ 1139, the Court of Appeal emphasised that, in a factual sense, it was for the minister to decide what was the proportionate response to the problem to be addressed. The court's function was supervisory only and was fulfilled by asking whether the minister, acting within the discretionary area of judgment accorded to him, could have reasonably concluded that his action struck a fair balance between the relevant interests and was necessary to achieve one of the legitimate public interests pursued.

It has also been made clear that reviewing decisions in this context the courts should allow the decision-maker a 'margin of discretion', the extent of which should be determined principally by the status of the decision-maker and the context in which the particular decision was made. Some of the principles applicable and their rationale were set out by Laws LJ in *International Transport Roth GmbH and Others* v *Home Secretary* [2002] EWCA Civ 158. These were:

* greater deference should be paid to an Act of Parliament than to a decision of the executive;
* 'there is more scope for deference where the Convention itself requires a balance to be struck, much less to where the right is stated in terms which are unqualified';
* 'greater deference will be due to the democratic powers where the subject-matter in hand is peculiarly within their constitutional responsibility [e.g. defence, security, social and economic policy] and less when it lies peculiarly within the constitutional responsibility of the courts [e.g. maintenance of the rule of law, criminal justice]'.

This was not the same, it was made clear, as applying the Strasbourg concept of the margin of appreciation due to individual states in the exercise of their powers of government:

> We do not apply the Strasbourg margin of appreciation because we are a domestic not an international tribunal...Being a domestic tribunal, our judgments as to the deference owed to the democratic powers will reflect the culture and traditions of the British states.

The application of the concept was well illustrated by the Court of Appeal in *R (on the application of Farrakhan)* v *Home Secretary* [2002] EWCA Civ 606. The case concerned the Home Secretary's refusal to admit to the United Kingdom the black

Muslim leader, Louis Farrakhan. The decision was taken on the basis of the applicant's previously expressed racial views and the fear that if he was allowed to speak in the United Kingdom disorder could occur. The court was in no doubt that Art 10 was engaged by the Home Secretary's decision but felt that, for the following reasons, the decision lay within the margin of discretion which should be allowed to him without judicial interference:

* the Strasbourg Court attaches considerable weight to the right under international law of a state to control immigration into its territory;
* the decision was the personal decision of the minister;
* the minister was far better placed than the court to assess the consequences of the applicant's entrance to the UK;
* the minister was democratically answerable for his decision.

APPLICATION OF THE HUMAN RIGHTS ACT

At the time of writing many other cases had been decided domestically on the basis of the requirements of the 1998 Act. Some of the more significant are set out below and arranged by reference to the particular Convention right which was in issue.

Article 2: Right to life

The extent of this most basic right had already been considered in relation to such controversial and sensitive topics as the withdrawal of medical treatment and the separation of conjoined twins when this would inevitably lead to the death of one of them.

In *Re A (Children)* [2001] 2 WLR 480, the Court of Appeal ruled that Art 2 did not render unlawful an operation to separate conjoined twins when both could not be saved and where both would die if the operation was not performed. The court's view was that the requirement that 'no one should be deprived of his/her life intentionally' must be given its natural and ordinary meaning and construed in that way applied only to cases where the prohibited act was the cause of death. Hence, in the medical circumstances in issue, it did not impart any prohibition to an operation other than those already contained in the common law of necessity which were satisfied by the facts of the case.

The issue of withdrawal of treatment from a person in a permanent vegetative state was raised in *NHS Trust A v M; NHS Trust B v H* [2001] 1 All ER 801. This was also found not to be an intentional deprivation of life for the purposes of Art 2 since the real cause of the person's death would be the original illness or injury and not the decision to cease to administer treatment. The court was also satisfied that such decision would not violate the state's positive duty to protect life providing it was made in accordance with the law and, in the view of a respectable body of medical opinion, was in the patient's best interests.

This was not the same, however, as recognising a right to die at the time of one's own choosing. Article 3 protects the right to live with as much dignity as possible until life reaches its natural end. The position appears to be that it may be lawful, under certain circumstances, to allow a person to die but it is not lawful to kill regardless of the individual's wishes (*R (on the application of Pretty) v DPP* [2001] UKHL 61).

A further interesting and positive application of the right to life occurred in *Venables v Mirror Group Newspapers Ltd, Times*, 9 December 1998, where it was held that, in exceptional circumstances, the equitable doctrine of confidentiality could be ruled on to prohibit the publication of information relating to a person's whereabouts and identity where that person's life and safety would otherwise be at risk.

Article 5: Right to liberty and security of the person

In this context it has been held that due to the loss of liberty involved, Art 5 was held to be engaged by a secure accommodation order made under the Children Act 1989, s 25 (in *Re K (A Child)* [2001] 2 All ER 719). Such deprivation did not amount to an abuse of Convention rights, however, as it fell within Art 5(1)(d) which permits 'the detention of a minor by lawful order for the purpose of educational supervision'.

Article 5 was found not to be applicable, however, to an extension of a prisoner's sentence resulting from disciplinary proceedings for the use of drugs. Any other interpretation of the Convention, it was felt, would seriously prejudice the maintenance of a swift and effective disciplinary system and that the award of additional days for disciplinary purposes should be viewed as part of the original sentence imposed by the court (*R v Home Secretary, ex parte Greenfield*, Smith Bernal Casetrack, 22 February 2001).

Article 5 was used successfully in relation to the penal system in *R (Noorkoiv) v Home Secretary* [2002] EWCA Civ 770, where it was held that a delay of two months between the end of the tariff period of a prisoner's sentence and consideration by the Parole Board of his eligibility for relief was a breach of Art 5(4).

Successful use has also been made of Art 5 by persons refused political asylum. Here it has been held that detention of such persons pending deportation should not exceed that period within which it would have been reasonable to exercise the power (see *R (on the application of I) v Home Secretary* [2002] EWCA Civ 888: twelve months not a reasonable period).

Article 6: Right to a fair trial

To date it has been aspects of this Convention right, more than any other, which have been at issue in any of the proceedings which have been commenced under the terms of the 1998 Act.

A number of cases have dealt with some of the various and well-documented limitations on fair trial rights, including limitations placed on the presumption of innocence and the rule against self-incrimination which have been imposed by Parliament in recent years to deal with the threats caused by such matters as drink-driving and the increase in drug related offences.

The general approach taken by the domestic courts has been founded on the principle, often stated by the Strasbourg court, that the rights in Art 6 are not absolute and may be subjected to moderate and proportionate restrictions in pursuit of clear legitimate aims. Thus in relation to drink-driving legislation it has been held that the rule against self-incrimination is not violated by the requirement that the owner of a vehicle should provide information concerning the identity of its driver at the time of an alleged offence. A legislative obligation to answer a simple question, on pain of a moderate non-custodial penalty, particularly where this was not part of the process of interrogation and could not lead to incrimination for the original offence, could not be regarded, it was felt, as a disproportionate response to the public danger caused by drinking and driving (*Procurator Fiscal of Dunfermline* v *Brown* 2000 SCCR 314).

A similar approach was taken to the irrebuttable presumption in the road traffic legislation to the effect that the amount of alcohol in a person's blood at the time the specimen was taken was no less than that present at the time of the offences. Since the legislation existed to control the amount of alcohol consumed before a vehicle was driven the court could find no serious intrusion upon the presumption of innocence in an assumption which, being based on a test taken some time after the alleged offence had been committed, would often operate in the suspect's favour (*Parker* v *Director of Public Prosecutions, The Times*, 26 January 2001).

Questions relating to the presumption of innocence have also been raised in the context of anti-drugs legislation. In *HM Advocate* v *McIntosh* 2001 SCCR 191, the Privy Council considered the provision which allows a court to assume, in the absence of viable explanation, that any discrepancy between the income and assets of a person convicted of a drug-trafficking offence was the product of that offence empowering it to make a confiscation order. The approach taken by the court was that, as the making of such order did not involve any fresh accusation and followed from the original offence, it was something which should properly be regarded as a part of the sentencing process. Hence, although the proceedings were to be conducted in accordance with the requirements for determinations affecting civil rights, they did not import the elements of Art 6 relating to the trial of criminal charges including the presumption of innocence in Art 6(2).

Article 6 was also in issue in the controversial case involving the government's attempts to reduce the number of illegal immigrants gaining entry to the country by concealing themselves in lorries and containers (*International Transport Roth GmbH* v *Home Secretary* [2002] EWCA Civ 158). The government's attempt to deal with the problem was contained in the Immigration and Asylum Act 1999. This consisted of a legislative scheme whereby a carrier found to be carrying an illegal immigrant was liable to pay a fixed penalty of £2000 for each such individual. According to Lord Simon Brown LJ, the scheme was criminal in nature and offended Art 6(1), (2) and (3). This was because:

(a)   it imposed a reverse burden of proof, in that the carrier could only avoid such penalty by showing that he did not know or could not reasonably have been expected to know of the person's presence;
(b)   the lorry in question could be detained pending determination of these issues;
(c)   the penalty was fixed, therefore precluding the imposition of penalties proportionate to the facts.

The hallowed principle that the punishment must fit the crime is irreconcilable with the notion of a substantial fixed penalty...the fixed penalty cannot stand unless it can be judged proportionate in all cases having regard to the culpability involved.

Further significant developments have resulted from the application of Art 6 to the law relating to applications for judicial review. In particular this has led to the adoption of the Convention's jurisprudence concerning the test of bias. The test would appear to be similar to that of reasonable suspicion of bias, frequently referred to in domestic courts, at least until the decision in *R v Gough* (above), and is satisfied where this is a legitimate reason to fear lack of impartiality in the decision-maker (*Director of Fair Trading v Proprietary Association of Great Britain* [2001] 1 WLR 700).

Other findings of note in relation to domestic applications of Art 6 have included decisions that a fair trial may be prejudiced through gross incompetence by legal advisers (*R v Nangle, The Independent*, 8 November 2000); that although trial *in absentia* is generally compatible with Art 6, a defendant may waive his right to be present if, aware of the trial date, he knowingly and deliberately absents himself from the proceedings (*R v Hayward; R v Jones; R v Purvis* [2001] 3 WLR 125); and that, providing the balancing exercise between the private and public interests was carried out by a judge, no breach of Art 6 was committed where, in a criminal trial, the lawfulness of the defendant's arrest was established on the basis of material put to the judge in an *ex parte* public interest immunity application (*R v Smith* [2001] 1 WLR 1031).

Article 8: Right to respect for private and family life

Increased use of methods of electronic surveillance by police and security forces will inevitably be one of the issues with which domestic courts will have to grapple in the context of seeking a proper balance between the public and private interests in the application of Art 8. This and related issues were raised in *R v P* [2001] 2 All ER 58, where the House of Lords ruled that telephone intercepts effected in another state could be admitted as evidence in a criminal trial in the United Kingdom. The House made clear that the Interception of Communications Act 1985, s 9, which precluded the use of such evidence, applies only to intercept evidence obtained in the country (see new RIPA, s 17). It could not operate, therefore, to exclude such evidence obtained abroad. Whether the interception violated Art 8 was a matter to be determined by reference to the law of the state in which it was done and the compatibility of that law with Convention requirements. Hence the fact that the method of interception may have failed to comply with the requirements of English law did not mean it had not been effected according to law for Convention purposes. Where the method of interception fell short of Art 8's requirements this did not, of itself, render its content to be inadmissible. The essential question was whether the proceedings as a whole were fair and whether the defendant had been given a proper opportunity to question the admission of the evidence in question.

The meaning and extent of the concept of family life was at issue in *R v Secretary of State for Health, ex parte L (M)* (2001) 1 FLR 406. The case involved a challenge to the policy of restricting child visits to patients in secure hospitals to circumstances where the visit was deemed to be in the child's best interests and, in the case of patients convicted of very serious offences, where a close family relationship existed between the prisoner and the child. In the instant case this had been relied on to prohibit the applicant, a convicted murderer detained in Rampton hospital, from being visited by his niece. The challenge failed on two grounds. First, the court felt that the policy was not disproportionate to the legitimate aims of protecting children from the danger of exposure to certain types of serious offenders. Second, as a general principle, it was not prepared to accept that Art 8 extended to the normal relationship between uncle and the niece.

In *R (on the application of Robertson)* v *City of Wakefield Metropolitan Council* [2001] EWCA Admin 915, a breach of Art 8 was held to have been committed by the sale of information in an electoral register to commercial concerns without affording those affected an opportunity to object.

Article 10: Right to freedom of expression

Some of the initial applications of Art 10 have related to an issue which will no doubt engage the attention of the domestic courts on future occasions, i.e. the relationship between the right to freedom of expression and the power of the court in the Contempt of Court Act 1981, s 10, enabling a court to order a journalist to reveal his or her sources of information where this is deemed to be necessary in the interests of justice, national security or the prevention of crime. In *Ashworth Security Hospital* v *MGN Ltd* [2001] 1 WLR 515, the Court of Appeal felt that no breach of Art 10 had occurred where the power was used to order disclosure of the identity of the person responsible for passing to a journalist information derived from the medical records of the 'moors murderer', Ian Brady. In the court's view the disclosure of confidential medical records to the press was 'an attack on an area of confidentiality which should be safeguarded in any democratic society' and of sufficient severity to override the public interest in the protection of journalistic sources.

In both this case and in *John* v *Express Newspapers* [2000] 3 All ER 257, it was also emphasised that the proportionality of any such order for disclosure, i.e. whether it was 'necessary in a democratic society', would depend, *inter alia*, on whether the party seeking disclosure had shown that all other reasonable means had been taken to identify the source.

Reference

Loveland (1996) *Constitutional Law: A Critical Introduction*, London: Butterworths.

Chapter 20

POLICE POWERS, PERSONAL LIBERTY AND PRIVACY

PERSONAL FREEDOM: INTRODUCTION

In a free society it is generally assumed that the individuals should be able to go about their business without fear of arbitrary arrest and detention or other forms of capricious interference with their personal liberty. Impositions on personal liberty should have a clear legal foundation, should not be a matter of wide executive discretion and, in normal circumstances, should exist only where this is reasonably necessary for the prevention of crime and the preservation of public order.

Personal freedom in the United Kingdom is restricted by a variety of statutory and common law rules. The principal statutory provision operating in this context is the Police and Criminal Evidence Act 1984 (PACE). This confers power on the police to stop and search, to arrest without warrant, to detain for questioning, to enter private premises to arrest suspects and persons unlawfully at large, and to search both persons and premises for evidence of offences. The 1984 Act also provides the individual with various safeguards and rights (e.g. the right to legal advice) which the police are required to observe in the exercise of these powers.

The principal rules empowering and regulating police conduct in the Police and Criminal Evidence Act 1984 are supplemented by five Codes of Practice (CoP) made under ss 60 and 66. These are Code A, stop and search; Code B, entry to premises; Code C, detention and questioning; Code D, identification; and Code E, tape-recording of interviews. These may be revised from time to time and provide a detailed practical framework for the exercise of the powers already referred to. The Codes are not, however, directly enforceable. Hence no civil or criminal proceedings may be founded solely on a police officer's failure to comply with them (s 67). This should not be taken as meaning that the Codes are purely advisory or that they can be ignored with impunity. Hence, abuse of the Codes is made an express ground of police disciplinary proceedings (s 67(8)). A further pressure for compliance is the power of the trial court to rule that evidence gained in breach of Code requirements may be regarded as inadmissible.

THE POWER TO STOP AND SEARCH

Before PACE

Prior to the 1984 Act the police possessed a variety of specific stop–search powers. These included powers to stop and search for firearms (Firearms Act 1968) and drugs

(Misuse of Drugs Act 1971). Some police forces also possessed additional stop–search powers, usually for stolen property, contained in local Acts of Parliament (e.g. Metropolitan Police Act 1839, s 66). No general power existed, however, to stop and search persons or vehicles for stolen goods or that which might be used to cause injury or to commit offences.

The position at common law

No common law power exists allowing a police officer to physically stop and detain an individual, even for a short period, either for the purpose of search or questioning. Hence, short of arrest, or where the statutory powers of stop–search are available, a police officer may stop, search and/or question only with the individual's consent. In *Rice* v *Connolly* [1966] 2 QB 414, it was held that, although every citizen had a moral duty to assist the police, there was no legal duty to that effect. It follows that a failure to stop and answer police questions does not, *per se*, amount to an obstruction of a police officer in the execution of his/her duty. It is also no obstruction to tell a person not to answer police questions (*Green* v *DPP* [1991] Crim LR 781).

Technically, therefore, every non-consensual physical contact between a police officer and a member of the public would appear to amount to a trespass. It has been held, however, that a police officer, in order to do his/her duty, may do that which is reasonable in the circumstances to attract a person's attention and that this may include physical touching such as a tap on the shoulder (*Donnelly* v *Jackman* [1970] 1 All ER 987). In *Collins* v *Wilcox* [1984] 3 All ER 374, however, it was held that a police officer who wished to talk to a woman had no power to take hold of her arm to prevent her walking away. The court expressed the view that in each case the test must be 'whether the physical conduct so persisted in has, in the circumstances, gone beyond generally accepted standards of conduct; and the answer to that question will depend on the facts of the particular case' (per Goff LJ). In *Mepstead* v *DPP* [1996] Crim LR 111, therefore, taking hold of a person's arm in order to get him to calm down and listen to what was being said to him did not take the police officer outside his course of duty. In this instance a limited degree of physical force was justified in order to enable the officer involved to gain control of the situation and convey information to the individual about the nature and consequences of his behaviour. This may be further contrasted with *Bently* v *Brudzinski* (1982) Crim App Rep 217, where the unlawful physical taking hold of the individual to prevent his departure, took place after he had stopped and, in a calm and orderly way, answered the questions which had been put to him.

Stop and search in PACE

The extent of the power (s 1(2))

Section 1 of the Act confers a general power to stop and search 'any person or vehicle' for 'stolen or prohibited articles' (s 1(2)). Prohibited articles include anything made or adapted for use in connection with certain offences (burglary, theft, taking and driving away, obtaining by deception) or intended for use in relation to these offences. Hence, providing the article was made or adapted for any of the prescribed purposes, the power exists, even though the possession is 'innocent' in the sense that there is no intention to use the thing for an illegal purpose. Also, the possession of ostensibly innocent articles (e.g. a screwdriver), if intended for use in connection with any of the specified offences, would also provide grounds for lawful exercise of the power.

In addition to the above, the term prohibited articles also applies to 'offensive weapons'. These include any article made or adapted for causing injury to persons (therefore, presumably, not animals) or intended for such use by the person in possession or any other person (e.g. an accomplice).

Hence, as with articles related to the commission of offences, stop–search would be justified even though the person in possession did not intend to use the thing to cause injury. Thus, for example, possession of an item of Second World War memorabilia (i.e. bayonet, grenade, pistol, etc.) would probably provide grounds for search. In similar fashion, use of the power would also appear to be justified where the article would normally be regarded as harmless (e.g. knitting needles), but the person in possession intends to cause injury with it.

Where the power may be used (s 1(1))

The power may be used in any place to which members of the public have a right of access 'on payment or otherwise' or by express or implied permission. This would include, therefore, pubs, cinemas, sports stadia, etc. The power may also be exercised in 'any place to which people have a ready access…and which is not a dwelling'. This includes places where members of the public have no right to go but which it is easy for them to gain access – e.g. private premises and buildings, but not dwellings – without fear of interference and open spaces such as playing fields where no significant effort is made to keep the public out.

If the person is in the garden or yard of an occupied dwelling, the power may not be used unless the police officer reasonably believes that the person does not live there or does not have express or implied permission to be there.

Reasonable grounds (s 1(3) and CoP A, paras 1.6–1.7 A)

There must be reasonable grounds for suspecting that stolen or prohibited articles will be revealed by the search. It would appear that reasonable grounds may exist even though the person was in 'innocent' possession – i.e. did not know that they were in possession or did know but was not aware that the item was stolen or prohibited. Reasonable grounds should not be based on purely 'personal factors', e.g. colour, hairstyle, dress, age, previous convictions or stereotyped images of certain persons (CoP A, paras 1.6, 1.7).

Before the search (s 2 and CoP A, para 2)

The person may be detained for as long as is reasonably necessary for the purposes of the search (s 2). The grounds for suspicion must exist before this is done. In the absence of such pre-existing grounds there is no power to stop and question to see if any can be found. Where grounds to stop and search do exist, the person may be questioned to see if he/she has a satisfactory explanation sufficient to remove the officer's suspicion. If so the search should not take place.

Before any search reasonable steps should be taken to inform the person to be searched (or in charge of the vehicle) of the following:

(a) the officer's name (except in terrorist investigations) and the station to which he/she is attached and, if not in uniform, his/her warrant card;
(b) the object of the search;
(c) the right to a copy of the written record of the search;
(d) the reason for the stop and search (*R v Fennerlley* [1989] Crim LR 142).

Failure to provide the information in (a) has been held to render the search unlawful (*Osman v DPP* Lexis Transcript, 1 July 1999).

Conduct of the search (s 2 and CoP A, para 3)

The search should be carried out at the place where the person or vehicle was detained or 'nearby'. The meaning of 'nearby' is not defined by the Act but the following may be a reasonable representation of Parliament's intention:

> it is submitted that it should be interpreted quite narrowly. To move a vehicle from a congested spot into a side street, or a person from the public gaze into an alley, would be a reasonable action to take and would not prevent the search from being 'nearby' (Card and English, *Butterworths' Police Law*).

The person or vehicle should not be detained for longer than is reasonably necessary to complete the search. The extent of the search should be determined by what is reasonably necessary to achieve its objective – i.e. if the person is reasonably believed to have put a stolen or prohibited article into his pocket then the search should be limited to that pocket.

If the search is conducted in public it should be restricted to a superficial examination of outer clothing. Other garments such as an outer coat, gloves and jacket may not be required to be moved, although this may be requested. Where reasonable grounds exist for a more thorough search (e.g. removal of shirt), this should be done out of public view – in police van, for example - and by an officer of the same sex without an officer of the other sex being present unless the person to be searched so requests. A search in an empty street is in public.

In every case the police should seek to carry out the search with the individual's cooperation. A forcible search may be made only where the person refuses to cooperate or resists. In this case reasonable force may be used.

Voluntary searches (CoP A, para 1D)

Nothing in the Act or relevant Code of Practice affects the ability of a police officer to search a person in the street with his/her consent where no legal power of search exists. The Code of Practice requires an officer attempting to effect a voluntary search to make it clear that he/she is 'seeking the co-operation of the person concerned'. It is hard to see, however, how this differs from making every effort to secure 'voluntary production' when using the statutory power. Hence, unless the officer actually tells the person that the search is not being conducted under PACE and is purely voluntary, the person may often not have a clear understanding of his/her exact legal position, i.e. whether submission is compulsory.

A voluntary search will be invalidated (i.e. rendered tortious and possible criminal) if the officer acts in an 'improper manner' (not defined). Presumably, however, if the search is voluntary, this would include force of any kind or detention. Mentally handicapped or disordered persons or those who appear not capable of consent should not be searched voluntarily.

After the search (s 3 and CoP A, para 4)

A written record must be completed on the spot or as soon as reasonably practicable afterwards. This should include the person's name or description and ethnic type, the registration and description of any vehicle searched, the officer's identity, the object and grounds for the search, the date, time and place it occurred, and any injury or damage to property caused.

Note that there is no power to require the person to reveal their name or other personal details (it is a power to search not to question). As this is stated expressly in the Code of Practice, failure to supply such information could not amount to an obstruction or a ground for arrest under s 25.

Searching vehicles (ss 1 and 2 and CoP A, para 4)

The power extends to anything which is in or on the vehicle, the contents of a roof rack or containers or packages on the back of an open lorry.

If the vehicle is in a yard or garden attached to and used in connection with an occupied dwelling, the officer may not search unless he/she reasonably believes that the person in charge of the vehicle does not live in the dwelling or the vehicle is there without the occupier's permission.

After searching an unattended vehicle the officer should leave a notice stating that he/she has searched it, the name of the police station to which he/she is attached, that an application may be made for compensation for any damage caused and where a copy of the search record may be obtained. The notice should be left inside the vehicle if reasonably practicable without causing damage. Where practicable the vehicle should be left secure (CoP, para 4.10).

Stopping vehicles

Note that the provisions in the 1984 Act relating to the searching of vehicles do not contain any express power to stop a vehicle for this purpose. There is, of course, nothing to prevent an officer signalling or requesting that a vehicle be brought to rest preparatory to using the stop–search power.

Otherwise, powers to stop vehicles may be found elsewhere in both statute and the common law. The most significant statutory power is contained in the Road Traffic Act 1988 (RTA), s 163(1). This provides that a person driving a motor vehicle must stop when ordered to do so by a police officer in uniform. Section 163(2) makes similar provision in relation to cyclists. It is an offence to disobey (s 163(3)). It would appear that this power may be used to facilitate performance of any of the officer's legitimate duties. Hence, if after using the power, the officer formed reasonable grounds for searching either the vehicle or the driver he could proceed to exercise the stop–search power. It would, however, probably be an abuse of s 163 for the officer to stop a vehicle for no better reason than to discover if grounds for a search could be found.

Section 163 is generally regarded as containing an implied obligation on the driver to remain at rest for a reasonable period to enable the officer to carry out his duty but confers no power to detain either the vehicle or the driver unless some specific suspicion of an offence exists (e.g. that the vehicle is stolen) or arises immediately after the vehicle has been brought to rest (see *Lodwick v Sanders* [1985] 1 WLR 382).

There would also appear to be a common law power to stop a vehicle as part of the officer's duty to investigate and prevent crime (see *Steel v Goacher* [1983] RTR 98).

A vehicle or vehicles may also be stopped where this is reasonably believed to be necessary to prevent a breach of the peace (see *Moss v McLachlan* (1984) 149 JP 167).

Road checks (s 4)

The 1984 Act also seeks to regulate the use of RTA, s 163 for general road checks – i.e. where, for the period of the check, all or selected vehicles in a particular locality are stopped. Section 4 provides that such general checks may be authorised by a superintendent or above where the police:

- are investigating a serious arrestable offence which has been or may be committed and have reasonable grounds for suspecting the suspect to be in the locality;
- are looking for a witness to such an offence;
- are looking for a person unlawfully at large.

A road check may be authorised by an officer below the rank of superintendent where this 'appears to him' (subjective) to be a matter of urgency for any of the above purposes.

A road check should not continue beyond seven days. This is a power to stop at random without any particular suspicion relating to the vehicle in question or its occupants.

Stop and search in the Criminal Justice and Public Order Act 1994

The power in the 1994 Act is contained in s 60. This allows a police officer of the rank of superintendent or above to authorise the stopping and searching of persons and vehicles for offensive weapons or dangerous instruments where he/she reasonably believes that incidents of serious violence may take place in his/her police area and it is expedient to use the power to prevent their occurrence. If it is reasonably believed that incidents of serious violence are imminent and no superintendent is available, the power may be exercised by a chief inspector or inspector. Such authorisation may be for any period up to 24 hours and may be extended for a further six hours by a superintendent or the officer responsible for the original authorisation.

It will be noted that this section permits the searching of any person or vehicle even though no specific suspicion exists relating thereto.

> A constable may, in the exercise of those powers, stop any person or vehicle and make any search he thinks fit whether or not he has any reasonable grounds for suspecting that the person or vehicle is carrying weapons or articles of that kind (s 60(5)).

This has not been the only relatively recent extension of stop and search powers. Other powers of this type for the purpose of controlling specific types of illegal activity may be found in the Crossbows Act 1987, the Deer Act 1991, the Badgers Act 1992 (also see, in the context of wildlife preservation, the stop–search powers in the Poaching Prevention Act 1862, the Conservation of Seals Act 1970 and the Wildlife and Countryside Act 1981), the Prevention of Terrorism Acts 1989, 1996 and the Terrorism Act 2000.

THE POWER OF ARREST

Some general comments

Powers of arrest in the United Kingdom may be found in a variety of statutory and common law provisions. A statute may authorise an individual's arrest:

- only after a warrant has been issued by a magistrate;
- without a warrant in specified circumstances – usually for the apprehension of someone suspected of one of the more serious types of criminal offence (i.e. an 'arrestable offence').

A person may also be arrested without warrant under a number of surviving common law powers – principally to prevent breaches of the peace and, in certain circumstances, for obstruction of a police officer in the course of his/her duty.

In practice most arrests are now effected under statutory powers and without warrant – the principal powers being those contained in PACE, ss 24 and 25. One of the objectives of the Act was to introduce some order and clarity into the wide range of statutory and common law powers of arrest hitherto existing. Hence, subject to certain exceptions listed in Sched 2, all such previous powers were repealed (see s 26) and replaced by the general powers of arrest in the above sections.

The purpose of an arrest

Until relatively recent times it was assumed that the power of arrest existed principally to allow the authorities to bring a person before a court to answer charges of a criminal nature. It is now accepted, however, that a person who is suspected of an offence may be arrested and brought into custody for the purpose of questioning related thereto (*Holgate-Mohammed v Duke* [1984] AC 437). Also, an arrest is probably not unlawful if the requisite suspicion exists and the correct reasons for it are given albeit that the arrest has been effected in the course of the investigation of other more serious offences, i.e. as a 'holding charge', and does not represent, therefore, the primary motivation for taking the suspect into custody (*R* v *Chalkley*; *R* v *Jeffries* [1998] 2 All ER 155).

Arrest without warrant

Section 24 of PACE authorises a police officer to arrest without warrant any person:

- who is about to commit an arrestable offence;
- who is reasonably suspected to be about to commit an arrestable offence;
- who is committing an arrestable offence;
- who is reasonably suspected to be committing an arrestable offence;
- who has committed an arrestable offence;
- who is reasonably suspected to have committed an arrestable offence.

The same section defines an arrestable offence as:

- any offence for which the sentence is fixed by law (i.e. murder and treason);
- any offence for which a person could be sentenced to a term of imprisonment of five years or more;
- offences not imprisonable for five years created by other statutes as specified in s 24(2).

Section 25 permits a police officer to arrest without warrant any person who is committing or is reasonably suspected of having committed a non-arrestable offence. This may be done where the usual method of dealing with this less serious type of offence – i.e. by obtaining the person's details and summoning them to appear in court – appears to be inappropriate because one of the 'general arrest conditions' has been satisfied. The arrest conditions are:

(a) that the person's name and address is unknown and cannot be readily ascertained or the officer has reasonable grounds for doubting whether the person has given his or her real name;

(b) the address provided is not satisfactory for the service of a summons (e.g. a temporary lodging house) or the officer has reasonable grounds for doubting whether it is satisfactory;

(c) the officer has reasonable grounds for believing that it is necessary to arrest the person to prevent him or her –

- causing physical harm
- suffering physical injury
- causing loss or damage to property
- committing an offence against public decency
- causing an unlawful obstruction of the highway;

(d) the officer has reasonable grounds for believing that the person's arrest is necessary to protect a child or other vulnerable person.

Note that s 25 does not authorise a police officer to arrest a person who has done nothing more than refuse to give his/her name and address. The officer must first see or suspect the commission of an offence. If the person then refuses to provide the relevant information or one of the other arrest conditions appears to be present, the power of arrest may then be activated. In G v *Director of Public Prosecutions* [1989] Crim LR 150, G and others went into a police station to make a complaint. The police officer dealing with the matter believed that persons of G's type seldom told the truth to the police and that the personal details G had provided were, therefore, probably not reliable. The situation then became disorderly. G was arrested for committing a non-arrestable offence (disorderly behaviour in a police station: Town Police Clauses Act 1847). It was held that G's arrest had been unlawful and that his resistance to it did not amount, therefore, to an obstruction of the officer in the course of his duties. The arrest was defective because no offence had been committed when the arrest condition was satisfied, viz. at the time when the officer doubted the truth of G's personal details.

Ingredients of a valid arrest

An arrest is not lawful simply because a police officer is executing a power vested in him by statute or common law. A number of other important requirements exist. In many circumstances, for example, valid exercise of the powers in ss 24 and 25 will be dependent on the existence of reasonable suspicion. Also PACE, s 28 requires that the officer effecting the arrest gives the reasons for it and makes it clear to the individual that he/she is no longer at liberty.

Reasonable suspicion

Powers of arrest unqualified by the need for reasonable suspicion are not compatible with the European Convention on Human Rights, Art 5 (*Fox, Campbell and Hartley* v *United Kingdom* (1990) 13 EHRR 157). Reasonable suspicion must be based on something more than a person's previous record or the officer's personal prejudices in matters of personal appearance, lifestyle, race, etc. (Code of Practice A, paras 1.6–1.7).

The cases indicate, however, that – in terms of the amount of relevant evidence or information which a police officer must possess in order to justify an arrest – this is not a particularly demanding requirement. The test is satisfied if a police officer acts on the basis of evidence or information which enables a plausible connection to be made between the suspect and a particular offence. It is not necessary that sufficient evidence exists to charge the person with an offence. Nor is it the case that the information on which the suspicion is based is something which could be put before a court as evidence (*Holtham* v *Metropolitan Police Commissioner*, *The Times*, 8 January 1987).

Note that other powers in PACE may be used only where there is a reasonable *belief* in the existence of certain facts. Hence the power to enter private premises without warrant for the purpose of effecting an arrest exists where it is reasonably believed, *inter alia*, that a person who has committed an arrestable offence may be found there (s 17). It is generally accepted that 'reasonable belief' denotes a state of mind which has progressed well beyond mere suspicion to a point which approaches certainty or conviction. Such state of conviction is not, therefore, a prerequisite of a valid arrest. It is enough that sufficient evidence exists to raise sufficient doubt in the officer's mind to justify further inquiries.

In *Castorina* v *Chief Constable of Surrey* [1988] NLJ 180, police officers went to investigate a burglary at the premises of the plaintiff's former employer. The plaintiff had been 'sacked' a short time before the offence was committed. The evidence suggested that it was an 'inside job' and may have been the work of someone bearing a grudge. On this basis the plaintiff was arrested and detained for questioning in police custody for nearly four hours. She was then released without charge.

Her action for false arrest and imprisonment was upheld in the county court. The arrest could not have been lawful, it was held, unless the officers 'had an honest belief founded on a reasonable suspicion leading an ordinary cautious man to the conclusion that the person arrested was guilty of the offence'. The court did not accept that on the small amount of evidence available to the officers they could have reached such a conclusion. On appeal, however, the Court of Appeal rejected this test as being too severe. It was not necessary that the arresting officers had evidence which led them to believe or conclude that the suspect was guilty. All that was required was that they had acted on evidence which would have caused a reasonable person to *suspect* the plaintiff (see also *Bull* v *Chief Constable of Sussex* (1995) 159 LG Rev 893).

The reasonable grounds for an arrest must be in the mind of the officer who effects it. These need not, however, be based on his/her own observations or inquiries but may, for example, be founded on information supplied by other officers or informers (*O'Hara* v *Chief Constable of Royal Ulster Constabulary* [1997] 1 All ER 129) or on that supplied by police computer records (*Hough* v *Chief Constable of Staffordshire Police* [2001] EWCA Civ 39).

Fact of arrest

Section 28(1) of PACE provides that an arrest is not lawful unless the person is told that he or she is under arrest at the time of the arrest or as soon as reasonably practicable afterwards. No precise linguistic formula is required but the words and/or actions of the officer must be such that an ordinary reasonable person would be in no doubt that an arrest has taken place (*Wheatley* v *Lodge* [1971] 1 All ER 173). Statements such as 'I shall have to ask you to come to the police station' would appear to be inadequate to convey the necessary degree of compulsion (*Alderson* v *Booth* [1969] 3 QB 216). In another case the words 'you must come with me' were held to be sufficient (*Times* v *John Lewis and Co Ltd* [1952] AC 676).

Reasons for arrest

An arrest is also not lawful unless the person is informed of the grounds for arrest. Again this information should be given at the time of the arrest or as soon as reasonably practicable afterwards (PACE, s 28(3)). The arresting officer must give the grounds or reason even though obvious. He/she need not, however, explain that reason in the precise legal terminology of the particular statute or common law offence. In *Abassy* v *Metropolitan Police Commissioner* [1990] 1 WLR 385, telling a person he had been arrested for 'unlawful possession' of a motor car was sufficient reason to support a valid arrest for taking a motor vehicle without consent under the Theft Act 1968. In *Gelberg v Miller* [1961] 2 All ER 291, G parked his car in a narrow street where parking was restricted. He was asked to move it by a police officer. When G refused, he was told he was being arrested for obstructing the officer by not moving his car. The officer's intention was to arrest G for obstructing him in the course of his duty. On the facts no power of arrest without warrant for this offence existed. G could have been arrested, however, for obstructing the highway. The court decided that the officer had not acted unlawfully. In the circumstances an offence arrestable without warrant had been committed, and the words used by the officer were sufficient to convey the general nature of that offence to G. It did not matter that the officer had an alternative offence in his mind nor that he had failed to use the precise terminology of obstruction of the highway.

> The whole point of the law is that the citizen must be told what the constable suspects he has done wrong. It does not have to be done in any technically precise way but…it must convey to the individual enough to show that the arrest is lawful. I have no difficulty with the proposition that technical or formal words are unnecessary. Although no constable ever admits to saying 'You're knicked for handling this gear' or 'I'm having you for two-cing this motor', either will do and, I have no doubt, frequently does (Sedley LJ, *Clarke v Chief Constable of North Wales* [2000] All ER 477).

If reasons are not given at the time of arrest when it would have been reasonable to do so, the arrest is unlawful and the person affected has a right of action for unlawful arrest and imprisonment. The arrest becomes lawful, however, if and when reasons are given at some later stage (*Lewis v Chief Constable of South Wales* [1991] 2 All ER 206). Similarly, if reasons are not given at the time of arrest because this would not have been reasonably practicable, and are still not given when it becomes reasonably practicable, the arrest becomes unlawful from that moment but again becomes lawful if and when the reasons are given (*DPP v Hawkins* [1988] 1 WLR 1166).

The use of force

The Criminal Law Act 1967, s 3 permits as much force as is reasonable in the making of an arrest; PACE, s 117 permits the use of similar force in the exercise of other powers conferred by the Act. The use of excessive force does not invalidate an arrest but may be the cause of a civil action or criminal prosecution for assault (*Simpson v Chief Constable of South Yorkshire Police* (1991) 135 SLJ 383).

Search after arrest

Under PACE, s 32 a person who has been arrested may be searched if a police officer has reasonable grounds for believing that he/she:

- may present a danger to himself or others;
- may be in possession of something which may be used to effect an escape;
- may be in possession of something which might be evidence of an offence.

Section 32 also empowers the police to search any premises where the arrested person was immediately before, or at the time of, the arrest. Section 18 provides a further power to search any premises occupied or controlled by a person under arrest.

Citizen's arrest

The wording of PACE, s 24 makes it clear that the power of arrest without warrant is not confined to police officers. The power is extended to private citizens where a person:

- is committing an arrestable offence;
- is reasonably suspected to be committing an arrestable offence;
- has committed an arrestable offence;
- is reasonably suspected of being guilty of an arrestable offence which has been committed.

The citizen's power of arrest is narrower than that of the police officer in the following respects. First, the private citizen has no power to arrest any person who is, or who is reasonably suspected to be, about to commit an arrestable offence. Second, the private citizen has no power to arrest a person who is reasonably suspected of being guilty of an arrestable offence if that offence has not been committed.

Hence, if A, a private citizen, reasonably suspects B of theft, and the particular theft has been committed by B or some other person, the arrest of B is lawful. If, however, A reasonably suspects B of theft but the particular theft has not been committed, either by B or anyone else, the arrest of B would be unlawful. Note that in the latter situation the arrest of B by a police officer with the requisite suspicion would be perfectly lawful. As explained above, a police officer may arrest without warrant any person reasonably suspected of having committed an arrestable offence. The legality of the arrest is not affected in any way by the fact that the offence has not been committed.

In *R v Self* [1992] 1 WLR 657, S was suspected of the theft of a bar of chocolate. He was followed from the shop and challenged by a shop assistant and store detective. They accused him of theft and told him he would have to return to the shop. A scuffle ensued and S ran away. A bystander who had witnessed all of this gave chase. After some resistance he managed to arrest S. S was then charged with theft and two counts of assault with intent to resist arrest. He was found not guilty of the theft. This meant that, although the shop assistant, store detective and bystander may have had reasonable grounds for suspecting S of being guilty of an arrestable offence, no such offence had been committed. In these circumstances, therefore, no citizen's power of arrest existed. From this it followed that S had been justified in acting as he did and could not be guilty of trying to resist a lawful arrest:

> section 24 (5) makes it abundantly clear that the powers of arrest without warrant where an arrestable offence has been committed require as a condition precedent an offence committed. The power of arrest is confined to the person guilty of the offence or anyone who the person making the arrest has reasonable grounds for suspecting to be guilty of it (per Garland J).

The procedural requirements for a valid citizen's arrest are similar to those for arrest by a police officer. Hence, both the fact of and the grounds for the arrest must be communicated to the arrested person at the time of the arrest or as soon as is reasonably practicable afterwards. In the case of a citizen's arrest, however, the reasons or grounds for the arrest need not be given if these are obvious.

Arrest with warrant

There are a variety of statutory powers of arrest with warrant. Of these the most significant is the power contained in the Magistrates' Court Act 1980, s 1. The procedure commences by the person seeking the warrant – usually a police officer – laying information before a magistrate. This is a sworn statement identifying the particular offence a person is suspected of having committed. A warrant may only be issued in respect of a person over seventeen years of age suspected of having committed an indictable offence or an offence punishable by imprisonment or whose particulars are insufficiently well known to enable a summons to be served.

To be valid the warrant must contain the name of the person to be arrested and the offence of which he/she is suspected. Where a police officer executes a warrant which the magistrate had no power to issue, the officer is protected from civil action by the Constables' Protection Act 1750 provided they acted in good faith.

The officer effecting the arrest need not have the warrant in their possession at the time but the arrested person has the right to see the warrant on demand as soon as possible (Magistrates' Courts Act 1980, s 125(3)).

Arrest at common law

Any person may arrest without warrant:

- a person whom he/she has reasonable cause to believe will commit a breach of the peace if not apprehended;
- a person who is committing a breach of the peace in his/her presence;
- any person who it is reasonably suspected has committed a breach of the peace which, unless the person is arrested, will reoccur in the immediate future.

A breach of the peace is committed 'when harm is done or is likely to be done to a person or, in his presence, to his property or a person is put in fear of being harmed through an assault, an affray, a riot, unlawful assembly or other disturbance' (R v Howell [1982] QB 416). This is the only remaining common law power of arrest.

DETENTION

Designated and non-designated police stations

For the purpose of the reception and detention of persons who have been arrested, the 1984 Act distinguishes between designated and non-designated police stations. A designated police station is one which has the necessary facilities for the detention and interviewing of suspects. Stations without these facilities are non-designated police stations. Designation is a function of the chief constable for the police district in question (s 35).

An arrested person should be taken to a designated police station unless:

(a) there is none in the locality;
(b) the arrest has been effected without assistance and it appears to the officer that he/she will be unable to take the arrested person to a designated police station without that person causing injury to himself, the officer or some other person (s 30).

In either case, if the police wish to detain a person beyond six hours from the time of their arrival at a non-designated police station, that person should be taken to a designated station.

On arrival at the police station

When the arrested person arrives at the police station he/she should be taken before the custody officer as soon as practicable. This will usually be an officer of the rank of sergeant (s 35). The custody officer is responsible for ensuring that persons in detention are treated in accordance with the Act and its Codes of Practice and, in particular, that due observance is given to the rights and safeguards intended for those in police custody. The custody officer will decide whether there is sufficient evidence to charge the person with an offence. If so, the arrested person should be charged forthwith. If the custody officer is not so convinced he/she may order that the person be released or detained for questioning. A decision to detain for questioning may be made only if the custody officer has reasonable grounds for believing that this is 'necessary to secure or preserve evidence relating to an offence for which [the suspect] is under arrest or to obtain such evidence by questioning him' (s 37). The suspect should be informed of:

- the grounds for detention;
- the right to have a friend, relative or other interested person know of his arrest;
- the right to consult privately with a solicitor;
- the right to see the Codes of Practice (s 38).

The custody officer is also responsible for ascertaining what property a detained person had with him/her when brought into custody and may conduct a search of the person for that purpose (CoP C, para 4).

The first 24 hours

The arrested person may then be detained for questioning for up to 24 hours calculated from the time he/she first arrived at the police station (s 41). The custody officer's decision authorising such detention must be reviewed within six hours of its making and thereafter at intervals of not less than nine hours. If this is not done the detention becomes unlawful (*Roberts v Jones* [1999] 1 WLR 662). The questioning should cease, however, once the investigating officer believes that enough evidence has been obtained to charge the person with an offence. The person should then be taken before the custody officer for that purpose (CoP C, para 11.4).

After 24 hours (continued detention)

If at the expiry of 24 hours the person has not been charged, he/she should be released unless an officer of the rank of superintendent or above has reasonable grounds for believing that the person may have committed a 'serious arrestable offence' and that the person's continued detention for questioning for any period of up to twelve hours is necessary to secure evidence relating thereto (s 42). The person should be given the grounds for continued detention and be given the opportunity to make representations personally or through a solicitor. Failure to do so may result in the continued detention being held to be illegal (*Re an Application for a Warrant of Further Detention* [1988] Crim LR 296). In effect, therefore, the police are authorised to keep a person suspected of a serious offence in custody without charge for up to 36 hours.

Serious arrestable offences are defined by PACE, s 116 and Sched 5, Pt 1. A number of arrestable offences are classified as 'always' being 'serious'. These include murder, manslaughter, rape and kidnapping. Other arrestable offences may be treated as serious if they were likely or were intended to result in:

- serious harm to public order or national security;
- serious interference with the administration of justice or investigation of crime;
- the death of any person;
- serious injury to any person;
- substantial financial gain or serious financial loss to any person.

Theft may be a serious arrestable offence, therefore, depending on whether the financial gain to the offender or the loss to the victim may be classified as significant. In *R v McIvor* [1987] Crim LR 409, the theft of 28 dogs collectively worth £800 and owned by the members of a hunt was held not to have occasioned substantial financial loss and did not amount, therefore, to a serious arrestable offence. Similarly, in *R v Smith (Eric)* [1987] Crim LR 579, the theft of cash and goods worth £516 from a chainstore was found not to have caused any great financial loss to the owners or significant financial gain to the thieves.

This approach introduces a degree of uncertainty into the precise definition of offences and, in circumstances similar to those in the above two cases, may present the police with difficulties in determining whether the various extra powers available to them in relation to persons suspected of serious arrestable offences can be safely relied upon.

After 36 hours (further detention)

Should the police wish to hold the person in custody for longer than 36 hours they must apply to a magistrate for a warrant of further detention (s 43). The application must be made before the 36 hours has elapsed unless it is not practicable for the court to which the application is to be made to sit before the expiry time. In this case a further six hours is permitted within which the application can be made. The police must satisfy the magistrate that they are investigating a serious arrestable offence and that further questioning of the detained person is necessary to secure, preserve or obtain relevant evidence. If so satisfied a warrant may be issued authorising the police to keep the person in detention for whatever further period the court deems fit, up to a maximum of 36 hours.

This could bring the total period for which the person has been held since arriving at the police station up to 72 hours. The detained person has the right to be present at the hearing and to be legally represented. Should an application of a warrant of further detention be made after the elapse of 36 hours in circumstances where it would have been practicable to deal with the matter within the specified time, the warrant is invalid and the person's further detention is unlawful (R v *Slough Magistrates, ex parte Stirling* [1987] Crim LR 576; R v *Sedgefield Justices, ex parte Milne* (1981) unreported).

Extension of further detention

Prior to the expiry of the warrant of further detention the police may apply for an extension of the permitted time (s 44). The grounds and procedure for making such application are the same as those for granting further detention. The period of extension may be for any time the magistrates deem appropriate provided that this does not take the total period for which the person has been in detention to above 96 hours. This, therefore, is the maximum period for which a person may be held in custody without charge (save, that is, for the special provision in the Prevention of Terrorism Acts).

Conditions of detention

Code of Practice C, para 8 provides that persons in detention must be held in conditions of reasonable comfort. Food and drink must be provided at regular intervals and the opportunity given for outdoor exercise if practicable. The detained person should be visited on at least an hourly basis. Medical attention should be provided if the person's condition gives cause for concern. Failure to comply with any of these requirements may result in any statement or confession being regarded as unsafe and, therefore, inadmissible as evidence.

Right to contact a friend or relative

A person being held in police custody has the right to have a friend or relative informed as to his/her whereabouts as soon as is practicable (s 56). The exercise of this right may be delayed for up to 36 hours where the person is suspected of a serious arrestable offence and an officer of the rank of superintendent or above reasonably believes that such contact would lead to:

- interference with relevant evidence;
- interference with or physical injury to other persons;
- the alerting of other suspects;
- the recovery of property obtained as the result of such offence being hindered.

INTERVIEWING SUSPECTS

The Police and Criminal Evidence Act 1984 and Code of Practice C provide a number of key safeguards designed to minimise the possibility of malpractice during the process of questioning. The use of improper methods which are calculated to 'make the suspect talk' may often seek to achieve this by undermining his/her free will. However, this only serves to cast doubt on the credibility of any statement or confession the suspect may have made. Such material is, therefore, of little use as evidence.

The principal safeguards are:

- that a contemporaneous tape-recorded or written record must be kept of the conduct and content of the interview;
- that the suspect should be cautioned before being questioned about any offence they are suspected of committing;
- that the suspect should be given access to legal advice;
- that the suspect should not be subjected to continuous questioning without breaks for rest and refreshment.

The interview record

Code of Practice C, para 11 provides that 'an interview is the questioning of a person regarding his involvement or suspected involvement in a criminal offence'. The Code further provides that such interview should take place at a police station unless this would be likely to result in any of those consequences prejudicial to the investigation set out above in the context of delaying contact with a friend or relative. The detained person should be told or reminded of his/her rights before the interview begins (see below, the caution and the rights contained in ss 56 and 58). The interview should cease as soon as the investigating officer believes that there is enough evidence to enable a prosecution to succeed.

An accurate written or tape-recorded record should be kept. This should be made during the course of the interview unless this is not practicable or would interfere with the course of the interview. If the record is not made contemporaneously, it should be compiled as soon as is practicable afterwards. These requirements apply to all interviews whether conducted at the police station or elsewhere.

Where a written record is kept, the detained person should be given the opportunity to read and sign it thus verifying that it represents a true record of what took place. If the interview was tape-recorded, the tape should be sealed in the detained person's presence and the detained person should be asked to sign the seal.

Compliance with these requirements gives the trial court a reasonable degree of assurance that statements and confessions given during police questioning may be relied upon. By definition, therefore, statements and confessions acquired in breach of these requirements have reduced credibility and may not be admitted as evidence (R v Chung [1991] Crim LR 622).

The caution

A person who refuses to answer police questions does not commit an offence, e.g. obstruction of a police officer in the course of his/her duty. A trial court may, however, place an 'adverse influence' on a suspect's silence if he/she seeks to rely on any facts by way of defence which were not mentioned during questioning by the police

(Criminal Justice and Public Order Act 1994, ss 34–37, applied in *R v Argent* [1997] 2 Crim App Rep 27).

The wording of the caution reflects these basic principles: You do not have to say anything. But it may harm your defence if you do not mention when questioned something which you later rely on in court. Anything you do say may be given in evidence (CoP C, para 10).

Where a police officer is questioning a person merely for the purpose of acquiring information and does not suspect that person of an offence, the caution need not be administered (*R v Shah* [1994] Crim LR 125; *R v Marsh* [1992] Crim LR 455). The caution should be administered, however:

- as soon as there is a ground for suspecting that the person may have committed an offence (*R v Rouf*, Smith Bernal Casetrack, 13 May 1999);
- at the time of the arrest unless it is impracticable to do so because of the person's behaviour or the person has already been questioned immediately before the arrest;
- if and when the person is charged with an offence.

The person should be reminded that he/she is under caution before being interviewed and after any breaks in such interview.

Failure to administer the caution as required may result in any statements the suspect has made being ruled to be inadmissible as evidence (*R v Saunders* [1988] Crim LR 521; *R v Hunt* [1992] Crim LR 582).

The right to legal advice

Every person in police custody must be informed of their right to consult a solicitor in private and must be allowed to exercise such right unless its delay for up to 36 hours is authorised according to the same criteria as for delay in informing a friend or relative of the person's whereabouts (s 56, see above) – i.e. the person is suspected of a serious arrestable offence and a superintendent or higher rank has reasonable grounds for believing that contact with a solicitor might lead to interference with evidence, harm being done to other persons, the alerting of suspects or the 'fruits of the crime' not being recovered.

The courts regard the right articulated by s 58 as fundamental. Clear words must be used when informing the suspect of his/her entitlement in this regard (*R v Beycan* [1990] Crim LR 185). Also, although the right of access to legal advice may be delayed, fulfilment of the obligation to tell the suspect that the right exists may not (*R v Absolam* (1989) 88 Crim App Rep 332).

Delay of access may not be authorised simply because it is believed that contact with any solicitor might lead to any of the negative consequences specified. The officer authorising the delay must have reasonable grounds to believe that access to the particular solicitor named would result in such consequence(s) (*R v Samuel* [1988] 2 All ER 135). In *R v Davison* [1988] Crim LR 442, a detained person asked to see a solicitor but did not name one. Permission was refused as others involved in the crime under investigation were still at large. This was a breach of s 58. The suspect having failed to specify which solicitor he wished to see, the authorising officer could not, at this stage, have had any grounds for believing that allowing access to a particular legal adviser would have had any of the consequences justifying delay.

> In the light of *R v Samuel*...it is clear that the police must be near certain that a solicitor granted access to the defendant would warn off an inside man or get rid of the proceeds of the robbery. No solicitor having been nominated by the defendant, the police could have no reasonable fear relating to an individual solicitor passing a message on from the defendant (*R v Davison*, above).

Where delay is justified, the detained person should be given reasons for it and should be informed forthwith if and when those reasons have ceased to exist (*R v Cochrane* [1988] Crim LR 449).

The general rule is that if a detained person has asked for legal advice the interview should not begin until he/she has received it (CoP C, para 6.6). The detained person must also be allowed to have his/her solicitor present while the interview takes place (CoP C, para 6.8).

Given the importance attached to this right by the courts, improper refusal of it will often be treated as sufficient ground for refusing to admit the detained person's statement as evidence.

Rest and refreshments

Code of Practice C, para 12 seeks to ensure that the detained person is not subject to any unacceptable degree of physical or emotional discomfort during the interview process. It provides that in any period of 24 hours the detained person must be allowed a continuous period of rest for at least eight hours. This should normally be at night and free from any unnecessary interruption. Interviews should be conducted in rooms which are adequately heated, lit and ventilated. The detained person should be allowed to sit while being questioned. Breaks from questioning should be allowed at meal times and short breaks should be allowed at intervals of approximately two hours.

The requirements that the detained person be allowed eight hours of rest and breaks from questioning may be departed from if there are reasonable grounds for believing that such delay would:

- involve a risk of harm to any person or serious damage to, or a loss of, property;
- delay unnecessarily the detained person's release;
- otherwise prejudice the outcome of the investigation.

INADMISSIBLE EVIDENCE

As already indicated, ill-treatment or malpractice in relation to those in detention or breach of the rules regulating the process of questioning may lead to any confession or statements made by the detained person being ruled to be inadmissible by the trial court. This issue is regulated by PACE, ss 76 and 78.

Exclusion of confessions under s 76

The effect of s 76 is to place the trial court under a legal duty to exclude any confession which has been obtained by oppression or any other means which makes it unreliable. Oppression includes torture, inhuman or degrading treatment or the use of threats of violence. If oppression is alleged it is for the prosecution to prove beyond reasonable doubt that such techniques were not used. One of the most frequent reasons for confessions being held to be unreliable is that they were made in response to some kind of inducement – i.e. a holding out to the suspected person that, in return for a confession, he/she will be given some sort of advantage, benefit or concession. Thus, in *R v Howden-Simpson* [1991] Crim LR 49, the defendant's confession was ruled inadmissible because it had been given in response to a promise that if he confessed to two offences he would not be charged with others which he was also suspected of having committed.

Note that where oppression or unreliability is established under s 76, the court has no discretion: it must exclude the confession. Also note that the section applies to confessions only and not to other statements.

Exclusion under s 78

This section gives the trial court a discretion to exclude both confessions and other statements if 'having regard to all the circumstances, including the circumstances in which the evidence was obtained, the admission of the evidence would have…an adverse effect on the fairness of the proceedings'. Although worded obscurely, its practical effect is to allow the court to exclude:

* confessions obtained by improper means not covered by s 76 (*R v Mason* [1987] 3 All ER 481);
* other statements which may have been obtained by force, pressure, threats, inducements or where some other improper act has been committed.

The cases suggest a general judicial opinion that evidence obtained from a person in police custody whose treatment was in 'significant and substantial' breach of the rules regulating detention and questioning should not be admitted (*R v Walsh* [1988] Crim LR 449). Evidence has been excluded under this provision in the following circumstances:

* no contemporaneous record made of interview (*R v Maloney and Doherty* [1988] Crim LR 523);
* access to solicitor refused improperly (*R v Davison*, above; *R v Samuel*, above; *R v Alladice* (1988) 87 Crim App Rep 380);
* continuous questioning without adequate rest or breaks (*R v Trussler* [1988] Crim LR 446).

In many cases evidence has been excluded because a variety of the relevant rules have been transgressed (e.g. *R v Saunders* (above): suspect not cautioned properly and no contemporaneous record kept; *R v Walsh* (above): suspect improperly refused access to solicitor and no contemporaneous record kept). Indeed, in one case it was suggested that an accumulation of serious breaches of the rules could amount to oppression within the meaning of s 76 (*R v Davison*, above).

Admissibility and the European Court of Human Rights

Whether evidence, particularly unlawfully obtained evidence, is admissible or not is now a matter which may also engage Art 6 (right to a fair trial). The position taken by the European Court of Human Rights on this issue has not differed greatly from that of the domestic law, i.e. that the crucial test is not the legality of the way the evidence was obtained but the overall effect its admission would have on the fairness of the proceedings. In *R* v *Mason* [2002] EWCA Crim 385, police officers placed listening devices in prisoners' cells without legal authority, thus not 'according to law'. This was found to be a breach of Art 8 (right to privacy). This did not mean, however, that the evidence gained thereby was automatically inadmissible under Art 6. The Court of Appeal quoted from the judgment of the Court of Human Rights in *PG and JH* v *United Kingdom* (2001) *Times*, 19 October:

> Whilst Art 6 guarantees the right to a fair hearing, it does not lay down any rules on the admissibility of evidence as such which is, therefore, primarily a matter for regulation under national law...It is not the role of the court to determine...whether particular types of evidence – for example, unlawfully obtained evidence – may be admissible...The question which must be answered is whether the proceedings as a whole, including the way in which the evidence was obtained, were fair.

In *Mason*, the defendants not having been tricked or induced into making statements, the covertly obtained evidence was found to be admissible. If aggrieved, it remained open to them to seek a remedy for breach of Art 8 (see also *R* v *Bailey* [2001] EWCA Crim 733).

ENTRY, SEARCH AND SEIZURE

Introduction

The Police and Criminal Evidence Act 1984 left untouched those powers to search premises for evidence of specific offences contained in previous enactments (e.g. Misuse of Drugs Act 1971, s 23(3); Obscene Publications Act 1959, s 3). In addition to these, PACE created two general powers of entry and search to assist the police with the investigation of more serious criminal offences. The principal powers of search conferred by the Act are found in ss 8 and 9. Further general powers of entry for a variety of purposes are contained in s 17.

Search with warrant from a magistrate

Section 8 of the 1984 Act permits a magistrate to issue a warrant authorising the search of premises if he or she is satisfied, pursuant to an application by a constable, that there are reasonable grounds for believing that a serious arrestable offence has been committed and that there is material in the specified premises which is likely to be admissible evidence of substantial value to the investigation of that offence(s). In addition, one of the following further conditions must be satisfied:

- it is not practicable to communicate with any person entitled to grant access to the premises;
- although it is practicable to communicate with someone entitled to grant access to the premises, it is not practicable to communicate with any person entitled to grant access to the evidence;
- entry to the premises will not be granted without a warrant;
- the purpose of the search may be frustrated or seriously prejudiced unless the police can gain immediate access to the premises.

The police officer applying for a warrant must state: the ground for making the application; the enactment under which the application is made; the premises to be searched; and the object of the search (s 15). If the application is refused, no further application may be made for a warrant to search the same premises unless supported by fresh evidence (Code B, para 2.8).

A warrant may not be issued under s 8 to search for material which is subject to legal privilege, excluded material or special procedure material (see below). The procedure both for applying for a search warrant and executing the same is contained in PACE, ss 15 and 16.

The same procedure governs the issuing of warrants under any other enactment.

Contents of the warrant

A valid search warrant must contain the following information:

- the name of the applicant;
- the date of issue;
- the statute under which it is issued;
- the premises to be searched;
- as far as is practicable, the articles or persons sought.

A warrant which fails to specify any of the above, or does not do so adequately, or which purports to authorise the seizure of materials not permitted by the enabling Act, is invalid (*R v Reading Justices, ex parte South West Meat Ltd* [1992] Crim LR 672; *R v Hunt* [1992] Crim LR 747; *Darbo v DPP* [1992] Crim LR 56). If the building to be searched is divided into flats or separate dwellings, the warrant should specify which flat is to be searched (*R v South Western Magistrates' Court, ex parte Cofie* [1997] 1 WLR 885).

Executing the warrant

A warrant to enter and search remains valid for one month from the date of issue (s 16(3)). It may be executed by any police officer and may authorise them to be accompanied by other persons who may or may not be other police officers (s 16(1) and (2)). Only one entry and search is permitted. Hence the warrant may not be used for repeated searches of the named premises (s 15(5)). Execution of the warrant should be at a 'reasonable hour' unless this would frustrate the purpose of the search (s 16(4)).

The occupier's consent to entry should be sought unless: the premises are known to be unoccupied; there is no person present authorised to grant entry; or there are reasonable grounds for believing that such communication would frustrate the objects of the search or endanger the officers (Code B, para 5.4). Reasonable force may be used to effect entry where any of the above conditions apply or access has been refused (Code B, para 5.6). Reasons for resort to the use of force should be given if the owner/occupier is present (*Lineham* v *DPP* [1999] All ER 1080). Where the occupier of the premises is present the officer executing the warrant should identify him/herself and produce his/her warrant card if not in uniform (s 16(5)). He/she should produce the warrant and supply the occupier with a copy (*ibid.*). If the occupier is not present, the same rules apply to any person who appears to be in charge of the premises. If no such person is present, a copy of the warrant must be left in a prominent place on the premises (s 16(5), (6) and (7)).

A failure to show the original warrant or any part of it to the occupier or other person present, or a failure to provide a correct copy of the same, will render the entry and search to be unlawful and deprive the police of any lawful authority to retain possession of any items which were seized (*R* v *Chief Constable of Lancashire, ex parte Parker* [1992] 2 All ER 56). Code of Practice B, para 5.7 provides that the officer should also produce a notice specifying, *inter alia*, whether the search is made with warrant or with consent, the extent of the powers of search and seizure in the authorising Act, and the rights of both the occupier and the owner of any property seized.

As a general rule the officer should provide the necessary identification, the warrant, and the above notice before the search begins. This is not necessary, however, if to do so would frustrate the object of the search (Code B, para 5.8, as confirmed by the Court of Appeal in *R* v *Longman* [1988] 1 WLR 619).

Premises should be searched only to the extent which is necessary to secure the items specified in the warrant 'having regard to the size and nature of whatever is sought' (Code B, para 5.9). The search should be conducted 'with due consideration for the property and privacy of the occupier... and with no more disturbance than necessary' (Code B, para 5.10). Reasonable force may be used to implement the search where the 'co-operation of the occupier cannot be obtained or is insufficient for the purpose' (Code B, para 5.11). The officer may seize any items covered by the warrant (s 8(2)) and other items which he/she has reasonable grounds for believing to be evidence of any offence or to have been obtained in consequence of such offence (s 19). This includes information in a computer (s 20).

Once the warrant has been executed it should be endorsed to show the date of execution, whether any items were seized, the names of the officers who executed it, and whether a copy and the other required information was given to the occupier or left on the premises (Code B, para 7.1). The warrant should then be returned to the court which issued it. Unused warrants should be returned before the expiry of one month from the date of issue (Code B, para 7.3). Returned warrants are retained for one year and affected occupiers have the right to inspect them.

Proceedings for abuse of powers provided by a search warrant should be pursued by an action for trespass and not by way of judicial review (*R* v *Chief Constable of Warwickshire, The Independent*, 13 October 1997).

Legally privileged, excluded and special procedure materials

General comment

Sections 9–14 of PACE deals with the procedure for and the extent of police access to various types of confidential information held, perhaps, by solicitors, doctors, accountants, banks, social workers, etc. The general rule is that legally privileged material is never obtainable. Access to excluded and special procedure materials cannot be given by the issue of a warrant by a magistrate under s 8. Under s 9, however, those in possession of such material may, in specified circumstances, be required to deliver them up to the police pursuant to an order of a circuit judge. The procedure for issue of the same is found in PACE, Sched 1.

Legally privileged material (PACE, s 10)

This consists of:

(a) communications in the form of legal advice between professional legal adviser and client whether or not related to legal proceedings;
(b) other communications between professional legal adviser and client and between the latter and any other person which do relate to actual or contemplated legal proceedings.

As already indicated, no warrant or other order may be issued authorising premises to be searched for the same unless the materials are held for a criminal purpose (s 10(2)).

The general purpose of the provision is to ensure that the individual is able to speak freely to his/her legal adviser without the danger of incriminating him or herself by records of such conversations falling into the hands of the police. This does not mean, however, that everything held in a solicitor's office is privileged and unobtainable. The privilege applies only to that related to legal advice or legal proceedings. Hence, in *R v Inner London Crown Court, ex parte Baines and Baines* [1987] 3 All ER 1025, it was held that documents held by a solicitor which related purely to certain commercial activities (i.e. the financing and purchase of a house), were not legally privileged.

Material held for a criminal purpose is excluded from the privilege (s 10(2)). The criminal purpose may be that of the solicitor, the client, or some other person and it matters not that the person in possession – usually the solicitor – is innocent of that purpose. In *R v Central Criminal Court, ex parte Francis and Francis* [1988] 3 All ER 775, access was sought to information held by a solicitor relating to certain property transactions. The police believed that the moneys to finance the same had been supplied by a relative of the client and were derived from drug-trafficking. Both the solicitor and the client were thought to be unaware of the moneys' dubious origins. By a majority, the House of Lords decided that otherwise legally privileged materials could be held for a criminal purpose albeit that such purpose could not be attributed to the person in possession of them. Hence, in the case itself, the criminal purpose of a third party was sufficient to negate any privilege which might otherwise have attached to the material in question, thereby rendering it subject to production according to the procedure in PACE, Sched 1 (see below).

Excluded material (PACE, s 11)

This is defined as:

(a) personal records acquired or created in a trade, business, profession, or other occupation or for the purposes of diagnosis or medical treatment, or
(b) human tissue or tissue fluid taken for the purpose of diagnosis or medical treatment, or
(c) journalistic materials consisting of documents or records held in confidence.

Special procedure material (PACE, s 14)

This consists of:

(a) any journalistic material which does not fall within the definition of excluded material – i.e. documents and records not held in confidence or other materials, held in confidence or not, compiled or acquired for the purpose of journalism;
(b) material which is neither legally privileged nor excluded material acquired or created in any trade, business, profession or occupation which is held in confidence, i.e. subject to an express or implied undertaking or statutory requirement to restrict disclosure or maintain secrecy. Examples of this category of special procedure materials would include the accounts of a Youth Association (*R v Central Criminal Court, ex parte Adegbesan* [1986] 3 All ER 113); conveyancing documents held by a solicitor (*R v Inner London Crown Court, ex parte Baines and Baines*, above); bank accounts (*R v Leicester Crown Court, ex parte DPP* [1987] 3 All ER 654).

Journalistic materials are protected in the interests of a free press. Hence journalists are enabled to collect information about criminal activities without having to worry that – save in exceptional circumstances – their premises may be searched by the police (see Contempt of Court Act 1981, s 10).

Procedure for access to excluded and special procedure materials (PACE, Sched 1)

The process begins by the police making an *inter partes* application to a circuit judge. Notice of application for production should be served on the person believed to be in possession of the requisite materials. Notice need not be served on the person under investigation if he/she is in possession (*R v Leicester Crown Court, ex parte DPP*, above). The notice should specify the premises where the material is believed to be and the nature of the offence being investigated – e.g. 'robbery', 'fraud' (*R v Central Criminal Court, ex parte Carr, The Independent,* 5 March 1987). The material sought should also be identified to avoid contravention of Sched

1, para 11 to the effect that it should not be concealed, destroyed, altered or disposed of.

At the hearing the police must satisfy the judge that one of the two sets of access conditions has been met. The person in possession has a right to be heard and the court has a discretion to hear also the person under investigation (*R* v *Lewes Crown Court, ex parte Hill* (1990) 93 Cri App R 60).

The first set of access conditions applies to special procedure material only. These are that there are reasonable grounds for believing:

- that a serious arrestable offence has been committed;
- that there is special procedure material in the specified premises;
- that the material is likely to be of substantial evidential value to the offence being investigated;

and that,

- other methods of obtaining the material have been tried without success or have not been tried because they were likely to fail;
- because of the material's likely benefit to the investigation the public interest in its production outweighs the public interest in confidentiality.

The second set of access conditions applies to both excluded and special procedure material. These are:

- that a warrant to search for the material could have been granted under a pre-PACE enactment (all such powers having been repealed by PACE, s 9(2));
- that there are reasonable grounds for believing that excluded or special procedure material may be found in the premises specified.

If either set of access conditions is satisfied the judge may order that the materials sought be delivered up to the police within seven days or that they be allowed access to them. Failure to comply constitutes contempt of court. In the event of such failure a warrant may be issued authorising the police to enter and search. A search warrant may also be issued by a circuit judge in respect of excluded or special procedure material where either set of access conditions is satisfied and:

- it is not practicable to communicate with any person entitled to grant access to the premises in question;
- the above is practicable but it is not practicable to communicate with any person entitled to grant access to the materials;
- disclosure of, or access to, the material is restricted by statute and is, therefore, unlikely to be given unless in compliance with a warrant;
- notice of an application for an order is likely to seriously prejudice the investigation.

Such warrants are subject to the general provisions applying to search with warrant considered above.

Other statutory powers of entry

Section 17 of PACE specifies the circumstances in which a police officer may enter premises without a search warrant. All pre-existing powers of entry without warrant were repealed (s 17(5)). The specified circumstances are:

(a) to execute a warrant of arrest;

(b) to arrest a person for an arrestable offence;

(c) to arrest a person under s 1 of the Public Order Act 1936 (wearing a uniform denoting membership of a political organisation in a public place) or s 4 of the Public Order Act 1986 (causing fear or provocation of violence);

(d) to arrest for any offence under ss 6–10 of the Criminal Law Act 1977 (squatting);

(e) to recapture a person unlawfully at large whom the officer is pursuing (i.e. in 'hot-pursuit' of, see *De Souza* v *DPP* [1992] 4 All ER 545);

(f) to save life or limb or prevent serious damage to property.

Except in the case of (f), the officer must have reasonable grounds for believing that the person is in the property.

Entry at common law

In addition to the above, the common-law power to enter private premises without warrant to deal with actual or apprehended breaches of the peace is preserved expressly by s 17(6). In *McLeod* v *Metropolitan Police Commissioner* [1994] 4 All ER 553, the Court of Appeal's view was that this 'was a power to enter premises to prevent a breach of the peace as a form of preventative justice' where there is 'a real and imminent risk' of such breach being committed.

Note that the above are principally powers of entry only. Section 17 confers no general power of search beyond that of effecting the purpose for which entry was made – i.e. to find the person to be arrested or recaptured or to deal with the danger specified in (f). As explained above, however, s 32 allows a police officer to search any premises where a person was immediately before or at the time of arrest (for evidence of the offence for which he/she was arrested). Section 18 permits the officer to search any premises occupied or controlled by a person under arrest (for evidence of the offence or any other offences that person may have committed).

Seizure

The extent of the power of seizure available to a police officer who is lawfully in private premises is governed by PACE, s 19. The power is to seize anything the officer has reasonable grounds for believing to have been obtained through the commission of an offence or to be evidence of any offence and, in either case, which it is necessary to seize in order to prevent it being concealed, lost, damaged, altered or destroyed. This is a power of seizure only and confers no authority to enter and search for such items. However, used in conjunction with the powers of entry and search discussed above, s 19 has the following practical consequences:

- a police officer lawfully on premises in order to execute a search warrant may seize any items covered by s 19 which they 'happen upon' in search for the articles specified in the warrant (*R v Southwark Crown Court and HM Customs, ex parte Sorsky Defries* [1996] Crim LR 195);
- a police officer lawfully on premises to effect an arrest or recapture a person unlawfully at large whom they are pursuing may seize any items covered by s 19 which they 'happen upon' while looking for the person in question;
- a police officer on premises with the occupier's consent may seize any items covered by s 19 which they happen to see there while acting within that consent.

For practical operational reasons, the power of seizure in s 19 was extended by the Criminal Justice and Police Act 2001, s 50. This allows that a person lawfully on premises may seize:

(a) anything he has reasonable grounds for believing may be contained in something for which he is authorised to search the premises;

(b) anything he would be entitled to seize 'but for its being comprised in something else that he has no power to seize'.

These powers may be used where, in all the circumstances, ascertaining the seizable property on the premises would not be reasonably practicable due to constraints of time, the number of persons needed, or technology.

Such difficulties may arise for the law enforcement agencies perhaps because of the bulk of the material or because it is contained within a set of documents which may also contain privileged material. It may also be the case that the material is held on computer. Hence it may be impossible to establish which material is relevant and seizable unless all the information stored is examined forensically. This may require removing the computer and/or imaging the entire contents of its hard disks and/or removing CD Roms or floppy disks.

The new provision allows the police and law enforcement agencies to do two things to circumvent these problems. First, they may remove entire collections of documents or information, however stored, so that these can be examined elsewhere. Second, it is recognised that, with the advance of technology, it may be perfectly possible to keep material for which there may be a power of seizure within the same physical object as perfectly innocent material or that which may be privileged.

A power of seizure from the person in similar circumstances is given by s 51. The explanatory notes to the Act say that this is necessary because, for example, individuals might have on them hand-held computers or computer disks which might contain electronic data which the police might wish to seize. Alternatively, they could be carrying a suitcase containing a bulk of correspondence which could not be examined in the street (para 165).

The use of force

Section 117 of PACE permits an officer to use reasonable force, where necessary, in order to exercise any of the powers conferred by the Act.

In the case of powers of entry, the general principle is that force should only be used 'if need be' (per Waller LJ, *Lunt* v *DPP* [1993] Crim LR 534). Otherwise, the officer should take all reasonable steps to secure the occupier's consent (subject to the exceptions dealt with above in the context of search with warrant). Where that consent is refused, unless circumstances make it 'impossible and impracticable or undesirable', the occupant should be given reasons for any forced entry (*O'Loughlin* v *Chief Constable of Essex* [1998] 1 WLR 374).

REMEDIES FOR POLICE MALPRACTICE

A person arrested unlawfully, either because no power of arrest existed or because any of the requirements of a valid arrest was not complied with, may sue for the tort of false arrest and imprisonment. The tort of assault and battery might also apply both to the above and to abuse of the power of stop and search. An action for false imprisonment would also be available to a person who was detained for a longer period than that permitted by PACE, ss 41–43. The issue whether otherwise lawful detention may be rendered actionable by breaches of the rules relating to the treatment of detainees and the conditions of detention remains a matter of some uncertainty. The probability is that it is not rendered actionable (*Weldon* v *Home Office* [1991] 3 WLR 340; cf. *Middleweek* v *Chief Constable of Merseyside* [1990] 3 All ER 62). Failure to comply with any requirement in the Codes of Practice in relation to a person in detention is not actionable in itself. It is conceivable, however, that an action for breach of statutory duty might lie if one of the statutory requirements has not been honoured (e.g. the right of access to a solicitor (s 58)).

A person who believes he/she has been detained unlawfully – or another person on his/her behalf – may also apply to the Divisional Court of the Queen's Bench Division for a prerogative writ of habeas corpus. If the court accepts the allegation as set out in the applicant's affidavit, the writ is issued requiring the detained person to be brought before the court. The issue is then decided on its merits and, if those holding the detained person cannot provide satisfactory authority or justification, his/her release will be ordered.

An action for trespass to land and/or goods may be used where a person's premises have been searched and perhaps items seized if there was no legal authority for such intrusion or if any of the requirements for valid search were not complied with. An entry which is lawful initially (either with a warrant to search or under s 17) may be rendered unlawful *ab initio* and, therefore, a trespass from the beginning if a police officer does something in the premises which exceeds the purpose for which the power of entry was given. In *Harrison and Hope* v *Chief Constable of Greater Manchester*, unreported, 14 August 1994, the police entered premises lawfully under s 17 to arrest a person believed to have committed an arrestable offence. The suspect was not there. However, the police searched the premises, including a wardrobe and drawers in a bedroom belonging to an eleven-year-old boy. The plaintiffs were awarded £2,000 for trespass.

A person aggrieved by the actions of a police officer also has the option of making a complaint according to the police complaints procedure now contained in the

Police Act 1997, Pt IV. This may result in the officer being disciplined but does not provide the complainant with any right of redress in the form of financial compensation.

LEGAL REGULATION OF INVESTIGATORY POWERS

Introduction

Effective policing and the protection of national security depends on information and intelligence. Much useful material can be gained by listening to or intercepting communications between individuals, by accessing information systems and by the more traditional means of watching and listening to people in their domestic and working environments. Any such activities by law enforcement agencies have, however, serious implications for the rights of individuals, particularly those relating to respect for private life, home and correspondence as contained in Art 8 of the European Convention on Human Rights.

For most of the twentieth century the law in the United Kingdom paid little heed to these aspects of criminal investigations. Hence, to the extent these sorts of activities were engaged in by the police and intelligence services, this was not based on any clear legal foundation.

Legislation to provide for and to regulate the interception of communications by post and telephone was finally introduced by the Interception of Communications Act 1985. This followed the decision in *Malone* v *United Kingdom* (1985) 7 EHRR 14 where the European Court of Human Rights decided that the previous practice in the United Kingdom, whereby telephone tapping was regulated by the Home Office guidelines only, did not comply with the Convention requirement that interference with the right to privacy (Art 8) should be:

(i) 'in accordance with the law', i.e. founded on easily accessible and comprehensible legal rules; and,

(ii) limited to circumstances where this could be related to one of the Convention's 'legitimate aims' or permissible public interests, e.g. the prevention of disorder or crime.

Interception of postal communications was already subject to the rather minimal requirements of the Post Office Act 1953. This provided that the opening of a postal packet was an offence unless pursuant to a warrant issued by the Home Secretary (s 58). The procedure and criteria for grant of such warrants were again, however, contained on Home Office rules which had no formal basis in law.

The first statutory provision for, and regulation of, intrusive electronic surveillance by the police was effected by the Police Act 1997. This permits interference with rights of private property for surveillance purposes for the detection of 'serious crime' pursuant to authorisation by a senior officer (Assistant Chief Constable or above). 'Serious crime' was defined by the Interception of Communications Act 1985, s 10, as any offence which involved, *inter alia*, the use of violence or results in substantial financial gain or for which a person with no previous convictions might reasonably be expected to be sentenced to a term of imprisonment of three years or more. Prior to the 1997 Act this type of surveillance, as with the interception of postal and telecommunications before the 1985 Act, was governed by Home Office rules only.

Legal authority for similar intrusive electronic surveillance by the Security Service (MI5) for the investigation of terrorism and espionage, or by the Secret Intelligence Service (MI6) for investigating threats to defence and national security, had previously been provided by the Intelligence Services Act 1994. The extent of the authority conferred by this and by the Police Act 1997 is considered further below.

Despite the relative modernity of much of the above legislation, continuing and rapid developments in information and communications technology meant that, for certain purposes, the legal framework it provided soon proved no longer adequate either as a sufficient legal basis for the activities of the law enforcement agencies or for the proper protection of the rights of the individual. In particular, none of the legislation mentioned contained any specific provisions relating to private telecommunications systems nor was any of it designed to deal with such developments as pagers, mobile phones, emails, the internet or the protection of information by encryption. The government's response to these difficulties, and its attempt to modernise the law in this context for both law enforcement and human rights purposes, was provided by the Regulation of Investigatory Powers Act (RIPA) 2000.

Objectives and general content

The stated purpose of the Act was to consolidate the law relating to the use of investigatory powers and to ensure that these are used in compliance with the Human Rights Act 1998. The powers to which the Act is directed are:

(i)   the interception of communications;
(ii) the acquisition of communications data;
(iii) intrusive surveillance of residential premises;
(iv) covert surveillance in the course of specific operations;
(v)   the use of covert human intelligence sources (informants, etc.);
(vi) giving access to information protected by encryption.

The Act makes clear the purposes for which each of these powers may be used, which of the law enforcement agencies may use them, the procedure for their activation and the uses which may be made of the information acquired.

The interception of communications

Part 1, chapter 1 of RIPA sets out:

(a)   the circumstances in which postal and electronic communications may be intercepted lawfully with and without warrant (ss 1–5);
(b)   who may apply for an interception warrant (s 6);
(c)   the information to be included in such warrant (s 8);
(d)   the period of time for which a warrant remains valid (s 9).

Section 3 permits interception without warrant where:

(i)   both parties to the communication have consented to it or, with one party's consent, where the intercept has been authorised for surveillance purposes, e.g. where the conversation takes place between a kidnapper and a relative of the hostage;

(ii) it is effected by the provider of the communications system for technical or operational reasons;

(iii) it is carried out for the purposes of the Wireless Telegraphy Act 1949 including the detention and prevention of anything that interferes with transmissions regulated by that Act.

Intercept without warrant under s 4 may be effected according to:

(a)   regulations made by the Home Secretary to give effect to international agreements relating to crime prevention and, in particular, the EU Convention on Mutual Assistance in Criminal Matters;

(b)   regulations made by the Home Secretary to permit intercepts in the course of lawful business practice, e.g. for recording transactions with call centres;

(c)   rules made by the Home Secretary for the management and maintenance of order and discipline in prisons;

(d)   directions made under the NHS Act 1977, s 17, concerning the provision of high security psychiatric units.

Interception with warrant is regulated by s 5. The Home Secretary may issue an interception warrant where 'he believes ... it is necessary' and that the conduct authorised is proportionate to what is sought to be achieved in the interests of:

- national security;
- preventing or detecting serious crime;
- safeguarding the economic well-being of the United Kingdom;
- to facilitate compliance with international agreements for crime prevention in circumstances where the detection or prevention of serious crime might be involved.

The persons who may apply for an interception warrant include chief officers of police, the Director-Generals of the Security and Intelligence Services (MI5 and MI6), GCHQ and the National Criminal Intelligence Service (s 6).

An interception warrant must contain details of the person or organisation which is the subject of the intercept or the premises in which it is to take place and should be accompanied by one or more schedules describing the communications which are to be intercepted, e.g. by citing telephone or email numbers/addresses (s 8).

As a general rule an interception warrant will remain valid for three months. Renewal for successive periods of three months is permitted for warrants issued for the detection or prevention of crime and for periods of six months where related to national security or the economic well-being of the country. Should the grounds on which the warrant was issued cease to exist, the warrant should be cancelled (s 9).

The Home Secretary is under a duty to ensure that the use of intercepted material is restricted to the minimum necessary for the authorised purposes (s 15). It is to be similarly restricted in terms of the extent of its disclosure and distribution within the agencies involved. Also, as a general rule, such material is not available for use in legal proceedings (s 17). It would appear, however, that material intercepted outside the state, providing this was done according to the law of the state in which the intercept was effected, is not covered by this domestic prohibition and may, therefore, be admitted as evidence (*R v P* [2001] 2 All ER 58). Unauthorised disclosure of information in or relating to an interception warrant or the intercepted material itself is an offence (s 19). Where such material ceases to be relevant for the purpose for which it was acquired it should be destroyed (s 13).

Acquisition and disclosure of communications data

Part 1, chapter 2 of RIPA regulates the acquisition and use of communications data. This is information relating to the use of a communications system but not the contents of communications transmitted through it. Such information would include data showing that certain communications have taken place, between whom, and how often, e.g. the details of telephone numbers called from a particular phone or extension (s 21).

Authorisation to acquire such information may be given where a person designated in regulations believes that the means to be used are proportionate to what is sought to be achieved and are necessary for the purposes of:

- national security;
- the prevention or detection of crime and the prevention of disorder;
- the economic well-being of the country;
- public safety;
- the protection of public health;
- the assessment or collection of taxes;
- the needs of an emergency or for preventing death or injury;
- purposes otherwise specified in regulations made by the Home Secretary (s 22).

The data may be acquired by a person authorised for that purpose by serving a notice on the particular service provider to deliver up whatever is specified (*ibid.*). Such authority or requirement remains valid for one month from the time it was given. The duty to provide the data or information is enforceable in civil proceedings by the Secretary of State (*ibid.*).

Surveillance and covert human intelligence sources

These matters are dealt with in Part 2 of the Act, ss 26–48.

Three types of activity are defined. These are:

(a) directed surveillance;
(b) the use of covert human intelligence sources;
(c) intrusive surveillance (s 26).

Directed surveillance is covert surveillance related to a particular investigation which is likely to result in the obtaining of private information about any person.

The use of human intelligence sources occurs where a member of a law enforcement agency establishes a personal or other relationship with a person for the covert purpose of persuading that person to obtain or provide information.

Intrusive surveillance is that which is carried out covertly in relation to anything taking place in residential premises or a private vehicle. It may be undertaken by placing a person or device inside the premises or by placing the same outside in a way which produces information of equivalent quality.

In all cases the person granting the authority must believe that the conduct which he/she has sanctioned is necessary for, and proportionate to, what is sought to be achieved (ss 28 and 29).

Authorisation for direct surveillance or the use of covert human intelligence sources may be given by police superintendents and above and by such other persons as are designated by the Home Secretary (s 30). The purposes for which such authority may be granted are as those cited above for the acquisition of communications data save that the permitted surveillance purposes do not include a provision relating to the needs of emergencies or the prevention of death or injury (*ibid.*).

In the case of intrusive surveillance, authorisation may be given by a chief officer of police or by the heads of the National Criminal Intelligence Services or the National Crime Squad (s 32) in the interest of:

- national security;
- preventing or detecting serious crime;
- the economic well-being of the United Kingdom (*ibid.*).

Except in urgent cases such authorisation will not take effect until approved by a surveillance commissioner appointed under the Police Act 1997, s 91.

Authorisation for intrusive intelligence by a member of the intelligence services, armed forces or Ministry of Defence must be given by the Home Secretary. In the case of the Ministry of Defence this may be given for the purposes of national security and the prevention/detection of serious crime only (s 41).

Authorisation for intrusive surveillance by any of the intelligence services must be in the form of a warrant. For the purposes of the Security Service (MI5) such warrants may extend to matters of:

- national security;
- the prevention/detection of serious crime;
- the economic well-being of the United Kingdom (s 42).

Warrants granted to the Secret Intelligence Service (MI6) or GCHQ must be limited to matters of:

- national security;
- the economic well-being of the United Kingdom.

Access to encrypted data

Encryption refers to the process of turning computer data into a series of letters and/or numbers which cannot be deciphered or 'unscrambled' except with the correct password or key. The practice has developed for the purposes of confidentiality and transaction security in e-commerce.

Where encrypted information has been obtained by a law enforcement agency through the exercise of one of its powers, e.g. the execution of a warrant under this or other statutory provision, s 49 of RIPA enables a properly authorised person to serve a notice on a specified individual or organisation requiring such to deliver up the information in intelligible form or supply the key necessary to decrypt it. Failure to comply with such notice is an offence (s 53).

An encryption notice may be served in the interests of:

- national security;
- preventing or detecting crime;
- the economic well-being of the United Kingdom.

The person serving the notice must have reasonable grounds for believing that:

(i)   the protected information is in possession of the persons on whom the notice is served;
(ii) its service is necessary in any of the interests cited above;
(iii) its service is proportionate to what is sought to be achieved;
(iv) an intelligible version of the information cannot be obtained otherwise (s 47).

Permission to serve an encryption notice must be granted by a judge or by the Home Secretary in the case of an application by a member of the intelligence services (Sched 2).

Scrutiny of the exercise and use of investigatory powers

The Act provides for the appointment of an:

(a) Interception of Communications Commissioner;
(b) Intelligence Services Commissioner (s 57).

The functions of the Interception Communications Commissioner are to keep under review, *inter alia*, the role of the Secretary of State in granting interception warrants and authorisation for encryption notices and the general operation of the scheme for acquiring communications data (*ibid.*). The Commission is to make an annual report on these matters to the Prime Minister (s 58).

The Intelligence Services Commissioner is to keep under review the exercise of the minister's powers in relation to those services including the granting of authorisation for surveillance and decryption purposes and the action taken to carry out those authorisations (s 59). He is also required to make an annual report to the Prime Minister concerning the exercise and use of the powers within his remit (s 60). The reports of both Commissioners are to be laid before Parliament (ss 58 and 60).

The Act concludes its substantive provisions by establishing a tribunal to hear proceedings for alleged abuse of human rights and complaints generally. The key elements of the Tribunal's jurisdiction are as follows:

(a) any proceedings alleging actions incompatible with Convention rights
   (i) by any of the intelligence services,
   (ii) which concern the use of the Act's investigatory powers or any entry or interference with the property or wireless telegraphy;
(b) any complaint that a person has been subjected to the use of the Act's investigatory powers or any entry or interference with property or wireless telegraphy by the intelligence services;
(c) any complaint that a person has been affected prejudicially in civil proceedings by the provision in s 17 precluding the use of intercepted material as evidence;
(d) any other proceedings against any of the intelligence services concerning the use of powers under this Act or the Intelligence Services Act 1994.

Other powers of electronic surveillance

The Regulation of Investigatory Powers Act will operate alongside the Police Act 1997 and the Intelligence Services Act 1994. These were the first pieces of legislation to authorise interference with private rights or a property for the purposes of electronic surveillance. The 1997 Act, s 93, conferred the relevant powers on the police while the 1994 Act, s 5, provided the necessary legal basis for similar activities by the Security Service (MI5), the Secret Intelligence Service (MI6) and GCHQ.

In the case of the Security Service, the Secret Intelligence Service or GCHQ, the authority to exercise the power must be in the form of a warrant issued by the Secretary of State. Such warrant should identify the premises or property concerned. In relation to the police, authorisation may be given by an officer of the rank of assistant chief constable or above but in certain cases must be approved by one of a number of commissioners appointed by the Prime Minister. This is required where:

• the property in question is a dwelling house, a hotel room or office premises;
• execution of the authorisation could result in the acquisition of legally privileged material, confidential personal information or confidential journalistic material (ss 93 and 97).

A warrant or authorisation should not be issued unless it is believed that the action permitted thereby is necessary and proportionate to the achievement of any of the agency's functions.

The functions of the Security Service are:

(a) the protection of national security
   • in general,
   • from threats of espionage, terrorism or sabotage by foreign agents or powers,

- from any other acts intended to undermine parliamentary democracy by political, industrial or violent means;
(b) the safeguarding of the economic well-being of the United Kingdom against threats posed by persons outside the United Kingdom;
(c) the support of the police in the prevention and detection of 'serious crime' (Security Service Act 1989, s 1).

The functions of the Secret Intelligence Service are to 'obtain information' and to 'perform other tasks' in relation to persons outside the United Kingdom in the interests of:

(a) national security, with particular reference to defence and foreign policy;
(b) the economic well-being of the United Kingdom;
(c) the prevention or detection of serious crime (Intelligence Services Act 1994).

The principal stated function of GCHQ is to monitor and interfere with communications signals and to use the information acquired thereby in the interests of (a)–(c) above (*ibid.*).

The function of the police for the purpose of the powers in the 1997 Act is the prevention or detection of 'serious crime' (as defined by the Interception of Communications Act 1985, s 10 now RIPA, s 81).

A warrant relating to property in the United Kingdom may not be issued to the Secret Intelligence Service or GCHQ for the purpose of investigating or detecting serious crime. A warrant for this purpose may, however, be issued to the Security Service.

Other points of interest and, perhaps, controversy arising out of these Acts are as follows:

- they recognise the existence of, and confer statutory powers upon, the 'covert' security forces, viz. MI5, MI6 and GCHQ;
- they authorise such forces or agencies to act in support of the police in dealing with serious or organised crime;
- they confer on these forces and on the police extensive powers to enter and interfere with private property without a judicial warrant.

References

Casey (1992) *Constitutional Law in Ireland* (2nd edn), London: Sweet & Maxwell.

Card and English (1998) *Butterworths' Police Law* (5th edn), London: Butterworths.

Stone (1997) *Textbook on Civil Liberties* (2nd edn), London: Blackstone.

Further reading

Allen and Thompson (1996) *Cases and Materials on Constitutional and Administrative Law* (4th edn), London: Blackstone, Ch 7.

Bailey, Harris and Jones (2001) *Civil Liberties: Cases and Materials* (5th edn), London: Butterworths, Chs 1–2.

Feldman (1993) *Civil Liberties and Human Rights in England and Wales*, Oxford: Clarendon Press, Chs 1 and 5.

Robertson (1993) *Freedom, the Individual and the Law* (7th edn), London: Penguin, Ch 1.

Zander (1995) *The Police and Criminal Evidence Act 1984* (3rd edn), London: Sweet & Maxwell.

Chapter 21

RESTRICTIONS ON THE RIGHTS OF FREEDOM OF ASSEMBLY AND ASSOCIATION

INTRODUCTION: THE FREEDOMS DEFINED

The freedom of association and assembly encapsulates two related but not entirely identical concepts. The freedom of association refers to the right of the individual to join whichever organisations they wish (e.g. political parties, cause groups, etc.), and implies that the state shall not impose unjustified restrictions on the existence of such groups. The freedom of assembly deals with the right of the individual to meet with others in public or private and, in concert with them, to march or demonstrate in support of whichever cause they may wish to further.

Freedom of association

English law imposes few restrictions on the freedom to form and join organisations for political or other purposes. The freedom does not extend, however, to those groups which would seek to achieve their objectives by overtly violent means. Hence the Terrorism Act 2000 gives the Home Secretary the power to proscribe any organisation he or she believes 'commits, participates, prepares, promotes or is otherwise engaged in acts of terrorism' (s 3).

Other restrictions related to the freedom of association include the provision in the Public Order Act 1936, s 1 making it an offence to wear any uniform in a public place or at a public meeting signifying association with a political organisation. Mention might also be made of the practice of excluding persons believed to have subversive sympathies or connections from senior positions in the public services.

Freedom of assembly

This is subject to a wide range of statutory and common law restrictions. Most of the relevant statutory rules are to be found in the Public Order Act 1986 and the Criminal Justice and Public Order Act 1994. The common law power to do all that is reasonably necessary to prevent breaches of the peace is also of considerable practical significance in this context.

The Public Order Act 1986 gave the police extensive powers to regulate the conduct of both processions (i.e. gatherings which move from A to B) and public assemblies (i.e. gatherings which stay in one place). The Act also contains a range of offences with which those who endanger public order may be charged. The Criminal Justice and Public Order Act 1994 supplemented the 1986 Act, principally by providing additional preventative powers to deal with types of assemblies not covered by the latter.

Marches and processions

The 1986 Act contains three main powers or requirements in relation to the above. These are:

- the need to give advance notice;
- the power to impose conditions;
- the power to ban.

Advance notice

Section 11 requires that the organisers of certain types of public procession must give the police at least six days' advance notice of their intentions. The types of processions affected are those which are intended:

(a) to show 'support for or opposition to the views or actions of any person or body of persons';
(b) 'to publicise a cause or campaign';
(c) 'to mark or commemorate an event'.

The requirement does not apply to processions which are 'customarily held in the police area' or to funeral processions. Nor does it apply where it is not reasonably practicable for advance notice to be given – i.e. where the procession is an immediate response to a very recent event. In this case notice should be given as soon as is reasonably practicable.

The notice should specify the date, time and proposed route of the procession. The name and address of one of the organisers should also be included. It should be delivered to a police station in the district where the procession is to take place. Failure to comply with any of these requirements renders the organisers guilty of an offence.

Section 11 does not require that the police give consent to a proposed march. It is solely concerned with the giving of notice. It does, however, forewarn the police so that the powers in ss 12 and 13 may be activated as is appropriate.

Conditions

Section 12 of the 1986 Act allows the police to impose conditions on the conduct of a procession where it is reasonably believed that:

(a) it may result in serious public disorder, serious damage to property or serious disruption to the life of the community, or
(b) the purpose of the organisers is to intimidate other persons so as to prevent them doing what they have a right to do or to make them do what they have a right not to do.

The power may be exercised in advance of the procession by the chief constable of the police district in question or 'on the spot' by the senior officer present (which could be an ordinary constable if no more senior officer is in the vicinity). Such conditions may be imposed as appear to be necessary to prevent any of the dangers listed above. On-the-spot conditions may be imposed verbally. Those imposed in advance should be in writing. These could relate to the route to be taken, the numbers taking part, the display of banners or emblems, etc.

Any person who organises or takes part in a procession and who knowingly fails to comply with such conditions – except where this is due to circumstances beyond the person's control – commits an offence and may be arrested without warrant.

Bans

Section 13 provides that if the chief constable for the police district where a procession is due to take place 'reasonably believes' that the powers in s 12 will not be sufficient to prevent 'serious public order', he/she may apply to the local council for an order prohibiting all public processions or any class of the same in the area for a period not exceeding three months. The council may make such order only after receiving the consent of the Home Secretary. In the Metropolitan Police District such bans may be imposed by the Metropolitan Police Commissioner with the Home Secretary's consent.

Any person who organises or takes part in a procession which he or she knows is prohibited commits an offence and may be arrested without warrant.

Section 13 has attracted controversy because it does not permit the police to ban a specific march. Its terms make it clear that only 'blanket bans' (i.e. those affecting all or any class of procession) may be imposed. Inevitably, therefore, where such ban is made, as well as prohibiting those processions which might endanger public order, it will affect processions not thought to represent any such danger whatsoever. The validity of a s 13 ban will not be questioned by a court unless it is unreasonable or capricious (*Kent v Metropolitan Police Commissioner*, *The Times*, 15 May 1981). This is consistent with the general reluctance of the courts to interfere with the exercise of discretion conferred on chief officers of police except in the most extreme cases where a power is used in a way which could never have been within Parliament's contemplation.

Meetings and assemblies

These are defined as 'an assembly of 20 or more...in a public place which is wholly or partly open to the air' (s 16). The Public Order Act 1986 provided the police with a power to impose conditions on the holding of such gatherings but did not give any power to impose a ban. A power to ban trespassory assemblies was, however, inserted into the 1986 Act by the Criminal Justice and Public Order Act 1994.

Conditions

The power to impose conditions on a public assembly is contained in s 14 of the 1986 Act. The grounds on which such conditions may be imposed are exactly the same as those applying to processions (see above). The power may be exercised by the chief constable of the police district in which the assembly is to take place or by the senior officer 'on the spot'.

An offence is committed by any person who organises or participates in such assembly and who knowingly fails to comply with any condition(s) applying thereto. That person may be arrested without warrant.

A conviction for failure to comply with a s 14 condition cannot be upheld if, on the facts, the ground on which the condition(s) was imposed did not exist or the person accused did not know, and could not reasonably have been expected to know, that the condition had been imposed. In *Police* v *Reid* [1981] Crim LR 702, a crowd gathered outside the South African embassy in London to protest against apartheid. Some of the demonstrators shouted and made insulting gestures at persons who were gathering for a reception which was being held at the embassy. A police officer using a loud hailer told the demonstrators to move away from the front of the embassy building. In the officer's view this was justified on the ground of intimidation. The defendant and others who did not comply were arrested and charged with an offence under s 14. In the stipendiary magistrate's opinion, however, causing discomfort did not amount to intimidation. Intimidation could only occur where a threat or violence was used to compel a person to act in a way inconsistent with his/her legal rights. *Brickley and Kitson* v *The Police,* unreported, July 1988, was also concerned with a demonstration outside the South African embassy. Again the demonstrators were instructed to move away from the embassy and, on this occasion, to hold their protest in a nearby street. The appellants' conviction for failure to comply was reversed by the Crown Court as, given the noisy and disorderly conditions which prevailed, the Court was not satisfied that they were fully aware either that conditions had been imposed or what those conditions were.

Bans and trespassory assemblies

Section 14A of the 1986 Act contains a power to ban trespassory assemblies. A trespassory assembly is one held on land to which the public has no, or only a restricted, right of access without the permission of the occupier. The procedure for prohibiting such assemblies is the same as that in s 13 relating to processions. The appropriate chief constable may apply to the local council for an order banning all such assemblies 'in the district or a part of it' where he/she reasonably believes that a trespassory assembly is intended to be held which may lead to serious disruption of the life of the community or may do significant damage to land, or to a building or monument which is of historical, archaeological, architectural or scientific interest. Such ban may then be imposed with the consent of the Home Secretary. In the Metropolis the banning order is made by the Metropolitan Police Commissioner, again with the Home Secretary's consent.

Any person who takes part in such an assembly knowing that it has been prohibited commits an offence (s 14B).

The wording of s 14A makes it clear that a trespassory assembly may take place on a public highway since this is a place to which the public have 'only a limited right of access' (i.e. to pass and repass). Hence, should a gathering of twenty or more take place on a highway within an area to which a banning order applies, those knowingly assembled in contravention of it commit an offence under s 14B except where the assembly does not cause unreasonable interference to the public's primary right of passage (*DPP* v *Jones* [1997] 2 ALL ER 119).

Other statutory preventative powers

The above represent the principal statutory powers designed to prevent public processions and assemblies from becoming disorderly. As the terms of the various provisions make clear, they have general application to the type of public demonstration often seen on the streets and in public places in the United Kingdom. In addition to these, the Criminal Justice and Public Order Act 1994 has given the police and public authorities a range of other preventative powers to deal with three types of gathering in particular, usually occurring on private property and about which, in the years immediately prior to the Act, there had been considerable political controversy – viz. assemblies and convoys of 'new age travellers', anti-blood sport demonstrations, and 'raves'.

Power to remove trespassers on land

Section 61 of the 1994 Act allows the police to order persons trespassing on land to leave if certain conditions are satisfied. These are that the senior officer present reasonably believes that two or more persons are trespassing on land with a common purpose to reside there for any period, that the occupier has taken reasonable steps to ask them to leave and:

(a) a damage has been caused to the land or property or threatening, abusive or insulting words have been used towards the occupier or anyone acting on his behalf; or
(b) there are six or more vehicles on the land.

   Where an order to leave has been given any person who fails to comply with it as soon as is reasonably practicable may be arrested without warrant and charged with an offence. A conviction will only follow, however, if the court is satisfied that the trespassers knew or should have known that they had been requested to leave. In *Krumpa and Anderson* v *DPP* [1989] Crim LR 295, K and A were living in converted buses on land belonging to a Tesco store. A Tesco representative told them that bulldozers would soon be arriving on the site to prepare it for development. Three weeks later the police ordered K and A to leave the site. It was held that the information conveyed by the Tesco representative to K and A did not amount to a request to leave. The police were not empowered, therefore, to order them to leave the site. It followed that K and A committed no offence when they failed to comply with the instruction.

   A further power to deal with trespasses not involving damage or the danger of disorder is contained in ss 77 and 78. This allows the appropriate local authority to direct persons residing in vehicles:

* on land forming part of a highway,
* on any unoccupied land, or
* on any occupied land without the occupier's permission,

to leave the land in question. Failure to comply constitutes an offence but is not arrestable without warrant. In addition, a magistrate's court may authorise the authority to take such steps as are reasonably necessary to ensure that the trespassers and their vehicles are removed (s 78).

Before issuing any such directions the local authority is under a duty to have regard to the individual circumstances of the persons affected and any duties which may be owed to them under any relevant Children, Education, Social Services and Housing Acts (R v *Lincolnshire County Council, ex parte Atkinson* [1996] Admin LR 529). Only those on the land when the directions are served are affected by them. Hence, such directions do not apply to those who arrive at a later date (*ibid.*).

Powers to deal with aggravated trespass

A trespass becomes an aggravated trespass if the intention of those involved is to intimidate those taking part in a lawful activity (e.g. hunting) on land in the open air (excluding highways) or to obstruct or disrupt that activity (s 68). Aggravated trespass is an offence and is arrestable without warrant. Where an aggravated trespass is committed the police may order those involved to leave the land as soon as is practicable and may arrest without warrant those who refuse to do so (s 69).

Powers to deal with raves

Section 63 of the 1994 Act provides that a police officer of the rank of superintendent or above may direct persons who it is reasonably believed have come to prepare, wait for, or attend a 'rave', to leave the land in question and remove any vehicles or other property they have with them. A 'rave' is defined as 'a gathering on land in the open air of 100 or more persons...at which amplified music is played during the night...and is such as, by reason of its loudness and duration and the time at which it is played...likely to cause serious distress to the inhabitants of the locality'. Any person who fails to comply with such direction commits an offence and may be arrested without warrant.

Section 64 gives the police a power to enter upon land without warrant to ascertain if a rave is taking place there or to enforce a direction issued under s 63. The police may also stop persons proceeding to a rave providing the power is exercised within five miles of the site of the gathering. Disobedience of police instructions would amount to an obstruction of the particular officer in the course of their duty. The essential principle that a breach of the peace must involve violence or the threat of it was confirmed in *Percy* v *DPP* [1995] 3 All ER 124. The appellant trespassed on a military base on a number of occasions and had been bound over to keep the peace. She did not commit or threaten any violence. The Divisional Court took the view that mere civil trespass does not amount to a breach of the peace. It followed that the magistrates had no power to bind her over.

The position in Northern Ireland

For Northern Ireland different provisions for marches and processions were introduced by the Public Processions (Northern Ireland) Act 1998.

Persons organising a public procession are required to give the police at least 28 days' notice of their intentions (s 6). Conditions may then be imposed, not by the police, but by a body known as the Parades Commission for Northern Ireland (s 1). The members of the Commission are appointed by the Secretary of State for Northern Ireland. The Commission is, however, 'not to be regarded as the servant or agent of the Crown' (s 1 and Sched 1). The Commission will be empowered to impose such conditions as it 'considers necessary' (s 8). In so doing the Commission will be required 'to have regard to' *inter alia*:

- any public disorder or damage to property which may result from the procession;
- any disruption to the life of the community which the procession may cause;
- any impact which the procession may have on relationships within the community; and
- the desirability of allowing a procession customarily held along a particular route to be held along that route.

Failure to comply with any such condition, unless because of circumstances beyond the person's control, will constitute an offence punishable by a maximum sentence of six months' imprisonment.

Note that the power to impose conditions on processions in Northern Ireland will not be dependent on the Commission having a *reasonable* belief that any of the above consequences might result from a particular procession. It will be sufficient that the Commission has directed its attention towards these possibilities.

The power to ban processions in Northern Ireland will be vested in the Secretary of State. The power may be exercised where the minister 'is of the opinion' that a ban is 'necessary in the public interest' having regard to the possible consequences of the procession in terms of serious public disorder; serious damage to property; serious disruption to the life of the community; serious impact on relationships within the community; or any undue demands which may be placed on the police or military forces (s 11). The Secretary of State will also be empowered to ban all or any class of processions in a particular area for a period not exceeding 28 days based on consideration of similar criteria.

The above provisions will leave the Northern Ireland Police Service with responsibility for policing public processions but will remove them from the politically-charged process of deciding whether such processions should take place and, if so, whether restrictions should be imposed on them. This, in theory, should help to reduce suspicions of police bias in the use of public order powers.

COMMON LAW PREVENTATIVE POWERS

Breach of the peace

It is the duty of every police officer to do all that is reasonably necessary to prevent an actual or reasonably apprehended and imminent breach of the peace. The concept has already been defined in the context of common law powers of arrest (see *R v Howell*, above).

In relation to the preservation of order during processions and at public and private meetings, the obligation to prevent breaches of the peace provides the police with a variety of powers. These have been held to include the following.

Arrest

A police officer may arrest without warrant any person who:

(a) has committed a breach of the peace in his/her presence;
(b) he/she reasonably believes is about to commit a breach of the peace;
(c) he/she reasonably believes is about to renew a breach of the peace which has been committed or is reasonably believed to have been committed (*R* v *Howell*, above; *Lain* v *Chief Constable of Cambridgeshire*, 14 October 1999, unreported).

Detention

The House of Lords, in *Albert* v *Lavin* [1982] AC 546, held that the reasonable steps which a police officer may take to prevent a person breaching the peace included the power to detain that person against his/her will without arresting them for so long as the necessity exists.

The power to detain to prevent a further breach of the peace is limited to circumstances where there is a real, rather than a fanciful, apprehension based on all the circumstances that if released the prisoner will commit or renew his breach of the peace within a short time (*McGrogan* v *Chief Constable of Cleveland Police* [2002] EWCA Civ 86).

Stop

A person may be stopped from proceeding to any place for the purpose of participating in any procession or assembly if it is reasonably believed that breaches of the peace will be occasioned by the same. The power to stop may be used in circumstances where 'there is a real risk of a breach of the peace in the sense that it is in close proximity both in place and time' (per Skinner J, *Moss* v *McLachlan* (1984) 149 JP 167). In this case, which arose out of the 1984 Miners' Strike, the power was held to provide sufficient justification for stopping a group of miners from travelling to various collieries to join fellow strikers on the picket lines. The miners in question were stopped as they left the motorway at a point within five miles of the pits to which they were travelling. Breaches of the peace had already occurred on the picket lines which they intended to join. The court was in no doubt that in these circumstances the police possessed the power to stop and that those miners who had refused to do so were guilty of obstruction.

Desist and disperse

Where a procession or meeting which it is reasonably believed may result in a breach of the peace is in progress or is about to commence any person organising, conducting or addressing the meeting may be ordered to desist and those taking part may be ordered to disperse. Any person may be arrested for obstruction if such instruction is ignored. Two famous cases illustrate the point. *O'Kelly* v *Harvey* (1883) 14 LR Ir

105, concerned a public meeting in Co. Fermanagh to protest about the rents imposed on Irish tenant farmers. The meeting was to be addressed by Parnell, then leader of the Irish Nationalist Party. It was believed that the meeting would be attended and disrupted by loyalists. The defendant, a justice of the peace, ordered the plaintiff, one of the organisers, to disperse the meeting. When the plaintiff refused, the defendant took hold of him and gave him into the custody of a police officer. The plaintiff's action for assault and battery was unsuccessful. The court's reasoning was as follows:

> even assuming that the danger to the public peace arose altogether from the threatened attack of another body on the plaintiff and his friends, still; if the defendant...had just grounds for believing that the peace could only be preserved by withdrawing the plaintiff and his friends from the attack with which they were threatened it was...the duty of the defendant to take that course (per Law CJ).

In *Duncan* v *Jones* [1936] 1 KB 218, D was one of the organisers of the National Unemployed Workers Movement. She wished to hold and address a meeting outside a centre for unemployed persons. Disturbances had occurred at meetings she had conducted there in the past. Accordingly, she was instructed by J, a police officer, to move away from the centre and to hold the meeting in a street at a distance of some 175 yards. It was held that D had been rightly arrested for obstruction when she refused to do so.

It might also be appropriate to mention under this subheading the power of the police to order the numbers participating in a particular gathering to be reduced. In *Piddington* v *Bates* [1960] 3 All ER 660, eighteen persons gathered to picket a works premises where an industrial dispute was going on. Eight of the 24 employees were still working. It was held that the police were entitled to direct the number of pickets to be reduced and to arrest for obstruction those who did not comply. The court found that, although there had been no violence on the picket line, 'the police reasonably anticipated that a breach of the peace might occur' (per Parke CJ).

Seizure of provocative emblems

In *Humphries* v *Connor* (1864) 17 ICLR 1, the defendant was a police officer in Co. Cavan, Ireland. He stopped the plaintiff and took from her an orange lily (a loyalist emblem) which she was wearing on her coat. The plaintiff's action for assault did not succeed. The court felt that the officer was entitled to believe that the wearing of the emblem might provoke a violent reaction from persons of a nationalist persuasion. It would have been 'absurd to hold that a constable may arrest a person whom he finds committing a breach of the peace but that he must not interfere with the individual who has provoked him...' (per Hayes J).

Entry without warrant

The authority for the police power to enter private premises where an imminent breach of the peace is reasonably anticipated, and to remain there until the danger has passed, is usually assumed to be *Thomas* v *Sawkins* [1935] 2 KB 249. The power has already been mentioned in the context of PACE, s 17. The power may be used to deal with domestic disputes (*McCleod* v *Metropolitan Police Commissioner*, above) or anticipated disorder at a meeting to be held in private premises (as was the case in *Thomas* v *Sawkins*). The police may remain on the premises for so long as the danger exists.

Restricting lawful conduct

The above case law has been used to support the proposition that the police in the UK had the authority to prevent a lawful and peaceful meeting from taking place if it was reasonably believed that the meeting would be opposed by those prepared to use violence or behave in a way which produced a risk of it. This, in turn, appeared to mean that, according to English law, the freedom of assembly must always give way to the perceived needs of public order and that the authorities were under no specific legal obligation to defend the freedom against those bent on using whatever means they deemed appropriate to prevent demonstrations of support for causes to which they were opposed.

All of this must now, however, be read subject to a series of decisions in the 1990s suggesting a clear judicial intent to limit the circumstances in which the police may interfere with and restrict lawful behaviour to situations where the conduct:

(a) interferes with the lawful rights of others; and
(b) its natural conseqence would be to provoke violence which, in the circumstances, although unlawful, would not be entirely reasonable.

> It is only if otherwise lawful conduct gives rise to a reasonable apprehension that it will, by interfering with the rights and liberties of others, provoke violence which, though unlawful, would not be entirely unreasonable that a constable is empowered to take steps to prevent (Sedley LJ, *Redmond-Bate* v *DPP* [1999] All ER (D) 864).

The *Redmond-Bate* decision was approved by the Court of Appeal in *Bibby* v *Chief Constable of Essex* [2000] RA 384. The effect is to bring English law in this context into closer compliance with the right to freedom of assembly as protected by the European Convention on Human Rights, Art 11.

This is achieved by:

(a) giving genuine legal protection to those wishing to meet or demonstrate peacefully and within the law;
(b) requiring the police, if the peace is to be kept, to direct their attentions to those who would oppose and disrupt the lawful conduct of others.

STATUTORY PUBLIC ORDER OFFENCES

Introduction

Should the above preventative powers prove inadequate to keep the peace at a public procession or assembly, those suspected of disorderly conduct may be charged with a range of public order offences. As with the preventative powers, the principal source of the relevant provisions is the Public Order Act 1986. It will be seen that these offences are worded in sufficiently expansive terms to encompass disorderly behaviour in public places which may not be related to any procession or assembly.

Riot

Section 1 of the 1986 Act provides that, where there are twelve or more persons present together using or threatening violence for a common purpose such as would cause a reasonably firm person present at the scene to fear for his/her safety, each person using violence intentionally is guilty of riot.

The offence may be committed in a public or private place. The common purpose requirement means that the offence cannot be used to deal with brawls or general mêlée. The common purpose need not be pre-arranged. Hence, in *R v Jefferson and Others* [1994] 1 All ER 271, riot was committed when a crowd of about three hundred youths went 'on the rampage' in the centre of Bedford to celebrate a victory by the English football team. It is not necessary for the prosecution to prove that a reasonably firm person witnessed the defendants' actions and was put in fear by them. The test is objective. It is sufficient, therefore, to show that the behaviour of those involved would have had such effect on a reasonably firm person had one been present (*R v Davison* [1992] Crim LR 31). Note that only persons using violence may be charged with riot. Those merely threatening violence may be charged with one of the lesser offences dealt with below. Riot is the most serious of the public law offences. It is arrestable and carries a maximum sentence of ten years' imprisonment.

Violent disorder

This offence is contained in the 1986 Act, s 2. It is committed where three or more persons use or threaten unlawful violence intentionally such as would cause a reasonably firm person present to fear for his/her safety. Each person using or threatening violence is guilty of the offence.

No common purpose need be proved and it is enough for a conviction that the defendant was merely threatening violence.

Where three or more persons are charged with violent disorder less than three may be convicted provided 'there is evidence before the jury that there were three people involved in the criminal behaviour, though not necessarily those named in the indictment and the defence are apprised of what it is they have to meet' (*R v Mahroof* (1988) 88 Crim App Rep 317).

The offence is arrestable and may be committed in public or private. A person convicted of violent disorder may be sentenced to five years' imprisonment.

Affray

Section 3 of the 1986 Act created the statutory offence of affray. It is committed by any person who uses or threatens unlawful violence intentionally such as would cause a reasonably firm person present to fear for his/her safety.

The offence is directed at unlawful fighting. For the purposes of this offence the threat of unlawful violence cannot be made by words alone. Some threatening action must be used. In *R v Robinson* [1993] Crim LR 581, the defendant told the driver of a car that, unless he gave the defendant a lift, the defendant would simply take his car. It was held that affray had not been committed as the threat consisted entirely of words. Affray was committed, however, in *R v Dixon* [1993] Crim LR 579, where the defendant ordered his alsatian dog to attack two police officers ('go on, kill'). The Court of Appeal took the view that the dog had, in effect, been used as a weapon with which to threaten the officers. Affray was also committed in *R v Davison*, above, where the defendant brandished a knife at police officers and said, 'I'll have you'.

A person who commits affray may be arrested without warrant. The offence may be committed in a public or private place and carries a maximum sentence of three years' imprisonment.

Fear or provocation of violence

By virtue of s 4 of the 1986 Act it is an offence to use threatening, abusive or insulting words or behaviour towards another person or to display any threatening, abusive or insulting writing, sign or other visual representation. The words, behaviour, or display must be intended or be likely to provoke or cause fear of immediate violence (i.e. violence which is not necessarily instantaneous but which may occur in a short time: *Valentine* v *DPP*, Current Law, June 1997). The offence may be committed in a public or private place. A person may not be charged under s 4, however, if he/she used the words or behaviour, or displayed the sign, inside a dwelling house to another person inside that or another dwelling house. Hence, in *R v Va Kun Hau* [1990] Crim LR 518, where a bailiff and police officer were in the defendant's house to collect unpaid parking fines, no offence was committed when the defendant brandished a knife at them. The decision might have been different if the defendant had stood in his doorway brandishing the knife at the bailiff and police officers as they approached his premises. Given that the offence does not apply where both parties are in a dwelling house, it cannot be used in the context of domestic disputes.

The words, behaviour, or sign must be used or shown in the presence of the person who it is claimed was put in fear of violence. In *R v Atkin* [1989] Crim LR 581, customs officers and a bailiff went to the defendant's premises in connection with unpaid VAT. The bailiff remained in the car while the officers went inside to talk to the defendant. The defendant had a gun in his hand and said that if the bailiff got out of the car he was 'a dead 'un'. The customs officers relayed this message to the bailiff. The defendant was acquitted of the s 4 offence as words could not be threatening, etc. unless used in the presence of the person claimed to have been put in fear of immediate violence.

The words or behaviour must carry a threat of immediate violence. An allegation that they might lead or contribute to violence at some indeterminate time in the future is not enough. Hence, where a bookshop displayed a copy of the book *Satanic Verses* in its window, no offence was committed. Although this might have contributed to a general climate of resentment which may have manifested itself in violence, the display itself was not something which was either intended or likely to cause or provoke an immediate violent reaction (*R v Horseferry Road Stipendiary Magistrate, ex parte Siadatan* [1991] 1 QB 260).

A person who commits the offence may be arrested without warrant and sentenced to six months' imprisonment.

Causing intentional harassment, alarm or distress

This offence is found in the 1986 Act, s 4A. It was inserted by the Criminal Justice and Public Order Act 1994, s 154. Its terminology is similar to the offence of causing fear or provocation of violence, save that the s 4A offence is committed by words, behaviour or signs (which are threatening, abusive or insulting) that cause a person 'harassment, alarm or distress' and were intended to have that effect. Hence, both the intent and the requisite consequences must be proved. As with the s 4 offence, it may be committed in public or private but not if the parties are in the same or different dwelling houses. It is a defence to show that the accused was inside a dwelling and had no reason to believe that what was said, done or displayed would be seen or heard by another person. It is also a defence if it can be shown that the accused's conduct was reasonable – e.g. that he/she intentionally harassed or caused alarm to another person to prevent the latter from committing a crime.

Any person reasonably suspected of committing the offence may be arrested without warrant and sentenced to a term of imprisonment of up to six months.

Causing harassment, alarm or distress

The offence in s 5 of the 1986 Act is linguistically very similar to that in s 4A. Here, however, it is sufficient if the threatening, abusive or insulting words, behaviour or display (sign, writing or other visual representation) were used 'within the hearing or sight of a person likely to be caused harassment, alarm or distress'. Hence it does not have to be shown that actual harassment, alarm or distress was caused. The defendant must intend his/her action to be harassing, alarming or distressing or be aware that it may be so interpreted.

The offence, unlike those in ss 4 and 4A, may also be committed by 'disorderly behaviour' which is likely to cause the specified reactions. The same defences are available as those in s 4A. In addition, it is a defence to show that the accused had no reason to believe that there was any person within hearing or sight likely to have been harassed, alarmed or distressed by his/her behaviour.

If the offensive conduct is witnessed by police officers only, it is not open to the defendant to argue that it is unlikely that they would have been harassed, alarmed or distressed by it. Police officers, it has been held, are just as likely as members of the public to experience these emotions (*DPP v Orum* [1988] 3 All ER 449). The offensive conduct need not be directed at the person likely to suffer from it. Hence the offence was committed by a person seen to be staggering about in the middle of a busy road (also shouting and gesticulating) thereby putting those nearby in fear that an accident would be caused (*Lodge v DPP, The Times*, 26 October 1988). The offence may also be committed by threatening telephone calls and letters (*DPP v Mills, The Times*, 26 April 1996).

Note that the offence only becomes arrestable if the person carries on with the behaviour after being ordered to desist by a police officer. In *DPP* v *Hancock and Tuttle* [1995] Crim LR 139, the court was of the view that the power of arrest was limited to the officer who gave the warning. However, the Public Order (Amendment) Act 1996 makes it clear that the power of arrest extends to any officer and is not restricted as suggested above. In *Groom* v *DPP* [1991] Crim LR 711, G swore and made racist remarks at H. A police officer told G to apologise. G continued to be abusive and was arrested. The court's view was that to tell a person to apologise necessarily implied that the offensive behaviour should be discontinued. G's arrest was, therefore, lawful.

Despite its apparent width, s 5 should not be used to impinge upon the freedom of expression guaranteed by the European Convention on Human Rights.

> A peaceful protest will only come within the terms of section 5 and constitute an offence where the conduct goes beyond legitimate protest and moves into the realms of threatening, abusive or insulting behaviour, which is calculated to insult either intentionally or recklessly, and which is unreasonable (per Hallett J, *Percy* v *DPP* [2001] EWHC Admin 1125).

The concept of 'harassment' as a criminal offence was further extended by the Protection from Harassment Act 1997. This was Parliament's response to the type of activity generally referred to as 'stalking'. The Act makes it an offence for any person to pursue a course of conduct which he/she knew or ought to have known 'amounts to harassment of another' (s 1). Note, however, the decision of the High Court in *Huntingdon Life Sciences Ltd* v *Curtin, The Times*, 11 December 1997, to the effect that Parliament could not have intended the Act to be used to prosecute those engaged in protesting about a matter of public interest – in this case anti-vivisectionists protesting against the activities of a company engaged in the use of animals for research purposes.

The Crime and Disorder Act 1998 provides that sentences in excess of those provided for in the 1986 Act will be available to the courts in respect of offences under ss 4, 4A and 5 of the latter Act where such offences are shown to have been 'racially aggravated', i.e. where the offence was motivated by racial hostility, and such hostility was demonstrated to the victim.

Stirring up racial hatred

Sections 18–24 of the 1986 Act are concerned with the control of actions and materials which may be racially inflammatory. The following actions are an offence if they are done with the intent to stir up racial hatred or are likely to have that result:

- the use of threatening, abusive or insulting words, behaviour or visual representations in a public or private place (s 18);
- the publication of threatening, abusive or insulting written material (s 19);
- the public performance of any play which involves the use of threatening, abusive or insulting language (s 20);
- the distribution, showing or playing of any threatening, abusive or insulting recorded visual images or sounds (e.g. films, videos, records, CDs, etc.) (s 21);
- the broadcasting of any threatening, abusive or insulting material (s 21).

The Act also makes it an offence to possess racially inflammatory material (s 23) and provides that the police may apply for a warrant to search premises reasonably suspected of containing the same (s 24).

OTHER RELEVANT STATUTORY OFFENCES

Obstruction of the highway

Prima facie the right of each individual on a public highway is to pass and repass along it in the course of their lawful business and to stop for rest or to make necessary repairs (*Hickman* v *Maisey* [1900] 1 QB 753). In theory, therefore, any other use – including public assemblies – represents a trespass against the highway authority and an offence against the Highways Act 1980, s 137. This section makes it an offence to wilfully obstruct free passage along the highway without lawful authority or excuse.

In practice, however, the courts have generally sought to strike a balance between the public right of passage and that of freedom of assembly. Hence, the cases suggest that a conviction under the 1980 Act is unlikely unless it can be shown that the defendant's use of the highway was unreasonable (*Hirst and Agu* v *Chief Constable of West Yorkshire* (1986) 85 Crim App Rep 143). This is a question of fact in each case and will depend on such matters as the duration of the obstruction, its purpose, the place where it occurred and its extent – i.e. whether the highway was totally or only partially obstructed (*Nagy* v *Weston* [1965] 1 All ER 78).

Obstruction of a police officer

The Police Act 1996, s 89(2) provides that it is an offence to resist or wilfully obstruct a police officer in the execution of his/her duty. The offence is arrestable without warrant where the person's behaviour interferes with a lawful arrest or may lead to a breach of the peace (*Wershof* v *Metropolitan Police Commissioner* [1978] 3 All ER 540).

The offence is of general application but has particular utility in the public order context. Given that police officers are under a common law obligation to preserve the peace, it is an arrestable obstruction to impede any reasonable course of action or any directions given for that purpose. Hence, should the police reasonably believe that an assembly may lead to disorder, they may do or direct that which is reasonably necessary to prevent that eventuality and arrest for obstruction those who refuse to cooperate.

COMMON LAW OFFENCES

Public nuisance

Obstruction of the highway as a result of a public assembly or otherwise may amount to the indictable common law offence of public nuisance. For a conviction to be sustained the obstruction must have constituted an 'unreasonable user' of the stretch of highway in issue (*R* v *Clarke (No. 2)* [1964] 2 QB 315).

Public nuisance is also actionable in tort by a person who has suffered damage over and above that inflicted on the rest of the public (e.g. the road obstructed led to the plaintiff's premises).

Reference

Robertson (1995) *Freedom, the Individual and the Law* (3rd edn), London: Sweet & Maxwell.

Further reading

Bailey, Harris and Jones (2001) *Civil Liberties: Cases and Materials* (5th edn), London: Butterworths, Ch 3.

Feldman (1993) *Civil Liberties and Human Rights in England and Wales*, Oxford: Clarendon Press, Ch 17.

Marston and Ward (1997) *Cases and Commentary on Constitutional and Administrative Law* (4th edn), London: Pitman Publishing, Ch 18.

Robertson (1995) *Freedom, the Individual and the Law* (7th edn), London: Penguin, Ch 2.

Stone (1997) *Textbook on Civil Liberties* (2nd edn), London: Blackstone, Ch 8.

Chapter 22

RESTRICTIONS ON THE RIGHTS OF FREEDOM OF EXPRESSION AND INFORMATION

INTRODUCTION

The principal justifications for restraints operating in this context would appear to be that these are the minimum necessary to:

- preserve social harmony and public order;
- safeguard certain fundamental standards of public morality;
- ensure the proper administration of justice;
- enable the state to function effectively in the fulfilment of the various public interests for which it is responsible.

The restraints themselves consist of:

- statutory and non-statutory complaints procedures and codes of practice relating to the press and broadcast media;
- an extensive range of statutory and common law offences relating to, *inter alia*, sedition, blasphemy, obscene publications, contempt of court and official secrecy;
- civil wrongs such as breach of confidence and defamation.

Defamation is, of course a significant restriction on the freedom of expression of both the individual and the media. Given, however, that it will be explained in detail in any standard textbook on the law of tort, defamation is not dealt with in the pages that follow. Note in passing, however, that it is not possible to defame a local council (*Derbyshire County Council v Times Newspapers* [1993] 1 All ER 1011) or a political party (*Goldsmith v Bhoyrul* [1998] 2 WLR 435).

The freedom of expression is, of course, essential for the practice of democracy. Without it there can be no meaningful political debate and no effective monitoring and criticism of the activities of government. It is no coincidence that the burning of books and the prohibition of the free exchange of views has been one of the first steps taken by many of the most oppressive regimes which have held power in various parts of the world.

> It is unacceptable in our democratic society that there should be a restraint on the publication of information relating to government when the only vice of that information is that it enables the public to discuss, review and criticise government action (per Mason J, *Commonwealth of Australia v John Fairfax and Sons Ltd* (1980) 147 CLR 39).

In a democracy, therefore, the function of the law-maker must be to achieve a workable balance between the right to freedom of expression and such restrictions as are necessary for the protection and well-being of the whole community.

FREEDOM OF EXPRESSION AND THE MASS MEDIA

The press

It is often claimed that the United Kingdom has a 'free' press. By this it is meant that the publication of newspapers and magazines is not subject to any direct political control. No prior official consent is needed for publication of the same nor does the government have any legal authority to influence editorial policy (i.e. the content of such publications). The law does not require press reporting to be fair or impartial or to achieve any sort of balance in the way particular topics, political or otherwise, are treated. As a result, great power and responsibility is left in the hands of newspaper editors and proprietors.

Fair Trading Act 1973

By way of recognition of the influence of newspaper proprietors and the potential for abuse, the 1973 Act sought to strike a balance between the free market in the ownership of newspapers and the public interest in the maintenance of a newspaper industry which reflects a range of political perspectives. The Act provides that the consent of the Secretary of State for Trade and Industry must be given before the proprietor of any newspaper can acquire the ownership of another paper where the joint circulation of the two would be in excess of 500,000 copies. Such provision does not, of course, ensure apolitical protection of the public interest since it is not unknown for ministers to equate such interest with the advancement of their own particular political party and its advocates. The 1973 Act further provides, therefore, that as a general rule ministerial consent to a newspaper takeover should not be given until the effect on the public interest has been considered by the Competition Commission (Monopolies and Mergers Commission). Ministerial consent without such reference should be given only where the newspaper in question has become uneconomic and the takeover is a matter of urgency if the paper is to survive.

Laudable as their intentions may have been, however, these provisions have not been sufficient to prevent a very small number of newspaper 'moguls' from gaining control and ownership of the majority of the main newspaper titles.

The Press Complaints Commission

This was created in 1991 following the recommendations of the Calcutta Committee (*Report of the Committee on Privacy and Related Matters*, Cm 1102, 1990). It replaced the much-criticised Press Council which had been in existence since 1953. The Press Council was a non-statutory body funded by the newspaper industry from which half of its members were drawn. It dealt with complaints from the public about press abuses (invasions of privacy, inaccuracy, etc.) and could censure editors and recommend the publication of apologies. It had no legal authority, however, to insist on compliance with its decisions and proved ineffective to prevent some sections of the press from indulging in the type of vulgarity and offensive intrusions into people's private lives which became a cause of increasing public concern in the 1970s and 1980s.

The Press Complaints Commission is also a non-statutory body. It has an independent chairperson and fifteen other members. Ten of these are from the newspaper industry. It deals with complaints alleging violation of the Press Code of Practice. This contains detailed guidelines dealing with matters such as accuracy, privacy, misrepresentation, harassment, intrusion into grief or shock, and the interviewing of children and victims of crime.

Like its predecessor, however, the Commission has no coercive or preventive powers and cannot insist on the payment of compensation. It may censure an editor or recommend that an apology or right of reply be published but has no legal authority to ensure compliance with its decisions. It is widely held that it has had little obvious effect on the behaviour of the less scrupulous newspaper editors and reporters. It has been described as a 'confidence trick which has failed to inspire confidence' and a further example of the fact that press self-regulation is an 'oxymoron' (Robertson, *Freedom, the Individual and the Law*).

The ineffectiveness of press self-regulation is compounded by the lack of any right to privacy in English law. This was graphically exemplified by the facts and decision in *Kaye v Robertson* [1991] FSR 62. Press photographers entered a hospital bedroom and photographed the actor Gordon Kaye who was recovering from brain surgery after suffering serious injury in a motoring accident. On the facts the court concluded that there had been a 'monstrous invasion of privacy' but explained that it was powerless to prevent the photographs from being published. Photographing a person at close range did not amount to a trespass to the person. Also, an invasion of privacy, *per se*, was not an actionable tort.

The result is that the person who suffers this sort of intrusion has a right of action only if actual physical interference is done or threatened (trespass to the person) or there has been an unlawful entry on to the victim's property (trespass to land). In certain circumstances invasions of privacy are now actionable under the Human Rights Act 1998.

Broadcasting

Initially this was the sole responsibility of the BBC. The BBC was established under Royal Charter in 1926 and broadcasts according to the terms of a licence granted to it by the government acting through the Home Secretary under the Wireless Telegraphy Acts. It is controlled by a Board of Governors who are appointed (and may be dismissed) by the Crown on the advice of the Prime Minister. It is a non-profit-making organisation and is financed by parliamentary grant equivalent to the net revenue from TV licence fees.

Despite its much vaunted and justified reputation for political independence, the licensing provisions under which the BBC operates give considerable powers of control to the Home Secretary. These include powers to:

- take over the BBC in times of emergency;
- direct that any material or class of material specified in a written notice should not be broadcast.

The BBC has also undertaken:

- not to broadcast that which could offend against good taste or decency, or be likely to encourage crime or disorder, or be offensive to public feeling;
- to comply with the statutory duties imposed on independent television by the Broadcasting Acts 1990 and 1996 including the obligation to observe due impartiality and balance in its coverage of political issues.

The Home Secretary is empowered to revoke the BBC's licence should the Corporation act in breach of it or any ministerial directions imposed thereunder.

The regulation of independent television broadcasting (i.e. everything not controlled by the BBC) is the function of the Independent Television Commission (ITC) established by the Broadcasting Act 1990. This function previously resided with the Independent Broadcasting Authority which dates back to the Independent Broadcasting Act 1954 as amended in 1973. The 1990 Act also established the Independent Radio Authority which is the licensing authority for commercial radio.

All independent television networks, including Channels 3, 4, 5 and all satellite, cable, multiplex and digital services broadcasting in the United Kingdom must be licensed by the ITC (Broadcasting Acts 1990 and 1996).

Note that the 1996 Act prevents any person who runs or controls a national newspaper having a national circulation of 20 per cent or above from holding a licence to provide a national or regional channel 3 or channel 5 service or a national or local radio service (Sched 2). The Act also provides that no person having control of a local newspaper which has in excess of a 20 per cent share of the readership in its locality may provide a regional channel 3 service or digital programme service. Furthermore, no person having a local newspaper with a market share of over 50 per cent of the local readership shall be licensed to provide a local radio service (Sched 2).

Section 6 of the Broadcasting Act 1990 requires the ITC to do all that it can to ensure that all licensed networks:

- do not include in any programme that which 'offends against good taste or decency or is likely to encourage...crime or lead to disorder or to be offensive to public feeling';
- observe 'due impartiality' in the presentation of news programmes and those dealing with 'matters of industrial or political controversy or relating to current public policy';
- observe 'due responsibility' in regard to the content of religious programmes and avoid 'abusive treatment of the religious views...of those belonging to a particular religion or...denomination'.

The Commission is also charged with formulating and keeping under review Codes of Practice containing rules relating to, *inter alia*:

- the meaning and application of the due impartiality requirement;
- the showing of violence, particularly when children and young persons may be watching;
- the control of advertising and the avoidance of advertisements with political content or objectives.

As to government control of programme content, the 1990 Act, s 10 provides that at any time the Home Secretary may direct any licensed network not to include any matter which they may specify by notice. Should a licence holder act in breach of the Codes of Practice it may be required by the ITC or Radio Authority to:

- broadcast a correction or apology;
- refrain from repeating the offending item or material;
- pay a fine.

The licence, which is normally for a ten-year period, may be reduced for up to two years or, in the final analysis, be revoked altogether.

The Independent Radio Authority is required to apply similar provisions to the licensing of commercial radio stations (Broadcasting Act 1990, ss 83–97).

It is thus apparent that the Home Secretary acting on behalf of the government has the legal authority to exert extensive control over both state and independent broadcasting. These powers are, however, seldom resorted to – probably because their use usually attracts considerable political controversy. Hence, the government was criticised when, in 1988, it directed both the BBC and the independent networks not to broadcast words being spoken by representatives of Sinn Fein and other paramilitary organisations proscribed under the emergency legislation in force in Northern Ireland. The directions were subsequently rescinded to allow Sinn Fein and spokespersons for loyalist organisations to participate in the Northern Ireland peace process.

The Broadcasting Standards Council

This was set up in 1988 and was governed by the Broadcasting Act 1990, ss 152–56. It was charged by the Act with formulating and keeping under review a Code of Practice relating to the portrayal of violence, sexual conduct and to 'standards of taste and decency...generally'. Its remit extended to both the BBC and independent TV networks.

The Broadcasting Standards Council (BSC) dealt with complaints from members of the public concerning those matters covered by the Code of Practice. It could require that a complaint and its findings on the same were broadcast by the particular broadcasting authority or licence holder against which the complaint had been made.

The Broadcasting Complaints Commission

This dealt with complaints of unfair or unjust treatment, or of invasion of privacy, in either television or radio programmes. It was created by the Broadcasting Act 1981 and its powers were subsequently derived from the Broadcasting Act 1990, ss 142–50. It had jurisdiction over radio and television broadcasting whether by the BBC or independent companies.

Like the BSC, it could direct that the broadcaster against whom a complaint was made should broadcast the complaint and the Commission's findings upon it. The right to complain to the Commission was restricted to those having a 'direct interest' in the subject matter of the complaint.

In *R v Broadcasting Complaints Commission, ex parte Channel Four Television Corporation, The Times*, 4 January 1995, the Divisional Court said that the term should be given a broad meaning. Hence the Commission had jurisdiction to entertain a complaint from the parish council of a village in Derbyshire about a Channel Four programme which alleged that many of the villagers were racially prejudiced. The parish council, the court felt, had a direct interest in media comment about racial attitudes amongst its local population. By contrast, however, in *R v Broadcasting Complaints Commission, ex parte BBC, The Times*, 24 February 1995, the Divisional Court felt that the National Council for One-Parent Families had no direct interest to complain about a BBC *Panorama* programme ('Babies on Benefit') which appeared to have dealt unfairly with 1.3 million lone parents.

The new Broadcasting Complaints Commission

This was created by the Broadcasting Act 1996, s 106, and replaced the existing Broadcasting Standards Council and the Broadcasting Complaints Commission. The Commission consists of up to fifteen members appointed by the Secretary of State. It is charged with the preparation of codes of conduct for:

(a) the avoidance of 'unwarranted infringement of privacy' in the preparation of any programme, or unjust or unfair treatment in such programmes (s 107);
(b) giving guidance in relation to programmes portraying violence, sexual conduct and as to standards of taste and decency generally (s 108).

It is also required to monitor and report on the same.

The Commission is further empowered to consider and adjudicate upon complaints relating to any of the above matters submitted by 'the person affected or by a person authorised by him' (ss 110–11). Where a complaint is upheld, the Commission may require the particular broadcasting body or licence holder to publish its findings as the Commission may direct. The Commission has no power to order payment of compensation.

Theatres

Censorship of the theatre was brought to an end by the Theatres Act 1968. Prior to that time a play could not be performed in public unless a licence had been granted by the Lord Chancellor.

A theatre cannot operate unless licensed by a local authority. An authority may attach conditions to the licence in relation to 'physical safety or health only'. It may not attach any conditions which seek to regulate 'the nature of plays which may be performed' (Theatres Act 1968, s 1). The 1968 Act does, however, make it an offence to present or direct a performance of a play which is obscene or which contains threatening, abusive or insulting words or behaviour intended or likely to cause a breach of the peace (Theatres Act, ss 1 and 3).

As with the offence under the Obscene Publications Act 1959, dealt with below, a play is obscene if, taken as a whole, it would tend to deprave and corrupt those likely to see it (Theatres Act 1968, s 2). No offence is committed, however, if it can be proved that performing the play was for the public good in the interests of drama, opera, ballet, literature, learning or any other art (s 3). No prosecution under the 1968 Act may be commenced without the Attorney-General's consent.

It is an offence under the Public Order Act 1986 to present or direct any public performance of a play which is intended or likely to stir up racial hatred (s 20).

Cinema

Cinemas Act 1985

Premises may not be used for the showing of films unless licensed by the appropriate district council or borough council in London (Cinemas Act 1985, s 1). The Act gives district councils the power to attach conditions to the licence specifying the types of films which may be shown. It is the practice of local councils to view potentially controversial films and to instruct licence holders (i.e. cinema owners) whether the film contravenes the standards imposed by the council's licensing conditions. The showing of a film in breach of the licensing conditions could result in the licence being withdrawn.

British Board of Film Classification

In deciding whether to allow a film to be shown in its district a local council will usually place great reliance on the recommendations of the BBFC. This was established in 1912 and was originally known as the British Board of Film Censors. It is a non-statutory body that was created, and is financed, by the film industry itself. It is concerned principally with explicit portrayal of sexual and violent conduct, and classifies each film within a range of six categories ranging from 'U' (suitable for all) to '18R' (distribution restricted to specially licensed premises to which persons of under 18 years are not permitted).

As a result of its non-statutory nature, the Board's classifications are not legally enforceable, nor are they binding on local authorities. It is open, therefore, for a local council to ban a film which the BBFC has classified as fit for general distribution or, alternatively, to allow a film to be shown which the BBFC felt was unsuitable for classification even within the '18R' category.

The Obscene Publications Act 1959 did not apply to the public showing of films. This was changed by the Criminal Law Act 1977, s 53. The public showing of a film may amount, therefore, to the offence of publishing an obscene article contrary to the 1959 Act, s 2(1). It is a defence to prove that the showing of the film was for the public good in the interests of 'drama, opera, ballet, literature, learning or any other art' (*ibid.*, s 4(1A)).

The Video Recordings Act 1984

This makes it an offence to supply or to be in possession of a video for the purposes of supply which has not been classified by the BBFC. It is also an offence to supply a video in breach of the terms of its classification. The 1984 Act does not apply to video games or video works:

• designed to 'inform, educate or instruct';
• 'concerned with sport, religion or music' (s 2).

In making a classification the BBFC is bound to consider the 'harm that may be caused to potential viewers, or through their behaviour, to society' by the manner in which the work deals with:

- criminal behaviour;
- drugs;
- violent behaviour or incidents;
- horrific behaviour or incidents; or
- human sexual activity (s 4A).

The meanings of the terms 'video work' and 'video recording' in the 1984 Act were amended by the Criminal Justice and Public Order Act 1994 to include 'any other device capable of storing data electronically' (Sched 9, para 22).

FREEDOM OF EXPRESSION, OBSCENITY AND PORNOGRAPHY

Obscene publications

The Obscene Publications Act 1959

Section 2(1) of the 1959 Act made it an indictable offence to publish an obscene article whether for gain or not. The offence thus stated contains a number of key words which require further definition.

Publish

For the purposes of the Act this has a much wider meaning than the publication of books and magazines by publishing companies. The Act states that a person publishes an article if he/she 'distributes, circulates, sells, lets on hire, gives, lends or offers it for sale or letting for hire' or, in the case of recorded material, 'shows, plays or projects it'. The 1959 Act has since been amended by the Criminal Justice and Public Order Act 1994, s 84 so that the definition of 'publishes' now extends to the transmission of data which is stored electronically. Hence, the transmission of material contained in a computer database, bulletin board or disk may constitute an obscene publication. *R v Fellows*; *R v Arnold* [1997] 2 All ER 548, was one of the first convictions under the 1959 Act resulting from the transmission of obscene material by computer. The defendants committed the offence by compiling a database of child pornography which they made available on the internet.

Article

This term is defined by the Act as extending to anything 'containing or embodying matter to be read or looked at...any sound record, and any film or other record of a picture or pictures' (s 1(2)). Books, pictures, records, films, compact discs, video cassettes, tapes, television and sound broadcasts, and computer images have all been held to fall within the definition as have those articles from which the images are to be reproduced (e.g. photographic negatives and floppy disks).

Obscene

An article is obscene if, taken as a whole, it would tend to deprave and corrupt those likely to see, hear or read it. The phrase 'deprave and corrupt' was not defined by the Act. In *R v Penguin Books* [1961] Crim LR 176, Byrne J said that to deprave meant 'to make morally bad, to pervert, or debase, or corrupt morally'. To corrupt, he continued, meant 'to render morally unsound or rotten, to destroy the moral purity or chastity of, to pervert or ruin a good quality, to debase, to defile...'.

Whether an article is obscene or not is a question of fact which should be left to the jury to decide. Expert evidence is admissible in exceptional circumstances only, as where obscene material relates to matters outside the experience of the ordinary jury member – e.g. evidence of child psychiatrists as to the possible effects on children of cards sold in chewing gum packets depicting graphic scenes of violence (*DPP v A and BC Chewing Gum Ltd* [1968] 1 QB 159) and medical evidence concerning the effects of taking cocaine (*R v Skirving* [1985] QB 819).

The requirement that the effect of the allegedly obscene article be judged 'as a whole' means that it is not open to the prosecution to base its case on particular parts or extracts drawn from it, e.g. those containing particularly graphic descriptions or depictions of sexual activity. Such material must not be considered, therefore, out of the context in which it is used. Hence, in the famous trial concerning D H Lawrence's book *Lady Chatterley's Lover*, jurors were told to read and base their decisions on the potential effects of the complete work and not to concentrate on, or be influenced unduly by, the 'purple passages' contained therein (*R v Penguin Books*).

If the article contains a number of distinct items, as might be the case with a magazine, then each item must be judged individually. If any one is found to be obscene this taints the whole of the article or publication (*R v Anderson* [1972] 1 QB 354).

It does not have to be proved that the defendant intended to deprave and corrupt his/her potential audience. 'Obscenity depends on the article and not upon the author' (*Shaw v DPP* [1962] AC 220). Nor is it necessary to show that any overt, depraved or corrupt behaviour resulted from the publication. The intention to publish material which a reasonable person might have been expected to know could have a tendency to deprave and corrupt is sufficient.

An article is not obscene simply because it could have a tendency to deprave and corrupt a person or persons of a particularly sensitive or gullible disposition. If the article is published to one person only then it must be shown that that person was likely to be depraved and corrupted. Hence, in *R v Clayton and Halsey* [1963] 1 QB 163, no offence was committed when the only proven publication of allegedly obscene photographs was to two policemen experienced in dealing with this sort of material.

When the publication is more general or wide reaching the requirement is that the article would tend to have the stipulated effect on a 'significant proportion' of the audience to which it is directed (*R v Calder and Boyars Ltd* [1969] 1 QB 151). The Act imposes, therefore, a relative test. An article cannot be judged to be obscene without reference to its likely readers: 'in every case the magistrates or the jury is called upon to ascertain who are the likely readers and then to consider whether the article is likely to deprave and corrupt them' (per Lord Wilberforce, *DPP v Whyte* [1972] AC 849). A significant proportion of a particular audience means 'a part which is not numerically negligible but which may be less than half' (*ibid.*).

It is no defence to argue that the article is only likely to be seen or heard by those who have already been depraved and corrupted: 'The Act is not merely concerned with the once for all corruption of the wholly innocent; it equally protects the less innocent from further corruption, the addict from feeding or increasing his addiction' (*ibid.*).

Obscene material is not confined to that dealing with sexual conduct. In *Calder (John) Publications Ltd* v *Powell* [1965] 1 QB 509, it was held that a book could be obscene if it 'highlighted...the favourable effects of drug-taking' so that there was 'a real danger that those into whose hands the book came might be tempted to experiment with drugs'. This was confirmed in *R* v *Skirving*, above. It has also been held that that which has a tendency to induce violence may be regarded as obscene (*DPP* v *A and BC Chewing Gum Ltd*, above).

The Obscene Publications Act 1964

Under the 1959 Act no offence is committed unless the obscene article was published. Hence, mere possession – albeit of large stocks of potentially obscene material for commercial purposes – was not rendered unlawful. Accordingly, the 1964 Act (s 1(1)) amended the 1959 Act and added to the offence of publishing an obscene article that of possessing an obscene article 'for publication for gain' (s 2(1)). This gives the police the power to search for and seize obscene material and to charge the possessor with an offence without having to wait for and prove publication. The offence thus phrased avoids the difficulties encountered in cases such as *Mella* v *Monehan* [1961] Crim LR 175, where the display of pornographic magazines in a shop window was held not to be a publication within the meaning of the 1959 Act. Although the Act specified that to offer an article for sale was to publish it, the court felt bound to apply the contractual rule that a display of goods in a shop window was merely an invitation to treat.

Forfeiture proceedings

If an information is laid before a magistrate that there are reasonable grounds for believing that obscene materials are being kept on specified premises for publication for gain, a warrant may be issued authorising the police to search for and seize the same (1959 Act, s 3). Following such seizure the occupier may be summoned to show cause why the material should not be forfeited. The right to contest forfeiture proceedings also extends to any others responsible for producing the article (author, publisher, etc.) or 'through whose hands' it has passed prior to seizure.

Such proceedings do not involve bringing any charge against the person in possession. Accordingly, the only sanction he or she might suffer is the loss of the material in question and any profit that it might have returned. As, however, it has proved difficult to secure convictions for publishing or possessing obscene articles, there is statistical evidence to suggest that, for practical purposes, the police favour the forfeiture procedure. It is apparently easier to persuade a magistrate that a thing is obscene than it is to convince a jury.

Defences

(a) Aversion

In a number of cases it has been held that, if the likely effect of a particular article is to be so revolting as to turn its audience against the type of activity depicted, then it cannot be said to have any tendency to deprave and corrupt. Thus the conviction of the publishers of *Last Exit to Brooklyn*, a book which contained 'graphic descriptions of the depths of depravity and degradation in which life was lived in Brooklyn', was overturned by the Court of Appeal because the trial judge in summing up had failed to emphasise that, although the book was 'intentionally disgusting, shocking and out-rageous, it made the reader share in the horror it described and thereby...being aware of the truth, he would do what he could to irradicate those evils' (per Salmon LJ, *R* v *Calder and Boyars*, above). The overwhelmingly repulsive nature of the material in question was also held to be a ground for overturning a conviction for obscenity in *R* v *Anderson*, above.

(b) Innocent publication

By virtue of s 2(5) of the 1959 Act it is a defence for a person charged with publishing or possessing an obscene article to prove that he/she had not examined the article and had no reason to suspect that it might be obscene. The defence is designed primarily to protect booksellers, newsagents, etc. in circumstances where there is nothing about a particular article – e.g. in the case of a magazine, its usual content or, if the article is a book, its title or the reputation of the author, etc. – which would have alerted a reasonable person to its possibly obscene content.

(c) Public good

The 1959 Act, s 4 provides that a person should not be convicted of publishing or possessing an obscene article, nor be subject to forfeiture proceedings under s 3, if it is proved that publication of the article in question is in the public good 'in the interests of science, literature, art or learning, or of other objects of general concern'. The defence exists to ensure that the 1959 Act cannot be used to prevent the publication of that which has significant and obvious literary or artistic merit whether conventional or unconventional.

Where reliance is made on the defence the function of the court is to determine, first, whether the article is obscene and second, and only if so, whether its publication is for the public good (*DPP* v *Jordan* [1976] 3 All ER 775). It has been held that the potentially open-ended phrase 'other objects of public concern' should be interpreted *ejusdem generis* or as relating to the type of subject matter indicated by the words 'science, literature, art or learning'. Thus, it was held in *R* v *Jordan*, above, that the possible therapeutic effects of pornographic literature for those unable to satisfy their sexual desires within heterosexual or homosexual relationships could not be related to the objects of public concern with which s 4 was concerned. Nor have the courts been prepared to accept that sexually explicit material is protected by s 4 because it may be expected to contribute to the 'learning' process of its audience. The type of learning meant by s 4 is that which has some conventional scholastic value (*Attorney-General's Reference (No. 3 of 1977)* [1978] 3 All ER 1166).

Other relevant statutory restrictions

Post Office Act 1953

Section 11 of the 1953 Act provides that it is an offence to send any 'indecent or obscene' material through the post. Unlike the Obscene Publications Act 1959, no definition of the word 'obscene' is provided. Hence it would appear that the ordinary dictionary meaning should be applied. The same goes for the word 'indecent'. In *R v Stanley* [1965] 2 QB 327, Lord Parker CJ said that 'the words "indecent or obscene" convey one idea, namely, offending against the recognised standards of propriety, indecent being at the lower end of the scale and obscene at the upper end of the scale'.

This is a summary offence and the 1953 Act does not include any public good defence.

Unsolicited Goods and Services Act 1971

It is an offence under this Act to send to any person unsolicited matter describing human sexual techniques or material advertising such matter. The offence so defined is of sufficient scope to criminalise the sending of matter which might not be thought to be indecent or obscene for the purpose of the Post Office Act 1953.

Children and Young Persons (Harmful Publications) Act 1955

The Act was passed in response to the perceived dangers for children of reading 'horror comics'. The offence thereby created (s 1) has a number of elements which consist of the following:

* publishing, printing or selling any book, magazine or like work consisting wholly or mainly of stories told in pictures;
* dealing with the commission of crimes, acts of violence or cruelty, or of a horrible or repulsive nature; and
* which is likely to fall into the hands of children, and to corrupt any child into whose hands it does fall.

The Act has rarely been invoked. Any prosecution requires the consent of the Attorney-General. No public good defence is made available.

Protection of Children Act 1978

The Act was passed in response to growing concerns about child pornography. It made it an offence to take, show or distribute any indecent photograph or film of a person under sixteen years. Possession of such material was made an offence by the Criminal Justice Act 1988, s 160.

To keep pace with computer technology the meaning of 'photograph' in the 1978 Act, s 7, has been extended by amendments contained in the Criminal Justice and Public Order Act 1994, s 84. As a result, the offence set out above now applies to any indecent 'pseudo-photograph', viz. 'an image whether made by computer graphics or otherwise howsoever which appears to be a photograph' and to any 'data stored on a computer disc or by other electronic means which is capable of conversion into a pseudo-photograph'.

In *R v Smith* (2002) *Times*, 23 April, the Court of Appeal held that the act of voluntary downloading an indecent image from a web page was an act of making a photograph or pseudo-photograph providing it was a deliberate and intentional act with the knowledge that the image was, or was likely to be, an indecent photograph or pseudo-photograph of a child.

No offence is committed by any person who, with legitimate reason, distributes, or is in possession of, such indecent photographs, but who has not seen them and does not know and has no reason to suspect that they are indecent (1978 Act, s 1(4)).

Where s 1(4) does not apply it is no defence for a person who has been charged with distribution or possession to plead that they did not know that the person depicted in the photographs was under sixteen years of age (*R v Land* [1998] 1 All ER 403).

Customs Consolidation Act 1876 and Customs and Excise Management Act 1979

The 1876 Act prohibits the importation of 'indecent or obscene prints, paintings, photographs, books, cards, lithographic and other engravings, or any other indecent or obscene articles'. The 1979 Act provides that any such 'goods...shall be liable to forfeiture'. No definition of the words indecent or obscene is given, nor are defendants able to plead a public good defence.

By virtue of EC law, import restrictions or trade with other EC states may not be imposed unless, *inter alia*, for the purpose of public morality and providing that the restrictions are not a means of 'arbitrary discrimination...between Member States' (Arts 30 and 36). It has been seen that English law regards that which is obscene as offensive to public morality and trading in such material is prohibited. To this extent, therefore, the import restrictions explained above would appear to be consistent with EC requirements. English law does not, however, impose similar restrictions on that which is merely indecent. Hence it could be argued that restricting its importation is not required to uphold public morality and discriminates against those wishing to send to and trade in such material in the United Kingdom.

Indecent Displays (Control) Act 1981

Section 1 of the Act introduced the offence of displaying publicly any indecent material. The Act was passed in response to public concerns about the open display of pornography in sex shops and some newsagents. A display is public if it is visible from a place to which the public have access. No offence is committed if the display is accessible only on payment of a fee by an adult or is in a part of a shop to which access can be gained only after passing an adequate warning notice.

British Telecommunications Act 1981

While the Post Office Act 1953 dealt with the sending of indecent material by post, the 1981 Act introduced the offence of sending any message by telephone which is 'grossly offensive or of an indecent, obscene, or menacing character' (s 49). This offence may be used to prosecute those who make available erotic recorded messages for an increased dialling rate.

Relevant common law offences

Conspiracy to corrupt public morals

In *Shaw* v *DPP* [1962] AC 220, S published a magazine entitled *The Ladies Directory*. This contained telephone numbers and descriptions of the services offered by prostitutes. S was convicted of the offence of conspiracy to corrupt public morals. The case remains controversial because the offence was previously unknown. It represents, therefore, an example of judicial law-making. Lord Simons (in the House of Lords) justified this as follows:

> In the sphere of criminal law I entertain no doubt that there remains in the courts a residual power to enforce the supreme and fundamental purpose of the law, to conserve not only the safety and order but also the moral welfare of the state and that it is their duty to guard it against attacks which may be the more insidious because they are novel and unprepared for.

He went on to say that a conviction for the offence was appropriate only where the defendant's behaviour was 'destructive of the very fabric of society'.

Conspiracy to outrage public decency

In *Knuller* v *DPP* [1973] AC 435, K published a contact magazine for homosexuals. The House of Lords upheld a conviction for conspiracy to corrupt public morals. K's conviction for conspiracy to outrage public decency was quashed only on the grounds of a misdirection by the trial judge. This represented another example of judicial law-making in this controversial context. Lord Simon explained the nature of the offence as follows: 'Outraging public decency goes considerably beyond offending the standards, susceptibilities of, or even shocking reasonable people...The offence is concerned with recognised minimum standards of decency, which are likely to vary from time to time'. The essence of the offence was said to be inserting outrageously indecent matter on the inside pages of magazines sold in public.

More recently, in *R* v *Gibson* [1990] 2 QB 619, the Court of Appeal confirmed that it was an indictable offence 'to do or exhibit anything in public which outrages public decency, whether or not it also tends to deprave and corrupt those who see or hear it'.

Where common law offences such as the above are used to found prosecutions in relation to obscene articles, no public good defence may be relied upon.

Also, note *R* v *Johnson* [1997] 1 WLR 367, where it was held that obscene telephone calls may amount to a public nuisance.

FREEDOM OF EXPRESSION AND THE ADMINISTRATION OF JUSTICE

General nature of contempt of court

Contempt of court may be either civil or criminal in nature. Civil contempt is committed by refusal to comply with an order of the court, e.g. failure to act in accordance with the terms of an injunction or a decree of specific performance. Although a civil obligation, a person who commits this type of contempt may be sentenced to up to two years' imprisonment (Contempt of Court Act 1981, s 14).

Criminal contempt is committed by words or actions which interfere with or obstruct the proper administration of justice or which bring the judicial system into disrepute. Obvious examples would include interference with jurors or witnesses, misbehaviour during judicial proceedings and refusal to give evidence or to attend court when ordered to do so.

Certain other types of criminal contempt are of more direct relevance to the issue of freedom of expression. These are:

- scandalising the court,
- publishing matter prejudicial to the course of justice.

Scandalising the court

It is a criminal contempt to utter or publish words which amount to scurrilous attacks on the integrity and impartiality of a judge or court of law. Reasoned criticism of the same made in good faith without abuse or malice is permissible. The line between this and criticism that is contemptuous is crossed where some improper purpose or motive in the exercise of the judicial function is alleged (*R v Metropolitan Police Commissioner, ex parte Blackburn (No. 2)* [1968] 2 QB 150).

Proceedings for this type of contempt are rare. One of the most famous cases is *R v New Statesman, ex parte DPP* (1928) 44 TLR 301. Criminal contempt was held to have been committed by the publication of an article which alleged that any person who believed in birth control would not receive a fair trial before Mr Justice Avery.

Publications prejudicial to the course of justice

Prima facie, the publication of material that might tend to affect the outcome of civil or criminal proceedings amounts to a contempt. Every person has the right to a fair trial regardless of past history, reputation or the allegations made against them and to a decision based solely on an objective and dispassionate assessment of the evidence given in court. It is thus a contempt, for example, to publish material which suggests that a person is guilty of an offence after that person has been charged but before the trial has begun.

The law of contempt in this context is now governed by the Contempt of Court Act 1981. This creates an offence of strict liability 'whereby conduct may be treated as a contempt of court as tending to interfere with the course of justice...regardless of intent to do so' (s 1).

The offence may be committed only when proceedings are 'active' (s 2). A criminal case becomes active when:

- a person is arrested without warrant;
- a warrant for arrest is issued;
- a summons is issued;
- a person is charged orally with an offence.

In the case of a civil matter the proceedings are active from the moment when the action is set down for trial ('from the time when arrangements for the hearing are made'). The serving of a writ, therefore, does not make a civil case active for the purpose of the law of contempt.

The content of the publication must be such that it creates 'a substantial risk that the course of justice in the proceedings in question will be seriously impeded or prejudiced' (s 2). The judicial view would appear to be that appellate courts are seldom likely to be affected in this way by media comment on particular proceedings:

> it is difficult to envisage circumstances in which any court in the United Kingdom exercising appellate jurisdiction would be in the least likely to be influenced by public discussions of the merits of a decision appealed against or of the parties' conduct in the proceedings (*Re Lonrho plc* [1980] 2 AC 154).

Many of the recent cases on contempt have been concerned with the type of publicity given by certain newspapers to trials which have attracted the public interest. *Attorney-General* v *Mirror Group Newspapers* [1997] 1 All ER 456, dealt with a newspaper's coverage of the trial of Mr Geoffrey Knights, who was charged with assault on a well-known actress. Schiemann LJ explained that, in determining whether a publication has created a substantial risk of seriously affecting the course of justice, the following matters should be taken into consideration:

- the likelihood of the publication coming to the attention of a potential juror;
- the likely impact of the publication on an ordinary reader at the time of publication;
- the residual impact of the publication on a notional juror at the time of the trial.

Defences

The 1981 Act exempts three types of publication from the strict liability rule. Hence, in these circumstances, no contempt is committed without proof of intent:

- where the defendant, having taken all reasonable care, is unaware that the proceedings to which the publication relates have become 'active' within the meaning explained above (s 3);
- where the publication in question represents 'a fair and accurate report of legal proceedings held in public, published contemporaneously and in good faith' (s 4);
- where the publication represents 'a discussion in good faith of public affairs or other matters of general public interest' and the 'risk of ... prejudice to particular legal proceedings is merely incidental to the discussion' (s 5).

Other relevant restrictions

In those rare circumstances where a court decides that justice will be best served by holding proceedings in private, publication of information relating thereto may amount to a contempt where, *inter alia*:

- the proceedings relate to the care, welfare or upbringing of an infant;
- the proceedings relate to national security;
- the publication of information relating to the proceedings has been prohibited by the court (Administration of Justice Act 1960, s 12).

Restrictions may also apply to proceedings held in public. Hence a court may order the postponement of the reporting of particular proceedings for such period as appears necessary to avoid 'a risk of substantial prejudice to the administration of justice' (1981 Act, s 4(2)). It is also a contempt:

- to publish the name of the complainant in a rape case without the court's consent (Sexual Offences Act 1976, s 4);
- to publish the name of any child involved in any legal proceedings contrary to a direction given by the court (Children and Young Persons Act 1933, s 39);
- to publish the name of any witness contrary to a direction by the court (this is a common law power).

Contempt and journalists' sources

Where a party seeks disclosure of a journalist's sources of information, perhaps for the purpose of bringing or defending legal proceedings or protecting a legal right (e.g. confidentiality), a court may make an order requiring production of that information only if satisfied that this is necessary in the interests of national security, the prevention of disorder, the prevention of crime or the administration of justice (Contempt of Court Act 1981, s 10). The justification for the protection of journalists' sources was explained by the European Court of Human Rights in *Goodwin* v *United Kingdom* (1996) 22 EHRR 123:

> Protection of journalistic sources is one of the basic conditions for press freedom... Without such freedom sources may be deterred from assisting the press in informing the public on matters of public interest. As a result the vital public watchdog role of the press may be undermined and the ability of the press to provide accurate and reliable information may be adversely affected.

The meaning of the word 'necessary' in s 10 was considered by the House of Lords in *Re an Inquiry under the Companies Securities (Insider Dealing) Act 1985* [1988] 1 All ER 208, where Lord Griffiths said:

> I doubt if it is possible to go further than to say that 'necessary' has a meaning that lies somewhere between 'indispensable', on the one hand, and 'useful' or 'expedient', on the other, and to leave it to the judge to decide which end of the scale of meaning he will place it on the facts of any particular case. The nearest paraphrase I can suggest is 'really needed'.

Disclosure in the interests of national security was ordered in the well-known case of *Secretary of State for Defence* v *Guardian Newspapers Ltd* [1985] AC 339, after a junior civil servant at the Ministry of Defence delivered highly confidential information to the *Guardian* newspaper detailing the schedule for the arrival of American nuclear missiles ('Cruise') at the Greenham Common airbase. The court's view was that to uphold journalistic privilege in these circumstances could have serious consequences for the ability of the United Kingdom government to enter into arrangements with friendly states which were essential for the preservation of national security and the proper defence of the realm. The civil servant in question was later convicted of offences against the Official Secrets Act 1911 and sentenced to six months' imprisonment (*R v Tisdall, The Times*, 26 March 1984).

A number of other, more recent cases have been concerned with attempts by private companies to discover the identities of employees allegedly responsible for 'leaking' confidential information which could have been damaging to the company concerned if published. In these cases it has been established that information necessary for the administration of justice is not confined to that which is required for proper disposal of actual legal proceedings but extends to that which is needed to protect a legal right, e.g. confidentiality. Hence, in a number of instances, and not without adverse academic comment, journalists have been ordered to reveal their sources purely to preserve commercial confidentiality in circumstances where, the court felt, publication could have done substantial damage to commercial interests and was not justified by any countervailing public interest, e.g. the need to expose corruption or 'iniquity' (see *X Ltd v Morgan Grampian (Publishers) Ltd* [1990] 2 All ER 1; *Camelot Group plc v Centaur Communications Ltd* [1998] 1 All ER 251).

FREEDOM OF EXPRESSION, PUBLIC ORDER AND NATIONAL SECURITY

Introduction

The principal objectives of the provisions operating in this context are to restrict the utterance and dissemination of words that:

- could incite persons to violence or be seriously detrimental to the maintenance of social harmony and public order;
- could reveal information which might prejudice the competence of the state to protect vital national interests.

Sedition

To utter or publish words which are intended to incite violence or public disorder for the purpose of obstructing, undermining or overthrowing the established order of government, or the institutions through which it is effected, constitutes the common law offence of sedition or seditious libel (*R v Chief Metropolitan Magistrate, ex parte Choudhury* [1991] 1 QB 429).

Prior to *Choudhury* the offence had been defined more extensively and could be committed by the use of words intended to have the above consequences or to stir up feelings of ill will between different classes of Her Majesty's subjects (*R v Burns* (1886) 16 Cox CC 355). It is now generally accepted that the narrower version of the offence is to be preferred.

The offence is seldom charged. One of the few modern examples of its use was in the unreported case of *R v Callinan, Quinn and Marcantonio* (1972), where the defendants made speeches at Hyde Park Corner urging their audience to take up arms to overthrow the British government in Northern Ireland.

Blasphemy

This is also a common law offence. It is committed where words are uttered or published which are likely to outrage and shock the general body of Christian believers (*ex parte Choudhury*, above). It is not necessary to prove that the words were intended to have that effect or that the defendant was reckless as to their consequences. Nor need it be shown that the words were so offensive as to be likely to cause a breach of the peace. The offence was found proved in *R v Lemon* [1979] AC 617, where the magazine *Gay News* published a poem which described sexual acts with the crucified body of Jesus Christ and ascribed homosexual activities to Him during His life. Since the United Kingdom is now a multicultural society, the offence is controversial in that it seeks to protect the Christian religion only.

Incitement to disaffection

It is an offence to 'maliciously and advisedly...seduce any member of Her Majesty's Forces from his duty or allegiance to Her Majesty' (Incitement to Disaffection Act 1934, s 1) or to be in possession of any document for that purpose (s 2). It follows that a relatively trivial act, such as persuading a soldier to overstay his leave, would satisfy the requirements of the offence. Mere proof that the words were likely to have the above effect is not sufficient. The defendant must be shown to have acted 'wilfully and intentionally' for the above purposes (*R v Arrowsmith* [1975] QB 678).

Prosecutions for this offence are rare and require the consent of the Director of Public Prosecutions. In *Arrowsmith* the defendant was convicted of the offence in s 2 after she had distributed leaflets at army barracks urging soldiers billeted there not to serve in Northern Ireland if so ordered.

The Police Act 1997, s 91 contains a similar provision making it an offence to 'cause disaffection amongst members of any police force' or to induce any police officer to withhold his/her services or commit breaches of discipline (originally Police Act 1964, s 53).

The Official Secrets Act

Reasons for official secrecy

Even a democratic government requires a measure of secrecy for some of its functions, as a means whereby it can better carry out its duties on behalf of the people. Among the primary tasks of the government are the defence of the nation from external threats, the maintenance of relations with the rest of the world and the preservation of law and order. Defence against external attack would be severely prejudiced if the potential enemies had access...to the details of our plans and weapons. It would be impossible to negotiate with other countries if all discussion, however delicate, was conducted completely in the open. Some measures for the prevention of crime would be ineffective if they were known to criminals. Some of the internal processes of government should be conducted in confidence if they are to result in effective policies. The presentation of clear issues to Parliament and the electorate depends upon ministers and administrators being able...to argue out all possibilities with complete frankness and free from the temptation to strike public attitudes (Departmental Committee on Section 2 of the Official Secrets Act 1911, Cmnd 5104: 'The Franks Committee').

More cynical commentators have suggested that official secrecy has had more to do with:

- the traditional 'establishment' view that the process of government is too important and complicated to be understood or appreciated by the general populace;
- the 'covering up' of mistakes made by civil servants and politicians and preserving the facade of government unity.

Official Secrets Act 1911

Section 1 provides that it is an offence if any person for a purpose prejudicial to the safety or interests of the state:

(a) obtains, publishes or communicates any information which might be useful to an enemy;

(b) enters, approaches or is found in the vicinity of a prohibited place (e.g. military establishment or property).

It would appear that it is not within the competence of a court to decide on the basis of evidence whether a particular act might be prejudicial to the interests of the state. This is a matter of political judgement falling within the Crown's non-justiciable prerogatives. Hence, once the prosecution has proved that the defendant intended the consequence of his actions, it is for the Crown to decide whether those consequences were prejudicial to its interests and to advise the court accordingly (*Chandler* v *DPP* [1964] AC 763).

Section 2 of the 1911 Act contained what was to become the Act's most controversial provision. This made it an offence to make any unauthorised communication of information gained in the service of the Crown to any unauthorised person. Hence the offence extended to relatively innocuous information having nothing to do with defence, national security, the investigation of crime, etc. It was also an offence to receive such information or to fail to take reasonable care of it. As a result of considerable criticism and political pressure from across the party divide, s 2 was eventually repealed and replaced by the Official Secrets Act 1989.

Official Secrets Act 1989

This limits the protection of the criminal law to certain specified classes of official information.

Section 1 deals with information relating to security and related intelligence. It provides that it is an offence for any member of the security forces or any person who has been notified that he or she is subject to the Act to disclose, without lawful authority, any information or document 'relating to security or intelligence which is or has been in his possession by virtue of his position as a member of...these services or in the course of his work' after being notified that this is subject to the section's requirements. It is a defence for the accused person to show that they 'did not know, and had no reasonable cause to believe, that the information...related to security or intelligence' (s 1(5)).

Note that the section covers all information relating to the security forces. It matters not whether the information revealed is particularly sensitive or wholly innocuous. Section 1(3) creates the offence of making a 'damaging disclosure of any information...relating to security or intelligence' without lawful authority. This applies to all past or present Crown servants, government contractors, and police officers. It is, therefore, a lifelong duty. The defence in s 1(5), explained above, is also available to any person charged with this offence.

It is probable that a court would not be prepared to consider evidence as to whether the disclosure of particular information was 'damaging' to the interests of the state (i.e. the Crown). Again, it is likely that this would be viewed as a political question relating to that element of the royal prerogative remaining beyond the scope of judicial comment.

Section 2 deals with disclosures of information relating to the defence of the realm. The offence consists of making a 'damaging disclosure of any information...relating to defence without lawful authority'. A damaging disclosure is that which:

(a) 'damages the capability of...the armed forces...or leads to loss of life or injury to members of those forces or serious damage to the equipment or installations of those forces' (s 2(2)(a));
(b) 'damages the interests of the United Kingdom abroad, seriously obstructs the promotion or protection...of those interests or endangers the safety of British citizens abroad' (s 2(2)(b)).

It is a defence for the accused to show that he did not know and had no reasonable cause to believe that disclosure of the information would be damaging in any of the above senses (s 2(3)). For the reasons already given, however, the willingness of a court to hear evidence on what is or is not damaging to the state remains open to question.

Section 3 makes it an offence for any past or present Crown servant or government contractor, without lawful authority, to make a damaging disclosure of any information relating to international relations or any confidential information which was obtained from a state other than the United Kingdom. The meaning of damaging is that given in s 2(2). Again, it is a defence to show lack of knowledge or reasonable cause to believe that the disclosure was damaging.

Section 4 identifies the last principal category of protected information, viz. that relating to crime and its investigation. The relevant offence is committed by a past or present Crown servant without lawful authority disclosing information which is likely to or results in 'the commission of an offence or facilitates an escape from custody...or impedes the prevention or detection of offence or the apprehension or prosecution of suspected offenders'. As with the preceding two categories of information, the defence of innocent publication is available (s 4(4)).

Any further disclosure by the recipient of information falling into any of the above categories is an offence providing that the recipient knew or should have known that the information fell within one of the protected categories (s 5).

The Act also creates the further offence of making, without lawful authority, a damaging disclosure of information relating to security, intelligence, defence or international relations which has been communicated in confidence to another state and which has come into the person's possession without that state's authority (s 6).

All of the above offences are committed only where the disclosure is made 'without lawful authority'. Such lawful authority to disclose information exists where:

- the disclosure is made by a Crown servant 'in accordance with his official duty';
- the disclosure is made by a government contractor 'in accordance with official authorisation' or for the purposes for which he is a government contractor 'without contravening an official restriction';
- the disclosure is made by a person who is neither of the above to a Crown servant or with official authorisation.

No public interest defence is included in the Act in respect of any of the categories of unlawful disclosure created by it. A defendant is not entitled to be acquitted, therefore, simply because he/she believed it was in the public interest to make the disclosure in question (*R v Shayler* [2002] 2 UKHL 11). The same case also decided that the 1989 Act was not incompatible with the European Convention, Art 10 on the grounds that it:

(a) is directed towards legitimate aims;
(b) contains internal review mechanisms for those concerned by the work or actions of the security services;
(c) allows disclosures with appropriate authorisation, which decisions are subject to judicial review.

Breach of confidence

A person may also be under an obligation not to disclose information which has been given in confidence or acquired against the wishes of those to whom it relates by an invasion of their privacy. Until the Court of Appeal's decision in *Douglas v Hello! Ltd* [2002] 2 All ER 289, it was generally accepted that such duty of confidence was limited to that which derived from:

(a) express or implied contractual terms;
(b) the special nature of the relationship between the parties.

In general, equity required exchanges of information to be treated confidentially where:

(a) the particular relationship cannot function effectively without it;
(b) in all the circumstances, the public interest in protecting the relationship clearly outweighs any countervailing public interest(s), e.g. that of freedom of information and expression.

Thus it was established that an action for breach of confidence could be used to prevent an employee from revealing or exploiting trade secrets confided by an employer (*Seager* v *Copydex Ltd* [1967] 1 WLR 923), or to prevent the disclosure of personal secrets exchanged between husband and wife during marriage (*Argyll* v *Argyll* [1967] Ch 302). Other examples of relationships which have been recognised as giving rise to a duty of confidence would include doctor and patient, priest and penitent, solicitor and client, and banker and customer.

The *Hello!* case involved proceedings for an injunction to restrain the proprietors of a popular magazine from publishing unauthorised photographs taken at a celebrity wedding. No contractual or prior relationship of a type previously held to import a duty of confidentiality existed between the parties claiming breach of confidence and the magazine proprietors. This was not something, however, which the court felt should be fatal to the claimants' case. Sedley LJ's opinion was that 'the law no longer needs to construct an artificial relationship of confidentiality between intruder and victim; it can recognise privacy itself as a legal principle drawn from the fundamental value of human authority'.

The restrictions on the freedom of expression discussed above have all been imposed by the criminal law. Hence the law is only brought to bear after the offensive words have been used or published. Breach of confidence, however, is a civil concept with the remedy sought usually being an injunction to prevent the disclosure or publication in question. It is a valuable means, therefore, of stopping the dissemination of information before damage has been caused rather than simply punishing the perpetrator after it has been done.

It is also now clear that in certain contexts the duty applies to the relationship between the Crown and those who work in its service whether these be ministers, civil servants or members of the intelligence and security services. This will be the case where the revelation of information could do serious damage to any of those public interests for which the government is directly responsible.

> In some instances disclosure of confidential information entrusted to a servant of the Crown may result in a financial loss to the public. In other instances such disclosure might tend to harm the public interest by impeding the efficient attainment of proper government ends and the revelation of defence or intelligence secrets certainly falls into that category (per Lord Keith, *Attorney-General* v *Guardian Newspapers Ltd (No. 2)* [1990] 1 AC 109).

Hence, an action for breach of confidence will lie to prevent an ex-member of the intelligence and security services from publishing memoirs which contain sensitive information about the activities of those services and the identities of their personnel (*ibid.*).

Where the Crown is the plaintiff in an action for breach of confidence this will involve the court in a delicate balancing exercise between the competing public interests:

> disclosure...will serve the public interest in keeping the community informed and in promoting discussion of public affairs. If, however, it appears that disclosure will be inimical to the public interest because national security, relations with foreign countries or the ordinary business of government will be prejudiced, disclosure will be restrained. There will be cases in which the conflicting considerations will be finely balanced, where it is difficult to decide whether the public's interest in knowing and expressing its opinion, outweighs the need to protect confidentiality (per Mason J, *Commonwealth of Australia* v *John Fairfax and Sons Ltd*, above).

The requirement that disclosure must do substantial damage to a public interest for which the Crown is responsible means that an injunction will not be granted to prevent disclosure of any and all information entrusted to a Crown servant in confidence. It has been said that the 'court will not prevent the publication of information which merely throws light on the past workings of government, even if it be not public property, so long as it does not prejudice the community in other respects' (*ibid.*).

In *Attorney-General* v *Jonathan Cape Ltd* [1975] QB 752, the government sought to prevent publication of an ex-Cabinet minister's memoirs. These contained details of Cabinet discussions some ten to twelve years previously. The court accepted that, as a general principle, there was a public interest in maintaining confidentiality of Cabinet proceedings but that, given the nature of the proposed disclosures and the length of time which had passed since they were current, any damage they might do did not outweigh the public interest in the freedom of information.

It also follows, as a further general principle, that a court will be unlikely to injunct disclosure of information, whatever its source and nature, if this is already widely available. Hence, in the *Spycatcher* case the House of Lords felt that injunctions could not be used to prevent newspapers from publishing highly sensitive security-related information contained in a book written by an ex-spy which was not yet on sale in the United Kingdom. The publication of the book in other parts of the English-speaking world (e.g. Ireland and the USA), meant that the information in question was already in the public domain so that the damage had already been done (*Attorney-General* v *Guardian Newspapers*, above).

There are dicta to the effect, however, that this should not apply to a member or ex-member of the security and intelligence services and that there is an overriding public interest in making such persons subject to a lifelong duty of confidence regardless of whether the public already has access to the information which he/she may wish to publish. Thus in *Attorney-General* v *Blake* [2000] 3 WLR 635, the House of Lords ruled that the Crown had a legitimate interest in preventing an ex-member of the Secret Intelligence Service who had defected to the USSR from profiting from disclosure of official information, whether classified or not, acquired while a member of the secret service and thereafter. According to Lord Nichols the disclosure of such information undermined the morale and trust of those engaged in secret and dangerous operations. In his view 'an absolute rule against disclosure, visible to all, made good sense'. The Crown was, therefore, entitled to whatever profits had been derived from the breach of confidentiality owed to it.

It would also appear to be the case that even though information is of the type that could damage a vital public interest, no breach of confidence is committed by its disclosure if this reveals serious abuses of power by the government:

> The press has a legitimate role in disclosing scandals by government. An open democratic society requires that that be so. If an allegation be made by an insider that, if true, would be a scandalous abuse by officers of the Crown of their powers and functions...the duty of the confidence...cannot be used to prevent the press from repeating the allegation (per Scott J, *Attorney-General* v *Guardian Newspapers*, above).

In a democracy, in such circumstances, the public interest in the freedom of information would outweigh the public interest in confidentiality.

The enactment of the Human Rights Act 1998 means that the requirements of Art 10 of the European Convention on Human Rights must now be considered where a government seeks to injunct information to prevent it coming into the public domain. It will be necessary, therefore, to show that the injunction serves a legitimate aim and is a proportionate response to the danger posed by publication. Where the injunction is sought by an individual to protect their privacy, Art 8 will also be brought into play. In these circumstances the court's function will be to reach a decision for or against publication which represents a fair and reasonable balance between the competing interests of privacy and the need for freedom of expression (*Campbell* v *Mirror Group Newspapers Ltd* [2002] EWHC 499). Thus by 'absorbing the rights which Articles 8 and 10 protect into the long-established action for breach of confidence', the courts are able to develop the concept in a way which complies with their duty in the Human Rights Act, s 6, not to act in a way which is incompatible with a Convention right (see Lord Woolf CJ, *A* v *B (a company)* [2002] EWCA Civ 337).

Interception of telecommunications

Prior to 1985 the executive's power to 'tap' telephone conversations and open letters was assumed to be derived from the royal prerogative. It was not authorised by statute or regulated by any specific legal rules. In *Malone* v *United Kingdom*, above, this lack of specificity in terms of when such practices were permissible was held to constitute a breach of Art 8 of the European Convention on Human Rights. This resulted in the enactment of the Interception of Communications Act 1985.

The 1985 Act provides that intentional interception of such communications is an offence unless done pursuant to a warrant issued by the Home Secretary. A warrant could be issued where this was considered necessary in the interests of:

- national security;
- preventing or detecting serious crime;
- safeguarding the economic well-being of the United Kingdom (s 2).

Section 9(1) of the Act rendered information obtained in this way to be inadmissible as evidence in any criminal or civil proceedings. Such infraction must, however, be disclosed to the defence (*R* v *Preston* [1993] 3 WLR 891).

The 1985 Act did not apply to cordless telephones as these are not connected to the public telecommunications system (*R* v *Effik* [1994] 3 WLR 583).

The key provisions of the 1985 Act were repealed and replaced by the Regulation of Investigatory Powers Act 2000 (RIPA). This permits the lawful interception of postal or telecommunications pursuant to a warrant of authority granted by the Home Secretary (s 5). The Act applies to both public and private telecommunications systems (s 2). The grounds on which such warrant may be issued are broadly the same as those specified by the Interception of Communications Act, s 2. It is, however, no longer sufficient that the minister considers the interception to be 'necessary' for a particular public interest. According to RIPA he or she must also 'believe' that the proposed action is a proportionate means of achieving the desired objective (s 5). It remains the case that information obtained through the statutory powers of interception cannot be used or referred to in legal proceedings (s 17).

D-notices

The publication or broadcasting of material sensitive to national security may also be restrained by the issue of a D-notice. These notices seek to prevent the dissemination of information relating to the following where this would be damaging to the public interest:

- defence plans, operational capability, state of readiness and training;
- defence equipment;
- nuclear weapons;
- defence communications technology;
- the security and intelligence services;
- contingency plans for war or national emergency;
- information relating to the defence and security establishments and installations.

D-notices are issued by the Defence, Press and Broadcasting Committee, composed of representatives from the Ministry of Defence and the media. Such notices tend to be issued only after more informal methods of communication have failed to achieve the desired result. The material not to be published will be specified therein.

The Committee was not created by statute or under the royal prerogative. Hence, D-notices have no legal force or sanctions attached to them. The system attempts to achieve a degree of self-regulation. There is always the possibility, however, that the publication of information in contravention of such notice may amount to a breach of the Official Secrets Acts.

FREEDOM OF INFORMATION AND DATA PROTECTION

Introduction

The state in its various guises both central and local, collects and holds a mass of detailed information about, and relating to, the lives of most of its citizens. Until the Data Protection Act 1984, which was concerned with personal information held on computer, this was not a matter subject to any legal regulation either in terms of giving any right of access to such information or of regulating its use and disclosure to third parties.

In December 1997 the government issued a White Paper, *Your Right to Know* (Cm 3818). This stated that 'unnecessary *secrecy in government* leads to arrogance...and defective decision-making' (para 1.1). The White Paper was followed by a draft Bill as part of a consultation exercise (Cm 4355, 1999). The stated intention of the Bill was to 'extend professionally the right of the public to have access to official information held by public authorities and, in so doing, to promote:

(a) 'better informed discussion of public affairs';
(b) 'greater accountability of public authorities';
(c) 'more effective participation in the making and administration of laws and policies'.

After considerable public and parliamentary debate (and amendment) this led to the Freedom of Information Act 2000. The Act provides a general right of access to information held by public authorities subject to a fairly lengthy catalogue of exemptions.

Any person applying for access to information is entitled to be informed whether the authority holds the information in question and, if it does, to have it communicated to him/her 'promptly' and within twenty working days (ss 1 and 10). The right to know whether certain information is held by a particular authority does not apply to, *inter alia*:

(i)   that relating to the formation of government policy;
(ii) ministerial communications;
(iii) advice given or requested by any of the Crown's law officers;
(iv) the operation of any ministerial private office (s 35).

The principal classes of information exempt from the duty of disclosure are:

(a) that which is reasonably accessible by other means (s 21) or which is to be published (s 22);
(b) that which relates to the security or intelligence services (s 23) or to the royal household (s 37);
(c) personal information (s 40) or that provided to the authority in confidence (s 41);
(d) that to which legal or professional privilege applies (s 42);
(e) that which might prejudice:

- the safeguarding of national security (s 24), defence or the effectiveness of the armed forces (s 26);
- relations between the United Kingdom and any other state or international organisation (s 27) or between any two administrations in the United Kingdom (s 28);
- the United Kingdom's economic interests (s 28);
- criminal investigations or proceedings (s 30);
- law enforcement (s 31);
- the effective conduct of public affairs (s 36);
- the physical or mental health of any individual (s 38);
- trade secrets or commercial interests (s 43).

The Act also provides for the creation of an Information Commissioner (s 18) to investigate any complaint that an authority is not complying with the Act. Where non-compliance is found the Commissioner may serve an information notice on the authority concerned enforceable by proceedings in a county court (s 54).

The Freedom of Information Act will operate alongside the Data Protection Act 1998. This provides the individual with rights in relation to 'personal data' against any person or body falling within the definition of a 'data controller'. Personal data is that which relates to a living individual and from which that individual may be identified (s 1). A data controller is a person who 'determines the purpose for which...any personal data...are to be processed' (*ibid.*).

The principal rights given to the individual are:

(a) to be informed whether any personal data relating to them is being processed by the data controller, the purposes for which it is to be used and the persons to whom it may be disclosed;
(b) to have the data communicated to them (s 7).

The rights are enforceable by court order where a valid request is not complied with (*ibid*). They are not absolute rights, however, and do not apply where disclosure could, *inter alia*, prejudice national security, the prevention or detection of crime or the apprehension or prosecution of offenders (ss 28 and 29).

The meaning of 'data' in the 1998 Act is wider than in the original Data Protection Act 1984 and extends beyond that held in computers to include that which is:

(i)   recorded with the intention that it should be processed by means of such equipment;
(ii) recorded as part of a filing system (s 1).

The Act imposes a duty on a data controller to discharge his/her functions in relation to personal data in accordance with prescribed data protection principles; these are that the data shall be:

- processed lawfully and fairly and only with the individual's consent or in performance of a legal duty, the administration of justice, a statutory or other function of a public nature;
- obtained for specified and lawful purposes;
- adequate, relevant and not excessive to those purposes;
- kept accurate and up to date;
- kept only for so long as is necessary;
- processed in accordance with the rights of the data subject;
- protected against unauthorised processing, loss or damage;
- not transferred to a country outside the European Economic Area unless that country has adequate protection for the rights of data subjects (s 4 and Sched 1).

Overall supervision of the Act's requirements is given to the Data Protection Commissioner (s 51). The Commissioner may serve an enforcement notice on any data controller alleged not to be acting in accordance with the data protection principles (s 40). Failure to comply with such notice is an offence (s 47).

The Commissioner must lay an annual general report before Parliament on the exercise of his/her functions and such periodic specific reports as he/she thinks appropriate (s 52).

Reference

Robertson (1995) *Freedom, the Individual and the Law* (3rd edn), London: Sweet & Maxwell.

Further reading

Bailey, Harris and Jones (1995) *Civil Liberties: Cases and Materials* (4th edn), London: Butterworths, Chs 5–7.

Feldman (1993) *Civil Liberties and Human Rights in England and Wales*, Oxford: Clarendon Press, Chs 12–16.

Pollard, Parpworth and Hughes (1997) *Constitutional and Administrative Law: Text with Materials* (2nd edn), London: Butterworths, Ch 10.

Robertson (1995) *Freedom of the Individual and the Law* (7th edn), London: Penguin, Chs 4–7.

Robertson (1993) *Media Law* (3rd edn), London: Penguin.

Stone (1997) *Textbook on Civil Liberties* (2nd edn), London: Blackstone, Chs 5–7.

Chapter 23

FREEDOM AND EMERGENCY POWERS

EMERGENCY POWERS IN GENERAL

Emergency powers may be defined as those which give the state the legal competence to deal with extraordinary and immediate threats to political, social and economic stability. Such threats may come in the form of:

- external aggression by another state(s);
- political terrorism for the purpose of changing the domestic political order or that of a foreign state;
- widespread disruption to the normal life of the community resulting from natural disasters or other causes of serious civil disruption, e.g. strikes in essential services.

The powers to deal with such contingencies will be contained principally in Acts of Parliament. Relevant common law powers may also be found in the royal prerogative (see Chapter 12). The existence of emergency powers on a more permanent basis, particularly when designed to deal with terrorism, may suggest a significant lack of social consensus concerning the legitimacy of the state. Such legislation will be likely to impose those restrictions on the liberties of the subject as are deemed appropriate to deal with the threat.

EMERGENCY POWERS IN WARTIME

On both occasions in the twentieth century when the very existence of the state was threatened by external aggression, Parliament responded by conferring extensive emergency powers on the executive. The principal enactments of this type were, for the First World War, the Defence of the Realm Acts 1914–15, and, for the Second World War, the Emergency Powers (Defence) Acts 1939–40. These gave the executive government the authority to control almost every aspect of national life and, in particular, to make such regulations as were deemed necessary for the defence of the realm, public safety and the successful prosecution of the war.

In both wars these Acts contained powers to, *inter alia*:

- conscript persons into military and industrial service;
- intern enemy aliens without trial;
- regulate the supply and distribution of food (rationing).

Although access to the courts to challenge alleged abuses of such powers was not excluded expressly, reference has already been made to the obvious judicial reluctance to review the exercise of discretionary powers in such times of national difficulty (see R v *Halliday, ex parte Zadig* [1917] AC 260; *Liversidge* v *Anderson* [1942] AC 206).

The principal two enactments containing powers to deal with terrorist activities currently in force in the United Kingdom are the Prevention of Terrorism Act 1989 and the Northern Ireland (Emergency Provisions) Act 1996. With the exception of ss 1–3, dealing with the proscription and membership of terrorist organisations, the 1989 Act has effect throughout the United Kingdom (i.e. including Northern Ireland). The 1996 Act, however, as its name indicates, has effect in Northern Ireland only.

EMERGENCY POWERS AND TERRORISM

Prevention of Terrorism Acts 1974–89 and Northern Ireland (Emergency Provisions) Acts 1973–96

The Prevention of Terrorism Act (PTA) 1974 was the United Kingdom's first piece of modern, generally applicable, anti-terrorist legislation. It was introduced as a 'temporary' response to increased IRA activity on the mainland of the United Kingdom in the early 1970s. Its specific timing was a direct result of the Birmingham pub bombings of 1974 in which 21 people were killed and 162 injured. Such was the political mood at the time, that the Act passed through nearly all its parliamentary stages in a single day notwithstanding that it contained a wide array of security powers beyond those normally available, or indeed generally held to be acceptable, for the investigation and prosecution of 'ordinary' criminal activities. Its provisions were directed principally at terrorism connected with Irish affairs. The Act was revised and re-enacted on a number of occasions, most recently in 1989. Amongst its core provisions were powers authorising police to:

(a) stop and search vehicles, their occupants and pedestrians, for articles which could be used for the purposes of terrorism (ss 13A and 13B, inserted by the Criminal Justice and Public Order Act 1994, s 81 and the Prevention of Terrorism (Additional Powers) Act 1996);

(b) arrest and detain any person reasonably suspected of involvement in specified terrorist offences and to detain such persons for questioning for 48 hours and for a further five days with the Home Secretary's consent (s 14);

(c) enter and search premises, with warrant, reasonably believed to contain a terrorist suspect on evidence of substantial value to a terrorist investigation (s 14);

(d) conduct such searches without warrant on the authority of an officer of the rank of superintendent or above where the investigation was reasonably believed to be one of great urgency necessitating immediate action in the interests of the state (Sched 7(7)).

These were in addition to the powers conferred on the Home Secretary to:

(a) proscribe any organisation appearing to him/her to be concerned in terrorism occurring in the United Kingdom in connection with affairs in Northern Ireland (s 1) (membership of such organisation being an offence under s 2);

(b) exclude from or prevent any person entering or remaining in any part of the United Kingdom if satisfied that such person had been concerned in acts of terrorism relating to Northern Ireland (ss 4–7).

For the purposes of the civil and military security forces on the ground in Northern Ireland itself, these powers were complemented by those contained in the Northern Ireland (Emergency Provisions) Acts, an important feature of which was that many of the powers found therein were exercisable by members of the armed forces as well as by police officers. The original Northern Ireland (Emergency Provisions) Act 1973, as with the first PTA, was also revised and re-enacted on several occasions. It was also subject to annual renewal by Parliament. The most recent complete version of these was the Northern Ireland (Emergency Provisions) Act 1996. In addition to authorising the Secretary of State for Northern Ireland to proscribe organisations appearing to him/her to be engaged in or promoting acts of terrorism and making membership of such organisations an offence (ss 30–31), the Act contained powers permitting:

(a) any member of the security forces (i.e. either police or army) to stop any person for as long as was necessary to obtain information concerning that person's identity, movements, and knowledge of any recent explosions or fatal or life-threatening incidents – all of this on pain of arrest without warrant (s 25);

(b) any member of the RUC to arrest without warrant any person he/she had reasonable grounds to suspect of any offence under the Act (s 18);

(c) any member of the armed forces to arrest without warrant any person he/she had reasonable grounds to suspect of 'any offence' (s 19);

(d) any member of the security forces to stop and search any person for possession of weapons, explosives or radio transmitters without need for reasonable suspicion (s 20 (6));

(e) any member of the RUC to enter and search any premises without warrant where it was suspected on reasonable grounds that any person suspected of a terrorist offence might be found (s 18);

(f) any member of the security forces to enter and search any premises without warrant either for weapons or explosives (s 19); or where it was considered necessary to do so in the 'course of operations for the preservation of peace or the maintenance of order' (s 26).

In addition, and although not used since 1976, the Northern Ireland emergency power legislation retained the power of indefinite detention without trial or internment available to the Northern Ireland Secretary in relation to any person he/she was 'satisfied' had been engaged in the planning or commission of acts of terrorism and whose detention was 'necessary for the protection of the public' (s 36 and Sched 3). The provisions containing this power were eventually repealed by the Northern Ireland (Emergency Provisions) Act 1998.

The Terrorism Act 2000

Background

The Act is based on the proposals contained in the government's consultation paper *Legislation Against Terrorism* (Cm 4178, 1998) which, in turn, were influenced considerably by Lord Lloyd's report of the Inquiry into Legislation Against Terrorism (Cm 3420, 1996). It is intended to be a comprehensive, all purpose instrument of anti-terrorist legislation applicable throughout the United Kingdom and to terrorism in general whatever its source or purpose. It thus repeals and replaces the Prevention of Terrorism Acts and the Northern Ireland (Emergency Provisions) Acts and is not subject to annual or periodic parliamentary renewal. According to the government's consultation paper, its aim has been 'to create legislation which is both effective and proportionate to the threat which the United Kingdom faces from all forms of terrorism – Irish, international and domestic – which is sufficiently flexible to respond to a changing threat, which ensures that individual rights are protected and which fulfils the United Kingdom's international commitments' (above, para 8).

The case set out by Lord Lloyd in his 1996 report for maintaining a different legal framework for dealing with terrorism than that applicable to 'ordinary crime' included the following:

- terrorism frequently involves the use of lethal force directed at, or capable of, causing extensive and indiscriminate casualties and is designed to create fear amongst the civilian population generally;
- its purpose is to secure political or ideological objectives by violence or threat of violence and thus to subvert the democratic process;
- it is perpetrated by highly trained and committed individuals, usually well-armed, acting on behalf of well-resourced organisations;
- terrorists have proved particularly difficult to catch and convict without special offences and additional police powers;
- the overall decline of terrorist incidents in recent years has been more than offset by the trend towards more deadly weapons and higher casualties.

Such arguments have, however, not proved sufficient to stifle all criticism of the new legislation and, particularly, the allegation that legislation of this type should be regarded as an extraordinary and temporary expedient for dealing with a pressing emergency or threat to social and political stability and that the enactment of permanent 'special powers' legislation, particularly at a time when the principal cause of terrorism in the United Kingdom appears to have been diminished, threatens the credibility of the United Kingdom's claim to be a genuinely free, liberal democracy.

The definition of terrorism

For the purposes of the Prevention of Terrorism and the Northern Ireland (Emergency Provisions) Acts this meant 'the use of violence for political ends' and included 'any use of violence for the purpose of putting the public or section of the public in fear'. Application of the concept in the Prevention of Terrorism legislation was limited, in the case of some powers and offences (including proscription and exclusion) to action in connection with the affairs of Northern Ireland and, in relation to others (including stop and search, arrest, search and seizure), to terrorism directed towards either the affairs of Northern Ireland or those of states beyond the United Kingdom. It did not apply, therefore, to acts of political violence relating to the internal affairs of those parts of the United Kingdom other than Northern Ireland.

In the Terrorism Act 2000 terrorism is expressed as the use or threat of certain types of action in or outside the United Kingdom designed to influence the government of the United Kingdom or any government, and intimidate the public or section of the public, for the purpose of advancing a political, religious or ideological cause (s 1). The types of action referred to are those which:

(i)   involve serious violence against a person;
(ii) involve serious damage to property;
(iii) endanger a person's life (other than that of the perpetrator of the act);
(iv) create a serious risk to the health or safety of the public;
(v)   are designed to interfere with or seriously disrupt an electronic system (s 1(4)).

If firearms or explosives are used in the commission of any of (i) to (v) above the action amounts to terrorism whether or not it is designed to influence the/a government or intimidate the public (s 1(3)).

Hence, although the new definition eschews the rather vague notion of 'violence for political ends', it seeks to extend the ambit and application of the term in a variety of ways and will apply to:

- acts falling within the definition wherever these are committed including those concerned purely with affairs in England, Scotland or Wales;
- acts directed to religious or ideological issues rather than overtly political causes;
- acts which may not cause or threaten any direct risk of personal violence or injury but which are directed towards property, or such matters as the workings of public services and utilities or telecommunications and computer systems.

As so phrased, therefore, it is conceivable that terrorism could now encompass, in pure legal terms at least, those forms of direct action or protest sometimes engaged in by, for example, environmental and animal rights groups and by trade unions where such activities might have an impact on public health or safety. It would also appear to extend to groups supporting struggles against repressive régimes in other jurisdictions.

Proscription and deproscription

The Act proscribes all organisations listed in Sched 2 and enables the Home Secretary to add or remove organisations to or from the Schedule (s 3(1)–(3)). The minister may take such action 'only if he believes' that an organisation commits, participates, prepares, promotes or is otherwise concerned in acts of terrorism (s 3(4)–(5)). Unlike its predecessors this new power of proscription is not limited to organisations using violence in connection with the affairs of Northern Ireland. Note also the lack of any express requirement that the minister's decision be based on reasonable grounds.

A major new departure in the 2000 Act is the provision of a procedure enabling a proscribed organisation to appeal against the proscription decision. An application may be made to the minister to exercise their power to remove an organisation from Sched 2 by the organisation or any person affected by its proscription (s 4(1)–(2)). Should such application be refused, a right of appeal is given to a Proscribed Organisation Appeals Commission (POAC) (s 5(1)–(2)). The Commission is to allow an appeal against a refusal of an application to deproscribe an organisation if it considers that the decision 'was flawed when considered in the light of the principles applicable on an application for judicial review' (s 5(3)). Where the Commission allows an appeal this determines that the minister has acted in contra-vention of the Human Rights Act. He/she is required, therefore, either to lay a deproscription order before Parliament subject to the affirmative resolution procedure or, in more urgent cases, make an order removing the organisation from Sched 2 which will lapse within 40 days unless approved by resolution passed by both Houses within that period (ss 5(5), 123 and 124). Decisions of the Commission may be appealed on a point of law to the Court of Appeal (s 6). Following the deproscription of an organisation, a right of appeal becomes available to any person convicted of any of the various offences in the Act relating to the membership or financing of it (s 7). These offences are contained in ss 11–13, 15–19 and 56 as set out below.

Members of the POAC are to be appointed by the Lord Chancellor who is also empowered to make rules regulating its procedure and workings (Sched 3). Three members must attend its proceedings one of whom must be a person who holds or has held high judicial office within the meaning of the Appellate Jurisdiction Act 1876 (ibid.). The rules made by the Lord Chancellor for the conduct of the Commission's proceedings may provide that, in certain circumstances:

(i)   its business may be conducted without an oral hearing;
(ii) reasons for proscription may be withheld;
(iii) legal representatives may be excluded (ibid.).

Terrorist and related offences

The principal offences contained in the Terrorism Act are:

- belonging or professing to belong to a proscribed organisation unless the person can prove that he/she did not take part in the activities of the organisation at any time during which it was proscribed (s 11);
- inviting support for a proscribed organisation or arranging a meeting to further that organisation's objectives or to be addressed by a person who belongs or pro-fesses to belong to a proscribed organisation (s 12);
- addressing a meeting for the purpose of encouraging support for a proscribed organisation (ibid.);
- wearing items of clothing or otherwise wearing, carrying or displaying any article in a public place in a way which arouses reasonable suspicion that he/she is a member or supporter of a proscribed organisation (s 13);
- raising or providing money or other property intended or reasonably suspected to be for the purposes of terrorism (s 15);

- possessing money intending it to be used for the purposes of terrorism or in circumstances where there is reasonable cause to suspect that it might be so used (s 16);
- entering into arrangements by which terrorist property is placed under the control of another for the purposes, *inter alia*, of concealment, removal from the jurisdiction or transfer to nominees (s 18, money 'laundering');
- failing to disclose as soon as reasonably practicable any belief or suspicion based on information gained in the course of employment or any trade, business or profession that a person has committed any of the offences in ss 15–18 (s 19);
- prejudicing a terrorist investigation either by disclosing information about it to another ('tipping off') or by concealing relevant material (s 39);
- giving, receiving, or inviting another to receive, instruction or training in the making or use of firearms, explosives or chemical, biological or nuclear weapons (s 54);
- directing at any level the activities of an organisation concerned in terrorism (s 56);
- possessing an article in circumstances which give rise to a reasonable suspicion that it is possessed for a terrorist purpose (s 57);
- making or possessing records of information likely to be useful to a person committing or preparing an act of terrorism (s 58);
- inciting another person to commit an act of terrorism wholly or partly outside the United Kingdom (ss 59–61);
- doing anything outside the United Kingdom as an act of or for the purposes of terrorism where the action would have amounted to the commission of certain offences involving causing explosions, using biological or chemical weapons (s 62);
- doing anything outside the United Kingdom amounting to an offence under ss 15–18 of the Act if committed in the United Kingdom (s 63).

Note that no offence is committed under ss 15–18 above (the fund-raising offences) if a person's involvement is with the express permission of a police officer or any suspicion that the money may be used for terrorist purposes is revealed to the police as soon as reasonably practicable (s 21). This provides protection for undercover agents and police informants.

Terrorist property

This is defined as money or other property which is:

(a) likely to be used for the purposes of terrorism;
(b) the proceeds of the commission of acts of terrorism or acts carried out for the purposes of terrorism (s 14).

The disclosure to a police officer of a belief or suspicion that money or other property is terrorist property or is derived from such property does not contravene any statutory or common law provision restricting the disclosure of information (s 20). A court which convicts a person of any of the offences in ss 15–18 (also 11–12 in Northern Ireland) may order forfeiture of any money or property in that person's possession or control which, at the time of the offence, was intended, or reasonably suspected as being for use for terrorist purposes (ss 23 and 111). That which is reasonably suspected to be terrorist property and is being imported or exported from the United Kingdom or moved between Northern Ireland and Great Britain may be seized and detained for 48 hours by police, immigration or customs officers (s 25). Continued detention of the same for periods of up to three months to a maximum of two years may be authorised by a magistrate (s 26). An application to a magistrates' court for forfeiture of the property may be made under s 28.

The provisions in the 2000 Act, ss 24–31, relating to the seizure and detention of terrorist cash were replaced by extended provisions in the Anti-Terrorism, Crime and Security Act 2001, s 1 and Sched 1. The principal difference effected by these later provisions was to allow the power of seizure to be used anywhere in the United Kingdom and not just at border crossings as envisaged by s 25 of the 2000 Act.

Terrorist investigations and related powers

A terrorist investigation is one which is concerned with:

(a) the commission, instigation or preparation of acts of terrorism;
(b) an act which appears to have been done for a terrorist purpose;
(c) the resources of a terrorist organisation;
(d) the possibility of proscribing or deproscribing an organisation;
(e) the commission, preparation or instigation of an offence under the Act (s 32).

A terrorist is a person who has committed any of the offences in ss 11, 12, 15–18, 54 or 56–63 or who has been concerned in the commission, preparation or instigation of acts of terrorism (s 40).

For the purposes of such investigations and for preventing terrorist activities, the Act entrusts the police with an extensive array of powers of stop and search, arrest, detention, entry, search and seizure and restriction of movements. For Northern Ireland these powers are supplemented with powers to stop and question and generally to override private and public property rights where this is thought to be in the interests of peace and order.

Arrest and detention

A police officer may arrest without warrant any person whom he/she reasonably suspects to be a terrorist (s 41). The arrested person may be searched to discover if he/she has anything in his/her possession which might constitute evidence that he/she is a terrorist (s 43) and may be detained by the police for up to 48 hours (s 41). Further detention may be authorised by a judicial authority up to a maximum of seven days from the time of the arrest providing there are reasonable grounds for believing that further detention is necessary to obtain or preserve relevant evidence and that the investigation is being conducted diligently and expeditiously (s 41 and Sched 8). The detained person has the right to appear and be legally represented before the judicial authority to whom the application for the warrant of further detention is made (*ibid.*). The judicial authority is, however, given powers to exclude both from any part of the hearing and to order that any information on which the application is based be withheld from them (*ibid.*).

Stop and search

The Act contains two principal powers of stop and search. The first authorises any police officer to stop and search any person reasonably suspected to be a terrorist to discover whether the person is in possession of anything which could constitute evidence that he/she is a terrorist (s 43). The second power is conferred on officers in uniform. It is a power to stop and search vehicles, their occupants and contents, or any pedestrian in a specified area, pursuant to authorisation given by an officer of at least the rank of Assistant Chief Constable or Commander in the City of London or Metropolitan police forces (s 44). Such authorisation may be given if it is considered 'expedient for the prevention of terrorism' (ibid.). An officer acting under such authorisation should stop and search only for the purpose of discovering articles which could be used for a terrorist purpose but need not have any suspicion of the possession of such articles before exercising the power (s 45). The person or vehicle may be detained for such time as is reasonably required to carry out the search. A person may not be required to remove anything other than outer clothing in public (ibid.). The officer may seize and retain any article he/she reasonably suspects is to be used in connection with terrorism (ibid.). A grant of authorisation for the use of the power may be made for renewable periods up to 28 days but will cease to have effect after 48 hours if not confirmed by the Home Secretary (s 46). Any obstruction of an officer in the exercise of the power constitutes an offence (s 47).

Entry and search of premises

The powers of entry and search provided by the Act relate to both evidence of terrorism and those suspected of it. Section 37 authorises a police officer to enter and search premises with warrant from a magistrate for the purposes of a terrorist investigation and to seize and retain any relevant material found there likely to be of substantial value to any such investigation and not merely the one for which the warrant was granted. A further power is given to a circuit judge to order a person to provide an explanation for any articles found in the course of the search. In cases of urgency both the search warrant and any order for explanation may be issued by a superintendent of police (s 37 and Sched 5, paras 13–16). Entry and search of any premises with warrant may also be made where there are reasonable grounds for suspecting that a person who is or has been involved in acts of terrorism may be found there (s 42).

Cordons and parking restrictions

Sections 33–36 and 48–52 give police wide powers to regulate the movement and use of vehicles and the movement of persons in designated areas to further a terrorist investigation or for the purposes of preventing terrorism.

By virtue of ss 33 and 34 an area may be designated as a cordoned area for the conduct of a terrorist investigation. Pursuant to such designation movements of vehicles and persons in and out of that area, and within it, may be restricted. It is an offence to refuse to comply with police instructions (s 36). A designation under s 33 may not exceed 28 days (s 35).

Authorisation to restrict parking on a specified road or roads where this is expedient to prevent acts of terrorism may be given by an officer of the rank of Assistant Chief Constable or Commander in the City of London or Metropolitan area (s 48).

Parking in contravention of the restrictions imposed without reasonable excuse is an offence (s 51). An authorisation under s 46 may be imposed for renewal periods of 28 days (s 50).

Powers applicable to Northern Ireland only

Part V of the Terrorism Act relates to Northern Ireland only and provides, *inter alia*, a range of additional powers to police officers there generally and to military personnel on duty in the province.

Stop and question

Any member of the police service or member of the armed forces on duty may stop and question any person for so long as necessary to ascertain:

(i)   his identity and movements;
(ii) what he knows about a recent explosion or other recent incident endangering life;
(iii) what he knows about a person killed in a recent explosion or incident (s 89).

A person who refuses to stop or to answer any questions to the best of his/her ability commits an offence (*ibid.*).

Arrest

Failure to comply with, or obstruction of the exercise of, any of the above powers is an offence contained in ss 82 and 83. Section 82 applies to the police and allows any officer to arrest without warrant on reasonable suspicion that a person is about to, is committing, or has committed an offence under the Act. Section 83 contains the more broadly worded power available to members of the armed forces. The power is to arrest any person reasonably suspected of 'any offence' and to detain such person for up to four hours.

The requirement resting on police officers to give reasons for arrest does not apply to arrest by military personnel under s 83. It is sufficient that the soldier states that he is 'making the arrest as a member of Her Majesty's forces' (s 83(2)).

Port and border controls

Although the power of exclusion in the Prevention of Terrorism Acts is not retained, s 53 and Sched 7 of the Terrorism Act seek to ensure that 'examining officers' (police, immigration and customs officers) at borders, ports and airports are possessed of sufficient array of security powers to minimise the movements of terrorists and their equipment to and from the United Kingdom and within it. To this end examining officers at all such points of entry and departure are authorised to:

• stop, search, detain and question for up to nine hours any person to determine whether he/she is a terrorist suspect (no need for reasonable suspicion);
• require persons questioned to provide the information required and to produce identification on pain of prosecution;

- search any ship or aircraft or luggage for or from such to discover whether these are persons travelling whom the officer may wish to question (again no requirement for any type of suspicion);
- search any vehicle at a border crossing.

Any property seized may be detained for seven days to determine whether it may be needed for criminal proceedings or in relation to a decision to deport.

Entry, search and seizure

Extensive powers of this type are conferred on both the police and military in order to facilitate effective exercise of the above power of arrest.

A police officer may enter and search any premises without warrant where he/she reasonably suspects that a terrorist or a person guilty of any offence under the Act may be (ss 81 and 82). Anything reasonably suspected of being for commission of any such offence may be seized (s 82).

A member of the armed forces may enter and search any premises without warrant in which they reasonably suspect that a person who has committed any offence or who is a terrorist may be found (s 83). Any items found which are reasonably suspected to be for the purpose of disrupting the exercise of the powers in ss 93 or 94 (see below) may be seized and detained for up to four hours.

In addition to the above both police and military may enter any premises without warrant:

(i) where it is reasonably believed that a person is detained in such circumstances that their life is in danger (s 86);
(ii) where it is considered necessary in the course of operations for the preservation of the peace or the maintenance of order (s 90).

Powers in relation to property

Beyond the specifically directed provisions for entry and search, the Act provides further powers which may have other substantial effects on private and public property rights. Thus where he/she 'considers it necessary for the preservation of the peace or the maintenance of public order', the Secretary of State for Northern Ireland may authorise police or military personnel to do anything which interferes with a private or public property right including:

(i) take possession of any land or property;
(ii) place buildings or other structures in a state of defence;
(iii) detain any property or cause it to be moved or destroyed;
(iv) carry out any works on land which has been taken possession of (s 91).

Rights of passage on the highway may also be restricted by closure of roads or the direction of the Secretary of State, again where he/she considers it necessary for the preservation of the peace, or, for the same reason, by police and military personnel where this is considered 'immediately necessary' (s 92).

Making further provision for the preservation of the peace

Should the above be insufficient for the preservation of the peace and maintenance of order in Northern Ireland, the Secretary of State may make further law enforcement provisions by regulation (s 96). The power to do so is not qualified by any requirement that these be 'necessary' or reasonably related to the purpose for which they are made.

Criticisms of the Act

Apart from the implications of the extended definition of terrorism already referred to and the very enactment of a comprehensive piece of anti-terrorist legislation at a time of significant reduction in domestic terrorist activity, the following represent just some of the other concerns which have been expressed about the 2000 Act.

(a) The offence of membership of a proscribed organisation has been retained despite there having been no convictions for this in Great Britain since 1990 (195 in Northern Ireland for the same period). The offence of directing the activities of a proscribed organisation for which there have been only two convictions under the prevention of terrorism legislation is also retained.

(b) The offence of membership of a proscribed organisation may be committed by a person who merely professes to be a member.

(c) The power of proscription coupled with the extended definition of terrorism vests the Home Secretary with a wide but subjective power to declare unlawful organisations whose objectives are not directed towards the police or legitimacy of particular governments or constitutional orders.

(d) The wording of some provisions is so imprecise as to admit of possibly absurd applications. Thus s 12(2) provides, *inter alia*, that an offence is committed by a person who organises a meeting to be addressed by a person who is or professes to be a member of a proscribed organisation. No reference is made, however, to the subject matter of the meeting or speech. This may mean, therefore, that it is an offence to organise a meeting at which such person is to speak about an entirely innocuous topic.

(e) A number of the Act's provisions would appear incompatible with the presumption of innocence. Thus, conviction for possession of an article for terrorist purposes under s 57 may be based on a reasonable suspicion, rather than proof, of the article's intended use. It is for the defendant, therefore, to show that the purpose for possession did not offend the Act. Similarly, under s 13 a person may be convicted for wearing items which cause reasonable suspicion, but do not prove, membership or support for a proscribed organisation. Again, therefore, to avoid conviction, the defendant is put to the test of disproving the suspicion against them.

(f) By virtue of ss 40 and 41 a person may be arrested on suspicion of being 'concerned' in acts of terrorism which is not, of itself, an offence.

(g) A number of the Act's powers may be exercised without need for reasonable suspicion or belief. In those parts of the Act applying throughout the United Kingdom these would include the power of prescription and the powers to set up cordons (s 33) and to search vehicles and their occupants (s 44).

The Anti-Terrorism, Crime and Security Act 2001

The stated purpose of the Act was to build on existing anti-terrorist and related legislation 'to ensure that the Government, in the light of the new situation arising from the September 11 terrorist attacks on New York and Washington, have the necessary powers to counter the threat to the UK' (Explanatory Notes to 2001 Act, para 3). The Act contains a miscellany of powers directed towards the above objective. The following represent some of its major provisions:

- the power to seize terrorist cash or property found at any place in the United Kingdom (s 1 and Sched 1);
- the power to freeze any assets which might otherwise be made available to a person or government involved in actions threatening the life or property of United Kingdom nationals or residents or the United Kingdom's economy (ss 4–16);
- extension of the existing statutory powers authorising disclosure of information by public authorities to include that which may assist in criminal investigations or proceedings and, in relation to such proceedings, removing any obligation of secrecy, other than contained in the Data Protection Act 1998, otherwise falling on the Inland Revenue and Customs and Excise (ss 17–20);
- the power to detain a suspected international terrorist under the terms of the Immigration Act 1971, i.e. for deportation, notwithstanding that the person cannot be removed from the United Kingdom because of a point of law, an international agreement or practical considerations (ss 21–36);
- extensions of both the meaning of racial hatred in the Public Order Act 1986, s 17, to include hatred directed at a group outside the United Kingdom and of the provisions concerning increased sentences for racially aggravated offences to include religiously aggravated acts (ss 37–42);
- making it an offence to transfer any biological agent or toxin to another person if it is likely to be kept or used otherwise than for prophylactic, protective or other peaceful purposes (ss 43–44);
- making it an offence to knowingly cause a nuclear explosion or develop a nuclear device except where authorised by the Secretary of State (ss 47–48);
- extension of police powers of search of persons in detention for the purposes of ascertaining their identity including whether the person 'has any mark' that would tend to identify him as a person involved in the commission of an offence (s 90);
- the power to remove disguises if reasonably believed to being worn to conceal a person's identity (s 94).

EMERGENCY POWERS IN PEACETIME

The principal powers in this context are to be found in the Emergency Powers Act 1920, as amended by the Emergency Powers Act 1964. These enable the Crown to make a proclamation of emergency where events have occurred which have so interfered with the supply and provision of food, water, fuel, light or transport as to deprive at least a substantial part of the community of the essentials of life (e.g. strikes, natural disasters). Where such proclamation is in force the government is empowered to make such regulations as are deemed necessary to deal with those exigencies to which the

Act relates (ss 1–2). Such regulations may confer extensive powers on the armed forces and police provided that these can be related to preserving the peace, the general safety of the community, and ensuring the necessaries of life. It may also be provided that breach of such regulations is an offence triable summarily and punishable by fine or imprisonment. Regulations may not be made, however, which:

- seek to impose military or industrial conscription;
- make it an offence to take part, or peacefully persuade others to take part, in a strike;
- confer powers of imprisonment without trial;
- seek to change the rules of criminal procedure.

Regulations made under the Acts must be laid before and approved by both Houses of Parliament if they are to remain effective.

The Emergency Powers Act 1964 permits the employment of members of the armed forces in any urgent work of national importance without a proclamation of emergency under the 1920 Act.

EMERGENCIES AND THE COMMON LAW

In addition to the prerogative powers dealt with in Chapter 12 which relate to the maintenance of law and order and the defence of the realm, the common law also appears to vest in the 'civil authority' (i.e. the Home Secretary) the power to use such force as is reasonably necessary to quell riots or insurrection. This may be effected by calling in the aid of military personnel providing that they remain under the civil authority's control. The taking of life by the police or the military may be justified in circumstances of grave disorder.

In the most extreme circumstances of civil insurrection – as occurred in Ireland during the period 1919–21 – the courts may accept that the country is in a state of war sufficient to justify resort to martial law. In effect, this means that the ordinary process of law and government are suspended and that responsibility for the restoration of law and order is transferred to the military authorities. In these circumstances the military authorities may:

- make law by decree;
- take such action as is deemed fit to enforce the same;
- use military tribunals to try those alleged to be guilty of any transgressions.

Where the judiciary have accepted that the country is in a state of war or civil insurrection, it would appear that redress may not be given in an ordinary court of law in respect of the way in which the military authorities have exercised their responsibilities.

Further reading

Bailey, Harris and Jones (2001) *Civil Liberties: Cases and Materials* (5th edn), London: Butterworths, Ch 4.

Bradley and Ewing (1997) *Constitutional and Administrative Law* (12th edn), London: Longman, Ch 25.

Walker (1992) *The Prevention of Terrorism in British Law* (2nd edn), Manchester: Manchester University Press.

Part 7

TRIBUNALS, INQUIRIES AND COMPLAINTS PROCEDURES

Chapter 24

TRIBUNALS AND INQUIRIES

INTRODUCTION

Administrative tribunals

Figures show that there are in excess of 3,000 tribunals currently operating in England and Wales. According to the 1996/97 Report of the Council on Tribunals these were of 68 different types. In the year covered by the above report, tribunals disposed of some 895,107 cases. It is now more likely that an individual seeking adjudication of a dispute will appear before a tribunal than a court of law. The importance of tribunals in the English legal system cannot, therefore, be overstated.

Most tribunals are a product of the welfare state and have been established to deal with the myriad of disputes arising out of decisions relating to eligibility for benefits, services, grants, licences, etc.

> The welfare state could not function without an elaborate judicial system of its own. Claims for benefit, applications for licences, disputes about controlled rents, planning appeals, compulsory purchase of land – there are a host of such matters which have to be adjudicated upon from day to day and which are, for the most part, unsuitable for the regular courts. In the background are the courts of law with supervisory and often, also, appellate functions. But the front line judicial authorities for administrative purposes are bodies created *ad hoc* (Schartz and Wade, *Legal Control of Government*).

Many tribunals make decisions by applying legal rules to the facts of particular cases. To this extent, therefore, their function is not dissimilar to courts of law. On the other hand, tribunals are deliberately designed to provide a speedier and cheaper means of adjudication which is accessible and comprehensible to ordinary individuals.

Although some tribunals exercise an important first-instance jurisdiction (e.g. the licensing function of the Civil Aviation Authority), most are appellate bodies dealing with appeals against the decisions of central and local government officials. A tribunal of this type may overrule an official's decision and substitute its own findings where:

- there has been a mistake of fact;
- there has been a mistake of law;
- the official's discretion has been exercised in a way which is incompatible with the policy of the enabling legislation.

While tribunals typically deal with disputes between the individual and the state, it should be noted that some adjudicate between one individual and another. The most well known amongst these would be industrial tribunals which have jurisdiction over, *inter alia*, claims for unfair dismissal, and rent assessment committees.

Public inquiries

These also may be attributed to the increase in the regulatory powers of the state, particularly in the context of land use. Their primary function is to gather information and allow individuals an opportunity to make representation before an executive decision is taken which may have adverse consequences for private rights and/or wider public concerns (e.g. whether to proceed with a slum clearance scheme).

In a general sense, inquiries may be distinguished from tribunals in that they were not designed primarily for the purpose of making decisions but rather to provide the factual basis on which the decision-maker (usually a minister) could reach a conclusion which, in his/her opinion, represented the best compromise between the private and public interests in issue. Public inquiries have long been, therefore, a typical procedural facet of those decision-making powers which involve the application of public policy to local facts or circumstances. Hence, it will be usual for a public inquiry to be convened before a ministerial decision is made to proceed with any major scheme of development involving the compulsory purchase of land (e.g. for the construction of motorways, power stations, airports or extensions to the same). Also, on a smaller and less controversial scale, thousands of local public inquiries will be convened annually to hear appeals against refusals of planning permission or the serving of compulsory purchase orders by local authorities.

ADMINISTRATIVE TRIBUNALS

In addition to the virtues of speed and economy, a variety of other related reasons are often put forward to explain the legislators' preference for tribunals as the principal means of resolving disputes in the social welfare context. These include the following:

(a) Some of those politically responsible for the creation and development of the welfare state, particularly after World War II, were not convinced that judges steeped in the individualism of the common law were best qualified to identify and apply the social policy objectives behind the legislation upon which the welfare state was founded.

(b) The creation of tribunals with narrow and specific jurisdictional remits (e.g. social security entitlements) enables them to be staffed by experts in the sphere of activity in which they operate. Thus mental health review tribunals will include persons with appropriate medical knowledge. The Revenue Commissioners dealing with appeals against local tax officials will be persons qualified in the law and practice of taxation. This contributes to the speed of proceedings by obviating the need for expert testimony and to their quality by increasing the likelihood that the relevant legislative rules will be applied in a functionally practical way.

(c) The sheer volume of disputes arising out of the administration of the welfare state could not have been dealt with by the courts as presently constituted: 'if all decisions arising from new legislation were automatically vested in the ordinary courts, the judiciary would by now have been grossly overburdened' (Report of the Committee on Administrative Tribunals and Inquiries, Cmnd 218, 1957, the 'Franks Committee').

(d) Tribunals attempt to minimise the formality and procedural technicality typical of courts of law. This helps persons to more readily understand the conduct of the proceedings and thus to represent themselves more effectively.

(e) Public confidence in the welfare state would be diminished if persons claiming to be in need of benefit were kept waiting for long periods while related disputes were resolved.

(f) The administrative efficiency of government departments is improved by removing the resolution of disputes from their responsibilities.

(g) Tribunals generate an impression that government offices are answerable for their decisions and provide a forum in which 'feelings of having been treated unfairly or unjustly can be diffused' (Cane, *Administrative Law*).

(h) Tribunals also enable ministers to 'off load responsibility for certain politically contentious decisions to a body immune from political criticism' (*ibid.*).

All of this indicates that tribunals represent an attempt to give the resolution of disputes within the welfare state that degree of procedural justice which is consistent with the administrative efficiency necessary to best secure the social objectives of the welfare state.

Composition and independence

There is no general principle requiring all tribunals to be similarly constituted. The composition of each type depends on its enabling legislation and subject matter. Some consist of one person only (e.g. immigration adjudicators). More usually, however, there will be a legally qualified chairperson with two other members appropriately qualified. In some cases these will be experts in the relevant subject matter; in others, the members may possess some representative quality. Thus, industrial tribunals consist of a legally qualified chair sitting with two others, representative of employers' and employees' organisations respectively.

Despite the diversity of practice in relation to the membership of tribunals, the following general principles may be extrapolated.

(a) Civil servants or other public officials are not appointed. Hence the vast majority of tribunal members have no direct links with government departments or officials.

(b) In the majority of cases the chairpersons of tribunals are appointed directly by the Lord Chancellor (i.e. chairs of mental health tribunals) or by the relevant minister usually from panels of suitably qualified people compiled by the Lord Chancellor.

(c) The members of most tribunals are appointed in one of the following ways:

- by the relevant minister or government department;
- by the Lord Chancellor;
- in some cases – for example, social security appeals tribunals and industrial tribunals – by the president of the particular category of tribunal.

(d) Removal of a member of a tribunal usually requires the consent of the Lord Chancellor (Tribunals and Inquiries Act 1992, s 7).

(e) In the matter of the appointment of members of tribunals, ministers are bound to have regard to the recommendations of the Council on Tribunals (*ibid.* s 5).

The above rules and practices do not guarantee the degree of independence and freedom from executive influence for tribunals that is expected of courts of law. In addition, the public conception of the independence of tribunals is not helped by the fact that many conduct their proceedings in government premises. There is, however, no record of actual or attempted executive inference with their activities or members. Were this to be alleged in any particular case, the complainant could seek redress by way of judicial review for illegality (acting under dictation). The matter would also be likely to have adverse political consequences for the minister involved, whether personally or through their departmental officials.

Procedure

The proceedings in tribunals tend to be conducted according to the adversarial model. There is an expectation, therefore, that everything will be done in accordance with the rules of natural justice. This does not mean, however, that tribunals have to act as if they were courts of law. Greater informality and procedural flexibility is the norm.

There is no generally applicable set of procedural rules. The degree of procedural formality observed by a particular type of tribunal will usually be determined by the nature of the subject matter with which it deals. Hence, those empowered to make decisions affecting the liberty of the subject – e.g. mental health review tribunals, the immigration appeals tribunal – operate according to relatively strict procedural requirements. Others, whose decisions have less significant consequences (e.g. education appeals committees), are expected to function with the minimum degree of procedural technicality as is compatible with efficiency and fairness.

A set of model rules on general procedural guidelines was issued by the Council on Tribunals in 1993. These provide that:

> the Tribunal shall conduct the hearing in such manner as it considers most suited to the clarification of the issues before it, and generally to the just handling of proceedings; it shall so far as to it appears appropriate seek to avoid formality in its proceedings.

As with the rules relating to composition and membership, although there is considerable diversity of practice, certain general rules may be identified.

(a) Where a person has a right of appeal to a tribunal from an official's decision, he/she will normally be informed of this at the time the decision is made.

(b) Most tribunals afford a public oral hearing at which it is possible to call and cross-examine witnesses. Some, however, with the consent of the claimant, may deal with routine, non-controversial cases through written submissions.

   Also, most tribunals have a discretion to hold closed sessions where this would appear to be appropriate (e.g. where intimate personal or financial details may be revealed).

(c) The strict rules of evidence are generally not applicable. Hence, probative hearsay evidence will usually be admitted provided the contesting party is given a proper opportunity to challenge it (*Kavanagh* v *Chief Constable of Devon and Cornwall* [1994] 1 QB 624). Tribunal members may also rely on their own knowledge and experience and are not limited to the facts adduced at the hearing. Again, however, natural justice requires that, if such additional considerations are to be taken into account, the party affected should be informed and given an opportunity to make a response (*Dugdale* v *Kraft Foods Ltd* [1977] 1 ICR 48).

(d) Although seldom used, all tribunals have an inherent power to take evidence on oath. Some also have powers to summon witnesses and order production of documents (e.g. industrial tribunals). Where this is not the case, persons may be subpoenaed to appear by the High Court.

(e) Statements made before and by tribunals are protected by qualified privilege. Whether absolute privilege extends to tribunal proceedings has not been decided conclusively. The answer would appear to depend on whether the tribunal in question may be regarded as exercising a judicial function (*Royal Aquarium Society* v *Parkinson* [1892] 1 QB 431; *Trapp* v *Mackie* [1979] 1 All ER 489).

(f) Unless judicially recognised to have the status of a court (e.g. the Employment Appeals Tribunal and the Mental Health Appeals Tribunal), tribunals have no power to punish for contempt.

(g) Legal representation is generally permitted but there is no general entitlement to legal aid to finance it (legal aid is available, however, for proceedings before the Lands Tribunal, Employment Appeals Tribunals, Mental Health Tribunals, and the Revenue Commissioners). The Council on Tribunals has made frequent reference to the exclusion of tribunals from the legal aid scheme. In its 1994/95 Report the Council suggested that legal aid for tribunal representation might be appropriate where:

   - 'a significant point of law arises';
   - 'the evidence is likely to be so technical or specialised that the average laymen could reasonably wish for expert help in assembling and evaluating the evidence and in its testing and interpretation';
   - 'a test case arises';
   - 'deprivation of liberty or the ability of an individual to follow his or her occupation is at stake'.

(h) Subject to a limited number of exceptions, tribunals must give reasons for their decisions save where this would be detrimental to national security (Tribunals and Inquiries Act, 1992, s 10).

(i) Tribunals are not bound to apply the doctrine of precedent. There is, however, a perhaps inevitable tendency to build on previous decisions. However, tribunals do have a greater freedom than courts of law to avoid decisions which are no longer relevant or appropriate.

(j)   There is no inherent right to appeal against a tribunal's decision. Whether a right of appeal exists will depend on the legislation under which the particular category of tribunal was established. Hence, any one of the following three circumstances may apply.

- The enabling Act provides no right of appeal whatsoever (e.g. Education Appeals Committees created by the Education Act 1980).
- The enabling Act provides a right of appeal on a point of law only (e.g. industrial tribunals with jurisdiction under various Acts, including the Employment Rights Act 1996, the Equal Pay Act 1970, the Race Relations Act 1976, and the Health and Safety at Work etc. Act 1974).
- The enabling Act gives a right of appeal on fact and law to a higher tribunal and perhaps thence to a court on a point of law (e.g. from social security appeals tribunals to a Social Security Commissioner and then to the High Court; from immigration adjudicators to the Immigration Appeals Tribunal and then to the Court of Appeal).

SOME PARTICULAR TRIBUNALS

The Appeals Service

The Social Security Act 1998 laid the foundation for a new system of first tier tribunals dealing with a wide range of welfare matters. These 'unified tribunals' replace Social Security Appeals Tribunals, Disability Appeals Tribunals and Medical Appeals Tribunals. The new Appeals Service hears appeals on security, child support, housing benefit, council tax benefit, vaccine damage, tax credit, and compensation recovery. The service became fully operational in April 2000.

Appeals are heard in a network of locally based tribunals in over 140 venues in England, Scotland and Wales.

Each local tribunal consists of one, two or three members depending on which benefit is involved. Thus, for example, for industrial injuries disablement benefit the tribunal will consist of a legally qualified chairperson and one or two doctors. For income support and job seekers allowance, appeals will usually be decided by a person who will be legally qualified. All tribunal members are drawn from panels appointed by the Lord Chancellor. The overall functioning of the system is the responsibility of the President of Appeals Tribunals, who is also appointed by the Lord Chancellor.

An appellant is given the option of an oral hearing on the papers. Oral hearings are conducted in public and legal representation is allowed.

An appeal on a point of law lies from a tribunal decision to a Soci Security Commission or Child Support Commission.

Immigration adjudications and the Immigration Appeals Tribunal

The current immigration appeals and tribunal system was created by the Immigration Act 1971, ss 12–18. Appeals against decisions of immigration officers may be made to an immigration adjudicator. The appeal may relate, *inter alia*, to refusal of entry, to variation of conditions of entry, or to the country to which an excluded or deported person is to be sent. Such appeal may be allowed where the decision:

- was wrong in law;
- was contrary to the immigration rules;
- involved a use of discretion which 'should have been exercised differently' (s 19).

An appeal lies from an adjudication officer to the Immigration Appeals Tribunal. Its members are appointed by the Lord Chancellor. It has a legally qualified chairperson. A further appeal on a point of law, with leave, lies to the Court of Appeal (Asylum and Immigration Appeals Act 1993, s 9). Note that an appeal against a deportation order lies direct to the Immigration Appeals Tribunal except where the order was made by a court.

Prior to 1997, no right of appeal of any sort lay against:

- a refusal of entry where this was for the public good (Immigration Act 1971, s 13(5));
- a deportation order where this was for the 'public good as being in the interests of national security or the relations between the United Kingdom and any other country or for reasons of a political nature' (*ibid.* s 15(3)).

A person wishing to appeal against any decision falling within s 15(3) was permitted to make representations to a panel of advisers consisting of three persons (often referred to as 'the three wise men'). This was a purely administrative concession made in response to parliamentary criticism of the lack of any related statutory right of appeal. Whether a person was given full details of the allegations to be met or was allowed to cross-examine witnesses and to be legally represented was entirely at the panel's discretion. Furthermore, although both the reasonableness and procedural propriety of the panel's decisions were, in theory, susceptible to judicial review, the courts were generally reluctant to intervene because of the apparently sensitive political and national security issues which the executive would usually claim were involved.

This rather unsatisfactory situation has, to some extent, been addressed by the Special Immigration Appeals Commission Act 1997. Persons refused entry or deported on the grounds of national security, etc. may now appeal to the Special Immigration Appeals Commission. This body consists of such numbers of persons appointed by the Lord Chancellor as he/she may determine (1997 Act, s 1 and Sched 1). The Act specifically authorises the Lord Chancellor to make procedural rules permitting proceedings to take place before the Commission without the appellant being given 'full particulars of the reasons for the decision which is the subject of the appeal' (s 5) and proceedings may be held in the 'absence of...the appellant and any legal representation appointed by him' (*ibid.*).

Persons refused political asylum may appeal to a Special Immigration Adjudicator and from thence, with leave, to the Immigration Appeals Tribunal (Asylum and Immigration Appeals Act 1993, ss 8–9). An appeal may be made on the grounds that removal from the United Kingdom would be contrary to the Geneva Convention Relating to the Status of Refugees 1951. A refugee is thereby defined as a person who 'owing to a well-founded fear of being persecuted for reasons of race, religion, nationality, membership of a particular social group or political opinion' has left his or her particular country of nationality and is afraid to return to it.

PUBLIC INQUIRIES

Various statutes provide for the holding of public inquiries to deal with either local or national issues. This is a usual feature of legislation concerned with regulating the use of land. Under such legislation inquiries may be convened to:

- hear objections to proposals for the compulsory acquisition of land or property (usually by a local authority);
- appeal against refusals of planning permission (again, in most cases, by a local authority).

Thousands of such inquiries are held each year. Most deal with issues of no great public concern and receive little political or media interest. Those attracting attention tend to be concerned with proposals which may have significant and far-reaching environmental or social consequences – e.g. the construction or extension of a motorway, airport or nuclear power station.

Less frequently, 'one-off' public inquiries may be convened to look into:

- the causes of major accidents (e.g. the sinking of the car ferry, *Herald of Free Enterprise*, in 1987);
- other incidents or issues of major public concern (e.g. the Aberfan Disaster, 1966; Arms to Iraq, 1996).

Inquiries of this type may be convened under statutory powers (e.g. Merchant Shipping Act 1894, Tribunals of Inquiry (Evidence) Act 1921) or may simply be set up by a minister acting administratively (also note the view that the creation of such non-statutory inquiries may derive legal authority from the royal prerogative).

Land use inquiries

An Englishman's home is no longer 'his castle'. Private rights over land and property are now subject to the overriding needs of the public interest as expressed through the actions and decisions of central and local government. Thus, throughout the twentieth century numerous pieces of legislation were enacted conferring on public authorities powers to acquire land compulsorily and to control development by the grant or refusal of planning permission. From the outset, it was standard procedural practice to provide that disputes arising out of the use of such powers should be heard before a local public inquiry.

The current procedure for the acquisition of land is contained in the Acquisition of Land Act 1981. Where the acquisition (compulsory purchase) is effected by a local authority the procedure is as follows:

(a) service of the compulsory purchase order on all persons whose property rights are affected;
(b) publication of the order in local newspapers;
(c) the lodging of objections (if there are any) by the parties affected;
(d) where objections have been lodged, the convening of a local public inquiry by the Secretary of State;
(e) the inquiry to be presided over by an inspector (appointed by the minister);

(f) at the conclusion of the inquiry, the submission to the minister of the inspector's report containing his/her recommendations and findings of fact;

(g) the minister's decision whether or not to confirm the order, based on the inspector's report and government policy.

The procedure for dealing with appeals against a local planning authority's refusal of planning permission (or against grants of permission subject to conditions) is contained in the Town and Country Planning Act 1990 and the Town and Country Planning (Inquiries Procedure) Rules 1992.

Where such appeal has been lodged it may be disposed of in a variety of ways. Routine cases may be decided by an inspector appointed by and acting on behalf of the Secretary of State for the Environment. Either party may insist on a public hearing. This may be by local public inquiry or a more informal hearing limited to the parties to the dispute. Otherwise, with the parties' consent, the inspector may decide the appeal purely on the basis of written submissions (over 80 per cent of cases are decided in this way).

In more controversial cases, however – as where the proposed development may have a major environmental or social impact – the minister may reserve the right to make the final decision (i.e. whether to allow the appeal). In such cases a local public inquiry will normally be held. This will be presided over by an inspector. As with inquiries concerned with the acquisition of land, the inspector will submit a report to the minister who will then make a final decision based on this and policy considerations.

There is considerable similarity between the way both compulsory purchase and planning inquiries are conducted. In both cases parties directly affected must be given six weeks' notice of the holding of the inquiry and four weeks' notice of the authority's case.

The procedure to be adopted at the inquiry is, to a considerable extent, within the discretion of the presiding inspector. This discretion is subject, however, to relevant statutory rules and the requirements of natural justice. In general, these may be said to impose the following procedural strictures.

(a) Persons directly affected are entitled to appear, to be legally represented and to call evidence and cross-examine witnesses.

(b) Written representations from parties not present may be admitted provided that these are put before the inquiry and an opportunity is provided to comment on them (*Miller* v *Minister of Housing and Local Government* [1968] 2 All ER 633).

(c) The parties to the inquiry should also be appraised of other evidence not adduced at the inquiry but upon which the inspector intends to rely, e.g. that derived from the inspector's previous experience of the subject matter or from his/her inspection of the land or property in issue (*Fairmount Investments* v *Secretary of State for the Environment* [1976] 2 All ER 865).

(d) The inspector may rule inadmissible any testimony which:

- proposes alternatives to the particular development in issue (*Wednesbury Corporation* v *Minister of Housing and Local Government (No. 2)* [1966] 2 QB 275);
- seeks to question relevant government policy (*Bushell* v *Secretary of State for the Environment* [1981] AC 75).

(e) After the inquiry the minister must not hear one side 'behind the back' of the other (*Errington* v *Minister of Health* [1935] 1 KB 249). He or she is bound to consider the inspector's report and to allow the parties an opportunity to comment on any fresh evidence he/she intends to consider (*Rea* v *Minister of Transport* [1984] JPL 876).

(f) The final decision should be accompanied by reasons (Tribunals and Inquiries Act 1992, s 10).

Problems associated with land use inquiries

(a) The way public inquiries are conducted may sometimes cause misconceptions as to their exact role and function. To the uninitiated it may appear that the inspector is adjudicating between the two sides of a dispute and that the decision whether to proceed with the proposed development will be determined according to which party has presented the most convincing arguments. In reality the inquiry's principal function is to assist the decision-maker (whether an inspector or the minister) in the exercise of their discretion. This it does by providing him/her with all the relevant factual information so that this, along with government perceptions of wider public interests, may all be brought to bear on the final decision. The facts as elucidated at the inquiry must be taken into account but are not conclusive. Hence, it is perfectly possible for a decision to be made in favour of a particular development mainly on the basis of policy considerations notwithstanding that the opposing case was presented most convincingly at the inquiry.

> It may well be that on considering the objections, the minister may find that they are reasonable and that the facts alleged in them are true, but, nevertheless he may decide that he will overrule them. His action in so deciding is purely administrative action, based on his conceptions as to what public policy demands. The objections, in other words, may fail to produce the result desired by the objector, not because the objector has been defeated by the local authority in a sort of litigation, but because the objections have been overruled by the minister's decision as to what the public interest demands (per Lord Greene MR, *Johnson (B) and Co (Builders) Ltd* v *Minister of Health* [1947] 2 All ER 395).

(b) The remit of a public inquiry is limited to information relating to the effect a particular development will have on the locality for which it is proposed. As already mentioned, therefore, wider considerations of relevant government policy (e.g. the national policy for motorways and road building) which, as indicated in (a), may be of overriding effect, cannot be raised or challenged.

> A decision to construct a nationwide network of motorways is clearly one of government policy... Any proposal to alter it is appropriate to be the subject-matter of debate in Parliament, not of separate investigations in each of scores of local public inquiries... up and down the country upon whatever material happens to be presented (per Lord Diplock, *Bushell* v *Secretary of State for the Environment*, above).

(c) Major public inquiries – e.g. into the construction or extension of a nuclear power station – may raise issues of considerable technical and scientific complexity. Such inquiries may also take many months to be completed. This may cause difficulties for individual objectors and interest groups both in terms of regular attendance and finding the necessary resources to pay for expert advice and perhaps legal representation. The Sizewell B Inquiry, for example, lasted 26 months. Of that inquiry it has been said: 'To anyone watching the proceedings, the contrast was startling: sometimes a single person was faced by the CEGB's team of four barristers, several solicitors and other legal and administrative assistants' (Armstrong, 'The Sizewell Inquiry', 1985 JPEL 686).

(d) The procedural format used in public inquiries is primarily adversarial rather than inquisitorial. As a result, the only facts considered by the decision-maker are those put forward in argument. Relevant information of which the parties are unaware, or which one party may not wish to use (e.g. the finding of some recent research), may not, therefore, be taken into account to the detriment of the overall quality of the decision-making exercise.

(e) The inspectors who preside over land use inquiries are members of the Planning Inspectorate which is an Executive Agency of the Department of Environment (now DEFRA). They are appointed by the Secretary of State and may often have a background in engineering, surveying or some related expertise. Also, where an appeal is to be decided by an inspector, he/she is bound to apply government policy. Despite appearances and public conceptions, therefore, inspectors cannot be regarded as performing an entirely independent role within the inquiry process.

All of this suggests that, although land use inquiries may be an appropriate forum for hearing objections to small-scale development or routine appeals against refusals of planning permission, they may not be best suited for dealing with issues of national importance where government policy will inevitably have a major impact on the final decision. Indeed, more cynical commentators have suggested that large-scale public inquiries should really be seen as little more than 'a means to neutralising public opinion, doing something about local hostility and resentment or allowing the public to let off steam' (Drapking, 'Development, Electricity and Power Stations' [1974] PL 220).

By way of response to the above criticisms, the Town and Country Planning Act 1990 provided for the creation of planning inquiry commissions to deal with proposed developments which raise issues of 'national or regional importance' or of great scientific or technical complexity (s 101). Such commissions will consist of three to five persons appointed by the Secretary of State. They are empowered to commission relevant research, to convene local public inquiries and to generally identify and investigate all matters relevant to the proposed development. Having completed their task, such commissions should submit a report to the minister.

Tribunals of inquiry

These are appointed by resolutions of both Houses of Parliament under the Tribunals of Inquiry (Evidence) Act 1921. Such tribunals may be constituted to inquire into any matter 'of urgent public importance' (s 1). To date, only twenty such inquiries have been appointed. These have dealt with, *inter alia,* the leaking of Budget secrets (1936), the Aberfan Disaster in 1966 and the events of 'Bloody Sunday' in 1972.

Tribunals of inquiry have all the powers of the High Court in terms of requiring the attendance of witnesses and the production of documents. They sit in public unless this is against the public interest. Legal representation is at the discretion of the tribunal and proceedings are absolutely privileged.

Such tribunals are normally chaired by a judge (or senior member of the legal profession) sitting with two others. The issue to be investigated is presented by a law officer of the Crown who is also responsible for the calling of witnesses. Proceedings are inquisitorial in nature. Witnesses may be questioned, therefore, both by counsel for other persons summoned to appear and by members of the tribunal itself.

Recent practice, however, appears to favour the non-statutory inquiry, often chaired by a senior judge, as the means of investigating matters of national importance. Thus, for example, this was the method chosen to look into the collapse of BCCI (chaired by Bingham LJ) and the Matrix Churchill – Arms to Iraq Affair (chaired by Scott LJ).

THE FRANKS COMMITTEE

Post-war concerns about the *ad hoc* proliferation of tribunals and inquiries, their procedural standards, and the extent to which they appeared to be usurping the functions of the courts led to the creation of the Committee on Tribunals and Inquiries (the Franks Committee) in 1955. The Committee reported in 1958.

The principal findings of the Committee were:

(a) that tribunals and inquiries should be conducted with 'openness, fairness, and impartiality';
(b) that there should be a permanent body (the Council on Tribunals) to oversee their workings and attempt to ensure observance of the above standards in practical terms.

The Franks Committee and tribunals

The particular problems the Committee were asked to consider in relation to tribunals included:

* the varying standards of procedural fairness and the lack of any procedural uniformity between different types of tribunals;
* the extent to which tribunal members who were all executive appointees could be seen as performing an independent function;
* the lack of any general requirement to a right of appeal from tribunal decisions.

Perhaps the most important conclusion of the Committee in this context was that tribunals should be seen as a genuine means of independent adjudication and not simply as a device to improve the efficiency of administration and give it an appearance of procedural fairness. On this basis, the Committee's more specific recommendations for tribunals were as follows:

(a) the chairpersons of tribunals should be appointed and removed by the Lord Chancellor;

(b) members of tribunals should be appointed by the Council on Tribunals and removed by the Lord Chancellor;
(c) in general such chairpersons should be legally qualified;
(d) procedural rules for administrative tribunals should be formulated by the Council on Tribunals and should seek some degree of uniformity;
(e) apart from very exceptional circumstances, tribunals should conduct their hearings in public;
(f) legal representation should normally be allowed;
(g) reasons should be given for decisions;
(h) rights of appeal to a higher tribunal on both facts and law should normally be available with a further right of appeal on a point of law to a court.

The Committee's report was followed by the Tribunals and Inquiries Act 1958. This has subsequently been amended and consolidated by the Tribunals and Inquiries Acts of 1971 and 1992. These have given effect to some, but not all, of the Franks Committee's recommendations. Most importantly, however, the 1958 Act did create the proposed Council on Tribunals (dealt with below). Otherwise, the extent to which the Committee's proposals were implemented may be seen in the text above dealing with the current principles relating to the composition and procedure of tribunals. It is worth noting, though, that to date (more than 40 years on from the Franks report), no legislative action has been taken in relation to the proposals that tribunal members should be chosen by the Council on Tribunals and that there should be a general right of appeal on fact and law from all tribunal decisions.

The Franks Committee and public inquiries

The major concern in this context related to the perceived role of public inquiries and whether these should be regarded primarily as an administrative mechanism designed to assist in the exercise of executive discretion or as a quasi-judicial process for the purpose of giving full and open hearings of the cases for and against particular government schemes and projects.

The Committee decided against both extremes and sought a compromise, which should be reflected in procedural practice:

> If the administrative view is dominant the public inquiry cannot play its full part in the total process, and there is a danger that the rights and interest of the individual citizens affected will not be sufficiently protected...If the judicial view is prominent there is a danger that people will regard the person before whom they state their case as a kind of judge provisionally deciding the matter, subject to an appeal to the minister. This view overlooks the true nature of the proceedings, the form of which is necessitated by the fact that the minister himself, who is responsible to Parliament for the ultimate decision, cannot conduct the inquiry in person (paras 273–74).

The detailed proposals of the Committee in relation to inquiries were directed to achieving the best possible workable balance between these two perspectives. These were:

(a) before an inquiry, the public authority involved should be required to give full details of its case to those affected;

(b) also before the inquiry, parties affected should be given a statement of relevant government policy;

(c) the main body of inspectors for land use and related inquiries should be appointed by the Lord Chancellor and should be under the control of his department;

(d) the authority's case should be fully explained at the inquiry and supported by oral evidence;

(e) inspectors should have the power to compel the attendance of witnesses and administer the oath;

(f) the inspector's report compiled at the inquiry's conclusion should accompany the letter of decision to the parties affected and be made available both centrally and locally;

(g) evidence received after the inquiry should be submitted to the parties for their comments;

(h) the final decision should be accompanied by a statement of reasons.

Most of these recommendations have since been implemented by administrative action or statutory rules. Particular exceptions, however, have been those relating to pre-inquiry statements of government policy and the status of the inspectorate.

THE COUNCIL ON TRIBUNALS

The Council consists of ten to fifteen members appointed by the Lord Chancellor. In addition, the Parliamentary Commissioner is an *ex officio* member (1992 Act, s 2).

The principal functions of the Council are:

(a) to keep under review and report on the constitutions and working of those tribunals specified in Sched 1 to the Act (currently the Tribunals and Inquiries Act 1992);

(b) to consider and report on any other matters as may be referred to the Council concerning any tribunal, whether or not specified in Sched 1 (see recommendations relating to non-statutory inquiries in 1995/96 Report);

(c) to consider and report on such matters as may be referred to it or considered by the Council to be of special importance with respect to administrative procedures which may involve the holding of a statutory inquiry by or on behalf of the minister (1992 Act, s 1).

These functions are underpinned, to a certain extent, by statutory provisions including in particular:

• the Council's right to make recommendations concerning the membership of tribunals (*ibid.*, s 5);

• the obligation imposed on ministers to consult with the Council when making procedural rules for most types of tribunals and inquiries.

In practice, the Council is also consulted when government departments are formulating legislation that seeks to introduce a new system of tribunals or make changes affecting an existing system.

The Council meets once per month. Detailed work and related recommendations are effected through a number of committees dealing with specific topics (e.g. planning procedures, social security appeals, etc.). Members visit and observe tribunals and inquiries in action and receive complaints from members of the public. Note, however, that the Council has no executive powers whatsoever and does not operate as some sort of court of appeal from tribunal decisions or those following the holding of a public inquiry. Nor has it any authority to investigate specific complaints or to initiate its own investigations. Its 'powers' are limited to making recommendations and being consulted but in neither case need its views be acted upon.

The Council's priorities were evident in some of the comments contained in its 1980 special report (*The Functions of the Council on Tribunals*, Cmd 7805):

- 'our most important contribution over the years have been...our constant efforts to translate the general principles of the Franks Committee into workable codes of principle and practice' (para 6.3);
- 'we seek to influence the shape of prospective legislation which may establish new tribunal or inquiry procedures...we welcome, and indeed have come to expect, consultation by government departments while new procedures are still in the formative stage' (para 6.4);
- 'we are vigilant in seeking to ensure that people are given a hearing as of right in suitable cases, and are not denied one if they request it; that rights of appeal are granted whenever appropriate...and that parties to tribunal proceedings are treated equitably, neither side being given an unfair advantage' (para 6.7);
- 'tribunal procedures should be such as to make it fairly simple for people to appear on their own behalf, if they prefer to do so, or to appoint a representative' (para 6.12).

Whatever its achievements, the Council on Tribunals has not been without its critics. Wade and Forsyth (*Administrative Law*), in particular, have listed a series of alleged weaknesses which have had, it is claimed, a negative effect on the Council's effectiveness. These are:

- 'its weak political position and scanty resources';
- 'the Council has proved relatively impotent in securing attention for its recommendations except in minor matters';
- 'it has not succeeded in establishing any connection with Parliament of the kind which gives such strength to the Parliamentary Commissioner';
- 'its heterogeneous membership...is not well suited to its work, much of which requires the ability to handle technical legal material and also some systematic knowledge of administrative law'.

Their overall conclusion on the utility of the Council is that it 'remains an inconspicuous advisory Committee'.

THE LEGGAT REVIEW

The first major review of the tribunal system since the Franks Committee was announced by the Lord Chancellor in May 2000. The review committee was to be chaired by Sir Andrew Leggat, formerly of the Court of Appeal. The review was to encompass all aspects of the workings of tribunals including their structure, jurisdiction, procedures, remedies and processes of appeal.

The review's terms of reference were 'to review the delivery of justice through tribunals other than ordinary courts of law, constituted under an Act of Parliament by a Minister of the Crown or for the purpose of a Minister's functions; in resolving disputes, whether between citizens and the state, or between other parties'. The Leggatt Review appeared in March 2001. It identified a series of key problems with the United Kingdom's tribunal network. These included:

(a) The lack of any coherent structure or system in the evolution and development of tribunals:

> ...the present collection of tribunals has grown up in an almost entirely haphazard way. Individual tribunals were set up and usually administered by departments, with wide variations of practice and approach, and almost no coherence. The current arrangements seem to us to have been developed to meet the needs of the departments which run tribunals, rather than the need of the user (para 1.3).

(b) The lack of any clear separation between tribunals and the departments they hear appeals against:

> There is no question of the Government attempting to influence individual decisions. In that sense, tribunal decisions appear to us clearly impartial. But it cannot be said with confidence that they are demonstrably independent. Indeed the evidence is to the contrary. In most tribunals, departments provide administrative support, pay the salaries of members, pay their expenses, provide accommodation, provide IT support...are responsible for some appointments and promote the legislation which prescribes the procedures to be followed. At best, such arrangements result in tribunals and the department being, or appearing to be, common enterprises. At worst they make the members of a tribunal feel that they have become identified with its sponsoring department, and they foster a culture in which the members feel that their prospects of more interesting work, of progression in the tribunal, and of appointments elsewhere depend on the department against which the cases that they hear are brought (para 2.20).

(c) There is insufficient support and advice from tribunal staff and other agencies to enable individuals to present cases as effectively as possible:

> ...the widest current theme in current tribunals is the aim that users should be able to prepare and present their own cases effectively, if helped by good quality, imaginatively presented information, and by expert procedural help from tribunal staff and substantive assistance from advice agencies...We have found, however, that in almost all areas the decision-making processes, and the administrative support that underlies them, do not meet the peculiar challenges the overall aim imposes (para 1.11).

(d) The lack of any right of appeal from some tribunals.

Principal recommendations

Independence

The Lord Chancellor should assume responsibility for both the administration of the tribunals system and for all appointments within it.

Structure

There should be a single tribunals system. This should be arranged into nine divisions which would group first tier tribunals by subject matter, e.g. Social Security and Pensions, Land and Valuation, Health and Social Services. There would be a right of appeal on a point of law from tribunals in each division to an appropriate tribunal in an appellate division and from appellate tribunals to the Court of Appeal.

Information and assistance

Basic information which should be provided to individuals should include that explaining the tribunal's jurisdiction, its procedure and any further right of appeal.

The basic agency for legal advice and assistance with tribunal hearings should be the Community Legal Service. Legal help beyond this may be provided by the contract scheme administered by the Legal Services Commission by solicitors or advice agencies. The Community Legal Service contract scheme should be extended to key advice agencies and 'the Lord Chancellor's department should consider whether the CLS's financial constraints should be adjusted so that it can fulfil the requirements of tribunal work' (para 4.20).

Tenure

All appointments to tribunals should be for five or seven years. Renewal for further such periods should be automatic except for cause. Grounds for removal should be prescribed by the Lord Chancellor.

References

Armstrong (1985) 'The Sizewell B Inquiry', 1985 JPEL 686.

Cane (1996) *An Introduction to Administrative Law* (3rd edn), Oxford: Clarendon Press.

Drapking (1974) 'Development, Electricity and the Power Stations' [1974] PL 220.

Schwartz and Wade (1972) *The Legal Control of Government*, Oxford: Clarendon Press.

Wade and Forsyth (1994) *Administrative Law* (7th edn), Oxford: Clarendon Press.

Further reading

Allen and Thompson (1996) *Cases and Materials on Constitutional and Administrative Law* (4th edn), London: Blackstone, Ch 11.

Bailey, Jones and Mowbray (1997) *Cases and Materials on Administrative Law* (3rd edn), London: Sweet & Maxwell, Chs 2–3.

Craig (1994) *Administrative Law* (3rd edn), London: Sweet & Maxwell, Ch 4.

Wade and Forsyth (1994) *Administrative Law* (7th edn), Oxford: Clarendon Press, Chs 23–24.

Chapter 25

OMBUDSMEN

BACKGROUND

In the immediate aftermath of the Second World War a further increase in the size and activities of government took place. The welfare state was expanded, giving greater rights of access to state benefits and services. Additional regulatory powers – particularly for the purposes of planning and urban renewal – were also entrusted to the government. Much of this was motivated by altruistic political principles and a desire to improve the quality of life of the wider community.

However, despite these overall laudable intentions, greater contact between the individual and the state and, in some cases, dependence on it, led to an increased incidence of complaints and disputes concerning the conduct of public officials and their treatment of individuals.

The creation of appropriate mechanisms to deal with grievances did not go hand in hand with the granting of powers. In some contexts (e.g. national assistance) tribunals were established to deal with complaints relating to the way an official had interpreted the relevant regulations or applied them to the facts of a particular case. Beyond this the traditional methods of dealing with a grievance against the state remained available. Hence, an individual could complain to an MP and ask for his/her intervention with the government department concerned or for the matter to be raised in Parliament. Also, where it appeared that a government department or official may have acted illegally, redress could be sought in the courts.

The general position was, however, unsatisfactory. Often the type of grievance felt by an individual would fall outside the jurisdiction of any tribunal and would not involve any breach of law. Examples would include such matters as rudeness, inattention, delay, inadequate or incomprehensible advice, or simply downright incompetence. The right to complain to an MP could not be regarded as a generally satisfactory or adequate means of dealing with the volume and variety of complaints arising out of the relationship between members of the public and government departments. Members of Parliament did not, and do not, have the time, resources or expertise required to deal with all such matters effectively, nor are such individual grievances matters to which Parliament can hope to devote any significant amount of time.

In the 1950s, therefore, an awareness began to develop – principally among academics and lawyers – of the need to provide the ordinary citizen with some more effective means of pursuing the type of complaint which might seem trivial in the general context of the administration of public policy but which might be of considerable importance to the individual affected.

In 1961 the British section of the International Commission of Jurists (Justice) recommended the introduction of a complaints procedure modelled on that already in use in some Scandinavian countries, i.e. an independent complaints commissioner ('ombudsman') equipped with the power to investigate and secure redress for the type of grievance against officialdom not easily remedied through more traditional procedures.

Initially, the official response to the proposal was not encouraging. In particular, it was argued that investigating and reporting on the activities of civil servants would be inconsistent with, and might undermine, the convention of individual ministerial responsibility (i.e. that everything done inside a government department is done in the name of the minister, who is answerable for the same to Parliament). Eventually, however, wiser counsels prevailed, and the incoming Labour government of 1964 gave an assurance that legislation would be formulated to deal with the problem. Their proposals were embodied in the Parliamentary Commissioner Act 1967 (subsequent references in this chapter relate to the 1967 Act, unless stated otherwise).

Since then other ombudsmen or complaints procedures have been established in both the public and private sectors. The principal public sector procedures were created as follows:

- the Health Service Commissioner (National Health Service Reorganisation Act 1973);
- the Commissions for Local Administration in England, Wales (Local Government Act 1974) and Scotland (Local Government (Scotland) Act 1975);
- the Northern Ireland Parliamentary Commissioner for Administration (Parliamentary Commissioner (Northern Ireland) Act 1969);
- the Northern Ireland Commissioner for Complaints (Commissioner for Complaints (Northern Ireland) Act 1969);
- the Pensions Commissioner (Social Security Act 1990);
- the Courts and Legal Services Ombudsman (Courts and Legal Services Act 1990);
- the Prisons Ombudsman (created administratively in 1994).

THE PARLIAMENTARY COMMISSIONER

Appointment

The Parliamentary Commissioner or Ombudsman is appointed by the Monarch on the advice of the government. The Monarch may also exercise the power of dismissal but only pursuant to resolutions of both Houses of Parliament (s 1). This gives the Commissioner a degree of independence and security of tenure similar to that accorded to senior judges. The Commissioner should retire at 65. He or she is an *ex officio* member of the Council on Tribunals and the Commissions for Local Administration but is disqualified from membership of the House of Commons.

Jurisdiction

The Commissioner is authorised to investigate written complaints from individuals who claim to have suffered 'injustice in consequence of maladministration' in dealings with any of the government agencies or departments specified originally in the 1967

Act, Sched 2, and now contained in Sched 1 of the Parliamentary and Health Service Commissioners Act 1987 as amended by the Parliamentary Commission Act 1994.

Maladministration

The term maladministration was not defined in the Act. At the time of the Act's introduction, however, the minister responsible for it said that the term would at least include 'bias, neglect, inattention, delay, incompetence, ineptitude, perversity, turpitude and arbitrariness' (Richard Crossman, 1966). More recently the following matters were specified by the Commissioner as falling within the definition:

> ...rudeness...; unwillingness to treat the complainant as a person with rights; refusal to answer reasonable questions; neglecting to inform a complainant on request of his or her rights to entitlement; knowingly giving advice which is misleading or inadequate; ignoring valid advice or overrating considerations which would produce an uncomfortable result for the overruler; offering no redress or manifestly disproportionate redress; showing bias whether because of colour, sex, or any other grounds; omission to notify those who thereby lose a right of appeal; faulty procedures; failure by management to monitor compliance with adequate procedures; cavalier disregard of guidance which is intended to be followed in the interest of equitable treatment of those who use a service; partiality; failure to mitigate the effects of rigid adherence to the letter of the law where that produces manifestly inequitable treatment (PCA, Annual Report, 1993, para 7).

Notwithstanding this extensive definition of the term, it is generally accepted that the formation of policy and legislation do not fall within it. Hence it is not open to an individual to complain that a particular policy or legislative rule might have been different if the department concerned had consulted more widely or taken additional considerations into account. Maladministration may occur, however, if a particular policy or legislative rule appears to be causing hardship and the department responsible refuses to review its interpretation of the rule or the way it is being applied.

The 1967 Act does make clear that the Parliamentary Commissioner was not created to act in an appellate capacity in matters of fact. The Commissioner's inquiries should concentrate, therefore, on the conduct of officials and the quality of the administrative processes through which official actions and decisions are taken. The Commissioner is thus expressly forbidden to entertain complaints relating solely to the merits of particular decisions (s 12).

Excluded matters

A considerable range of activities in which central government departments are involved were, from the outset, put beyond the Commissioner's powers of investigation. The principal exclusions and the reasons given for them were as follows:

(a) Any matter in respect of which a complainant may appeal to a tribunal or seek redress in the courts (s 5) (e.g. by applying for judicial review). This was based on the principle that the Commissioner was not introduced to replace existing grievance procedures but to supplement these in areas where adequate protection for the citizen in dealings with the executive would not otherwise exist.

Note, however, that the Commissioner has a discretion to waive this exclusion if satisfied that in the particular circumstances it would not be reasonable to expect the complainant to go before a court or tribunal, e.g. where the relevant law is uncertain or the cost of proceedings is prohibitive.

(b) Any matter or grievance which arose more than twelve months before the complaint was made ('stale' complaints) unless there are special circumstances for making an exception (s 6). This was designed to prevent a grievance being referred to the Commissioner where this did not have sufficient impact on the complainant to cause the matter to be raised at an earlier stage.

(c) Matters relating to the contractual or commercial dealings of a government department (Sched 3, para 9).

The original reason for this exclusion was that the PCA was intended to operate in the field of relationships between the government and the governed. Commercial judgements are by nature discriminatory...and so allowing the commercial judgements of departments to be open to examination by private interests while leaving those interests themselves free from investigation would amount to putting departments, and with them the taxpayer, at a disadvantage (Select Committee on the Parliamentary Commissioner for Administration, 1993/4).

(d) Matters relating to personnel issues in the public services or armed forces (Sched 3, para 10). It was felt that it would be unfair and illogical to give public sector employees a grievance procedure not available to their private sector counterparts. Also, in the case of the armed forces, it was believed that access to the Commissioner would be inimical to the maintenance of authority and discipline.

(e) Matters relating to the government's dealings with any other government or international organisation (Sched 3, para 1). Here it was argued that a decision whether or not to pursue a complaint which might involve a foreign government could often raise political considerations outwith the Parliamentary Commissioner's proper sphere of competence. Also, it was felt that, in this context, pursuit of an individual's concerns might not always be synonymous with effective protection of the wider public interest.

(f) Action taken by British diplomats outside the United Kingdom. The two reasons offered for this exclusion were that such actions might well be determined by local circumstances over which such officials had no control and that the investigation of any matter arising within the territory of a foreign state would be beset with practical difficulties (particularly in terms of access to information and official cooperation generally).

(g) Action taken relating to the investigation of crime and the protection of national security (Sched 3, para 5). It was felt that allowing information relating to the same to come into the public domain could be detrimental to the effectiveness of the law enforcement agencies and could put at risk some key prerequisites of good criminal intelligence, e.g. anonymity and confidentiality.

(h) The exercise of the prerogative of mercy (Sched 3, para 7). This was justified on the ground that royal clemency was not thought to be an appropriate issue for investigation and that, in the normal course of events, problem cases of this type would most probably have already been referred to a court for reconsideration.

(i) The grant of honours (Sched 3, para 11). Again, it was felt that it would be constitutionally improper to subject the exercise of the Monarch's powers to investigation and that, since the conferment of an honour was a privilege, nobody aggrieved in such matter could be said to have suffered injustice.

(j) The extradition process.

> In the exercise of extradition orders, the Secretary of State is acting in a quasi-judicial capacity as a final appellate authority. Adding, in effect, a further appeal – an investigation by the PCA – would, the argument ran, be inappropriate and inconsistent with the government's responsibility for compliance with international obligations (1993/94 Report).

Excluded bodies

As stated, the PCA's investigative jurisdiction extends only to those government agencies and bodies listed in Sched 2 to the 1967 Act, as amended by the Parliamentary and Health Service Commissioners Act 1987. The Schedule lists some 115 of the same. Significant amongst those excluded and, therefore, not within the PCA's remit would be: the remaining public corporations, e.g. the Post Office, the Civil Aviation Authority and the Atomic Energy Authority; the Criminal Injuries Compensation Board; parole boards; the Bank of England; the then Monopolies and Mergers Commission (now Competition Commission); and various bodies operating in the sphere of education, e.g. the Higher Education Funding Council, the National Curriculum Council and the School Examinations and Assessment Council.

Open government

The subject matter falling within this aspect of the Parliamentary Commissioner's jurisdiction was extended as a result of the government's White Paper on Open Government published in 1993 (Cm 2290). This promised 'to establish a more disciplined framework for publishing factual and analytical information about new policies and reasons for administrative decisions'. A Code of Practice on Access to Information was introduced to secure implementation of these good intentions. A failure to supply information according to the Code's requirements amounts to injustice as a consequence of maladministration and may, therefore, be investigated by the Commissioner.

The Code of Practice divides official information into fifteen categories. Some of these are completely exempt from disclosure: communications with the royal household, public employment, public appointments and honours. Information in the other categories (e.g. defence and national security) should be disclosed unless this would harm the national interest to a degree which outweighs the national interest in making information available. The onus is, therefore, on disclosure unless it can be shown that the information falls into one of the exempted categories or there are good grounds for believing that its disclosure would do unacceptable damage to a public interest. Such official judgements may be questioned by the Commissioner – i.e. it is open to the Commissioner to dispute a government conclusion concerning the degree of harm that the disclosure of a particular piece of information might do.

The Commissioner's remit in this context extends only to those departments and bodies coming within his/her jurisdiction as determined by the 1967 Act.

Procedure

The 1967 Act, s 5 provided that each complaint must be made initially to an MP (not necessarily that of the complainant). This requirement is known as the 'MP filter'. It reflects the fact that the office of Parliamentary Commissioner was created to make departmental accountability to Parliament more effective rather than to replace it with an alternative mechanism. It is for the MP to decide whether the complaint should be referred to the Commissioner. Obvious considerations would be whether the complaint falls within the PCA's jurisdiction and whether it raises an issue worthy of investigation. Also, it is open to the MP to take up the complaint and pursue it personally if in his/her opinion this would appear to be an appropriate way of dealing with the problem. The Commissioner has no authority, therefore, to entertain a complaint which has been made to him directly by a member of the public. He may, however, communicate such complaint to an appropriate MP so that it may, at the MP's discretion, be referred back to the Commissioner and, therefore, not simply 'lost'. It should also be emphasised that the Commissioner has no authority to initiate an investigation. All is entirely dependent on a complaint being raised by an individual and being referred to the Commissioner by an MP.

Each investigation should be conducted in private (s 7). The head of the department or agency and those within it who are the subject of an investigation should be given an opportunity to comment on the complainant's allegations (*ibid.*). The same persons and the minister who referred the complaint are entitled to a report of the Commissioner's findings (*ibid.*).

A general report on the performance of his/her functions must be laid before each House of Parliament on an annual basis (s 10). Other special reports may be laid from time to time as the Commissioner thinks fit (*ibid.*). These may relate, *inter alia*, to particularly important inquiries or to instances where government departments found guilty of maladministration have refused to respond to the Commissioner's recommendations. Since 1997 such reports have been considered by the House of Commons Select Committee on Public Administration which makes recommendations concerning the Commissioner's jurisdiction, powers and investigative methods. It may also suggest changes in the administrative procedures of the government departments and bodies falling within the Commissioner's jurisdiction. This function was performed previously by the Select Committee on the Parliamentary Commissioner.

Powers and remedies

Apart from that relating to proceedings in Cabinet or Cabinet Committees, any information relevant to an investigation, whether in the possession of a minister, civil servant or any other person, must be submitted to the Commissioner on request (s 8). This includes information which is subject to the Official Secrets Acts or any other legal restriction relating to its disclosure, e.g. a duty of confidentiality or public interest immunity (*ibid.*). Refusal to comply with such a request, or any other obstruction of an investigation, may be referred to the High Court and dealt with as if it were a contempt of court (s 9). The Commissioner is also empowered to demand the attendance of any person for the purpose of obtaining oral testimony and may administer the oath (s 8).

These extensive powers of access to official information are subject to the provision that the Commissioner may not include in a report anything which a minister has certified would be damaging to the national security (s 8).

Where the Commissioner finds maladministration he/she may recommend remedial action – e.g. payment of compensation, altering of decisions or procedures, or the giving of an apology – but has no power to insist on official compliance, the sole weapon being to report the matter to the MP concerned and, in particular cases, to lay a special report before Parliament. This is another illustration that the primary purpose of the office is to assist MPs in the task of supervising the activities of government departments and agencies. It is only in relatively rare cases, however, that a government body will not respond in an appropriate fashion to an adverse finding by the Commissioner.

Evaluation

Publicity

The number of complaints submitted to the PCA each year would suggest that public awareness of the office is not great. In ten years, from 1982 to 1991, the average annual figures were as follows:

Number of cases referred	746
Number of cases investigated	188
Number of cases where maladministration found	73

More recent figures have shown something of an increase in the Commissioner's workload. Figures for complaints received in 1997/98, 1998/99 and 1999/2000 were 1,459, 1,506, and 1,612 respectively. In 1998/99 372 complaints were investigated and 312 in 1999/2000. This would suggest that qualms about public awareness have not entirely been put to rest – even the more recent figures do not compare well with those recorded in other countries having similar complaints systems for smaller populations. It is not uncommon, for example, for the ombudsman in Australia to receive in excess of 15,000 complaints per annum or for his counterpart in New Zealand to receive in excess of 4,000. In 1992 the number of complaints received by the French Médiateur was 35,123.

In its 1993/94 Report, the Select Committee for the Parliamentary Commissioner suggested that the problem of a lack of public awareness might be diminished to some extent if the Commissioner's reports were to be debated on the floor of the House of Commons. Currently such debates are not obligatory and are infrequent.

Time taken for investigation

The Commissioner's record here has not always been impressive. In the early 1990s the average time taken for an investigation was in excess of eighteen months. After criticism by the Select Committee, the Ombudsman's 1999/2000 report recorded that this had been reduced to, on average, 44 weeks.

The MP filter

Since the inception of the PCA in 1967 debate has continued concerning the lack of direct access and the need for a complaint to be channelled to the Commissioner through an MP. The supposed benefits of the requirement were summarised as follows in the Select Committee's Report for 1978:

- the complainant's problem could often be solved by an MP's intervention without the need for a reference to a lengthy investigation by the Commissioner;
- it helps MPs to keep in touch with the problems of constituents in the 'daily contact with the machinery of the State';
- it restricts the Commissioner's attentions to those complaints which MPs feel they would not be able to deal with competently through lack of time, expertise or resources.

It has also been emphasised that the MP filter was designed 'to allay the fears of those who thought that the Ombudsman system would detract from the traditional constitutional role of Parliament in its scrutiny of the executive' (Select Committee Report 1993/94).

Arguments against the filter include the following:

- it lowers the profile of the office of Parliamentary Commissioner and, therefore, public awareness of its existence;
- potential complainants may suspect that an MP 'of a different colour from their own political persuasion will not help them' (ibid.);
- it imposes an additional administrative burden on MPs which some may be reluctant or unable to discharge as expeditiously as possible;
- because MPs have differing views concerning the utility of the Parliamentary Commissioner as a means of dealing with an individual's grievances, some are more likely to refer complaints to the Commissioner than others;
- 'the filter is an anomaly, almost unknown in other Ombudsmen systems' (ibid.).

To date, however, the Select Committee has remained unconvinced of the need for change and has continued to assert the benefit of maintaining the MP's involvement in dealing with complaints against the executive.

> We continue to believe that the Member has an irreplaceable role in pursuing the complaints of the public against the Executive...The work of the Parliamentary Ombudsman, acting at the behest of MPs and reporting to them the details of his investigations has a vital role in equipping Members for the tasks of Parliament. The knowledge of the details of any problems in administration has an important part in any effective scrutiny of the Executive. The publication of anonymised reports can never be a genuine substitute for direct involvement in the case which the Member has referred. Direct access will result in the denial to Members of the expertise in the problems facing their constituents as they come into contact with the Executive. This is to impoverish parliamentary and thus political life (ibid.).

Jurisdiction

Many criticisms have been made of the wide range of matters and government bodies excluded from the Commissioner's jurisdiction. The Select Committee has suggested that there should be a presumption that 'all decisions of civil servants and others within departments and appropriate public bodies involving maladministration should be subject to investigation...unless any constitutional principle such as independence of the judiciary dictated otherwise'. In evidence to the Select Committee in 1993, Justice's proposal was that the Commissioner's jurisdiction should extend to 'all who perform a public duty and to all areas of central government administration, save of those for whom exclusion can be justified'.

The work of the Parliamentary Commissioner

The most complained about departments are the Department of Social Security and the Inland Revenue. The DSS has been described as the Commissioner's 'best customer'. In 1999/2000 complaints relating to the DSS constituted 41 per cent of the Commissioner's workload. Complaints concerning the Inland Revenue amounted to 8 per cent with the Department of the Environment, Transport and the Regions not far behind with a score of 7.5 per cent. A significant number of complaints relating to the DSS concerned the activities and decisions of the Child Support Agency. Figures contained in the 1994 Report showed that one of the most common complaints against the Agency concerned misidentification of absent parents. The Commissioner found 70 cases of this type of injustice to have been committed and recommended remedies by way of *ex gratia* payments.

The following are typical examples of the types of complaints dealt with by the Commissioner.

Department	Case Reference	Title
Ministry of Agriculture, Fisheries and Food	1. C.1380/9999	Incorrect guidance regarding the level of veterinary supervision in abattoirs
Charity Commission	2. C.406/99	Mishandling of an application for National Lottery funding
Department of Health	3. C.1274/00	Delay in removing a name from their police notification list
Home Office	4. C.429/00	Improper disclosure of information about a member of a prison Board of Visitors
	5. G.1304/00	Delay in arranging the issue of entry clearance to enter the United Kingdom
	6. C.1441/00	Delay and mishandling in processing applications for indefinite leave to remain in the United Kingdom and for travel documents
Inland Revenue	7. C.61/00	Mishandling of a company valuation for capital gains tax purposes
	8. C.951/99	Unnecessarily protracted enquiries
Legal Services Commission	9. C.1262/00	Failure to supply accurate information about a legal aid debt

Department of Social Security	10. C.1059/00	Benefits Agency and Appeals Service: error by Benefits Agency when completing a claim form; delay by Benefits Agency and errors by Appeals Service in resolving matters
	11. C.1075/00	Benefits Agency: refusal to pay the equivalent of benefit lost between 1991 and 1995
	12. C.1286/00	Benefits Agency: administrative failings led to the arrest of a woman on warrant
	13. C.423/00	Child Support Agency: poor handling leading to gross inconvenience, worry and distress

The Parliamentary Commissioner and judicial review

From the institution of the office it was probable that the actions and decisions of the Commissioner were reviewable for simple *ultra vires* (e.g. investigating a matter not within his/her jurisdiction) and for procedural impropriety. As yet, the matter has not been settled definitively (see, however, *R v Parliamentary Commissioner for Administration, ex parte Balchin* [1997] JPL 917). As to the willingness of a court to review a decision of the Commissioner for abuse of discretion, the matter was shrouded in considerable uncertainty.

The first case to shed any light on the matter was *Re Fletcher's Application* [1970] 2 All ER 527, where it was held that the exercise of the Commissioner's discretion as to which complaints should be investigated could not be questioned in the courts. Once, however, the Commissioner has embarked upon an investigation it would appear that decisions relating to the conduct of the inquiry may be susceptible to review if *Wednesbury* unreasonableness of a serious or gross nature can be established (*R v Parliamentary Commissioner for Administration, ex parte Dyer* [1994] 1 WLR 621). It is interesting to note that the court in the *Dyer* case refused to accept the argument that since the Commissioner is an officer of the House of Commons he should be answerable to Parliament, and to Parliament only, for the way he performs his functions.

THE HEALTH SERVICE COMMISSIONER

Creation

The National Health Service was excluded from the jurisdiction of the Parliamentary Commissioner. This was because, at the time, some elements of the health service were under local government control. Central government responsibility for the entire health service was effected by the National Health Service Reorganisation Act 1973. This also established Health Commissioners for England and Wales (the office of

Health Commissioner for Scotland was created by the National Health Service (Scotland) Act 1972). To date the practice has been to appoint the same person who holds the post of Parliamentary Commissioner to the offices of Health Commissioner for England, Wales and Scotland.

Matters relating to the Health Commissioner's appointment, jurisdiction and powers are currently governed by the Health Service Commissioners Act 1993. Like the Parliamentary Commissioner, the Health Service Commissioner is an independent officer of Parliament appointed by the Crown but dismissible only pursuant to resolutions of both Houses of Parliament.

Jurisdiction

The Health Service Commissioner was originally empowered to investigate hardship or injustice arising from maladministration in the National Health Service or from the provision of, or failure to provide, any aspect of such service. He was not given jurisdiction, however, over complaints relating to clinical judgements or to the services provided by GPs and other family practitioners (e.g. dentists, pharmacists, opticians). These restrictions on his jurisdiction have since been removed by the Health Service Commissioners (Amendment) Act 1996.

Procedure

The MP filter does not operate in relation to the Health Service Commissioner. Hence, a complaint may be made directly to the Commissioner providing all internal health service complaints procedures have been exhausted. The Commissioner's reports are submitted to the Secretary of State for Health who is obliged to lay them before Parliament. Such reports are scrutinised by the Select Committee for the Parliamentary Commissioner.

Powers and remedies

The Health Commissioner's powers in the matters of access to information and the taking of oral testimony are as those of the Parliamentary Commissioner. Similarly, the assumption is that the adverse publicity caused by his reports will be sufficient to produce the necessary remedial action to secure compliance with his recommendations.

The work of the Health Commissioner

The number of complaints received by the Commissioner have been increasing in recent years. Thus, while 1,784 complaints were made in 1995/96, of which 199 were accepted for investigation, by 1999/2000 the figure had risen to 2,526 complaints with 212 accepted for investigation.

THE COMMISSIONS FOR LOCAL ADMINISTRATION

Creation and appointment

Complaints relating to local government are made to a commissioner for local administration. Each commissioner belongs to a commission for local administration. There are three such commissions. The Commissions for England and Wales were established by the Local Government Act 1974 and the Scottish Commission by the Local Government (Scotland) Act 1975. Commissioners are appointed by the Crown and hold office during good behaviour, retiring at 65 (s 23).

Jurisdiction

A complaint may be made to a commissioner by any person who claims to have 'sustained injustice in consequence of maladministration in connection with action taken by...an authority...in exercise of [its] administrative functions'. The complaint must be lodged within twelve months from the day on which the complainant became aware of the subject matter of the complaint.

A local government commissioner has no jurisdiction to investigate:

- matters for which redress may be granted by a court, tribunal or by appeal to a minister unless it would be unreasonable to expect the complainant to use one of these remedies;
- actions or decisions which affect all or most of the inhabitants of the authority in question (s 26) (e.g. the level of council tax);
- matters relating to the prevention and investigation of crime;
- actions taken in relation to civil or criminal proceedings in which an authority is involved;
- commercial or contractual transactions;
- personnel and disciplinary matters;
- the internal affairs of educational institutions.

Procedure

A complaint may be made directly to a commissioner or to a local councillor who may refer it to a commissioner with the complainant's consent (s 26). Prior to this the complaint should have been brought to the attention of the local authority to which it relates and the authority must have been given a reasonable opportunity to respond to it (ibid.).

Each investigation should be conducted in private (s 28). An opportunity to comment on the complaint should be given to the authority concerned and to any person alleged to have taken the action complained about (ibid.). At the conclusion of an investigation a report of the commissioner's findings should be given to the complainant, the authority, and to any local councillor through whom the complaint was referred (s 30).

Each commissioner must submit an annual report to his/her local commission and each commission must report to a body designated by the Secretary of State as representative of the local authorities subject to its investigative powers (s 24).

Powers and remedies

A local commissioner may require any person in possession of information relevant to an investigation to furnish them with the same. They may require the attendance of witnesses and take evidence on oath. No statutory or common law rule protecting information from disclosure (e.g. confidentiality, public interest immunity, official secrecy) may be used to deny a commissioner access to information they consider relevant (s 29).

A local commissioner has no power to insist on compliance with his/her reports. Where, however, a report contains a finding of maladministration, the local authority concerned must, within a reasonable time, notify the commissioner of the action it has taken or proposes to take (s 31). If the commissioner is not satisfied with such response they may make a further report to the authority containing specific recommendations (*ibid.*). A decision not to comply with such a report must be taken by the full council of the authority. Compliance is the norm.

Between 1974 and 1993 local government commissioners issued 3,548 reports which identified injustice arising from maladministration. Lack of satisfactory response occurred in 202 cases (less than 6 per cent). If a council persists in refusing to implement a commissioner's recommendations it must publish those recommendations and its reasons for non-compliance in a local newspaper (s 31).

Some criticisms

(a) In 1994 the Local Commission for England reported that the average time to complete an investigation was 70.5 weeks.
(b) It has also conceded that 'it is extremely doubtful whether the service is known to many of those who might be able to make use of it' (Memorandum to Select Committee on the Parliamentary Commissioners, 1993).
(c) Although the local government commissioners at times become aware of issues which call for investigation 'they are powerless... unless they receive a complaint from a citizen'.
(d) Recommendations of a local commissioner are not legally enforceable.

Judicial review

A challenge may be made to the legality of the actions or decisions of a local government commissioner where:

- the commissioner has entertained a complaint which does not relate to a matter within his/her jurisdiction (*R* v *Commissioner for Local Administration, ex parte Eastleigh Borough Council* [1988] QB 855);
- the commissioner has made findings for which there was no reasonable factual basis (*R* v *Commissioner for Local Administration, ex parte Croydon London Borough Council* [1989] 1 All ER 1033);
- the commissioner has been guilty of procedural impropriety.

THE NORTHERN IRELAND OMBUDSMAN

Complaints about action taken by government departments for which the Secretary of State for Northern Ireland is responsible are dealt with by the Northern Ireland Parliamentary Commissioner for Administration (NIPCA) and must be made through an MP. Complaints relating to the activities of local authorities and other public bodies are investigated by the Northern Ireland Commissioner for Complaints (NICC). Such complaints may be made to the Commissioner directly. Since 1973 both offices have been held by the same person. The NIPCA was created by the Parliamentary Commissioner (Northern Ireland) Act 1969. The office of NICC was established by the Commissioner for Complaints (Northern Ireland) Act 1969.

Subject to the following exceptions, the jurisdiction and powers of Northern Ireland's two Commissioners are similar to those possessed by their English counterparts:

(a) in both central and local government capacities the Commissioners may deal with complaints relating to personnel matters;
(b) in the local government context, the Commissioner may entertain complaints relating to commercial and contractual matters;
(c) findings of maladministration in relation to local government may be referred to a county court for enforcement by way of an appropriate remedy (e.g. damages or mandatory or other injunction).

In 1997 the number of complaints made to the NIPCA was 327. The number of complaints to the NICC was 432. The average time taken for a full investigation was between eight and ten months. A public awareness survey in 1994 showed that only 10 per cent of the population of Northern Ireland were aware of the existence and functions of the two complaints procedures.

A further ombudsman procedure for Northern Ireland was established by the enactment of the Police (Northern Ireland) Act 1997. This created the Police Ombudsman for Northern Ireland which replaced the Independent Commission for Police Complaints for Northern Ireland.

THE PENSIONS OMBUDSMAN

The office was created by the Social Security Act 1990. The Ombudsman has authority to investigate allegations of injustice arising from maladministration in occupational or personal health schemes. Awards made by the Ombudsman are legally enforceable and his/her decisions are subject to a right of appeal on a point of law to the High Court. The Pensions Ombudsman's activities are subject to review by the Council on Tribunals.

THE LEGAL SERVICES OMBUDSMAN

The Legal Services Ombudsman deals with complaints about the way allegations against members of the legal profession have been dealt with by the appropriate professional body. He or she has no jurisdiction, however, in relation to decisions made by a court, the Solicitors' Disciplinary Tribunal or the Disciplinary Tribunal of the Council of the Inns of Court. A report of the Ombudsman's findings in any particular case goes to the complainant, the person against whom the allegation was made and the professional body concerned. The Ombudsman may recommend the taking of disciplinary action or the payment of compensation. The complaints scheme was established by the Courts and Legal Services Act 1990.

THE PRISONS OMBUDSMAN

The office of Prisons Ombudsman was created in 1994 by administrative action (i.e. appointment by the Home Secretary) and not pursuant to any primary legislation as in the cases of all of the above.

The jurisdiction of the Prisons Ombudsman extends to all matters affecting prisoners except:

(a) those relating to litigation or criminal proceedings;
(b) those relating to persons or bodies outside the prison service – e.g. the police, courts, immigration service, the parole board;
(c) ministerial decisions concerning the release of mandatory life prisoners.

Unlike other ombudsmen, the Prisons Ombudsman may investigate the merits of decisions as well as the administrative processes through which they were made.

The government has undertaken to give the Prisons Ombudsman unfettered access to prison documents, establishments and individuals, subject to the need to withhold from complainants, and not make public, information which could be damaging to national security, to security in prisons or to the protection of individuals.

Any recommendations made by the Ombudsman pursuant to an investigation must be submitted to the Director-General of the Prison Service. The Ombudsman is also obliged to report annually to the Home Secretary, who is to lay a shortened version of the full report before Parliament.

During the period from October 1994 to December 1995, 2,050 complaints were submitted by prisoners; 424 full investigations were carried out. The complaint was upheld in 44 per cent of fully investigated cases.

Further reading

Bailey, Jones and Mowbray (1997) *Cases and Materials on Constitutional and Administrative Law* (3rd edn), London: Sweet & Maxwell, Ch 4.

Birkinshaw (1995) *Grievances, Remedies and the State* (2nd edn), London: Sweet & Maxwell.

Hawke (1993) *The Ombudsman: Twenty Five Years On*, London: Cavendish.

Pollard, Parpworth and Hughes (1997) *Constitutional and Administrative Law, Text with Materials* (2nd edn), London: Butterworths, Ch 7.

Seneviratne (1994) *Ombudsman in the Public Sector*, Buckingham: Open University Press.

INDEX